Modern Socio-Technical Perspectives on Privacy

Bart P. Knijnenburg • Xinru Page •
Pamela Wisniewski • Heather Richter Lipford •
Nicholas Proferes • Jennifer Romano
Editors

Modern Socio-Technical Perspectives on Privacy

 Springer

Editors
Bart P. Knijnenburg
Clemson University
Clemson, SC, USA

Xinru Page
Brigham Young University
Provo, UT, USA

Pamela Wisniewski
University of Central Florida
Orlando, FL, USA

Heather Richter Lipford
University of North Carolina at Charlotte
Charlotte, NC, USA

Nicholas Proferes
School of Social and Behavioral Sciences
Arizona State University
Tempe, AZ, USA

Jennifer Romano
Bridgewater Associates
Westport, CT, USA

ISBN 978-3-030-82788-5   ISBN 978-3-030-82786-1   (eBook)
https://doi.org/10.1007/978-3-030-82786-1

This Springer imprint is published by the registered company Springer Nature Switzerland AG.
The registered company address is: Gewerbestrasse 11, 6330 Cham, Switzerland

Foreword

This book reflects an explosive interest in privacy, which, until a few decades ago, was a niche issue too often relegated to the domain of the Luddite and paranoid. Skeptics have suggested that privacy is a newfangled idea, antithetical to other more important, more relevant, and less selfish ethical and political values. I suspect the authors in this impressive volume would disagree, for although the concept and value of privacy have gathered widespread attention only in the past few decades, it's not because privacy is a recent idea. Instead, like clean air and untainted drinking water, the value of privacy to human life and healthy societies is now acutely acknowledged as, increasingly, it has come under siege and we are reckoning with the dire consequences of its loss. Privacy threatened by careless and exploitative, if not venal, human and corporate industry, abetted by a veil of regulatory neglect, has also lacked the illumination of a coordinated body of scientific research. This book marks an ambitious reversal.

There was a time, not so long ago, when someone entering the field of privacy research could reasonably take in the entire state of the art. The methods and disciplinary approaches were diverse, to be sure, including philosophical, sociological, policy, and law, but the work was sparse, a large tract of land holding only a few buildings. By contrast, this tract of land now holds a vast metropolis. Leading conferences in computer and information science include burgeoning sections devoted to privacy, the leading law and policy conferences can no longer accommodate all comers, and conferences dedicated to privacy have rapidly achieved enviable rejection rates (a poignant sign of success). The greatest burgeoning of work, to my eye, has occurred, generally, in areas of empirical social, cognitive, and behavioral sciences, much of it spurred by imperatives of design and usability, in academia as well as industry. If we are to situate this book somewhere in the disciplinary space, these would be its coordinates.

A single volume, however, even as capacious as this one, cannot provide a sampling of all that is important. Accordingly, the review style of many of the articles is useful for anyone wishing a bird's-eye view of key areas of work. Many of us, tired of uninformed challenges—"Young people don't care about privacy!" or "Privacy is not universally valued!"—will particularly appreciate the volume's review of privacy across cultures, and privacy in adolescence, which meet these challenges head-on. Similarly, readers will be pleased to see well-documented articles on tracking technologies, such as Internet of Things, and the privacy implications of personalization, one among a growing set of mind-boggling, data-intensive practices that simultaneously are exciting and sinister. They will find it useful to read articles about privacy for people with special needs—the disabled and vulnerable—and people in special circumstances, such as healthcare. In search of insight into the past and ongoing work in the revealing work on privacy in behavioral economics, which has had a significant impact on the making of policy around the globe, they will not be disappointed.

"Privacy Frameworks," the first substantive chapter, held my attention. It offers a grand sweep of the conceptions of privacy that explicitly or implicitly lie behind the privacy research represented in this volume and beyond. The chapter is not judgmental: it seeks to portray the different conceptions of privacy as different perspectives, different ways of focusing, different approaches united, however, toward a common end. While admiring the scope and inclusivity of this chapter, my own view is less sanguine. In my view, not all of these conceptions and approaches can play nicely together; they are not all mutually compatible. Some will have to give way to others if the field of privacy research is to develop and mature into greater coherence and exert more power on the normative and regulatory stage. The beauty of this volume is not that it is the last word on this critical journey toward coherence and efficacy but that it sets a definitive course toward it.

One of the most valuable contributions of this volume, in my view, is the framework around which the articles and reviews are organized—Theory and Methods, Domains, Audiences, and Moving Forward. Obviously, any cut through the complex metropolis of privacy research is going to raise questions about edge cases, intersectionality, fuzzy borders, and proverbial misfits. Despite exposing themselves to these hazards, placing a distinctive stamp on their structuration of the field, the volume editors reveal a well-deserved confidence based on their respective research accomplishments, their long-standing participation in and contribution to the disparate professional communities—in academia and industry—represented by the works in this volume, and an abiding passion, collectively, for seeing beyond their individual positioning within the metropolis of privacy research.

Insistence on seeing beyond, and in between silos that already have sprung up in this relatively new field, is a hallmark of this volume, reflected in articles that readers might not expect in a book primarily devoted to the empirical social sciences of privacy design and usability. I refer to articles on the relevance of the European Union's General Data Protection Regulation to creation of digital systems; privacy's value beyond the individual, not always recognized even by staunch defenders; and distinctive ethical challenges confronting those who pursue empirical studies of privacy. Those who know my work will not be surprised to learn that I particularly welcomed the chapter on contextual integrity and privacy norms. Acknowledging norms imparts gravitas to privacy, which frequently is relegated to the status of taste: "I like chocolate, you like vanilla." Tastes may be accommodated, but they are not guaranteed. Norms, especially ethical norms, may embody a great deal of wisdom;

they may reveal majority expectations and settled accommodations among warring interests, but they may also reveal oppressive victories of some interests over others. They tell of the past and potentially serve as a guide to the future—if only we would pay attention!

Information Science Department   Helen Nissenbaum
Cornell Tech, New York, USA
June 29, 2021

Acknowledgement

Co-editor Knijnenburg was partially supported by Department of Defense award W911QY-16-C-0105. Co-editor Wisniewski was partially supported by the U.S. National Science Foundation under grants #IIP-1827700 and #IIS-1844881 and by the William T. Grant Foundation grant #187941. Any opinions, findings, and conclusions or recommendations expressed in this material are those of the authors/editors and do not necessarily reflect the views of the research sponsors.

Contents

Chapter 1
Introduction and Overview

Bart P. Knijnenburg, Xinru Page, Pamela Wisniewski,
Heather Richter Lipford, Nicholas Proferes, and Jennifer Romano

Abstract This chapter introduces the book *Modern Socio-Technical Perspectives on Privacy*. The book informs academic researchers and industry professionals about the socio-technical privacy challenges related to modern networked technologies. This chapter provides a working definition of privacy, describes the envisioned audiences of this book, and summarizes the key aspects covered in each chapter. The chapter concludes with an invitation to join our community of privacy researchers and practitioners at modern-privacy.org.

B. P. Knijnenburg (✉)
School of Computing, Clemson University, Clemson, SC, USA
e-mail: bartk@clemson.edu

X. Page
Brigham Young University, Provo, UT, USA
e-mail: xinru@cs.byu.edu

P. Wisniewski
College of Engineering and Computer Science, University of Central Florida, Orlando, FL, USA
e-mail: pamela.wisniewski@ucf.edu

H. R. Lipford
College of Computing and Informatics, UNC Charlotte, Charlotte, NC, USA
e-mail: richter@uncc.edu

N. Proferes
School of Social and Behavioral Sciences, Arizona State University, Tempe, AZ, USA
e-mail: nicholas.proferes@asu.edu

J. Romano
Google, New York City, NY, USA
e-mail: jennifer@romanocog.com

© The Author(s) 2022
B. P. Knijnenburg et al. (eds.), *Modern Socio-Technical Perspectives on Privacy*,
https://doi.org/10.1007/978-3-030-82786-1_1

1.1 Introduction

Privacy issues are intricately tied to real-world implementations of modern online systems, with many users lamenting a lack of understanding about and control over the personal data collected by online entities [1]. Academics and industry professionals who wish to address these issues must familiarize themselves with the various socio-technical aspects of privacy that affect the user experience of modern networked technologies. This book gives researchers and professionals a foundational understanding of online privacy as well as insight into the issues that are most pertinent to modern information systems, covering several modern topics (e.g., privacy in social media, IoT) and underexplored areas (e.g., privacy accessibility, privacy for vulnerable populations, cross-cultural privacy). It draws upon the latest works by authors in the networked privacy research community (c.f., [2–7]), which is growing quickly as the discourse about and around privacy is becoming increasingly prominent in academia and in the public.

The consensus among this research community is that the term "privacy" is complex, misunderstood, and often misused in empirical human-computer interaction (HCI) research as well as in public discourse [8]. Thus, this introductory chapter starts by exploring the question of "What is Privacy?" With a baseline definition of privacy in place, this chapter then provides a description of the structure of the book, highlighting the key takeaways of each chapter in the context of this volume as a whole. We conclude this chapter with an invitation to join our growing community of researchers and professionals seeking to address the privacy challenges that lie ahead.

Who should read this book? While we purposefully present this book as an academic text, with arguments backed up by a vast and carefully cited body of academic literature, it was written and compiled with the explicit aim of bridging the divide between academia and practice. As such, our primary goal is to inform IT students, researchers, and professionals about both the fundamentals of online privacy and the issues that are most pertinent to modern information systems. It consists of short chapters that provide an overview on each topic and gives concrete advice for researchers and practitioners. Particularly, we envision the following audiences:

- **Teachers of undergraduate IT students** can assign (parts of) this book for a "professional issues" course or assign specific chapters in the "domains" section as part of a course on said domains (e.g., IoT, social media, healthcare, or personalization). We particularly recommend the "Privacy Frameworks" (Chap. 2), as it introduces the various lenses through which privacy can be discussed.
- **IT professionals** are encouraged to select chapters covering domains and audiences relevant to their field of work, as well as the "Moving Forward" chapters that cover ethical and legal aspects. Each chapter contains a number of bullet-point lists that serve as a shortcut to the content presented in the preceding or subsequent section.

- **User researchers in the IT industry** are advised to start with the "Privacy Frameworks" (Chap. 2) and should subsequently focus on those chapters in the "audiences" section that fit their target user profiles. The "Moving Forward" section will help them provide an ethical and legal context to their work, and the final "Bridging Privacy to Practice" (Chap. 19) will help them understand the main privacy-related issues that are currently being discussed in the industry.
- **Academics outside the field of privacy** who are interested in studying privacy or privacy-related topics will likely be most interested in the chapters in the "theory and methods" section of this book, as these chapters cover the most prominent academic approaches to the study of privacy. Their selection of subsequent chapters will depend on their particular area of research.

1.2 What Is Privacy?

There is a wide range of privacy theories and frameworks that approach the topic in different ways. Some classify information types by sensitivity [9, 10], others focus on privacy as awareness and control of information [11], and still others approach it from a state-based perspective where there are different privacy states that affect how we engage with others (e.g., anonymity, intimacy) [12]. Underlying these various approaches are some fundamental differences in how privacy is conceptualized. For instance, much of European law frames privacy as a fundamental human right that must be protected [11]. However, American society often treats privacy as a commodity that can be bought and sold and that can be weighed against other benefits and drawbacks [11]. In terms of benefits, privacy is not only an important right for individuals but also crucial to freedom of speech and democracy [13]. Hand in hand with this debate is whether privacy is a means toward other goals (e.g., creativity, democracy, character development) or whether privacy is a desirable end-state in itself, as assumed in some frameworks where the goal is a state of privacy (e.g., solitude) [14]. There are also more technical definitions of privacy, such as those used for differential privacy, which treats privacy as the level of obfuscation of algorithmically generated noise in data [15]. As one can see, defining privacy is not a simple matter.

Another debate about privacy is whether it is an individual good or a societal good [11]. For instance, interface designers may treat privacy as an individual-level decision, where a user defines what is the right level of privacy by customizing a setting or choosing a permission default [10, 16]. However, recent research recognizes that privacy also serves a societal goal, and more collective conceptualizations of privacy (see Chap. 6) should be used in the design of systems [17, 18]. This leads to tensions between satisfying the desires of an individual versus the needs of groups, or even societies as a whole.

While we have left the authors of each chapter to select their own specific definition of privacy and theoretical lens through which it is studied, we acknowledge that most existing works on socio-technical aspects of privacy employ one of the frameworks that is covered in the "Privacy Frameworks" (Chap. 2) in this book. Fundamentally, we want to make the readers of this book aware of the ephemeral nature of the concept of privacy, specifically the following:

- **Privacy is a complex, multifaceted concept** that has been defined in numerous ways—from legal to normative definitions—that uncover important and differing aspects of networked privacy. Whereas technical definitions of privacy tend to be precise but narrow, the broad and complex nature of privacy is a defining characteristic of the concept as a socio-technical phenomenon.
- **Being aware of different privacy theories and frameworks** is the first step toward advancing modern privacy. Since no single definition can adequately capture every facet of privacy, we have asked the authors of individual chapters to emphasize the theoretical lens through which they view their work. Readers are advised to study the relevant theoretical lenses so as to gain a more fundamental understanding of the presented material.
- **Privacy is contextual**—this is a shared element of all existing privacy theories and frameworks (cf. [19]). Hence, the second step toward advancing modern privacy is to avail oneself of the key concerns in different contexts and the privacy norms and needs for different populations.
- **Being aware of diverse privacy perspectives** can help researchers, practitioners, and policy-makers ensure that they are considering privacy holistically and not unintentionally missing key components.

The remainder of this chapter briefly discusses the broad spectrum of privacy perspectives covered in the rest of this book.

1.3   Privacy Theory and Methods

There is no single theory that covers the concept of privacy as it shapes—and is shaped by—our everyday experiences. The "theory and methods" section of this book therefore covers a range of theoretical lenses through which one can view the concept of privacy. The chapters in this section relate to "modern" privacy phenomena, thus emphasizing its relevance to our digital, networked lives, but they can equally be applied to "real-world" situations (which, of course, rarely escape the influence of the digital world anyway).

"Privacy Frameworks" (Chap. 2) is an overview chapter that demonstrates how research frameworks developed in academia can support privacy research, design, and product development. It covers definitional perspectives on privacy as information disclosure, as interpersonal boundary regulation processes, and as prescriptive reflections on information flows. Furthermore, it explains how privacy can be construed as a design objective or a target for personalization. This chapter is foundational and will help the reader deepen their understanding of subsequent chapters.

"Revisiting APCO" (which stands for Antecedents, Privacy Concerns, and Outcomes) introduces the most prominent perspective on privacy from the field of Information Systems. This model was first developed in a foundational literature review by Smith et al. [20] and later updated by Dinev et al. [21]. The model was specifically developed to theorize how root causes of users' privacy concerns connect to specific behavioral outcomes and actions. The chapter focuses on the model's use in research and its applicability to design processes while simultaneously highlighting the limits of the model in explaining user behavior.

"Privacy and Behavioral Economics" (Chap. 4) examines the different streams of research in the area of judgment and decision-making that attempt to study complex privacy behaviors in different scenarios. It focuses on three themes in this research: (1) individuals' uncertainty about their own preferences and desires in terms of privacy, as well as the uncertainty and difficulty they face in predicting the consequences of particular information disclosures, (2) the context dependence of individuals' privacy concern, and (3) the degree to which privacy concerns are malleable and prone to manipulations by different actors.

"The Development of Privacy Norms" (Chap. 5) presents a social-theoretical perspective on privacy. This chapter examines how what we consider appropriate information flows in any given situation is shaped by particular norms. Privacy norms are socially constructed and evolve over time, particularly as new networked and persistently listening technologies have been introduced into society. The chapter details how we develop, revisit, and negotiate norms around privacy when faced with new technologies.

The final chapter in this section covers "Privacy Beyond the Individual Level" (Chap. 6). Acknowledging that privacy increasingly revolves around the actions of multiple actors, this chapter discusses several contemporary situations where "group privacy" is relevant, such as tagging on social networks, privacy in workplace teams, life logging, and AI-based inference technologies. The chapter details the dynamics of the multi-stakeholder privacy decisions that occur in these situations, examining potential tensions that exist between the rights and preferences of individual group members or between individuals and the group as a whole. Finally, the chapter outlines tools and other mechanisms that can support collaborative privacy management and group privacy protection.

1.4 Domains

While privacy permeates all aspects of modern life, there are a number of domains in which privacy concerns and implications are particularly salient. The "domains" section of this book covers a number of these domains—some of which are well established, while others are emergent. We want to emphasize that these domains (and their privacy implications) are continually evolving and that the emergence of novel socio-technical domains is a regular occasion. Hence, we advise readers to treat these chapters as introductions to their respective topic areas and encourage them to conduct a subsequent investigation into the state of the art.

"Social Media Privacy" (Chap. 7) describes various types of social privacy concerns, covering public versus private information disclosure, imagined audiences and context collapse, self-presentation and impression management, and issues of availability and physical access. Furthermore, the chapter explains how social media users regulate different interpersonal boundaries on social media: relationship (regulating appropriate interactions with others based on relationship type), network (who is in my network), territorial (where content can be posted), disclosure (what information is shared), and interactional boundaries (what social interactions are acceptable). The chapter emphasizes the importance of designing social media with individual differences between users in mind and ends by pointing out the negative consequences of not addressing social media users' privacy concerns.

The chapter on "Privacy Enhancing Technologies" (Chap. 8) covers technological solutions that can prevent or limit privacy violations. It covers protocols that can be used to secure communication channels (secure messaging, email, and HTTPS), authenticate data access (two-factor authentication), and anonymize our interactions on the Internet (Tor). It presents existing work from the usable security community describing users' issues with these technologies and outlines research directions to help improve their usability and support their adoption.

"Tracking and Personalization" (Chap. 9) are at the heart of many modern mobile and online experiences. This chapter covers the various uses of personalization— ranging from recommender systems and intelligent user interfaces to user-tailored and context-aware advertisements—and discusses how user tracking powers these use cases. It then covers the downsides of user tracking and the various ways in which companies can misuse tracking to infer private information about users and/or engage in price discrimination or invasive advertising practices. The chapter concludes with a discussion of recent and potential future work to improve the balance between personalization benefits and concerns about tracking. This includes practical considerations around state-of-the-art privacy-preserving personalization practices for system developers willing to strike this balance.

The chapter on "Healthcare Privacy" (Chap. 10) describes sources of privacy threats that have accompanied digitization of healthcare. It emphasizes the complex environment in which health information is shared, involving practitioners, labs, clinics, hospitals, medical organizations, health insurance companies, as well as the patients themselves and their family members. It also notes how health information is often dispersed, not only in official health records repositories but on mobile devices, as it is transferred to different stakeholders and even shared on personal or public social media and online forums. The chapter describes a range of applicable policies and legal regulations, including HIPAA, and the type and location of data that is regulated under these various policies. It acknowledges an important deficiency of existing policies: they regulate neither the data collected by health monitoring and fitness sensors nor the data that is shared via social media, online communities, and mobile apps. The chapter highlights genetic data as a novel area that is not well regulated, especially given that it is difficult to anticipate the privacy issues that may arise from such data. Throughout the chapter, the reader will find practical recommendations, tailored to different stakeholders, touching on how to share information appropriately using adequate technical protections.

The "domains" section ends with a chapter on "Privacy and the Internet of Things (IoT)" (Chap. 11). It covers household IoT (smarthomes), public IoT (smart cities, smart buildings, and self-driving cars), and wearable IoT (fitness trackers, smartwatches). It covers how these technologies are used for security and safety, remote access and automation, resource management, wellness monitoring, and entertainment. It subsequently covers the main problems that particularly apply to (or are particularly prominent in) the IoT domain. Particularly, it discusses the fact that many IoT systems operate outside the user's awareness, making privacy issues less salient. Moreover, most IoT devices give those who are being observed by them little (household/wearable IoT) or no (public IoT) control over their privacy settings. Even when such settings are available, interacting with them is particularly difficult due to the lack of a visible interface. Aside from this, the active presence of IoT devices intrudes upon our daily lives and may alter our behavior, and their always-on nature means that they accumulate a lot of data that can be used to make far-reaching inferences about the user and/or be vulnerable to hackers. Finally, the chapter acknowledges that IoT systems may reveal personal information to its multiple users (e.g., households) and that they may face difficulties in reconciling the privacy preferences of their multiple users.

1.5 Audiences

Recurring privacy surveys that started in the early 1980s have consistently found a substantial diversity in privacy concerns and behaviors across the population [12]. Taking this diversity of concerns and practices into account is a major challenge for corporations that wish to respect the privacy preferences of the audiences that use their platforms or services. The "audiences" section of this book highlights audiences that have traditionally been ignored when creating privacy-preserving experiences: people from other (non-Western) cultures, people with accessibility needs, adolescents, and people who are underrepresented in terms of their race, class, gender or sexual identity, religion, or some combination.

The first chapter in this section covers "Cross-Cultural Privacy Differences" (Chap. 12). The increasingly global nature of social networking sites as well as the broader information economy has revealed an urgent need to study how users in different cultures manage their privacy differently. This chapter offers practical tips that can inform the privacy design for technologies that are used globally. The chapter highlights important differences in privacy decision-making between people in individualistic cultures and collectivistic cultures and makes recommendations for global social networks and global e-commerce companies based on these differences. Regarding social networks, the chapter recommends investing more effort to support collective privacy management in collectivistic countries, differentiating mechanisms for audience control in different cultures, providing users more privacy support to protect others' privacy in collectivistic countries, and emphasizing mechanisms to support individual privacy in individualistic countries. Regarding e-commerce, the chapter recommends customizing data collection strategies and enabling different options to control personal data flow in different countries, as well as differentiating relationships between privacy perceptions and privacy decisions.

The chapter on "Accessible Privacy" (Chap. 13) focuses on the intersection of accessibility and privacy, paying particular attention to the privacy needs and challenges of people with disabilities. The chapter opens by acknowledging that people with disabilities face heightened challenges in managing their privacy. For example, people with visual impairments are more vulnerable to shoulder surfing and aural eavesdropping. Moreover, their use of assistive technologies and their need to ask others for help (in person or virtually) open them up to additional vulnerabilities. The chapter further covers how existing end-user privacy tools (e.g., CAPTCHA, authentication tools) are often inaccessible to people with disabilities, making them more vulnerable to privacy threats. In response, the chapter calls for design guidelines that support the creation of more accessible privacy tools and addresses how such guidelines should incorporate the variances among users with disabilities.

The chapter on "Privacy in Adolescence" (Chap. 14) covers the unique developmental life stage where teens transition between childhood and emerging adulthood, distancing themselves from their parents. It acknowledges that teenage years are characterized by increased sociality and peer pressure, the need for more autonomy and privacy, as well as heightened risk-seeking behaviors. The chapter addresses how existing tools for monitoring teens online are heavily focused on parental control, using authoritarian restriction and privacy-invasive monitoring that negate the developmental needs of teens. It emphasizes that the fallacy of these tools is that they assume that teens do not care about privacy. The chapter subsequently outlines how, instead, teens' strategies are often just different from adults' privacy management strategies, requiring a different set of tools that support teen self-regulation. In particular, such tools should emphasize collaborative practices and open communication within families and give teens some leeway to make mistakes, learn from them, and be able to recover.

The final chapter in the "audiences" section covers "Privacy and Vulnerable Populations" (Chap. 15), which are defined as groups of individuals who are more susceptible to privacy violations because of their race, class, gender or sexual identity, religion, or other intersectional characteristics or circumstances. This chapter explores the role that social norms play in shaping privacy theory and how this can disadvantage members of vulnerable populations. It also covers how technologies exacerbate existing inequalities, including in terms of privacy. The chapter outlines what the specific privacy concerns and needs of certain vulnerable populations might encompass and proposes intersectional approaches to some of the biggest challenges for vulnerable communities. Finally, it explains how technologists can identify and incorporate vulnerable populations into requirements-gathering, testing, and policy-making, including a thought experiment to help guide readers as they consider how to incorporate vulnerable users into their design process.

1.6 Moving Forward

In the "Moving Forward" section of this book, we take a higher-level, systemic perspective on the field of privacy. The chapters in this section outline approaches to privacy that move beyond one-size-fits-all solutions, explore ethical considerations, and describe the regulatory landscape that governs privacy through laws and policies. Perhaps even more so than the other chapters in this book, the chapters in this section are forward-looking, in that they use current personalized, ethical, and legal approaches as a starting point for potentially groundbreaking reconceptualizations of privacy to serve the modern technological landscape. The section ends with a chapter that is the product of a series of interviews with industry professionals who were asked to comment upon the topics covered in this book.

The chapter on "User-Tailored Privacy" (Chap. 16) describes an approach to privacy that provides adaptive privacy decision support that fits the preferences and concerns of each individual user. This chapter outlines the measure-model-adapt framework that underlies user-tailored privacy. The chapter acknowledges that the plurality and multidimensionality of people's privacy decision-making practices can only be captured via direct observation of their behaviors or via inference from their attitudes. It outlines how, depending on the situation, a user-tailored privacy system can automate people's existing privacy practices, recommend complementary practices, or aim to move people beyond their current practices. It highlights opportunities for personalization that exist in adapting the privacy settings of an application, the means of justifying certain information requests, the interface for setting one's privacy settings, or the tracking and personalization practices that the application employs.

The second chapter in this section is titled "The Ethics of Privacy in Research and Design: Principles, Practices, and Potential" (Chap. 17). The chapter starts with a retrospective on the past 50 years of privacy research, in which privacy contexts expanded from the individual to Internet, interdependence, intelligences, and artificiality. It discusses how each expansion has broadened the field of ethical concerns. The chapter then introduces a principlist framework to guide ethical decision-making and uses this framework to assess the challenges posed by several emerging technologies from the perspective of five ethical principles: autonomy, justice, nonmaleficence, beneficence, and explicability. The chapter ends by identifying a number of resources that codify the reasoning outcomes of ethics, including technical standards, codes of conduct, curricular programs, and statements of principles.

The next chapter complements this perspective with a policy analysis. Titled "EU GDPR: Towards a Regulatory Initiative for Deploying a Private Digital Era" (Chap. 18), it examines the global privacy policy landscape, with a particular focus on Europe's General Data Protection Regulation (GDPR). The chapter both explains the GDPR, its evolution from previous EU privacy policies and standards, what the law requires of companies, and how it is becoming a "gold standard" globally for privacy regulation. The chapter concludes by examining other national policies which are modeled on some of the key requirements of the GDPR.

Our book concludes with a chapter titled "Reflections: Bringing Privacy to Practice" (Chap. 19). This chapter reflects on the topics covered in this book from the perspective of a number of industry professionals who were interviewed on these topics. The chapter indicates how industry researchers can benefit from academic research—specifically its longer-term perspective and its opportunity to study a broader population. Conversely, it highlights how academic researchers can look toward industry researchers to find potential areas of impact and to verify theories with a large sample in an ecologically valid setting. At the same time, the chapter acknowledges that the timelines of academic and industry research often do not match and that there are several legal and ethical barriers that preclude the sharing of industry data with academic partners. The chapter ends on a call to action, encouraging academic and industry researchers to engage in collaborative events and projects to share research ideas, outcomes, and best practices.

1.7   Conclusion

In line with the final chapter's call to action, we end the current chapter with an invitation to join the community of editors, authors, and readers of this book at modern-privacy.org. On this Web site, we track research publications related to the topics of this book, maintain useful resources related to privacy-enhancing design, and announce upcoming events that connect privacy researchers across industry and academia. Through this site, we aim to connect you to the growing community of researchers and professionals seeking to address the privacy challenges that lie ahead. We hope that you enjoy this book and look forward to your participation!

References

1. Auxier, Brooke, Rainie Lee, Monica Anderson, Andrew Perrin, Madhu Kumar, and Erica Turner. 2019. *Americans and Privacy: Concerned, Confused and Feeling Lack of Control Over Their Personal Information.* Pew Research Center.
2. Ayalon, Oshrat, and Eran Toch. 2017. Not even past: Information aging and temporal privacy in online social networks. *Human Computer Interaction* 32 (2): 73–102.
3. Lampinen, Airi, Fred Stutzman, and Markus Bylund. 2011. Privacy for a networked world: Bridging theory and design. In *CHI'11 Extended Abstracts on Human Factors in Computing Systems*, ACM, 2441–2444.
4. Lipford, Heather Richter, Pamela J. Wisniewski, Cliff Lampe, Lorraine Kisselburgh, and Kelly Caine. 2012. Reconciling privacy with social media. In *Proceedings of the ACM 2012 conference on Computer Supported Cooperative Work Companion*, ACM, 19–20.
5. Stark, Luke, Jen King, Xinru Page, et al. 2016. Bridging the gap between privacy by design and privacy in practice. In *Proceedings of the 2016 CHI Conference Extended Abstracts on Human Factors in Computing Systems*, ACM, 3415–3422.
6. Vitak, Jessica, Pamela Wisniewski, Xinru Page, et al. 2015. The future of networked privacy: Challenges and opportunities. In *Proceedings of the 18th ACM Conference Companion on Computer Supported Cooperative Work & Social Computing*, ACM, 267–272.

7. Wilkinson, Daricia, Moses Namara, Karla Badillo-Urquiola, et al. 2018. Moving beyond a "One-size Fits All": Exploring individual differences in privacy. In *Extended Abstracts of the 2018 CHI Conference on Human Factors in Computing Systems*, ACM, W16:1–W16:8.

8. Barkhuus, Louise. 2012. The mismeasurement of privacy: Using contextual integrity to reconsider privacy in HCI. In *Proceedings of the 2012 ACM annual conference on Human Factors in Computing Systems*, ACM, 367–376.

9. Ackerman, Mark S., Lorrie Faith Cranor, and Joseph Reagle. 1999. Privacy in e-commerce: Examining user scenarios and privacy preferences. In *Proceedings of the 1st ACM conference on electronic commerce*, ACM Press, 1–8.

10. Pamela Wisniewski, A. K. M., Najmul Islam, Bart P. Knijnenburg, and Sameer Patil. 2015. Give social network users the privacy they want. In *Proceedings of the 18th ACM Conference on Computer Supported Cooperative Work & Social Computing*, ACM, 1427–1441.

11. Solove, Daniel J. 2008. *Understanding Privacy*. Cambridge, MA: Harvard University Press.

12. Westin, Alan F. 1967. *Privacy and Freedom*. New York, NY: Atheneum.

13. Solove, Daniel J. 2007. "I've Got Nothing to Hide" and other misunderstandings of privacy. *San Diego Law Review* 44: 745.

14. ———. 2006. A taxonomy of privacy. *University of Pennsylvania Law Review* 154 (3): 477–564.

15. Dwork, Cynthia, and Aaron Roth. 2014. The algorithmic foundations of differential privacy. *Foundations and Trends® in Theoretical Computer Science* 9 (3–4): 211–407.

16. Wisniewski, Pamela J., Bart P. Knijnenburg, and Heather Richter Lipford. 2017. Making privacy personal: Profiling social network users to inform privacy education and nudging. *International Journal of Human-Computer Studies* 98: 95–108.

17. Dourish, Paul, and Ken Anderson. 2006. Collective information practice: Emploring privacy and security as social and cultural phenomena. *Human Computer Interaction* 21 (3): 319–342.

18. Jia, Haiyan, and Xu. Heng. 2016. Measuring individuals' concerns over collective privacy on social networking sites. *Cyberpsychology: Journal of Psychosocial Research on Cyberspace* 10: 1.

19. Nissenbaum, Helen. 2009. *Privacy in Context: Technology, Policy, and the Integrity of Social Life*. Stanford, CA: Stanford Law Books.

20. Smith, H. Jeff, Sandra J. Milberg, and Sandra J. Burke. 1996. Information privacy: Measuring individuals' concerns about organizational practices. *MIS Quarterly* 20 (2): 167–196.

21. Dinev, Tamara, Allen R. McConnell, and H. Jeff Smith. 2015. Research Commentary—Informing privacy research through information systems, psychology, and behavioral economics: Thinking outside the "APCO" box. *Information Systems Research* 26 (4): 639–655.

Part I
Privacy Theory and Methods

Chapter 2
Privacy Theories and Frameworks

Pamela J. Wisniewski and Xinru Page

Abstract This chapter introduces relevant privacy frameworks from academic literature that can be useful to practitioners and researchers who want to better understand privacy and how to apply it in their own contexts. We retrace the history of how networked privacy research first began by focusing on privacy as information disclosure. Privacy frameworks have since evolved into conceptualizing privacy as a process of interpersonal boundary regulation, appropriate information flows, design-based frameworks, and, finally, user-centered privacy that accounts for individual differences. These frameworks can be used to identify privacy needs and violations, as well as inform design. This chapter provides actionable guidelines for how these different frameworks can be applied in research, design, and product development.

2.1 Introduction

Since privacy is a complex, multifaceted concept, it is unlikely that a single theory or framework can provide the foundation for all privacy research. Yet, a comprehensive understanding of the relevant privacy theories can lead to better connections between research and practice. In this chapter, we provide an overview of some of the most prominent privacy frameworks in the human-computer interaction (HCI) networked privacy literature. One way to solve the problem of the often fragmented and erratic use of the term privacy is to converge on a set of core privacy theories and frameworks that can meaningfully inform our scholarly work and provide a common foundation in which to move our field forward.

P. J. Wisniewski (✉)
Department of Computer Science, University of Central Florida, Orlando, FL, USA
e-mail: pamwis@ucf.edu

X. Page
Brigham Young University, Provo, UT, USA
e-mail: xinrupage@byu.edu

© The Author(s) 2022
B. P. Knijnenburg et al. (eds.), *Modern Socio-Technical Perspectives on Privacy*,
https://doi.org/10.1007/978-3-030-82786-1_2

In this chapter, we provide an overview of the following:

- Privacy as information disclosure
- Privacy as interpersonal boundary regulation
- Privacy as contextual norms
- Privacy as affordances and design
- User-centered privacy and individual differences

By consolidating this knowledge and providing practical guidelines on how to apply these theories, this chapter will also help researchers and practitioners ascertain which privacy theories and/or frameworks may be useful when conducting empirical social computing research in HCI or when attempting to translate this research into practice. In the following sections, we compare and contrast four primary ways in which privacy frameworks have been constructed and studied in the human-computer interaction and computing literature: (1) privacy as information disclosure, (2) privacy as interpersonal boundary regulation, (3) privacy as context and norms, and (4) privacy as design. We present the case that modern privacy research is moving toward more user-centered and proactive approaches, which attempt to consider individual differences (see Chaps. 7 and 16), including the needs of vulnerable populations (see Chap. 15). By applying these frameworks, researchers and practitioners will be more equipped to meet users' privacy needs in an era of intense public scrutiny around networked technologies and privacy protection.

2.2   Privacy as Information Disclosure

Section Highlights

- Before the advent of social media, **networked privacy was viewed as a form of information disclosure** in which individuals control what personal information to withhold from others.
- **Privacy concern** has been studied as a key factor in individuals' information disclosure decisions, and people have been shown to perform a **privacy calculus** to weigh the **benefit versus the cost** of disclosing personal information.
- Yet, **privacy paradox** research has shown that there is often a **disconnect between an individual's privacy concern and their information disclosure behavior**.

Privacy, particularly within the Information Systems (IS) field, is often defined as "the ability of individuals to control when, to what extent, and how information about the self is communicated to others" [1]. Even with the different conceptualizations of privacy, one commonality among many fields is the unilateral emphasis on privacy as it relates to *information disclosures*. Viewing privacy as control over one's information disclosures treats privacy as a somewhat dichotomous boundary between private and public information disclosures [2]. As such, several information privacy models have been developed; a commonality among these frameworks is that the focus has been on privacy as withholding or divulging information [3]. For example, Smith et al. (1996) [4] developed the **concern for information privacy** (CFIP) scale in the context of offline direct marketing. It consisted of 15 items and 4 dimensions: collection, errors, secondary use, and unauthorized access to information. Each dimension represented a privacy concern for a type of information misuse. People differed in their concern for (1) data collection, (2) whether the data was represented faithfully, (3) whether data was used for its originally intended purpose, and (4) if data was used by an unauthorized third party. They used this scale to measure an individual's concern about organizational information privacy practices, as they considered information privacy one of the most important ethical concerns of the information age.

Malhotra et al. (2004) [5] extended this work from organizational contexts to the online world to develop the **Internet users' information privacy concerns** (IUIPC) scale. This scale consisted of three dimensions identified as the most pressing for online privacy concerns: collection, control, and awareness of privacy practices. Anton et al. (2010) [6] provided a more fine-grained version of IUIPC by including access/participation, information collection, information storage, information transfer, notice/awareness, and personalization as additional factors to consider. CFIP and IUIPC have been and continue to be widely used in many studies as a way to characterize privacy concerns. Xu et al. [3] also studied information privacy online and developed their "information boundary theory" by studying privacy attitudes on information disclosure across e-commerce, finance, healthcare, and social networking websites. They found that privacy intrusion, risk, and control were all important factors related to privacy concerns in the context of social networking websites. This provided guidance on the common elements to be considered when studying information privacy across various online contexts.

In 2011, Smith et al. [7] created a comprehensive framework widely used for understanding information privacy research, called the Antecedents-Privacy Concerns-Outcomes model (or "APCO" model; see Chap. 3). It considers not only the privacy concerns that people have but also the antecedents that shape those concerns, as well as the consequences or outcomes of such concerns. Antecedents such as personal traits, contextual factors, regulatory forces, and technology attributes have been connected to increased or decreased privacy concerns [8, 9]. Consequences resulting from privacy concerns include fewer disclosures or reduced technology use [10]. Much of the privacy research in this space unpacks how heightened privacy concerns can adversely affect users' online engagement. In fact, researchers have studied in detail how people translate their privacy appraisals into information disclosure behaviors across multiple domains from retail online consumerism, social networking, to healthcare. In the next section, we introduce this decision-making process, which is called privacy calculus.

2.2.1   Privacy Calculus: Assessing the Benefit vs. Cost of Information Disclosures

When privacy is framed as withholding or disclosing personal information, researchers have found that people often undergo a cost-benefit analysis to make privacy decisions. In other words, they consider the tradeoff between the cost and gain of disclosing their personal information to a particular source, a phenomenon known as "privacy calculus" [11]. This view of privacy decision-making explains how, despite privacy concerns, people may still disclose information if they perceive that the benefits outweigh the risks. Conversely, the absence of privacy concern is not enough to lead to disclosure when there is no perceived benefit. This aligns with a commodity view of privacy where it can be given up for some sort of benefit. Much of the privacy economic research community takes this view on privacy, putting a monetary value on the cost of giving up one's privacy versus a monetary value on the benefits reaped by doing so [12, 13].

Over the past decade, researchers have identified both positive and negative outcomes associated with online personal information disclosures, ranging from how disclosure facilitates access to social support and resources [14–16] to how it may make some users more vulnerable to harassment [17–19]. Much research has focused on how disclosing on social networking sites allows users to gain social capital [16, 20], strengthen their relationships with others [15], improve their well-being [21], and even increase employee performance [22] and innovation [23]. However, there is also research that has uncovered drawbacks of disclosure, including reputational harm, losing one's job, and financial harm [24, 25].

In terms of systematically assessing the drawbacks of information disclosures, there are various types of activities that can pose threats to one's privacy. Most notably, Solove developed a framework consisting of privacy violations that can arise from information disclosure. Solove's **taxonomy of privacy threats** identifies four types of threats [26]. *Information collection* describes threats resulting from collecting sensitive information (e.g., financial or location information) about someone. *Information processing* threats arise from how collected data is used or stored and often can occur when data is used in a way that differs from its originally intended usage. *Information dissemination* threats arise from sharing collected information with others not originally intended to have access to the data. *Invasion*-type threats have to do with disturbing one's solitude or tranquility (e.g., inundating them with too much information or constantly interrupting them).

Another theoretical lens commonly used in information privacy research is **uses and gratification theory** [27, 28]. This theory focuses on user goals and ties user behaviors to those goals. Disclosure is not driven purely by degree of privacy sensitivity; it is rather driven by higher-level motivations of use and the associated privacy concerns that may impact technology use [29]. In fact, different ways of disclosing information often stem from different goals; for instance, posting a status on a Facebook timeline is not the same as sharing through a different mechanism, despite similar capabilities [30]. In practice, people are likely to differ in terms of what kinds of privacy benefits and violations they consider important for themselves. For instance, Page et al. [31] point out that collecting one's location data might unsettle some people but not others. Namely, some users avoid posting information about themselves online because of privacy concerns, while others consider it a matter of convenience to be able to do so [32].

Yet, while individual differences are to be expected, research has uncovered inconsistencies at the individual level, where some claims to be privacy concerned, yet their behavior seems to reflect a lack of this concern [33]. As such, the disconnect between an individual's stated privacy concerns and the privacy calculus people use to make information disclosure decisions gave rise to a new body of research on the privacy paradox, which we cover next.

2.2.2   Privacy Paradox: The Discrepancy Between Users' Privacy Concerns and Information Disclosure Behavior

Studies that have tried to predict users' information disclosure behavior have produced mixed results, often showing an individual's information disclosure behavior does not reflect their stated privacy concerns [13, 34, 35]. This mismatch between stated concerns and actual behavior has been called the "privacy paradox" [34, 36]. This research concludes that users may not always weigh costs and benefits in what one might consider to be a rational way. Some scholars explain how limits on human memory and reasoning capabilities lead to a *bounded rationality*, where people resort to satisficing behaviors and heuristics to make decisions [37]. For example, privacy research shows hyperbolic discounting, where future consequences are not weighted as heavily as immediate gratifications [38]. Research also shows that certain individuals are more likely to rely on heuristics than others [39]. Moreover, while users claim to *want* full control over their data (c.f., [40–48]), they do not actually exploit this control, which also creates a paradox between privacy and control [33, 49].

As user interactions and transactions increasingly move online [50], people must learn how to manage their online privacy, which requires more intentional and explicit disclosure decisions. Indeed, networked social interactions can be much more difficult to navigate when one's audience and social contexts shift often and blur [13, 51]. The nuance of nonverbal and social cues that people have acquired and mastered in offline contexts over the years and the ambiguity and fleeting nature of interactions possible offline give way to explicit online actions and digitized representations [52]. Being able to anticipate audience and subsequent consequence of a disclosure can be extremely challenging and difficult, given the design and properties of online technologies. Thus, people often imagine they are disclosing to a given audience, but this does not match up with the reality of who is privy to that information [40, 53]. This disconnect may partially explain why people's expressed privacy concerns do not always match up with their information disclosure behaviors.

2.2.3 Westin's Privacy Taxonomy: The Classification of Consumers' Privacy Knowledge and Preferences

Many scholars have attempted to classify people based on their information disclosure behaviors and/or preferences. One of the most commonly cited is the **Westin classification of consumers' privacy knowledge and preferences**, which maintains that people can be categorized as *privacy fundamentalists* who highly value protecting their privacy, *privacy pragmatists* who are willing to weigh pros and cons of disclosure, and *privacy unconcerned* who do not value privacy [54–56]. However, these classifications lack empirical support, and recent work has questioned their effectiveness for predicting online behavior [57]. In fact, research shows that classification may need to consider not just the amount of disclosure that one is willing to make but also the type of information that people are willing to share [57, 58]. Furthermore, even types of online activity may differ. Rather than looking just at disclosure, scholars should consider the use of privacy protecting measures, feature use, and type of interactions [30, 59, 60].

As Westin's taxonomy suggests, there are many individual differences that can help explain seemingly paradoxical information disclosure behaviors. Studies have uncovered differences in gender [61–63], age [51], and prior experiences [64] as well as varying social norms [65, 66] and network compositions [67] that shape whether and how people choose to disclose information, leverage privacy features, and manage their privacy. And while people may deal with the context collapse of their many social circles colliding (e.g., boss, friend, and family) by adjusting what they disclose or using privacy features, others may not for fear of harming their relationships [60] or may lack digital literacy to realize the issue or how to fix it, leading to regrets [18, 24, 68]. Researchers continue to identify other individual and group-level factors and social contexts that help explain the privacy paradox [52, 69]. These factors involve understanding social norms and context, as well as viewing privacy behaviors at a dyadic level by honing in on interpersonal relationships [70]. We discuss these approaches in more detail in the sections that follow.

2.3 Privacy as an Interpersonal Boundary Regulation Process

Section Highlights

- Privacy has been conceptualized as a **dialectical process of managing interpersonal boundaries with others**. In other words, it is a dynamic and ongoing process of setting boundaries between, e.g., what is shared or withheld, being accessible or inaccessible to interaction with others, presenting a certain identity and not others.

- **Altman saw boundary regulation as a process of opening and closing oneself to others**, which could lead to a state of social isolation on one extreme or social crowding on the other extreme, when boundary mechanisms did not allow people to achieve their desired level of privacy.
- **Petronio created a framework of communication privacy management**, which is the process of disclosing or withholding personal information. When information is shared, it becomes co-owned by others who then are participants in privacy management.

The networked privacy research community has studied the type of information people share online and the factors that influence what they share [71, 72]. However, privacy is not limited to what people share online. Privacy, as a construct for social contexts, extends beyond information disclosure decisions to a broader range of social interactions that require regulating interpersonal boundaries. It also involves the management of interpersonal boundaries that help regulate users' interactions, both positive and negative [73]. This includes physical and communicative accessibility, emotional and psychological well-being, and reputation and impression management boundaries. As such, scholars have drawn from a broader *social privacy* perspective to explain privacy as a process of boundary regulation. We describe some of the most prominently used theories below.

2.3.1 Altman's Conceptualization of Privacy

Social psychologist Irwin Altman defined privacy as "an **interpersonal boundary process** by which a person or group regulates interaction with others," by altering the degree of openness of the self to others [74]. This process is dialectic in nature, balancing both the restriction and seeking of social interaction with others. Interpersonal boundaries are important because they help users define self, give protection (physically and emotionally), help manage our personal resources, and forge deeper relationships with others [74]. The boundary regulation process allows for feedback and readjustment along with a dynamic need for varying levels of separateness and togetherness. According to Altman, boundary mechanisms are behaviors (e.g., body language, eye contact, physical distance) employed in combination and adjusted over time to achieve one's desired level of privacy. Individuals have different mechanisms for erecting boundaries, and they adjust these mechanisms as their needs change [74].

Although Altman's work on boundary regulation was initially confined to the physical world, it has been used heavily to frame research in privacy in social media [2, 75, 76], which will be covered in more detail in Chap. 7. For instance, Stutzman and Hartzog [75] examined the creation of multiple profiles on social media websites, primarily Facebook, as an information regulation mechanism. They identified three types of boundary regulation within this context: (1) *pseudonymity*, a profile that was fully disassociated from personally identifiable information as to conceal one's identity; (2) *practical obscurity*, an alternate profile created by obscuring some aspect of personally identifiable information to make it harder to find; and (3) *transparent separations*, no attempt to obscure or conceal information but multiple profiles for the sake of practical separation (e.g., personal versus professional) [75]. Lampinen et al. [2] likewise focused on boundary management strategies and created a framework for managing private versus public disclosures. Their framework defined three dimensions by which strategies differed: behavioral vs. mental, individual vs. collaborative, and preventative vs. corrective. For instance, a preventative strategy would be sharing content to a limited audience, while a corrective strategy would be deleting content after the fact. Wisniewski et al. [77] also built upon Altman's theory to empirically show how different social media users have different privacy management strategies (which they refer to as "profiles") on Facebook. A user's privacy strategy related to their awareness of the privacy settings and features available to manage privacy desires. The concept of creating privacy profiles for user-tailored privacy will be covered in more depth in Chap. 16.

Most notably, Palen and Dourish [78] explain how extending Altman's work to the networked world manifests in more than the boundary regulation of disclosures. It also manifests as other privacy boundaries, such as identity (i.e., choosing who you appear as to others and how you behave toward them) and temporality (i.e., the persistence of content and performing actions based on perceptions of the past or future). Furthermore, while disclosing or withholding information is commonly recognized as a privacy boundary that, respectively, lowers or increases privacy, the authors point out that each of these mechanisms can serve the opposite privacy goal. For example, disclosing information can actually serve to increase privacy. Posting information might be a way to prevent people from asking for the information and protect the discloser from interruptions and a deluge of requests. In the next section, we introduce Petronio's communication privacy management theory, which was an extension of Altman's earlier work.

2.3.2 Petronio's Communication Privacy Management Theory

Building on Altman's conceptualization of privacy, Petronio's **communication privacy management** (CPM) **theory** [79] outlined five suppositions related to disclosure boundaries. First, a boundary exists between private and public information. Second, disclosure privacy deals specifically with the disclosure of private information (as opposed to information that is not considered private). Third, individuals have a sense of ownership or control regarding this private information. Fourth, a rule-based system defines how individuals manage this privacy boundary. Namely, Petronio defines boundary linkages, which are "connections that form boundary alliances" [79]. These are the people who have come to know this private information, whether it be an intentional disclosure or someone overhearing a conversation. The idea of co-ownership deals with the privilege to have joint ownership of one's private information, and permeability deals with "how opened or closed the collective boundaries are once they are formed" [79]. If only a single person knows, the boundary is very thick and less permeable than if many people know, and there is more of a chance of disclosure. Therefore, disclosure boundaries require a coordination process between co-owners of private information. Fifth, this process is dialectical in nature. In other words, Petronio drew from Altman's theory to reiterate that an individual's desire for information privacy may change over time.

CPM also delineated between two different interpersonal boundaries: personal and collective. *Personal boundaries* deal with how one shares private information about one's self, while *collective boundaries* involve private information shared with others. "A boundary is transformed from a personal to a collective when someone self-discloses to a confidant," [79] explained Petronio. Child and Agyeman-Budu [80] applied Petronio's CPM to blogging disclosures made by young adults on websites such as MySpace, Facebook, and LiveJournal. They found that high self-monitoring bloggers displayed more privacy-oriented management practices than bloggers who were low self-monitors, but high self-monitors also tended to blog more often. They further found support that individuals with higher Concern for Appropriateness (CFA), aka cared more about whether they come across appropriately, had more permeable privacy boundaries, so they disclosed in more detail and with higher frequency than bloggers with low CFA [80]. A number of other researchers have extended Petronio's CPM theory into the domain of HCI by trying to design interfaces and create models to help users understand and alleviate collective privacy concerns [81, 82]. For example, Jia and Xu developed the SNS collective privacy concerns (SNSCPC) scale to measure an individual's collective privacy concerns across three dimensions: collective information control, access, and diffusion [82].

In contrast to treating privacy as information disclosure, viewing privacy as a process of interpersonal boundary regulation broadens the conceptualization of privacy to include varying aspects of human behavior. For instance, Wisniewski et al. [69] identified and measured the multidimensional facets of interpersonal privacy preferences for social networking site users. They found that privacy boundaries included self-disclosure decisions but went beyond self-disclosure to also include confidant disclosures (co-owned information shared by others), relationship boundaries (e.g., deciding with whom to connect), network boundaries (e.g., giving others access to one's connections), territorial boundaries (e.g., managing content and interactions across public, semipublic, and private spaces), and interactional boundaries (e.g., the ability to make oneself unavailable to others). Taking this more interpersonal perspective to modern privacy acknowledges that people are inherently social, and privacy must be considered in relation to sociality rather than in isolation.

In the next section, we discuss how researchers have started to embed privacy more fully within social contexts by considering contextual factors beyond information and interpersonal relationships. They also consider how social contexts, norms, and values shape privacy outcomes.

2.4   Privacy as Social Context, Norms, and Values

Section Highlights

- **Nissenbaum's framework of contextual integrity describes privacy as the appropriate flow of information** based on contextual factors, such as social norms.
- **Privacy decisions cannot be made optimally without considering context**, which includes the type of information being shared, the actors involved, and the mechanisms and purpose in which information sharing occurs.
- **Social norms and values are critically important when identifying appropriate information flows** and whether privacy violations are likely to occur.

Most recently, a norm-based theory of privacy has gained traction. Nissenbaum's **contextual integrity** (CI) has been used to identify privacy violations in diverse situations. In fact, the theory recognizes that people interact within a wide variety of contexts, where each context is associated with expectations for who should share what type of information to whom and in what circumstances. Privacy management is a process of negotiating these social norms and assumptions held by the individuals [83].

More specifically, the CI framework defines elements that should be considered in determining or defining privacy violations [84]. First, the *context* (e.g., school, work) is the social space that sets the stage for privacy expectations. Next, there are several *actors* involved, such as the information sender, recipient, and the individual who is the subject of the information. Also relevant is the *type* of the information being shared (e.g., medical, academic records). Finally, there are *transmission principles* which are rules for how the information can be transferred from actor to actor.

Often a change in one element causes privacy expectations to be violated. For example, a school sending a student's parents their academic records through a password-protected parent portal may be appropriate. However, once any of those actors change, there can be problems. If it is a different student's records, or if the recipient is a journalist, these are all privacy violations. Or if the transmission mechanism changes, such as using a publicly accessible website, again a privacy violation occurs. In fact, when we apply this framework to the latest developments in personalized and algorithmically driven technologies, we see that there may be ambiguity and uncertainty about social norms. Sometimes the actor is not human but an autonomous agent acting on behalf of someone or some organizational entity. Considering whether these are appropriate flows of information is crucial when defining how information should flow in a privacy-sensitive way.

In the following sections, we elaborate on how to apply the CI framework when designing new technologies or studying the use of existing ones. It can serve as a set of heuristics that can be used systematically to guide researchers and practitioners toward the elements important to privacy. We first describe how social contexts need to be considered in designing for privacy. Then, we can turn to the privacy norms and human values [84]. Finally, we discuss how to put CI into practice.

2.4.1   Considering Social Contexts

Information sharing and interpretation and interpersonal interaction occur within a broader social context (e.g., at school, doctor's office, at home). These social contexts are what shape and define social life, each consisting of "canonical activities, roles, relationships, norms (or rules), and internal values (goals, ends, purposes)" [84]. The roles and activities that occur at school are different than the ones found in a doctor's office. Thus, sharing one's weight with the doctor will be interpreted and used for different purposes by the physician than if it were disclosed in a class setting with classmates and the teacher. While much past privacy research has emphasized giving users control over their data, the CI framework asserts that people are more interested in *appropriate* information disclosures. Social contexts provide an existing social structure for determining appropriate information sharing (i.e., sharing for what purpose, in what way, and by, to, and about whom). Being able to rely on these social contexts that have shaped our collective expectations of appropriate behavior and information sharing allows people to establish shared expectations around what values are being furthered and thus what is the appropriate behavior. In an educational setting, information sharing and behaviors should be aimed at student growth and learning. In this context, a common technique is identifying mistakes, so that students can learn from these mistakes and demonstrate mastery by the end of the course. This could be contrasted with the workplace value of productivity where the employee may be expected to have a high level of performance and identifying a mistake instead negatively impacts the employee's performance evaluation. Information that serves a helpful purpose in one social context may be harmful in another. Similarly, in a healthcare context, sharing accurate details about patient behavior and health habits may help physicians hone in on a more accurate diagnosis, improving quality of life. Yet, the same information may be considered incriminating in a workplace context if health information can lead to discrimination against those whose are perceived as having less healthy habits. These examples illustrate how social context sets the backdrop for interpreting appropriateness of information sharing. While many social contexts are now facilitated online, such as patient portals in healthcare, we can still draw on those values and norms that are implicit in these social contexts to understand expectations of privacy online.

2.4.2   Identifying Privacy Norms and Human Values in Design

Given a social context, there are privacy norms around who can share what information about whom and with whom and under what circumstances (i.e., when, where, how, for what purpose). All these factors can play a part in determining "appropriate information flows," namely, when it is acceptable to share information. Probing on these various dimensions of who, what, where, when, why, and how can give a fuller picture of privacy norms. For example, a common factor that determines appropriateness is the recipient of information. Medical records shared with one's doctor may be appropriate, while sharing with one's employer may be less so. Other research has found that revealing one's location to people located in the same city may be more acceptable than doing so to those further away [85]. Another important dimension that is relevant to privacy norms is the type of information being shared. For instance, studies have shown that people may worry about inferences made based on their past purchases, web browsing history, or emails [58]. Especially without an understanding of the context in which these behaviors occurred, the information could prove embarrassing when shared with certain audiences [86] or be perceived by an employer in a way that could threaten one's employment. As such, norms around privacy are an important consideration across different contexts, groups, individuals, and cultures.

Understanding the norms that are considered appropriate across different social contexts allows us to identify the expectations that people have established around privacy. However, when introducing new technologies, there may be new factors to consider such as competing values embedded by the technology, new information dissemination mechanisms, and human and nonhuman actors. Online technologies may even create new social contexts or allow disparate ones to converge into one virtual space. This convergence of values and technology capabilities can lead to conflicts between actors and make it difficult to anticipate what the privacy norms should be. Friedman et al.'s value-sensitive design framework identifies how considering different values can uncover these tensions and should be a part of the design process [87]. Value sensitive design is a theoretically grounded approach to systems design that accounts for human values in a principled manner throughout the design process, including conceptual, empirical, and technical investigations. Value sensitive design helps researchers and designs both reflectively identify and proactively embed values that are of moral importance in the design of systems [87].

Privacy norms and values go together. Identifying the appropriate privacy norms involves answering questions around appropriate ways to collect information and what type of data is necessary to support the values of the given social context in a technology-mediated form. Considering the feature capabilities and data format preferences of users is also relevant for uncovering factors that could affect attitudes about appropriateness of information flows. Although users commonly provide systems with feedback about their preferences [88], they may not be able to accurately anticipate and express their data collection preferences [89], given the complexity of understanding how information is collected, stored, processed, and used [90]. To determine appropriate data collection and information flow, starting by observing people's disclosure behaviors [91] can allow designers to discover expectations of appropriate information sharing for a social context. Then, they must work to uphold those expectations in the way the data is handled by the system, being sensitive to the social context and not letting technology capabilities override the values and norms of that context. For instance, one of the values emphasized in healthcare is confidentiality, an underlying principle of the Hippocratic Oath: "I will respect the privacy of my patients, for their problems are not disclosed to me that the world may know" [92]. However, healthcare technologies may have the default values of storing information indefinitely and making it easily accessible to anyone. Thus, the conflicting capabilities and norms around the social context and the medium through which information is conveyed (and recorded) must be reconciled. Designers can decide to respect the norms of the social context and build strict access limitations so that the principle of confidentiality is supported.

Next, we give an example how the framework of CI can be applied in practice.

2.4.3 Applying Contextual Integrity to Practice

Empirical research has shown that people's contextual privacy concerns align well with the CI framework. Wang et al.'s study on drone bystanders' privacy shows that people's privacy concerns about drone usage are highly dependent on context and purpose (e.g., using a drone in a friend's party for personal recording use causes less concerns) [93]. In another example, Ayalon and Toch concluded that users were less willing to share older content on online social networks as a result of norm changes [94]. Yet, some research suggests that the CI framework (as well as other theoretical and conceptual frameworks) is often mentioned within empirical privacy research without a strong integration of the theory [95]. For instance, Badillo-Urquiola et al.'s [38] initial review of the recent HCI literature that invoked CI as a privacy framework found that most of these studies did not deeply engage with CI beyond mentioning it in the background or discussion sections either to motivate or explain their findings.

Figure 2.1 summarizes the key dimensions of contextual integrity, and we use this framework to unpack two examples of how CI could be applied to understand recent privacy violations that surfaced in the news media.

In 2018, Uber and Lyft garnered negative press from news media as some drivers were caught livestreaming their rides over the Internet [96]. By applying the framework of contextual integrity, we can understand why this was considered a violation of privacy and trust. The type of information being shared was a video/audio feed. The actors involved included the passengers (subject), driver (sender), and the public (recipient). The transmission principle involved sending this information without the consent of the subject and for the profit of the recipient. Given that notice and informed consent are often social norms around sharing personal content about an individual, this was clearly a violation of privacy. However, what if the recipient of the information and transmission principle changed, while all other factors remained constant? For instance, if Lyft or Uber (sender) made it standard policy that all drivers post a notice that video recording was implemented for security purposes (transmission principle) and only shared with the security company (recipient) who was contractually hired by the company, the public discourse around this issue would be very different. Instead of outcries about privacy violations, it is possible that Uber or Lyft could have been lauded for their efforts in protecting the physical safety of both drivers and passengers.

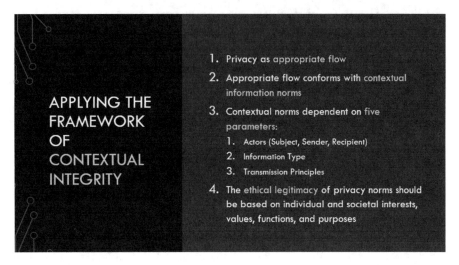

Fig. 2.1 Summary of the framework of contextual integrity

While many of the examples in the previous sections involve data connected to a readily identifiable individual, note that privacy threats still exist even when data is collected from anonymous users [97]. The data can still lead to identification of an individual because of inferences made from the content or the record of the user's social connections [98]. Thus, context is key to the interpretability of any given information, and simply removing typical personal identifiers does not guarantee privacy.

In short, context matters when it comes to the appropriate flow of information. As such, future research could benefit from using CI to inform the design of their study, system, or even their qualitative codebooks. Meanwhile, some researchers have chosen to focus on more tangible elements of privacy, such as design.

2.5 A Privacy Affordance and Design Perspective

Section Highlights

- **Affordances** are perceptions of what the user can do with a technical object, e.g., deleting information or recording a conversation.
- **Privacy expectations** and behaviors are shaped by affordances of technology.
- **Privacy by Design** is a set of principles for translating privacy concepts proactively into the **design of systems**.

The end goal of developing privacy theories and frameworks is often to translate these principles into actionable design guidelines or system specifications that meet end users' needs. Given that networked privacy hails primarily from the HCI research community, privacy affordances and design are two major streams of research that are useful to this end. Unlike the previous frameworks and theories, the affordance and design perspectives focus more on tangible outcomes toward implementation. Therefore, it might be beneficial to apply the former research when conducting formative analyses of users' needs and the approaches below when further down the systems developmental life cycle. In other words, combining these multiple perspectives can both inform what users' needs should be considered, how design can meet these needs, and how systems can be built and deployed in a privacy conscious way.

2.5.1 Privacy Affordances

Several researchers [99–102] have taken an affordance perspective on privacy. **Technological affordances** represent "relationship between a technical object and a specified user (or user group) that identifies what the user may be able to do with the object, given the user's capabilities and goals" (p. 622) [103]. In other words, objects can be used by people in certain ways based on their physical or technical properties. In the offline world, a dial is designed to be turnable and a button pushable, which is perceived by the user and facilitated by the physical properties of the object. Similarly, in the digital realm, technology affordances support certain tasks, such as allowing users to share content with a broader audience at a lower cost than offline. Privacy researchers have started to investigate how the affordances of digital technologies shape privacy behaviors, attitudes, and expectations [104, 105]. Affordances, such as editability and persistence of data, impact privacy practices [102, 106]. Namely, if people can share information online and have the ability later to edit or delete it, then they have the ability to manipulate disclosure on a temporal dimension. Users can share something temporarily and then revoke that access. However, if others can copy that information and save it, then there may never be a guarantee of revocability once information has been shared. All these technology affordances (e.g., editing, deletion, copying, saving) shape user's privacy practices and expectation of privacy.

Research has indeed shown that the affordances of an interface affect people's privacy behaviors. Vitak and Kim [102] revealed how the high visibility of content and its persistence on social media platforms made it much easier to locate content about an individual, prompting people to think harder about making self-disclosures online. In face-to-face conversations and other more ephemeral communication medium, people did not worry as much about information being available after the fact or to as wide of an audience. On the other hand, Trepte et al. [101] found that by introducing the affordance of *association* to social media, they could manipulate users' self-disclosures. By showing that many other similar social media users were self-disclosing, they could increase a user's self-disclosures. This leveraged the principle of association by showing that if people felt others who were similar to them were less privacy concerned, they were also less privacy concerned and more likely to disclose. Introducing features, such as those that enable people to associate with other users, enables new affordances that can shape people's perceptions and subsequently their privacy behaviors. Next, we turn to discuss the proactive practice of Privacy by Design (PbD).

2.5.2 Privacy by Design

While much research has focused on uncovering privacy issues, there has been more effort recently to integrate privacy insights into the design of information systems from the get-go. One set of principles for integrating privacy into design was promoted by Ann Cavoukian, former privacy commissioner of Ontario, Canada. The set of principles and strategies referred to as "Privacy by Design" (PbD) aims to incorporate the value of privacy into the design of systems from beginning to end [40, 95, 107]. PbD engages perspectives from industry, academia, as well as civil society. There has been a lot of work incorporating principles of legal compliance and data protection into requirements engineering, but there is still a need for PbD to provide more concrete guidance on how to design for privacy in the actual design of systems [99]. Indeed, the Federal Trade Commission's 2012 consumer privacy report encouraged companies to utilize PbD, but there was not much guidance for how to address privacy in the design process [40]. Other attempts to incorporate privacy into the design process, such as with privacy-enhancing technologies (PETs) and privacy-preserving technologies (PPTs), have also encountered such challenges and have met with mixed success [38, 42].

The next challenge for PbD to tackle is to make privacy principles and guidelines that can be readily implemented by design practitioners. There has been a widening gap between academic work, which involves identifying theoretical privacy principles, and having a set of principles that are useful at a practical level [41]. One challenge is that privacy design is relevant at all levels of product development, not just at the user-visible interface. The data representation and the protocols used to communicate between different aspects of the system can all have privacy implications. Furthermore, the fast-paced change characteristic of today's technologies makes it difficult to track implications to privacy. The movement toward algorithmic transparency could be a move in the right direction, enabling outsiders to access the way information is processed and how decisions are made. This could be a promising direction to help people understand how the data is being collected, processed, and used.

Designing for privacy is a difficult challenge, but users are demanding more contextual understanding and nuance and the ability to keep certain aspects of their lives separate rather than the trend toward online social contexts all colliding [85, 108]. People are losing trust toward systems which reach beyond the data and responsibilities that are appropriate for their social context, and collecting unnecessary data or encroaching on other life domains [109]. However, in designing to regain user trust in systems, it is important to do so ethically and to make sure the system is supporting appropriate privacy practices that are in the interest of the user.

Masking potentially privacy-invasive data flows just to avoid user alarm would not be in line with the principles of PbD.

In summary, modern privacy perspectives have shifted and matured over time from viewing privacy as a transactional process of information disclosure, to making privacy interpersonal, to viewing privacy as a socially constructed phenomenon that we continually strive to embed in the design of the technologies we use daily. In the next section, we show how this progression has become more human-centered over time and is, what we believe, the future of modern privacy.

2.6   The Future of Modern Privacy: Individual Differences and User-Centered Privacy

Section Highlights

- **Individual** differences play a key role in users' privacy preferences, goals, and outcomes.
- However, individual **differences are rarely accounted for** in the design of systems.
- As modern privacy research advances, **it will be critical to develop solutions that take individual differences into consideration**, so that those who are the most vulnerable to privacy violations are protected.

Modern privacy research is increasingly focusing on applying user-centered principles to privacy research and design, such as helping users achieve a level of privacy relative to their own desires [110, 111]. Because privacy is a complex and highly normative construct [112], individual differences have been shown to play a key role in shaping attitudes related to various privacy concerns (e.g., interactional preferences on social media [113]) and influence subsequent on- or offline behaviors [114]. As such, we discuss why individual differences are important to consider when thinking about privacy and how we might design for them.

Research suggests that privacy preferences vary drastically from individual to individual, can change over time, and are based on context [83]. Individuals also have different privacy preferences that are influenced by contextual factors (e.g., [41, 84, 115]) that significantly affect their privacy decisions and their interaction with others online [41, 107, 116]. An individual's digital privacy behavior and preferences are influenced by personal factors, such as time available [41, 107], recipient [85], age [62, 63], gender [61, 117, 118], personality [119], network compositions [67, 102], social norms [84], culture [115], and previous experiences [108, 120]. Several chapters in this book unpack salient individual differences, including privacy with respect to cross-cultural contexts (Chap. 12), adolescents (Chap. 14), the elderly (Chap. 13), and other vulnerable populations (Chap. 15).

Despite recent research on the importance of individual differences in privacy, this scholarship has yet to make a major impact on product design and software development [121]. The disconnect between academic research and the work of practitioners suggests a need for collaborative conversations to help ensure that research on individual privacy differences is taken into consideration in the design of networked platforms. For example, communication style, which has been a strong predictor of behavior in the offline world, also influences online privacy behaviors. Recent research shows how an "FYI communication style" trait strongly predicts privacy attitudes and resulting behaviors in social media [32]. Generally, privacy behaviors and levels of privacy feature awareness vary among end users along informational boundaries (e.g., what I share), interactional boundaries (e.g., blocking other users or hiding one's online status to avoid unwanted chats on social networks), and territorial boundaries (e.g., untagging posts or photos or deleting unwanted content posted by others on social networks) [69, 73]. Users can therefore be categorized by their disclosure styles, management strategies, and proficiency. However, there is a need to further unpack the most important contributing factors that lead to individual privacy differences, thereby allowing us to better design for them and offer more personalized user privacy support.

While recent privacy research has shown that accounting for individual differences in privacy preferences and behaviors can have a positive impact [122], there is still little work done on designing systems that support these individual differences. Part of the issue is that there is little consensus on which of the individual differences are the ones most influential when it comes to privacy concerns and behaviors [123]. Furthermore, it may not be practical to expect users to fully understand the privacy implications of every action on every technology, given the complexities and many differences between the various systems they use. One promising avenue could be to extend privacy nudging solutions, which prompt users toward more privacy-sensitive behaviors and currently do not yet account for individual differences [124, 125].

Along these lines, a more recent paradigm is that of "user-tailored privacy" [110, 111, 126] (see Chap. 16), which provides nudges (e.g., automatic initial default settings) that are tailored to users' individual differences. In this approach, the user is no longer solely responsible for their own privacy management; instead, an algorithm will support this practice, taking individual differences (e.g., the context, the user's known characteristics, their decision history, and the decision history of like-minded other users) into account. Several researchers have developed "intelligent" privacy designs to meet users' privacy needs in light of their individual differences, but they are yet to be fully utilized in the information systems we use in our daily lives. In the subsequent chapters of this book, we will further unpack modern privacy research that will help future researchers and practitioners achieve these goals.

Next, we will provide actionable guidelines for how existing privacy theories, frameworks, and paradigms can be immediately applied in practice.

2.7   Guidelines for Applying Privacy Frameworks in Practice

Section Highlights

- Identify **framework(s) relevant to the context** of your product.
- **Use the framework to uncover privacy norms and privacy threats**. Take special note of **individual differences** that are relevant to privacy expectations and preferences for your target market.
- **Design affordances into the technology that will support privacy.** Convey those affordances to the user.

Privacy frameworks can help you understand existing and potential networked privacy concerns and violations. But how do you use them? Here is a practical guideline for selecting and applying different frameworks:

Choose a privacy framework that is relevant to your design space. This chapter presented several frameworks describing the concept of privacy. Analyzing your users and their context using a framework can help you uncover potential issues. Or if you start with complaints from users, you could use a framework to reverse-engineer why they might be upset. For example, if your product supports interpersonal communication and interaction between small groups of individuals, it may make sense to draw on communication privacy management theory. The framework could guide you to ask a user (or look for evidence of) the set of people that they feel should be co-owners of their private information. It can also sensitize you to probe on the rules around when it is appropriate for co-owners to share that information. If there is not a clear theory that maps to your design space, a more general framework, such as contextual integrity, can be applied. Analyze user behaviors to understand what people feel comfortable sharing and to whom. This can help you understand the norms of privacy behaviors in your user base. Break your data down by contextual integrity factors, such as data subject and data type. Also take product maturity into consideration. If you are designing something from scratch, privacy by design would be a useful approach. If you are evaluating an existing product, you may want to consider the privacy paradox and not only ask users about their concerns but measure their behaviors to see if those concerns map to behaviors.

Apply the framework in a way that is relevant to the maturity of your product/problem space. If you are exploring a new market or problem space, you may use a framework to guide your research questions at a high level (e.g., what are people's expectations of privacy in this social context). The questions you ask people and the phenomenon you take note of during observations or analysis of materials (e.g., written and digital artifacts) should also be informed by the privacy framework. For example, drawing on privacy calculus would guide you toward probing on both benefits and drawbacks that may be playing into user's decisions. In identifying the pros and cons, you may have a better understanding of the tradeoffs people are making and the relative importance of focusing on one problem over another. If the exploratory research has already been conducted, you can still use the framework to guide your analysis of the situation. It can uncover patterns in situations that are considered privacy violations. If you are designing a solution, you can use the framework to guide your design principles. For instance, focusing on affordances and making sure that your user interface communicates the privacy abilities that you want to communicate to the user is key. It is often important to make sure that the user understands *who* can see *what* and *when* (and even communicating *why* can help users internalize the privacy rules of your product). After you've deployed a product, you can still leverage a framework to evaluate whether user privacy needs are being met or to identify the cause of issues that arise.

Operationalizing the framework. Once you have decided on the framework and how to apply it, you will need to get down to low-level details such as what survey instruments to use to measure the privacy concepts embedded in these frameworks. Research in this area is ongoing, and new instruments, methods, and processes are constantly being developed.

2.8   Chapter Summary

We have given an overview of various conceptualizations of privacy which has guided privacy research. Some frameworks have been heavily utilized in the research community while others have yet to be widely applied but could potentially uncover new insights into how privacy is perceived and enacted. It is important that those researching networked privacy take time to consider how systems, norms, and behaviors may evolve in the future. However, platforms are constantly emerging, restructuring, and disappearing. Users flock from one site to the next, interact across platforms, and may develop distinct or overlapping networks and identities based on their primary goals. The increasingly blurry distinction between public and private spheres further complicates privacy management, with platforms only now beginning to consider solutions to make privacy and disclosure easier to manage. It will only become more important to understand users' mental models of privacy, which shape individual and group behavior around privacy in unexpected and often underappreciated ways. User mental models that understand privacy as control [27], privacy as contextual integrity [21], privacy as an emotional variable [34, 49, 70], privacy as a commodity [15], or privacy as a universal right [68] are just a few possible ways of evaluating privacy needs and explaining concerns and behaviors. Drawing on these privacy conceptualizations can guide researchers, designers, and policymakers even as technologies continually change and social norms evolve.

References

1. Ellison, N.B., J. Vitak, C. Steinfield, R. Gray, and C. Lampe. 2011. Negotiating privacy concerns and social capital needs in a social media environments. In *Privacy Online*, ed. S. Trepte and L. Reinecke, 19–32. Berlin: Springer.

2. Lampinen, Airi, Vilma Lehtinen, Asko Lehmuskallio, and Sakari Tamminen. 2011. We're in it together: Interpersonal management of disclosure in social network services. In *SIGCHI Conference on Human Factors in Computing Systems*: 3217–3226.
3. Xu, Heng, Tamara Dinev, H. Jeff Smith, and Paul Hart. 2008. *Examining the Formation of Individual's Privacy Concerns: Toward an Integrative View.*
4. Smith, H.J., J.S. Milberg, and J.S. Burke. 1996. Information privacy: Measuring individuals' concerns about organizational practices. *MIS Quarterly* 20 (2): 167–196.
5. Malhotra, Naresh K., Sung S. Kim, and James Agarwal. 2004. Internet users' information privacy concerns (IUIPC): The construct, the scale, and a causal model. *Information Systems Research* 15 (4): 336–355.
6. Anton, Annie I., Julia B. Earp, and Jessica D. Young. 2010. How Internet users' privacy concerns have evolved since 2002. *IEEE Security and Privacy* 8 (1): 21–27.
7. Smith, H. Jeff, Tamara Dinev, and Xu. Heng. 2011. Information privacy research: An interdisciplinary review. *MIS Quarterly* 35 (4): 989–1016.
8. Krasnova, Hanna, Natasha F. Veltri, and Oliver Günther. 2012. Self-disclosure and privacy calculus on social networking sites: The role of culture. *Business & Information Systems Engineering* 4 (3): 127–135.
9. Xu, Heng, Hock-Hai Teo, Bernard C.Y. Tan, and Ritu Agarwal. 2012. Research Note—Effects of individual self-protection, industry self-regulation, and government regulation on privacy concerns: A study of location-based services. *Information Systems Research* 23 (4): 1342–1363.
10. Vitak, Jessica. 2012. The impact of context collapse and privacy on social network site disclosures. *Journal of Broadcasting & Electronic Media* 56 (4): 451–470.
11. Laufer, Robert S., and Maxine Wolfe. 2010. Privacy as a concept and a social issue: A multidimensional developmental theory. *Journal of Social Issues* 33 (3): 22–42.
12. Acquisti, A., and J. Grossklags. 2008. What can behavioral economics teach us about privacy? *Digital Privacy: Theory, Technologies, and Practices*: 363–377.
13. Acquisti, Alessandro, and Ralph Gross. 2006. Imagined communities: Awareness, information sharing, and privacy on the Facebook. In *Privacy enhancing technologies*. 36–58.
14. Burke, Moira, and Mike Develin. 2016. Once more with feeling: Supportive responses to social sharing on Facebook. In *Proceedings of the 19th ACM Conference on Computer-Supported Cooperative Work & Social Computing*, Association for Computing Machinery, 1462–1474.
15. Burke, Moira, Robert Kraut, and Cameron Marlow. 2011. Social capital on Facebook: Differentiating uses and users. In *Proceedings of the SIGCHI Conference on Human Factors in Computing Systems*, ACM, 571–580.
16. Ellison, Nicole B., Jessica Vitak, Rebecca Gray, and Cliff Lampe. 2014. Cultivating social resources on social network sites: Facebook relationship maintenance behaviors and their role in social capital processes. *Journal of Computer-Mediated Communication* 19 (4): 855–870.
17. Page, Xinru, Bart P. Knijnenburg, Pamela Wisniewski, and Moses Namara. 2018. Avoiding online harassment: The socially disenfranchised. In *Online Harassment*, ed. J. Golbeck, 243–268. Cham: Springer International Publishing.
18. Page, Xinru, Pamela Wisniewski, Bart P. Knijnenburg, and Moses Namara. 2018. Social media's have-nots: An era of social disenfranchisement. *Internet Research*: 00.
19. Sengupta, Anirban, and Anoshua Chaudhuri. 2014. Simply having a social media profile does not make teens more likely to be bullied online. Demographics and online behavior play a larger role. In *LSE American Politics and Policy*. Retrieved Sept 16, 2016 from http://blogs.lse.ac.uk/usappblog/.
20. Ellison, N.B., C. Steinfield, and C. Lampe. 2007. The benefits of Facebook "Friends:" Social capital and college students' use of online social network sites. *Journal of Computer-Mediated Communication* 12 (4): 1143–1168.
21. Burke, Moira, and Robert E. Kraut. 2016. The relationship between Facebook use and well-being depends on communication type and tie strength. *Journal of Computer-Mediated Communication* 21 (4): 265–281.

22. Kuegler, Maurice, Stefan Smolnik, and Gerald Kane. 2015. What's in IT for employees? Understanding the relationship between use and performance in enterprise social software. *The Journal of Strategic Information Systems* 24 (2): 90–112.
23. Newell, Sue. 2015. Managing knowledge and managing knowledge work: What we know and what the future holds. *Journal of Information Technology*.
24. Wang, Yang, Pedro Giovanni Leon, Xiaoxuan Chen, et al. 2013. From Facebook regrets to Facebook privacy nudges.
25. Wisniewski, Pamela, Heather Lipford, and David Wilson. 2012. Fighting for my space: Coping mechanisms for Sns boundary regulation. In *Proceedings of the SIGCHI Conference on Human Factors in Computing Systems*, ACM, 609–618.
26. Solove, Daniel J. 2006. A taxonomy of privacy. *University of Pennsylvania Law Review* 154 (3): 477–560.
27. Coursaris, Constantinos, Wietske Van Osch, Jieun Sung, and Younghwa Yun. 2013. Disentangling Twitter's adoption and use (dis)continuance: A theoretical and empirical amalgamation of uses and gratifications and diffusion of innovations. *AIS Transactions on Human-Computer Interaction* 5 (1): 57–83.
28. Park, Namsu, Kerk F. Kee, and Sebastián Valenzuela. 2009. Being immersed in social networking environment: Facebook groups, uses and gratifications, and social outcomes. *CyberPsychology & Behavior* 12 (6): 729–733.
29. Sutanto, Juliana, Elia Palme, Chuan-Hoo Tan, and Chee Wei Phang. 2013. Addressing the personalization–privacy paradox: An empirical assessment from a field experiment on smartphone users. *Management Information Systems Quarterly* 37 (4): 1141–1164.
30. Smock, Andrew D., Nicole B. Ellison, Cliff Lampe, and Donghee Yvette Wohn. 2011. Facebook as a toolkit: A uses and gratification approach to unbundling feature use. *Computers in Human Behavior* 27 (6): 2322–2329.
31. Page, Xinru, Alfred Kobsa, and Bart P. Knijnenburg. 2012. Don't disturb my circles! Boundary preservation is at the center of location-sharing concerns. In *Sixth International AAAI Conference on Weblogs and Social Media*.
32. Page, Xinru, Reza Ghaiumy Anaraky, and Bart P. Knijnenburg. 2019. How communication style shapes relationship boundary regulation and social media adoption. In *Proceedings of the 10th International Conference on Social Media and Society*, Association for Computing Machinery, 126–135.
33. Spiekermann, Sarah, Jens Grossklags, and Bettina Berendt. 2001. E-privacy in 2nd generation e-commerce: Privacy preferences versus actual behavior. In *Proceedings of the 3rd ACM conference on Electronic Commerce*, Association for Computing Machinery, 38–47.
34. Barnes, Susan B. 2006. A privacy paradox: Social networking in the United States. *First Monday* 11: 9.
35. Tufekci, Zeynep. 2008. Can you see me now? Audience and disclosure regulation in online social network sites. *Bulletin of Science, Technology & Society* 28 (1): 20–36.
36. Norberg, Patricia A., Daniel R. Horne, and David A. Horne. 2007. The privacy paradox: Personal information disclosure intentions versus behaviors. *Journal of Consumer Affairs* 41 (1): 100–126.
37. Simon, Herbert A. 1990. Bounded rationality. In *Utility and Probability*, ed. J. Eatwell, M. Milgate, and P. Newman, 15–18. London: Palgrave Macmillan UK.
38. Acquisti, Alessandro, and Jens Grossklags. 2006. Privacy and rationality. In K.J. Strandburg and D.S. Raicu, eds., *Privacy and Technologies of Identity: A Cross-Disciplinary Conversation*. Springer US, 15–29.
39. Ghaiumy, Reza, Kaileigh A. Byrne, Pamela Wisniewski, Xinru Page, and Bart P. Knijnenburg. 2021. To disclose or not to disclose: Examining the privacy decision-making processes of older vs. younger adults. In *Proceedings of the 2021 ACM conference on Human Factors in Computing Systems*.
40. Acquisti, Alessandro, and Ralph Gross. 2006. *Imagined Communities: Awareness, Information Sharing, and Privacy on the Facebook*. Berlin: Springer.

41. Benisch, Michael, Patrick Gage Kelley, Norman Sadeh, and Lorrie Faith Cranor. 2011. Capturing location-privacy preferences: Quantifying accuracy and user-burden tradeoffs. *Personal Ubiquitous Computing* 15: 679–694.
42. Brodie, C., C. M. Karat, and J. Karat. 2004. Creating an E-commerce environment where consumers are willing to share personal information. *Designing Personalized User Experiences in eCommerce*: 185–206.
43. Kolter, Jan and Günther Pernul. 2009. *Generating User-Understandable Privacy Preferences.* 299–306.
44. Pavlou, Paul A., Huigang Liang, and Yajiong Xue. 2007. Understanding and mitigating uncertainty in online exchange relationships: A principal-agent perspective. *MIS Quartely* 31 (1): 105–136.
45. Tang, Karen, Jialiu Lin, Jason Hong, Daniel Siewiorek, and Norman Sadeh. 2010. Rethinking Location Sharing: Exploring the Implications of Social-Driven vs. Purpose-Driven Location Sharing. ACM Press, 85–94.
46. Toch, Eran, Justin Cranshaw, Paul Hankes Drielsma, et al. 2010. Empirical Models of Privacy in Location Sharing. ACM Press, 129–138.
47. Wenning, Rigo, and Matthias Schunter. 2006. *The Platform for Privacy Preferences 1.1 (P3P1.1) Specification.* W3C Working Group Note.
48. Xu, H. 2007. *The Effects of Self-Construal and Perceived Control on Privacy Concerns.* Paper 125.
49. Compañó, Ramón, and Wainer Lusoli. 2010. The policy maker's anguish: Regulating personal data behavior between paradoxes and dilemmas. In *Economics of Information Security and Privacy*, ed. T. Moore, D. Pym, and C. Ioannidis, 169–185. New York, NY: Springer US.
50. Smith, Aaron, and Monica Anderson. 2018. Social media use in 2018. *Pew Research Center: Internet, Science & Tech.* Retrieved Sept 16, 2018 from http://www.pewinternet.org/2018/03/01/social-media-use-in-2018/.
51. Marwick, A.E., and D. Boyd. 2014. Networked privacy: How teenagers negotiate context in social media. *New Media & Society* 16 (7): 1051–1067.
52. Wisniewski, Pamela. 2012. *Understanding and Designing for Interactional Privacy Needs Within Social Networking Sites.*
53. Lipford, H. R., A. Besmer, and J. Watson. 2008. *Understanding Privacy Settings in Facebook with an Audience View.*
54. Harris, Louis, Associates, and Alan F Westin. 1997. *Commerce, Communications, and Privacy Online: A National Survey of Computer Users.*
55. Harris, Louis, Alan F Westin, and Associates. 2003. *Consumer Privacy Attitudes: A Major Shift Since 2000 and Why.* Harris Interactive, Inc.
56. Westin, Alan F., Louis Harris, and Associates. 1981. *The Dimensions of Privacy: A National Opinion Research Survey of Attitudes Toward Privacy.* New York: Garland Publishing.
57. Woodruff, Allison, Vasyl Pihur, Sunny Consolvo, Lauren Schmidt, Laura Brandimarte, and Alessandro Acquisti. 2014. Would a privacy fundamentalist sell their DNA for $1000... if nothing bad happened as a result? The Westin categories, behavioral intentions, and consequences.
58. Knijnenburg, Bart P., Alfred Kobsa, and Hongxia Jin. 2013. Dimensionality of information disclosure behavior. *International Journal of Human-Computer Studies* 71: 1144–1162.
59. Joinson, Adam N., Carina Paine, Tom Buchanan, and Ulf-Dietrich Reips. 2008. Measuring self-disclosure online: Blurring and non-response to sensitive items in web-based surveys. *Computers in Human Behavior* 24 (5): 2158–2171.
60. Page, Xinru, Reza Ghaiumy Anaraky, Bart P. Knijnenburg, and Pamela J. Wisniewski. 2019. Pragmatic tool vs. relational hindrance: Exploring why some social media users avoid privacy features. In *Proceedings of the ACM on Human-Computer Interaction* 3, CSCW: 110:1–110:23.
61. Hoy, Mariea Grubbs, and George Milne. 2010. Gender differences in privacy-related measures for young adult Facebook users. *Journal of Interactive Advertising* 10 (2): 28–45.

62. Litt, Eden. 2012. Knock, knock. who's there? The imagined audience. *Journal of Broadcasting & Electronic Media* 56 (3): 330–345.
63. Madden, Mary. 2012. *Privacy Management on Social Media Sites.* Pew Internet & American Life Project, Pew Research Center, Washington, DC.
64. Wang, Yang, Gregory Norcie, Saranga Komanduri, Alessandro Acquisti, Pedro Giovanni Leon, and Lorrie Faith Cranor. 2011. *"I regretted the minute I pressed share": A Qualitative Study of Regrets on Facebook.* ACM, 10:1–10:16.
65. Abaquita, Denielle, Paritosh Bahirat, Karla A. Badillo-Urquiola, and Pamela Wisniewski. 2020. Privacy norms within the internet of things using contextual integrity. In *Companion of the 2020 ACM International Conference on Supporting Group Work*, Association for Computing Machinery, 131–134.
66. Fono, David, and Kate Raynes-Goldie. 2006. Hyperfriendship and beyond: Friends and social norms on LiveJournal. *Internet Research Annual* 4.
67. Vitak, Jessica, and Nicole B. Ellison. 2013. 'There's a network out there you might as well tap': Exploring the benefits of and barriers to exchanging informational and support-based resources on Facebook. *New Media & Society* 15 (2): 243–259.
68. Davis, Katie, David P. Randall, Anthony Ambrose, and Mania Orand. 2015. 'I was bullied too': Stories of bullying and coping in an online community. *Information, Communication & Society* 18 (4): 357–375.
69. Wisniewski, Pamela, A.K.M. Islam, Heather Richter Lipford, and David Wilson. 2016. Framing and measuring multi-dimensional interpersonal privacy preferences of social networking site users. *Communications of the Association for Information Systems* 38: 1.
70. Barkhuus, Louise. 2012. The mismeasurement of privacy: using contextual integrity to reconsider privacy in HCI. In *Proceedings of the SIGCHI Conference on Human Factors in Computing Systems*, ACM 367–376.
71. Hargittai, Eszter, and Alice Marwick. 2016. "What Can I Really Do?" Explaining the privacy paradox with online apathy. *International Journal of Communication* 10: 21.
72. Page, Xinru, and Marco Marabelli. 2017. Changes in social media behavior during life periods of uncertainty. In *Eleventh International AAAI Conference on Web and Social Media*.
73. Karr-Wisniewski, Pamela, David C. Wilson, and Heather Richter-Lipford. 2011. A new social order: Mechanisms for social network site boundary regulation. In *AMCIS 2011 Proceedings*, Paper 101.
74. Altman, I. 1975. *The Environment and Social Behavior: Privacy, Personal Space, Territory, and Crowding.* Monterey, CA: Brooks/Cole Publishing.
75. Stutzman, Fred, and W Hartzog. 2009. *Boundary Regulation in Social Media.*
76. Tufekci, Zeynep. 2008. Can you see me now? Audience and disclosure regulation in online social network sites. *Bulletin of Science, Technology & Society* 28 (1): 20–36.
77. Wisniewski, Pamela J., Bart P. Knijnenburg, and Heather Richter Lipford. 2017. Making privacy personal. *International Journal of Human-Computer Studies* 98 (C): 95–108.
78. Palen, Leysia, and Paul Dourish. 2003. *Unpacking "Privacy" for a Networked World.* ACM, 129–136.
79. Petronio, Sandra Sporbert. 2002. *Boundaries of Privacy: Dialects of Disclosure.* SUNY Press.
80. Child, Jeffrey T., and Esther A. Agyeman-Budu. 2010. Blogging privacy management rule development: The impact of self-monitoring skills, concern for appropriateness, and blogging frequency. *Computers in Human Behavior* 26 (5): 957–963.
81. Dourish, Paul, and Ken Anderson. 2006. Collective Information practice: Exploring privacy and security as social and cultural phenomena. *Human–Computer Interaction* 21 (3): 319–342.
82. Jia, Haiyan, and Xu. Heng. 2016. Measuring individuals' concerns over collective privacy on social networking sites. *Cyberpsychology: Journal of Psychosocial Research on Cyberspace* 10: 1.
83. Nissenbaum, Helen. 2004. Privacy as contextual integrity. *Washington Law Review* 79: 119.

84. ———. 2009. *Privacy in Context: Technology, Policy, and the Integrity of Social Life.* Stanford University Press.
85. Consolvo, Sunny, Ian E. Smith, Tara Matthews, Anthony LaMarca, Jason Tabert, and Pauline Powledge. 2005. Location disclosure to social relations: Why, when, & what people want to share. In *Proceedings of the SIGCHI Conference on Human Factors in Computing Systems,* Association for Computing Machinery, 81–90.
86. Page, Xinru Woo. 2014. *Factors that Influence Adoption and Use of Location-Sharing Social Media.* Retrieved Jan 21, 2021 from http://search.proquest.com/docview/1493902213/abstract/DA0CC637A21947B3PQ/1.
87. Friedman, Batya, Peter H. Kahn, and Alan Borning. 2006. Value sensitive design and information systems. In *Human-Computer Interaction and Management Information Systems: Foundations.* M.E. Sharpe, 348–372.
88. Lerato, Masupha, Omobayo A. Esan, Ashley-Dejo Ebunoluwa, S. M. Ngwira, and Tranos Zuva. 2015. A survey of recommender system feedback techniques, comparison and evaluation metrics. In *2015 International Conference on Computing, Communication and Security (ICCCS),* IEEE, 1–4.
89. Knijnenburg, Bart P., Martijn C. Willemsen, and Stefan Hirtbach. 2010. Receiving recommendations and providing feedback: The user-experience of a recommender system. In *E-Commerce and Web Technologies,* ed. F. Buccafurri and G. Semeraro, 207–216. Berlin: Springer.
90. Knijnenburg, Bart P., Niels J.M. Reijmer, and Martijn C. Willemsen. 2011. Each to his own: How different users call for different interaction methods in recommender systems. In *Proceedings of the fifth ACM conference on Recommender systems,* ACM Press, 141–148.
91. Gardner, Damian, and John Marzillier. 1996. Day to day maintenance of confidentiality: Practices and beliefs of trainee and qualified clinical psychologists in the UK. *Clinical Psychology & Psychotherapy* 3 (1): 35–45.
92. Tyson, Peter. 2001. *The Hippocratic Oath Today — NOVA | PBS.* Retrieved Apr 3, 2018 from http://www.pbs.org/wgbh/nova/body/hippocratic-oath-today.html.
93. Wang, Yang, Huichuan Xia, Yaxing Yao, and Yun Huang. 2016. Flying eyes and hidden controllers: A qualitative study of people's privacy perceptions of civilian drones in the US. *Proceedings on Privacy Enhancing Technologies* 2016 (3): 172–190.
94. Ayalon, Oshrat, and Eran Toch. 2017. Not even past: Information aging and temporal privacy in online social networks. *Human-Computer Interaction* 32 (2): 73–102.
95. Badillo-Urquiola, Karla, Yaxing Yao, Oshrat Ayalon, et al. 2018. Privacy in Context: Critically Engaging with theory to guide privacy research and design. In *Companion of the 2018 ACM Conference on Computer Supported Cooperative Work and Social Computing,* ACM, 425–431.
96. Dakin Andone CNN. Uber and Lyft drop driver for livestreaming passengers on Twitch. *CNN.* Retrieved Feb 20, 2020 from https://www.cnn.com/2018/07/22/us/uber-lyft-driver-recording-passengers/index.html.
97. Narayanan, Arvind, and Edward W. Felten. 2014. *No Silver Bullet: De-identification Still Doesn't Work.*
98. Zheleva, Elena, and Lise Getoor. 2009. To join or not to join: The illusion of privacy in social networks with mixed public and private user profiles. In *Proceedings of the 18th International Conference on World Wide Web,* Association for Computing Machinery, 531–540.
99. Boyd, Danah. 2010. *Social Network Sites as Networked Publics: Affordances, Dynamics, and Implications.* Routledge.
100. Trepte, Sabine. 2020. The social media privacy model: Privacy and communication in the light of social media affordances. *Communication Theory* qtz035.
101. Trepte, Sabine, Michael Scharkow, and Tobias Dienlin. 2020. The privacy calculus contextualized: The influence of affordances. *Computers in Human Behavior* 104.
102. Vitak, Jessica, and Jinyoung Kim. 2014. "You Can't Block People Offline": Examining how Facebook's affordances shape the disclosure process. In *Proceedings of the 17th ACM Conference on Computer Supported Cooperative Work & Social Computing,* ACM, 461–474.

103. Lynne Markus, M., and Mark Silver. 2008. A foundation for the study of IT effects: A new look at DeSanctis and Poole's concepts of structural features and spirit. *Journal of the Association for Information Systems* 9 (10): 609–632.
104. Gibson, James J. 2014. *The Ecological Approach to Visual Perception: Classic Edition*. New York, London: Psychology Press.
105. Leonardi, Paul M. 2011. When flexible routines meet flexible technologies: Affordance, constraint, and the imbrication of human and material agencies. *MIS Quarterly* 35 (1): 147–167.
106. Treem, Jeffrey W., and Paul M. Leonardi. 2013. Social media use in organizations: Exploring the affordances of visibility, editability, persistence, and association. *Annals of the International Communication Association* 36 (1): 143–189.
107. Dong, Cailing, Hongxia Jin, and Bart P. Knijnenburg. 2015. Predicting privacy behavior on online social networks. In *Ninth International AAAI Conference on Web and Social Media*, AAAI Publications, 91–100.
108. Chen, Hongliang, Christopher E. Beaudoin, and Traci Hong. 2016. Protecting oneself online: The effects of negative privacy experiences on privacy protective behaviors. *Journalism & Mass Communication Quarterly* 93 (2): 409–429.
109. Badillo-Urquiola, Karla, Xinru Page, and Pamela Wisniewski. 2018. Literature Review: Examining contextual integrity within human-computer interaction.
110. Knijnenburg, B. P. 2015. *A User-Tailored Approach to Privacy Decision Support*. http://search.proquest.com/docview/1725139739/abstract.
111. Wilkinson, Daricia, Saadhika Sivakumar, David Cherry, et al. 2017. User-tailored privacy by design. In *Proceedings of the Usable Security Mini Conference*, Internet Society.
112. Turkington, Richard C., and Anita L. Allen. 2002. *Privacy Law: Cases and Materials*. West Academic Publishing.
113. Fogel, Joshua, and Elham Nehmad. 2009. Internet social network communities: Risk taking, trust, and privacy concerns. *Computers in Human Behavior* 25 (1): 153–160.
114. Solove, Daniel J. 2008. *Understanding Privacy*. Rochester, NY: Social Science Research Network.
115. Li, Yao, Alfred Kobsa, Bart P. Knijnenburg, and M.H. Carolyn Nguyen. 2017. Cross-cultural privacy prediction. *Proceedings on Privacy Enhancing Technologies* 2: 93–112.
116. Xie, Jierui, Bart Piet Knijnenburg, and Hongxia Jin. 2014. Location sharing privacy preference: Analysis and personalized recommendation. In *Proceedings of the 19th International Conference on Intelligent User Interfaces*, ACM, 189–198.
117. Hargittai, Eszter. 2010. Facebook privacy settings: Who cares? *First Monday*.
118. Sheehan, Kim Bartel. 1999. An investigation of gender differences in on-line privacy concerns and resultant behaviors. *Journal of Interactive Marketing* 13 (4): 24–38.
119. Weiser, Eric B. 2015. # Me: Narcissism and its facets as predictors of selfie-posting frequency. *Personality and Individual Differences* 86: 477–481.
120. Ramokapane, Kopo M., Gaurav Misra, Jose M. Such, and Sören Preibusch. 2021. *Truth or Dare: Understanding and Predicting How Users Lie and Provide Untruthful Data Online*.
121. Rubinstein, Ira S., and Nathaniel Good. 2013. Privacy by design: A counterfactual analysis of google and facebook privacy incidents. *Berkeley Technology Law Journal* 28: 1333–1414.
122. Wilkinson, Daricia, Moses Namara, Karla Badillo-Urquiola, et al. 2018. Moving beyond a "One-size Fits All": Exploring individual differences in privacy. In *Extended Abstracts of the 2018 CHI Conference on Human Factors in Computing Systems*, ACM, W16:1–W16:8.
123. Yao, Mike Z., Ronald E. Rice, and Kier Wallis. 2007. Predicting user concerns about online privacy. *Journal of the Association for Information Science and Technology* 58 (5): 710–722.
124. Wang, Yang, Pedro Giovanni Leon, Kevin Scott, Xiaoxuan Chen, Alessandro Acquisti, and Lorrie Faith Cranor. 2013. Privacy nudges for social media: An exploratory Facebook study. In *Second International Workshop on Privacy and Security in Online Social Media*, 763–770.

125. Wisniewski, Pamela J., Bart P. Knijnenburg, and Heather Richter Lipford. 2017. Making privacy personal: Profiling social network users to inform privacy education and nudging. *International Journal of Human-Computer Studies* 98: 95–108.
126. Knijnenburg, B.P. 2017. Privacy? I Can't Even! Making a case for user-tailored privacy. *IEEE Security Privacy* 15 (4): 62–67.

Chapter 3
Revisiting APCO

Christoph Buck, Tamara Dinev, and Reza Ghaiumy Anaraky

Abstract Imagine that you are a product manager at a software company. When users disclose some information to your product, they can use all the great features you and your team have integrated into the software. Utilizing these features is essential for the success of your product: it makes users satisfied and encourages others to use the software as well. Furthermore, the user and usage data can be used to improve the product and help implementing new features over time. However, since your product collects users' data, you are worried about privacy-related issues. What causes users' privacy concerns, and what are the potential consequences of those concerns? The APCO (**A**ntecedents → **P**rivacy **C**oncerns → **O**utcomes) and enhanced APCO models provide a summary of the current scientific findings related to these questions and present them in a conceptual model. The APCO framework will help practitioners and scholars to bring different privacy-related aspects of a product to their attention and suggests how these aspects can interrelate. Throughout this chapter, we will consider a use case scenario of a fitness tracker application and discuss how APCO applies to this scenario.

3.1 Introduction

In 2011, *Management Information Systems Quarterly (MISQ)* published three papers reviewing literature on privacy—the articles of Li [1], Bélanger and Crossler [2], and Smith et al. [3]—which continue to be regarded as central works of the more

C. Buck (✉)
University of Bayreuth, Bayreuth, Germany
e-mail: christoph.buck@uni-bayreuth.de

T. Dinev
Florida Atlantic University, Boca Raton, FL, USA
e-mail: tdinev@fau.edu

R. G. Anaraky
Clemson University, Clemson, SC, USA
e-mail: rghaium@clemson.edu

© The Author(s) 2022   43
B. P. Knijnenburg et al. (eds.), *Modern Socio-Technical Perspectives on Privacy*,
https://doi.org/10.1007/978-3-030-82786-1_3

recent Information Systems (IS)-driven privacy research. All three publications reviewed existing literature on the basis of a structured literature overview and derived comprehensive research models from it. Their common thread is the identification of privacy concerns as a proxy for measuring privacy and a central construct of current privacy research.

The often cited theoretical review of Smith et al. [3], titled "Information Privacy Research: An Interdisciplinary Review," gained a lot of attention in research and practice. The authors performed an integrated interdisciplinary review of privacy and privacy-related concepts, which included 320 research papers and 128 books [3]. By their work, they proposed a widely discussed framework for information privacy research—the APCO model—which has an intuitive appeal and can be easily understood by researchers and practitioners [4]. The APCO model presents a macro-model of privacy-related concepts and is divided into three main categories: the Antecedents (A), the Privacy Concerns (PC), and the Outcomes (O).

In this chapter, we provide a summary of the conceptualization of privacy and the integrated APCO model, one of the central macro-models in the scientific privacy discourse, as well as its more recent derivatives such as in Dinev et al. [5]. We discuss practical relevance and future opportunities in the post-APCO research landscape.

3.2   The APCO Model

As a result of an integrated interdisciplinary review of privacy and privacy-related concepts, Smith et al. [3] proposed the so-called APCO model—a framework for information privacy research—shown in Fig. 3.1.

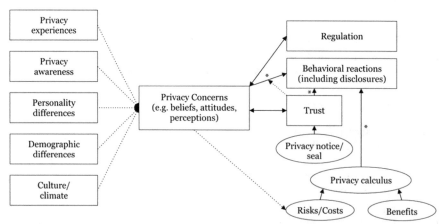

Dotted lines indicate that the relationship is tenuous (i.e, has not been confrimed through repeated studies).

Not shown: Possible two-way loop, in which some actions on the right may impact some constructs on the left.

*Results threatened by privacy paradox, since usually intentions (not behaviors) have been measured.

Fig. 3.1 APCO model [3]

APCO unifies information privacy literature by incorporating predominant variables used in different studies beginning with privacy concerns, the most commonly studied variable in the field. Although not as a steadfast rule [6, 7], most privacy studies suggest a negative relationship between privacy concerns and behavioral outcomes (**Privacy Concerns** → **Outcomes**). When considering the use of a fitness app, high privacy concerns can prevent users from disclosing their data or even using the application altogether. Privacy concern, itself, is shown to be a function of personal and situational cues [8]. In the APCO model, Smith et al. [3] categorize these cues as different antecedents and mark them as independent variables predicting privacy concerns (**Antecedents** → **Privacy Concerns**). In addition, APCO also discusses trust and privacy calculus as two established predictors of privacy-behavioral outcomes.

3.2.1 The Antecedents of Privacy Concerns

Investigations of the antecedents of privacy concerns have been studied in a somewhat disjointed manner and were rarely replicated in research studies until today. The existing research today suggests that privacy concerns are influenced by the following factors:

- **Privacy experiences:** Negative privacy experiences can lead to an increase in privacy concerns [4, 9]. Thereby, if users of our fitness app had previously fallen prey to a hacker attack or a phishing attack, even if this occurred within *other* apps, they are expected to have higher levels of concern.
- **Privacy awareness:** Users' knowledge about organizational privacy practices is referred to as privacy awareness [10]. Awareness particularly increases concerns when users learn that the company used their personal data without their consent [11]. If users of our fitness tracking app know that their vital signs are being stored and sent to their physician prior to data collection, it will likely not affect their concerns [12]. However, if this data sharing initially occurs outside of their awareness, and they suddenly receive a feedback from their physician about their vital signs, this surprising revelation will likely increase their concerns.
- **Personality differences**: Various studies suggest that personality traits can affect privacy concerns. Agreeableness (being trusting, sympathetic, straightforward, and selfless) [13], for example, is shown to increase privacy concerns [14]. Other aspects of the "big five" personality traits (particularly introversion/extraversion) and independence/interdependence are also suggested to influence privacy concerns [15–17]. The privacy setting of our fitness app will likely have to be flexible enough to support a body of users that runs the gamut on these various traits.
- **Demographic differences:** Demographics are another parameter that can affect privacy concerns [18, 19]. Females and older users have higher privacy concerns than males and younger users, respectively [20, 21]. For our fitness app scenario,

we should consider gender and age in how we manage users' privacy and present privacy features to the user.

- **Culture:** Cultural values can result in different privacy concerns. For example, high masculinity cultures who prioritize material success over caring relationships (e.g., Japan) show higher concerns for unauthorized secondary usages of their personal data than low masculinity cultures (e.g., Sweden) [22]. Therefore, our fitness app may need different privacy settings or presentations in different cultures. More detailed information on cultural differences in privacy concerns and behaviors can be found in Chap. 12.

3.2.2 Privacy Concerns

Privacy concerns, the most researched construct and proxy for the investigation of privacy issues, are put at the heart of the APCO model. It acts as a dependent variable of the privacy concerns' antecedents (A) and, at the same time, as an independent variable of the privacy-related outcomes (O).

The right side of the APCO model, in which privacy concerns function as an independent variable, has so far been at the center of privacy research. First and foremost, the connection between privacy concerns and behavioral reactions was investigated in this area: a high privacy concern will lead to low levels of disclosure. However, a common drawback of this work is that it has mostly investigated behavioral intention (usually a questionnaire on willingness to disclose) rather than actual behavior (actual disclosure in a real-life scenario). According to the theory of reasoned action (TRA) [23], actual behaviors align with intentions. In the context of privacy, however, a number of researchers have demonstrated that users often disclose vast amounts of information despite their high privacy concerns [6, 24]. Privacy behaviors not being aligned to privacy concerns and intentions are referred to as privacy paradox [7]. Varian [25] describes the paradox (without naming it that way) in his work titled "Economic Aspects of Personal Privacy." According to the paradox, users articulate high privacy concerns and do not intend to purchase services that could violate their privacy (their intention) but behave in the opposite way [7, 26]. Accordingly, users show a high level of attention to data misuse, but do not change their behavior with regard to data disclosure and potential misuse. A theory-based and uniform model to explain the dichotomy described by the privacy paradox is still lacking [24]. Due to this privacy paradox, measuring the actual behavior instead of relying on a behavioral intention questionnaire seems necessary since they can be contradictory.

3.2.3   *Measuring Privacy Concerns*

Despite the omnipresence of privacy, research faces the challenge of measuring the vaguely defined, individually expressed, and subjectively perceptible construct. Privacy itself is based on insights, perceptions, and experiences and cannot always be rationalized [3]. The lack of a well-accepted and a clear definition of privacy makes the measurement of privacy difficult to operationalize.

Concerns about privacy or, shorter, privacy concerns have been an established IS research variable and are a widely recognized proxy for privacy [1, 3, 27]. Due to the broad application of privacy concerns, different perspectives and definitions of privacy concerns have developed in the scientific discourse as well. Privacy concerns can be defined as user concerns about a possible future loss of privacy as a result of voluntary or involuntary disclosure of personal data [28]. This definitional approach is followed by a broader definition of privacy per se, according to which privacy is defined as the subjective view of the users regarding fairness in the handling of personal data [10]. Many researchers use a narrower definition of privacy concerns and define them as concerns users have about the way companies and organizations handle personal information [9].

Empirical research uses mainly two constructs for privacy concerns. In the following, we discuss these two constructs as well as a third approach, which accommodates the context in measuring privacy concerns:

1. The Concern for Information Privacy (CFIP) is the first developed and verified construct for measuring informational privacy [9, 29]. This construct discusses four overall themes in privacy concern:

    (a) **Collection concerns** arise when an extensive amount of user data is being collected and stored (e.g., "It usually bothers me when companies ask me for personal information"). For our fitness app scenario, asking users for excessive amounts of information might increase collection concerns.
    (b) **Unauthorized secondary use concern** captures users' worriedness on potential unauthorized usages of their data (e.g., "Companies should never share personal information with other companies unless it has been authorized by the individual who provided the information"). For instance, users of our fitness application might willingly disclose some data to receive better trainings but at the same time might be worried about their data being shared with commercial or insurance companies.
    (c) **Improper access** reflects users' concerns about unauthorized individuals accessing their data (e.g., "Companies should devote more time and effort to preventing unauthorized access to personal information"). For example, who has the permissions to see user data in the fitness application? Is it just a machine or are there employees who can check user data too?
    (d) **Errors** capture users' concerns on accidental and deliberate errors (e.g., "companies should devote more time and effort to verifying the accuracy of the personal information in their databases"). If users of our fitness app

know that the company takes adequate precautions to minimize problems from errors, they will have less error concerns.

2. The Internet Users' Information Privacy Concerns (IUIPC) model is a further three-dimensional measurement instrument for privacy concerns, which was developed to deal more specifically with the technological conditions of the Internet [10]:

    (a) **Collection**: Similar to Smith et al. [9], collection comes first in the IUIPC dimensions.

    (b) **Control**: Users are less worried about personal data collection if they are given some degrees of control over this disclosure, e.g., if they are able to opt out [12]. If users of our fitness app are easily able to stop location tracking, and even delete the data that is already being collected, they perceive more control and thereby will have less control concerns (i.e., "Consumer online privacy is really a matter of consumers' right to exercise control and autonomy over decisions about how their information is collected, used, and shared.").

    (c) **Awareness**: Users who are not aware of how companies use their data are less likely to share information [30]. Informing users about the procedures will give them the ability to utilize *control* and choose whether they want to disclose their data or not (i.e., "It is very important to me that I am aware and knowledgeable about how my personal information will be used.").

The technological realities and the research landscape after the publication of the APCO model have offered more diverse perspectives and treatments of privacy concerns. Through this new work, privacy concerns have been studied more closely in the specific contexts. For example, the Mobile Users' Information Privacy Concerns (MUIPC) model developed constructs that account for the context and peculiarities of privacy concerns in the context of mobile systems [31]. MUIPC captures privacy concerns by secondary use of personal data, presided surveillance (similar to collection concerns discussed earlier, i.e., "I am concerned that mobile apps may monitor my activities on my mobile device."), and perceived intrusion (similar to improper access discussed earlier, i.e., "I feel that as a result of my using mobile apps, information about me is out there that, if used, will invade my privacy.").

3.2.4 Trust and Privacy Calculus

Trust is cited as one of the most important variables in the context of privacy concerns and privacy behavior. However, we believe that a clear relationship in terms of nature and direction has still not been proven. Although trust is presented as a predictor of behavioral reactions, studies also describe trust as moderator of the relationship between privacy concerns and behavioral reactions and demonstrate a reciprocal relationship to privacy concerns. Users' trust can play an important role in our fitness tracker scenario. If we consider a direct effect of trust on behavioral reactions, increasing users' trust will result in more disclosure and in turn using more features. On the other hand, considering trust as a moderator for the effect of privacy concerns on disclosure will have different implications. In that case, trust will be less important when users have low privacy concerns. For those users with higher privacy concerns, however, trust can play an important role since a high trust can mitigate their tendencies for withholding data.

Privacy calculus is a term used to describe the privacy trade-off between the risks and the benefits of disclosure [32]. Hence, APCO considers privacy calculus as a function of perceived risks and benefits and a predictor of behavioral intention. It is worth noting that the APCO model recognizes the role of privacy calculus but treats it as a part of a more integrative process that goes on when a user decides to reveal private information. In our fitness scenario, users make a trade-off between the risk of (and maybe embarrassments resulting from) disclosing their daily intake calories and the merits of learning about the quantity of the exercise they need to undergo. This process is ongoing at least until user discloses the data or hits the next button while leaving the "daily intake calories" field empty.

The privacy calculus perspective suggests that when individuals are asked to reveal personal information to others, they deliberate on the risks involved and the potential benefits received [28]. However, this description may not paint the full picture of users' behaviors, because of bounded rationality [33]. Users may not be able to fully deliberate on risks and benefits of a disclosure decision due to cognitive limitations and a finite amount of time to make the decision. Furthermore, behavioral economics suggests that uncertainty, ambiguity, and behavioral biases also play a role in behavioral outcomes [34]. Users fall prey to nudges such as framing and default effects [35, 36]. Chapter 4 of this book will elaborate more on the behavioral economics aspect of privacy decisions.

While the influence of behavioral economic factors is evident in privacy decisions (behavioral outcome), APCO does not take such factors into account. This has prompted scholars to propose the enhanced APCO model [5], which introduces behavioral economics concepts into the APCO model.

3.3 Enhanced APCO: An Expanded View on Privacy Research

An interesting aspect of the published literature since the appearance of the APCO model can be seen in the integration of new theoretical frameworks, the incorporation of findings, effects and results from other research domains, and the application of experimental research methodologies. Already in 2015, Dinev et al. [5] reacted with a critique of the existing macro-models of privacy research and the APCO model in particular, which assume that "responses to external stimuli result

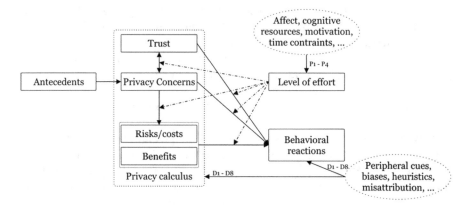

Fig. 3.2 The enhanced APCO model [5]

in deliberate analyses, which lead to fully informed privacy-related attitudes and behaviors" [5]. The scientific discourse is increasingly responding to the criticism of the assumption of complete cognitively controlled "high-effort" privacy decisions that are made under complete information [5, 25, 37], suggesting that the decisions are neither made with completely high cognitive effort nor are fully informed. Dinev et al. [5] called for an enhanced APCO model that addresses those criticisms by including concepts from behavioral economics and psychological research on cognitive processing (Fig. 3.2). In this new framework, the level of effort is specified as a moderating variable (M1) of the APCO relationships. They argue that the level of effort is influenced by factors such as affect, motivations, and temporal restrictions (P1–P4). The authors also emphasize the contextual and situational influences on privacy decisions, which have rarely been researched in IS literature but may influence the constructs of the APCO model (D1–D8). With the enhanced APCO model, Dinev et al. [5] provide a framework for further research efforts.

These ideas seemed to have caught the interests of more and more researchers. In the IS domain, for example, Adjerid et al. [38] introduce the distinction between objective and relative risks in privacy decisions, while Kehr et al. [39] examine limited cognitive resources and heuristic thinking as well as preexisting attitudes and dispositions in the situation-specific evaluation of risks and benefits in privacy decisions. Special attention in the area of "low-effort" decisions was paid to affect heuristics and the influence of affect and affective commitment [39–41]. With his study, Wakefield [42] shows that positive and negative affect has a significant effect on users' trust in websites and their privacy beliefs, which motivates the disclosure of information. Interestingly, Wakefield [42] can underline the impact intensity of affect by emphasizing that this effect is pronounced for users with high privacy concerns. Similarly, Gerlach et al. [43] investigated how users' stereotypical thinking can cause systematic judgment errors when individuals form their beliefs about an online service. In addition, they explored the effectiveness of counterstereotypic privacy statements in preventing such judgment errors [43].

Since the appearance of the APCO model and its enhanced version, numerous researchers have taken up this call for research and expanded privacy research in various directions. Due to the large contextual and situational dependence of privacy decisions, numerous approaches have been integrated into privacy research such as social cognitive theory [44], gratification theory [45], information boundary theory [45, 46], impression formation theory [47], social identity theory [48], direct causation theory and affect heuristic theory [41], and the theory of psychological ownership [49].

3.4 The Research Landscape After APCO

3.4.1 Evolution of Technology and Personalization of Services

Since the publication of the APCO model in Smith et al. [3], the importance of privacy research has continued to grow, at least due to the rapid development of digital technologies, social media, and consumer-friendly applications [4, 50]. Due to the increasing penetration of businesses in consumers' everyday life facilitated by IS, further areas of application and research have developed in many diverse contexts.

A driving factor for the increasing relevance of privacy issues is the development of mobile digital ecosystems, invisible computing, and the Internet of Things, which resulted in profound integration of IS into people's everyday life. Modern IS enable users to gain experiences that go far beyond the functional and practical applications of operationally motivated IS [51]. They can share content, experiences, knowledge, and skills as well as opportunities and even technology themselves [51]. This illustrates the changing role that products and services play in satisfying users' needs [52]. The user-centric offerings integrate the user as the co-creator of the value propositions [53]. It is the personal user data that enable these types of co-created and integrated value offerings.

The APCO model, which managed to place the individual behavior in the overall context of privacy research in an intuitive but structured way, has not lost its relevance in the scientific discourse. Although only a few authors actively classify their research work within the APCO model, its application helps to establish references to related scientific results and insights, especially in recent works.

Privacy concerns continue to serve as a central construct for measuring privacy. The majority of privacy literature includes (different forms of) privacy concerns in its considerations as a proxy for measuring privacy. Although many studies use existing and past developed measurement tools for privacy concerns, few authors began to expand or vary the spectrum of measurement instruments. Dinev et al. [54], for example, define privacy as a state and thereby establish the dependent variable perceived privacy. Other related constructs not explicitly mentioned in the APCO model include, for example, privacy self-efficacy [42] and privacy beliefs [55].

Due to the high individuality, the high contextual complexity, and the subjective perception of privacy as a personal value, it seems only sensible to strengthen the further development and adaptation of measuring instruments in the field of privacy research.

A more diverse level of analysis of APCO-related constructs and models is still desired. The majority of the studies continue to relate to the individual privacy level. Only a few studies extend this perspective to other privacy levels. Kim et al. [56], for example, point to the high level of release of group privacy based on an exploratory literature review. Although there are regulations in modern societies regarding individual privacy, this is rarely the case regarding group privacy. Societies may find a need to close this gap quickly, as, for example, social networks and virtual worlds threaten individual privacy by disregarding group privacy [56].

Two exciting and highly relevant privacy perspectives have developed in the scientific discourse in recent years: the cause and direction of privacy abuse and privacy as a serious management issue for companies. Choi et al. [57] and Teubner and Flath [58] extend the perspective of the use of personal data to the peer-to-peer (P2P) area. On P2P platforms, such as social media platforms or sharing economy platforms, personal data is no longer necessarily released or distributed by the user himself but also by other peers [4, 57]. On social media platforms, for example, friends disseminate information about users who do not necessarily want to disclose it themselves. Choi et al. [57] demonstrate in such a relationship the influence of information dissemination and network commonality on perceived privacy invasion and perceived privacy bonding.

With almost every company using personal data, privacy research is increasingly developing as a management issue for the companies. The resulting issues can be described as opportunities (exploitation) and risks (regulation, attacks). How companies deal with these challenges is the focus of a few publications, such as Greenaway et al. [59] and Oetzel and Spiekermann [60]. These works highlight the risks for companies arising from the storage of personal data and provide a tool for systematic privacy impact assessment and "privacy by design" (in European regulatory context). Privacy impact assessments (PIAs) are systematic risk assessments and scrutinize privacy implications of organizations' operations and personal data handling. The European Commission integrated PIAs into the new regulation proposal for legal data protection [61], and both European Data Protection and the US Federal Trade Commission are endorsing PIAs. Oetzel and Spiekermann [60] suggest a model for systematic step-by-step PIAs for organizations—early in the development of new products—to identify privacy risks upfront and address them accordingly. In their approach, for a new system or with a change in the system, PIA should elaborate on the characteristics of the new system, define privacy targets, and identify threats aiming those targets. Then, the PIA team should find control mechanisms to shield targets from the identified threats and document the whole process.

As already pointed by Smith et al. [3], research on the relationship between antecedents and privacy concerns (A-PC) continues to be very limited. However, Ozdemir et al. [4] demonstrate a relation between privacy awareness, privacy experiences, and privacy concerns. Xu et al. [62], on the other hand, focus on perceived control in their work and show a relationship between the perceived control of personal information and context-specific privacy concerns. Meanwhile, Miltgen and Peyrat-Guillard [63] contributed to intercultural differences in EU countries and show that younger people feel more responsible and have more positive attitudes toward the management of personal data [63].

The post-APCO academic research continues to focus on the relationship between privacy concerns (or correlates) and outcomes (PC-O). Numerous papers focus on the interaction between trust and privacy concerns. Bansal et al. [64] show a strong correlation between privacy assurance mechanisms and trust, with privacy concerns acting as a moderating variable. In the context of location-based services, Keith et al. [44] demonstrate an effect of mobile computing self-efficacy on the confidence of users in the application as well as on the perceived risks on the disclosure of personal data. Especially in the context of mobile applications, however, classic indicators such as application quality, trust-building measures, brand recognition, and the moderating effect of privacy concerns seem to have a lower impact on the adoption of mobile services [44].

Privacy calculus and variants of costs-benefits analysis in a privacy decision continue to be a subject of intense privacy research, extending to social media. Spiekermann and Korunovska [49] provide a basic consideration of the privacy calculus through the lens of "user-centered value theory for personal data".... Further, Karwatzki et al. [46] show that the evaluation of privacy by users is a major obstacle to the disclosure of personal data. Richey et al. [65] consider the publication of personal data and profiles via social media platforms. Interestingly, while earlier works assume a clear separation of private and professional spheres and consider the publication of private profiles as a threat to privacy, Richey et al. [65] show a contrasting effect: the respondents consciously use their private social media account to become visible to potential employers. On social network websites, Choi et al. [47] show that the expected privacy risks and social capital gains can be seen as the strongest predictors for non-acceptance or acceptance of friendship requests. For more information, please refer to Chap. 7.

The academic discussion of the personalization of IS or applications is seen through the lens of the privacy calculus in which the personalization of services usually represents an added value for the user [48]. Although the personalization of services requires the release and use of personal data, this data leads to an improved customer experience, a higher product-market fit, and an improved value proposition design. Thus, Li and Unger [66] show in the context of news and financial services that higher perceived quality and personalization can lead to an equalization of privacy concerns (see Chap. 9). Karwatzki et al. [46] and Albashrawi and Motiwalla [67], on the other hand, come to different conclusions, as they are unable to determine a significantly higher willingness to disclose data due to personalization advantages and transparency features.

3.5   Conclusion and Avenues of Future Research

Although privacy research has continued to develop positively in recent years, the APCO model has not lost its topicality in terms of structuring the research landscape. At the latest, through its extension to the enhanced APCO model, it allows both researchers and practitioners to classify questions relating to privacy decisions. The model can be used to derive references to related research work and to relate findings to one another. For example, APCO can alleviate the privacy paradox issue. To better explain privacy behaviors, rather than merely focusing on privacy concerns and risks, APCO also accounts for disclosure benefits. When disclosure results in considerable gratifications for the users, they may disclose their data even when privacy concerns are high [28, 68]. In addition, the enhanced APCO addresses the privacy paradox further by considering heuristics, since heuristics can nudge users to disclose data, regardless of their privacy concerns [26]. Overall, the IS-driven privacy research is slowly opening up to approaches from other research domains, such as psychology, behavioral economics, or marketing. There are numerous areas and opportunities for new approaches for future research work.

First and foremost, the IS research community should introduce a new term for "user." With the most recent development of ubiquitous and invisible computing, users themselves have become central actors in the digital ecosystems. They interact with IS, use networked smart everyday objects, and expand the existing system through their everyday use [69]. Since users actively contribute to value creation, they do not necessarily perceive themselves as users of a service with reference to a defined exchange relationship. For example, users of the fitness app can be content generators (e.g., by sharing success stories of reaching their goals and responding to their training experience), and their data can be used to improve the product and help others benefit from it further (e.g., to study what exercise routine results in optimal outcome for each demographic population). Therefore, the users of these IS can no longer be understood as atomistic users focused on functionality and practicability in the operational work environment. Rather, invisible computing can be explored by the users. With this new perspective, the motivation to use a system can no longer be limited to a mere fulfillment of a task but rather a contribution to the whole [51, 70]. Since invisible computing is seen as a post-desktop era in which users interact in smart environments and with smart everyday objects (Salinas Segura and Thiesse; [71]), the perspective on users should be changed [69, 72].

Building on the new user concept, future work would need to increasingly focus on the actual situation of privacy decisions and the resulting behavior. Thus, situational decisions and individual contexts represent central adjusting screws and influencing variables of human action, without which privacy decisions cannot be adequately described and researched.

Another opportunity for future research would be the focus on the antecedents of privacy and the emergence of privacy-relevant attitudes and concerns after previous work has focused predominantly on outcomes. As discussed earlier, privacy decisions are situational and contextual. Hence, it's best to measure antecedents and privacy concerns in the context.

The assumption of rising privacy concerns, inherent in numerous research projects, needs to be reexamined. The increasing use of services that pose a serious threat to the privacy of users coupled with the increasingly careless use of IS leads to the assumption that the reported growing privacy concerns are not valid. It is possible that today's complex, fully networked, and integrated IS and processes are no longer understood by the average user, who can no longer critically question or examine the ways their personal information and activity are used by various companies and stakeholders. This can raise a case for user-tailored privacy, which utilizes adaptive tools to personalize privacy to each user (Chap. 16). There may also be some sense of resignation among the users. Today, they are faced with the choice of using modern IS that intrudes their privacy or, not using it at all, with negative consequences such as technological and social exclusion.

Following the call for research by Dinev et al. [5], IS research should increasingly open up to methodological research approaches and findings from related research domains. Since digital IS are deeply and invisibly integrated into the everyday life, the social life, and social actions of groups and societies, the behavior, attitudes, and perceptions of users should be investigated in various situations that inform decision-making. Proven effects and findings from related research domains, e.g., behavioral economics, marketing, consumer behavior, or social psychology [73, 74], should be examined against the background of the digital decision-making environment, and, if necessary, new mechanisms or IS specific effects should be researched using behavioral research methods [5, 37]. As IS are user-centric and intuitive designed services, they foster low involvement and habitual buying and downloading decisions [75–77]. These environmental factors, driven by a high degree of convenience and usability, can lead to peripheral cues, heuristics and mental shortcuts, biases, and misattributions, which can affect the privacy behavior [78, 79]. Further research should consider the digital context that supports decision-making with low cognitive load. Preliminary results show a significant impact of cognitive load experiments on privacy concerns, privacy attitudes, and privacy behavior [80]. As users more and more decide, interact, and behave through the usage of complex IS, we believe that intensified research efforts in this domain will lead to progress in our understanding of privacy.

References

1. Li, Y. (2011) Empirical studies on online information privacy concerns: Literature review and an integrative framework. *CAIS* 28. https://doi.org/10.17705/1CAIS.02828
2. Bélanger, F., and R.E. Crossler. 2011. Privacy in the digital age: A review of information privacy research in information systems. *MIS Quarterly* 35: 1017–1A36.
3. Smith, H.J., T. Dinev, and H. Xu. 2011. Information privacy research: An interdisciplinary review. *MIS Quarterly* 35: 989–1015.
4. Ozdemir, Z.D., H. Jeff Smith, and J.H. Benamati. 2017. Antecedents and outcomes of information privacy concerns in a peer context: An exploratory study. *European Journal of Information Systems* 26: 642–660. https://doi.org/10.1057/s41303-017-0056-z.

5. Dinev, T., A.R. McConnell, and H.J. Smith. 2015. Research Commentary—Informing privacy research through information systems, psychology, and behavioral economics: Thinking outside the "APCO" box. *Information Systems Research* 26: 639–655. https://doi.org/10.1287/isre.2015.0600.
6. Barnes, S.B. 2006. A privacy paradox: Social networking in the United States. *First Monday*.
7. Norberg, P.A., D.R. Horne, and D.A. Horne. 2007. The privacy paradox: Personal information disclosure intentions versus behaviors. *Journal of Consumer Affairs* 41: 100–126.
8. Xu, H., T. Dinev, H.J. Smith, and P. Hart. 2008. Examining the formation of individual's privacy concerns: Toward an integrative view. In *ICIS 2008 Proceedings*.
9. Smith, H.J., S.J. Milberg, and S.J. Burke. 1996. Information privacy: Measuring individuals' concerns about organizational practices. *MIS Quarterly* 20: 167. https://doi.org/10.2307/249477.
10. Malhotra, N.K., S.S. Kim, and J. Agarwal. 2004. Internet Users' Information Privacy Concerns (IUIPC): The construct, the scale, and a causal model. *Information Systems Research* 15: 336–355. https://doi.org/10.1287/isre.1040.0032.
11. Cespedes, F.V., and H. Jeff Smith. 1993. Database marketing: New rules for policy and practice. *Sloan Management Review* 34. https://www.proquest.com/openview/8ce0a3e960946f7a684c13badd19eb89/1?pq-origsite=gscholar&cbl=26142.
12. Nowak, G.J., and J. Phelps. 1995. Direct marketing and the use of individual-level consumer information: Determining how and when "privacy" matters. *Journal of Direct Marketing* 9 (3): 46–60. https://doi.org/10.1002/dir.4000090307.
13. Terracciano, A., R.R. McCrae, D. Hagemann, and P.T. Costa Jr. 2003. Individual difference variables, affective differentiation, and the structures of affect. *Journal of Personality* 71 (5): 669–704. https://doi.org/10.1111/1467-6494.7105001.
14. Korzaan, M.L., and K.T. Boswell. 2008. The influence of personality traits and information privacy concerns on behavioral intentions. *Journal of Computer Information Systems* 48 (4): 15–24. https://doi.org/10.1080/08874417.2008.11646031.
15. Xu, H. 2007. The effects of self-construal and perceived control on privacy concerns. In *ICIS 2007 Proceedings*, 125. http://aisel.aisnet.org/icis2007/125.
16. Bansal, G., and D. Gefen. 2015. The role of privacy assurance mechanisms in building trust and the moderating role of privacy concern. *European Journal of Information Systems* 24 (6): 624–644. https://doi.org/10.1057/ejis.2014.41.
17. Lu, Y., B. Tan, and K.-L. Hui. 2004. Inducing customers to disclose personal information to internet businesses with social adjustment benefits. In *ICIS 2004 Proceedings*, 45. https://aisel.aisnet.org/icis2004/45.
18. Culnan, M.J., and P.K. Armstrong. 1999. Information privacy concerns, procedural fairness, and impersonal trust: An empirical investigation. *Organization Science* 10: 104–115. https://doi.org/10.1287/orsc.10.1.104.
19. Chen, K., and A.I. Rea Jr. 2004. Protecting personal information online: A survey of user privacy concerns and control techniques. *Journal of Computer Information Systems* 44 (4): 85–92. https://doi.org/10.1080/08874417.2004.11647599.
20. Youn, S., and K. Hall. 2008. Gender and online privacy among teens: Risk perception, privacy concerns, and protection behaviors. *Cyberpsychology and Behavior* 11 (6): 763–765. https://doi.org/10.1089/cpb.2007.0240.
21. Hoy, M.G., and G. Milne. 2010. Gender differences in privacy-related measures for young adult Facebook users. *Journal of Interactive Advertising* 10 (2): 28–45. https://doi.org/10.1080/15252019.2010.10722168.
22. Bellman, S., E.J. Johnson, S.J. Kobrin, and G.L. Lohse. 2004. International differences in information privacy concerns: A global survey of consumers. *The Information Society* 20 (5): 313–324. https://doi.org/10.1080/01972240490507956.
23. Fishbein, M, and I. Ajzen. 1975. *Belief, Attitude, Intention, and Behavior: An Introduction to Theory and Research*.

24. Kokolakis, S. 2017. Privacy attitudes and privacy behaviour: A review of current research on the privacy paradox phenomenon. *Computers & Security* 64: 122–134. https://doi.org/10.1016/j.cose.2015.07.002.
25. Varian, H.R. 2009. Economic aspects of personal privacy. In *Internet Policy and Economics*, ed. L.M. Pupillo and W.H. Lehr, 2nd ed., 101–109. Dordrecht: Springer.
26. Acquisti, A., and J. Grossklags. 2005. Privacy and rationality in individual decision making. *IEEE Security & Privacy Magazine* 3: 26–33. https://doi.org/10.1109/MSP.2005.22.
27. Hong, W., and J.Y.L. Thong. 2013. Internet privacy concerns: An integrated conceptualization and four empirical studies. *MIS Quarterly* 37: 275–298.
28. Dinev, T., and P. Hart. 2006. An extended privacy calculus model for e-commerce transactions. *Information systems research* 17: 61–80. https://doi.org/10.1287/isre.1060.0080.
29. Stewart, K.A., and A.H. Segars. 2002. An empirical examination of the concern for information privacy instrument. *Information systems research* 13: 36–49. https://doi.org/10.1287/isre.13.1.36.97.
30. Hoffman, D.L., T.P. Novak, and M. Peralta. 1999. Building consumer trust online. *Communications of the ACM* 42 (4): 80–85. https://doi.org/10.1145/299157.299175.
31. Xu, H., S. Gupta, M. Rosson, and J. Carroll. 2012. Measuring mobile users' concerns for information privacy. In *ICIS 2012 Proceedings*.
32. Laufer, R.S., and M. Wolfe. 1977. Privacy as a concept and a social issue: A multidimensional developmental theory. *Journal of Social Issues* 33: 22–42. https://doi.org/10.1111/j.1540-4560.1977.tb01880.x.
33. Simon, H.A. 1955. A behavioral model of rational choice. *The Quarterly Journal of Economics* 69 (1): 99–118. https://doi.org/10.2307/1884852.
34. Grossklags, J., and A. Acquisti. 2007. When 25 cents is too much: An experiment on willingness-to-sell and willingness-to-protect personal information. In *WEIS*. https://econinfosec.org/archive/weis2007/papers/66.pdf.
35. Johnson, E.J., S. Bellman, and G.L. Lohse. 2002. Defaults, framing and privacy: Why opting in-opting out 1. *Marketing Letters* 13 (1): 5–15. https://doi.org/10.1023/A:1015044207315.
36. Bahirat, P., Q. Sun, and B.P. Knijnenburg. 2018. Scenario context V/s framing and defaults in managing privacy in household IoT. In *Proceedings of the 23rd International Conference on Intelligent User Interfaces Companion*, 1–2.
37. Goes, P.B. 2013. Editor's Comments: Information systems research and behavioral economics. *MIS Quarterly* 37: iii–viii.
38. Adjerid, I., E. Peer, A. Acquisti. 2016. *Beyond the Privacy Paradox: Objective Versus Relative Risk in Privacy Decision Making.*
39. Kehr, F., T. Kowatsch, D. Wentzel, and E. Fleisch. 2015. Blissfully ignorant: The effects of general privacy concerns, general institutional trust, and affect in the privacy calculus. *Information Systems Journal* 25: 607–635. https://doi.org/10.1111/isj.12062.
40. Kordzadeh, N., and J. Warren. 2014. Communicating personal health information in virtual health communities: A theoretical framework. In *IEEE 8th International Symposium on Service-Oriented System Engineering (SOSE), Oxford, United Kingdom, 7–11 April 2014 [including workshop/symposium papers]*, 636–645. Piscataway, NJ: IEEE.
41. Yu, J., P.J.-H. Hu, and T.-H. Cheng. 2015. Role of affect in self-disclosure on social network websites: A test of two competing models. *Journal of Management Information Systems* 32: 239–277. https://doi.org/10.1080/07421222.2015.1063305.
42. Wakefield, R. 2013. The influence of user affect in online information disclosure. *The Journal of Strategic Information Systems* 22: 157–174. https://doi.org/10.1016/j.jsis.2013.01.003.
43. Gerlach, J., P. Buxmann, and T. Dinev. 2018. 'They're All the Same!' Stereotypical thinking and systematic errors in users' privacy-related judgments about online services. *Journal of the Association for Information Systems* 19: 247–265.
44. Keith, M.J., J.S. Babb, P.B. Lowry, C.P. Furner, and A. Abdullat. 2015. The role of mobile-computing self-efficacy in consumer information disclosure. *Information Systems Journal* 25: 637–667. https://doi.org/10.1111/isj.12082.

45. Sutanto, J., E. Palme, C.-H. Tan, and C.W. Phang. 2013. Addressing the personalization–privacy paradox: An empirical assessment from a field experiment on smartphone users. *MIS Quarterly* 37: 1141–1164.
46. Karwatzki, S., O. Dytynko, M. Trenz, and D. Veit. 2017. Beyond the personalization–privacy paradox: Privacy valuation, transparency features, and service personalization. *Journal of Management Information Systems* 34: 369–400. https://doi.org/10.1080/07421222.2017.1334467.
47. Choi, B., Y. Wu, J. Yu, and L. Land. 2018. *Love at First Sight: The Interplay Between Privacy Dispositions and Privacy Calculus in Online Social Connectivity Management.* 1536–9323
48. Shih, H.-P., K.-h. Lai, and T.C.E. Cheng. 2017. Constraint-based and dedication-based mechanisms for encouraging online self-disclosure: Is personalization the only thing that matters? *European Journal of Information Systems* 26: 432–450. https://doi.org/10.1057/s41303-016-0031-0.
49. Spiekermann, S., and J. Korunovska. 2017. Towards a value theory for personal data. *Journal of Information Technology* 32: 62–84. https://doi.org/10.1057/jit.2016.4.
50. Lowry, P.B., T. Dinev, and R. Willison. 2017. Why security and privacy research lies at the centre of the information systems (IS) artefact: Proposing a bold research agenda. *European Journal of Information Systems* 26: 546–563. https://doi.org/10.1057/s41303-017-0066-x.
51. Sullivan, J., R. Scheepers, and C. Middleton. 2009. Conceptualizing user satisfaction in the ubiquitous computing era. In *ICIS 2009 Proceedings*.
52. Merli, G. 2013. The transformation of the business model: Business modelling. In *New Business Models and Value Creation: A Service Science Perspective*, ed. L. Cinquini, A. Di Minin, and R. Varaldo, 67–86. Milan: Springer.
53. Vargo, S.L., and R.F. Lusch. 2008. Service-dominant logic: Continuing the evolution. *Journal of the Academy of Marketing Science* 36: 1–10. https://doi.org/10.1007/s11747-007-0069-6.
54. Dinev, T., H. Xu, J.H. Smith, and P. Hart. 2013. Information privacy and correlates: An empirical attempt to bridge and distinguish privacy-related concepts. *European Journal of Information Systems* 22: 295–316. https://doi.org/10.1057/ejis.2012.23.
55. Gerlach, J., T. Widjaja, and P. Buxmann. 2015. Handle with care: How online social network providers' privacy policies impact users' information sharing behavior. *The Journal of Strategic Information Systems* 24: 33–43. https://doi.org/10.1016/j.jsis.2014.09.001.
56. Kim, J., R.L. Baskerville, and Y. Ding. 2018. Breaking the privacy kill chain: Protecting individual and group privacy online. *Information Systems Frontiers*. https://doi.org/10.1007/s10796-018-9856-5.
57. Choi, B.C.F., Z. Jiang, B. Xiao, and S.S. Kim. 2015. Embarrassing exposures in online social networks: An integrated perspective of privacy invasion and relationship bonding. *Information Systems Research* 26: 675–694. https://doi.org/10.1287/isre.2015.0602.
58. Teubner, T., and C. Flath. 2019. Privacy in the sharing economy. *Journal of the Association for Information Systems* 20. https://doi.org/10.17705/1jais.00534.
59. Greenaway, K.E., Y.E. Chan, and R.E. Crossler. 2015. Company information privacy orientation: A conceptual framework. *Information Systems Journal* 25: 579–606. https://doi.org/10.1111/isj.12080.
60. Oetzel, M.C., and S. Spiekermann. 2014. A systematic methodology for privacy impact assessments: A design science approach. *European Journal of Information Systems* 23: 126–150. https://doi.org/10.1057/ejis.2013.18.
61. Gutwirth, S., R. Leenes, P. De Hert, and (Eds.). 2015. *Reforming European Data Protection Law*. Vol. 20. Dordrecht: Springer. https://doi.org/10.1016/B978-0-12-802122-4.00002-X.
62. Xu, H., H.-H. Teo, B.C.Y. Tan, and R. Agarwal. 2012b. Research Note —Effects of individual self-protection, industry self-regulation, and government regulation on privacy concerns: A study of location-based services. *Information Systems Research* 23: 1342–1363. https://doi.org/10.1287/isre.1120.0416.
63. Miltgen, C.L., and D. Peyrat-Guillard. 2014. Cultural and generational influences on privacy concerns: A qualitative study in seven European countries. *European Journal of Information Systems* 23: 103–125. https://doi.org/10.1057/ejis.2013.17.

64. Bansal, G., F.M. Zahedi, and D. Gefen. 2015. The role of privacy assurance mechanisms in building trust and the moderating role of privacy concern. *European Journal of Information Systems* 24: 624–644. https://doi.org/10.1057/ejis.2014.41.
65. Richey, M., A. Gonibeed, and M.N. Ravishankar. 2018. The perils and promises of self-disclosure on social media. *Information Systems Frontiers* 20: 425–437. https://doi.org/10.1007/s10796-017-9806-7.
66. Li, T., and T. Unger. 2012. Willing to pay for quality personalization? Trade-off between quality and privacy. *European Journal of Information Systems* 21: 621–642. https://doi.org/10.1057/ejis.2012.13.
67. Albashrawi, M., and L. Motiwalla. 2017. Privacy and personalization in continued usage intention of mobile banking: An integrative perspective. *Information Systems Frontiers*. https://doi.org/10.1007/s10796-017-9814-7.
68. Debatin, B., Lovejoy, J. P., Horn, A.-K., & Hughes, B. N. (2009). Facebook and online privacy: Attitudes, behaviors, and unintended consequences. *Journal of Computer-Mediated Communication*, 83–108.
69. Yoo. 2010. Computing in everyday life: A call for research on experiential computing. *MIS Quarterly* 34: 213. https://doi.org/10.2307/20721425.
70. Borriello, G. 2008. Invisible computing: Automatically using the many bits of data we create. *Philosophical Transactions of the Royal Society A: Mathematical, Physical and Engineering Sciences* 366: 3669–3683. https://doi.org/10.1098/rsta.2008.0128.
71. Zhao, R., and J. Wang. 2011. Visualizing the research on pervasive and ubiquitous computing. *Scientometrics* 86: 593–612. https://doi.org/10.1007/s11192-010-0283-8.
72. Lamb, R., and R. Kling. 2003. Reconceptualizing users as social actors in information systems research. *MIS Quarterly* 27: 197. https://doi.org/10.2307/30036529.
73. Acquisti, A., L. Brandimarte, and G. Loewenstein. 2015. Privacy and human behavior in the age of information. *Science* 347: 509–514. https://doi.org/10.1126/science.aaa1465.
74. Ariely, D. 2009. The end of rational econonmics. *Harvard Business Review* 87: 78–84.
75. Aarts, H., and A.P. Dijksterhuis. 2000. The automatic activation of goal-directed behaviour: The case of travel habit. *Journal of Environmental Psychology* 20: 75–82.
76. Buck, C., C. Horbel, T. Kessler, and C. Christian. 2014. Mobile consumer apps: Big data brother is watching you. *Marketing Review St. Gallen* 31: 26–35. https://doi.org/10.1365/s11621-014-0318-2.
77. Dijksterhuis, A., P.K. Smith, R.B. van Baaren, and D.H.J. Wigboldus. 2005. The unconscious consumer: Effects of environment on consumer behavior. *Journal of Consumer Psychology* 15: 193–202. https://doi.org/10.1207/s15327663jcp1503_3.
78. Anaraky, R., B.P. Knijnenburg, and M. Risius. 2020. Exacerbating mindless compliance: The danger of justifications during privacy decision making in the context of Facebook applications. *AIS Transactions on Human-Computer Interaction*: 70–95.
79. Buck, C., S. Burster, and T. Eymann. 2018. An experiment series on app information privacy concerns. In *26th European Conference on Information Systems (ECIS)*.
80. Buck, C., and T. Dinev. 2019. Verifying effects and findings of behavioral economics and social psychology in information systems and digital decision-making environments using experimental research approaches. *Research in Progress*.

Chapter 4
Privacy and Behavioral Economics

Alessandro Acquisti, Laura Brandimarte, and George Loewenstein

Abstract There are diverse streams of empirical research attempting to study complex privacy behaviors in different scenarios. In this chapter, we connect those streams and present them under three themes: (1) individuals' uncertainty about their own preferences as well as their uncertainty about the consequences of information disclosure; (2) the context-dependence of individuals' concern, or lack thereof, about privacy; (3) the degree to which privacy concerns are malleable and prone to manipulations by commercial and government entities. Building on these themes, we discuss the role of public policy in the protection of privacy in the information age.

4.1 Introduction

If this is the age of information, then privacy is the issue of our times. Activities that were once private or shared with the few now leave trails of data that expose our interests, traits, beliefs, and intentions. We communicate using e-mails, texts, and social media; find partners on dating sites; learn via online courses; seek responses to mundane and sensitive questions using search engines; read news and books in the cloud; navigate streets with geotracking systems; and celebrate our newborns, and mourn our dead, on social media profiles. Through these and other activities, we reveal information—both knowingly and unwittingly—to one another, to commercial entities, and to our governments. The monitoring of personal

A. Acquisti (✉)
H. John Heinz III College, Carnegie Mellon University, Pittsburgh, PA, USA
e-mail: acquisti@andrew.cmu.edu

L. Brandimarte
Eller College of Management, University of Arizona, Tucson, AZ, USA
e-mail: lbrandimarte@arizona.edu

G. Loewenstein
Dietrich College, Social and Decision Sciences, Carnegie Mellon University, Pittsburgh, PA, USA
e-mail: gl20@andrew.cmu.edu

© The Author(s) 2022

B. P. Knijnenburg et al. (eds.), *Modern Socio-Technical Perspectives on Privacy*,
https://doi.org/10.1007/978-3-030-82786-1_4

information is ubiquitous; its storage is so durable as to render one's past undeletable [1], a modern digital skeleton in the closet. Accompanying the acceleration in data collection are steady advancements in the ability to aggregate, analyze, and draw sensitive inferences from individuals' data [2].

Both firms and individuals can benefit from the sharing of once hidden data and from the application of increasingly sophisticated analytics to larger and more interconnected databases [3]. So too can society as a whole; for instance, when electronic medical records are combined to observe novel drug interactions [4]. On the other hand, analytics of this data can pose risks to individuals; not many years ago, it was possible to predict one's social security number using their location and date of birth [5]. Such risks are not limited to individuals; the potential for personal data to be abused for economic and social discrimination, hidden influence and manipulation, coercion, or censorship is alarming. The erosion of privacy can threaten our autonomy, not merely as consumers but as citizens [6]. Sharing more personal data does not necessarily always translate into more progress, efficiency, or equality [7].

Because of the seismic nature of these developments, there has been considerable debate about individuals' ability to navigate a rapidly evolving privacy landscape, and about what, if anything, should be done about privacy at a policy level. Some trust people's ability to make self-interested decisions about information disclosing and withholding. Those holding this view tend to see regulatory protection of privacy as interfering with the fundamentally benign trajectory of information technologies and the benefits such technologies may unlock [8]. Others are concerned about the ability of individuals to manage privacy amid increasingly complex trade-offs. Traditional tools for privacy decision-making such as choice and consent, according to this perspective, no longer provide adequate protection [9]. Instead of individual responsibility, regulatory intervention may be needed to balance the interests of the subjects of data against the power of commercial entities and governments holding that data.

Are individuals up to the challenge of navigating privacy in the information age? To address this question, we review diverse streams of empirical privacy research from the social and behavioral sciences. We highlight factors that influence decisions to protect or surrender privacy and how, in turn, privacy protections or violations affect people's behavior. Information technologies have progressively become part of every aspect of our personal and professional lives. Thus, the problem of control over personal data has become inextricably linked to problems of personal choice, autonomy, and socioeconomic power. Accordingly, this chapter focuses on the concept of, and literature around, informational privacy (i.e., privacy of personal data) but also touches on other conceptions of privacy, such as anonymity or seclusion. Such notions all ultimately relate to the permeable yet pivotal boundaries between public and private [10].

We use three themes to organize and draw connections between streams of privacy research that, in many cases, have unfolded independently.

- **Uncertainty**: The first theme is people's uncertainty about the nature of privacy trade-offs, and their own preferences over them.
- **Context-dependence**: The second theme is the powerful context-dependence aspect of privacy preferences; the same person can in some situations be oblivious to, but in other situations be acutely concerned about, issues of privacy.
- **Malleability and influence**: The third theme is the malleability of privacy preferences, by which we mean that privacy preferences are subject to influence by those possessing greater insight into their determinants. Although most individuals are probably unaware of the diverse influences on their concern about privacy, entities whose interests depend on information revelation by others are not. The manipulation of subtle factors that activate or suppress privacy concern can be seen in myriad realms such as the choice of sharing defaults on social networks, or the provision of greater control on social media which creates an illusion of safety and encourages greater sharing.

Uncertainty, context-dependence, and malleability are closely connected. Context dependence is amplified by uncertainty. Because people are often "at sea" when it comes to the consequences of, and their feelings about, privacy, they cast around for cues to guide their behavior. Privacy preferences and behaviors are, in turn, malleable and subject to influence in large part because they are context-dependent and because those with an interest in information divulgence are able to manipulate context to their advantage.

4.2 Uncertainty

Individuals manage the boundaries between their private and public spheres in numerous ways: via separateness (separation from others), reserve (creating barriers against unwanted intrusion), or anonymity [11], by protecting personal information, but also through deception and dissimulation [12]. People establish such boundaries for many reasons, including the need for intimacy and psychological respite and the desire for protection from social influence and control [13]. Sometimes, these motivations are so visceral and primal that privacy-seeking behavior emerges swiftly and naturally. This is often the case when physical privacy is intruded such as when a stranger encroaches in one's personal space [14–16] or demonstratively eavesdrops on a conversation. However, at other times (often including when informational privacy is at stake), people experience considerable uncertainty about whether, and to what degree, they should be concerned about privacy.

A first and most obvious source of privacy uncertainty arises from incomplete and asymmetric information. Advancements in information technology have made the collection and usage of personal data often invisible. As a result, individuals rarely have clear knowledge of what information other people, firms, and governments have about them or how that information is used and with what consequences. To the extent that people lack such information, or are aware of their ignorance, they are likely to be uncertain about how much information to share.

Two factors exacerbate the difficulty of ascertaining the potential consequences of privacy behavior:

1. **It is hard to think about privacy.** Whereas some privacy harms are tangible, such as the financial costs associated with identity theft, many others, such as having strangers become aware of one's life history, are intangible.
2. **Privacy is rarely an unalloyed good.** It typically involves trade-offs [17]. For example, ensuring the privacy of a consumer's purchases may protect them from price discrimination but also deny the potential benefits of targeted advertisements.

Elements that mitigate one or both of these exacerbating factors, by either increasing the tangibility of privacy harms or making trade-offs explicit and simple to understand, will generally affect privacy-related decisions. This is illustrated by one laboratory experiment in which participants were asked to use a specially designed search engine to find online merchants and purchase from them, with their own credit cards, either a set of batteries or a sex toy [18]. When the search engine only provided links to the merchants' sites and a comparison of the products' prices from the different sellers, a majority of participants did not pay any attention to the merchants' privacy policies; they purchased from those offering the lowest price. However, when the search engine also provided participants with salient, easily accessible information about the differences in privacy protection afforded by the various merchants, a majority of participants paid a roughly 5% premium to buy products from (and share their credit card information with) more privacy-protecting merchants.

A second source of privacy uncertainty relates to preferences. Even when aware of the consequences of privacy decisions, people are still likely to be uncertain about their own privacy preferences. Research on preference uncertainty [19] shows that individuals often have little sense of how much they like goods, services, or other people. Privacy does not seem to be an exception. This can be illustrated by research in which people were asked sensitive and potentially incriminating questions either point-blank, or followed by credible assurances of confidentiality [20]. Although logically such assurances should lead to greater divulgence, they often had the opposite effect because they elevated respondents' privacy concerns, which without assurances would have remained dormant. The remarkable uncertainty of privacy preferences comes into play in efforts to measure individual and group differences in preference for privacy [21]. For example, Westin [22] famously used broad (i.e., not contextually specific) privacy questions in surveys to cluster individuals into privacy segments: privacy fundamentalists, pragmatists, and unconcerned. When asked directly, many people fall in the first segment: They profess to care a lot about privacy and express particular concern over losing control of their personal information or others gaining unauthorized access to it [23, 24]. However, doubts about the power of attitudinal scales to predict actual privacy behavior arose early in the literature [25]. This discrepancy between attitudes and behaviors has become known as the "privacy paradox."

In one early study illustrating the paradox, participants were first classified into categories of privacy concern inspired by Westin's categorization based on their responses to a survey dealing with attitudes toward sharing data [26]. Next, they were presented with products to purchase at a discount with the assistance of an anthropomorphic shopping agent. Few, regardless of the group they were categorized in, exhibited much reluctance to answering the increasingly sensitive questions the agent plied them with.

Why do people who claim to care about privacy often show little concern about it in their daily behavior? One possibility is that the paradox is illusory—that privacy attitudes, which are defined broadly, and intentions and behaviors, which are defined narrowly, should not be expected to be closely related [27, 28]. Thus, one might care deeply about privacy in general but, depending on the costs and benefits prevailing in a specific situation, seek or not seek privacy protection [29].

This explanation for the privacy paradox, however, is not entirely satisfactory for two reasons. The first is that it fails to account for situations in which attitude-behavior dichotomies arise under high correspondence between expressed concerns and behavioral actions. For example, one study compared attitudinal survey answers to actual social media behavior [30]. Even within the subset of participants who expressed the highest degree of concern over strangers being able to easily find out their sexual orientation, political views, and partners' names, 48% did in fact publicly reveal their sexual orientation online, 47% revealed their political orientation, and 21% revealed their current partner's name. The second reason is that privacy decision-making is only in part the result of a rational "calculus" of costs and benefits [17, 29]; it is also affected by misperceptions of those costs and benefits, as well as social norms, emotions, and heuristics. Any of these factors may affect behavior differently from how they affect attitudes. For instance, present-bias can cause even the privacy-conscious to engage in risky revelations of information, if the immediate gratification from disclosure trumps the delayed, and hence discounted, future consequences [31].

Preference uncertainty is evident not only in studies that compare stated attitudes with behaviors but also in those that estimate monetary valuations of privacy. "Explicit" investigations ask people to make direct trade-offs, typically between privacy of data and money. For instance, in a study conducted both in Singapore and the United States, students made a series of hypothetical choices about sharing information with websites that differed in protection of personal information and prices for accessing services [32]. Using conjoint analysis, the authors concluded that subjects valued protection against errors, improper access, and secondary use of personal information between $30.49 and $44.62. Similar to direct questions about attitudes and intentions, such explicit investigations of privacy valuation spotlight privacy as an issue that respondents should take account of and, as a result, increase the weight they place on privacy in their responses.

Implicit investigations, in contrast, infer valuations of privacy from day-to-day decisions in which privacy is only one of many considerations and is typically not highlighted. Individuals engage in privacy-related transactions all the time, even when the privacy trade-offs may be intangible or when the exchange of personal data may not be a visible or primary component of a transaction. For instance, completing a query on a search engine is akin to selling personal data (one's preferences and contextual interests) to the engine in exchange for a service (search results). "Revealed preference" economic arguments would then conclude that because technologies for information sharing have been enormously successful, whereas technologies for information protection have not, individuals hold overall low valuations of privacy. However, that is not always the case: Although individuals at times give up personal data for small benefits or discounts, at other times they voluntarily incur substantial costs to protect their privacy. Context, as further discussed in the next section, matters.

In fact, attempts to pinpoint exact valuations that people assign to privacy may be misguided, as suggested by research calling into question the stability, and hence validity, of privacy estimates. In one field experiment inspired by the literature on endowment effects [33], shoppers at a mall were offered gift cards for participating in a nonsensitive survey. The cards could be used online or in stores, just like debit cards. Participants were either given a $10 "anonymous" gift card (transactions done with that card would not be traceable to the subject) or a $12 trackable card (transactions done with that card would be linked to the name of the subject). Initially, half of the participants were given one type of card, and half the other. Then, they were all offered the opportunity to switch. Some shoppers, for example, were given the anonymous $10 card and were asked whether they would accept $2 to "allow my name to be linked to transactions done with the card"; other subjects were asked whether they would accept a card with $2 less value to "prevent my name from being linked to transactions done with the card." Of the subjects who originally held the less valuable but anonymous card, five times as many (52.1%) chose it and kept it over the other card than did those who originally held the more valuable card (9.7%). This suggests that people value privacy more when they have it than when they do not.

The consistency of preferences for privacy is also complicated by the existence of a powerful countervailing motivation: the desire to be public, share, and disclose. Humans are social animals, and information sharing is a central feature of human connection. Social penetration theory [34] suggests that progressively increasing levels of self-disclosure are an essential feature of the natural and desirable evolution of interpersonal relationships from superficial to intimate. Such a progression is only possible when people begin social interactions with a baseline level of privacy. Paradoxically, therefore, privacy provides an essential foundation for intimate disclosure. Similar to privacy, self-disclosure confers numerous objective and subjective benefits, including psychological and physical health [35, 36]. The desire for interaction, socialization, disclosure, and recognition or fame (and, conversely, the fear of anonymous unimportance) are human motives no less fundamental than the need for privacy. The electronic media of the current age provide unprecedented opportunities for acting on them. Through social media, disclosures can build social capital, increase self-esteem [37], and fulfill ego needs [38]. In a series of functional magnetic resonance imaging experiments, self-disclosure was even found to engage neural mechanisms associated with reward; people highly value the ability to share thoughts and feelings with others. Indeed, subjects in one of the experiments were willing to forgo money in order to disclose about themselves [39].

To summarize, there can be several reasons contributing to uncertainty in privacy decision-making. It is a good practice for system providers to acknowledge these factors and try to address them.

- **Users are rarely aware of the information that others might have about them.** Trade-offs associated with privacy decisions with intangible risks even worsen the situation. A potential remedy is to make trade-offs explicit, so that users will have less difficulty understanding them—however, that may not always be possible.
- **Users are uncertain about their privacy preferences.** Their preference can indeed be constructed at the moment. Continuing consent may be a potential solution to this problem—unfortunately, a system can ask for consent only every so often.

4.3 Context-Dependence

Much evidence suggests that privacy is a universal human need [40]. However, when people are uncertain about their preferences, they often search for cues in their environment to provide guidance. And because cues are a function of context, behavior is as well. Applied to privacy, context-dependence means that individuals can, depending on the situation, exhibit anything ranging from extreme concern to apathy about privacy. Adopting the terminology of Westin, we are all privacy pragmatists, privacy fundamentalists, or privacy unconcerned, depending on time and place [41].

The way we construe and negotiate public and private spheres is context-dependent because the boundaries between the two are murky [42]: The rules people follow for managing privacy vary by situation, are learned over time, and are based on cultural, motivational, and purely situational criteria. For instance, usually we may be more comfortable sharing secrets with friends, but at times we may reveal surprisingly personal information to a stranger on a plane [43]. The theory of contextual "integrity" posits that social expectations affect our beliefs regarding what is private and what is public and that such expectations vary with specific contexts [44]. Thus, seeking privacy in public is not a contradiction; individuals can manage privacy even while sharing information, and even on social media [45]. For instance, Fig. 4.1 shows the results of actual disclosure behavior of online social network users in a longitudinal study [46]. The results suggest that over time, many users increased the amount of personal information revealed to their friends (those connected to them on the network) while simultaneously decreasing the amounts revealed to strangers (those unconnected to them). In 2005 over 89% of profiles publicly revealed their birthday, while in 2011 just 20% of the profiles were public. Decreasing disclosures for several years, the percentage of profiles that publicly

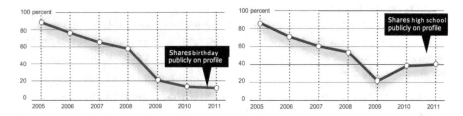

Fig. 4.1 Privacy behavior is affected both by endogenous motivations (i.e., subjective preferences: downtrend on the graphs suggests users disclose less as the time passes) and exogenous factors (i.e., changes in user interfaces: Facebook changed the default visibility settings for various fields on its profiles, including high school (bottom) but not birthday (top)) [46]

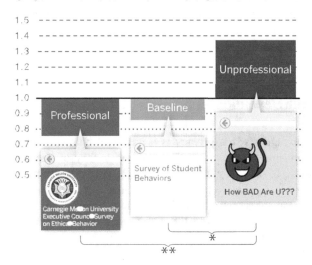

Fig. 4.2 The impact of cues on disclosure behavior. Subjects revealed more personal and even incriminating information on the website with a more casual design rather than a professionally developed website. The y axis captures the mean affirmative admission rates (AARs) normed, question by question, on the overall average AAR for the question

revealed their high school roughly doubled between 2009 and 2010 after Facebook changed the default visibility settings for various fields on its profiles, including high school (bottom), but not birthday (top).

The cues that people use to judge the importance of privacy sometimes result in sensible behavior. For instance, the presence of government regulation has been shown to reduce consumer concern and increase trust; it is a cue that people use to infer the existence of some degree of privacy protection [47]. In other situations, however, cues can be unrelated, or even negatively related, to normative bases of decision-making. For example, in one online experiment [48], individuals were more likely to reveal personal and even incriminating information on a website with an unprofessional and casual design with the banner "How Bad R U" than on a site with a formal interface even though the site with the formal interface was judged by other respondents to be much safer (Fig. 4.2). The study illustrates how cues can influence privacy behavior in a fashion that is unrelated, or even negatively related, to normative bases of decision-making. Yet in other situations, it is the physical environment that influences privacy concern and associated behavior [49], sometimes even unconsciously. For instance, all else being equal, intimacy of self-disclosure is higher in warm, comfortable rooms, with soft lighting, than in cold rooms with bare cement and overhead fluorescent lighting [50].

Some of the cues that influence perceptions of privacy are one's culture and the behavior of other people, either through the mechanism of descriptive norms (imitation) or via reciprocity [51]. Observing other people reveal information increases the likelihood that one will reveal it oneself [52]. In one study, survey-takers were asked a series of sensitive personal questions regarding their engagement in illegal or ethically questionable behaviors. After answering each question, participants were provided with information, manipulated unbeknownst to them, about the percentage of other participants who in the same survey had admitted to having engaged in a given behavior. Being provided with information that suggested that a majority of survey takers had admitted a certain questionable behavior increased participants' willingness to disclose their engagement in other, also sensitive, behaviors. Other studies have found that the tendency to reciprocate information disclosure is so ingrained that people will reveal more information even to a computer agent that provides information about itself [53]. Findings such as this may help to explain the escalating amounts of self-disclosure we witness online: If others are doing it, people seem to reason unconsciously, doing so oneself must be desirable or safe.

Other people's behavior affects privacy concerns in other ways, too. Sharing personal information with others makes them "co-owners" of that information [54] and, as such, responsible for its protection. Mismanagement of shared information by one or more co-owners causes "turbulence" of the privacy boundaries and, consequently, negative reactions, including anger or mistrust. In a study of undergraduate Facebook users [55], for instance, turbulence of privacy boundaries, as a result of having one's profile exposed to unintended audiences, dramatically increased the odds that a user would restrict profile visibility to friends-only.

Likewise, privacy concerns are often a function of past experiences. When something in an environment changes, such as the introduction of a camera or other monitoring devices, privacy concern is likely to be activated. For instance, surveillance can produce discomfort [56] and negatively affect worker productivity [57]. However, privacy concern, like other motivations, is adaptive; people get used to levels of intrusion that do not change over time. In an experiment conducted in Helsinki [58], the installation of sensing and monitoring technology in households led family members initially to change their behavior, particularly in relation to conversations, nudity, and sex. And yet, if they accidentally performed an activity, such as walking naked into the kitchen in front of the sensors, it seemed to have the effect of "breaking the ice"; participants then showed less concern about repeating the behavior. More generally, participants became inured to the presence of the technology over time.

The context-dependence of privacy concern has major implications for the risks associated with modern information and communication technology [59]. With online interactions, we no longer have a clear sense of the spatial boundaries of our listeners. Who is reading our blog post? Who is looking at our photos online? Adding complexity to privacy decision-making, boundaries between public and private become even less defined in the online world [60] where we become social media friends with our coworkers and post pictures to an indistinct flock of followers. With different social groups mixing on the Internet, separating online and offline identities and meeting our and others' expectations regarding privacy becomes more difficult and consequential [61]. Hence, it is important for system designers to account for context-dependence aspect of privacy. There might not be a global solution that fully addresses the issues caused by context-dependence aspect of privacy decisions, but being aware of that might lead to some best practice approaches to empower users' decisions. As a summary:

- **Privacy is context-dependent.** People might have different preferences based on a myriad of different, even inconspicuous factors. For instance, self-disclosure may be higher in a warm and comfortable room, compared to a cold and dark room.
- **Privacy concern is a function of users' past experiences in an environment.** Such concerns can change in response to changes in the environment (i.e., when setting up a surveillance camera for the first time). However, users can adapt to the new environment and get used to it too.

4.4   Malleability and Influence

Whereas individuals are often unaware of the diverse factors that determine their concern about privacy in a particular situation, entities whose prosperity depends on information revelation by others are much more sophisticated. With the emergence of the information age, growing institutional and economic interests have developed around disclosure of personal information, from online social networks to behavioral advertising. It is not surprising, therefore, that some entities have an interest in, and have developed expertise in, exploiting behavioral and psychological processes to promote disclosure [62]. Such efforts play on the malleability of privacy preferences, a term we use to refer to the observation that various, some- times subtle, factors can be used to activate or suppress privacy concerns, which in turn affect behavior.

Default settings are an important tool used by different entities to affect information disclosure. A large body of research has shown that default settings matter for decisions as important as organ donation and retirement saving [63]. Sticking to default settings is convenient, and people often interpret default settings as implicit recommendations [64]. Thus, it is not surprising that default settings for one's profile's visibility on social networks [65], or the existence of opt-in or opt-out privacy policies on websites [66], affect individuals' privacy behavior. Figure 4.3 shows how default visibility settings became more revelatory between 2005 and

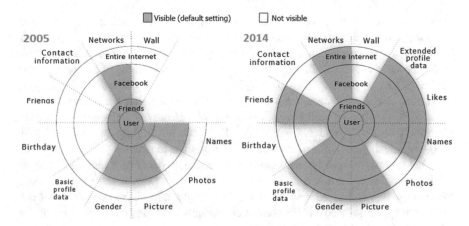

Fig. 4.3 Changes in Facebook default profile visibility settings over time (2005–2014). Fields such as "Likes" and "Extended Profile Data" did not exist in 2005. This figure is based on the authors' data and the original visualization created by M. McKeon, available at http://mattmckeon. com/facebook-privacy

2014, disclosing more personal information to larger audiences, unless the user manually overrode the defaults.

In addition to default settings, websites can also use design features that frustrate or even confuse users into disclosing personal information [67], a practice that has been referred to as "malicious interface design" [68]. Another obvious strategy that commercial entities can use to avoid raising privacy concerns is not to "ring alarm bells" when it comes to data collection. When companies do ring them—for example, by using overly fine-tuned personalized advertisements—consumers are alerted [69] and can respond with negative "reactance" [70].

Various so-called antecedents [71] affect privacy concerns and can be used to influence privacy behavior. For instance, trust in the entity receiving one's personal data soothes concerns. Moreover, because some interventions that are intended to protect privacy can establish trust, concerns can be muted by the very interventions intended to protect privacy. Perversely, 62% of respondents to a survey believed (incorrectly) that the existence of a privacy policy implied that a site could not share their personal information without permission [41], which suggests that simply posting a policy that consumers do not read may lead to misplaced feelings of being protected.

Control is another feature that can inculcate trust and produce paradoxical effects. Perhaps because of its lack of controversiality, control has been one of the capstones of the focus of both industry and policy-makers in attempts to balance privacy needs against the value of sharing. Control over personal information is often perceived as a critical feature of privacy protection [40]. In principle, it does provide users with the means to manage access to their personal information. Research, however, shows that control can reduce privacy concern [47], which in turn can have unintended effects. For instance, one study found that participants who were provided with greater explicit control over whether and how much of their personal information researchers could publish ended up sharing more sensitive information with a broader audience, the opposite of the ostensible purpose of providing such control [72].

Similar to the normative perspective on control, increasing the transparency of firms' data practices would seem to be desirable. However, transparency mechanisms can be easily rendered ineffective. Research has highlighted not only that an overwhelming majority of Internet users do not read privacy policies [73], but also that few users would benefit from doing so; nearly half of a sample of online privacy policies were found to be written in language beyond the grasp of most Internet users [74]. Indeed, and somewhat amusingly, it has been estimated that the aggregate opportunity cost if US consumers actually read the privacy policies of the sites they visit would be $781 billion/year [75].

Although uncertainty and context-dependence lead naturally to malleability and manipulation, not all malleability is necessarily sinister. Consider monitoring. Although monitoring can cause discomfort and reduce productivity, the feeling of being observed and accountable can induce people to engage in prosocial behaviors or (for better or for worse) adhere to social norms [76]. Prosocial behavior can be heightened by monitoring cues as simple as three dots in a stylized face configuration [77]. By the same token, the depersonalization induced by computer-mediated interaction [78], either in the form of lack of identifiability or of visual anonymity [79], can have beneficial effects, such as increasing truthful responses to sensitive surveys [80, 81]. Whether elevating or suppressing privacy concerns is socially beneficial critically depends, yet again, on context [a meta-analysis of the impact of de-identification on behavior is provided in [82]]. For example, perceptions of anonymity can alternatively lead to dishonest or prosocial behavior. Illusory anonymity induced by darkness caused participants in an experiment [83] to cheat in order to gain more money. This can be interpreted as a form of disinhibition effect [84], by which perceived anonymity licenses people to act in ways that they would otherwise not even consider. In other circumstances, though, anonymity leads to prosocial behavior for instance, higher willingness to share money in a dictator game, when coupled with priming of religiosity [85].

As a summary, in contrast to unintentional effects of uncertainty and context-dependence which can lead to malleability, in this section we discussed intentional interventions that can nudge people towards disclosing more than what they really want to:

- **Default effects can lead to over-disclosure.** People might interpret default as the recommended option.
- **Malicious interface design is a design practice that aims to influence user behavior**, including nudging the user towards increased disclosures.
- **Having a sense of control can lead to over-disclosure.** Users are more likely to disclosure information in a system that provides granular control. A granular control induces a higher sense of control and in turn decreases privacy concerns.

4.5 Conclusions

Norms and behaviors regarding private and public realms greatly differ across cultures [86]. Americans, for example, are reputed to be more open about sexual matters than are the Chinese, whereas the latter are more open about financial matters (such as income, cost of home, and possessions). And even within cultures, people differ substantially in how much they care about privacy and what information they treat as private. And as we have sought to highlight in this chapter, privacy concerns can vary dramatically for the same individual, and for societies, over time.

If privacy behaviors are culture- and context-dependent, however, the dilemma of what to share and what to keep private is universal across societies and over human history. The task of navigating those boundaries and the consequences of mismanaging them have grown increasingly complex and fateful in the information age, to the point that our natural instincts seem not nearly adequate.

In this chapter, we used three themes to organize and draw connections between the social and behavioral science literature on privacy and behavior. We end the chapter with a brief discussion of the reviewed literature's relevance to privacy policy.

- **Uncertainty and context-dependence** imply that people cannot always be counted on to navigate the complex trade-offs involving privacy in a self-interested fashion. People are often unaware of the information they are sharing, unaware of how it can be used, and even in the rare situations when they have full knowledge of the consequences of sharing, **uncertain** about their own preferences.
- **Malleability**, in turn, implies that people are easily influenced in what and how much they disclose. Moreover, what they share can be used to influence their emotions, thoughts, and behaviors in many aspects of their lives, as individuals, consumers, and citizens. Although such influence is not always or necessarily malevolent or dangerous, relinquishing control over one's personal data and over one's privacy alters the balance of power between those holding the data and those who are the subjects of that data.

Insights from the social and behavioral empirical research on privacy reviewed here suggest that policy approaches that rely exclusively on informing or "empowering" the individual are unlikely to provide adequate protection against the risks posed by recent information technologies. Consider transparency and control, two principles conceived as necessary conditions for privacy protection. The research we highlighted shows that they may provide insufficient protections and even backfire when used apart from other principles of privacy protection.

The research reviewed here suggests that if the goal of policy is to adequately protect privacy (as we believe it should be), then we need policies that protect individuals with minimal requirement of informed and rational decision-making—policies that include a baseline framework of protection, such as the principles embedded in the so-called fair information practices [87]. People need assistance and even protection to aid in navigating what is otherwise a very uneven playing field. As highlighted by our discussion, a goal of public policy should be to achieve a more even equity of power between individuals, consumers, and citizens on the one hand and, on the other, the data holders such as governments and corporations that currently have the upper hand. To be effective, privacy policy should protect real people—who are naive, uncertain, and vulnerable—and should be sufficiently flexible to evolve with the emerging unpredictable complexities of the information age.

Acknowledgments The authors gratefully acknowledge the American Association for the Advancement of Science for allowing the use of previously published materials [88] and Reza Ghaiumy Anaraky for excellent editing.

References

1. Mayer-Schönberger, V. 2011. *Delete: The Virtue of Forgetting in the Digital Age*. Princeton: Princeton University Press.
2. Sweeney, L. 2002. k-anonymity: A model for protecting privacy. *International Journal of Uncertainty, Fuzziness and Knowledge-Based Systems* 10 (05): 557–570.
3. McAfee, A., E. Brynjolfsson, T.H. Davenport, D. Patil, and D. Barton 2012. Big data: The management revolution. *Harvard Business Review* 90 (10): 60–68.
4. Tatonetti, N.P., P.Y. Patrick, R. Daneshjou, and R.B. Altman. 2012. Data-driven prediction of drug effects and interactions. *Science Translational Medicine* 4 (125): 125ra31–125ra31.
5. Acquisti, A., and R. Gross. 2009. Predicting social security numbers from public data. *Proceedings of the National Academy of Sciences* 106 (27): 10975–10980.
6. Cohen, J.E. 1999. Examined lives: Informational privacy and the subject as object. *Stanford Law Review* 52: 1373.
7. Crawford, K., M.L. Gray, and K. Miltner. 2014. Big data— critiquing big data: Politics, ethics, epistemology—special section introduction. *International Journal of Communication* 8: 10.
8. Posner, R.A. 1981. The economics of privacy. *The American Economic Review* 71 (2): 405–409.
9. Solove, D.J. 2012. Introduction: Privacy self-management and the consent dilemma. *Harvard Law Review* 126: 1880.
10. Solove, D.J. 2005. A taxonomy of privacy. *University of Pennsylvania Law Review* 154: 477.
11. Schoeman, F.D. 1984. *Philosophical Dimensions of Privacy: An Anthology*. Cambridge: Cambridge University Press.
12. DePaulo, B.M., C. Wetzel, R. Weylin Sternglanz, and M.J.W. Wilson. 2003. Verbal and nonverbal dynamics of privacy, secrecy, and deceit. *Journal of Social Issues* 59 (2): 391–410.
13. Margulis, S.T. 2003. Privacy as a social issue and behavioral concept. *Journal of Social Issues* 59 (2): 243–261.
14. Goffman, E. 1971. *Relations in Public: Microstudies of the Public Order*. Milton Park: Routledge.
15. Sundstrom, E., and I. Altman. 1976. Interpersonal relationships and personal space: Research review and theoretical model. *Human Ecology* 4 (1): 47–67.
16. Schwartz, B. 1968. The social psychology of privacy. *American Journal of Sociology* 73 (6): 741–752.
17. Laufer, R.S., and M. Wolfe. 1977. Privacy as a concept and a social issue: A multidimensional developmental theory. *Journal of Social Issues* 33 (3): 22–42.
18. Tsai, J.Y., S. Egelman, L. Cranor, and A. Acquisti. 2011. The effect of online privacy information on purchasing behavior: An experimental study. *Information Systems Research* 22 (2): 254–268.

19. Slovic, P. 1995. The construction of preference. *American Psychologist* 50 (5): 364.
20. Singer, E., H.J. Hippler, and N. Schwarz. 1992. Confidentiality assurances in surveys: Reassurance or threat? *International Journal of Public Opinion Research* 4 (3): 256–268. (1992)
21. Skotko, V.P., and D. Langmeyer. 1977. The effects of interaction distance and gender on self-disclosure in the dyad. *Sociometry* 40: 178–182.
22. Louis Harris and Associates, Inc. 1991. Equifax-Harris consumer privacy survey. Equifax, Inc. https://hdl.handle.net/1902.29/H-912046
23. Culnan, M.J., and P.K. Armstrong. 1999. Information privacy concerns, procedural fairness, and impersonal trust: An empirical investigation. *Organization Science* 10 (1): 104–115.
24. Smith, H.J., S.J. Milberg, and S.J. Burke. 1996. Information privacy: Measuring individuals' concerns about organizational practices. *MIS Quarterly* 20: 167–196.
25. Lubin, B., and R.L. Harrison. 1964. Predicting small group behavior with the self-disclosure inventory. *Psychological Reports* 15 (1): 77–78.
26. Spiekermann, S., J. Grossklags, and B. Berendt. 2001. E-privacy in 2nd generation e-commerce: privacy preferences versus actual behavior. In *Proceedings of the 3rd ACM Conference on Electronic Commerce*, 38–47. New York: ACM.
27. Norberg, P.A., D.R. Horne, and D.A. Horne. 2007. The privacy paradox: Personal information disclosure intentions versus behaviors. *Journal of Consumer Affairs* 41 (1): 100–126.
28. Ajzen, I., and M. Fishbein. 1997. Attitude-behavior relations: A theoretical analysis and review of empirical research. *Psychological Bulletin* 84 (5): 888.
29. Klopfer, P.H., and D.I. Rubenstein. 1977. The concept privacy and its biological basis. *Journal of Social Issues* 33 (3): 52–65.
30. Acquisti, A., and R. Gross. 2006. Imagined communities: Awareness, information sharing, and privacy on the facebook. In *International Workshop on Privacy Enhancing Technologies*, 36–58. Berlin: Springer.
31. Acquisti, A. 2004. Privacy in electronic commerce and the economics of immediate gratification. In *Proceedings of the 5th ACM Conference on Electronic Commerce*, 21–29. New York: ACM.
32. Hann, I.H., K.L. Hui, S.Y.T. Lee, and I.P. Png 2007. Overcoming online information privacy concerns: An information-processing theory approach. *Journal of Management Information Systems* 24 (2): 13–42.
33. Acquisti, A., L.K. John, and G. Loewenstein. 2013, What is privacy worth? *The Journal of Legal Studies* 42 (2): 249–274.
34. Altman, I., and D.A. Taylor. 1973. *Social Penetration: The Development of Interpersonal Relationships*. New York: Holt, Rinehart & Winston.
35. Frattaroli, J. 2006. Experimental disclosure and its moderators: A meta-analysis. *Psychological Bulletin* 132 (6): 823.
36. Pennebaker, J.W. 1993. Putting stress into words: Health, linguistic, and therapeutic implications. *Behaviour Research and Therapy* 31 (6): 539–548.
37. Steinfield, C., N.B. Ellison, and C. Lampe. 2008. Social capital, self-esteem, and use of online social network sites: A longitudinal analysis. *Journal of Applied Developmental Psychology* 29 (6): 434–445.
38. Toma, C.L., and J.T. Hancock. 2013. Self-affirmation underlies facebook use. *Personality and Social Psychology Bulletin* 39 (3): 321–331.
39. Tamir, D.I., and J.P. Mitchell. 2012. Disclosing information about the self is intrinsically rewarding. *Proceedings of the National Academy of Sciences* 109 (21): 8038–8043.
40. Westin, A.F. 1967. Privacy and freedom atheneum. *New York* 7: 431–453.
41. Hoofnagle, C.J., and J.M. Urban. 2014 Alan Westin's privacy homo economicus. *Wake Forest Law Review* 49: 261.
42. Marx, G.T. 2001. Murky conceptual waters: The public and the private. *Ethics and Information Technology* 3 (3): 157–169.
43. Thibaut, J.W., and H.H. Kelley. 1959. *The Social Psychology of Groups*. Milton Park: Routledge.

44. Nissenbaum, H. 2009. *Privacy in Context: Technology, Policy, and the Integrity of Social Life.* Palo Alto: Stanford University Press
45. Boyd, D. 2014. *It's Complicated: The Social Lives of Networked Teens.* New Haven: Yale University Press.
46. Stutzman, F.D., R. Gross, and A. Acquisti. 2013. Silent listeners: The evolution of privacy and disclosure on facebook. *Journal of Privacy and Confidentiality* 4 (2): 2.
47. Xu, H., H.H. Teo, B.C. Tan, and R. Agarwal. 2009. The role of push-pull technology in privacy calculus: The case of location-based services. *Journal of Management Information Systems* 26 (3): 135–174.
48. John, L.K., A. Acquisti, and G. Loewenstein. 2010. Strangers on a plane: Context-dependent willingness to divulge sensitive information. *Journal of Consumer Research* 37 (5): 858–873.
49. Altman, I. 1975. *The Environment and Social Behavior: Privacy, Personal Space, Territory, and Crowding.* Pacific Grove: Brooks/Cole.
50. Chaikin, A.L., V.J. Derlega, and S.J. Miller. 1976. Effects of room environment on self-disclosure in a counseling analogue. *Journal of Counseling Psychology* 23 (5): 479.
51. Derlega, V.J., and A.L. Chaikin 1977. Privacy and self-disclosure in social relationships. *Journal of Social Issues* 33 (3): 102–115.
52. Acquisti, A., L.K. John, and G. Loewenstein. 2012. The impact of relative standards on the propensity to disclose. *Journal of Marketing Research* 49 (2): 160–174.
53. Moon, Y. 2000. Intimate exchanges: Using computers to elicit self-disclosure from consumers. *Journal of Consumer Research* 26 (4): 323–339.
54. Petronio, S. 2002. *Boundaries of Privacy: Dialectics of Disclosure.* Albany: State University of New York Press.
55. Stutzman, F., and J. Kramer-Duffield. 2010. Friends only: examining a privacy-enhancing behavior in facebook. In *Proceedings of the SIGCHI Conference on Human Factors in Computing Systems*, 1553–1562. New York: ACM.
56. Honess, T., and E. Charman. 1992. *Closed Circuit Television in Public Places: Its Acceptability and Perceived Effectiveness.* Home Office Police Research Group.
57. Gagné, M., and E.L. Deci. 2005. Self-determination theory and work motivation. *Journal of Organizational Behavior* 26 (4): 331–362.
58. Oulasvirta, A., A. Pihlajamaa, J. Perkiö, D. Ray, T. Vähäkangas, T. Hasu, N. Vainio, and P. Myllymäki. 2012. Long-term effects of ubiquitous surveillance in the home. In *Proceedings of the 2012 ACM Conference on Ubiquitous Computing*, 41–50. New York: ACM.
59. Palen, L., and P. Dourish. 2003. Unpacking privacy for a networked world. In *Proceedings of the SIGCHI Conference on Human Factors in Computing Systems*, 129–136. New York: ACM.
60. Tufekci, Z. 2008. Can you see me now? audience and disclosure regulation in online social network sites. *Bulletin of Science, Technology & Society* 28 (1): 20–36.
61. Bargh, J.A., K.Y. McKenna, and G.M. Fitzsimons. 2002. Can you see the real me? activation and expression of the true self on the internet. *Journal of Social Issues* 58 (1): 33–48.
62. Calo, R. 2013. Digital market manipulation. *The George Washington Law Review* 82:995.
63. Johnson, E.J., and D. Goldstein 2003. Do defaults save lives? *Science* 302: 1338–1339.
64. McKenzie, C.R., M.J. Liersch, and S.R. Finkelstein. 2006. Recommendations implicit in policy defaults. *Psychological Science* 17 (5): 414–420.
65. Gross, R., and A. Acquisti 2005. Information revelation and privacy in online social networks. In *Proceedings of the 2005 ACM Workshop on Privacy in the Electronic Society*, 71–80. New York: ACM.
66. Johnson, E.J., S. Bellman, and G.L. Lohse. 2002. Defaults, framing and privacy: Why opting in-opting out. *Marketing Letters* 13 (1): 5–15.
67. Hartzog, W. 2010. Website design as contract. *American University Law Review* 60: 1635.
68. Conti, G., and E. Sobiesk 2010. Malicious interface design: exploiting the user. In *Proceedings of the 19th International Conference on World Wide Web*, 271–280. New York: ACM.
69. Goldfarb, A., and C. Tucker. 2011. Online display advertising: Targeting and obtrusiveness. *Marketing Science* 30 (3): 389–404.
70. White, T.B., D.L. Zahay, H. Thorbjørnsen, and S. Shavitt. 2008. Getting too personal: Reactance to highly personalized email solicitations. *Marketing Letters* 19 (1): 39–50.

71. Smith, H.J., T. Dinev, and H. Xu. 2011. Information privacy research: An interdisciplinary review. *MIS Quarterly* 35 (4): 989–1016.
72. Brandimarte, L., A. Acquisti, and G. Loewenstein. 2013. Misplaced confidences: Privacy and the control paradox. *Social Psychological and Personality Science* 4 (3): 340–347.
73. Jensen, C., C. Potts, and C. Jensen. 2005. Privacy practices of internet users: Self-reports versus observed behavior. *International Journal of Human-Computer Studies* 63 (1–2): 203–227.
74. Jensen, C., and C. Potts 2004. Privacy policies as decision-making tools: An evaluation of online privacy notices. In *Proceedings of the SIGCHI Conference on Human Factors in Computing Systems*, 471–478. New York: ACM.
75. McDonald, A., and L. Cranor. 2008. *I/S: A Journal of Law and Policy for the Information Society* 4: 540–565.
76. Wedekind, C., and M. Milinski. Cooperation through image scoring in humans. *Science* 288 (5467): 850–852.
77. Rigdon, M., K. Ishii, M. Watabe, and S. Kitayama. 2009. Minimal social cues in the dictator game. *Journal of Economic Psychology* 30 (3): 358–367.
78. Kiesler, S., J. Siegel, and T.W. McGuire. 1984. Social psychological aspects of computer-mediated communication. *American Psychologist* 39 (10): 1123.
79. Joinson, A.N. 2001. Self-disclosure in computer-mediated communication: The role of self-awareness and visual anonymity. *European Journal of Social Psychology* 31 (2): 177–192.
80. Weisband, S., and S. Kiesler. 1996. Self disclosure on computer forms: Meta-analysis and implications. In *Proceedings of the SIGCHI Conference on Human Factors in Computing Systems*, 3–10. New York: ACM.
81. Tourangeau, R., and T. Yan. 2007. Sensitive questions in surveys. *Psychological Bulletin* 133 (5): 859.
82. Postmes, T., and R. Spears. 1998. Deindividuation and antinormative behavior: A meta-analysis. *Psychological Bulletin* 123 (3): 238.
83. Zhong, C.B., V.K. Bohns, and F. Gino. 2010. Good lamps are the best police: Darkness increases dishonesty and self-interested behavior. *Psychological Science* 21 (3): 311–314.
84. Suler, J. 2004. The online disinhibition effect. *Cyberpsychology & Behavior* 7 (3): 321–326.
85. Shariff, A.F., and A. Norenzayan. 2007. God is watching you: Priming god concepts increases prosocial behavior in an anonymous economic game. *Psychological Science* 18 (9): 803–809.
86. Moore Jr, B. 1984. *Privacy: Studies in Social and Cultural History, Armonk, NY: Me Sharpe*. Milton Park: Routledge.
87. Welfare Secretary's Advisory Committee on Automated Personal Data Systems. 1973. Records, computers, and the rights of citizens: report. United States Department of Health, Education, and Welfare; for for sale by the Superintendent of Documents, US.
88. Acquisti, A., L. Brandimarte, and G. Loewenstein. 2015. Privacy and human behavior in the age of information. *Science* 347 (6221): 509–514. https://doi.org/10.1126/science.aaa1465. http://science.sciencemag.org/content/347/6221/509

Chapter 5
The Development of Privacy Norms

Nicholas Proferes

Abstract This chapter addresses how we develop, revisit, and negotiate norms around privacy when confronted with new technologies. The chapter first examines Nissenbaum's (Washington Law Review 79(1):119–157, 2004) theory of privacy as contextual integrity, a framework that helps unpack how context-relevant norms for appropriateness and transmission can be challenged by new technologies. It then reviews how social norms develop as we build mental models of how a technology works during its diffusion process. The chapter concludes with suggestions for designers about approaches for thinking through implications when a design may challenge a preexisting social norm, or where there is no socially agreed upon norm. This includes careful reflection on who challenges to the current social norms may benefit and who they may hurt.

5.1 Introduction

Privacy norms shape what we consider appropriate information flow in any given situation. For example, while we might voluntarily share sensitive health information about ourselves with a friend, it would likely violate our sense of privacy for that friend to turn around and tell our boss the same information. As new technologies such as cellphone cameras, social media platforms, and persistently listening technologies such as digital personal assistants have been introduced into society, prior privacy norms have been thrown into question. This chapter addresses how we develop, revisit, and negotiate norms around privacy when faced with new technologies.

Privacy norms have evolved over time. Historically, we defined privacy as relating to a narrow set of situations and circumstances. However, novel inventions challenged these prior privacy regimes, throwing both the norms and the concept

N. Proferes (✉)
School of Social and Behavioral Sciences, Arizona State University, Tempe, AZ, USA
e-mail: nicholas.proferes@asu.edu

of privacy itself into disarray. This chapter introduces Nissenbaum's [1] model of privacy as contextual integrity as a way to help us make sense of these challenges. Nissenbaum posits that, in a given setting, contextual integrity is maintained when the norms of information appropriateness and norms of information transmission are respected; when it's not, our sense of privacy is violated. The contextual integrity framework helps unpack how context-relevant norms for appropriateness and transmission can be challenged by new technologies.

Next, the chapter details how we develop and evaluate social norms for information appropriateness and transmission in relation to new technologies. First, we build an internal mental model of how a technology works, the kinds of information it collects and transmits, and the kinds of actions and outcomes it can afford us. We then take that picture and paste it to our understandings of particular social situations. In each of these social situations, we consider the social roles associated with a given context, our own expectations and those of others, and the possible actions and practices of others, as informed by history, culture, law, and social convention. Based on this, we engage in a kind of calculus, weighing the benefits of particular technological ends afforded to us versus any challenges to established norms. Thus, at the individual level, social privacy norms are continuously revised in relation to the perceived benefits of particular uses of a technology. As we will see, this is not always a rational process and is often filled with risk and uncertainty. This process of social negotiation scales as a technology diffuses and begins to involve not just users but also social leaders, policy-makers, and designers.

The chapter concludes with suggestions for designers about approaches for thinking through implications when a design may challenge a preexisting social norm, or where there is no socially agreed upon norm. This includes careful reflection on who challenges to the current social norms may benefit and who they may hurt.

Key Takeaways

- Privacy norms shape our expectations for what's appropriate in a given situation.
- Privacy norms are socially constructed and evolve overtime. This means they may vary culturally and may change, even within a culture.
- A new technology can create new social contexts, which challenge preexisting norms. Our beliefs about how a given technology works are a key component of how we build and adapt our privacy norms.

5.2 Privacy and Challenges in Relation to Technology

In the United States, the regulatory genesis for privacy rights can be found in rules meant to protect people from government agents (such as rights against unreasonable search and seizure), restricting access to specific kinds of information about one's self (such as rights against being forced to testify against one's self), and the establishment of particular physical locations that could be considered private (such as the privacy of one's home) [1]. These frameworks have historically helped create certain baseline expectations for privacy. For more on how privacy laws and frameworks vary internationally, see Chap. 2. However, the relevance and applicability of these frameworks have also been challenged by the development of new technologies.

Smith [2] traces the conceptualization of privacy as it has existed from the founding of the United States to contemporary outlooks, noting, "each time when there was renewed interest in protecting privacy it was in reaction to new technology" (p. 6). For example, when the handheld snap camera become widely available in the late 1800s, it became more readily possible to invade the privacy of others from a distance and to use someone else's likeness without their permission, challenging both our previous beliefs about what privacy should protect and the norms of what is appropriate. New practices emerged, such as newspaper photographers "feeding an 'unseemly gossip' industry by taking and publishing candid shots of people without their consent" [3]. In response to these practices, Brandeis and Warren [4] argued "solitude and privacy have become more essential to the individual; but modern enterprise and invention have, through invasions upon his privacy, subjected him to mental pain and distress, far greater than could be inflicted by mere bodily injury" (p. 263). As part of their seminal *Harvard Law Review* article, "The Right to Privacy," the pair argued for a new vision of privacy as the right to be "let alone."

Smith [2] observes that as computer databases meant for commercial usages became more ubiquitous in the 1960s, public concern about privacy grew rapidly. Digital technologies were increasing the ability for actors to collect, store, aggregate, and transmit information in ways that extended beyond the interruption of another's seclusion. Americans became particularly concerned with "informational privacy" (p. 6). New policies emerged in response to demand from a worried public. For example, the 1973 issuance of the Fair Information Practice Principles (FIPPs) and a US Secretary Advisory Committee report entitled Records, Computers, and the Rights of Citizens and the 1974 Privacy Act were enacted to try to put some controls on commercial practices [5]. At the same time, researchers such as Alan Westin [6, 7] began to push for what are some of the basic underpinnings of online privacy protections used today, such as informed consent for transmission of personal information.

Today, privacy scholars such as Solove [8] have argued that privacy is a concept in disarray. Older models have failed to keep pace with the actual practices enabled by contemporary tech [9]. Technologies such as cellphone cameras, social media platforms, and persistently listening digital personal assistants have complicated our earlier notions of what privacy should protect and what is normatively appropriate. For example, cellphone cameras have raised questions about whether or not the practice of taking pictures of strangers in public places and then circulating them online for entertainment—a practice known as posting "strangershots" [10]—is a violation of one's privacy. Social media platforms such as Facebook have raised questions about the kinds of information resharing with third parties that are socially permissible (for more on this, read [11] on the Cambridge Analytica scandal). And Internet of Things assistive technologies such as Alexa rely on human workers that often listen to voice recordings captured in Echo owners' homes and offices, "as part of an effort to eliminate gaps in Alexa's understanding of human speech and help it better respond to commands" [12], a practice not always known to users.

We have collectively struggled with questions about whether or not these technological practices violate our privacy and what appropriate social norms are for activities involving these technologies. Each new tool creates a new social context which complicates our reliance on earlier privacy practices. Nissenbaum's [1] conceptualization of privacy as contextual integrity offers an alternative framework that helps us understand not just why new technologies constantly cause us to revisit our privacy norms but additionally offers insights into where the norms for privacy come from.

Key Takeaways

- Our understanding of what privacy is and what it should protect has historically evolved in response to the introduction of new technologies.
- Narrow definitions of privacy, such as only considering it "the right to be let alone," are being challenged by new technologies, such as cellphone cameras, social media platforms, and persistently listening digital personal assistants.
- Nissenbaum's theory of privacy as "contextual integrity" can help unpack why new technology uses challenge privacy.

5.3   Privacy as Contextual Integrity

Nissenbaum's [1] contextual integrity framework allows us to unpack how context-relevant norms for information gathering and information flow form a basis for prescriptive evaluations of privacy-related situations. One of the main premises of contextual integrity is that, rather than only having specific areas of life where privacy is a concern, there are "no arenas of life not governed by norms of information flow, no information or spheres of life for which 'anything goes.' Almost everything—things that we do, events that occur, transactions that take place—happens in a context not only of place but of politics, convention, and cultural expectation" (p. 119). Importantly for our conversation, social norms around information flow are always in play because we always exist in some kind of contextual position. We are never outside of the social. Each life situation we find ourselves in contains its own distinct norms, which are dictated by our social role, expectations, actions, and practices. For example, we may find ourselves in the social role of "patient seeing their doctor." The norms of information for these social roles are defined by history, culture, law, and convention. Information flow in this situation is dictated by norms of how the medical field has historically treated patient information, standardized medical practices, and various laws that govern how medical information is collected.

Nissenbaum argues that there are two primary types of informational privacy norms: norms of informational appropriateness and norms of information flow.

Contextual integrity, and our underlying sense of privacy, is upheld when **both** types of norms are upheld. Norms of information appropriateness generally govern the match between the type of information being requested and the context of the request. For example, it would be perfectly reasonable for a doctor to ask a patient about their health condition. However, it might be unreasonable to go up to strangers in a park and ask them about the same question. Again, roles, expectations, actions, and practices as informed by history, culture, law, and social convention will tell us what is an appropriate request versus an inappropriate request. New technologies can challenge preexisting norms of information appropriateness. For example, a social media profile generator may make requests for information about things such as location, political affiliation, birthdays, tastes, etc. As the social media platform constitutes a new social context, users may struggle in determining what is normatively appropriate.

Norms of distribution govern "movement, or transfer of information from one party to another or others" (p. 122). It might be perfectly reasonable for our doctors to gather sensitive health information from us, but if they exchange it with our bosses without our consent, this would likely violate our normative expectations. Cellphone cameras have made it possible to record and rebroadcast the activities of others in public, challenging our earlier notions of "privacy via obscurity" [13]. However, in addition to these new information flows, what makes norms of distribution particularly tricky is that many of the information flows enabled by contemporary tools are not transparent to users. As a result, users may be broadly unaware that particular flows exist, and thus, when they are revealed, can cause considerable consternation.

Nissenbaum's framework helps us identify reasons why particular practices may violate our expectations for privacy. For example, new technologies might demand kinds of information that we are uncomfortable sharing, thus violating information appropriateness. A technology could also be used to transmit information in ways that violate our expectations for information transmission and our imagined audiences, such as when social media posts are shown to our bosses [14, 15]. However, new technologies can also create the potential for privacy harm when we have incomplete understandings of how they work and when norms of information appropriateness and transmission are still being socially negotiated. The next section talks about how we build expectations for technology that we then use to negotiate appropriate social norms.

Key Takeaways

- Contextual integrity argues that every moment of our lives is governed by situationally informed information norms (i.e., contexts).
- In contextual integrity, there are two types of informational norms that impact our privacy evaluations: norms of information appropriateness and norms of information flow. Both must be met for us not to feel our privacy has been violated.
- The norms we use to evaluate information appropriateness and information flow are influenced by our social roles, expectations, actions, and practices, which

are themselves shaped by history, culture, law, and convention. As a result, individuals may have different evaluations of whether or not the same practice is a privacy violation, depending on these factors.

5.4 Building Expectations

Contextually relevant social norms for information appropriateness and transmission do not fall from the sky. They have their genesis in individual expectations about how technologies work and what they can afford in terms of actions and outcomes, applied to social contexts (which, again, are made up social roles, expectations, actions, and practices, as shaped by history, culture, law, and convention). We develop our understandings of what a technology does and how it might enable certain information flows through three sources: our direct interactions with a technology, watching others use a technology, and consuming discourse about a technology (e.g., reading a newspaper article about a new technology) [16]. Once we have this "mental model" in place, we situate our understandings of these information flows against broader preexisting social norms. Social norms then develop out of scaled expectations about appropriate behavior that occurs in the context [17].

For technology designers, what is particularly important in this process is how individuals develop their mental models about what a technology affords in terms of information flows. The term "affordance" originally comes from the perceptual psychologist J. J. Gibson [18], who argues that the meanings of objects in an environment can be directly perceived and that these perceptions can then be mentally linked to the possible actions that can be taken in an environment. For example, in perceiving a large leafy tree, the individual may observe that this object creates shade on a sunny day. After perceiving this affordance within the environment, the individual may take the action of sitting down under the tree to cool off (realizing this affordance in action).

Norman [19] and Gaver [20] are the two authors who are generally credited for taking Gibson's concept from psychology and importing it into the study of technological artifacts and technological design. Gaver [20] observes that any given technology provides a set of affordances that exist in relationship with that technology's users. These affordances "are properties of the world that are compatible with and relevant for people's interactions" (p. 79). This is to say technologies can afford us certain interactions and outcomes within the world. For example, social media sites commonly afford various degrees of visibility to users [21]. However, for the individual to realize an affordance in action, the affordance must first be *perceptible*. It is only when technological affordances are perceptible to the individual that there can be a direct link between perception and action [20]. When the affordances of technology are not perceivable (such as when they are hidden) or are perceived incorrectly by an individual, this can lead to mistakes. Poor design choices can hinder the perceptibility of a technology's affordances and, hence, why badly designed technology is more likely to lead to user failures and frustration. Perceptibility of information collection and information transmission is critical for the social negotiation of appropriate norms.

Once an individual has perceived a technology, but before action, they often build a conceptual model for a technology [22]. These conceptual models are used to "test" how a technological object should work. When the individual adds in the context of the environment, themselves, and other objects in relationship with the technology to this internal picture, the individual arrives at what Norman [22] calls a mental model. Mental models are internal representations of the world that people use to model and predict the world around them. These models provide "predictive and explanatory power for understanding the interaction" ([22], p. 7).

Individuals' mental models facilitate prediction and realizing affordances in different scenarios. Yet, most of us operate without a fully developed mental model of every technology we use. In fact, an individual's mental models need not be fully accurate with respect to how a technology works to be functional. For example, an individual may not know the full details of how Google's PageRank algorithm works, but that individual can likely still use Google search bar to look for websites. But this is also where the potential for violating expectations around information appropriateness and information flow can crop up. If individuals do not actively perceive information flows made possible by certain technologies and have them incorporated into their mental models, they may feel as though their privacy is violated when those flows are later revealed. For example, with persistently listening digital personal assistants, individuals may believe that a device is constantly listening for trigger words that cause the device to "wake" for requests. They may not have it built into their mental models, however, that recordings can be made by these digital assistants outside of the "trigger word" scenarios and that these recording could be listened to by humans. This can result in their privacy feeling violated as expectations for information transmission are thrown into conflict.

There can be numerous reasons why users do not perceive particular information flows. Users have a tendency to develop understandings of how information flows from feedback mechanisms within a design interface that they directly experience. For example, Proferes [23] shows that Twitter users have more accurate understandings of how features such as hashtags, retweeting, following, and direct messaging work than Twitter's APIs or Twitter's data-gathering techniques that rely on the use of tracking cookies. In the absence of clear feedback mechanisms about how particular flows work, users will sometimes try to fill in gap, inferring, correctly or not. For example, Eslami et al. [24] found Facebook users "wrongly attributing the composition of their feeds to the habits or intent of their friends and family" (p. 161) rather than interventions made by the News Feed algorithm.

Outside of misunderstandings stemming from opaque design elements, users can also develop misunderstandings from the discourse that they consume. How a company talks to users about a product working is a critical part of the way individuals build mental models. For example, the messages about a company's products communicated by its founders, CEOs, or other representatives are often picked up in the media and rebroadcast. These become important framing mechanisms for people looking to make sense of a new tool [25]. If these speakers leave out key details (e.g., how they collect, share, or sell user data), users may develop incomplete mental models.

Once we have our mental model of the informational requests a technology makes and the kinds of information flows a technology enables, we situate these models against existing norms and engage in a kind of prescriptive evaluation. We may choose to not use a technology, use it only in certain ways, or use it wholesale and expect others to do the same. These social norms are developed out of expectations about appropriate behavior that occurs in social contexts and are built on our own beliefs about roles within the social context, our own expectations and the expectations of others, and practices, as informed by history, culture, law, and social convention. The whole-sale adoption of these norms depends on a longer process of social negotiation that takes place as the technology diffuses throughout society.

Key Takeaways

- People carry internal pictures of how they think technologies work, called "mental models."
- People develop their mental models of technology three ways: direct interaction with a technology, watching others use a technology, or consuming messages about a technology.
- When users' mental models don't match actual practices of information collection and transmission, this can violate contextual integrity and their sense of privacy.

5.5   Negotiating Norms and Negotiating Technology

Once individuals have a sense of what a technology is and what it affords, they may evaluate and interpret the use of a particular technology in light of extant social norms. Depending on what they perceive the particular benefits of the technology to be in the social context, they may choose to forgo, revise, or stick to earlier normative behaviors. For example, sharing certain kinds of information publicly on social media may have been seen as socially unfathomable 50 years ago but is seen as an acceptable social practice today. Many users find that the benefits they derive from such sharing outweigh what might have earlier been seen as violating norms of appropriateness. On the flipside, many individuals have chosen to forgo the use of digital personal assistants because of fears about the kinds of data they collect [26].

However, users' decisions about the adherence to privacy norms are not always rational. Early privacy analysis from behavioral economics often tried on the use of rational choice theory to explain why users make certain privacy decisions. In reality, users' decisions are often made for less than rational reasons [27]. For more on this, see Chap. 4. Complicating matters, there is often a high degree of information asymmetry at play, and users cannot see into the future to look at the actual end consequences of their use of particular technologies. Instead, they must assess risk and uncertainty and face ambiguity in deciding whether or not to adhere to particular norms. This is also where beliefs about roles within the social context, our own expectations and the expectations of others, and practices, as informed by history, culture, law, and social convention, come into play. For example, if we have diminished social power in our contextual roles, we may be more likely to rely on already established social norms rather than relying on our own normative evaluations for information disclosure. Or, if we are apprehensive about sharing data through a new tool because we aren't entirely aware of what the third-party data flows look like, being in a social context where regulatory frameworks punish companies who misuse user data can help give us that added bit of trust.

As technologies diffuse, social practices involving those technologies are negotiated, stabilized, and become more obdurate in nature. Individual choices about adoption and use scale within social groups and the meaning and rituals associated with a given technology either fall by the wayside or become adopted [28]. Once the meanings and uses of a given technology are socially agreed to through adoption practices, the meaning of the technological artifact becomes stabilized within the social setting, and normatively acceptable practices emerge.

While the arrow of time has seemed to have resulted in more relaxed privacy norms, so much so that some have called it the "death of privacy" (see, e.g., [29–31]), users can and will push back against technologies that fall too far outside of negotiated norms. For example, introduced in late 2007, Facebook's Beacon program tracked the purchases of Facebook users on third-party websites and subsequently broadcasted messages about those purchases to those users' friends. However, many users were unhappy with this development, finding it "an intrusive form of advertising that took online surveillance and targeted marketing too far" ([32], p. 12). Soon, users created a petition protesting the new feature, and soon after, amid public outcry, Facebook pulled the plug on the program.

When normative violations of information collection and information flows occur, different social actors with the social context will attempt to respond. Individuals will make choices about whether or not to use a particular technology or otherwise augment their behavior, social groups may express unease in the discursive field, policy-makers may consider passing new laws or regulations, and designers will consider whether or not to change the technology to more closely align with the perceived norm.

Key Takeaways

- Individuals weigh the value of benefits of challenges to existing privacy norms against the perceived benefits, but this process is often less than fully rational, and individuals are often having to make decisions with incomplete mental models.
- Our social position, expectations and the expectations of others, and practices as informed by history, culture, law, and social convention, all play a role in whether or not we adhere to existing norms.

- If a technology is too far out of joint with social norms around privacy, different social actors will "push back" in a myriad of ways, including non-adoption, augmented use, complaint, or regulation.

5.6 Conclusion

Privacy is an ever-evolving, contextually shaped phenomenon. Privacy norms are constantly evaluated and reevaluated in light of the new situations enabled by novel technology. Privacy norms are also not universal. This chapter has grounded much of its narrative in talking about privacy norms as they have existed and changed in the United States, which is a limitation. The stories and histories of evolving privacy norms vary both internationally, but also at the more microlevel.

It is important for designers to understand the multitude of situational, social dynamics at play, and not to consider their own experience with local privacy norms as universal. Hubs of innovation in Silicon Valley, for example, often considerably lack diversity [33], which can create a challenge for appreciating how different groups prioritize privacy and the need to protect themselves from certain kinds of information gathering and information flows. Privacy harms are not evenly distributed across the population. For example, the use of real-name policies on social media platforms can create the potential for privacy harms for transgender and gender-variant users, drag queens, Native Americans, abuse survivors, and others [34]. Designers must carefully reflect on who challenges to the current social norms may benefit and who they may hurt. Careful technology design must consider the ways in which challenging existing privacy norms carries with it ethical implications. For more on the ethical implications of privacy work, see Chap. 17.

Working with privacy advocates can help developers think through the challenges that a novel technology may raise. Collaborations between users, academics, nonprofits, and industry can further the responsible development of tech in ways that maximize benefit while minimizing potential harms. Doing so can help designers avoid "creepy" technology [35] and actions out of joint with the social context for which they are creating tools.

Key Takeaways

- Designers must be careful not to take their own privacy norms as universal and to consider the different social contexts in which a technology will be deployed.
- The impacts of changes to privacy norms are not evenly distributed and frequently present outsized risks to disenfranchised groups. Thus, ethical evaluation should be considered in the design process.
- Working with privacy advocates can benefit technology development.

References

1. Nissenbaum, H. 2004. Privacy as contextual integrity. *Washington Law Review* 79 (1): 119–157.
2. Smith, R.E. 2004. Ben Franklin's web site: Privacy and curiosity from plymouth rock to the internet. *Privacy Journal.*
3. Singer, N. 2010, December 11. Online privacy races against technology. *The New York Times.* Retrieved from https://www.nytimes.com/2010/12/12/business/12stream.html
4. Brandeis, L., and S. Warren. 1890. The right to privacy. *Harvard Law Review* 4 (5): 193–220.
5. Gellman, R. 2014. Fair information practices: A basic history. *SSRN Electronic Journal.* https://doi.org/10.2139/ssrn.2415020
6. Westin, A.F. 1970. *Privacy and freedom.* New York: Atheneum.
7. Westin, A.F., and M.A. Baker. 1972. *Databanks in a Free Society: Computers. Record Keeping and Privacy.* Times Books.
8. Solove, D.J. 2010. *Understanding Privacy.* Harvard University Press.
9. Cate, F.H. (2006). The failure of fair information practice principles. *Consumer Protection in the Age of the Information Economy.*
10. Cagle, L.E. 2019. Surveilling strangers: The disciplinary biopower of digital genre assemblages. *Computers and Composition* 52: 67–78. https://doi.org/10.1016/j.compcom.2019.01.006.
11. Isaak, J., and M.J. Hanna. 2018. User data privacy: Facebook, Cambridge analytica, and privacy protection. *Computer* 51 (8): 56–59.
12. Day, M., G. Turner, and N. Drozdiak. 2019. *Is Anyone Listening to You on Alexa? A Global Team Reviews Audio.* Retrieved May 10, 2019, from Bloomberg website: https://www.bloomberg.com/news/articles/2019-04-10/is-anyone-listening-to-you-on-alexa-a-global-team-reviews-audio
13. Zimmer, M. 2008. The externalities of Search 2.0: The emerging privacy threats when the drive for the perfect search engine meets Web 2.0. *First Monday* 13: 3. Retrieved from http://firstmonday.org/htbin/cgiwrap/bin/ojs/index.php/fm/article/view/2136/1944
14. Litt, E., and E. Hargittai. 2016. The imagined audience on social network sites. *Social Media+Society* 2 (1): 2056305116633482.
15. Marwick, A.E., and D. Boyd. 2010. I tweet honestly, I tweet passionately: Twitter users, context collapse, and the imagined audience. *New Media & Society* 13 (1): 114–133. https://doi.org/10.1177/1461444810365313.
16. Rogers, E.M. 2003. *Diffusion of Innovations.* 5th ed. New York, NY: Free Press.
17. McDonald, R.I., and C.S. Crandall. 2015. Social norms and social influence. *Current Opinion in Behavioral Sciences* 3: 147–151.
18. Gibson, J.J. 1977. The concept of affordances. *Perceiving, Acting, and Knowing*: 67–82.
19. Norman, D.A. 1988. *The Psychology of Everyday Things.* New York: Basic Books.
20. Gaver, W.W. 1991. Technology affordances. In *Proceedings of the SIGCHI Conference on Human Factors in Computing Systems*, 79–84.
21. Boyd, D. 2010. Social network sites as networked publics: Affordances, dynamics, and implications. In *A Networked Self*, pp. 47–66. Routledge.
22. Norman, D.A. 1983. Some observations on mental models. *Mental Models* 7 (112): 7–14.
23. Proferes, N. 2017. Information flow solipsism in an exploratory study of beliefs about Twitter. *Social Media + Society*, 3, 1. https://doi.org/10.1177/2056305117698493
24. Eslami, M., A. Rickman, K. Vaccaro, A. Aleyasen, A. Vuong, K. Karahalios, . . . C. Sandvig. 2015. "I always assumed that I wasn't really that close to [her]": Reasoning about invisible algorithms in the news feed. In *Proceedings of the 33rd Annual SIGCHI Conference on Human Factors in Computing Systems*, 153–162.
25. Hoffmann, A.L., N. Proferes, and M. Zimmer. 2018. "Making the world more open and connected": Mark Zuckerberg and the discursive construction of Facebook and its users. *New Media & Society* 20 (1): 199–218.

26. Shulevitz, J. 2018, November. Alexa, should we trust you? *The Atlantic*. Retrieved from https://www.theatlantic.com/magazine/archive/2018/11/alexa-how-will-you-change-us/570844/.
27. Acquisti, A., and J. Grossklags. 2007. What can behavioral economics teach us about privacy. *Digital Privacy: Theory, Technologies and Practices* 18: 363–377.
28. Bijker, W.E., Hughes, T., & Pinch, T. (1987). *The Social Construction of Technological Systems: New Directions in the Sociology and History of Technology*.
29. Andrews, L. 2012. *I Know Who You Are and I Saw What You Did: Social Networks and the Death of Privacy*. Simon and Schuster.
30. Froomkin, A.M. 2000. The death of privacy. *Stanford Law Review* 52 (5): 1461–1543.
31. Garfinkel, S. 2000. *Database Nation: The Death of Privacy in the 21st Century*. Sebastopol, CA: O'Reilly.
32. Cohen, N.S. 2008. The valorization of surveillance: Towards a political economy of Facebook. *Democratic Communiqué* 22 (1): 5–22.
33. Wong, J.C. 2017. Segregated Valley: The ugly truth about Google and diversity in tech. In *The Guardian*. https://www.theguardian.com/technology/2017/aug/07/silicon-valley-google-diversity-black-women-workers.
34. Haimson, O.L., and A.L. Hoffmann. 2016. Constructing and enforcing "authentic" identity online: Facebook, real names, and non-normative identities. *First Monday* 21 (6).
35. Tene, O., and J. Polonetsky. 2013. A theory of creepy: Technology, privacy and shifting social norms. *Yale JL & Technolgy*. 16: 59.

Chapter 6
Privacy Beyond the Individual Level

Jennifer Jiyoung Suh and Miriam J. Metzger

Abstract This chapter examines privacy as a multilevel concept. While current conceptualizations of privacy tend to focus on the individual level, technological advancements are making *group privacy* increasingly important to understand. This chapter offers a typology of both groups and group privacy to establish a framework for conceptualizing how privacy operates beyond the individual level. The chapter describes several contemporary practices that influence the privacy of multiple actors and considers the dynamics of multi-stakeholder privacy decision-making. Potential tensions that exist between the rights and preferences of individual group members or between individuals and the group as a whole are also examined. Finally, recommendations for tools and other mechanisms to support collaborative privacy management and group privacy protection are provided.

6.1 Introduction

Early privacy theorists conceptualized privacy in terms of control. Westin [1], for example, defined privacy as "the claim of individuals, groups, or institutions to determine for themselves when, how, and to what extent information about them is communicated to others" (p. 5), and Altman [2] defined it as "selective control of access to the self or to one's group" (p. 18). Despite these scholars' acknowledgment of groups and institutions, the vast majority of privacy scholarship that has accumulated since has focused on the individual level [2, 3]. Indeed, most conceptualizations of privacy view it as a matter for *individuals* to manage by controlling others' access to their personally identifying information. In line with this conceptualization, social, legal, and ethical paradigms that dominate discussions about privacy are also focused on individuals' interests—for example, individual autonomy and personal freedom from surveillance [4]. Consequently, the tools,

J. J. Suh (✉) · M. J. Metzger
Department of Communication, University of California at Santa Barbara, Santa Barbara, CA, USA
e-mail: suh@ucsb.edu; metzger@comm.ucsb.edu

© The Author(s) 2022
B. P. Knijnenburg et al. (eds.), *Modern Socio-Technical Perspectives on Privacy*,
https://doi.org/10.1007/978-3-030-82786-1_6

laws, and policies currently in place to help people manage privacy—such as offering privacy settings to control one's information in social media, ensuring anonymity to protect individual identity, or obtaining informed consent to collect and use personally identifiable information—rarely consider risks and threats that affect privacy beyond the individual level [5].

As a consequence of the emphasis on individual privacy, understanding privacy at the *group* level has received little attention in the research literature [2, 6]. However, the era of social media, big data, and data analytics poses new threats to privacy for groups and collectives, in addition to individuals [7, 8]. Advances in information and communication technologies over the last two decades have simultaneously increased opportunities for social sharing of information while diminishing control over that information (e.g., posting group photos in social media), often resulting in clashes between multiple stakeholders over protecting or revealing an image or piece of information. They have also spurred practices that not only acquire and collect individuals' data but also aggregate data to identify trends in human behavior for modelling and making predictions about groups and collectives. These practices are often invisible to individuals. For example, geolocation information collected via GPS signals, cell towers, Wi-Fi connections, or Bluetooth sensors can be used to identify and/or predict mobility of migrant groups [4, 9] or, in the case of data from a fitness app used by soldiers, to identify the locations of secret military operations [10]. Further, data from individuals can be aggregated for purposes of predictive analytics and group profiling, such as likely academic or job performance (used by admissions officers or employers), health or financial status (used by medical insurers or loan officers), or criminality (used by law enforcement), which may result in discrimination against particular groups of people [11, 12].

These new privacy threats to groups as well as to individuals make it clear that individuals alone cannot manage their privacy effectively through merely controlling the flow of their own information. Recognizing the limitations of viewing privacy only at the individual level is an important starting point for expanding current views about privacy, as well as its protection. But what exactly is group privacy? Does it differ from individual privacy, and if so, how? This chapter begins with discussing current conceptualizations of both groups and group privacy to establish a framework for understanding the complex landscape of privacy at multiple levels. It then describes practices that influence the privacy of multiple actors, who may or may not realize they are a part of a group. Next, it considers the dynamics of multi-stakeholder privacy decision-making and potential tensions that exist between the rights and preferences of individual group members or between a member and the group as a whole. Finally, the chapter concludes with recommendations for tools and other efforts that support collaborative privacy management and group privacy protection.

6.2   Types of Groups and Types of Group Privacy

Conceptualizations of groups can be conceived to lie along two axes or dimensions: (1) how the group is constituted and (2) whether people are aware of the group's existence or their group membership status. In addition, group privacy can be conceived either in terms of the privacy of the group as a whole or in terms of the privacy of group members. These distinctions have important implications for social, legal, and technological mechanisms to protect privacy and thus are explicated below.

6.2.1   Types of Groups: Self-Constituted Groups and Algorithmically Determined Groups

In discussing group privacy, Taylor [9] explains that how people understand group privacy likely depends on what they mean by "the group," and recent efforts to reconceptualize privacy illustrate that there are at least two different types of groups that must be distinguished: *self-constituted groups* and *algorithmically determined groups*. Most people are familiar with self-constituted groups, which refer to collectivities that are recognized as groups by their members or by outsiders (e.g., Girl Scouts, fan clubs for K-pop groups, Rotary Club, etc.). These groups tend to be stable over at least some period of time. Algorithmically determined groups, on the other hand, are often not self-constituted; rather they are identified by algorithms and typically are associated with group-level information that is obtained for some specific purpose, such as marketing (e.g., groups of people who buy natural hair care products and share demographic or geographic characteristics) or law enforcement (e.g., people who spend a lot of time at bars and night clubs in a specific neighborhood). Algorithmically constituted groups are also ad hoc and thus are usually less stable than self-constituted groups because group membership status may change with any tweak of the algorithm [13].

A further consideration for these two types of groups is the degree to which they are aware they are members of the group. In self-constituted groups, members usually know that the group exists and that they are members. As such, these groups are said to be "self-aware" [14]. In contrast, because algorithmically determined groups are discovered or "created" by data analytic technologies, group members are typically unaware of the group's existence. Such groups are increasingly prevalent and important because data analytic strategies, such as group profiling and data mining, are used across many sectors (businesses, education, health, government, military, etc.), so people can be part of these groups without being aware of the group itself or that they belong to them. See also [15] who use the terms "active" versus "passive" groups to differentiate groups that are self-aware from those that are not. An important implication of this for privacy is that group members are unable to protect themselves when they are not aware that algorithmic group profiling has occurred and/or when they cannot detect their own membership in a group.

6.2.2   Types of Group Privacy: "Their" Privacy and "Its" Privacy

When thinking about privacy risks for a group, both "their" privacy and "its" privacy must be considered [4]. The difference between these two types lies is in whether group privacy is constituted by concern for the "privacies" of individual group members ("their" privacy) or the privacy of a group as a whole ("its" privacy). In the first type, the privacy concern could be that revelations about a group would expose the identities of individual group members in a harmful way, for example, with members of a group of political dissidents. With the latter type, the privacy concern rests on the group's very existence being discovered by a nonmember. Protecting one type of group privacy does not necessarily protect the other. For example, while anonymization of individual-level data may protect "their privacy" (i.e., the privacy of individual group members), it does not protect "its privacy" (i.e., the privacy of the group as a whole) from being detected by outsiders.

The case of Strava illustrates this point well. Strava is a popular fitness app that allows users to record and share their exercise routines via smartphone and fitness trackers. The data are collected from individual users anonymously, but they are then aggregated to produce heatmaps of popular exercise routes. One group of heavy users turned out to be US military personnel, and in 2017, it was discovered that the heatmaps based on data from this user group could reveal the locations and patrol routines of secret military bases overseas to anyone, including our enemies [10]. The heatmap used data that were anonymized and thus did not reveal personal information about any individual. But while aggregating anonymized individual data can protect group members' identity, such data still have privacy implications for groups that are identified or profiled by the technology. The revelation of where a military group is located puts *both* the group as a whole, as well as individual members of that group, at risk. The lesson here is that protecting "their" group privacy through data anonymization does not necessarily protect "its" group privacy.

"Its" privacy and "their" privacy apply to both types of groups discussed in Sect. 6.2.1. Let's take the case of a self-constituted and self-aware group of political dissidents. People may be concerned about "its" privacy if they are worried that the group's existence may be discovered by the government, leading to the group's dissolution. At the same time, people may also be concerned about "their" privacy if they are afraid that the identities of group members can be discovered by leaders of a repressive regime, resulting in group members' imprisonment or worse. With an algorithmically determined group that is not self-aware, such as a collection of people who buy similar products and share demographic characteristics (e.g., women in San Francisco who like natural hair care products), people could be concerned about "their" privacy if they are afraid that individuals who are categorized as members of the group would receive unwanted targeted advertisements. One could also be concerned about "its" privacy here too if they are uncomfortable with the idea of algorithms being used by marketers to group people into this, or any other, group to send targeted advertisements based on algorithmically predicted preferences that were not directly shared with the marketers.

6.2.3   Distinguishing Between Types and Levels of Privacy

These conceptualizations of privacy have raised debates about the degree to which individual privacy and group privacy, including both "its" and "their" types, are distinct. Two issues arise here. The first is whether "their" privacy amounts to anything more than individual privacy. Some argue that "their" privacy is the collection or sum of the privacies of the individual group members and thus is simply individual privacy. Others, however, maintain that the "their" type of group privacy is more properly conceptualized in a gestalt manner, as a property over and above the collection of the privacies of the individuals comprising the group, and thus is not the same as individual privacy [12]. Adopting this perspective, Belanger and Crossler [6] define group information privacy concern as "group members' normalized view of information privacy concerns, which can be higher or lower than the individual members' concerns taken as a whole" (p. 1031).

Second, adding to the complexity, Floridi [16, p. 90] explains how the notions of "its" group privacy and individual privacy may also intersect by giving rise to the notion of groups as individuals:

> There are some kinds of rights that belong only to a group as a group, not to a group insofar as it is constituted by individual persons who enjoy those rights. In this case, it is important to understand that the group itself acts as an individual, to which a right is attributed.

While in most cases it may be easy to see the privacy of a group as a whole ("its" version of group privacy) and the individual privacy of group members as distinct (e.g., the right of a group not to be discovered by outsiders versus an individual's right not to be identified as a member of a group), recent empirical studies have shown that it is not so easy for people to psychologically differentiate individual privacy from the "their" version of group privacy [17]. However, algorithmically determined groups that are not self-aware argue that "their" (group) privacy and individual privacy are separable, at least in theory, because while people are incapable of defending their individual privacy in such groups, laws can do so by recognizing and protecting the "their" type of group privacy (e.g., class action lawsuits). So even if differentiating these categories is impossible at a psychological level, they can be meaningfully differentiated at a legal level. These debates have important implications for the privacy rights of groups and individuals, which will be discussed in Sect. 6.5. In any case, perhaps the best that can be said is that while privacy is a multilevel concept, individuals are always important [6].

6.3   Contemporary Practices That Influence the Privacy of Multiple Actors or Groups

Technological advancements in recent years have enabled new practices that draw group privacy to the foreground. Such practices span across small group, organizational, and societal levels, affecting social groups, teams, as well as larger organizations and collectives. In all cases, these practices influence the privacy of multiple actors, rendering individual-level privacy insufficient to fully understand or to protect privacy in these contexts. Below are some examples that affect privacy at these various levels of analysis:

Example 1   One common and relatable example that illustrates how privacy risk can influence multiple actors in small groups is the practice of sharing group photos and tagging other users in social media posts. Most popular social network sites (SNSs) allow one user to share information about other users by posting group photos or by tagging them (e.g., User A tags User B, which then associates User B with User A's posts). As a result of these practices, one user has control over other people's information because there is not yet an effective tool or strategy that allows everyone involved to contribute equally to the decision of sharing a post about a group of users. In this situation, if the user who posts information about a group does not care about the privacy—and by extension the public image—of other members in the group (e.g., posting a group photo in which User A is shown in a positive light, but the others in the photo are not), this user will share the post and other members in the group will lose control over their information [3, 18]. Everyone in a group photo could have opinions about whether and how they want the photo to be shared online, but their personal opinions, or the group's collective opinion for that matter, are not taken into account.

Example 2   Workplace teams often use communication platforms that are administered by their organizations. While individual employees can use personal devices for private conversations, teams that discuss work-related matters that are not ready to be shared with the entire organization (e.g., special projects, secret assignments, etc.) often create private channels on communication platforms provided by their organizations (e.g., Slack, Microsoft Teams, etc.). While using these private channels for group conversations is efficient, individual team members have limited control over group-level information. For example, while a team's private channel may appear as "closed" to other employees, the fact that private channels are visually labeled as closed to others means that group itself (i.e., its existence) can be easily discovered. Indeed, and perhaps as a result of this, Microsoft recently announced that moving forward "private teams" on Microsoft Teams cannot be set as discoverable [19].

While this change may help work groups remain hidden to other employees, these communication platforms are administered by their organizations, so private groups can still be discovered and exposed to administrators that monitor and regulate the use of these communication platforms across teams in the organization. One workaround is to use personal devices as an alternative private team channel. However, this is not enough to protect groups' privacy when employees are asked to install productivity monitoring software and/or security software to protect sensitive information about their organizations even on personal devices that are used to access work-related information (e.g., work email, etc.) [20, 21]. This example demonstrates how increasing workplace surveillance not only threatens personal privacy but also group privacy.

Example 3 The examples so far include people's decision to share information involving more than one person or a group of people, but individuals' actions to log data about their own personal behavior (e.g., lifelogging) can also affect group privacy. Lifelogging involves tracking personal data generated by our own behavioral activities. As more people use mobile and/or wearable devices, lifelogging has become very easy because many of these devices capture data about people's activities automatically (e.g., number of steps taken each day, details about workout routines or routes, etc.). Individuals' decision to log their lives may seem like it has nothing to do with group privacy, but the networked nature of individuals' data that are collected may expose lifeloggers to group privacy risks. A good example is Strava, the fitness app described earlier, which produced heatmaps that could compromise classified military information (e.g., strategic bases) and thus make groups and individuals, including military personnel and units on those bases, vulnerable to outside attacks. The Strava example is one of the few publicized cases, but it is not likely the only case because anonymized but aggregated location data are being used widely, and policy decisions based on such data could impact vulnerable groups that move with GPS-enabled devices, such as victims of natural disasters, patients fleeing from disease outbreaks, political asylum seekers and refugees, etc. [9].

Example 4 Lastly, emerging privacy threats from group inference technologies can even affect groups that have never shared anything about their group membership or information. Recent developments in AI-based group profiling and machine learning techniques enable marketers to not simply rely on data collected directly from their customers to design more effective targeted advertisements but by using technologies that make inferences about new potential consumer groups to target based on analyzing big data from a variety of sources. An example of these new techniques is a machine learning technology that correlates topics discussed on Twitter (e.g., #organicshampoo, #botanicalshampoo) with publicly available personal data of individuals who post about such topics (e.g., women who are in the ages of between 18 and 25 and live in San Francisco) [17]. This tool allows companies to make inferences about who and where they are likely to find new customers and thus to whom they should target their marketing messages. In other words, algorithmically determined groups could be used to draw inferences about potential customers for anyone who shares similar group (demographic and/or geographic) characteristics with the algorithmically discovered groups.

The important point to grasp here is that, based on this technology, groups of people who merely share particular demographic and geographic characteristics with other people who happen to discuss a topic in social media (e.g., natural hair care products) would receive targeted advertising or marketing messages about that topic. While sending targeted messages to people that share characteristics with a company's existing customer base may not seem like a new advertising or marketing strategy, the use of big data analytics makes the scale and reach of such messages both more invasive and pervasive than ever before. One seemingly benign hashtag that does not contain any personally identifiable information can, when aggregated, help companies extract group-level information that affects the lives of people who have never consented to sharing their group-level information with the data gatherer. While the information in this example is about hair products, the sensitivity of group-level information that is collected can vary, and the severity of negative consequences associated with different kinds of group-level information (e.g., identifiers for socially vulnerable groups, such as political protestors, sexual minorities, etc.) would vary accordingly.

The examples above illustrate why individuals cannot manage privacy by themselves, as well as when they should be concerned about privacy at the group level. And as technologies that enable group communication, creation, and discovery continue to advance, the number and types of practices that put the privacy of multiple stakeholders at risk will be even more far-reaching.

6.4   Dynamics of Multi-stakeholder Privacy Decision-Making

People are beginning to realize that they cannot effectively manage their own privacy by themselves because other group members' actions influence their own privacy, and in turn, they influence other group members' privacy. In other words, managing privacy is often not intrapersonal but *inter*personal [22, 23]. The example of photo sharing in social network sites discussed in Sect. 6.3 illustrates how individual users do not have full control over their information because a group photo is co-owned. Indeed, participants in a recent survey reported that they preferred not to be tagged at all in photos because they want to be able to control their information [8]. The interpersonal nature of privacy in these kinds of scenarios raises the question of how to coordinate group members' expectations about appropriate information flow. Yet ways to collectively manage privacy with other people is not sufficiently addressed by how most privacy management options currently work, namely, individually managing control over one's own information through privacy settings.

A common problem that people experience from content generated by others that includes information about their own group belonging is face threats [24]. Face threats are verbal or nonverbal communication acts that challenge a person's self-presentation, and their consequences can vary in severity. For example, a post with multiple users tagged might reveal an individual's association with a social issue that they had not been previously public about. Or, a group photo of teenagers at a party posted on social media might inadvertently reveal drug use. Research shows that people desire an effective way to manage privacy collaboratively in relation to face threats [25]. In fact, many people resort to relying on "mutual considerations" or "mental strategies" to do so. These strategies involve group members exerting mental effort during decision-making about whether to share information that they feel might cause face threats for other members and trusting that other members will do the same for them [26]. People often rely on these mental coping strategies to deal with privacy threats from others because they do not have alternative options.

However, while these mental strategies involve thinking about others' desired self-presentation, relying on one person's assumptions about what other group members would want is not always successful in reducing face threats because of misunderstanding, miscommunication, and mistaken assumptions [26]. Moreover, group members themselves may be concerned about whether they or others could actually succeed in living up to mutual expectations of making the right decision for each post and for everyone involved in a group [26].

Other studies show that people are starting to devise collaborative strategies to manage group privacy as co-owners of group-related information [27, 28]. Research by De Wolf et al. [28] suggests that members of groups may take the time to communicate, negotiate, and agree on what type of co-owned group information can be shared. For example, these researchers found that members of a youth organization in Flanders deal with group privacy management by employing a variety of communication strategies to coordinate privacy rules about their group, including *group privacy guidelines* (having explicit rules about what types of group information members can post on Facebook), *encryption* (interacting in a language that outsiders cannot understand), and *information management* (omitting information that one feels may anger other group members).

Cho and Filippova [27] aimed to create a comprehensive account of the types of privacy co-management strategies people use on Facebook. They found four strategies that people use to co-manage shared information. *Corrective strategies* include things like untagging or asking peers to remove content that allows users to control the visibility of content posted about them by others after the content has been published. *Preventive strategies* constrain the audience for shared information and may be enacted by using the friend lists feature to share content with a chosen group of people or by creating secret groups to share content. *Collaborative strategies* involve explicit coordination mechanisms to collectively manage each other's privacy through negotiation. Similar to the members of the Flemish youth organization in [28], participants in Cho and Filippov's study engaged in deliberate communication with each other about ways to manage their collective privacy. These included negotiating "rules of thumb" with their friends about sharing content concerning their group or discussing the appropriate privacy settings with their friends prior to disclosing content. Finally, *information control* is achieved by either self-censorship (as also found by [28]) or by making peace with the public nature of information sharing on social media. The most commonly applied privacy co-management strategy was information control, which was followed by preventive, collaborative, and corrective strategies.

Jia and Xu [25] studied adoption of collaborative privacy management strategies by groups of linked contacts in social network sites. They found evidence for three types of rules negotiated by co-owners of shared information:

1. *Ownership management* rules that "define who the co-owners of the shared information are, with the assumption that co-owners should be able to make decisions about future disclosure of the collectively owned information" (p. 4289). This includes group members negotiating which group-owned information may be disclosed to others.
2. *Access management* rules that regulate disclosure and concealment of shared information to outsiders, ranging from open access to closed access. This may include coordinated content removal, restricting the visibility of shared information, or collectively deciding to provide unrestricted access to group information.
3. *Extension management* rules that govern decisions about whether to allow outsiders into the group privacy boundary by, for example, re-sharing group information by one member to people outside the group or adding new members to the group. Adopting and upholding these privacy co-management rules was positively related to a group's collective value on privacy, the amount of disclosure of private information in the group, and group members' perceived collective privacy risk.

Most of the research discussed so far takes the perspective that group norms shape rules that are developed within groups about whether and how to reveal or conceal collectively held information. This notion is central to the Theory of Multilevel Information Privacy (TMIP) proposed by Belanger and James [7] to understand how groups and individual group members make decisions about co-owned information. The theory posits that different social units (e.g., groups or individuals) can have different sets of rules about how to manage the unit's information and interactions to protect privacy and also recognizes that people belong to multiple groups. Rule sets are thus activated according to the social identity that is salient in the decision moment. The social identity that is salient depends on the environment and specific situation or context. People will follow the normative rules of their social unit unless their privacy calculus (i.e., analysis of risks and benefits) indicates they should not. After a decision is made, positive and negative feedback shapes and refines their privacy rules and norms, which can affect future decisions. So, decisions about the same piece of co-owned information can be different in different environments, at different points in time, and if different social identities are made salient.

Engagement with the collaborative privacy management principles and strategies described in this section demonstrates that people are thinking about privacy at the group level and desire collaborative privacy management mechanisms. However, strategies that involve explicit group communication may not be enough to achieve effective group privacy management for many people because they are time-consuming and may be uncomfortable to negotiate [27]. And some group members may not see the need for group privacy management, which can put other members at risk [28]. In general, people are more likely to use group privacy management strategies if they sense a stronger common bond as a group or feel highly attached to other group members [28]. Moreover, when people experience face threats as a result of others' privacy decisions, they often do not address the issue because they do not want to instigate conflict or "create drama," which they feel may hurt group cohesion [25, 29]. Perhaps for these reasons, collaborative group privacy strategies are still not as easily or widely applied as individual privacy management strategies that focus on individuals' controlling their own personal information through privacy settings.

Jia and Xu [25] moreover point out that many of the strategies for collaborative privacy management are only functional at a small scale or with a limited number of groups and become impractical and cost-inefficient in large social networks and when people interact with a large number of different groups. Another critique is that these strategies focus mostly on protecting individual privacy or the "their" type of group privacy rather than the "its" type of group privacy. For instance, healthcare teams using shared electronic medical records have rules to protect a patient's information (individual privacy), and friend groups in social media negotiate rules to avoid face threats of fellow members ("their" privacy). Although some collaborative privacy management strategies can be implemented to protect "its" group privacy, such as entirely closed access management rules or using preventative strategies to create secret groups (e.g., "finstas"), more typically the rules and strategies described in this section are used to make some particular *piece* of group information invisible to outsiders rather than to make the entire group itself undiscoverable. And perhaps most important, all of the strategies described above can only be used by groups that are self-aware. The privacy protection options for groups that are not self-aware, such as most algorithmically determined groups, are extremely limited. This issue will be addressed in Sect. 6.5.

6.5   Tensions Between Privacy Rights of Individuals Versus Groups

Whenever information is collectively held, tensions can arise about how to manage privacy. For example, individuals within groups may clash over their privacy preferences regarding information about the group. Take the example where one member wants to publish a group photo and another member does not, or where one wants the group as whole to be discoverable by outsiders, but another member does not. There is also the issue of privacy preferences of individual group members versus the group as a whole. Here, the group has negotiated and agreed upon a privacy rule (e.g., "no one shares information about our group to outsiders"), but then one group member violates the rule. Communication Privacy Management theory [23] would discuss all of these examples in terms of privacy "boundary turbulence" among co-owners of information. Boundary turbulence is caused by a failure of privacy rule coordination between group members. It arouses negative emotions and has behavioral and relational consequences for co-owners [30].

Most of the research on boundary turbulence stays at the individual or at the "their" privacy levels, for example, by looking at how individual group members react to privacy breaches from other group members in terms of protecting their own (individual) or other group members' ("their") privacy. One example is when individual group member(s) withdraw from the member who caused the turbulence, through stonewalling, ignoring, or forcing the offending member out of the group [30]. Another example is if a group member withdraws their personal information from the group to protect their own privacy [16]. Turbulence also has group-level consequences, as it can prompt group members to collectively recalibrate, renegotiate, and re-coordinate their privacy rules [28, 31]. Much less research has examined the consequences of boundary turbulence in terms of individual group members' relationships to groups as a whole (e.g., a member deciding to leave a group due to an instance of turbulence) or how boundary turbulence impacts the "its" type of group privacy. Boundary turbulence can threaten "its" group privacy (privacy of the group as a whole, such as its existence), with consequences that may be severe, including group infiltration, hostile takeover, harassment, or dissolution if all members decide to withdraw from the group.

Beyond preferences that may not align between individual members of a group or between a group and its members, there is also the question of the privacy *rights* of group members versus the group as a whole. While it is clear that group members have a right to privacy, this right is no different from individual privacy rights. More interestingly, there is debate about whether a *group* can have a right to privacy, or if that right is any different from the privacy interests of its individual members. Excellent discussions of this debate are available from [13, 32] and [33] (see also [17]). Bloustein [34] was the first to propose that groups have an interest in privacy. This interest, he argues, stems from group members' desire to form associations privately with one another and legitimizes the idea of a group as a holder of privacy rights (rather than its members) because information about the existence of the group, and about the members who are associated with a group and with each other, can define a group's identity in some cases.

Passive groups—groups that are not self-aware—complicate matters because if group members do not know that a group has been identified or that they are members, they have no ability to protect the group from unwanted intrusions. In these cases, how can or should privacy rights be protected for groups that are not self-aware? Some perspectives hold that a minimal level of "entitativity," which is a perception of the extent to which a collection of people is perceived as a group by themselves or others, is a necessary condition for groups to have attitudinal and behavioral significance for people [35]. So clusters of individuals identified via an algorithm will not generate group privacy concerns if the individuals do not perceive themselves to constitute a group (see also [36]). In contrast, the minimal group paradigm in social psychology finds that mere categorization, even on an ad hoc basis, reliably produces group identification and may lead to discrimination against group members [37]. This suggests that algorithmically determined groups who are not self-aware may (or should in theory) produce group privacy concerns for people and thus warrant claims that groups can be viewed as holders of privacy rights (see also [12]). Or in Mittelstadt's [33] words, "Algorithmically grouped individuals have a collective interest in the creation of information about the group, and actions taken on its behalf" (p. 475).

Finally, lawmakers have acknowledged the need to protect groups, even when members are not aware of their own group membership. Similar to algorithmically constituted groups, groups of people involved in class action lawsuits are ad hoc, and members may not have ever met or interacted with each other, but rather the group is constituted by a third party (i.e., the plaintiff) for a specific purpose (i.e., the lawsuit), and individuals' membership in the group is unbeknownst to them until they are notified of the lawsuit. Class action lawsuits are accepted as a critical tool to protect the interest of groups who do not have the means or ability to protect themselves from harms imposed on them by others. As such, they provide a legal framework for the protection of "its" group privacy rights even in the case of groups that are not self-aware [13].

6.6 Recommendations for Tools and Mechanisms to Protect Privacy Beyond the Individual Level

Protecting privacy beyond the individual is challenging because several parties are necessarily involved, which means communication, coordination, and, in some cases, conflict resolution are required. While some might assume that protecting individual privacy will protect group privacy, this is a fallacy. The Strava case is a good example of how group privacy can be compromised even when individual privacy is protected via anonymization. Kammourieh et al. [15] moreover argue that any privacy protection remedy based on individual identifiability is ineffective when the goal of an attacker is to identify or profile a group rather than to identify individuals. Identifying individuals is not necessary for group profiling. People may be acted upon in harmful ways through the act of being grouped, even without their personal identity being revealed and without knowledge that they have been categorized as a member of a group [9]. Because of this, groups need to safeguard their collective privacy and data protection rights [12]. To do so, new privacy protection solutions that are not exclusively based on individual privacy rights are needed [9, 13]. The remainder of this section offers ideas for some possible solutions.

- *Communication-based strategies for multi-party privacy management*: As discussed in Sect. 6.4, groups can engage in explicit deliberation to negotiate shared rules concerning how to protect the privacy of the group and/or group members. Examples include devising group privacy guidelines where group members discuss whether and which content from a group event is appropriate to be shared on social media, encryption or using codewords and language that only group members know, and self-censorship [27, 28]. The downside to communication-based strategies to protect group privacy is that they are cumbersome and can be time-intensive, which likely explains why they are not widely used in practice. These strategies also do not apply to groups that are not self-aware.

- *Tools for multi-party privacy management*: While there are many tools available for people to protect personal privacy (e.g., privacy settings, anonymization and encryption of personal data, etc.), there are very few tools to protect group privacy. Yet such tools may help to overcome the overhead associated with adopting time-consuming collaborative group privacy management tactics, such as the communication-based strategies described above. Although still in their infancy, some prototypes exist for tools that allow multiple people to control content that involves more than one person [38–40]. For example, *CoPE* (Collaborative Privacy ManagEment) is an application developed to aid collective privacy management of group photos on Facebook [40]. This tool alerts users to photos that they have been tagged in, requests and grants co-ownership of these photos, allows co-owners to see and change the privacy policies of individual pictures (i.e., control access to each photo), and provides photo browsing history. One drawback of the CoPE tool is that each co-owner separately specifies her or his own privacy preference for the shared photo instead of accommodating all stakeholders' privacy preferences or facilitating active negotiation of control between co-owners.

  Another third-party Facebook application, *Retinue*, enables multiple associated users to specify their privacy concerns to co-control a shared group photo [38]. To resolve privacy conflicts caused by different privacy concerns of multiple users, a single data owner is specified who can take input from group members to make an appropriate privacy-sharing trade-off by adjusting the preference weights to balance the privacy risk and sharing loss for the group, taking all members' preferences into account. If a group member is not satisfied with the current level of privacy control, that user can adjust her/his privacy settings, ask the owner of the photo to change the weights for the privacy risk and the sharing loss, or report a privacy violation to request social network administrators to delete the photo.

  Both CoPE and Retinue present usability problems for users, as they require extra layers of manual setting and re-setting of privacy preferences for shared content. A different approach to managing the privacy of co-owned information is "privacy nudges." Nudges are short, on-screen, in situ messages that raise people's awareness of privacy issues. They are considered a "soft paternalistic approach" to increase user awareness of potential privacy risks and guide users to make more informed choices about their privacy management [41–43]. Although typically used to notify users about threats to their own privacy, nudges could be designed to help users become more aware about how their actions might impact group privacy. For example, a nudge might appear whenever users decide to tag another person to confirm that they are indeed willing to share the co-owned information. A similar approach was proposed by [44], where users install a software daemon called *LocBorg*, which resides on a their computer or phone and protects the user from privacy violations by reminding them about the risks to their own and their groups' privacy in real time as they use social media apps such as Twitter.

- *Group privacy by design*: Group privacy management should not reside only in the hands of group members. Private companies could voluntarily develop their technology to be more accountable for protecting group privacy. "Group privacy by design" means designing products that incorporate protecting group privacy by default. Embedding group privacy management or protection tools into products (e.g., social network sites) is one form of this. An interesting idea to achieve group privacy by design is to use nudges to alert software engineers of potential dangers to group privacy during the design process to increase their awareness of vulnerabilities and, ideally, prompt them to eliminate dangers or insert group privacy protections as they develop systems and applications.

  Group privacy by design is especially important for companies that use algorithms to identify groups from individuals' digital traces. Efforts to protect group privacy on the part of companies that use data analytic techniques to group people without their knowledge are needed because people who do not know they are being grouped cannot protect themselves from negative effects of such grouping. And companies stand to benefit from group privacy by design if it helps them avoid public outrage or boycotts from group privacy scandals. It is useful to recall that a good deal of the public outcry against Cambridge Analytica in 2018 was due to the company's failure to notify Facebook users that the company collected and processed not only individual users' data but also the data of users' linked contacts as well.

- *Self-regulation*: Companies should develop and then adhere to codes of ethical conduct to provide guidelines for responsible innovation, development, and usage of user data and algorithms to ensure the protection of both individual and group privacy. Rules surrounding the creation, accuracy, aggregation, deletion, storage, minimization, sharing, and other aspects of not just data collection but also its processing are important elements of such codes. Increasing transparency about classification and grouping algorithms, adopting policies that make clear to the public when and how group-related information is used, are also essential to effective self-regulation. Civil society groups such as consumer protection agencies and advocate organizations should be consulted during the development of ethical codes of conduct to help ensure privacy rights of groups are respected [45].

- *Government regulation*: Regulations governing data processing and the use of group-inference algorithms could prevent uses of data analytic techniques that profile and target groups and thus are another mechanism for protecting group privacy [15]. Specifically, policies that limit companies' use of sensitive information pertaining to groups or require companies that use group-inference algorithms to provide notice to data subjects about how their information will be processed and/or to obtain informed consent from groups could be implemented. Policies about obtaining consent not just for data collection but also for any data processing or algorithms that may be applied to the data, such as those that aggregate anonymized datasets or use machine learning to infer group memberships, are useful. That said, obtaining informed consent from groups is difficult and could likely only be applied to groups that are, or are made to be, self-aware. Government mandates for companies to report their data processing methods alongside their potential risks to the public, as well as requiring procedures to allow users to opt out of data collection or aggregation, would go a long way toward group privacy protection. Allowing legal redress for violations to such policies is also important.

• *Education:* One of the major hurdles for protecting privacy beyond the individual level is the lack of public awareness about threats to group privacy [46]. Demystifying how big data analytics threaten not only individual but also the "their" and "its" types of group privacy would motivate people to begin to demand solutions. There are several means to educate the public on issues of data privacy, including campaigns by consumer protection agencies and advocates to increase awareness about the range of dangers algorithms pose to both individuals and groups; classes on data ethics, law, privacy, and digital rights in high schools and universities, especially early in data science training curricula; and continuing education for software developers [15]. Media reports of privacy scandals such as Strava and Cambridge Analytica also help raise public awareness of privacy threats posed to groups and their members.

6.7   Conclusion

Advances in technology in recent years have made privacy beyond the individual more pressing than ever. Group privacy has become increasingly important in the age of big data because most analytics target people not as individuals but rather as groups [13]. Groups, not individuals, are the object of value for data processors, as they care much less about a particular individual than they do about extracting behavior from individuals to shed light about groups who, for example, eat at different types of restaurants, prefer certain film or music genres, buy certain models or brands of cars, vote for liberal versus conservative candidates, are likely to suffer from a particular health issue, and so on. The privacy literature has been slow to recognize this, focusing instead on individual privacy interests, rights, and protection. A major purpose of this chapter has been to point out that by only protecting individual privacy, group privacy is not protected, and by revealing group privacy, individual privacy can be compromised. The implication of this codependency is that *both* individual and group information must be protected in order to protect privacy effectively.

This chapter attempts to lay some of the groundwork for moving beyond the individual level in conceptualizing, theorizing about, and protecting privacy. By outlining how threats to privacy operate at multiple levels, providing examples of problems that people may experience as a result of threats to both "their" and "its" aspects of group privacy, and presenting recommendations for ways to resolve those problems, our hope is that this chapter will increase awareness and broaden the scope of scholarship on privacy that ultimately leads to more comprehensive and effective solutions to help both groups and individuals avoid privacy problems in the future.

References

1. Westin, A. 1967. *Privacy and Freedom*. New York: Atheneum.
2. Altman, I. 1975. *The Environment and Social Behavior: Privacy, Personal Space, Territory, Crowding*. Monterey, CA: Brooks/Cole Publishing Company.
3. Alsarkal, Y., N. Zhang, and H. Xu. 2018. Your privacy is your friend's privacy: Examining interdependent information disclosure on online social networks. In *Proceedings of the 51st Hawaii International Conference on System Sciences*, pp 1–10.
4. Taylor, L., L. Floridi, and B. Van Der Sloot. 2017. Introduction: A new perspective on privacy. In *Group Privacy: New Challenges of Data Technologies*, ed. L. Taylor, L. Floridi, and B. van der Sloot, 1–12. Cham: Springer.
5. Cohen, J.E. 2012. *Configuring the Networked Self: Law, Code, and the Play of Everyday Practice*. New Haven, CT: Yale University Press.
6. Bélanger, F., and R.E. Crossler. 2011. Privacy in the digital age: A review of information privacy research in information systems. *Management Information Systems Quarterly*.
7. Bélanger, F., and T.L. James. 2020. A theory of multilevel information privacy management for the digital era. *Information Systems Research*. https://doi.org/10.1287/isre.2019.0900.
8. Birnholtz, J., M. Burke, and A. Steele. 2017. Untagging on social media: Who untags, what do they untag, and why? *Computers in Human Behavior* 69: 166–173. https://doi.org/10.1016/j.chb.2016.12.008.
9. Taylor, L. 2017. Safety in numbers? Group privacy and big data analytics in the developing world. In *Group Privacy: New Challenges of Data Technologies*, ed. L. Taylor, L. Floridi, and B. van der Sloot, 13–36. Cham: Springer.
10. Tufekci, Z. 2018. The latest data privacy debacle. *New York Times*.
11. Barocas, S., and H. Nissenbaum. 2014. Big data's end run around anonymity and consent. In *Privacy, Big Data and the Public Good: Frameworks for Engagement*, ed. J. Lane, V. Stodden, S. Bender, and H. Nissenbaum, 44–75. New York, NY: Cambridge University Press.
12. Taylor, L., L. Floridi, and B. van der Sloot. 2017. *Group Privacy: New Challenges of Data Technologies*. Cham: Springer.
13. Floridi, L. 2017. Group privacy: A defence and an interpretation. In *Group Privacy*.
14. Taylor, L., B. van der Sloot, and L. Floridi. 2017. Conclusion: What do we know about group privacy? In *Group Privacy*.
15. Kammourieh, L., T. Baar, J. Berens, E. Letouzé, J. Manske, J. Palmer, D. Sangokoya, and P. Vinck. 2017. Group privacy in the age of big data. In *Group Privacy: New Challenges of Data Technologies*, ed. L. Taylor, L. Floridi, and B. van der Sloot, 37–66. Cham: Springer International Publishing.

16. Child, J.T., P.M. Haridakis, and S. Petronio. 2012. Blogging privacy rule orientations, privacy management, and content deletion practices: The variability of online privacy management activity at different stages of social media use. *Computers in Human Behavior* 28: 1859–1872.

17. Suh, J.J., M.J. Metzger, S.A. Reid, and A. El Abbadi. 2018. Distinguishing group privacy from personal privacy: The effect of group inference technologies on privacy perceptions and behaviors. *Proceedings of the ACM on Human Computer Interaction* 2: 1–22. https://doi.org/10.1145/3274437.

18. Yu, L., S.M. Motipalli, D. Lee, P. Liu, H. Xu, Q. Liu, J. Tan, and B. Luo. 2018. My friend leaks my privacy. In *Proceedings of the 23rd ACM Symposium on Access Control Models & Technologies (SACMAT)*, 93–104. New York, NY: ACM.

19. Microsoft. 2020. Manage discovery of private teams in Microsoft Teams. In *Microsoft Docs*. https://docs.microsoft.com/en-us/microsoftteams/manage-discovery-of-private-teams. Accessed 11 Aug 2020.

20. Chyi, N. 2020. The workplace-surveillance technology boom. *Slate*.

21. Roberts, J.J. 2020. Workplace privacy and surveillance software: What the law says | Fortune. *Fortune*.

22. Laufer, R.S., and M. Wolfe. 1977. Privacy as a social issue: A multidimensional development theory. *Journal of Social Issues*.

23. Petronio, S. 2002. *Boundaries of Privacy: Dialectics of Disclosure*. Albany, NY: State University of New York Press.

24. Litt, E., E. Spottswood, J. Birnholtz, J. Hancock, M.E. Smith, and L. Reynolds. 2014. Awkward encounters of an "other" kind: Collective self-presentation and face threat on facebook. In *Proceedings of the 17th ACM Conference on Computer-Supported Cooperative Work and Social Computing (CSCW'14)*. Baltimore, MD: ACM.

25. Jia, H., and H. Xu. 2016. Autonomous and interdependent: Collaborative privacy management on social network sites. In *Conference on Human Factors in Computing Systems – Proceedings*.

26. Lampinen, A., V. Lehtinen, A. Lehmuskallio, and S. Tamminen. 2011. We're in it together: Interpersonal management of disclosure in social network services. In *Annual Conference on Human Factors in Computing Systems*, 3217–3226. https://doi.org/10.1145/1978942.1979420.

27. Cho, H., and A. Filippova. 2016. Networked privacy management in Facebook: A mixed-methods and multinational study. In *Proceedings of the 19th ACM Conference on Computer-Supported Cooperative Work and Social Computing (CSCW '16)*, 503–514. San Francisco, CA: ACM.

28. De Wolf, R., K. Willaert, and J. Pierson. 2014. Managing privacy boundaries together: Exploring individual and group privacy management strategies in Facebook. *Computers in Human Behavior* 35: 444–454. https://doi.org/10.1016/j.chb.2014.03.010.

29. Wohn, D.Y., and E.L. Spottswood. 2016. Reactions to other-generated face threats on Facebook and their relational consequences. *Computers in Human Behavior* 57: 187–194. https://doi.org/10.1016/j.chb.2015.12.021.

30. Aloia, L.S. 2018. The emotional, behavioral, and cognitive experience of boundary turbulence. *Communication Studies*. https://doi.org/10.1080/10510974.2018.1426617.

31. Steuber, K.R., and R.M. McLaren. 2015. Privacy recalibration in personal relationships: Rule usage before and after an incident of privacy turbulence. *Communication Quarterly*. https://doi.org/10.1080/01463373.2015.1039717.

32. Floridi, L. 2014. Open data, data protection, and group privacy. *Philosophy and Technology* 27: 1–3. https://doi.org/10.1007/s13347-014-0157-8.

33. Mittelstadt, B. 2017. From Individual to group privacy in big data analytics. *Philosophy and Technology*. https://doi.org/10.1007/s13347-017-0253-7.

34. Bloustein, E.J. 1976. Group privacy: The right to huddle. *Rutgers-Camden Law Journal* 8: 219.

35. Campbell, D.T. 1960. Common fate, similarity and other indices of the status of aggregates of persons as social entities. In *Decisions, Values and Groups*.

36. Loi, M., and M. Christen. 2020. Two concepts of group privacy. *Philosophy and Technology*. https://doi.org/10.1007/s13347-019-00351-0.
37. Tajfel, H. 1970. Experiments in intergroup discrimination. *Scientific American*. https://doi.org/10.1038/scientificamerican1170-96.
38. Hu, H., Ahn, G.-J., and Jorgensen, J. 2011. Detecting and resolving privacy conflicts for collaborative data sharing in online social networks. In *Proceedings of the 27th Annual Computer Security Applications Conference – ACSAC '11*, 103. https://doi.org/10.1145/2076732.2076747
39. Squicciarini, A.C., M. Shehab, and F. Paci. 2009. Collective privacy management in social networks. In *Proceedings of the 18th International Conference on World Wide Web – WWW '09* 521. https://doi.org/10.1145/1526709.1526780.
40. Squicciarini, A.C., H. Xu, and X. Zhang. 2011. CoPE: Enabling collaborative privacy management in online social networks. *Journal of the American Society for Information Science and Technology* 63: 521–534. https://doi.org/10.1002/asi.21473.
41. Acquisti, A., I. Adjerid, R. Balebako, L. Brandimarte, L.F. Cranor, S. Komanduri, P.G. Leon, N. Sadeh, F. Schaub, M. Sleeper, Y. Wang, and S. Wilson. 2017. Nudges for privacy and security: Understanding and assisting users' choices online. *ACM Computing Surveys* 50. https://doi.org/10.1145/3054926.
42. Dogruel, L. 2019. Privacy nudges as policy interventions: Comparing US and German media users' evaluation of information privacy nudges. *Information, Communication & Society* 22: 1080–1095. https://doi.org/10.1080/1369118X.2017.1403642.
43. Solove, D.J. 2013. Introduction: Privacy self-management and the consent dilemma. *Harvard Law Review* 126: 1880–1903.
44. Zakhary, V., C. Sahin, T. Georgiou, and A.E. Abbadi. 2017. LocBorg: Hiding social media user location while maintaining online persona (vision paper). In *25th ACM SIGSPATIAL International Conference on Advances in Geographic Information Systems (ACM SIGSPATIAL 2017)*.
45. Zook, M., S. Barocas, D. Boyd, K. Crawford, E. Keller, S.P. Gangadharan, A. Goodman, R. Hollander, B.A. Koenig, J. Metcalf, A. Narayanan, A. Nelson, and F. Pasquale. 2017. Ten simple rules for responsible big data research. *PLoS Computational Biology*.
46. Metzger, M.J., J.J. Suh, S.A. Reid, and A. El Abbadi. 2021. What can fitness apps teach us about group privacy? In *Privacy Concerns Surrounding Personal Information Sharing on Health and Fitness Mobile Apps*, ed. D. Sen and R. Ahmed. IGI Global.

Part II
Domains

Chapter 7
Social Media and Privacy

Xinru Page, Sara Berrios, Daricia Wilkinson, and Pamela J. Wisniewski

Abstract With the popularity of social media, researchers and designers must consider a wide variety of privacy concerns while optimizing for meaningful social interactions and connection. While much of the privacy literature has focused on information disclosures, the interpersonal dynamics associated with being on social media make it important for us to look beyond informational privacy concerns to view privacy as a form of interpersonal boundary regulation. In other words, attaining the right level of privacy on social media is a process of negotiating how much, how little, or when we desire to interact with others, as well as the types of information we choose to share with them or allow them to share about us. We propose a framework for how researchers and practitioners can think about privacy as a form of interpersonal boundary regulation on social media by introducing five boundary types (i.e., relational, network, territorial, disclosure, and interactional) social media users manage. We conclude by providing tools for assessing privacy concerns in social media, as well as noting several challenges that must be overcome to help people to engage more fully and stay on social media.

7.1 Introduction

The way people communicate with one another in the twenty-first century has evolved rapidly. In the 1990s, if someone wanted to share a "how-to" video tutorial within their social networks, the dissemination options would be limited (e.g., email,

X. Page (✉) · S. Berrios
Brigham Young University, Provo, UT, USA
e-mail: xinru@cs.byu.edu; berrios@byu.edu

D. Wilkinson
Department of Computer Science, Clemson University, Clemson, SC, USA
e-mail: dariciw@g.clemson.edu

P. J. Wisniewski
Department of Computer Science, University of Central Florida, Orlando, FL, USA
e-mail: pamwis@ucf.edu

© The Author(s) 2022
B. P. Knijnenburg et al. (eds.), *Modern Socio-Technical Perspectives on Privacy*,
https://doi.org/10.1007/978-3-030-82786-1_7

floppy disk, or possibly a writeable compact disc). Now, social media platforms, such as TikTok, provide professional grade video editing and sharing capabilities that give users the potential to both create and disseminate such content to thousands of viewers within a matter of minutes. As such, social media has steadily become an integral component for how people capture aspects of their physical lives and share them with others. Social media platforms have gradually altered the way many people live [1], learn [2, 3], and maintain relationships with others [4].

Carr and Hayes define social media as "Internet-based channels that allow users to opportunistically interact and selectively self-present, either in real time or asynchronously, with both broad and narrow audiences who derive value from user-generated content and the perception of interaction with others" [5]. Social media platforms offer new avenues for expressing oneself, experiences, and emotions with broader online communities via posts, tweets, shares, likes, and reviews. People use these platforms to talk about major milestones that bring happiness (e.g., graduation, marriage, pregnancy announcements), but they also use social media as an outlet to express grief and challenges, and to cope with crises [6–8]. Many scholars have highlighted the host of positive outcomes from interpersonal interactions on social media including social capital, self-esteem, and personal well-being [9–12]. Likewise, researchers have also shed light on the increased concerns over unethical data collection and privacy abuses [13, 14].

This chapter highlights the privacy issues that must be addressed in the context of social media and provides guidance on how to study and design for social media privacy. We first provide an overview of the history of social media and its usage. Next, we highlight common social media privacy concerns that have arisen over the years. We also point out how scholars have identified and sought to predict privacy behavior, but many efforts have failed to adequately account for individual differences. By reconceptualizing privacy in social media as a boundary regulation, we can explain these gaps from previous one-size-fits-all approaches and provide tools for measuring and studying privacy violations. Finally, we conclude with a word of caution about the consequences of ignoring privacy concerns on social media.

7.2   A Brief History of Social Media

Section Highlights

- **Social media use has quickly increased** over the past decade and plays a key role in social, professional, and even civic realms. The rise of social media has led to **"networked individualism."**
- This enables people to access a **wider variety of specialized relationships**, making it more likely they can meet a variety of needs. It also allows people to **project their voice** to a wider audience.

- However, people have more **frequent turnover in their social networks**, and it takes much more **effort to maintain social relations** and **discern (mis)information** and **intention** behind communication.

The initial popularity of social media harkened back to the historical rise of *social network sites* (SNSs). The canonical definition of SNSs is attributed to Boyd and Ellison [15] who differentiate SNSs from other forms of computer-mediated communication. According to Boyd and Ellison, SNS consists of (1) profiles representing users and (2) explicit connections between these profiles that can be traversed and interacted with. A social networking profile is a self-constructed digital representation of oneself and one's social relationships. The content of these profiles varies by platform from profile pictures to personal information such as interests, demographics, and contact information. Visibility also varies by platform and often users have some control over who can see their profile (e.g., everyone or "friends"). Most SNSs also provide a way to leave messages on another's profile, such as posting to someone's timeline on Facebook or sending a mention or direct message to someone on Twitter.

Public interest and research initially focused on a small subset of SNSs (e.g., Friendster [16] and MySpace [17–19]), but the past decade has seen the proliferation of a much broader range of social networking technologies, as well as an evolution of SNSs into what Kane et al. term *social media networks* [20]. This extended definition emphasizes the reach of social media content beyond a single platform. It acknowledges how the boundedness of SNSs has become blurred as platform functionality that was once contained in a single platform, such as "likes," are now integrated across other websites, third parties, and mobile apps.

Over the past decade, SNSs and social media networks have quickly become embedded in many facets of personal, professional, and social life. In that time, these platforms became more commonly known as "social media." In the USA, only 5% of adults used social media in 2005. By 2011, half of the US adult population was using social media, and 72% were social users by 2019 [21]. MySpace and Facebook dominated SNS research about a decade ago, but now other social media platforms, such as YouTube, Instagram, Snapchat, Twitter, Kik, TikTok, and others, are popular choices among social media users. The intensity of use also has drastically increased. For example, half of Facebook users log on several times a day, and three-quarters of Facebook users are active on the platform at least daily [21]. Worldwide, Facebook alone has 1.59 billion users who use it on a daily basis and 2.41 billion using it at least monthly [22]. About half of the users of other popular platforms such as Snapchat, Instagram, Twitter, and YouTube also report visiting those sites daily. Around the world, there are 4.2 billion users who spend a cumulative 10 billion hours a day on social networking sites [23]. However, different social networking sites are dominant in different cultures. For example, the most popular social media in China, WeChat (inc. Wēixìn 微信), has 1.213 billion monthly users [23].

While SNS profiles started as a user-crafted representation of an individual user, these profiles now also often consist of information that is passively collected, aggregated, and filtered in ways that are ambiguous to the user. This passively collected information can include data accessed through other avenues (e.g., search engines, third-party apps) beyond the platform itself [24]. Many people fail to realize that their information is being stored and used elsewhere. Compared to tracking on the web, social media platforms have access to a plethora of rich data and fine-grained personally identifiable information (PII) which could be used to make inferences about users' behavior, socioeconomic status, and even their political leanings [25]. While online tracking might be valuable for social media companies to better understand how to target their consumers and personalize social media features to users' preferences, the lack of transparency regarding what and how data is collected has in more recent years led to heightened privacy concerns and skepticism around how social media platforms are using personal data [26–28]. This has, in turn, contributed to a loss of trust and changes in how people interact (or not) on social media, leading some users to abandon certain platforms altogether [26, 29] or to seek alternative social media platforms that are more privacy focused.

For example, WhatsApp, a popular messaging app, updated its privacy policy to allow its parent company, Facebook, and its subsidiaries to collect WhatsApp data [30]. Users were given the option to accept the terms or lose access to the app. Shortly after, WhatsApp rival Signal reported 7.5 million installs globally over 4 days. Recent and multiple social media data breaches have heightened people's awareness around potential inferences that could be made about them and the danger in sensitive privacy breaches. Considering the invasive nature of such practices, both consumers and companies are increasingly acknowledging the importance of privacy, control, and transparency in social media [31]. Similarly, as researchers and practitioners, we must acknowledge the importance of privacy on social media and design for the complex challenges associated with networked privacy. These types of intrusions and data privacy issues are akin to the informational privacy issues that have been investigated in the context of e-commerce, websites, and online tracking (see Chap. 9).

While early research into social media and privacy largely focused on these types of concerns, researchers have uncovered how the social dynamics surrounding social media have led to a broader array of social privacy issues that shape people's adoption of platforms and their usage behaviors. Rainie and Wellman explain how the rise of social technologies, combined with ubiquitous Internet and mobile access, has led to the rise of "networked individualism" [32]. People have access to a wider variety of relationships than they previously did offline in a geographically and time-bound world. These new opportunities make it more likely that people can foster relationships that meet their individual needs for havens (support and belonging), bandages (coping), safety nets (protect from crisis), and social capital (ability to survive and thrive through situation changes). Additionally, social media users can project their voice to an extended audience, including many weak ties (e.g., acquaintances and strangers). This enables individuals to meet their social, emotional, and economic needs by drawing on a myriad of specialized relationships (different individuals each particularly knowledgeable in a specific domain such as economics, politics, sports, caretaking). In this way, individuals are increasingly networked or embedded within multiple communities that serve their interests and needs.

Inversely, networked individualism has also made people less likely to have a single "home" community, dealing with more frequent turnover and change in their social networks. Rainie and Wellman describe how people's social routines are different from previous generations that were more geographically bound – today, only 10% of people's significant ties are their neighbors [32]. As such, researchers have questioned and studied the extent to which people can meaningfully maintain interpersonal relationships on social media. The upper limit for doing so has been estimated at 150 connections or "friends" [33], but social media connections often well exceed this number. With such large networks, it also takes users much more effort to distinguish (mis)information, when communication is intended for the user, and the intent behind that communication. The technical affordances of social media can also help or hinder their (in)ability to capture the nuances of the various relationships in their social network. On many social media platforms, relationships are flattened into friends and followers, making them homogenous and lacking differentiation between, for instance, casual acquaintance and trusted confidant [16, 34]. These characteristics of social media lead to a host of social privacy issues which are crucial to address. In the next section, we summarize some of the key privacy challenges that arise due to the unique characteristics of social media.

7.3   Privacy Challenges in Social Media

Section Highlights

- **Information disclosure** privacy issues have been a dominant focus in online technologies and the primary focus for social media. It focuses on **access to data** and defining **public vs. private disclosures**. It emphasizes user control over who sees what.
- With so many people from different social circles able to access a user's social media content, the issues of **context collapse** occur. Users may post to an **imagined audience** rather than realizing that people from multiple social contexts are privy to the same information.
- The issues of **self-presentation** jump to the foreground in social media. Being able to manage impressions is a part of privacy management.
- The social nature of social media also introduces the issues of **controlling access to oneself**, both in terms of **availability** and **physical** access.
- Despite all of these privacy concerns, there is a noted **privacy paradox** between what people say they are concerned about and their resulting behaviors online.

Early focus of social media privacy research was focused on helping individuals meet their privacy needs in light of four key challenges: (1) information disclosure, (2) context collapse, (3) reputation management, and (4) access to oneself. This section gives an overview of these privacy challenges and how research sought to overcome them. The remainder of this chapter shows how the research has moved beyond focusing on the individual when it comes to social media and privacy; rather, social media privacy has been reconceptualized as a dynamic process of interpersonal boundary regulation between individuals and groups.

7.3.1 Information Disclosure/Control over Who Sees What

A commonality among early social media privacy research is that the focus has been on information privacy and self-disclosure [35]. Self-disclosure is the information a person chooses to share with other people or websites, such as posting a status update on social media. Information privacy breaches occur when a website and/or person leaks private information about a user, sometimes unintentionally. Many studies have focused on informational privacy and on sharing information with, or withholding it from, the appropriate people [36–38] on social media. Privacy settings related to self-disclosure have also been studied in detail [39–41]. Generally, social media platforms help users control self-disclosure in two ways. First is the level of granularity or type of information that one can share with others. Facebook is the most complex, allowing users to disclose and control more granular information for profile categories such as bio, website, email addresses, and at least eight other categories at the time of writing this chapter. Others have fewer information groupings, which make user profiles chunkier, and thus self-disclosure boundaries less granular. The second dimension is one's access level permissions, or with whom one can share personal information. The most popular social media platforms err on the side of sharing more information to more people by allowing users to give access to categories such as "Everyone," "All Users," or "Public." Similarly, many social media platforms give the option for access for "friends" or "followers" only.

Many researchers have highlighted how disclosures can be shared more widely than intended. Tufekci examined disclosure mechanisms used by college students on MySpace and Facebook to manage the boundary between private and public. Findings suggest that students are more likely to adjust profile visibility rather than limiting their disclosures [42]. Other research points out how users may not want their posts to remain online indefinitely, but most social media platforms default to keeping past posts visible unless the user specifies otherwise [43]. Even when the platform offers ways to limit post sharing, there are often intentional and unintentional ways this content is shared that negates the users' wishes. For example, Twitter is a popular social media platform where users can choose to have their tweets available only to their followers. However, millions of private tweets have been retweeted, exposing private information to the public [44]. Even platforms like Snapchat, which make posts ephemeral by default, are susceptible to people taking screenshots of a snap and distributing through other channels. Thus, as social media companies continue to develop social media platforms, they should consider how to protect users from information disclosure and teach people to practice privacy protective habits.

Although some users adjust their privacy settings to limit information disclosures, they may be unaware of third-party sites that can still access their information. Scholars have emphasized the importance of educating users on the secondary use of their data, such as when third-party software takes information from their profiles [45]. Data surveillance continues to expand, and the business model of social media corporations tends to favor getting more information about users, which makes it difficult for users that want to control their disclosure [46]. Third-party apps can also access information about social media users' connections without consent of the person whose information is being stored [47].

7.3.2 Unique Considerations for Managing Disclosures Within Social Media

As mentioned earlier, social media can expand a person's network, but as that network expands and diversifies, users have less control over how their personal information is shared with others. Two unique privacy considerations for social media that arise from this tension are context collapse and imagined audiences, which we describe in more detail in the subsections below. For example, as Facebook has become a social gathering place for adults, one's "friends" may include family members, coworkers, colleagues, and acquaintances all in one virtual social sphere. Social media users may want to share information with these groups but are concerned about which audiences are appropriate for sharing what types of information. This is because these various social spheres that intersect on Facebook may not intersect as readily in the physical world (e.g., college buddies versus coworkers) [48]. These distinct social circles are brought together into one space due to social media. This concept is referred to as "context collapse" since a user's audience is no longer limited to one context (e.g., home, work, school) [15, 49, 50]. We highlight research on the phenomenon of the privacy paradox and explain how context collapse and imagined audiences may help explain the apparent disconnect between users' stated privacy concerns and their actual privacy behavior.

Context Collapse Nuanced differences between one's relationships are not fully represented on social media. While real-life relationships are notorious for being complex, one of the biggest criticisms of social media platforms is that they often simplify relationships to a "binary" [51] or "monolithic" [52] dimension of either friend or not friend. Many platforms just have one type of relationship such as a "friend," and all relationships are treated the same. Once a "friend" has been added to one's network, maintaining appropriate levels of social interactions in light of one's relationship context with this individual (and the many others within one's network) becomes even more problematic [53]. Since each friend may have different and, at times, mutually exclusive expectations, acting accordingly within a single space has become a challenge. As Boyd points out, for instance, teenagers cannot be simultaneously cool to their friends and to their parents [53]. Due to this collapsed context of relationships within social media, acquaintances, family, friends, coworkers, and significant others all have the same level of access to a social media user once added to one's network – unless appropriately managed.

Research reveals that the way people manage context collapses varies. Working professionals might deal with context collapse by limiting posts containing personal information, creating different accounts, and avoiding friending those they worked with [54]. As another example, many adolescents manage context collapse by keeping their family members separate from their personal accounts [55]. Other mechanisms for managing context collapse include access-level permission to request friendship, denying friend requests, and unfriending. While there is limited support for manually assigning different privileges to each friend, the default is to start out the same and many users never change those defaults.

Privacy incidents resulting from mixing work and social media show the importance of why context collapse must be addressed. Context collapse has been shown to negatively affect those seeking employment [56], as well as endangering those who are employed. For example, a teacher in Massachusetts lost her job because she did not realize her Facebook posts were public to those who were not her friends; her complaints about parents of students getting her sick led to her getting fired from her job [57]. Many others have shared anecdotes about being fired after controversial Facebook and Twitter posts [58, 59]. Even celebrities who live in the public eye can suffer from context collapse [60, 61]. Kim Kardashian, for example, received intense criticism from Internet fans when she posted a photo on social media of her daughter using a cellphone and wearing makeup while Kim was getting ready for hair and wardrobe [62]. Many online users criticized her parenting style for not limiting screen time and Kim subsequently shared a photo of a stack of books that the kids have access to while she works.

Nevertheless, context collapse can also increase bridging social capital, which is the potential social benefit that can come through having ties to a wider audience. Context collapse enables this to occur by allowing people to increase their connections to weak ties and creating serendipitous situations by sharing with people beyond whom one would normally share [60]. For example, job hunters may increase their chances of finding a job by using social media to network and connect with those they would not normally be associated with on a daily basis. Getting out a message or spreading the word can also be accomplished more easily. For instance, finding people to contribute to natural disaster funds can be effective on social media because multiple contexts can be easily reached from one account [63]. In addition to managing context collapse, social media users also have to anticipate whether they are sharing disclosures with their intended audiences.

Imagined Audiences The disconnect between the real audience and the imagined audience on social media poses privacy risks. Understanding who can see what content, how, when, and where is key to deciding what content to share and under what circumstances. Yet, research has consistently demonstrated how users do not accurately anticipate who can potentially see their posts. This manifests as wrongly anticipating that a certain person can see content (when they cannot), as well as not realizing when another person can access posted content. Users have an "imagined audience" [64, 65] to whom they are posting their content, but it often does not match the actual audience viewing the user's content. Social media users typically imagine that the audience for their social media posts are like-minded people, such as family or close friends [65]. Sometimes, online users think of specific people or groups when creating content such as a daughter, coworkers, people who need cleaning tips, or even one's deceased father [65]. Despite these imagined audiences, privacy settings may be set so that many more people can see these posts (acquaintances, strangers, etc.). While users do tend to limit who sees their profile to a defined audience [44, 66, 67], they still tend to believe their posts are more private than they actually are [49, 68].

Some users adopt privacy management strategies to counter potential mismatch in audience. Vitak identified several **privacy management tactics** users employ to disclose information to a limited audience [69]:

1. *Network-based*. Social media users decide who to friend or follow, therefore filtering their network of people. Some Facebook users avoid friending people they do not know. Others set friends' profiles to "hidden," so that they do not have to see their posts, but avoid the negative connotations associated with "unfriending."
2. *Platform-based*. Some users choose to use the social media sites' privacy settings to control who sees their posts. A common approach on Facebook is to change the setting to be "friends only," so that only a user's friends may see their posts.
3. *Content-based*. These users control their privacy by being careful about the information they post. If they knew that an employer could see their posts, then they would avoid posting when they were at work.
4. *Profile-based*. A less commonly used approach is to create multiple accounts (on a single platform or across platforms). For example, a professional, personal, and fun account.

As another example, teenagers often navigate public platforms by posting messages that parents or others would not understand their true meaning. For instance, by posting a song lyric or quote that is only recognized by specific individuals as a reference to a specific movie scene or ironic message, they therefore creatively limit their audience [49, 70]. Others manage their audience by using more self-limiting privacy tactics like self-censorship [70], choosing just to not post something they were considering in the first place. These various tactics allow users to control who can see what on social media in different ways.

7.3.3 Reputation Management Through Self-Presentation

Technology-mediated interactions have led to new ways of managing how we present ourselves to different groups of friends (e.g., using different profiles on the same platform based on the audience) [71]. Being able to control the way we come across to others can be a challenging privacy problem that social media users must learn to navigate. Features to limit audience can also help with managing self-presentation. Nonetheless, reputation or impression management is not just about avoiding posts or limiting access to content. Posting more content, such as selfies, is another approach used to control the way others perceive a user [72]. In this case, it is important to present the content that helps convey a certain image of oneself. Research has revealed that those who engage more in impression management tend to have more online friends and disclose more personal information [73]. Those who feel online disclosures could leave them vulnerable to negativity, such as individuals who identify as LGBTQ+, have also been found to put an emphasis on impression management in order to navigate their online presence [74]. However, studies still show that users have anxieties around not having control over how they are presented [75]. Social media users worry not only about what they post, but are concerned about how others' postings will reflect on them [42].

Another dimension that affects impression management attitudes is how social media platforms vary in their policies on whether user profiles must be consistent with their offline identities. Facebook's real name policy, for instance, requires that people use their real name and represent themselves as one person, corresponding to their offline identities. Research confirms that online profiles actually do reflect users' authentic personalities [76]. However, some platforms more easily facilitate identity exploration and have evolved norms encouraging it. For example, Finsta accounts popped up on Instagram a few years after the company started. These accounts are "Fake Instagram" accounts often sharing content that the user does not want to associate with their more public identity, allowing for more identity exploration. This may have arisen from the social norm that has evolved where Instagram users often feel like they need to present an ideal self. Scholars have observed such pressure on Instagram more than on other platforms like Snapchat [77]. While the ability to craft an online image separate from one's offline identity may be more prevalent on platforms like Instagram, certain types of social media such as location-sharing social networks are deeply tied to one's offline self, sharing actual physical location of its users. Users of Foursquare, a popular location-sharing app, have leveraged this tight coupling for impression management. Scholars have observed that users try to impress their friends or family members about the places they spend their time while skipping "check-in" at places like McDonald's or work for fear of appearing boring or unimpressive [78].

Regardless of how tightly one's online presence corresponds with their offline identity, concerns about self-presentation can arise. For example, users may lie about their location on location-sharing platforms as an impression management tactic and have concerns about harming their relationships with others [79]. On the other hand, Finstas are meant to help with self-presentation by hiding one's true identity. Ironically, the content posted may be even more representative of the user's attitudes and activities than the idealized images on one's public-facing account. These contrasting examples illustrate how self-presentation concerns are complicated.

What further complicates reputation management is that social media content is shared and consumed by a group of people and not just individuals or dyads. Thus, self-presentation is not only controlled by the individual, but by others who might post pictures and/or tag that individual. Even when friends/followers do not directly post about the user, their actions can reflect on the user just by virtue of being connected with them. The issues of co-owned data and how to negotiate disclosure rules are a key area of privacy research on the rise. We refer you to Chap. 6, which goes in-depth on this topic.

7.3.4   Access to Oneself

A final privacy challenge many social media users encounter is controlling accessibility others have to them. Some social media platforms automatically display when someone is online, which may invite interaction whether users want to be accessible or not. Controlling access to oneself is not as straightforward as limiting or blocking certain people's access. For instance, studies have also shown that social pressures influence individuals to accept friend requests from "weak ties" as well as true friends [53, 80]. As a result, the social dynamics on social media are becoming more complex, creating social anxiety and drama for many social media users [52, 53, 80]. Although a user may want to control who can interact with him or her, they may be worried about how using privacy features such as "blocking" other accounts may send the wrong signal to others and hurt their relationships [81]. In fact, an online social norm called "hyperfriending" [82] has developed where only 25% of a user's online connections represent true friendship [83]. This may undermine the privacy individuals wished they had over who interacts with them on their various accounts. Due to social norms or etiquette, users may feel compelled to interact with others online [84]. Even if users do not feel like they need to interact, they can sometimes get annoyed or overwhelmed by seeing too much information from others [85]. Their mental state is being bombarded by an overload of information, and they may feel their attention is being captured.

Many social media sites now include location-sharing features to be able to tell people where they are by checking in to various locations, tag photos or posts, or even share location in real time. Therefore, privacy issues may also arise when sharing one's location on social media and receiving undesirable attention. Studies point out user concerns about how others may use knowledge of that location to reach out and ask to meet up, or even to physically go find the person [86]. In fact, research has found that people may not be as concerned about the private nature of disclosing location as they are concerned for disturbing others or being disturbed oneself as a result of location sharing [87]. This makes sense given that analysis of mobile phone conversations reveals that describing one's location plays a big role in signaling availability and creating social awareness [87, 88].

Some scholars focus on the potential harm that may come because of sharing their location. Tsai et al. surveyed people about perceived risks and found that fear of potential stalkers is one of the biggest barriers to adopting location-sharing services [89]. Nevertheless, studies have also found that many individuals believe that the benefits of using location sharing outweigh the hypothetical costs. Foursquare users have expressed fears that strangers could use the application to stalk them [78]. These concerns may explain why users share their location more often with close relationships [37].

Geotagging is another area of privacy concern for online users. Geotagging is when media (photo, website, QR codes) contain metadata with geographical information. More often the information is longitudinal and latitudinal coordinates, but sometimes even time stamps are attached to photos people post. This poses a threat to individuals that post online without realizing that their photos can reveal sensitive information. For example, one study assessed Craigslist postings and demonstrated how they could extract location and hours a person would likely be home based on a photo the individual listed [90]. The study even pinpointed the exact home address of a celebrity TV host based on their posted Twitter photos. Researchers point out how many users are unaware that their physical safety is at risk when they post photos of themselves or indicate they are on vacation [22, 90, 91]. Doing so may make them easy targets for robbers or stalkers to know when and where to find them.

7.3.5   Privacy Paradox

While researchers have investigated these various privacy attitudes, perceptions, and behaviors, the privacy paradox (where behavior does not match with stated privacy concerns) has been especially salient on social media [92–97]. As a result, much research focuses on understanding the decision-making process behind self-disclosure [98]. Scholars that view disclosure as a result of weighing the costs and the benefits of disclosing information use the term "privacy calculus" to characterize this process [99]. Other research draws on the theory of bounded rationality to explain how people's actions are not fully rational [100]. They are often guided by heuristic cues which do not necessarily lead them to make the best privacy decisions [101]. Indeed, a large body of literature has tried to dispel or explain the privacy paradox [94, 102, 103].

7.4   Reconceptualizing Social Media Privacy as Boundary Regulation

Section Highlights

- By reconceptualizing privacy in social media as a **boundary regulation**, we can see that the seeming paradox in privacy is actually a balance between being too open or disclosing too much and being too inaccessible or disclosing too little. The latter can result in social isolation which is privacy regulation gone wrong.

- In the context of social media, there are **five different types of privacy boundaries** that should be considered.
- People use various methods of **coping with privacy violations**, many not tied to disclosing less information.

Drawing from Altman's theories of privacy in the offline world (see Chap. 2), Palen and Dourish describe how, just like in the real world, social media privacy is a boundary regulation process along various dimensions besides just disclosure [104]. Privacy can also involve regulating interactional boundaries with friends or followers online and the level of accessibility one desires to those people. For example, if a Facebook user wants to limit the people that can post on their wall, they can exclude certain people. Research has identified other threats to interpersonal boundary regulation that arise out of the unique nature of social media [42]. First, as mentioned previously, the threat to spatial boundaries occurs because our audiences are obscured so that we no longer have a good sense of whom we may be interacting with. Second, temporal boundaries are blurred because any interaction may now occur asynchronously at some time in the future due to the virtual persistence of data. Third, multiple interpersonal spaces are merging and overlapping in a way that has caused a "steady erosion of clearly situated action" [5]. Since each space may have different and, at times, mutually exclusive behavioral requirements, acting accordingly within those spaces has become more of a challenge to manage context collapses [42]. Along with these problems, a major interpersonal boundary regulation challenge is that social media environments often take control of boundary regulation away from the end users. For instance, Facebook's popular "Timeline" automatically (based on an obscure algorithm) broadcasts an individual's content and interactions to all of his or her friends [41]. Thus, Facebook users struggle to keep up to date on how to manage interactions within these spaces as Facebook, not the end user, controls what is shared with whom.

7.4.1 Boundary Regulation on Social Media

One conceptualization of privacy that has become popular in the recent literature is viewing privacy on social media as a form of interpersonal boundary regulation. These scholars have characterized privacy as finding the optimal or appropriate level of privacy rather than the act of withholding self-disclosures. That is, it is just as important to avoid over disclosing as it is to avoid under disclosing. Therefore, disclosure is considered a boundary that must be regulated so that it is not too much or too little. Petronio's communication privacy management (CPM) theory emphasizes how disclosing information (see Chap. 2) is vital for building relationships, creating closeness, and creating intimacy [105]. Thus, social isolation and loneliness resulting from under disclosure can be outcomes of privacy regulation gone wrong just as much as social crowding can be an issue. Similarly, the framework of contextual integrity explains that context-relative informational norms define privacy expectations and appropriate information flows and so a disclosure in one context (such as your doctor asking you for your personal medical details) may be perfectly appropriate in that context but not in another (such as your employer asking you for your personal medical details) [106]. Here it is not just about an information disclosure boundary but about a relationship boundary where the appropriate disclosure depends on the relationship between the discloser and the recipient.

Drawing on Altman's theory of boundary regulation, Wisniewski et al. created a useful taxonomy detailing the various types of privacy boundaries that are relevant for managing one's privacy on social media [107]. They identified five distinct privacy boundaries relevant to social media:

1. *Relationship*. This involves regulating who is in one's social network as well as appropriate interactions for each relationship type.
2. *Network*. This consists of regulating access to one's social connections as well as interactions between those connections.
3. *Territorial*. This has to do with regulating what content comes in for personal consumption and what is available in interactional spaces.
4. *Disclosure*. The literature commonly focuses on this aspect which consists of regulating what personal and co-owned information is disclosed to one's social network.
5. *Interactional*. This applies to regulating potential interaction with those within and outside of one's social network.

Of these boundary types, Wisniewski et al. emphasize the most important is maintaining relationship boundaries between people. Similarly, Child and Petronio note that "one of the most obvious issues emerging from the impact of social network site use is the challenge of drawing boundary lines that denote where relationships begin and end" [108]. Making sure that social media facilitates behavior appropriate to each of the user's relationships is a major challenge.

Each of these interpersonal boundaries can be further classified into regulation of more fine-grained dimensions. In Table 7.1, we summarize the different ways that each of these five interpersonal boundaries can be regulated on social media.

Next, we describe each of these interpersonal boundaries in more detail.

Self- and Confidant Disclosures The information disclosure concerns described in the previous "Privacy Challenges" section are the focus of privacy around disclosure boundaries. Posting norms on social media platforms often encourage the disclosure of one's personal information (e.g., age, sexual orientation, location, personal images) [109, 110]. Disclosing such information can leave one open to financial, personal, and professional risks such as identity theft [46, 111]. However, there are motivations for disclosing personal information. For example, research suggests that posting behaviors on social media platforms have a significant relationship with a desire for positive self-presentation [112, 113]. Privacy management is necessary for balancing the benefits of disclosure and its associated risks. This involves

Table 7.1 Description of the different privacy boundaries

Boundary	Dimensions	Description	Example
Disclosure	Self-disclosure	Regulating your own information disclosures	Limiting the audience of a post
	Confidant disclosure	Regulating the dissemination of co-owned information	Asking family not to post pictures of your baby until you consent
Relationship	Connection	Regulating the members of your network	Adding or deleting friends
	Context	Regulating various interactions depending on the nature of the relationship	Sharing specific content with colleagues versus college friends
Network	Discovery	Controlling the access others have to your network connections	Restricting your friend list to show mutual friends only
	Intersection	Managing interactions between groups or connections	Hiding a polarizing comment from your work friend
Territorial	Inward facing	Regulating content for consumption	Using filters for content
	Outward facing	Controlling the creation of semipublic content	Limiting who can post on your profile/wall
Interactional	Disabling	Managing interactions through the use or nonuse of platform features	Deactivating Messenger to avoid messages
	Blocking	Limiting access to specific persons	Blocking an unwanted friend

regulating both *self-disclosure* for information about one's self and *confidant-disclosure* boundaries for information that is "co-owned" with others [105] (e.g., a photograph that includes other people, or information about oneself that is shared with another in confidence).

There are a variety of disclosure boundary regulation mechanisms on social media interfaces. Many platforms offer users the freedom to selectively share various types of information, create personal biographies, share links to their websites, or post their birthday. Self-disclosure can also be maintained through privacy settings such as granular control over who has access to specific posts. The level of information one wishes to disclose could be managed by various privacy settings. Many social media platforms encourage multiparty participation with features such as tagging, subtweeting, or replying to others' posts. This level of engagement promotes the celebration of shared moments or co-owned information/content. At the same time, it increases possibilities for breaching confidentiality and can create unwanted situations such as posting congratulations to a pregnancy that has not yet been announced to most family members or friends. Some ways that people manage violations of disclosure boundaries are to reactively confront the violator in private or to stop using the platform after the unexpected disclosure [114].

Relationship Connection and Context Relationship boundaries have to do with who the user accepts into his or her "friend group" and consequently shapes the nature of online interactions within a person's social network. Social media platforms have embedded the idea of "friend-based privacy" where information and interactional access is primarily dependent on one's connections. The structure of one's network can affect the level of engagement and the types of disclosures made on a platform. Individuals with more open relationship boundaries may have higher instances of weak ties compared to others who may employ stricter rules for including people into their inner circles. For example, studies have found people who engage in "hyper-adding," namely, adding a significant number of persons to their network which could result in a higher distribution of "weak ties" [53, 82].

After users accept friends and make connections, they must manage overlapping contexts such as work, family, or acquaintances. This leads to the types of privacy issues discussed under "Context Collapse" in the previous "Privacy Challenges" section. Research shows that boundary violations are hardly remedied by blocking or unfriending unless in extreme cases [115]. Furthermore, users rarely organize their friends into groups (and some social media platforms do not offer that functionality) [114]. People are either unaware of the feature, think it takes too much time, or are concerned that the wrong person would still see their information. As a result, users often feel they have to sacrifice being authentic online to control their privacy.

Network Discovery and Interaction An individual's social media network is often public knowledge, and there are advantages and disadvantages of having friends being aware of one's social connections (aka friends list or followers). Network boundary mechanisms enable people to identify groups of people and manage interactions between the various groups. We highlight two types of network boundaries, namely, network discovery and network intersection boundaries. First, network discovery boundaries are primarily centered around the act of regulating the type of access others have to one's network connections. Implementing an open approach to network discovery boundaries may create problems that may arise including competition as competitors within the same industry could steal clients by carefully selecting from a publicly facing friend list. Another issue arises when a person's friend does not have a good reputation and that connection is negatively received by others within that social group. Sometimes the result is positive, for example, when friends or family find they have mutual connections, thus building social capital. Some social media platforms offer the ability to hide friend groups from everyone.

Network intersection boundaries involve the regulation of the interactions among different friend groups within one's social network. Social media users have expressed the benefits of engaging in discourse online with people who they may not personally know offline [116]. In contrast, clashes within one's friend list due to opposing political views or personal stances could create tensions that would make moderating a post difficult. These boundaries could be harder to control and sometimes lead to conflict if one is forced to choose which friends can participate in discussions.

Inward- and Outward-Facing Territories Territorial boundaries include "places and objects in the environment" to indicate "ownership, possession, and occasional active defense" [117]. Within social media, there are features that are either inward-facing territories or outward-facing territories. Inward-facing territories are commonly characterized as spaces where users could find updates on their friends and see the content their connections were posting (such as the "news feed" on Facebook or "updates" on LinkedIn). To control their inward-facing territories, individuals could hide posts from specific people, adjust their privacy settings, and use filters to find specific information.

These territories are constantly being updated with photos, videos, and news articles that are personalized and not public facing which contributes to an overall low priority for territorial management [114]. Most choose to ignore content that is irrelevant to them rather than employing privacy features. In addition, once privacy features are used to hide content from particular friends, users rarely revisit that decision to reconsider including content within that territory from that person.

It is important to note that the key characteristic of outward-facing territory management is the regulation of potentially unsatisfactory interactions rather than a fear of information exposure. One example of an outward-facing territory is Facebook's wall/timeline, where a person's friend may contribute to your social media presence. Outward-facing territories fall between a public and private place, which creates more risk of unintended boundary violations. Altman argues that "because of their semipublic quality [outward-facing territories] often have unclear rules regarding their use and are susceptible to encroachment by a variety of users, sometimes inappropriately and sometimes predisposing to social conflict" [117]. Similar to confidant disclosure described above, connections may post (unwanted) content on a user's wall that could lead to turbulence if that content is later deleted.

Interactional Disabling and Blocking Interactional boundaries limit the need for other boundary regulations discussed because a person reduces access to oneself by disabling features [114]. For example, a user may deactivate Facebook Messenger to avoid receiving messages but reactivate the app when they deem that interaction to be welcomed. In a similar regard, disabling semipublic features of the interface (such as the wall on Facebook) could assist users in having a greater sense of control. This manifestation of interaction withdrawal is typically not directed at reducing interaction with a specific person; rather, it may be motivated by a high desire to control one's online spaces. As such, disabling features are associated with perceptions of mistrust within one's network and a desire to limit interruptions [115]. On the more extreme end, blocking could also be employed to regulate interactional boundaries. Unlike other withdrawal mechanisms such as disabling your wall, picture tagging, or chat, blocking is inherently targeted. The act represents the rejection and revocation of access to oneself from a particular party. Some social media platforms allow users to block other people or pages, meaning that the blocked person may not contact or interact with the user in any form. Generally, blocking a person results from a negative experience such as stalking or being bombarded with unwanted content [118].

7.4.2 Coping with Social Media Privacy Violations

Overtime, many social media platforms have implemented new privacy features that attempt to address evolving privacy risks and users' need for more granular control online. While this effort is commendable, Ellison et al. argue that "privacy behaviors on social networking sites are not limited to privacy settings" [41]. Thus, social media users still venture outside the realm of privacy settings to achieve appropriate levels of social interactions. Coping mechanisms can be viewed as behaviors utilized to maintain or regain interpersonal boundaries [107]. Although these coping approaches may often be suboptimal, Wisniewski et al.'s framework of coping strategies for maintaining one's privacy provides insight into the struggles many social media users face in maintaining these boundaries.

Filtering This approach is often defined as the "reduction of intensity of inputs" [117]. Filtering includes selecting whom one will accept into their online social circle and is often used in the management of relational boundaries. Filtering techniques may include relying on social cues (e.g., viewing the profile picture or examining mutual friends) before confirming the addition of a new connection. Other methods leverage non-privacy-related features that are repurposed to manage interactions based on relation context, for example, creating multiple accounts on the same platform to separate professional connections from personal friends.

Ignoring The vast amount of information on social media could easily become overwhelming and difficult to consume. Therefore, social media users may opt to ignore posts or skim through information to decide which ones should receive priority for engagement. Ignoring is most common for inward-facing territories such as your "Feed" page. The overreliance on this approach might increase the chances of missing critical moments that connections shared.

Blocking Blocking is a more extreme approach to interactional boundary management compared to filtering and ignoring, which contributes to lower levels of reported usage [119]. As an alternative, users have developed other technology-supported mechanisms that would allow them to avoid unwanted interactions. As an example, Wisniewski et al. describe using pseudonyms on Facebook to make it more difficult to find a user on the platform [107]. Another method for blocking unwanted interactions is to use the account of a close friend or loved one to enjoy the benefits of the content on the platform without the hassle of expected interactions. Page et al. highlight this type of secondary use for those who avoid social media because of social anxieties, harassment, and other social barriers [120].

Withdrawal When some users feel they are losing control, they withdraw from social media by doing one of the following: deleting their account, censoring their posts, or avoiding confrontation. As a result, a common technique is limiting or adjusting the information shared (even avoiding posts that may be received negatively) [121]. Das and Kramer found that "people with more boundaries to regulate censor more; people who exercise more control over their audience censor more content; and, users with more politically and age diverse friends censor less, in general" [122]. Withdrawal suggests that some users think the risks outweigh the benefits of social media.

Aggression Unlike offensive coping mechanisms such as filtering, blocking, or withdrawal, social media users resort to more defensive mechanisms when the intention is to create interactions that may be confrontational. Aggressive behavior is displayed when the goal is to seek revenge or garner attention from specific people or groups. Some users may choose to exploit subliminal references in their posts to indirectly address or offend specific persons (e.g., an ex-partner, coworker, family member).

Compliance Compliance is giving in to pressures (external or internal) and adjusting one's interpersonal boundary preferences for others. Altman describes this as "repeated failures to achieve a balance between achieved and desired levels of privacy" [117]. Relinquishing one's interactional privacy needs to accommodate pressures of disclosure, nondisclosure, or friending preferences could result in a perceived loss of control over social interactions.

Compromise A healthy strategy for managing social media boundary violations is communicating with the other person involved and finding a resolution. Prior work indicates that most users that compromise do so offline [107]. These compromises are mostly with closer friends who the user can contact through email, phone call, or messaging. These more private scenarios avoid other people becoming involved online. Also, many compromises are about tagging someone in photos or sharing personal information about another user (i.e., confidant disclosure).

In addition to this coping framework for social media privacy, Stutzman examined the creation of multiple profiles on social media websites, primarily Facebook, as an information regulation mechanism. Through grounded theory, he identified three types of information boundary regulation within this context (pseudonymity, practical obscurity, and transparent separations) and four overarching motives for these mechanisms (privacy, identity, utility, and propriety) [71]. Lampinen et al. created a framework of strategies for managing private versus public disclosures. It defined three dimensions by which strategies differed: behavioral vs. mental, individual vs. collaborative, and preventative vs. corrective [71, 123]. The various coping frameworks conceptualize privacy as a process of interpersonal boundary regulation. However, they do not solve the problem of managing privacy on these platforms. They do attempt to model the complexity of privacy management in a way that better reflects the complex nature of interpersonal relationships rather than as a matter of withholding versus disclosing private information.

7.5 Addressing Privacy Challenges

Section Highlights

- Rather than just measuring privacy concerns, researchers and designers should focus on understanding attitudes towards boundary regulation. Validated tools for measuring **boundary preservation concern** and **boundary enhancement expectations** are provided in this chapter.
- **Privacy features** need to be designed to account for **individual differences** in how they are perceived and used. While some feel features like untag, unfriend, and delete are useful, others are worried about how using such features will impact their relationships.
- Unaddressed privacy concerns can serve as a barrier to using social media. It is crucial to design for not only **functional privacy concerns** (e.g., being overloaded by information, guarding from inappropriate data access) but **social privacy concerns** as well (e.g., unwelcome interactions, pressures surrounding appropriate self-presentation).

This section describes how to better identify privacy concerns by measuring them from a boundary regulation perspective. We also emphasize the importance of individual differences when designing privacy features. Finally, we elaborate on a crucial set of social privacy issues that we feel are a priority to address. While many social media users may feel these types of social pressures to some degree, these problems have pushed some of society's most vulnerable to complete abandonment of social media despite their desire for social connection. We call on social media designers and researchers to focus on these problems which are a side effect of the technologies we have created.

7.5.1 Understanding People and Their Privacy Concerns

Understanding social media privacy as a boundary regulation allows us to better conceptualize people's attitudes and behaviors. It helps us anticipate their concerns and balance between too little or too much privacy. However, many existing tools for measuring privacy come from the information privacy perspective [124–126] and focus on data collection by organizations, errors, secondary use, or technical control of data. In detailing the various types of privacy boundaries that are relevant for managing one's privacy on social media, Wisniewski et al. [114] emphasized that the most important is maintaining relationship boundaries between people.

Page et al. [86, 127] similarly found that concerns about damaging relationship boundaries are actually at the root of low-level privacy concerns such as worrying about who sees what, being too accessible, or being bothered or bothering others by sharing too much information. For instance, a typically cited privacy concern such as being worried about a stranger knowing one's current location turns out to be a privacy concern only if an individual expects that a stranger might violate typical relationship expectations. Their research revealed that many people were unconcerned about strangers knowing their location and explained that no one would care enough to use that information to come find them. They did not expect anyone to violate relationship boundaries and so were privacy unconcerned. On the other hand, those who felt there was a likelihood of someone using their location for nefarious purposes were privacy concerned. Social media enabling a negative change in relationship boundaries and the types of interactions that are now possible (such as strangers now being able to locate me) drives privacy concerns.

In fact, while scholars have used many lower-level privacy concerns such as being worried about sharing information to predict social media usage and adoption, they have met with mixed success leading to the commonly observed privacy paradox. However, research shows that preserving one's relationship boundaries is at the root of these low-level online privacy concerns (e.g., informational, psychological, interactional, and physical privacy concerns) and is a significant predictor of social media usage [86, 127]. In other words, concerns about social media damaging one's relationships (aka relationship boundary regulation) are what drives privacy concerns.

7.5.2   Measuring Privacy Concerns

Boundary regulation plays a key role in maintaining the right level of privacy on social media, but how do we evaluate whether a platform is adequately supporting it? A popular scale for testing users' awareness of secondary access is the Internet Users' Information Privacy Concerns (IUIPC) scale, which measures their perceptions of collection, control, and awareness of user data [125]. An important finding is that users "want to know and have control over their information stored in marketers' databases." This indicates that social media should be designed such that people know where their data goes. However, throughout this chapter, it is evident that research on social media privacy has found concerns about social privacy more salient. In fact, the focus on relationship boundaries is a key privacy boundary to consider and measure in evaluating privacy concerns. Thus, having a scale to measure relationship boundary regulation would allow researchers and designers to better evaluate social media privacy.

Here we present validated relationship boundary regulation survey items developed by Page et al. which predict adoption and usage for various social media including Facebook, Twitter, LinkedIn, Instagram, and location-sharing social media [127, 128]. These survey items can be used to evaluate privacy concerns for use of existing social media platforms, as well as capturing attitudes about new features or platforms. The survey items capture attitudes about one's ability to regulate relationship boundaries when using a social media platform and are administered with a 7-point Likert scale (-3 = Disagree Completely, -2 = Disagree Mostly, -1 Disagree Slightly, 0 = Neither agree nor disagree, 1 = Agree

Table 7.2 Survey items for relationship boundaries when using social media platforms

Attitude	Survey items
Relationship boundary preservation concerns (BPC)	I'm worried others will use <platform> in a way that is out of line with our relationship.
	<Platform> exposes information that will negatively affect my relationship with others.
	I'm concerned that using <platform> will trigger changes in behavior that hurt my relationships.
	It is likely that using <platform> will negatively impact my relationships with others.
Relationship boundary enhancement expectation (BEE)	Using <platform> will improve my relationships with others.
	<Platform> supports new behaviors that will improve my relationships.
	Using <platform> enhances my relationships with others by keeping us better informed.
	I feel others will use <platform> in a way that pushes our relationship in a positive direction.

Slightly, 2 = Agree Mostly, 3 = Agree Completely). These items measure both concerns and positive expectations.

When evaluating a new or existing social media platform, the *relationship boundary preservation concern (BPC)* items can be used to gauge user's concerns about harming their relationships. A higher score would indicate that more support for privacy management is needed on a given platform. The *relationship boundary enhancement expectation (BEE)* items can also be used to evaluate whether users expect that using the platform will improve the user's relationships. A high score is important to driving adoption and usage – having low concerns alone is not enough to drive usage. Along similar lines, even if users have high concerns, they may be counteracted by a perceived high level of benefits and so users remain frequent users of a platform. For instance, Facebook, one of the most widely used platforms, was shown to both invoke high levels of concern as well as high levels of enhancement expectation [127]. However, note that high frequency of use does not necessarily mean high levels of engagement (e.g., posting, commenting) or that users do not employ suboptimal workarounds (e.g., being vague in their posts) [81]. On the other hand, Twitter has a higher level of concerns compared to perceived enhancement and, accordingly, lower levels of usage [127].

In the validation studies, the set of survey items representing BPC were treated as a scale and factor analysis used to compute a single score. Similarly, the ones representing BEE were used to generate a single factor score to represent that construct. These could be used to evaluate new features or platforms in the lab or after deployment. For instance, after performing tasks on a new feature or platform, the user can answer these questions and the designer can compare the responses between different designs in A/B testing, or to predict usage frequency and adoption intentions (e.g., see [127, 129] for detailed examples). Moreover, by correlating BPC or BEE with demographics or other customer segmentations (e.g., age, whether they are new customers, purpose for using the platform), product designers may be able to identify attitudes that are connected with certain segments of their customer base and address it directly.

7.5.3   Designing Privacy Features

When designing for privacy features, a crucial aspect to consider is individual differences. Privacy is not one-size-fits-all: there are many variations in how people feel, what they expect, and how they behave. Because social media connects individuals with diverse needs and expectations, and from a myriad of contexts, a necessity in addressing social media privacy is understanding individual differences in privacy attitudes and behaviors. Many individual differences have been identified that shape privacy needs and preferences [15] and behaviors [6, 24, 99].

Scholars have established that privacy as a construct is not limited to informational privacy (i.e., understanding the flow of data) but also includes social privacy concerns that may be more interactional (e.g., accessibility) or psychological in nature (e.g., self-presentation) [111, 130]. Thus, a host of attitudes and experiences could shape an individual's view on what it means to have privacy online. For example, people's preferences for privacy tools could be heavily influenced by the type of data being shared or the recipient of that data [36, 131, 132]. Likewise, prior experiences (negative or positive) could shape how people interact online which could affect disclosure [133]. Context and relevance have also been found to significantly influence privacy behavior online. Drawing from the contextual integrity framework, many researchers argue that when people perceive data collection to be reasonable or appropriate, they are more likely to share information [134]. On the other hand, research has shown that when faced with uncomfortable scenarios, people employ privacy protective behaviors such as nondisclosure or falsifying information [135]. Research has also pointed to personal characteristics that could shape digital privacy behavior such as personality, culture, gender, age, and social norms [64, 106, 136–140].

While identifying concerns about damaging one's relationships is important to measure, understanding the individual differences that can lead someone to be concerned can provide insight into addressing these concerns. For instance, through a series of investigations, Page et al. uncovered a communication style that predicts concerns about preserving relationship boundaries on many different social media platforms [127–129]. This communication style is characterized by wanting to put information out there so that the individual does not need to proactively inform others. Those who prefer an FYI (For Your Information) communication style are less concerned about relationship boundary preservation and, as a result, exhibit higher levels of engagement, interactions, and use of social media than low FYI communicators. For example, the survey items that capture an FYI communication style preference for location-sharing social media are: "I want the people I know to be aware of my location, without having to bother to tell them," "I would prefer to make my location available to the people I know, so that they can see it whenever they need it," and "The people I know should be able to get my location whenever they feel they need it." Each item is administered with a 7-point Likert scale (Disagree strongly, Disagree moderately, Disagree slightly, Neutral, Agree slightly, Agree moderately, Agree strongly). For other social media platforms, the information type is adjusted (i.e., "what I'm up to" instead of "my location").

Consequently, this raises concern over implications for non-FYI communicators since the design of major social media platforms is catered to FYI communicators [127, 128]. Drawing on this insight, Page demonstrated how considering the user's communication style when designing location-sharing social media interfaces can alleviate boundary preservation concerns [129]. Certain design choices such as choosing a request-based location-sharing interaction can lower concerns for non-FYI communicators, while continuous location-sharing and check-in type interactions that are typical in social media may be fine for FYI communicators.

This demonstrates that researchers should consider in the design of social media individual differences that affect privacy attitudes. Another individual difference in attitudes towards privacy features is a user's apprehension that using common features such as untag, delete, or unfriend/unfollow can act as a hindrance in their relationships with others. Page et al. identified that while many use privacy features and perceive them as a tool useful for protecting their privacy, there are also many who are concerned about how using privacy features could hurt their relationships with others (e.g., being worried about offending others by untagging or unfriending) [81]. Instead, those individuals would use alternative privacy management tactics such as vaguebooking (not sharing specific details and using vague posts). Designers need to be aware that privacy features also need to be catered to individual variations in attitudes as well or else they may be ineffective and unused by certain segments of the user population.

7.5.4 Privacy Concerns and Social Disenfranchisement

A significant amount of research within the domain of social media nonuse has been focused on functional barriers that hinder adoption. In many cases, nonuse is traced to a lack of access (e.g., limited access to technology, financial resources, or the Internet). However, the push against adoption and subsequent usage can be voluntary [141] due to functional privacy concerns such as concerns about data breaches, information overload, or annoying posts [120]. Several social media companies have also implemented features such as time limits to help users counter overuse [142].

Likewise, it is equally important to consider social barriers that prevent social media engagement for people who really could use the social connection. Sharing about distressing experiences can be beneficial and reduce stigma, improve connection and interpersonal relationships with one's network, and enhance well-being

[6, 7, 143, 144]. However, Page et al. identified a class of barriers that highlight social privacy concerns rooted in social anxiety or concerns about being overly influenced by others on social media. This is in contrast to the prior school of thought that focused primarily on functional motivations as barriers that influence nonuse (see Fig. 7.1) [120]. They point out that many who are already vulnerable avoid social media due to social barriers such as online harassment or paralysis over making decisions pertaining to online social interactions. Yet, they are also the ones who could benefit greatly from social connection and who end up losing touch with friends and social support by being off social media. They term this lose-lose situation of negative social consequences that arise when using social media as well as consequences from not using it, *social disenfranchisement*. They call on designers to address such social barriers and to realize that in designing the user experience to connect users so well, they are implicitly designing the nonuser experience of being left out. Given that social media usage may not always be a viable option, designers should design to alleviate the negative consequences of nonuse.

7.5.5 Guidelines for Designing Privacy-Sensitive Social Media

Now that you have learned about various privacy problems related to social media use, how do you apply that to designing or studying social media? Here are some practical guidelines.

Identifying Privacy Attitudes Measuring privacy attitudes is a tricky task. Using existing informational privacy scales, users often say they are concerned, but this does not end up matching their actual behavior. By approaching it from a boundary regulation perspective, it will be easier to identify the proper balance between sharing too much and sharing too little. The survey items described in this chapter offer a way to measure concerns about boundary regulation as well as positive expectations. Considering both are key to more accurately predicting user behaviors.

Understanding Your Target Population Some key characteristics are described in this chapter. Identifying these in your target population can help you be aware of individual differences that might affect privacy preferences on social media. When you are measuring privacy concerns, matching the preferences of your audience makes it more likely that they will have a good user experience. Pay particular attention to traits that have been identified as being related to usage and adoption of social media platforms, such as the FYI communication style which can be measured using the survey items provided in this chapter.

Evaluating Privacy Features Focus on understanding whether users perceive your privacy features as useful or perhaps as posing a relational hindrance. The survey items provided in this chapter can help you do so. When anticipating privacy needs of your social media users, make sure you identify features that may impact boundary regulation both positively and negatively. You can compare attitudes

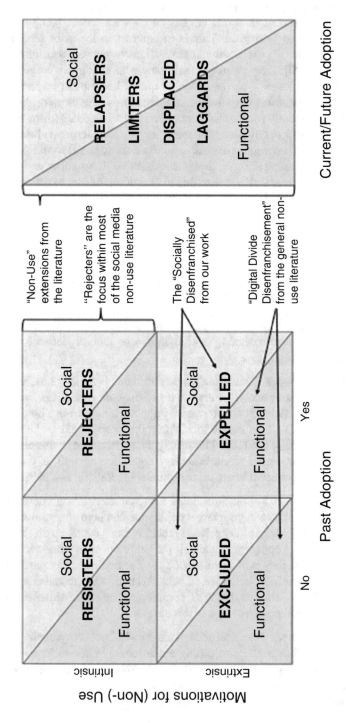

Fig. 7.1 Extension of Wyatt's frame that divided nonusers along the dimensions of whether someone has used the technology in the past and the motivation for adoption (extrinsic, e.g., organizationally imposed, versus intrinsic, e.g., desire to communicate through technology). Page et al. differentiate between functional motivations/barriers of use (which has been the focus of much research) versus social motivations/barriers to use. Other frameworks consider additional temporal states of adoption (whether they are currently using and whether they will in the future). See [120] for more detailed descriptions

between the existing feature and the newer version of the feature that will/has been deployed. You can also correlate attitudes towards privacy features with individual characteristics – some subpopulation of users may see privacy features as useful, while others may consider them a relational hindrance.

7.6 Chapter Summary

Social media has been widely adopted and quickly become an integral part of social, personal, economic, political, professional, and instrumental welfare. Understanding how mediated social interactions change the assumptions around audience management, disclosure, and self-presentation is key to working towards reconciling offline privacy assumptions with new realities. Moreover, given the rapidly changing landscape of widely available social media platforms, researchers and designers need to continually re-evaluate the privacy implications of new services, features, and interaction modalities.

With the rise of networked individualism, an especially strong emphasis must be placed on understanding individual characteristics and traits that can shape a user's privacy expectations and needs. Given the inherently social nature of social media, understanding social norms and the influence of larger cultural and structural factors is also important for interpreting expectations of privacy and the significance around various social media behaviors.

Privacy does not have a one-size-fits-all solution. It is a normative construct that is context dependent and can change over time, from culture to culture, and person to person. It needs to be weighed across different individuals and against other important goals and values of the larger group or society. Because people and their social interactions can be complex, designing for social media privacy is usually not a straightforward task. However, the consequences of not addressing privacy issues can range from irritating to devastating. Using this chapter as a guide and taking the steps to think through privacy needs and expectations of your social media users is an integral part of designing for social media.

References

1. Quan-Haase, Anabel, and Alyson L. Young. 2010. Uses and gratifications of social media: A comparison of Facebook and instant messaging. *Bulletin of Science, Technology & Society* 30 (5): 350–361.
2. Gruzd, Anatoliy, Drew Paulin, and Caroline Haythornthwaite. 2016. Analyzing social media and learning through content and social network analysis: A faceted methodological approach. *Journal of Learning Analytics* 3 (3): 46–71.
3. Yang, Huining. 2020. Secondary-school Students' Perspectives of Utilizing Tik Tok for English learning in and beyond the EFL classroom. In *2020 3rd International Conference on Education Technology and Social Science (ETSS 2020)*, 163–183.

4. Van Dijck, José. 2012. Facebook as a tool for producing sociality and connectivity. *Television & New Media* 13 (2): 160–176.
5. Grudin, Jonathan. 2001. Desituating action: Digital representation of context. *Human–Computer Interaction* 16 (2–4): 269–286.
6. Andalibi, Nazanin, Oliver L. Haimson, Munmun De Choudhury, and Andrea Forte. 2016. Understanding social media disclosures of sexual abuse through the lenses of support seeking and anonymity. In *Proceedings of the 2016 CHI conference on human factors in computing systems*, 3906–3918.
7. Andalibi, Nazanin, Pinar Ozturk, and Andrea Forte. 2017. Sensitive self-disclosures, responses, and social support on Instagram: The case of #depression. In *Proceedings of the 2017 ACM Conference on Computer Supported Cooperative Work and Social Computing*, 1485–1500.
8. Lin, Han, William Tov, and Qiu Lin. 2014. Emotional disclosure on social networking sites: The role of network structure and psychological needs. *Computers in Human Behavior* 41: 342–350.
9. Burke, Moira, Cameron Marlow, and Thomas Lento. 2010. Social network activity and social well-being. In *Proceedings of the SIGCHI Conference on Human Factors in Computing Systems*, ACM, 1909–1912.
10. Ellison, Nicole B., Charles Steinfield, and Cliff Lampe. 2007. The benefits of Facebook "Friends:" Social capital and college students' use of online social network sites. *Journal of Computer-Mediated Communication* 12 (4): 1143–1168.
11. ———. 2011. Connection strategies: social capital implications of Facebook-enabled communication practices. *New Media & Society* 13 (6): 873–892.
12. Koroleva, Ksenia, Hanna Krasnova, Natasha Veltri, and Oliver Günther. 2011. It's all about networking! Empirical investigation of social capital formation on social network sites. In *ICIS 2011 Proceedings*.
13. Fischer-Hübner, Simone, Julio Angulo, Farzaneh Karegar, and Tobias Pulls. 2016. Transparency, privacy and trust–technology for tracking and controlling my data disclosures: Does this work? In *IFIP International Conference on Trust Management*, Springer, 3–14.
14. Xu, Heng, Hock-Hai Teo, Bernard C.Y. Tan, and Ritu Agarwal. 2012. Research note-effects of individual self-protection, industry self-regulation, and government regulation on privacy concerns: A study of location-based services. *Information Systems Research* 23 (4): 1342–1363.
15. Boyd, Danah. 2002. *Faceted Id/Entity: Managing Representation in a Digital World.* Retrieved August 14, 2020 from https://dspace.mit.edu/handle/1721.1/39401.
16. Boyd, Danah M., and Nicole B. Ellison. 2007. Social network sites: Definition, history, and scholarship. *Journal of Computer-Mediated Communication* 13 (1): 210–230.
17. Dwyer, C., S.R. Hiltz, M.S. Poole, et al. 2010. Developing reliable measures of privacy management within social networking sites. In *System Sciences (HICSS), 2010 43rd Hawaii International Conference on*, 1–10.
18. Hargittai, E. 2007. Whose space? Differences among users and non-users of social network sites. *Journal of Computer-Mediated Communication* 13: 1.
19. Tufekci, Zeynep. 2008. Grooming, Gossip, Facebook and Myspace. *Information, Communication & Society* 11 (4): 544–564.
20. Kane, Gerald C., Maryam Alavi, Giuseppe Joe Labianca, and Stephen P. Borgatti. 2014. What's different about social media networks? A framework and research agenda. *MIS Quarterly* 38 (1): 275–304.
21. Pew Research Center. 2019. *Social Media Fact Sheet.* Pew Research Center: Internet, Science & Technology. Retrieved November 27, 2020 from https://www.pewresearch.org/internet/fact-sheet/social-media/.
22. Fire, M., R. Goldschmidt, and Y. Elovici. 2014. Online social networks: Threats and solutions. *IEEE Communications Surveys Tutorials* 16 (4): 2019–2036.
23. Social Media Users. *DataReportal – Global Digital Insights.* Retrieved March 16, 2021 from https://datareportal.com/social-media-users.

24. Alalwan, Ali Abdallah, Nripendra P. Rana, Yogesh K. Dwivedi, and Raed Algharabat. 2017. Social media in marketing: A review and analysis of the existing literature. *Telematics and Informatics* 34 (7): 1177–1190.
25. Binns, Reuben, Jun Zhao, Max Van Kleek, and Nigel Shadbolt. 2018. Measuring third-party tracker power across web and mobile. *ACM Transactions on Internet Technology* 18 (4): 52:1–52:22.
26. Barnard, Lisa. 2014. The cost of creepiness: How online behavioral advertising affects consumer purchase intention.
27. Dolin, Claire, Ben Weinshel, Shawn Shan, et al. 2018. Unpacking perceptions of data-driven inferences underlying online targeting and personalization. In *Proceedings of the 2018 CHI Conference on Human Factors in Computing Systems*, ACM, 493.
28. Ur, Blase, Pedro Giovanni Leon, Lorrie Faith Cranor, Richard Shay, and Yang Wang. 2012. Smart, useful, scary, creepy: Perceptions of online behavioral advertising. In *Proceedings of the eighth symposium on usable privacy and security*, ACM, 4.
29. Dogruel, Leyla. 2019. Too much information!? Examining the impact of different levels of transparency on consumers' evaluations of targeted advertising. *Communication Research Reports* 36 (5): 383–392.
30. Hamilton, Isobel Asher, and Dean Grace. Signal downloads skyrocketed 4,200% after WhatsApp announced it would force users to share personal data with Facebook. It's top of both Google and Apple's app stores. *Business Insider*. Retrieved February 1, 2021 from https://www.businessinsider.com/whatsapp-facebook-data-signal-download-telegram-encrypted-messaging-2021-1.
31. Wilkinson, Daricia, Moses Namara, Karishma Patil, Lijie Guo, Apoorva Manda, and Bart Knijnenburg. 2021. *The Pursuit of Transparency and Control: A Classification of Ad Explanations in Social Media.*
32. Lee, Rainie, and Barry Wellman. 2012. *Networked*. Cambridge, MA: MIT Press.
33. Dunbar, Robin. 2011. How many" friends" can you really have? *IEEE Spectrum* 48 (6): 81–83.
34. Carr, Caleb T., and Rebecca A. Hayes. 2015. Social media: Defining, developing, and divining. *Atlantic Journal of Communication* 23 (1): 46–65.
35. Xu, Heng, Tamara Dinev, H. Smith, and Paul Hart. 2008. *Examining the Formation of Individual's Privacy Concerns: Toward an Integrative View.*
36. Consolvo, Sunny, Ian E Smith, Tara Matthews, Anthony LaMarca, Jason Tabert, and Pauline Powledge. 2005. Location disclosure to social relations: Why, when, & what people want to share. 10.
37. Wiese, Jason, Patrick Gage Kelley, Lorrie Faith Cranor, Laura Dabbish, Jason I. Hong, and John Zimmerman. 2011. Are you close with me? Are you nearby?: Investigating social groups, closeness, and willingness to share. *UbiComp* 10.
38. Xu, Heng, and Sumeet Gupta. 2009. The effects of privacy concerns and personal innovativeness on potential and experienced customers' adoption of location-based services. *Electronic Markets* 19 (2–3): 137–149.
39. Acquisti, A., and R. Gross. 2006. Imagined communities: Awareness, information sharing, and privacy on the Facebook. *Privacy Enhancing Technologies*: 36–58.
40. Debatin, Bernhard, Jennette P. Lovejoy, Ann-Kathrin Horn, and Brittany N. Hughes. 2009. Facebook and online privacy: Attitudes, behaviors, and unintended consequences. *Journal of Computer-Mediated Communication* 15 (1): 83–108.
41. Ellison, Nicole B., Jessica Vitak, Charles Steinfield, Rebecca Gray, and Cliff Lampe. 2011. Negotiating privacy concerns and social capital needs in a social media environment. In *Privacy Online: Perspectives on Privacy and Self-Disclosure in the Social Web*, ed. S. Trepte and L. Reinecke, 19–32. Berlin: Springer.
42. Tufekci, Z. 2008. *Can You See Me Now? Audience and Disclosure Regulation in Online Social Network Sites*. Retrieved January 29, 2021 from https://journals.sagepub.com/doi/abs/10.1177/0270467607311484.

43. Ayalon, Oshrat and Eran Toch. 2013. Retrospective privacy: Managing longitudinal privacy in online social networks. In *Proceedings of the Ninth Symposium on Usable Privacy and Security – SOUPS '13*, ACM Press, 1.
44. Meeder, Brendan, Jennifer Tam, Patrick Gage Kelley, and Lorrie Faith Cranor. 2010. *RT @IWantPrivacy: Widespread Violation of Privacy Settings in the Twitter Social Network.* 12.
45. Padyab, Ali, and Tero Pã. *Facebook Users Attitudes towards Secondary Use of Personal Information.* 20.
46. van der Schyff, Karl, Stephen Flowerday, and Steven Furnell. 2020. Duplicitous social media and data surveillance: An evaluation of privacy risk. *Computers & Security* 94: 101822.
47. Symeonidis, Iraklis, Gergely Biczók, Fatemeh Shirazi, Cristina Pérez-Solà, Jessica Schroers, and Bart Preneel. 2018. Collateral damage of Facebook third-party applications: A comprehensive study. *Computers & Security* 77: 179–208.
48. Binder, Jens, Andrew Howes, and Alistair Sutcliffe. 2009. The problem of conflicting social spheres: Effects of network structure on experienced tension in social network sites. In *Proceedings of the 27th international conference on Human factors in computing systems – CHI 09*, ACM Press, 965.
49. Marwick, Alice E., and Danah Boyd. 2011. I tweet honestly, I tweet passionately: Twitter users, context collapse, and the imagined audience. *New Media & Society* 13 (1): 114–133.
50. Sibona, Christopher. 2014. Unfriending on Facebook: Context collapse and unfriending behaviors. In *2014 47th Hawaii International Conference on System Sciences*, 1676–1685.
51. Boyd, Danah Michele. 2004. Friendster and publicly articulated social networking. In *Extended Abstracts of the 2004 Conference on Human Factors and Computing Systems – CHI '04*, ACM Press, 1279.
52. Brzozowski, Michael J., Tad Hogg, and Gabor Szabo. 2008. Friends and foes: Ideological social networking. In *Proceeding of the Twenty-Sixth Annual CHI Conference on Human Factors in Computing Systems – CHI '08*, ACM Press, 817.
53. Boyd, Danah. 2006. Friends, Friendsters, and MySpace Top 8: Writing community into being on social network sites. *First Monday.*
54. Vitak, Jessica, Cliff Lampe, Rebecca Gray, and Nicole B Ellison. *"Why won't you be my Facebook friend?": Strategies for Managing Context Collapse in the Workplace.* 3.
55. Dennen, Vanessa P., Stacey A. Rutledge, Lauren M. Bagdy, Jerrica T. Rowlett, Shannon Burnick, and Sarah Joyce. 2017. Context collapse and student social media networks: Where life and high school collide. In *Proceedings of the 8th International Conference on Social Media & Society - #SMSociety17*, ACM Press, 1–5.
56. Pike, Jacqueline C., Patrick J. Bateman, and Brian S. Butler. 2018. Information from social networking sites: Context collapse and ambiguity in the hiring process. *Information Systems Journal* 28 (4): 729–758.
57. Heussner, Ki Mae and Dalia Fahmy. Teacher loses job after commenting about students, parents on Facebook. *ABC News.* Retrieved November 19, 2020 from https://abcnews.go.com/Technology/facebook-firing-teacher-loses-job-commenting-students-parents/story?id=11437248.
58. Torba, Andrew. 2019. High school teacher fired for tweets criticizing illegal immigration. *Gab News.* Retrieved November 19, 2020 from https://news.gab.com/2019/09/16/high-school-teacher-fired-for-tweets-criticizing-illegal-immigration/.
59. Hall, Gaynor, and Courtney Gousman. 2020. Suburban teacher's social media post sparks outrage, internal investigation | WGN-TV. *WGNTV.* Retrieved November 19, 2020 from https://wgntv.com/news/chicago-news/suburban-teachers-social-media-post-sparks-outrage-internal-investigation/.
60. Davis, Jenny L., and Nathan Jurgenson. 2014. Context collapse: Theorizing context collusions and collisions. *Information, Communication & Society* 17 (4): 476–485.
61. Kaul, Asha, and Vidhi Chaudhri. 2018. Do celebrities have it all? Context collapse and the networked publics. *Journal of Human Values* 24 (1): 1–10.

62. Donnelly, Erin. 2019. Kim Kardashian mom-shamed over photo of North staring at a phone: "Give her a book." *Yahoo! Entertainment*. Retrieved April 11, 2021 from https://www.yahoo.com/entertainment/kim-kardashian-mom-shamed-north-west-phone-book-151126429.html.
63. Sutton, Jeannette, Leysia Palen, and Irina Shklovski. 2008. *Backchannels on the Front Lines: Emergent Uses of Social Media in the 2007 Southern California Wildfires*. 9.
64. Litt, Eden. 2012. Knock, knock. Who's there? The imagined audience. *Journal of Broadcasting & Electronic Media* 56 (3): 330–345.
65. Litt, Eden, and Eszter Hargittai. 2016. The imagined audience on social network sites. *Social Media + Society* 2 (1): 2056305116633482.
66. Li, N., and G. Chen. 2010. Sharing location in online social networks. *IEEE Network* 24 (5): 20–25.
67. Stutzman, Fred, and Jacob Kramer-Duffield. 2010. Friends only: Examining a privacy-enhancing behavior in Facebook. In *Proceedings of the 28th international conference on Human factors in computing systems – CHI '10*, ACM Press, 1553.
68. Jung, Yumi, and Emilee Rader. 2016. The imagined audience and privacy concern on Facebook: Differences between producers and consumers. *Social Media + Society* 2 (2): 2056305116644615.
69. Vitak, Jessica. 2015. *Balancing Audience and Privacy Tensions on Social Network Sites*. 20.
70. Oolo, Egle, and Andra Siibak. 2013. Performing for one's imagined audience: Social steganography and other privacy strategies of Estonian teens on networked publics. *Institute of Journalism and Communication, University of Tartu, Tartu, Estonia* 7: 1.
71. Stutzman, Fred, and Woodrow Hartzog. 2012. *Boundary Regulation in Social Media*. 10.
72. Pounders, Kathrynn, Christine M. Kowalczyk, and Kirsten Stowers. 2016. Insight into the motivation of selfie postings: Impression management and self-esteem. *European Journal of Marketing* 50 (9/10): 1879–1892.
73. Krämer, Nicole C., and Stephan Winter. 2008. Impression Management 2.0: The relationship of self-esteem, extraversion, self-efficacy, and self-presentation within social networking sites. *Journal of Media Psychology* 20 (3): 106–116.
74. Duguay, Stefanie. 2016. "He has a way gayer Facebook than I do": Investigating sexual identity disclosure and context collapse on a social networking site. *New Media & Society* 18 (6): 891–907.
75. Tang, Karen P., Jialiu Lin, Jason I. Hong, Daniel P. Siewiorek, and Norman Sadeh. 2010. Rethinking location sharing: Exploring the implications of social-driven vs. purpose-driven location sharing. In *Proceedings of the 12th ACM International Conference on Ubiquitous Computing*, ACM, 85–94.
76. Back, Mitja D., Juliane M. Stopfer, Simine Vazire, et al. 2010. Facebook profiles reflect actual personality, not self-idealization. *Psychological Science* 21 (3): 372–374.
77. Choi, Tae Rang, and Yongjun Sung. 2018. Instagram versus Snapchat: Self-expression and privacy concern on social media. *Telematics and Informatics* 35 (8): 2289–2298.
78. Lindqvist, Janne, Justin Cranshaw, Jason Wiese, Jason Hong, and John Zimmerman. 2011. I'm the mayor of my house: Examining why people use foursquare – a social-driven location sharing application. In *Proceedings of the 2011 Annual Conference on Human Factors in Computing Systems – CHI '11*, ACM Press, 2409.
79. Page, Xinru, Bart P. Knijnenburg, and Alfred Kobsa. 2013. What a tangled web we weave: Lying backfires in location-sharing social media. In *Proceedings of the 2013 Conference on Computer Supported Cooperative Work – CSCW '13*, ACM Press, 273.
80. Hogg, Tad, and D Wilkinson. 2008. *Multiple Relationship Types in Online Communities and Social Networks*. 6.
81. Page, Xinru, Reza Ghaiumy Anaraky, Bart P. Knijnenburg, and Pamela J. Wisniewski. 2019. Pragmatic tool vs. relational hindrance: Exploring why some social media users avoid privacy features. In *Proceedings of the ACM on Human-Computer Interaction* 3, CSCW: 1–23.
82. Fono, D., and K. Raynes-Goldie. 2006. Hyperfriends and beyond: Friendship and social norms on Live Journal. *Internet Research Annual*.

83. Zinoviev, Dmitry, and Vy Duong. 2009. Toward understanding friendship in online social networks. *arXiv:0902.4658 [cs].*
84. Smith, Hilary, Yvonne Rogers, and Mark Brady. 2003. Managing one's social network: Does age make a difference. In *Proceedings of the Interact 2003,* IOS Press, 551–558.
85. Ehrlich, Kate, and N. Shami. 2010. Microblogging inside and outside the workplace. *Proceedings of the International AAAI Conference on Web and Social Media* 4: 1.
86. Page, Xinru, Alfred Kobsa, and Bart P. Knijnenburg. 2012. Don't disturb my circles! Boundary preservation is at the center of location-sharing concerns. In *Proceedings of the Sixth International AAAI Conference on Weblogs and Social Media,* 266–273.
87. Iachello, Giovanni, and Jason Hong. 2007. End-user privacy in human-computer interaction. *Foundations and Trends in Human-Computer Interaction* 1 (1): 1–137.
88. Bentley, Frank R., and Crysta J. Metcalf. 2008. Location and activity sharing in everyday mobile communication. In *Proceeding of the Twenty-Sixth Annual CHI Conference Extended Abstracts on Human Factors in Computing Systems – CHI '08,* ACM Press, 2453.
89. Tsai, Janice Y., Patrick Gage Kelley, Lorrie Faith Cranor, and Norman Sadeh. *Location-Sharing Technologies: Privacy Risks and Controls.* 34.
90. Friedland, Gerald, and Robin Sommer. 2010. *Cybercasing the Joint: On the Privacy Implications of Geo-Tagging.* 6.
91. Stefanidis, Anthony, Andrew Crooks, and Jacek Radzikowski. 2011. Harvesting ambient geospatial information from social media feeds.
92. Awad, Naveen Farag, and M.S. Krishnan. 2006. The personalization privacy paradox: An empirical evaluation of information transparency and the willingness to be profiled online for personalization. *MIS Quarterly* 30 (1): 13–28.
93. Chen, Xi, and Shuo Shi. 2009. A literature review of privacy research on social network sites. In *2009 International Conference on Multimedia Information Networking and Security,* IEEE, 93–97.
94. Gerber, Nina, Paul Gerber, and Melanie Volkamer. 2018. Explaining the privacy paradox: A systematic review of literature investigating privacy attitude and behavior. *Computers & Security* 77: 226–261.
95. Houghton, David J., and Adam N. Joinson. 2010. Privacy, social network sites, and social relations. *Journal of Technology in Human Services* 28 (1–2): 74–94.
96. Pavlou, Paul A. 2011. State of the information privacy literature: Where are we now and where should we go. *MIS Quarterly* 35 (4): 977–988.
97. Xu, Feng, Katina Michael, and Xi Chen. 2013. Factors affecting privacy disclosure on social network sites: An integrated model. *Electronic Commerce Research* 13 (2): 151–168.
98. Xu, Heng, Rachida Parks, Chao-Hsien Chu, and Xiaolong Luke Zhang. 2010. Information disclosure and online social networks: From the case of Facebook news feed controversy to a theoretical understanding. *AMCIS,* Citeseer, 503.
99. Dinev, Tamara, Massimo Bellotto, Paul Hart, Vincenzo Russo, Ilaria Serra, and Christian Colautti. 2006. Privacy calculus model in e-commerce – a study of Italy and the United States. *European Journal of Information Systems* 15 (4): 389–402.
100. Selten, Reinhard. 1990. Bounded rationality. *Journal of Institutional and Theoretical Economics (JITE)/Zeitschrift für die gesamte Staatswissenschaft* 146 (4): 649–658.
101. Knijnenburg, Bart P., Elaine M. Raybourn, David Cherry, Daricia Wilkinson, Saadhika Sivakumar, and Henry Sloan. 2017. Death to the privacy calculus? In *Proceedings of the 2017 Networked Privacy Workshop at CSCW,* Social Science Research Network.
102. Dienlin, Tobias, and Sabine Trepte. Is the privacy paradox a relic of the past? An in-depth analysis of privacy attitudes and privacy behaviors. *European Journal of Social Psychology* 45 (3): 285–297.
103. Kokolakis, Spyros. 2017. Privacy attitudes and privacy behaviour: A review of current research on the privacy paradox phenomenon. *Computers & Security* 64: 122–134.
104. Palen, Leysia, and Paul Dourish. 2003. Unpacking "Privacy" for a networked world. *NEW HORIZONS* 5: 8.

105. Petronio, Sandra. 1991. Communication boundary management: A theoretical model of managing disclosure of private information between marital couples. *Communication Theory* 1 (4): 311–335.
106. Nissenbaum, Helen. 2010. *Privacy in Context*. Stanford University Press.
107. Wisniewski, Pamela, Heather Lipford, and David Wilson. 2012. Fighting for my space: Coping mechanisms for SNS boundary regulation. In *Proceedings of the 2012 ACM annual conference on Human Factors in Computing Systems – CHI '12*, ACM Press, 609.
108. Petronio, S. 2010. Communication Privacy Management Theory: What Do We Know About Family Privacy Regulation? *Journal of Family Theory & Review* 2 (3): 175–196.
109. Clemens, Chris, David Atkin, and Archana Krishnan. 2015. The influence of biological and personality traits on gratifications obtained through online dating websites. *Computers in Human Behavior* 49: 120–129.
110. Vitak, Jessica, and Nicole B. Ellison. 2013. 'There's a network out there you might as well tap': Exploring the benefits of and barriers to exchanging informational and support-based resources on Facebook. *New Media & Society* 15 (2): 243–259.
111. Fogel, Joshua, and Elham Nehmad. 2009. Internet social network communities: Risk taking, trust, and privacy concerns. *Computers in Human Behavior* 25 (1): 153–160.
112. Agger, Ben. 2015. *Oversharing: Presentations of Self in the Internet Age*. Routledge.
113. Krämer, Nicole C., and Nina Haferkamp. 2011. Online self-presentation: Balancing privacy concerns and impression construction on social networking sites. In *Privacy Online: Perspectives on Privacy and Self-Disclosure in the Social Web*, ed. S. Trepte and L. Reinecke, 127–141. Berlin: Springer.
114. The University of Central Florida, Wisniewski Pamela, A.K.M. Najmul Islam, et al. 2016. Framing and measuring multi-dimensional interpersonal privacy preferences of social networking site users. *Communications of the Association for Information Systems* 38: 235–258.
115. Pamela Wisniewski, A.K.M. Najmul Islam, Bart P. Knijnenburg, and Sameer Patil. 2015. Give social network users the privacy they want. In *Proceedings of the 18th ACM Conference on Computer Supported Cooperative Work & Social Computing*, ACM, 1427–1441.
116. Bouvier, Gwen. 2015. What is a discourse approach to Twitter, Facebook, YouTube and other social media: Connecting with other academic fields? *Journal of Multicultural Discourses* 10 (2): 149–162.
117. Altman, Irwin. 1975. *The Environment and Social Behavior: Privacy, Personal Space, Territory, and Crowding*. Monterey, CA: Brooks/Cole Publishing Company.
118. Paasonen, Susanna, Ben Light, and Kylie Jarrett. 2019. The dick pic: Harassment, curation, and desire. *Social Media + Society* 5 (2): 2056305119826126.
119. Karr-Wisniewski, Pamela, David Wilson, and Heather Richter-Lipford. 2011. A new social order: Mechanisms for social network site boundary regulation. In *Americas Conference on Information Systems, AMCIS*.
120. Page, Xinru, Pamela Wisniewski, Bart P. Knijnenburg, and Moses Namara. 2018. Social media's have-nots: An era of social disenfranchisement. *Internet Research* 28: 5.
121. Sleeper, Manya, Rebecca Balebako, Sauvik Das, Amber Lynn McConahy, Jason Wiese, and Lorrie Faith Cranor. 2013. The post that wasn't: Exploring self-censorship on Facebook. In *Proceedings of the 2013 Conference on Computer Supported Cooperative Work*, ACM, 793–802.
122. Das, Sauvik, and Adam Kramer. 2013. Self-censorship on Facebook. *Proceedings of the International AAAI Conference on Web and Social Media* 7: 1.
123. Lampinen, Airi, Vilma Lehtinen, Asko Lehmuskallio, and Sakari Tamminen. 2011. We're in it together: Interpersonal management of disclosure in social network services. In *Proceedings of the 2011 Annual Conference on Human Factors in Computing Systems – CHI '11*, ACM Press, 3217.
124. Buchanan, Tom, Carina Paine, Adam N. Joinson, and Ulf-Dietrich Reips. 2007. Development of measures of online privacy concern and protection for use on the internet. *Journal of the American Society for Information Science & Technology* 58 (2): 157–165.

125. Malhotra, Naresh K., Sung S. Kim, and James Agarwal. 2004. Internet Users' Information Privacy Concerns (IUIPC): The construct, the scale, and a causal model. *Information Systems Research* 15 (4): 336–355.
126. Westin, Alan. 1991. *Harris-Equifax Consumer Privacy Survey*. Atlanta, GA: Equifax Inc.
127. Page, Xinru, Reza Ghaiumy Anaraky, and Bart P. Knijnenburg. 2019. How communication style shapes relationship boundary regulation and social media adoption. In *Proceedings of the 10th International Conference on Social Media and Society*, 126–135.
128. Page, Xinru, Bart P. Knijnenburg, and Alfred Kobsa. 2013. FYI: Communication style preferences underlie differences in location-sharing adoption and usage. In *Proceedings of the 2013 ACM International Joint Conference on Pervasive and Ubiquitous Computing*, ACM, 153–162.
129. Page, Xinru Woo. 2014. *Factors That Influence Adoption and Use of Location-Sharing Social Media*. Irvine: University of California.
130. Solove, Daniel. 2008. *Understanding Privacy*. Cambridge, MA: Harvard University Press.
131. Knijnenburg, B.P., Alfred Kobsa, and Hongxia Jin. 2013. Dimensionality of information disclosure behavior. *International Journal of Human-Computer Studies* 71 (12): 1144–1162.
132. Wilkinson, Daricia, Paritosh Bahirat, Moses Namara, et al. 2019. Privacy at a glance: Exploring the effectiveness of screensavers to improve privacy awareness. In *Proceedings of the ACM Conference on Human Factors in Computing Systems (CHI). Under Review*, ACM.
133. Joinson, Adam N., Ulf-Dietrich Reips, Tom Buchanan, and Carina B. Paine Schofield. 2010. Privacy, trust, and self-disclosure online. *Human–Computer Interaction* 25 (1): 1–24.
134. Nissenbaum, Helen. 2004. Privacy as contextual integrity. *Washington Law Review* 79: 119–157.
135. Ramokapane, Kopo M., Gaurav Misra, Jose M. Such, and Sören Preibusch. 2021. Truth or dare: Understanding and predicting how users lie and provide untruthful data online.
136. Barkhuus, Louise. 2012. The mismeasurement of privacy: Using contextual integrity to reconsider privacy in HCI. In *Proceedings of the SIGCHI Conference on Human Factors in Computing Systems*, ACM, 367–376.
137. Cho, Hichang, Bart Knijnenburg, Alfred Kobsa, and Yao Li. 2018. Collective privacy management in social media: A cross-cultural validation. *ACM Transactions on Computer-Human Interaction* 25 (3): 17:1–17:33.
138. Hoy, Mariea Grubbs, and George Milne. 2010. Gender differences in privacy-related measures for young adult Facebook users. *Journal of Interactive Advertising* 10 (2): 28–45.
139. Li, Yao, Bart P. Knijnenburg, Alfred Kobsa, and M-H. Carolyn Nguyen. 2015. Cross-cultural privacy prediction. In *Workshop "Privacy Personas and Segmentation", 11th Symposium On Usable Privacy and Security (SOUPS)*.
140. Sheehan, Kim Bartel. 1999. An investigation of gender differences in on-line privacy concerns and resultant behaviors. *Journal of Interactive Marketing* 13 (4): 24–38.
141. Wyatt, Sally M.E. 2003. Non-users also matter: The construction of users and non-users of the Internet. *Now Users Matter: The Co-construction of Users and Technology*: 67–79.
142. 2018. Facebook and Instagram introduce time limit tool. *BBC News*. Retrieved February 10, 2021 from https://www.bbc.com/news/newsbeat-45030712.
143. Andalibi, Nazanin. 2020. Disclosure, privacy, and stigma on social media: Examining non-disclosure of distressing experiences. *ACM Transactions on Computer-Human Interaction (TOCHI)* 27 (3): 1–43.
144. Gibbs, Martin, James Meese, Michael Arnold, Bjorn Nansen, and Marcus Carter. 2015. #Funeral and Instagram: Death, social media, and platform vernacular. *Information, Communication & Society* 18 (3): 255–268.

Chapter 8
Privacy-Enhancing Technologies

Kent Seamons

Abstract An increasing amount of sensitive information is being communicated and stored online. Frequent reports of data breaches and sensitive data disclosures underscore the need for effective technologies that users and administrators can deploy to protect sensitive data. Privacy-enhancing technologies can control access to sensitive information to prevent or limit privacy violations. This chapter focuses on some of the technologies that prevent unauthorized access to sensitive information. These technologies include secure messaging, secure email, HTTPS, two-factor authentication, and anonymous communication. Usability is an essential component of a security evaluation because human error or unwarranted inconvenience can render the strongest security guarantees meaningless. Quantitative and qualitative studies from the usable security research community evaluate privacy-enhancing technologies from a socio-technical viewpoint and provide insights for future efforts to design and develop practical techniques to safeguard privacy. This chapter discusses the primary privacy-enhancing technologies that the usable security research community has analyzed and identifies issues, recommendations, and future research directions.

8.1 Introduction

An increasing amount of sensitive information is being communicated, stored, and shared online. Unauthorized access to this information can lead to serious privacy violations. This chapter focuses on some privacy-enhancing technologies (PETS) that prevent unauthorized access to sensitive information.

The need for effective privacy-enhancing technologies has never been greater. The Snowden revelations in 2013 exposed a broad array of government surveillance programs and ignited renewed interest in privacy-preserving technologies that

K. Seamons (✉)
Brigham Young University, Provo, UT, USA
e-mail: seamons@cs.byu.edu

© The Author(s) 2022

B. P. Knijnenburg et al. (eds.), *Modern Socio-Technical Perspectives on Privacy*,
https://doi.org/10.1007/978-3-030-82786-1_8

prevent eavesdropping. The steady stream of data breaches underscores the risks of trusting third parties with sensitive information and the importance of robust defenses against unauthorized account access. Along with the risk of sensitive information disclosure, the rise of online social networks and other data-sharing cloud services presents increasing opportunities for privacy violations.

This chapter discusses several technologies that the usable security research community has analyzed and identifies issues, recommendations, and future research directions. For example, privacy-enhancing technologies protect sensitive information during transmission (HTTPS) and storage at untrusted third parties (end-to-end encryption in secure messaging and secure email). Technologies can also keep sensitive conversations private so that the fact that two parties are even communicating is not made public (Tor).

Usable security researchers explore the human-computer interaction aspects of PETS, an important socio-technical element beyond the formal security guarantees established by a security analysis. A security technology that is not usable can lead to reduced security or no security at all.

8.2 Secure Messaging

Instant messaging (IM) applications provide an online chat capability that allows users to communicate in real time. Without end-to-end encryption, the conversation is not private. Early IM applications did not provide any encryption, allowing eavesdropping by the service provider or anyone with access to the network during transmission. For instance, other users on a wireless network with the proper software could easily view the chat messages.

IM applications typically rely on a centralized server to relay messages between the users. If each user connects to the server using HTTPS, no network eavesdroppers can read the messages. However, the service provider has access to the entire chat conversation when the server relays or stores the plaintext messages.

A significant post-Snowden development was the creation of the Signal Protocol [1] by Moxie Marlinspike and Trevor Perrin. The protocol provides end-to-end encryption and is available in WhatsApp, the Signal app by Open Whisper Systems, and Facebook Messenger Secret Conversations. Together, these applications serve over a billion users. Moxie and Trevor received the 2017 Levchin Prize for Real-World Cryptography for the development and widespread deployment of the Signal Protocol.

The widespread adoption and use of the Signal Protocol may represent the largest, most rapid adoption of end-to-end encryption in history. Interestingly, privacy was not a driving motivation for users to adopt these systems [2]. Instead, adoption was based on the natural spread of messaging applications so that friends could communicate with their friends. The privacy benefits of encrypted conversations are a side benefit that did not drive adoption. Nonetheless, the result is that billions of users have private conversations protected against passive eavesdropping by the service provider, hackers, and governments without taking any action or even being aware of that protection.

With Signal, each user has a public and private key that the messaging app generates upon installation. Signal implementations rely on a server to relay messages and distribute public keys. When Alice and Bob want to communicate securely, they obtain each other's public key (sometimes referred to as their identity key) and jointly compute a shared key using their identity keys. As Alice and Bob exchange messages, they continue to calculate new shared keys to encrypt each message with a different encryption key. This approach provides *forward secrecy*, a significant privacy protection property in many state-of-the-art encryption systems. Even if the encryption key for a message is compromised, the attacker gains access to only a single message and cannot read any previous or future messages using the compromised key.

All deployments of the Signal Protocol rely on a centralized key server trust model. The messaging provider maintains a key server that stores and hands out public keys for all users. Reliance on a trusted key server means that even though Signal protects against passive eavesdropping, users are vulnerable to an active man-in-the-middle (MITM) attack.

An active MITM attack works as follows. Suppose Alice and Bob want to have a private conversation. A compromised key server can hand out fake keys for Alice and Bob. As Alice and Bob send messages to each other, the compromised server can decrypt and possibly modify each message as it flows through the provider. Alice and Bob are not even aware that their messages are not private.

To defend against an active MITM attack, users can complete an authentication ceremony with each contact to verify out-of-band that their device has the correct public key of their contact and not a fake key from an active MITM attacker. Key verification requires that a pair of users each navigate to an interface in their messaging client and confirm that both users have the same fingerprint (sometimes called a safety number) on their phone as their partner (see Fig. 8.1). There are two ways to accomplish key verification. First, if the users are physically co-located, the app provides each with a QR code that they each scan from their partner's phone to confirm that they have each other's correct public key. The QR code confirmation requires that the partners meet and conduct the ceremony in person. If they are remote, they can confirm that they each have the same. One partner can read the safety number to the other partner to confirm. If the numbers match, the conversation is private. If the numbers don't match, an active MITM attack is likely in progress.

The usable security research community has studied the effectiveness of the current authentication ceremony and proposed improvements based on usability study results. There have been studies that compare various methods for comparing fingerprints [3–5], along with studies that analyze the full authentication ceremony.

Early studies of Signal revealed that the ceremony was unusable, error-prone, and took too long [6, 7]. More recently, a redesign of the authentication ceremony interface using opinionated design resulted in fewer mistakes and reduced the average time to find and complete the ceremony from 11 to 2 min [8].

Fig. 8.1 Signal app authentication ceremony

Next, an approach to automate the ceremony by confirming key ownership using social media accounts removed the requirement that both participants be physically present or communicate online while confirming each other's keys. However, the results show that users do not trust social network providers as the third party to distribute their keys automatically [9].

Finally, Wu et al. [10] applied risk communication theory to test modifications to the Signal app authentication ceremony that showed increased user understanding and decreased usage of the authentication ceremony as users made choices based on risk assessments.

In summary, the authentication ceremony in secure messaging applications is broken [11]. Research reveals the problems and limitations of the current approach. It is unlikely that very many of the billions of secure messaging users will start using the ceremony. Hence, a better approach to obtaining assurance for the masses is to automatically detect attacks to distribute fake keys for users.

Issues

- **Lack of user understanding**—Users do not understand the need for the authentication ceremony to detect man-in-the-middle attacks.
- **Authentication ceremony is not usable**—Lab studies show that the authentication ceremony is time-consuming, error-prone, and hard to use.
- **No interoperability**—The current IM systems are walled gardens or silos. There is no interoperability between different providers. A WhatsApp user cannot communicate securely with a Facebook Messenger user.
- **Server must be trusted**—The secure messaging provider is trusted to deliver public keys and provide the client software. Even if a user has the assurance that a contact's correct key is in use, there is still the risk that compromised software can leak keys or sensitive information. The government could still coerce a company to update the software on a target's phone with a backdoor.

Recommendations

- **Use secure messengers for private communication**—For secure communication, the best option available today is for individuals to use an instant messenger client that supports the Signal Protocol for private conversations.
- **Vulnerable users should complete the authentication ceremony**—If you are a high-risk target or are communicating highly sensitive data, complete the authentication ceremony with each contact to ensure there is no MITM attack.

Research Directions

- **Nudge users to verify keys only when the risk is high**—Explore the use of machine learning to detect when a user is communicating sensitive information and then prompt the user to complete the authentication ceremony when the risk of data compromise is greatest. This approach enables users to make risk decisions at the moment the risk is present.
- **Automate key verification**—Design methods to automatically detect or prevent active MITM attacks that relieve users from the burden of the authentication ceremony.

- **Provide application-independent key management**—Provide centralized support for key management in the browser or operating system to enable interoperability between applications that support the Signal Protocol.
- **Better support for message deletion**—Study user behavior and attitudes in response to new features that allow them to forget or delete messages.
- **Safeguard encryption keys**—Design approaches utilizing secure enclaves to protect encryption keys and encryption software from compromise.

8.3   Secure Email

Email was not originally designed to be secure. Figure 8.2 illustrates the vulnerabilities in plaintext email, including (1) unsecured links, (2) message forgeries, (3) malicious content, and (4) untrusted servers. Without the use of encryption, sensitive email messages are vulnerable to eavesdroppers while in transit. In addition, sensitive messages stored in the server are also vulnerable to unauthorized access. Email messages are often stored indefinitely, and the long-term storage adds to the privacy risks even if the data is compromised well into the future.

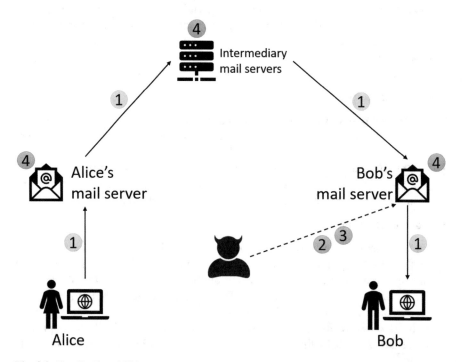

Fig. 8.2 Email vulnerabilities

Technologies exist to address some of these vulnerabilities [12]. Transport Layer Security (TLS) encrypts email messages during transmission between communication links. Sender Policy Framework (SPF) lets the domain owner specify the legitimate servers that send email messages for that domain. DomainKeys Identified Mail (DKIM) includes a signature on each email message from a domain to guard against message forgery. Recent studies show that these techniques are not universally deployed, leaving a significant gap in the secure email infrastructure [13–16]. Even if we close this gap, servers still have access to plaintext email messages, and the threat of disclosure to hackers or government surveillance remains.

End-to-end encryption addresses the issue of server access to plaintext email. The most well-known secure email systems are S/MIME and PGP. S/MIME supports a hierarchical, top-down trust model and is used mainly in corporations. PGP supports a grass-roots, bottom-up trust model that is suitable for individuals. Deployment of these technologies continues to languish after decades. The reasons are complex and nuanced, and center around a diverse set of stakeholders with competing interests that no one-size-fits-all solution can satisfy [12].

Secure email is one of the challenges that launched the field of usable security with the seminal paper *Why Johnny Can't Encrypt* [17]. The paper included a lab usability study of PGP that failed miserably and provided a wake-up call to the security community of the importance of user-centered design. Nearly 20 years later, a lab usability study of a modern PGP web client (Mailvelope) had similarly disappointing results when 9 of 10 participant pairs were unable to exchange a secure email message after 1 h of trying to use the system [18].

Despite the lack of a usable production PGP tool, recent research has produced several highly usable secure email interfaces (e.g., [19–21]). Figure 8.2 illustrates the interface for Private Webmail 2.0, a system that grew out of a series of studies (e.g., [22, 23]) over many years. The research shows that the following are essential properties for a usable, secure email interface:

1. *Tight Integration.* Users want secure email systems that enhance their existing email clients and fit within their existing workflows [20]. This integration is both visual and functional—that is, it looks like a part of the client application and has similar functionality, respectively (see Fig. 8.3). While visual integration is important, users should be able to clearly distinguish between emails protected with end-to-end encryption and emails that are not [22].

   While most users prefer integrated solutions, a small but consistent portion prefer standalone clients   [20, 21], believing that handling secure email in a separate client makes it more obvious to the user when encryption is in use.
2. *Inline, context-sensitive tutorials.* Tutorials are essential in helping users understand how to use secure email properly [22]. For users to pay attention and use these tutorials, the tutorial must be shown inline with the secure email system [22]. Additionally, the system should provide context-sensitive tutorials, walking first-time users through the process of sending and receiving secure email (see Fig. 8.3, left side).

3. *Streamlined onboarding.* Encrypted email should be designed to help recipients understand what they have received and what actions they need to take next [22] (see Fig. 8.3, right side). If the secure email system requires recipients first to generate a key pair, the system should automatically send an email explaining what the recipient needs to do [20]. Additionally, the system should save a draft of the sender's message to send automatically after the recipient generates and makes their public key available.

4. *Understandable and trustworthy design.* Interfaces need to help users understand how secure email is protecting them—for example, telling them whether the subject line is encrypted (it usually is not). Increased understanding allows users to make informed decisions and avoid mistakes [22, 24]. Additionally, system operation needs to conform to user expectations; otherwise, users reject the system. For example, studies show that if encryption happens too quickly, users assume that their messages were not encrypted and did not trust the tool [22].

5. *Easy-to-use key management.* Users struggle with managing their keys. Automation of key generation, uploading, and discovery significantly improve the user experience [19, 20, 24].

Studies show that systems applying (most of) these principles are perceived as highly usable, result in a low mistake rate, and help novice users begin sending encrypted email without expert assistance [20–24].

Secure email is a two-body problem, and Ruoti et al. [23] pioneered a novel two-person methodology where pairs of participants are brought into a user study to test a system. They found that participants were more relaxed during the study and

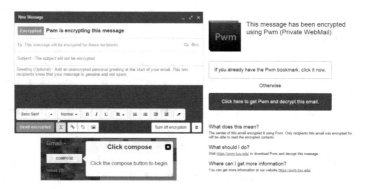

Top left—placeholder text that acts as an inline tutorial instructing users about how secure email works.

Bottom left—an inline, context-sensitive tutorial helping users send an encrypted email for the first time.

Right—the body of the encrypted email providing plaintext instructions to streamline onboarding.

Fig. 8.3 Interface for private webmail (Pwm) 2.0 [22], a modern usable secure email system

did not automatically assume that they were responsible for system mistakes. This methodology has been utilized in recent secure messaging studies [8, 10].

The storage of plaintext email at the server presents an attack surface in case of future account compromise. Research is beginning to explore email deletion capabilities that reduce the risk of future disclosure of sensitive messages that do not require long-term storage [25]. Another approach is to encrypt the plaintext email on the server with a locally stored encryption key and delete the plaintext copy [26]. The advantage of this approach is that a user can do this unilaterally without the cooperation of their communication partner. However, it does not safeguard the copy of the message in the original sender's outbox.

Multiple stakeholders with competing priorities for secure email make it difficult for a one-size-fits-all solution [27]. There needs to be more willingness by the various stakeholders to allow for alternatives that support the needs of only some of the stakeholders. There has been significant effort by the usable security research community to study the issues surrounding secure email, and usable system designs have been demonstrated in a laboratory setting [28].

Issues

- **PGP is dead**—PGP is a failed experiment. Even the proponents of secure email have been abandoning PGP recently. Modern PGP clients exhibit poor usability in laboratory user studies.
- **Secure email solutions are not interoperable**—The various approaches to secure email are not interoperable (PGP, S/MIME, proprietary web-based systems).
- **It is difficult to introduce a secure email solution that maintains ubiquity**— Email has a history emphasizing ubiquity and interoperability. Anyone can send an email to any other user if they have an email address for them. It is challenging to introduce secure email into this environment and maintain the same service guarantees.

Recommendations

- **Individuals should use secure messaging instead**—Given the current state of secure email, use a secure messaging client that supports the Signal Protocol for private conversations with friends and family.
- **Businesses should use S/MIME or secure webmail**—For sensitive business communications that must occur over email, enterprises can use S/MIME, and small businesses and individuals can use web-based secure email services such as ProtonMail and Tutanota.
- **All email providers should support TLS**—It is exasperating that all email is not protected from passive eavesdropping today. All email systems should support TLS for exchanging email between email systems.
- **Delete old sensitive email when possible**—Unless legally required to retain a copy, delete outdated sensitive email messages that could be problematic if made public following an account compromise.

Research Directions

- **Longitudinal studies are needed**—Previous secure email usability studies are all short-term lab studies. Longitudinal studies could confirm whether the above design principles are sufficient for email or whether more improvements are needed to support long-term usage.
- **Providers should only have access to encrypted messages**—Develop techniques to process encrypted data so the email provider can scan for malware and spam without having access to the plaintext.
- **Support easy deletion of old messages**—Analyze the usability of secure email deletion approaches.

8.4   HTTPS

The privacy of sensitive information is protected when it is encrypted during transmission over an insecure network. HTTPS is the protocol for encrypting data transmitted between browsers and web servers. It relies on a lower-level protocol known as Transport Layer Security (TLS), formerly known as the Secure Socket Layer (SSL). At a high level, HTTPS/TLS/SSL are synonymous—it is the most common protocol for encrypted communication on the Internet. As part of the HTTPS setup, a website authenticates to the browser using a certificate digitally signed by a trusted third party.

In 2010, the Firesheep browser extension demonstrated the risks of session hijacking for sites that used HTTPS only to protect the login page and sent browser cookies in the clear. The tool allowed an attacker sniffing traffic on a wireless network to easily hijack another user's session to gain unauthorized access to their social network or webmail. The publicity and ease of performing this attack contributed to major websites, like Google and Facebook, requiring HTTPS for all session traffic to their website.

More recently, there has been a significant uptick in the use of HTTPS for all web traffic, which provides increased protection against unauthorized access to browser activity. The increase in HTTPS has been mainly fueled by Let's Encrypt, a service that offers free digital certificates that are easy for admins to request and manage.

The most recent version of the protocol (TLS 1.3) supports only ciphers that provide the forward secrecy property described earlier in the secure messaging discussion. It also provides increased privacy protection by encrypting the server certificates transmitted to the client.

There are three aspects of HTTPS that have socio-technical implications: (1) HTTPS warning messages, (2) developer and administrator development and deployment hurdles, and (3) HTTPS inspection.

8.4.1 HTTPS Warning Messages

Users are sometimes faced with HTTPS warning messages when the browser encounters a website certificate that does not properly validate. The web server certificate authenticates a website to the browser. HTTPS warnings have been an area of significant usability studies and modification over the past decade.

Researchers at Google have been at the forefront of this effort[29–35]. Google is well-positioned to gather telemetry data from its users and conduct large-scale A/B tests comparing alternate designs. The results of these studies have shown a decrease in the click-through rate of HTTPS warning messages. It isn't clear that the reduction is due to increased user understanding as much as it is that the browsers make it more difficult to click through the warning message by adding additional steps that may discourage users from continuing.

Browsers display a lock icon whenever HTTPS is in use. Users interpret the lock icon as an indicator that the website is secure. Several studies show that users interpret the lock icon to mean that the website is secure [36]. The lock icon is unrelated to the website's security, and this misunderstanding is precisely the wrong interpretation when a phishing website impersonates a well-known company and employs HTTPS.

8.4.2 HTTPS Development and Deployment

Software developers that build HTTPS applications can make mistakes, such as introducing certificate validation errors that compromise user privacy [37–39].

Two recent research projects presented user-level and system-level approaches for automatically intercepting and verifying a website certificate, which overrides an application with broken HTTPS authentication [40, 41]. An approach that goes beyond intercepting broken HTTPS applications is to design a more straightforward, abstract interface to HTTPS applications that make it easier for developers to build reliable applications that encrypt network traffic. O'Neill et al. [42] proposed a simple extension to the existing POSIX secure socket API. They demonstrate how their approach can replace a 300+ line program using the complex OpenSSL library with a 16-line program using their simplified approach for creating a secure connection to a website.

Administrators of websites can misconfigure HTTPS and create privacy risks for users. A qualitative study examined mental models of users and administrators, and administrators did not understand protocol components and technical terms associated with HTTPS [36].

8.4.3   HTTPS Interception

HTTPS interception (also known as a TLS Proxy) often occurs within a corporation, library, or school so that the organization can monitor the security of their network and make sure clients are not unknowingly downloading malware or releasing sensitive business secrets from a compromised machine. Several studies measure how often HTTPS inspection occurs by using detection techniques from the server side [43–45]. A study of client-side HTTPS interception software shows that these systems can introduce privacy risks to users due to programmer error [46].

The same mechanisms utilized for inspection can also be the source of an active man-in-the-middle attack. Since the two options appear similar, it makes the task of informing the user all the more difficult.

A survey of user attitudes and opinions of HTTPS inspection showed that most users are unfamiliar with this practice and consider it an invasion of privacy [47, 48]. Some results of the survey are illustrated in Figs. 8.4 and 8.5. Although security proponents often object vehemently to the practice of HTTPS inspection, users were more moderate and accepting that a business or organization has the right to inspect the traffic on their network. Surveys show that users overwhelmingly want to be notified when HTTPS inspection is happening.

Issues

- **Companies perform HTTPS Interception to protect their network and systems.** Intermediate servers run by a company or organization can access a user's HTTPS web traffic, known as HTTPS inspection. Some users consider this a privacy breach, but they understand why a company must protect its network.
- **Users overwhelmingly desire notification** when an HTTPS proxy is operating.
- **Many HTTPS applications are broken.** Developers make mistakes when building HTTPS applications due to the complexity of HTTPS libraries.

Recommendations

- **Use HTTPS on all websites.** All owners of websites should be using HTTPS for all connections to their site. Certificates are inexpensive and easy to acquire using Let's Encrypt.
- **Website designers should not mix HTTP and HTTPS traffic** on a single web page since this has been a source of compromise in the past.

Research Directions

- **HTTPS warning redesign**—As we transition to a web where most sites support HTTPS, new approaches are needed for warning users when there is a risk of using an HTTP website and when they should not trust an HTTPS site.
- **HTTPS inspection detection**—We need improved techniques to detect when HTTPS inspection occurs and the associated risks.
- **Developer and administrator usability studies** can determine the effectiveness of recent advances in easy-to-use libraries for building and deploying HTTPS applications.

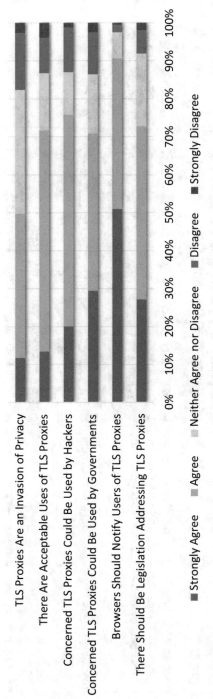

Fig. 8.4 Participant attitudes toward HTTPS inspection (N=1049)

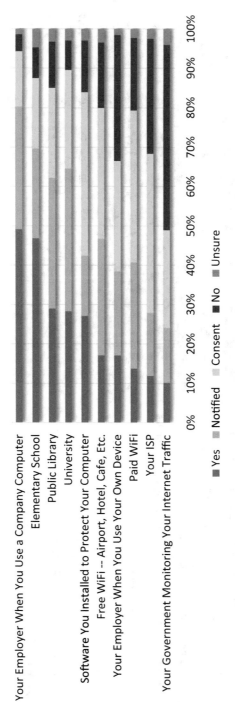

Fig. 8.5 Participant responses on scenarios—should the organization be allowed to inspect HTTPS traffic? (N=927)

8.5   Two-Factor Authentication

Controlling access to sensitive user data is paramount to privacy. Passwords remain the most common form of online user authentication today, despite the tremendous amount of research that demonstrates their security and usability weaknesses [49]. The number of data breaches is increasing rapidly [50], and most data breaches involve weak, compromised, or default passwords [51]. In response, many organizations and individuals turn to two-factor authentication (2FA) to protect against privacy violations that occur when user accounts are compromised.

2FA requires users to present two factors from *something they know* (such as a password or the answers to a set of security questions), *something they have* (such as a phone or hardware token), and *something they are* (a biometric such as a fingerprint or facial recognition). 2FA protects against remote attackers because attackers are not able to compromise user accounts using passwords alone.

Companies deploy 2FA internally to strengthen security. Lang et al. [52] report on Google's internal deployment of security keys to their employees. It was generally successful and reduced the number of authentication-related support tickets.

Later, two academic studies of security keys showed that the setup was challenging for some end-users who completed tasks without the aid of an IT support staff. Das et al. [53] performed two studies measuring both the usability and the acceptability of using the YubiKey (a type of FIDO U2F compliant hardware token) as a second factor in securing a Google account. Employing a think-aloud protocol, they made some recommendations to Yubico (the manufacturer of the YubiKey) based on common points of confusion. After 1 year, they repeated the study with a new group of users, finding that although many of the previous usability concerns had been addressed, many users still did not see much benefit in using the YubiKey. Das et al. postulated that this lack of acceptability was due partly to the lack of awareness of the risks mitigated through using the YubiKey. Reynolds et al. [54] describe two usability studies of YubiKeys. The study found many usability concerns with the setup process of the YubiKey but found that day-to-day usability was significantly higher.

Reese et al. [55] compared five types of 2FA over 2 weeks and found that users generally had a positive experience. The setup experience for users in this study was favorable compared to earlier setup studies, indicating that improved setup instructions make a difference.

Many universities in the United States are adopting Duo 2FA to reduce the risk of compromised student data. Two qualitative studies completed at CMU [56] and BYU [57] explored user attitudes toward Duo after being required to use it for some time. Both institutions report that some users are annoyed at being required to use 2FA on all university websites, even some that may not have personal information at risk. There is also evidence that users are frustrated with certain limitations that have potential solutions that they are unaware exist. For instance, some users are frustrated when they need access to the web when they have no Wi-Fi available, and they do not know that there are alternative 2FA options that work without any Wi-Fi, such as a phone app that generates one-time passwords.

Issues

- **Lack of user understanding**—Users do not understand how 2FA makes them more secure. Users also do not understand the pros and cons of various 2FA options.
- **No support for account sharing**—Studies show that account sharing occurs, and two-factor solutions are not easy to adapt to legitimate account-sharing scenarios such as for family members or a caregiver.
- **Weak backup authentication**—Many websites require a fallback authentication method in case a 2FA device is lost, effectively reducing security to the strength of the authentication method used for backup.

Recommendations

- A **standardized setup process** for 2FA devices across the major websites would make it easier for users to setup 2FA on multiple accounts easily.

Research Directions

- **Longitudinal studies with diverse populations**—We need longitudinal studies of 2FA technology with a broader population of users, not just university student populations. Some potential populations include the elderly, low-income, and disabled.
- **Integrate 2FA with password managers**—Password managers may be well-suited to help with easy 2FA registration and recovery.
- **Automate the 2FA setup process** to make mass 2FA enrollment simpler and to make it easy to transition to a new authenticator device when the old one is lost or stolen.

8.6 Anonymity

Anonymous communication aims to hide the identity of participants as they communicate to protect their privacy. The Onion Router (Tor) is a free software program supporting anonymous web browsing. It relies on multiple layers of encryption to hide the origin of a request from the website. As messages flow through multiple hops in the Tor network, each node in the random set of relay servers only knows the relay server immediately before and after it along the route through the network.

Qualitative studies consisting of semi-structured interviews with Tor users reveal that users have inaccurate mental models of Tor and Tor Onion services, which raises the risk that user mistakes could deanonymize them [58, 59]. Earlier studies examined the usability of the Tor Browser [60], the Tor Browser Bundle[61, 62], and the Tor Launcher [63]—about 78% of users failed to set up Tor correctly in a usability study of the Tor Launcher. Even though prior research has identified weaknesses and limitations in Tor implementations, proposed design recommendations have yet to be implemented and tested.

Bitcoin supports pseudonymity, meaning a user has a persistent alias unrelated to their real-world identity. To maintain pseudonymity, users can install and run Bitcoin client software on their own, but they run the risk of losing access to their Bitcoin if they forget their password or lose access to their wallet. Usability studies of Bitcoin also show that poor understanding can lead to mistakes that reveal a user's identity or a loss of their cryptocurrency [64–66].

Issues

- **Incorrect mental models**—Non-expert users have incorrect mental models of anonymity technology that increase the risk of mistakes that could deanonymize them.
- **Privacy technology can cause harm**—There are tensions between privacy capabilities that protect individuals from harm and the use of privacy tools to commit crimes and harm individuals.

Recommendations

- **Use tools to limit information collection**—Tools like Tor, private browsing modes, and VPNs can limit the information that is collected about your on-line activities.

Research Directions

- **Easier setup**—How can users easily install or configure Tor to protect their anonymity.
- **User education**—How can we educate or inform users about online privacy risks and ways to effectively mitigate those risks?
- **Tighter integration of privacy technology**—Tighter integration between anonymity technology and browsers or operating systems may increase usability and reduce the risk of errors.
- **Increase the benefits while reducing the potential for harm**—How can we provide users with tools that adequately protect their privacy while reducing the risks that criminals will use those tools to harm vulnerable users [67].

8.7 Summary

This chapter provides an overview of some of the privacy-enhancing technologies that protect access to sensitive data and the socio-technical challenges surrounding them. It discusses results from the usable security community that evaluates this technology and provides insight into future directions to make improvements. The following are some overarching themes and takeaways.

- **Key management presents a usability challenge** for PETs technology and is an essential focus of usable security research moving forward. Key management usability challenges exist for key recovery and key portability in applications that require encryption. Secure enclaves present new opportunities to protect keys and enable privacy-preserving applications.

- Usability research for PETs extends beyond non-technical end-users to include **developers and administrators**.
- Due to the variety of users and differing goals, **privacy solutions need to be adaptable** to the context, preferences, and goals of individual users.
- Lab user studies help identify when deficiencies are present that need to be corrected. However, once lab results are positive, **longitudinal studies with a general population** are necessary to determine whether an approach is suitable for the day-to-day use of typical users.
- The insights from usability studies in academia and research demonstrate the potential early gains that technology companies could realize by doing **more usability testing for new products**.
- Usability studies show that **users have misunderstandings** about most of the privacy-related software they encounter (e.g., end-to-end encryption, HTTPS inspection, two-factor authentication, anonymous services). Can automated solutions hide technical details and provide security benefits without making the user aware?
- The Signal Protocol is an example of a system that was able to introduce security that prevents eavesdropping without the user having to do anything to configure that protection. However, in most cases, there are options or potential false positives that require the user to decide how best to proceed. A hard question is how to **empower users to easily and conveniently make informed choices** when they face security and usability trade-offs.

Acknowledgments I want to thank Daniel Zappala and our students at BYU that participated in some of the research described in this chapter. This work was supported in part by the National Science Foundation under grants CNS-1528022 and CNS-1816929.

References

1. Systems, O. W. Signal. https://signal.org/. Accessed Feb 10 2018.
2. Abu-Salma, R., M. A. Sasse, J. Bonneau, A. Danilova, A. Naiakshina, and M. Smith. 2017. Obstacles to the adoption of secure communication tools. In *IEEE Symposium on Security and Privacy*. Piscatawy: IEEE.
3. Dechand, S., D. Schürmann, K. Busse, Y. Acar, S. Fahl, and M. Smith. 2016. An empirical study of textual key-fingerprint representations. In *USENIX Security Symposium*. Berkeley: USENIX Association.
4. Tan, J., L. Bauer, J. Bonneau, L. F. Cranor, J. Thomas, and B. Ur. 2017. Can unicorns help users compare crypto key fingerprints? In *Proceedings of the CHI Conference on Human Factors in Computing Systems*. New York: ACM.
5. Shirvanian, M., N. Saxena, and J. J. George. 2017. On the pitfalls of end-to-end encrypted communications: A study of remote key-fingerprint verification. In *Annual Computer Security Applications Conference (ACSAC)*. New York: ACM.

6. Herzberg, A., and H. Leibowitz. 2016. Can Johnny finally encrypt? Evaluating E2E-encryption in popular IM applications. In *Workshop on Socio-Technical Aspects in Security and Trust (STAST), Los Angeles.*

7. Vaziripour, E., J. Wu, M. O'Neill, R. Clinton, J. Whitehead, S. Heidbrink, K. Seamons, and D. Zappala. 2017. Is that you, Alice? A usability study of the authentication ceremony of secure messaging applications. In *Symposium on Usable Privacy and Security (SOUPS).*

8. Vaziripour, E., J. Wu, M. O'Neill, D. Metro, J. Cockrell, T. Moffett, J. Whitehead, N. Bonner, K. Seamons, and D. Zappala. 2018. Action needed! Helping users find and complete the authentication ceremony in Signal. In *Proceedings of the Fourteenth Symposium on Usable Privacy and Security.*

9. Vaziripour, E., D. Howard, J. Tyler, M. O'Neill, J. Wu, K. Seamons, and D. Zappala. 2019. I don't even have to bother them! Using social media to automate the authentication ceremony in secure messaging. In *Proceedings of the CHI Conference on Human Factors in Computing Systems.* New York: ACM.

10. Wu, J., C. Gattrell, D. Howard, J. Tyler, E. Vaziripour, K. Seamons, and D. Zappala. 2019. "Something isn't secure, but i'm not sure how that translates into a problem": Promoting autonomy by designing for understanding in signal. In *Symposium on Usable Privacy and Security (SOUPS).*

11. Herzberg, A., H. Leibowitz, K. Seamons, E. Vaziripour, J. Wu, and D. Zappala. 2020. Secure messaging authentication ceremonies are broken. *IEEE Security & Privacy* 19 (2): 29–37.

12. Clark, J., P. C. van Oorschot, S. Ruoti, K. E. Seamons, and D. Zappala. 2018. Securing email. CoRR abs/1804.07706.

13. Durumeric, Z., D. Adrian, A. Mirian, J. Kasten, E. Bursztein, N. Lidzborski, K. Thomas, V. Eranti, M. Bailey, and J. A. Halderman. 2015. Neither snow nor rain nor MITM...: An empirical analysis of email delivery security. In *Proceedings of the Internet Measurement Conference (IMC).* New York: ACM.

14. Foster, I. D., J. Larson, M. Masich, A. C. Snoeren, S. Savage, and K. Levchenko. 2015. Security by any other name: On the effectiveness of provider based email security. In *Proceedings of the 22nd ACM SIGSAC Conference on Computer and Communications Security (CCS).*

15. Holz, R., J. Amann, O. Mehani, M. Wachs, and M. A. Kaafar. 2016. TLS in the wild: An Internet-wide analysis of TLS-based protocols for electronic communication. In *Network and Distributed System Security Symposium (NDSS).*

16. Mayer, W., A. Zauner, M. Schmiedecker, and M. Huber. 2016. No need for black chambers: Testing TLS in the e-mail ecosystem at large. In *IEEE 11th International Conference on Availability, Reliability and Security (ARES).*

17. Whitten, A., and J. D. Tygar. 1999. Why Johnny can't encrypt: A usability evaluation of PGP 5.0. In *USENIX Security Symposium.*

18. Ruoti, S., J. Andersen, L. Dickinson, S. Heidbrink, T. Monson, M. O'Neill, K. Reese, B. Spendlove, E. Vaziripour, J. Wu, D. Zappala, and K. Seamons. 2019. A usability study of four secure email tools using paired participants. *ACM Transactions on Privacy and Security (TOPS)* 22 (2): 1–22.

19. Garfinkel, S. L., and R. C. Miller. 2005. Johnny 2: A user test of key continuity management with S/MIME and outlook express. In *Symposium on Usable Privacy and Security (SOUPS).* New York: ACM.

20. Atwater, E., C. Bocovich, U. Hengartner, E. Lank, and I. Goldberg. 2015. Leading Johnny to water: Designing for usability and trust. In *Symposium on Usable Privacy and Security (SOUPS).* New York: ACM.

21. Lerner, A., E. Zeng, and F. Roesner. 2017. Confidante: Usable encrypted email: A case study with lawyers and journalists. In *Proceedings of the IEEE European Symposium on Security and Privacy.* Piscataway: IEEE.

22. Ruoti, S., J. Andersen, T. Hendershot, D. Zappala, and K. Seamons. 2016. Private webmail 2.0: Simple and easy-to-use secure email. In *Proceedings of the 2016 Symposium on User Interface Software and Technology.* New York: ACM.

23. Ruoti, S., J. Andersen, S. Heidbrink, M. O'Neill, E. Vaziripour, J. Wu, D. Zappala, and K. Seamons. 2016. We're on the same page: A usability study of secure email using pairs of novice users. In *Proceedings of the CHI Conference on Human Factors in Computing Systems*. New York: ACM.

24. Bai, W., M. Namara, Y. Qian, P. G. Kelley, M. L. Mazurek, and D. Kim. 2016. An inconvenient trust: User attitudes toward security and usability tradeoffs for key-directory encryption systems. In *Symposium on Usable Privacy and Security (SOUPS)*. Berkeley: USENIX.

25. Monson, T., S. Ruoti, J. Reynolds, D. Zappala, T. Smith, and K. Seamons. 2018. A usability study of secure email deletion. In *European Workshop on Usable Security (EuroUSEC)*.

26. Koh, J. S., S. M. Bellovin, and J. Nieh. 2019. Why Joanie can encrypt: Easy email encryption with easy key management. In *Proceedings of the Fourteenth EuroSys Conference 2019*. New York: ACM.

27. Clark, J., P. van Oorschot, S. Ruoti, K. Seamons, and D. Zappala. 2021. SoK: Securing email— a stakeholder-based analysis. In *Proceedings of the 25th International Conference on Financial Cryptography and Data Security*.

28. Ruoti, S., and K. Seamons. 2019. Johnny's journey toward usable secure email. *IEEE Security Privacy* 17 (6): 72–76.

29. Reeder, R. W., A. P. Felt, S. Consolvo, N. Malkin, C. Thompson, and S. Egelman. 2018. An experience sampling study of user reactions to browser warnings in the field. In *Proceedings of the CHI Conference on Human Factors in Computing Systems*. New York: ACM.

30. Acer, M. E., E. Stark, A. P. Felt, S. Fahl, R. Bhargava, B. Dev, M. Braithwaite, R. Sleevi, and P. Tabriz. 2017. Where the wild warnings are: Root causes of Chrome HTTPS certificate errors. In *Proceedings of the ACM SIGSAC Conference on Computer and Communications Security*. New York: ACM.

31. Felt, A. P., R. W. Reeder, A. Ainslie, H. Harris, M. Walker, C. Thompson, M. E. Acer, E. Morant, and S. Consolvo. 2016. Rethinking connection security indicators. In *Symposium on Usable Privacy and Security (SOUPS)*.

32. Felt, A. P., A. Ainslie, R. W. Reeder, S. Consolvo, S. Thyagaraja, A. Bettes, H. Harris, and J. Grimes. 2015. Improving SSL warnings: Comprehension and adherence. In *Proceedings of the CHI Conference on Human Factors in Computing Systems*. New York: ACM.

33. Akhawe, D., and A. P. Felt. 2013. Alice in warningland: A large-scale field study of browser security warning effectiveness. In *USENIX Security Symposium*.

34. Akhawe, D., B. Amann, M. Vallentin, and R. Sommer. 2013. Here's my cert, so trust me, maybe? Understanding TLS errors on the web. In *Proceedings of the 22nd International Conference on World Wide Web*. New York: ACM.

35. Sunshine, J., S. Egelman, H. Almuhimedi, N. Atri, and L. F. Cranor. 2009. Crying wolf: An empirical study of SSL warning effectiveness. In *USENIX Security Symposium*.

36. Krombholz, K., K. Busse, K. Pfeffer, M. Smith, and E. von Zezschwitz. 2019. "if HTTPS were secure, i wouldn't need 2FA"-end user and administrator mental models of HTTPS. In *IEEE Symposium on Security and Privacy*.

37. Brubaker, C., S. Jana, B. Ray, S. Khurshid, and V. Shmatikov. 2014. Using frankencerts for automated adversarial testing of certificate validation in SSL/TLS implementations. In *IEEE Symposium on Security and Privacy*. Piscatawy: IEEE.

38. Fahl, S., M. Harbach, T. Muders, L. Baumgärtner, B. Freisleben, and M. Smith. 2012. Why Eve and Mallory love android: An analysis of android SSL (in) security. In *ACM Conference on Computer and Communications Security (CCS)*. New York: ACM.

39. Georgiev, M., S. Iyengar, S. Jana, R. Anubhai, D. Boneh, and V. Shmatikov. 2012. The most dangerous code in the world: Validating SSL certificates in non-browser software. In *ACM Conference on Computer and Communications Security (CCS)*, 38–49. New York: ACM.

40. Bates, A., J. Pletcher, T. Nichols, B. Hollembaek, D. Tian, K. R. Butler, and A. Alkhelaifi. 2014. Securing SSL certificate verification through dynamic linking. In *Proceedings of the 2014 ACM SIGSAC Conference on Computer and Communications Security*. New York: ACM.

41. O'Neill, M., S. Heidbrink, S. Ruoti, J. Whitehead, D. Bunker, L. Dickinson, T. Hendershot, J. Reynolds, K. Seamons, and D. Zappala. 2017. Trustbase: An architecture to repair and strengthen certificate-based authentication. In *USENIX Security Symposium*.
42. O'Neill, M., S. Heidbrink, J. Whitehead, T. Perdue, L. Dickinson, T. Collett, N. Bonner, K. Seamons, and D. Zappala. 2018. The secure socket API:TLS as an operating system service. In *USENIX Security Symposium*.
43. Huang, L. S., A. Rice, E. Ellingsen, and C. Jackson. 2014. Analyzing forged SSL certificates in the wild. In *IEEE Symposium on Security and Privacy*. Piscatawy: IEEE.
44. O'Neill, M., S. Ruoti, K. Seamons, and D. Zappala. 2016. TLS proxies: friend or foe? In *Proceedings of the Internet Measurement Conference (IMC)*. New York: ACM.
45. Durumeric, Z., Z. Ma, D. Springall, R. Barnes, N. Sullivan, E. Bursztein, M. Bailey, J. A. Halderman, and V. Paxson. 2017. The security impact of HTTPS interception. In *Network and Distributed Systems Symposium*.
46. de Carné de Carnavalet, X., and M. Mannan. 2016. Killed by proxy: Analyzing client-end TLS interception software. In *Network and Distributed System Security Symposium*.
47. O'Neill, M., S. Ruoti, K. Seamons, and D. Zappala. 2017. TLS inspection: How often and who cares? *IEEE Internet Computing* 21 (3): 22–29.
48. Ruoti, S., M. O'Neill, D. Zappala, and K. Seamons. 2016. User attitudes toward the inspection of encrypted traffic. In *Symposium on Usable Privacy and Security (SOUPS)*.
49. Bonneau, J., C. Herley, P. C. V. Oorschot, and F. Stajano. 2012. The quest to replace passwords: A framework for comparative evaluation of web authentication schemes. In *IEEE Symposium on Security and Privacy*.
50. ITRC Data Breach Overview 2007 to 2017, Identity Theft Resource Center, 2018. https://itrcold.cmctempsites.com/images/breach/Overview20052017.pdf.
51. 2017 Data Breach Investigations Report. Verizon. 2017. https://www.knowbe4.com/hubfs/rp_DBIR_2017_Report_execsummary_en_xg.pdf.
52. Lang, J., A. Czeskis, D. Balfanz, M. Schilder, and S. Srinivas. 2016. Security keys: Practical cryptographic second factors for the modern web. In *International Conference on Financial Cryptography and Data Security (FC)*.
53. Das, S., A. Dingman, and L. J. Camp. 2018. Why Johnny doesn't use two factor: A two-phase usability study of the FIDO U2F security key. In *2018 International Conference on Financial Cryptography and Data Security (FC)*.
54. Reynolds, J., T. Smith, K. Reese, L. Dickinson, S. Ruoti, and K. Seamons. 2018. A tale of two studies: The best and worst of yubikey usability. In *IEEE Symposium on Security and Privacy*.
55. Reese, K., T. Smith, J. Dutson, J. Armknecht, J. Cameron, and K. Seamons. 2019. A usability study of five two-factor authentication methods. In *Symposium on Usable Privacy and Security (SOUPS)*.
56. Colnago, J., S. Devlin, M. Oates, C. Swoopes, L. Bauer, L. Cranor, and N. Christin. 2018. "it's not actually that horrible": Exploring adoption of two-factor authentication at a university. In *Proceedings of the 2018 CHI Conference on Human Factors in Computing Systems*.
57. Dutson, J., D. Allen, D. Eggett, and K. Seamonsy. 2019. "Don't punish all of us": Measuring user attitudes about two-factor authentication. In *European Workshop on Usable Security (EuroUSEC)*.
58. Winter, P., A. Edmundson, L. M. Roberts, A. Dutkowska-Żuk, M. Chetty, and N. Feamster. 2018. How do Tor users interact with onion services? In *USENIX Security Symposium*.
59. Gallagher, K., S. Patil, and N. Memon. 2017. New me: Understanding expert and non-expert perceptions and usage of the Tor anonymity network. In *Symposium on Usable Privacy and Security (SOUPS)*.
60. Clark, J., P. C. Van Oorschot, and C. Adams. 2007. Usability of anonymous web browsing: An examination of Tor interfaces and deployability. In *Symposium on Usable Privacy and Security (SOUPS)*. New York: ACM.
61. Norcie, G., K. Caine, and L. J. Camp. 2012. Eliminating stop-points in the installation and use of anonymity systems: A usability evaluation of the Tor browser bundle. In *5th Workshop on Hot Topics in Privacy Enhancing Technologies (HotPETS)*. Princeton: Citeseer.

62. Norcie, G., J. Blythe, K. Caine, and L. J. Camp. 2014. Why Johnny can't blow the whistle: Identifying and reducing usability issues in anonymity systems. In *Proceedings 2014 Workshop on Usable Security*. Princeton: Citeseer. https://doi.org/10.14722/usec

63. Lee, L., D. Fifield, N. Malkin, G. Iyer, S. Egelman, and D. Wagner. 2017. A usability evaluation of Tor launcher. *Proceedings on Privacy Enhancing Technologies* 2017 (3): 90–109.

64. Eskandari, S., J. Clark, D. Barrera, and E. Stobert. 2018. A first look at the usability of Bitcoin key management. arXiv:1802.04351.

65. Krombholz, K., A. Judmayer, M. Gusenbauer, and E. Weippl. 2016. The other side of the coin: User experiences with Bitcoin security and privacy. In *International Conference on Financial Cryptography and Data Security*. Berlin: Springer.

66. Gao, X., G. D. Clark, and J. Lindqvist. 2016. Of two minds, multiple addresses, and one ledger: Characterizing opinions, knowledge, and perceptions of Bitcoin across users and non-users. In *Proceedings of the CHI Conference on Human Factors in Computing Systems*. New York: ACM.

67. Levine, B. N., and B. Lynn. 2020. Tor hidden services are a failed technology, harming children, dissidents and journalists. In *Lawfare*.

Chapter 9
Tracking and Personalization

Rahat Masood, Shlomo Berkovsky, and Mohamed Ali Kaafar

Abstract This chapter studies the relationship between two important, often conflicting paradigms of online services: personalization and tracking. The chapter initially focuses on the categories and levels of online personalization, briefly overviewing algorithmic methods applied to achieve these. Then, the chapter turns to online tracking specific to mobile and web technologies, as well as the more advanced behavioral tracking. Following this, the chapter ties the streams of personalization and tracking together and discusses various aspects of their relationships, including the currently deployed tracking methods for personalization. Privacy implications of personalization via online tracking, highlighted by organizations and researchers, are also illustrated. Lastly, this chapter discusses the ways to balance personalization benefits and privacy concerns. This includes the state-of-the-art practices, current challenges, and practical recommendations for system developers willing to strike this balance.

9.1 Introduction

The ever-changing technological landscape, high user involvement, increased societal visibility, and amalgamation of services have made privacy challenging to maintain in a digital world. In recent years, we have witnessed many privacy violation incidents where tech-giant companies (e.g., Google, Facebook, LinkedIn) were involved. For instance, at Princeton University, computer-science researchers

R. Masood (✉)
Data61-CSIRO, University of New South Wales (UNSW), Sydney, NSW, Australia
e-mail: rahat.masood@data61.csiro.au

S. Berkovsky
Macquarie University, Sydney, NSW, Australia
e-mail: shlomo.berkovsky@mq.edu.au

M. A. Kaafar
Macquarie University and Data61-CSIRO, Sydney, NSW, Australia
e-mail: dali.kaafar@mq.edu.au

© The Author(s) 2022
B. P. Knijnenburg et al. (eds.), *Modern Socio-Technical Perspectives on Privacy*,
https://doi.org/10.1007/978-3-030-82786-1_9

confirmed that Google services on Android devices and iPhones store users' location data, even if users set their privacy settings to prevent Google from (geo)locating a user [1]. Similarly, Facebook has often been involved in scandals such as the Cambridge Analytica data harvesting [2], suspicions of Russian and Iranian meddling in the US elections [3], and several data-exposing "bugs" [4]. According to [5], roughly 17,000 Android apps collect identifying information about a user by setting persistent identifiers on mobile phones. These identifiers are the unique numbers that allow companies to learn about user's activities on a mobile phone. These examples indicate that a growing number of service providers use several techniques to collect a wide variety of data about end-users, from basic socio-demographic details to a complete history of a user's searches, clicks, locations, and details of the device used.

One apparent reason to collect such information is to create a personalized user experience to increase revenue, but at the same time, this information may also be used for different purposes, such as to build user profiles to strengthen user engagement and loyalty. Moreover, in some cases, this information may be shared with third parties to assist in various tasks such as sharing on social platforms, hosting and maintenance, or customer care [6]. The plethora of cases where companies collect as much information about end users as possible, sometimes unknowingly to them, and then using it for personalization, has raised the awareness of various issues associated with the need to preserve and maintain users' privacy. This chapter details the various aspects of the relationship between online tracking and personalization, including the currently deployed tracking methods for personalization, and existing solutions to balance personalization benefits and privacy concerns.

9.2 Aspects of Personalization

Personalized technologies are deployed nowadays by virtually every website and mobile app. These technologies facilitate the "provision of content and services tailored to individuals based on knowledge about their preferences and behavior" [7]. While personalized services started two decades ago with use cases like web content filtering and eCommerce recommendations, they have since spread to applications like music, tourism, eHealth, and more [8]. In this subsection we initially overview the goals and benefits of personalized technologies and then discuss their applications in the web and mobile environments.

9.2.1 Goals of Personalization

Naturally, the tailoring of services offered by personalization can benefit both the service provider and the end user. For the former, it allows to increase the quality of the service, as it gets adjusted to the needs and preferences of the user. This can lead to tangible improvements in various metrics, such as user engagement, click-through rate, returning users, positive feedback, and, in consequence, to increased revenues for the service. Likewise, users also benefit from the personalization, as the overall user experience is improved. For example, personalization can shorten the discovery of a desired content or reduce the costs of buying a product.

Many algorithmic approaches for personalization have been developed, evaluated, and deployed. Some of them rely on statistical correlations of past user behavior [9], while others capitalize on extensive domain knowledge [10]. Regardless of the underlying personalization algorithm, a necessary precondition for personalized services is the availability of reliable and up-to-date representation of the user, that is, their interests, preferences, and needs, as encapsulated by the user model [11].

User models typically reflect the goals and domain of the personalized service. For example, an email filtering plugin should be able to distinguish between genuine senders and spammers, while a movie recommender should know what movie genres are liked and disliked by the user. Thus, no one-size-fits-all representation of the user model can be conceived, and the target data is learned implicitly from observable user interactions with the system and other users.

Moreover, the information collected for personalizing the service is closely related to the underlying personalization algorithm. For example, collaborative methods rely on identifying similar users and deriving predictions for the target user from the behavior of the identified similar users. As such, collaborative methods naturally require knowledge about numerous users and the privacy concerns are harder to enforce in this case [12]. On the contrary, content-based methods require only the model of the target user and additional domain knowledge. The privacy of the latter is easier to protect than in the collaborative case, as the domain knowledge typically does not include any personal data [13].

9.2.2 Personalization Environments

The increasing use of mobile technologies has led to multi-modality (cross platforms), which allows users to access content and services through the web as well as through apps and mobile devices. In this section, we briefly describe these modalities with respect to personalization technologies.

9.2.2.1 Web Personalization

User modeling for web personalization purposes typically involves making sense of users' past information access and their interactions with online systems and other users. The facets of user data that can be modeled are diverse; for instance, they may include users' knowledge level, interests, goals and motivation, personality, and language. Potential sources of such user modeling data include past visited pages, launched search queries, purchased products, played songs and video clips, friended social network users, liked content, and more [11].

Note that, if accessible, these sources allow the personalized services not only to populate the desired user model facets but also to derive additional sensitive information that may undermine users' privacy [14]. Depending on the richness and reliability of the user models, the service can either be truly personalized or just tailored, for example, according to the group to which the user belongs.

9.2.2.2 Mobile Personalization

The use case of mobile personalization adds another layer of information, often referred to as the *context*. The most prominent example of the contextual user model is users' location. This can be leveraged for a range of location-aware personalized services, such as recommendations of places of interest, weather and traffic alerts, presence of other people nearby, and so on. Within such services, either the user modeling data or the personalized options are preselected according to the user's current location [15].

Other available sources of mobile user modeling data are various sensors deployed by the mobile device. These include accelerometers and gyroscopes that track movement, biometric sensors that recognize faces as well as scan eye iris and fingerprints, light sensors that detect the ambient illumination level, microphones that can detect background noises, and more. Add to these the plethora of behavioral and interaction data that can potentially be extracted from the installed mobile apps, such as browsing logs, social media friends, physical activity data, commute and driving patterns, and so forth. In combination, mobile phones can collect a large variety of user data and allow constructing detailed user models [16].

Having obtained and processed this information, various adaptive services and suggestions can be tailored to the users' preferences and interests. For example, recommended retailers can be restricted to the user's current location [17], screen brightness can be adjusted to the ambient light intensity [18], timing and frequency of reminders can be tuned according to interactions with similar reminders [19], and driving route can be modified if traffic to the desired location is slow [20]. In the next section, we focus on tracking techniques and discuss in detail the relevant entities and mechanisms that facilitate personalization.

9.3   Online Tracking

Research has shown that desktops and mobile devices and associated web browsers and mobile apps contain subtle information that allows them to be "fingerprinted or tracked." Online tracking has several meanings, but one of the most valid general definition is "following the trails and movements of someone on the Internet through means such as mobile phones, desktop, and smart devices, in order to gain unique information about them for incentives such as target advertising, profiling, and data exchange" [21]. Online tracking has various types and extensions: from detecting user interests when visiting a web page to recording various detailed aspects about the user, including their location, social relations, health, and political beliefs. A combination of such information increases the chances of identifying and appropriately tracking a user online. In Fig. 9.1, we show the ecosystem of online tracking. Additionally, the increasing use of IoT devices, such as SmartWatches, Fitbits, and SmartShoes, has made online tracking more aggravated as these devices collect, process, store, and disseminate sensitive users' data, such as health conditions, billing information, physical environment, and behavioral information. In Chap. 11, privacy issues in IoT devices are discussed in detail.

9.3.1   Tracking Contexts

There are several ways to achieve online tracking. In general, we contextualize them in four categories:

Web Tracking is one of the primary sources of the profiling that tracks users across different visits or sites. There are various design, implementation, and deployment methods that enable web tracking. For instance, for an externally hosted website, a service provider can embed third-party content or incorporate dynamic content like JavaScript snippets or libraries supplied by third party to implement the tracking functionality. In fact, more than 90% of Alexa's top-500 websites contain third-party tracking content [22], and that 70% of the cookies recorded were third-party cookies set by just 25 third-party domains [23]. That means the entities with whom the user may or may not have chosen to interact on the web may be recording their online behavior in unexpected ways.

Mobile Tracking identifies users through the devices equipped with sophisticated sensors, such as microphones, GPS, accelerometers, and cameras. These sensors generate highly sensitive data that can be used as unique fingerprints.[1] Like web tracking, mobile devices contain various identifiers that can be used (in isolation or in combination) to track or profile users. For example, researchers demonstrated how the use of WiFi SSID (the Service Set IDentifier representing the WiFi network devices connect to) in its active discovery mode could lead to revealing the geographical location of users [24] or distinguishing WiFi-enabled devices [25]. Others have shown how to infer the social relationship between mobile device owners by tracking their WiFi fingerprints [26]. Others have used motion sensor signals to identify devices or users [27–29]. The privacy concerns of mobile tracking are different from web tracking because of the diverse range of data available through sensors, apps, and mobile browsers. The high interconnectivity

---

[1] In privacy terminology, a fingerprint refers to a trace of information, often an observable characteristics of a device or a user, that is unique enough for identification or tracking purposes.

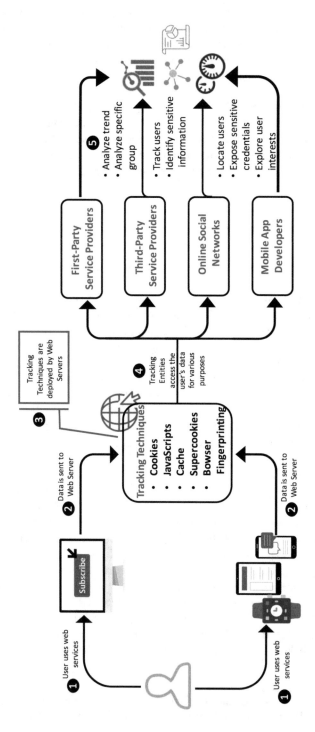

Fig. 9.1 Ecosystem of online tracking

and portability features of mobile devices have made them a perfect target for tracking.

Cross-Device Tracking is performed by many organizations today and can provide a more comprehensive view into users' behavior. There are several reasons to perform cross-device tracking. It allows consumers to log in to their email or social media accounts from multiple devices to maintain a "state" so they can pick up where they left off on a different device. It also facilitates companies to prevent fraud; for instance, if there is an unrecognized device, a company can take steps—such as sending an authentication code to an email address or phone number—to ensure that the new device belongs to the consumer who is trying to access an existing account. Companies also use cross-device tracking to improve user experience by personalizing the content on a website or an app and to accurately retarget a user on multiple devices by displaying relevant ads. Consider an example where a user searches for a movie ticket on a web browser of his desktop. He later used his mobile phone browser, which showed an advertisement of the same movie running in nearby cinemas.

Cross-App Tracking can be considered a particular form of cross-device tracking, where an app identifies other apps installed on the device and makes a link to a user [30]. For example, it was shown that user traits and whether or not the user is a parent of small children could be predicted from the installed mobile apps [31]. Similarly, a search of a discounted movie ticket on a Groupon app may result in ads for movies in theater on a Facebook app.

9.3.2 Tracking Entities

The abovementioned web and mobile tracking are used by *first-party* and *third-party* tracking entities, respectively. These entities perform tracking for purposes ranging from improved user experience to credit scoring or targeted political messages. We explain these two types of tracking below.

9.3.2.1 First-Party Tracking

First-party tracking is performed by the service providers with which the user interacts directly. This entity allows site owners to directly collect customer analytics data, remember language settings, and carry out other useful functions that help provide a good user experience. There are a variety of ways to perform first-party tracking, for example, user accounts, first-party cookies or caches. In first-party cookie tracking, site owners record user information such as username, passwords, and items added to the cart by attaching a unique string to the user browser. For example, Google tracks user interests via the search engine. When a user enters a query in the search bar, Google keeps a record of this entry through login credentials or information such as IP addresses, caches, or cookies. It then shows related links and advertisements in subsequent searches. A similar method is adopted by social networks such as Facebook, where a user could be tracked via interests shown through likes, comments, or posts. The user can control this tracking through security and privacy settings offered by these service providers.

Akin to websites, mobile app developers can also be considered first-party tracking entities as they have an ability to capture device data (e.g., sensors) and user information or activities through their apps. To capture device data, developers make API calls to multiple sensors like microphones, cameras, GPS, accelerometers, and touch. Similarly, device information such as phone numbers, current location, or unique phone ID number can also be extracted through APIs. However, in most cases, users' consent is required before extracting such information. The consent can be acquired by displaying app permissions and policies and getting explicit acknowledgment from a user.

First parties have several potential incentives to perform tracking. For instance, a first party wants to personalize user experience across sessions, detect frauds, or conform with law enforcement requiring websites to log user activities for fraud prevention and anti-laundering. However, there are cases where first-party websites voluntarily sell user identities. For example, Datalogix buys user information from companies, compile user dossiers, and then use it to target advertising [32]. Sometimes, a first party can also act as a third party (discussed in Sect. 9.3.2.2); for instance, logging in to a website using a third-party service such as Facebook or Google allows the website to request your data from them.

9.3.2.2   Third-Party Tracking

Third-party tracking is performed by the entities that track users across different services, for example, websites. It can also be an entity that provides resources while a page is being displayed. Typical resources are the content embedded in the page or external content accessed by a script running on the page. Third-party tracking offers several benefits to service providers, such as better audience targeting, boosting company recognition and reputation, or increasing its ROI. For instance, Google Analytics is a third-party entity used by more the half of the websites to gain aggregated statistics such as the business's performance, user experiences, user activities, and traffic records. This means that during any given browsing period, it is likely that at least some of that user's activity is being tracked by website owners, which is sent to Google Analytics for further processing. The processed data is then returned to the website owners to provide insights into their website traffic (e.g., geographic region and what type of device is being used) and user activity (e.g., page views and link clicks). Hence, aggregating data from various sources (e.g., websites, surveys, or publicly available information) can provide rich information in both breadth and depth. This allows a service provider to grow their targeted audience's size by including new prospects (e.g., who purchase similar or complementary products or services from a direct competitor or partner company).

Third parties have a range of motivations, which can be grouped into six main reasons, mentioned below:

- **Advertising** is one of the most common reasons to track and identify users online. In order to sell products, gain revenues, or increase product awareness, businesses and companies build associations with ad networks. However, it is essential to profile users and target the right ads on a website to be successful. For example, a user interested in buying a pair of shoes of a specific brand should be shown ads related to that brand.
- **Third-party measurement and analytics services** allow first-party websites to better understand their users by getting statistical information on demographics, content view distribution, and more. Third-party measurement services provide such analysis either using a paid or free analytics model. In a paid model, an analytics company takes precautions to silo data between clients, whereas in a free analytics model (e.g., Google Analytics), aggregated traffic statistics are sent to service providers to improve their content or enhance their services.
- **User engagement** can be increased via social networks, which allow service providers to offer personalized content and single sign-on services to their customers. These services either use cookies or require users to log in to their social network accounts and thus inevitably track and identify users. Examples include Facebook's like and comment widget and Google's like button. These features are offered for free to increase user engagement and to conduct market research. Moreover, there are social services that exist almost exclusively in a third-party context [33]. For instance, Disqus is a worldwide blog comment hosting service that offers features, such as social integration, social networking, user profiles, spam and moderation tools, analytics, and email notifications, to websites.
- Third-parties offer **Customized Content** such as video, maps, news, weather, stocks, and other media for embedding into websites. YouTube, for example, offers third-party widgets to generate revenue through in-widget advertising. Many others, such as the Associated Press, also charge for their content.
- **Content distribution** is yet another motivation for a third party to track and identify users. Content distribution networks, such as Akamai, help service providers distribute customized content to users based on their interests and profile.

There are potentially more intricate privacy issues with third-party tracking than with first-party tracking. For instance, users sometimes provide personal information such as contact details, email addresses, and billing information to a first party, which is sent to third parties for processing and detailed analysis. Hence, working across first-party providers, this third party then also has the ability to identify users across multiple website domains, thus providing much information about users, something they may be neither aware of nor comfortable with.

9.3.3 Tracking Techniques

In recent years, online tracking techniques have been extensively studied in academia. In contrast, only a few of them have been deployed online. We classify these tracking techniques into two categories: *(i) deployed tracking techniques* and *(ii) potential tracking techniques.* The deployed tracking techniques are widely used for online tracking and have been employed at a large scale in the mobile and web industries. On the other hand, potential tracking refers to the (advanced) mechanisms proposed by researchers in academia in an attempt to identify privacy leakages in mobile and web platforms.

9.3.3.1 Deployed Tracking Techniques

Deployed tracking techniques use IP addresses, cookies, Javascript, cache, and more for user identification purposes. In general, these tracking techniques operate as follows:

- **Cookies** are texts stored by a user's web browser and transmitted as part of an HTTP request. Cookies are essential to managing long user sessions, and they can be used to identify a user's browser uniquely. Service providers can use cookies to collect users' web activity. An example is Analytics Cookies (**_utma, _ga, _utmb**) that identify users or sessions and are used by website publishers to understand how people are using their website. Another particular form of cookie is a *persistent cookie*, which stores identifying information, such as user preferences, for an extended period. Similarly, *third-party cookies* are set while fetching website content, such as images, frames, and Javascript. *Cookie syncing* is another type of cookie where unique identifiers are correlated to identify a user in an external database for purposes discussed above. All these types of cookies are distributed and retrieved across multiple website domains allowing companies to build detailed profiles of users' interests, for example, spending history or frequently visited places such as restaurants. Intimate knowledge of users' personal preferences and private activities might eventually be used to brand them as members of a particular group, which could have serious privacy implications.
- **Javascript** codes can be loaded both from first- and third-party domains. They are widely used by ad networks, content distribution networks (CDNs), tracking services, analytics platforms, and online social networks [34]. They can track information about browsers such as cached objects, history of visited links, user-agent strings, or language preferences. In addition, they can read from and write to a cookie database or reconstruct user identifiers. Such information enables servers and third-party domains to track users using HTTP requests regularly. The dynamic nature of Javascript also allows service providers to construct a behavioral profile of a user. For example, through Javascript event handlers, it is

possible to obtain information about a user's mouse clicks and movements, and scrolls [35].

- **Caching** stores the content of webpages and other information in the browser to minimize latency and redundant network activity. This technique improves performance, as it becomes possible for a server to associate a unique tracking identifier with each client requesting content for the first time. A server can then use Javascript and standardized messages to check if the content is cached or not, to identify a user. This technique can be implemented for resources like images or fonts and is difficult to avoid unless the cached content is regularly cleared, for example, when closing the browser. For instance, Acar et al. [36] showed that 146 websites from Alexa's top 10,000 websites track users through fonts. Google was one of the domains that used fonts to track users to ensure quality and improve Google products and services [37].
- **Supercookies** also known as *unique identifier headers* inject user information into packets, which are then sent from a user device to a server. Some prominent supercookie types are *Flash Cookie* and *EverCookies*, where the former is maintained by the Adobe Flash plugin, and the latter is a combination of various tracking mechanisms. *Local Shared Objects (LSOs)* are supported by browser plugins, which can track users using unique identifiers. These objects are invisible to the browser, and therefore, it is impossible to examine their content. LSOs are retained in the browser even when the user deletes cookies and browser storage. For this reason, LSOs are used to store copies of browser cookies or other unique identifiers. All these types of supercookies contain unique identifiers allowing trackers to link records in their data to track browsing history and browsing behavior (e.g., visited websites including the length of stay). In 2014, Verizon and AT&T were found to be quietly tracking the Internet activity of more than 100 million cellular customers with "supercookies," which allowed the companies to monitor which sites their customers visit, cataloging their tastes and interests [38]. In other words, network providers (who are supposed to provide a content-agnostic service) were inspecting the contents of users' Internet traffic without their knowledge. Such tracking aimed to facilitate advertisers to display ads based on individual Internet behavior, however, considered against the GDPR.
- **Stateless tracking** allows websites to track users based on information such as user agent, fonts, screen resolution, and more. Standard techniques for stateless tracking are as follows: (i) canvas fingerprinting detects minor differences in display hardware by reading back rendered text from a storage area mapped to the display, (ii) font/plugin fingerprinting involves detection of fonts or plugins supported by a browser, (iii) MediaStream Fingerprinting is performed through Media Capture and Streams API that generates a unique stream identifier, (iv) WebRTC determines local IP address behind any firewall and can generate a unique tracking identifier, and (v) user agents/IP address in combination can be used to identify the user behind a browser. Although some of these techniques

individually produce medium-entropy identifiers, it has been shown that a combination of these is unique enough to generate a high-entropy identifier.[2]

We refer interested readers to [32], for a survey and in-depth study of online tracking mechanisms.

9.3.3.2 Potential Tracking Techniques

The abovementioned deployed tracking techniques have been extended by researchers either by using additional identifiers or by using advanced classification technologies, such as machine learning. The pioneering work in the threat of tracking dates back to Sweeney, who showed for the first time that coarse-grained information such as birthday, gender, and ZIP code could uniquely identify a person [39]. This work was followed by several studies that provided measurement insights into web and device tracking. The success of such methods is a clear indication that anonymization techniques to protect the privacy of individuals may fail if the collected data contains unique combinations of attributes relating to specific individuals. This section presents the online tracking technologies proposed by researchers and categorizes them based on the tracking medium: web browser, mobile phones, or other devices.

Web Browser-Based Tracking Techniques
In the past decade, several studies measured and analyzed web tracking. The authors of [40] provided an early insight into web tracking, followed by a continual increase in third-party tracking techniques. Also, [41] quantified the uniqueness of web browsers based on user agent and/or the browser configuration (plugins, fonts, cookies, screen resolution) and showed that 90% of browsers could be uniquely identified by the user agent, cookies, time zone, plugins, and fonts. The algorithm was able to detect returning browsers, even if some features changed over time.

Following this, [42] quantified the amount of information revealed by host identifiers, including IP addresses, cookies, and user login IDs. Authors used month-long datasets of a web-mail service and a search engine for the analyses. Further, they discussed the implications of cookie-churn on privacy and security, along with the utilization of host fingerprinting for improving security. An extended approach presented in [43] showed that cross-browser fingerprinting could achieve high uniqueness if the operating system collected enough data.

The authors of [44] performed a large-scale analysis of web browsing histories to track users. They were able to detect 97% of browsers by inspecting only four web pages in the browser history. Akin to this, [45] explored browser fingerprints

---

[2] Medium-entropy identifiers refer to the attributes/features that give limited information about a device or a user, that is, low information gain to the trackers. On the other hand, high-entropy identifiers refer to the attributes/features that contain rich information about users or devices, that is, high information gain.

validity by collecting more than 100K fingerprints composed of 17 attributes. Their results showed that HTML5 and Canvas API offer highly distinguishable features. A fingerprint technique based on the measurement of on-screen dimensions of font glyphs is proposed in [46].

A crawler-based measurement study of online tracking at 1M websites was reported in [47]. The analysis was based on stateful (cookies) and stateless (fingerprinting) tracking, the effect of browser privacy tools, and data exchange between different sites (cookie syncing). The authors developed an open-source privacy measurement tool, which simplifies data collection for privacy studies on a scale of millions of websites. Similarly, [48] studied the effect of third-party HTTP requests on the top 1M websites and showed that Google could track across 80% of websites through third-party domains. It has been shown that 80–90% of browsers can be uniquely identified. Besides HTTP cookies, other entities such as Flash cookies, WebGL, and HTML5 were also used as a tracking medium [22, 49].

It is important to mention that several side-channel and timing attacks have been launched on web browsers to leak the browser histories and cache information [50, 51]. These attacks can de-anonymize users in social networks, uncover user data, or reveal data to service providers or ad networks. Two different studies, [52] and [53], showed that usernames and online social profiles could uniquely identify user profiles and link users across different social platforms. In these works, fingerprinting was based on device configuration, device settings, and device hardware.

We summarize popular web-based tracking techniques as follows.

- **Web Tracking Measurement Studies** crawled data using Firefox extension and plugins [22, 40, 54] or open-source tools such as Open WPM [47, 55] and webXray [48, 56]. These mechanisms crawled attributes mainly including first- and third-party cookies, JavaScripts, canvas font, audio, JSON, PHP and CGI scripts, tracker-owned cookies, site-owned cookies, and HTML5 Local storage.
- **Web Browser Fingerprinting Techniques** used information gain, entropy, and k-anonymity to fingerprint the browsers [41, 45, 46, 49]. The attributes which contributed toward fingerprints mainly include user agent, cookies, timezone, screen resolution, MIME types, system fonts, WebGL, and HTTP headers.
- **Cross Browser Web Fingerprinting** used anonymity sets, entropy, and correlation as fingerprinting metrics [43]. The features used are user agent, OS, screen resolution, basic fonts, and timestamp.
- **Web-Based Device Fingerprinting** used host tracking graphs, entropy, and battery-reading techniques for fingerprinting [42, 44]. These techniques used attributes such as user agent, IP address, browser cookies, battery level, readouts, and charge/discharge time.
- **Online User Profiling** used information surprisal, entropy, and Markov chain as fingerprinting mechanisms [52, 53]. The information used for profiling includes gender, age, usernames, city and status.

Mobile-Based Tracking Techniques

Mobile device fingerprinting is a recent technique used by companies to profile device data or user interests. In general, the techniques mentioned above for browser fingerprinting can also be used for mobile tracking. However, studies revealed that mobile browsers do not have such distinguishable features as plugins and fonts; thus, requiring fingerprinting methods that are specifically designed for mobile devices or browsers [41]. Thus, several studies proposed alternative methods to fingerprint mobile devices. These techniques utilize different physical characteristics of a mobile device, for example, camera, sensors, microphones, and speakers. For instance, a study in [28] used the vibration motor to develop accelerometer fingerprints and then applied machine learning to extract the frequency and time-domain features. These features were able to distinguish mobile devices with 99% of accuracy.

Authors in [57] proposed a fingerprint mechanism to uniquely identify smartphones based on motion sensors (accelerometer and gyroscope) and inaudible audio stimulation, along with a mechanism to obfuscate the fingerprints by calibrating sensors. Noise-based sensor fingerprinting for mobile devices has also been discussed in [58–60], which focused on acoustic components such as speakers, microphones, or cameras. These techniques require access to the microphone, which needs separate permission. Authors in [61] utilized the noisy nature of hardware sensors such as accelerometer and microphones. Similarly, images taken by a mobile phone camera can derive a noise pattern that is considered to be different in each device sensor [62, 63].

A study conducted in [64] focused on mobile users' identification and tracking based on touch-based gestures. Their fingerprinting mechanism extracted statistical features from swipe, keystrokes, taps, and handwriting gestures and showed a true positive rate of 93% to detect returning users. Some studies have also focused on privacy-preserving online behavioral targeting for various purposes, including advertising, spamming, and political interests [65, 66]. Another work [67] analyzed 59 mobile device fingerprints and concluded that "the fingerprints taken from mobile devices are far from unique and targeting." However, they did not consider the canvas test for fingerprinting. Authors in [68] presented a new side-channel attack against smartphone keyboards that support gesture typing. They identified returning users with 97% accuracy using a set of 35 sentences, and the system also correctly predicted sentences.

A number of studies have focused on identifying mobile user traits and characteristics using the information provided by mobile SDKs to third-party apps, such as the running apps, device model, and operating system [31]. A study in [69] showed that mobile devices can be tracked through personalized configurations (e.g., installed apps, top 50 songs, device, WiFi name) without involving hardware identifiers such as Unique Device Identifier (UDID), International Mobile Station Equipment Identity (IMEI), and others. A work in [70] showed the existence of a diverse set of mobile users using clustering and feature ranking. Their results identified 382 categories of users based on their app usage patterns. We summarize popular mobile tracking techniques below:

- **Mobile Tracking based on Motion Sensors** used techniques such as bagged decision trees, machine learning classifiers, Gaussian mixture models, and k-nn classifier with common features such as spectral centroid, spectral skewness, spectral flatness, and average deviation [28, 57, 59, 71–73].
- **Mobile Tracking based on Audio Sensors** used Euclidean distance and L2 distance with main features such as sensitivity parameters, vector aptitude, feedback ratio of different frequencies and harmonics [60, 61].
- **Mobile Tracking based on Camera Sensors** used SVM, Photo-Response Non-Uniformity (PRNU), and Pearson correlation mechanisms [62, 63]. The techniques used 81 features (i.e., 3 RGB channel * 3 wavelet components * 9 central moments).
- **Mobile Tracking based on Touch Sensors** used cosine similarity, entropy, information gain, and recurrent neural network mechanism [64, 68]. Authors used 50 extracted touch features such as x-coordinate, y-coordinate, finger pressure, and finger area.
- **Mobile Tracking based on Mobile Browsers** used Open AM algorithm with features such as screen dimensions, color depth, installed plugins, user agents, and timezones [67].
- **Mobile Tracking based on Personalized Configurations** used Jaccard similarity coefficient, k-means clustering, entropy, and SVM as main mechanisms [31, 69, 70]. Features mainly include device model, device ID, username, installed apps, etc.

Device Tracking Based on Network Properties: Some of the fingerprinting techniques have also used properties, such as network configuration or traffic records, for a device or host tracking. One of the prominent works on remote device fingerprinting was presented in [74] that proposed a method to measure device clock skew using ICMP and TCP traffic. Some works also deal with wireless traffic; for example, radiometric analysis of 802.11 transmitters [75], signal phase identification of Bluetooth transmitters [76], or timing analysis of 802.11 probe request frames [25]. For example, [75] utilized manufacturing defects in hardware to identify the device and, by association, the end-user. Many efforts on tracking wireless devices focused on other hardware characteristics, such as radio frequency and drivers [77, 78]. While these techniques can also be used to identify smartphones, these calculations are also resource intensive and require user cooperation. In addition, identifiers such as network names and IP addresses also help in host fingerprinting [75].

9.3.4 Behavioral Tracking: State of the Art

Behavioral-based tracking refers to constructing user profiles and uniquely identifying the users through their gestures to perform certain activities [79]. Such gestures are collected via many modalities such as touch, motion, GPS, camera, mouse, search queries, writing pattern, and more. Examples of such information include the location of a user at a particular time, user-touchscreen interaction, duration of the calls, and dialed numbers. Such profiling could be used by data custodians, receivers, or consumers, in order to provide personalized services to their customers with the goal of increasing revenues. For instance, advertising companies use user behavior profiles, user interests, characteristics, or activities to display relevant advertisements to the user [80].

The ability to distinguish behavioral biometrics is a new form of tracking. Behavior-based tracking has the ability to continuously and surreptitiously track users while they are interacting with their devices. As opposed to "regular" tracking mechanisms based on cookies, browser fingerprints, logins, and similar, which track virtual identities or browser profiles, this type of tracking is subtle. First, while regular tracking deals with virtual identities and online profiles, behavior-based tracking has the potential to track and identify the actual (physical) person operating the device. It can track multiple users accessing the same device by profiling user behavioral activities such as touch gestures [81]. Second, behavior-based tracking has the ability to track users continuously. Third, it also leads to cross-device tracking, where the same user can be tracked on multiple devices, and user data can be collated and used to build more encompassing user profiles. However, implementing such tracking requires a more generalized approach, requiring, for example, to validate the stability of features across devices [64]. On the other hand, the ubiquity of smart devices and the fact that any web service can extract data from touch and motion sensors make behavioral-based tracking quite achievable. This not only represents a valuable source of information for analytics and ad services but also for app developers who can use the information to track individuals on a single device or across devices. Table 9.1 summarizes the distinction between behavioral tracking and other tracking methods.

Nevertheless, behavioral-based tracking is equally beneficial to users and service providers. Some argue the benefits of behavior-based tracking as a way of receiving useful information, for example, relevant ads or health monitoring. For instance, monitoring a phone's motion might reveal changes in gait, which could be indicators of ailments or depression [82]. Another benefit of behavioral tracking is continuous or implicit authentication of users on mobile and web platforms. Implicit authentication is a mechanism to continuously authenticate users while they perform activities on mobile or web platforms. This type of authentication continuously monitors users through behavioral biometrics such as touch swipes, taps, keystrokes, or stylometric features, to verify a user's legitimacy with high accuracy. The usability and deployability of implicit authentication schemes without compromising security have made them an attractive alternative to legacy password systems [82].

Table 9.1 Behavioral-based tracking versus other tracking methods

Behavioral-based tracking	Other tracking methods
Aims to identify or track user or his activities	Aims to identify devices or browsers
Constructs user profiles based on their gestures to perform certain activities	Constructs profiles based on device or browser configuration, specifications, or settings
Has a potential to track the physical identity of users	Has a potential to identify virtual identities of users
Continuously track users through their behavioral actions	Track device or browser only when a certain action is performed, for example, when a website is visited
Is ideal for cross-device or cross-system tracking	Is less suitable for cross-device or cross-system tracking

9.4   Personalization via Online Tracking

As mentioned earlier, Internet users are increasingly being tracked, and their personal data are extensively used in exchange for services. In the current era, when people use real identities to communicate on the Web, maintaining privacy has become a complicated challenge. Service providers are using a variety of personal information to personalize their content and services. The privacy challenge becomes more critical with the dissemination of smart phones and devices offering new possibilities for personalization. On the other hand, personalization algorithms and technologies are steadily improving, making behavioral profiling more powerful, yet raising a multitude of privacy challenges.

To understand the personalization system, Fig. 9.2 shows an exemplary working diagram of an advertisement network system. There are three main entities in an advertisement network system: the publisher, the advertiser, and the ad network. The publisher is an entity that owns a website or service; the advertiser is an entity that wants to advertise to users; and the ad network collects advertisements from an advertiser, displays them on a publisher's website, and connects advertisers to users with relevant demographics. If a user clicks on an advertisement, the ad network collects money from an advertiser and pays part of it to the publisher. It is thus important for the ad network to generate accurate and complete profiles of users, in order to increase the click chances and maximize the revenues. These three entities also exist in a mobile environment, where a mobile app developer acts as a publisher, while the roles of an advertiser and ad networks remain unchanged.

It should also be noted that, while the above example is tailored to the advertisement context, it is similarly applicable to other applications. Consider other scenarios, such as multimedia content consumption on YouTube or Spotify, a news dissemination platform, or even a student eLearning environment. In all of them, the three entities—content provider, content consumer, and the intermediate network—can be easily identified and the need for accurate user profiles for an enjoyable and engaging service is evident.

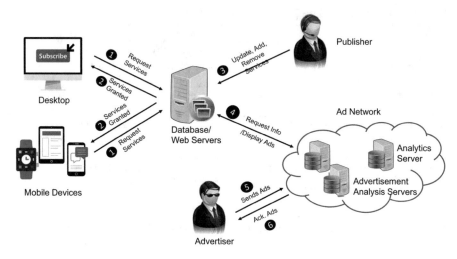

Fig. 9.2 Ecosystem of advertisement network

9.4.1 Relationship

Personalization is hard to achieve without losing privacy since a service provider needs users' personal information to tailor or customize services. Research has shown that users are willing to share their personal interests or information in exchange for the apparent benefits of using personalized products or services [83, 84]. To build trust, some service providers promise to ensure the anonymity of their customers for the usage of their services, and in some cases, the anonymity is guaranteed for a lifetime. On the contrary, research shows that it is difficult to guarantee anonymity as linking anonymized data to other databases with personally identifiable information leads to the (re)identification of a user [85]. Therefore, privacy risks are not just limited to a particular service provider, rather these risks are pervasive concerns where personal information provided by users to different services could be linked together to track/identify them ubiquitously. Authors of [14] discussed the risks associated with recommender systems. The authors argue that privacy breaches are either due to direct data access or due to data sharing with third parties. In both cases, the effects of privacy breaches can be significant, such as exposure of sensitive information, reidentification of anonymized data, leaks through the shared device, or service inference by the recommender.

In [86], authors link privacy to three different personalization categories: social, behavior, and mobile.

- In a **social-based personalization**, providing privacy is a major concern because of three main reasons: (i) users are willing to reveal more information, (ii) social networks compromise not only a single user's privacy but also their friends' privacy, and (iii) social networks can reveal potentially embarrassing information. There have been several cases where an employee's misuse of social media has led to their dismissal. For example, various incidents resulted in employee termination from firms based on their post or comments on social media [87, 88]. According to one survey, 17% of companies with 1000 or more employees report issues with employees' use of social media, whereas 8% of those companies fired employees because of information released on social networks [89].

- **Behavior-based personalization**, where information about observable user activity is longitudinally collected and harnessed for personalization purposes, poses several privacy risks. These include unsolicited marketing, personal information being shared with third-party providers without users' consent or knowledge, and in some cases, being inadvertently revealed to other users of the same device. For instance, users who share a computer and or a Web browser may view each other's ads if cookies are used by websites to identify users. Another risk involves linking behavioral profiles to server-side user accounts so that advertisers can target users across different devices.

- **Mobile-based personalization** has increased with the spread of smartphones and phone sensors. With this, the ability of service providers to continuously track users has also grown. Sensor data has been used in various ways for personalization. One way is the improvement of search results, such that search results displayed on a smartphone are tuned according to the user's location, highlighting nearby venues and services. Similarly, the installation of various apps on mobile phones conveys user interests, helping app developers to show targeted ads. Authors in [90] performed a measurement study of in-app advertisement and showed that GoogleAdMob has a higher proportion of targeted than generic ads. Privacy leakages in mobile-based personalization are more significant, mainly because mobile devices are carried around all the time and are increasingly being used for sensitive operations like personal communications, dating, and banking. Therefore, privacy concerns regarding what information is collected for ad personalization are rather serious.

9.4.2   Privacy Implications of Personalization

Although personalization via online tracking has been performed for a number of reasons that bring tremendous value, it also raises serious privacy concerns having subtle and far-reaching consequences. Researchers, civil organizations, and policy-makers have identified several ways tracking can cause privacy leaks.

Global surveillance, performed by the government for security reasons or by companies for commercial benefits, is one such privacy risk. Between January and June 2014, the US government made 12,539 requests for 21,576 persons' information from Google, including search history, and Google complied with 84% of them [91]. According to the internal National Security Agency (NSA) presentations [92], the American NSA and British GCHQ use cookies (one of them being Google PREFIDs) to investigate the online activity of users. The government agents are first granted access to Internet links, and then they use cookies to differentiate flows generated by different users within the same Internet connection. These cookies help them track user locations and denounce users who have unauthorized access to the network. The presentation also revealed that some NSA divisions engage with private companies and Internet service providers to collect data, which are later used for hacking into people. Another presentation revealed that the NSA uses DoubleClick cookies to identify TOR users [92]. A program named HAPPYFOOT by the NSA was designed to map users' Internet addresses to their physical locations. By capturing the Internet traffic, the NSA gathers almost five billion records a day on the locations of cellphones around the world. That also allows the NSA to track how particular people travel and gain knowledge about their mutual relations by revealing co-travelers [93]. Such surveillance is a threat to privacy, but there may be chances that collected information is distorted and leads to incorrect decisions. The potential dangers could be an error, abuse, and lack of transparency and accountability [32].

Unwanted profiling, performed by service providers to personalize content for users, is another risk. A news site may display news matching users' previous items, a merchant may propose products based on users' previous shopping, or a search engine may refine results based on users' previous queries. Often, such profiling may seriously impact users. For example, it was shown that a person discovered his teenage daughter was pregnant when she received advertisements for baby food. The teenager was profiled as pregnant based on her shopping behavior [94]. Similarly, Gmail was shown to use words from the sent and received emails to target ads. The emails were scanned without a user's explicit permission and used to identify the themes and trends for ad targeting [32]. The Facebook Beacon advertising program faced a federal class-action lawsuit because users were automatically opted into having purchases disclosed to friends and networks [95].

Reidentification of anonymized public data is required in several business applications and research studies to improve the provided services by utilizing the available information and rich user data. However, studies have shown that users could be identified even from anonymized datasets through inference analysis by an eavesdropper. A few examples involving such threats are the reidentification of users in the anonymized AOL search histories, Netflix training data that was attacked, and Massachusetts hospital discharge data [96–98]. For instance, in an open competition for the best collaborative filtering algorithm in 2009, Netflix disclosed data records of 480,000 customers "anonymously" in an attempt to create a smarter recommendation algorithm. The data contained subscribers' information, including gender, zip code, age, unique subscriber ID, the movie title, year of release, and the date on which the subscriber rated it. Despite being anonymous, researchers were able to reidentify sensitive information about people, as in the case of a closeted lesbian mother who sued Netflix for disclosing her sexuality to the public through rented movies such as Brokeback Mountain or Passion of the Christ. Similarly, when AOL released anonymized search queries of its customers, a 62-year-old widow was identified living in LilBurn GA, Georgia, United States. The lady frequently searched for her friend's medical ailment and loved her three dogs. These examples show that it is possible to violate the users' privacy by tracking their activities, thereby inferring their personal profiles. Thus, users' privacy is at risk when their data can be distinguished from other users and linked with high confidence based on the user's previous history.

Personalized search, which offers the benefit of presenting information that the user wants to see based on their queries, is another reason to track. However, it has been shown in [85] that even anonymized search queries could lead to the identification of users and their interests. The ability for a search company to efficiently track and record users' search habits and tie them directly to their identity has profound privacy implications. For instance, search engines may know the current situation of a user (e.g., illness, depression, studying, startup business, or looking for jobs) through their searches and show them results related to their situation (e.g., recruitment websites, training workshops, discounted medicine prices).

Lastly, tracking was found to be the reason for **price discrimination** based on geographical location, affluence of the user, and the referrer. Examples include credit card interest rates, hotel bookings, and insurance coverage. In [32], authors provided a detailed overview of how such implications occur. For instance, Capital One Financial Corporation differentiates car loans' interests based on the browser used by the prospective customer (3.5% for Firefox, 2.7% for Safari, 2.3% for Chrome, and 3.1% for Opera). Similarly, Orbitz Worldwide Inc. differently sorts out the hotel advertisements depending on the type of computer used by the customer. Orbitz found that Mac users tend to spend around 30% more on hotel bookings than PC users. Using this fact, more expensive hotels are advertised to Mac users, while the cheaper ones to the PC users.

9.4.3 Balancing Privacy and Personalization

It is reasonable to expect that users would be more inclined to share their data with service providers and use personalized services if the user information is collected and treated fairly. However, striking a balance between privacy and personalization is quite a challenge. Researchers, businesses, and nonprofit organizations have made a continuous effort to provide efficient solutions to overcome user privacy/tracking issues. Some of these efforts have resulted in privacy design principles, privacy tools, and features. In this section, we discuss the technological measures that could be taken to minimize tracking via personalization.

9.4.3.1 Privacy-by-Design

Privacy-by-Design is deemed an essential step toward better privacy protection. It is based on the idea that privacy requirements should be taken into account while designing a system. As with any process, privacy by design should have well-defined objectives, methodologies, and evaluation metrics.

Consent-Based Mechanisms Consent-based mechanisms are one way to obtain privacy-by-design. These mechanisms inform and obtain users' consent before collecting and processing the data. According to General Data Protection Regulation (GDPR), a consent is "any freely given, specific, informed and unambiguous indication of the data subject's wishes by which he or she, by a statement or by a clear affirmative action, signifies agreement to the processing of personal data relating to him or her" [21]. Therefore, it is necessary for a user to know which data is collected and for what purpose. The most widespread mechanism for user consent on the web is probably the cookie header banner, which is displayed on all web pages and invites user to make a choice of accepting or refusing cookies.

Another widespread mechanism is to take consent through browser settings which offer four options, that is, accept all cookies of a websites, accept cookies set or accessed by first party, accept cookies set by first party only, or accept no cookies. A "tag manager" is also a technical implementation of the cookie consent that could block third-party scripts if consent has not been obtained. One key issue with consent-based mechanisms is that the entity that informs users is often not the only entity to track users. For instance, third-party trackers also collect and share information about users, which the first party may be not be aware of. In this situation, some methods that are less often employed are first- and third-party consent tools, which are used to make an agreement between parties, explicitly stating what user data will be obtained and for what purpose.

Obfuscation Methods Several obfuscation methods have been proposed as the means to maintain user privacy in recommender systems. These mainly include distribution, aggregation, anonymization, identity management systems, privacy proxies, encryption mechanisms, and differential privacy. One strategy is to distribute user data across a set of machines; however, this solution aggravates personalization based on data of other users [99]. Another strategy is to use the encrypted aggregation of user data [100, 101]. Privacy-preserving approaches like differential privacy and k-anonymity are the widely used privacy-preserving solutions. Differential privacy mathematically guarantees that anyone seeing the result of a differentially private analysis will essentially make the same inference about any individual's private information, whether or not that individual's private information is included in the input to the analysis [102]. It provides a mathematically provable guarantee of privacy protection against a wide range of privacy attacks mainly including differencing attacks, linkage attacks, and reconstruction attacks [103]. Similar to DP, k-anonymity also guarantees privacy by holding a property that a released dataset is k-anonymous if the information for each person contained in the dataset cannot be distinguished from at least $k - 1$ individuals whose information also appear in the dataset [104].

A study in [105] investigated the effectiveness of different obfuscation strategies and policies for online social networks and proposed a novel obfuscation strategy that does not require knowledge about the adversary classifier. Authors of [106] and [107] proposed methodologies that prevent inference attacks by distorting data before making it publicly available. In [108], authors proposed a utility-aware obfuscation framework that limits the risk of disclosing sensitive information from sensors data. Similarly, work proposed in [109, 110], and [111] tried to protect user location data by generating fake privacy-preserved location traces. In another recent paper [112], author proposed an obfuscation scheme [27] to defeat fingerprinting based on motion sensors.

Pseudonymous personalization is a basic yet common approach to hide true user identity. It allows people to use the same pseudonym across different sessions and to create or maintain more than one pseudonym. This helps users separate different aspects of their online activity and control which service provider can access their persona [113, 114]. However, anonymity is difficult to maintain when payments or nonelectronic services are involved. It has also been shown that hiding explicit identities like usernames and emails are not sufficient to prevent tracking. There are cases where users have been identified through their anonymized data, hence revealing personal/sensitive information about them [85].

Client-side personalization is another way to prevent online tracking. This type of privacy preservation implies data storage and subsequent personalization processes to take place on the client-side [115]. Since data collection and processing occur at the client side rather than the server-side, users may perceive more control over their data and lower privacy risks. However, the challenge with this approach is that existing personalization algorithms need to be redesigned to fit the client-side model [12].

User controls and feedback is another way to preserve privacy in personalized systems. Studies conducted in [116, 117] suggested adding scrutability to user modeling and personalized systems. The term "scrutability" signifies the users' ability to understand and control what goes into their user models, what parts from their models are available to various services, and how the model is managed and maintained. This allows users to restrict service providers from accessing their sensitive data. However, achieving such a level of balance is currently challenging due to poor user understanding of these notions.

9.4.3.2   Privacy Tools

A number of browser tools and plugins have been developed to protect users from tracking. These tools perform various functionalities such as detecting or blocking lists of third-party trackers, informing users how much information is revealed to trackers, allowing only executable content from trusted domains to run, detecting flash cookies and deleting them, and more. ENISA provided a detailed analysis of online privacy tools in [118]. The study analyzed several web portals that are listing and/or recommending the use of specific online privacy tools (e.g., for secure messaging, anti-tracking, and encryption). There is also a Tracking Protection List (TPL) approach that contains addresses of misbehaving tracking sites published by various organizations. Other ways to protect information include tools like private browsing modes of major browsers and anonymity networks.

Do Not Track (DNT) Major browsers implement the DNT (Do Not Track) methodology to show websites that they are forbidden from tracking. DNT is a technology and policy proposal that enables users to opt out of tracking by all third-party websites they do not visit, including analytics services, advertising networks, and social platforms [119]. Technically, the implementation of DNT is simple; a browser sends a DNT header in every HTTP request to websites the users wish to opt out of tracking. This includes web pages and all the objects/scripts embedded within a page. However, it is up to the discretion of an advertiser to respect user preferences.

Similar to DNT, some other tools have also been proposed to anonymize web search queries. For example, TrackMeNot (TMN) [120] is proposed as a Firefox plugin to randomly issue dummy queries from predefined Rich Site Summary (RSS) feeds. GooPIR is a standalone application for noise addition to Google queries [121], which modifies the user queries by adding dummy keywords, and then the search results are re-ranked locally based on the original user queries. PRivAcy model for the Web (PRAW) [122] is another technique, which continuously generates fake queries in different topics of interest of the user. This is done by generating user profiles from user queries and corresponding responses and thus the fake queries added will be in the general area of interest of the user to make the distinction between real and fake queries difficult.

Decentralized Ad Platforms A few behavioral advertising systems, like Adnostic, PrivAd, and RePriv, consider privacy as a design requirement. The main objective of these systems is to limit tracking, while still serving behavioral advertisements. For instance, PrivAd preserves privacy by maintaining user profiles on the user's device, thus minimizing the information released to the ad network. A trusted third party anonymizes the network addresses of clients whereas encryption prevents the proxy from viewing client messages. As such, PrivAd offers privacy against profiling, ad dissemination, auctions, click fraud, view and click reporting, and click anonymization [65]. Similarly, in Adnostic, the browser continuously updates user profiles [66], allowing the ad network to offer several ads to the browser, where the browser picks the ad most relevant to the profile. In addition, the principle of privacy-by- design has also been introduced by some web browsers such as Brave, which is a free and open-source web browser that aims to block ads and website trackers [123]. Brave also introduced the first advertising platform that puts the user in control with privacy by design and does not leak the user's personal data from their device. The ad matching happens directly on the user's device, such that the user's data is never sent to anyone.

User Agents User agents prevent tracking by providing users with relevant choices. Most user agents include functionalities that allow users to examine cookies associated with a domain or a web page, showing expiration date duration, their contents, and the associated host domain [21]. Such information can be presented as user agent settings through a user interface to get valid consent from the user. This has already been implemented by a browser extension that uses the DNT Consent API to take consent from user before sending or receiving any data from the browser. Similarly, the Content-Security-Policy API (CSP) is another tracking prevention tool that prevents cross-site scripting, click-jacking, and other code injection attacks. CSP provides a standard method for first-party services to declare specific types of content that user agents should be allowed to load on that website—covered types are JavaScript, CSS, HTML frames, web workers, fonts, images, embeddable objects, etc. If any of these content types are provided in the source list within the CSP header, then user agent will load only that content type in a browser and block rest of the types. In this way, user agents can be told to block iframes from being loaded when they have not been explicitly allowed by the site designers or which refuse to respect the provided CSP. In general, user agents can prevent tracking at various granularity levels. This includes (1) items the user wants to block or take consent, like list of websites, tracking companies, (2) locations of blockage, (3) types of data, or (4) purpose of data.

Opt-Out Cookies Some tracking companies allow users to set opt-out cookies. If implemented properly, this option disables user tracking. However, opt-out cookies are not considered reliable, as they are not supported by all ad networks and are easy to interpret by those wishing to track users. Moreover, they have a limited lifetime, so they must be periodically renewed. These cookies are lost when the user cleans the cookies from their web browser.

Chapter 8 covers more details about privacy enhancing technologies, in a general sense. We recommend interested readers to go through the chapter for more information on privacy preserving solutions.

9.5 Conclusion

The ever-changing technological landscape, high user involvement, increased societal visibility, and amalgamation of services have made privacy difficult to maintain in a digital world. Preserving user identity from being tracked is a significant challenge nowadays and has become more complex with the advancement in technologies that have an ability to cross-link data sources to infer more information. Some examples aggravating the privacy concerns include location-based tracking, mobile sensors to identify location, behavioral features, interactions and gestures, and so on.

Moreover, the state-of-the-art data analysis methods and the exponentially growing computational resources available for data mining tasks are another potential obstacle for balancing privacy and personalization. For example, cloud-based data centers have the ability to process and compare user profiles among massive sets of records, to identify relevant information and make sense of it. As the user models and predictions become more accurate, and as the services increase their reliance on these predictions, user privacy concerns may further increase. The propagation of online social network in our daily life also poses new challenges, as personalization processes are targeting not only online user activities but also the physical environment.

The proposed solutions to preserve privacy and prevent tracking have practical limitations that often preclude their developers from striking the balance between privacy and utility goals. Nevertheless, we would like to emphasize the need for technically encompassing, while also user-friendly, policy-compliant, and transparent, solutions. We believe that tracking-related privacy concerns will take a more prominent role and will attract research works and practical industry attention alike.

References

1. AP. 2018. Google has been tracking your movements even if you told it not to. https://www.news.com.au/technology/gadgets/mobile-phones/google-has-been-tracking-your-movements-even-if-you-told-it-not-to/news-story/bb9eb906387ffd2295e8b17b24b7d883

2. ur Rehman, I. 2019. Facebook-cambridge analytica data harvesting: What you need to know. *Library Philosophy and Practice*, 2497: 1–11.

3. Wong, J. C. 2019. Facebook discloses operations by russia and iran to meddle in 2020 election. https://www.theguardian.com/technology/2019/oct/21/facebook-us-2020-elections-foreign-interference-russia

4. BBC. 2018. Facebook's data-sharing deals exposed. https://www.bbc.com/news/technology-46618582

5. Hautala, L. 2019. These android apps have been tracking you, even when you say stop. https://www.cnet.com/news/these-android-apps-have-been-tracking-you-even-when-you-say-stop/

6. Zhang, B., N. Wang, and H. Jin. 2014. Privacy concerns in online recommender systems: Influences of control and user data input. In *10th Symposium On Usable Privacy and Security ({SOUPS} 2014)*, 159–173.

7. Berkovsky, S., and J. Freyne. 2015. Web personalization and recommender systems. In *Proceedings of the 21th ACM SIGKDD International Conference on Knowledge Discovery and Data Mining*, 2307–2308.

8. Brusilovsky, P., A. Kobsa, and W. Nejdl. (Eds.) 2007. *The Adaptive Web, Methods and Strategies of Web Personalization. Lecture Notes in Computer Science*. Berlin: Springer.

9. Ning, X., C. Desrosiers, and G. Karypis. 2015. A comprehensive survey of neighborhood-based recommendation methods. In *Recommender Systems Handbook*, 37–76. Berlin: Springer.

10. De Gemmis, M., P. Lops, C. Musto, F. Narducci, and G. Semeraro. 2015. Semantics-aware content-based recommender systems. In *Recommender Systems Handbook*, 119–159. Berlin: Springer.

11. Berkovsky, S., T. Kuflik, and F. Ricci. 2008. Mediation of user models for enhanced personalization in recommender systems. *User Modeling and User-Adapted Interaction* 18 (3): 245–286.

12. Vallet, D., A. Friedman, and S. Berkovsky. 2014. Matrix factorization without user data retention. In *Advances in Knowledge Discovery and Data Mining - 18th Pacific-Asia Conference, PAKDD 2014, Tainan, May 13–16, 2014. Proceedings, Part I*, 569–580.

13. Erkin, Z., M. Beye, T. Veugen, and R. L. Lagendijk. 2012. *Privacy-Preserving Content-Based Recommender System*. New York: ACM.

14. Friedman, A., B. P. Knijnenburg, K. Vanhecke, L. Martens, and S. Berkovsky. 2015. Privacy aspects of recommender systems. In *Recommender Systems Handbook*, 649–688. Berlin: Springer.

15. Adomavicius, G., and A. Tuzhilin. 2011. Context-aware recommender systems. In *Recommender Systems Handbook*, 217–253. Berlin: Springer.

16. Lathia, N. 2015. The anatomy of mobile location-based recommender systems. In *Recommender Systems Handbook*, 493–510. Berlin: Springer.

17. Yang, W.-S., H.-C. Cheng, and J.-B. Dia. 2008. A location-aware recommender system for mobile shopping environments. *Expert Systems with Applications* 34 (1): 437–445.

18. Yu, J., J. Zhao, Y. Chen, and J. Yang. 2015. Sensing ambient light for user experience-oriented color scheme adaptation on smartphone displays. In *Proceedings of the 13th ACM Conference on Embedded Networked Sensor Systems*, 309–321.

19. Freyne, J., J. Yin, E. Brindal, G. A. Hendrie, S. Berkovsky, and M. Noakes. 2017. Push notifications in diet apps: Influencing engagement times and tasks. *International Journal of Human–Computer Interaction* 33 (10): 833–845.

20. Rogers, S., and P. Langley. 1998. Personalized driving route recommendations. In *Proceedings of the American Association of Artificial Intelligence Workshop on Recommender Systems*, 96–100.

21. Online tracking and user protection mechanisms. 2017. White paper, European Union Agency For Network and Information Security (ENISA).

22. Roesner, F., T. Kohno, and D. Wetherall. 2012. Detecting and defending against third-party tracking on the web. In *Proceedings of the 9th USENIX conference on Networked Systems Design and Implementation*, 12–12. Berkeley: USENIX Association.

23. European Commission (EU). 2016. Cookie sweep combined analysis report. https://ec.europa.eu/newsroom/article29/item-detail.cfm?item_id=640605

24. Rose, I., and M. Welsh. 2010. Mapping the urban wireless landscape with argos. In *Proceedings of the 8th ACM Conference on Embedded Networked Sensor Systems, SenSys'10, New York*, 323–336. New York: ACM.

25. Desmond, L. C. C., C. C. Yuan, T. C. Pheng, and R. S. Lee. 2008. Identifying unique devices through wireless fingerprinting. In *Proceedings of the First ACM Conference on Wireless Network Security - WiSec'08*, 46.

26. Cunche, M., Mohamed Ali Kaafar, and R. Boreli. 2012. I know who you will meet this evening! Linking wireless devices using wi-fi probe requests. In *2012 IEEE International Symposium on a World of Wireless, Mobile and Multimedia Networks (WoWMoM)*, 1–9.

27. Das, A., N. Borisov, and E. Chou. 2018. Every move you make: Exploring practical issues in smartphone motion sensor fingerprinting and countermeasures. *Proceedings on Privacy Enhancing Technologies* 2018 (1): 88–108.

28. Dey, S., N. Roy, W. Xu, R. R. Choudhury, and S. Nelakuditi. 2014. Accelprint: Imperfections of accelerometers make smartphones trackable. In *Network and Distributed System Security Symposium (NDSS)*.

29. Miluzzo, E., A. Varshavsky, S. Balakrishnan, and R. R. Choudhury. 2012. Tapprints: Your finger taps have fingerprints. In *MobiSys'12: Proceedings of the 10th International Conference on Mobile Systems, Applications, and Services, ACM*, 323.

30. Achara, J. P., G. Acs, and C. Castelluccia. 2015. On the unicity of smartphone applications. In *Proceedings of the 14th ACM Workshop on Privacy in the Electronic Society*, 27–36. New York: ACM.

31. Seneviratne, S., A. Seneviratne, P. Mohapatra, and A. Mahanti. 2014. Predicting user traits from a snapshot of apps installed on a smartphone. *ACM SIGMOBILE Mobile Computing and Communications Review* 18 (2): 1–8.

32. Bujlow, T., V. Carela-Español, J. Sole-Pareta, and P. Barlet-Ros. 2017. A survey on web tracking: Mechanisms, implications, and defenses. *Proceedings of the IEEE* 105 (8): 1476–1510.

33. Mayer, J. R., and J. C. Mitchell. 2012. Third-party web tracking: Policy and technology. In *2012 IEEE Symposium on Security and Privacy*, 413–427. Piscatawy: IEEE.

34. Ikram, M., H. J. Asghar, M. A. Kaafar, A. Mahanti, and B. Krishnamurthy. 2017. Towards seamless tracking-free web: Improved detection of trackers via one-class learning. *Proceedings on Privacy Enhancing Technologies* 2017 (1): 79–99.
35. Atterer, R., M. Wnuk, and A. Schmidt. 2006. Knowing the user's every move: User activity tracking for website usability evaluation and implicit interaction. In *Proceedings of the 15th International Conference on World Wide Web*, 203–212. New York: ACM.
36. Acar, G., M. Juarez, and N. Nikiforakis. 2013. FPDetective: Dusting the web for fingerprinters. In *Proceedings of the 2013 ACM SIGSAC Conference on Computer & Communications Security*, 1129–1140.
37. Ullrich, J. B. 2015. 11 ways to track your moves when using a web browser. https://isc.sans.edu/forums/diary/11+Ways+To+Track+Your+Moves+When+Using+a+Web+Browser/19369/
38. Timber, C. 2014. Verizon, AT&T tracking their users with 'supercookies'. https://www.washingtonpost.com/business/technology/verizon-atandt-tracking-their-users-with-super-cookies/2014/11/03/7bbbf382-6395-11e4-bb14-4cfea1e742d5_story.html
39. Sweeney, L. 2000. Simple demographics often identify people uniquely. Carnegie Mellon University, Data Privacy Working Paper 3. Pittsburgh 2000, 1–34.
40. Krishnamurthy, B., and C. Wills. 2009. Privacy diffusion on the web: a longitudinal perspective. In *Proceedings of the 18th International Conference on World Wide Web*, 541–550. New York: ACM.
41. Eckersley, P. 2010. How unique is your browser? In *Proceedings of the Privacy Enhancing Technologies Symposium (PETS)*, 1–18.
42. Yen, T.-F., Y. Xie, F. Yu, R. P. Yu, and M. Abadi. 2012. Host fingerprinting and tracking on the web: Privacy and security implications. In *Network and Distributed System Security Symposium*, 1–16.
43. Boda, K., A. M. Foeldes, G. G. Gulyas, and S. Imre. 2012. User tracking on the web via cross-browser fingerprinting. *Information Security Technology for Applications* 7161: 31–46.
44. Olejnik, Ł., G. Acar, C. Castelluccia, and C. Diaz. 2016. The leaking battery: A privacy analysis of the HTML5 battery status API. *Lecture Notes in Computer Science (including subseries Lecture Notes in Artificial Intelligence and Lecture Notes in Bioinformatics)* 9481: 254–263.
45. Laperdrix, P., W. Rudametkin, and B. Baudry. 2016. Beauty and the beast: Diverting modern web browsers to build unique browser fingerprints. In *2016 IEEE Symposium on Security and Privacy (SP)*, 878–894. Piscataway: IEEE.
46. Fifield, D., and S. Egelman. 2015. Fingerprinting web users through font metrics. *Lecture Notes in Computer Science (including subseries Lecture Notes in Artificial Intelligence and Lecture Notes in Bioinformatics)* 8975: 107–124.
47. Englehardt, S., and A. Narayanan. 2016. Online tracking: A 1-million-site measurement and analysis. In *Proceedings of the 2016 ACM SIGSAC Conference on Computer and Communications Security - CCS'16*, 1388–1401.
48. Libert, T. 2015. Exposing the hidden web: An analysis of third-party HTTP requests on 1 million websites. *International Journal of Communication* 9, 3544–3561.
49. Mowery, K., and H. Shacham. 2012. Pixel perfect : Fingerprinting canvas in HTML5. In *Web 2.0 Security & Privacy 20 (W2SP)*, 1–12.
50. Weinberg, Z., E. Y. Chen, P. R. Jayaraman, and C. Jackson. 2011. I still know what you visited last summer: Leaking browsing history via user interaction and side channel attacks. In *2011 IEEE Symposium on Security and Privacy*, 147–161. Piscatawy: IEEE.
51. Zalewski, M. 2008. Browser Security Handbook, Part 2. Mountain View: Google.
52. Chen, T., A. Chaabane, P. U. Tournoux, M.-A. Kaafar, and R. Boreli. 2013. How much is too much? Leveraging ADS audience estimation to evaluate public profile uniqueness. In *International Symposium on Privacy Enhancing Technologies Symposium*, 225–244. Berlin: Springer.

53. Perito, D., C. Castelluccia, M. A. Kaafar, and P. Manils. 2011. How unique and traceable are usernames? In *International Symposium on Privacy Enhancing Technologies Symposium*, 1–17. Berlin: Springer.
54. DeDeo, S. 2006. Pagestats. http://web.cs.wpi.edu/~cew/pagestats/.
55. Openwpm. 2019. https://github.com/mozilla/OpenWPM
56. Libert, T. webxray. https://webxray.org
57. Das, A., N. Borisov, and M. Caesar. 2016. Tracking mobile web users through motion sensors: Attacks and defenses. In *Network and Distributed System Security Symposium (NDSS)*.
58. Das, A., and N. Borisov. 2014. Poster: Fingerprinting smartphones through speaker. In *Poster at the IEEE Security and Privacy Symposium*. Princeton: Citeseer.
59. Das, A., N. Borisov, and M. Caesar. 2014. Do you hear what i hear? Fingerprinting smart devices through embedded acoustic components. In *Proceedings of the 2014 ACM SIGSAC Conference on Computer and Communications Security*, 441–452. New York: ACM.
60. Zhou, Z., W. Diao, X. Liu, and K. Zhang. 2014. Acoustic fingerprinting revisited: Generate stable device ID stealthily with inaudible sound. In *Proceedings of the 2014 ACM SIGSAC Conference on Computer and Communications Security - CCS'14*, 429–440.
61. Bojinov, H., Y. Michalevsky, G. Nakibly, and D. Boneh. 2014. Mobile device identification via sensor fingerprinting. arXiv:1408.1416.
62. Corripio, J., D. González, A. Orozco, L. Villalba, J. Hernandez-Castro, and S. Gibson. 2013. Source smartphone identification using sensor pattern noise and wavelet transform. In *5th International Conference on Imaging for Crime Detection and Prevention, ICDP 2013*.
63. Lukáš, J., J. Fridrich, and M. Goljan. 2006. Digital camera identification from sensor pattern noise. *IEEE Transactions on Information Forensics and Security* 1 (2): 205–214.
64. Masood, R., B. Z. H. Zhao, H. J. Asghar, and M. A. Kaafar. 2018. Touch and you're trapp (CK) ed: Quantifying the uniqueness of touch gestures for tracking. *Proceedings on Privacy Enhancing Technologies* 2018 (2): 122–142.
65. Fredrikson, M., and B. Livshits. 2011. Repriv: Re-imagining content personalization and in-browser privacy. In *32nd IEEE Symposium on Security and Privacy, S&P 2011, 22–25 May 2011, Berkeley*, 131–146.
66. Toubiana, V., A. Narayanan, D. Boneh, H. Nissenbaum, and S. Barocas. 2010. Adnostic: Privacy preserving targeted advertising. In *Proceedings Network and Distributed System Symposium*.
67. Spooren, J., D. Preuveneers, and W. Joosen. 2015. Mobile device fingerprinting considered harmful for risk-based authentication. In *Proceedings of the Eighth European Workshop on System Security*, 6. New York: ACM.
68. Simon, L., W. Xu, and R. Anderson. 2016. Don't interrupt me while i type: Inferring text entered through gesture typing on android keyboards. *Proceedings on Privacy Enhancing Technologies* 2016 (3): 136–154.
69. Kurtz, A., H. Gascon, T. Becker, K. Rieck, and F. Freiling. 2016. Fingerprinting mobile devices using personalized configurations. *Proceedings on Privacy Enhancing Technologies* 2016 (1): 4–19.
70. Zhao, S., J. Ramos, J. Tao, Z. Jiang, S. Li, Z. Wu, G. Pan, and A. K. Dey. 2016. Discovering different kinds of smartphone users through their application usage behaviors. In *Proceedings of the 2016 ACM International Joint Conference on Pervasive and Ubiquitous Computing - UbiComp'16*, 498–509.
71. Dey, S. 2014. Accelprint: Data and source code. http://sdey4.web.engr.illinois.edu/AccelPrintDataSourceCode.html
72. Das, A. 2018a. Collecting sensor data from smart devices. https://anupamdas.org/SensorDataCollection.html
73. Das, A. 2018b. Fingerprinting smartphones via microphones and speakers. https://anupamdas.org/acoustistic_fp.html
74. Kohno, T., A. Broido, and K. C. Claffy. 2005. Remote physical device fingerprinting. *IEEE Transactions on Dependable and Secure Computing* 2 (2): 93–108.

75. Pang, J., B. Greenstein, R. Gummadi, S. Srinivasan, and D. Wetherall. 2007. 802. 11 user fingerprinting. *Proceedings of the 13th Annual ACM International Conference on Mobile Computing and Networking* 9: 99–110.
76. Hall, J., M. Barbeau, and E. Kranakis. 2003. Detection of transient in radio frequency fingerprinting using signal phase. *Wireless and Optical Communications*, 13–18.
77. Nguyen, N. T., G. Zheng, Z. Han, and R. Zheng. 2011. Device fingerprinting to enhance wireless security using nonparametric Bayesian method. In *Proceedings of IEEE Infocom*, 1404–1412.
78. Acar, G., M. Juarez, N. Nikiforakis, C. Diaz, S. Gürses, F. Piessens, and B. Preneel. 2013. Fpdetective: Dusting the web for fingerprinters. In *Proceedings of the 2013 ACM SIGSAC Conference on Computer & Communications Security*, 1129–1140. New York: ACM.
79. Ruotsalo, T., K. Athukorala, D. Głowacka, K. Konyushkova, A. Oulasvirta, S. Kaipiainen, S. Kaski, and G. Jacucci. 2013. Supporting exploratory search tasks with interactive user modeling. *Proceedings of the American Society for Information Science and Technology* 50 (1), 1–10.
80. Ha, I., K.-J. Oh, and G.-S. Jo. 2015. Personalized advertisement system using social relationship based user modeling. *Multimedia Tools and Applications* 74 (20): 8801–8819.
81. Xue, B., L. Wu, K. Wang, X. Zhang, J. Cheng, X. Chen, and X. Chen. 2021. Multiuser gesture recognition using semg signals via canonical correlation analysis and optimal transport. *Computers in Biology and Medicine* 130: 104188.
82. Magrabi, F., I. Habli, M. Sujan, D. Wong, H. Thimbleby, M. Baker, and E. Coiera. 2019. Why is it so difficult to govern mobile apps in healthcare? *BMJ Health and Care Informatics* 26 (1): e100006.
83. Chellappa, R. K., and R. G. Sin. 2005. Personalization versus privacy: An empirical examination of the online consumer's dilemma. *Information Technology and Management* 6 (2–3): 181–202.
84. Berkovsky, S., N. Borisov, Y. Eytani, T. Kuflik, and F. Ricci. 2007. Examining users' attitude towards privacy preserving collaborative filtering. In *Workshop on Data Mining for User Modeling, Online Proceedings*, 28.
85. Masood, R., D. Vatsalan, M. Ikram, and M. A. Kaafar. 2018. Incognito: A method for obfuscating web data. In *WWW '18: Proceedings of the 2018 World Wide Web Conference*, 267–276.
86. Toch, E., Y. Wang, and L. F. Cranor. 2012. Personalization and privacy: A survey of privacy risks and remedies in personalization-based systems. *User Modeling and User-Adapted Interaction* 22 (1–2): 203–220.
87. Morrissey, P. 2018. 6 people who were fired for social media posts. https://www.smithslawyers.com.au/post/6-people-who-were-fired-for-social-media-posts
88. Schroeder, S. 2009. Domino's youtube video: Youtube can get you fired, too. https://mashable.com/2009/04/14/youtube-fired/
89. Ostrow, A. 2009. Facebook fired: 8% of us companies have sacked social media miscreants. https://mashable.com/2009/08/10/social-media-misuse/.
90. Ullah, I., R. Boreli, M. A. Kaafar, and S. S. Kanhere. 2014. Characterising user targeting for in-app mobile ads. In *2014 IEEE Conference on Computer Communications Workshops (INFOCOM WKSHPS)*, 547–552. Piscatawy: IEEE.
91. United states - google transparency report. 2014. https://transparencyreport.google.com/userdata/us-national-security?hl=en
92. Post, T. W. 2013b. NSA uses google cookies to pinpoint targets for hacking. http://www.washingtonpost.com/blogs/the-switch/wp/2013/12/10/nsa-uses-google-cookies-topinpoint-targets-for-hacking
93. Post, T. W. 2013a. NSA tracking cellphone locations worldwide, snowden documents show. https://www.washingtonpost.com/world/national-security/nsa-tracking-cellphone-locations-worldwide-snowden-documents-show/2013/12/04/5492873a-5cf2-11e3-bc56-c6ca94801fac_story.html

94. Duhigg, C. 2012. How companies learn your secrets. https://www.nytimes.com/2012/02/19/magazine/shopping-habits.html?pagewanted=all

95. Singel, R. 2008. Facebook beacon tracking program draws privacy lawsuit. https://www.wired.com/2008/08/facebook-beacon/

96. Hansell, S. 2006. Aol removes search data on vast group of web users. http://query.nytimes.com/gst/fullpage.html?res=9504e5d81e3ff93ba3575bc0a9609c8b63

97. Narayanan, A., and V. Shmatikov. 2008. Robust de-anonymization of large sparse datasets. In *Proceedings of the 2008 IEEE Symposium on Security and Privacy, SP'08, Washington*, 111–125. Piscatawy: IEEE.

98. Sweeney, L. 1997. Weaving technology and policy together to maintain confidentiality. *The Journal of Law, Medicine & Ethics* 25 (2–3): 98–110.

99. Canny, J. 2002. Collaborative filtering with privacy via factor analysis. In *Proceedings of the 25th Annual International ACM SIGIR Conference on Research and Development in Information Retrieval*, 238–245. New York: ACM.

100. Schafer, J. B., D. Frankowski, J. Herlocker, and S. Sen. 2007. Collaborative filtering recommender systems. In *The Adaptive Web*, 291–324. Berlin: Springer.

101. Canny, J. F. 2002. Collaborative filtering with privacy. In *2002 IEEE Symposium on Security and Privacy, Berkeley, California, May 12–15, 2002*, 45–57.

102. Nissim, K., T. Steinke, A. Wood, M. Altman, A. Bembenek, M. Bun, M. Gaboardi, D. R. O'Brien, and S. Vadhan. 2017. Differential privacy: A primer for a non-technical audience. In *Privacy Law Scholars Conference*.

103. Dwork, C., A. Roth, et al. 2014. The algorithmic foundations of differential privacy. *Foundations and Trends® in Theoretical Computer Science* 9 (3–4): 211–407.

104. Samarati, P., and L. Sweeney. 1998. Protecting privacy when disclosing information: k-anonymity and its enforcement through generalization and suppression. Technical Report, SRI International.

105. Chen, T., R. Boreli, M. A. Kâafar, and A. Friedman. 2014. On the effectiveness of obfuscation techniques in online social networks. In *Privacy Enhancing Technologies - 14th International Symposium, PETS 2014, Amsterdam, July 16–18, 2014. Proceedings*, 42–62.

106. Salamatian, S., A. Zhang, F. du Pin Calmon, S. Bhamidipati, N. Fawaz, B. Kveton, P. Oliveira, and N. Taft. 2013. How to hide the elephant- or the donkey- in the room: Practical privacy against statistical inference for large data. In *IEEE Global Conference on Signal and Information Processing, GlobalSIP 2013, Austin, December 3–5, 2013*, 269–272.

107. Li, C., H. Shirani-Mehr, and X. Yang. 2007. Protecting individual information against inference attacks in data publishing. In *Proceedings of the 12th International Conference on Database Systems for Advanced Applications, DASFAA'07, Berlin*, 422–433. Berlin: Springer.

108. Raval, N., A. Machanavajjhala, and J. Pan. 2019. Olympus: Sensor privacy through utility aware obfuscation. *Proceedings on Privacy Enhancing Technologies* 2019 (1): 5–25.

109. Bindschaedler, V., and R. Shokri. 2016. Synthesizing plausible privacy-preserving location traces. In *2016 IEEE Symposium on Security and Privacy (SP)*, 546–563. Piscatawy: IEEE.

110. Cerf, S., V. Primault, A. Boutet, S. B. Mokhtar, R. Birke, S. Bouchenak, L. Y. Chen, N. Marchand, and B. Robu. 2017. Pulp: Achieving privacy and utility trade-off in user mobility data. In *2017 IEEE 36th Symposium on Reliable Distributed Systems (SRDS)*, 164–173. Piscatawy: IEEE.

111. Boutet, A., and M. Cunche. 2018. A privacy-preserving mechanism for requesting location data provider with wi-fi access points. *International Journal of Applied Engineering Research*, 12 (9): 1982–1986

112. Das, A., G. Acar, N. Borisov, and A. Pradeep. 2018. The web's sixth sense: A study of scripts accessing smartphone sensors. In *Proceedings of the 2018 ACM SIGSAC Conference on Computer and Communications Security*, 1515–1532. New York: ACM.

113. Arlein, R. M., B. Jai, M. Jakobsson, F. Monrose, and M. K. Reiter. 2000. Privacy-preserving global customization. In *Proceedings of the 2nd ACM Conference on Electronic Commerce*, 176–184. New York: ACM.

114. Hitchens, M., J. Kay, B. Kummerfeld, and A. Brar. 2005. Secure identity management for pseudo-anonymous service access. In *International Conference on Security in Pervasive Computing*, 48–55. Berlin: Springer.
115. Gerber, S., M. Fry, J. Kay, B. Kummerfeld, G. Pink, and R. Wasinger. 2010. Personisj: Mobile, client-side user modelling. In *International Conference on User Modeling, Adaptation, and Personalization*, 111–122. Berlin: Springer.
116. Kay, J. 2006. Scrutable adaptation: Because we can and must. In *International Conference on Adaptive Hypermedia and Adaptive Web-Based Systems*, 11–19. Berlin: Springer.
117. Kay, J., B. Kummerfeld, and P. Lauder. 2003. Managing private user models and shared personas. In *UM03 Workshop on User Modeling for Ubiquitous Computing*, 1–11. Princeton: Citeseer.
118. Online privacy tools for the general public. 2015. White paper, European Union Agency For Network and Information Security (ENISA).
119. Electronic Frontier Foundation (EFF). Do not track (DNT). https://www.eff.org/issues/do-not-track
120. Howe, D. C., and H. Nissenbaum. 2009. Trackmenot: Resisting surveillance in web search. *Lessons from the Identity Trail: Anonymity, Privacy, and Identity in a Networked Society* 23: 417–436.
121. Domingo-Ferrer, J., A. Solanas, and J. Castellà-Roca. 2009. h (k)-private information retrieval from privacy-uncooperative queryable databases. *Online Information Review* 33 (4): 720–744.
122. Shapira, B., Y. Elovici, A. Meshiach, and T. Kuflik. 2005. PRAW - A privacy model for the web. *Journal of the American Society for Information Science and Technology (JASIST)* 56 (2): 159–172.
123. Brave. 2019. https://brave.com/

Chapter 10
Healthcare Privacy

Vivian Genaro Motti and Shlomo Berkovsky

Abstract As healthcare shifts towards the digital realm and healthcare delivery steers to patient-centric solutions, new privacy risks emerge. Such risks are acknowledged, but understanding and addressing them with privacy-enhanced technologies is practically challenging. This chapter describes privacy concerns and risks that emerge with the digitization of healthcare services, the availability of Internet-of-care-things, and the usage of online services for medical data. To ensure patients' privacy, collaborative efforts from stakeholders are necessary. Patients, practitioners, and family members play an important role, along with medical organizations, including hospitals, insurance companies, and clinics. Privacy-preserving mechanisms go beyond the protection of patients' data to the infrastructure of medical devices, networks, and systems. The data life cycle, from collection to disposal, must be considered when implementing privacy protections. Principles, policies, and regulations addressing privacy are limited and costly to implement, failing to cover novel technologies that collect and transmit medical data. In the USA, HIPAA is the de facto policy standard. Nevertheless, HIPAA disregards data collected by wearable sensors, fitness trackers, and smartwatches. It does not consider social media networks, mobile applications, and discussion forums where users share medical information. Lastly, genetic data available through online profiles rises privacy issues that are neither known nor regulated.

V. G. Motti (✉)
George Mason University, Fairfax, VA, USA
e-mail: vmotti@gmu.edu

S. Berkovsky
Macquarie University, Sydney, Australia
e-mail: shlomo.berkovsky@mq.edu.au

© The Author(s) 2022   203
B. P. Knijnenburg et al. (eds.), *Modern Socio-Technical Perspectives on Privacy*,
https://doi.org/10.1007/978-3-030-82786-1_10

10.1   Privacy in Healthcare

Privacy considerations for medical records aim at protecting patients and their data by preventing unauthorized access to personal health data by third parties [49]. To ensure privacy, access control mechanisms enforce authorized access to protected patient information. The goal of privacy in this case is to ensure that the patients' information is protected while facilitating the provision of healthcare services. Thus, privacy controls should be incorporated to prevent data misuse and exploitation as well as abusive and discriminatory practices. For instance, they can block a health insurance company from denying care or raising healthcare costs to a patient, or prevent an employer discriminating job applicants, who are more likely to become sick or disabled.

Privacy concerns are important regardless of the industry sector at stake or the profile of the user involved. Still, certain users may be more vulnerable to privacy risks, due to their limited awareness of threats or limited understanding of the intricate details of the technology. Specifically, users with cognitive impairments [1] and older adults may face higher risks due to quick technological changes and challenges to follow and understand updates in business models [2, 51]. They are also subject to remote monitoring by caregivers and practitioners [3], for instance, with self-trackers, robots, or smart home technologies that support older adults' ability to age in place [4, 5]. The continuous use of technology in such cases exacerbates risks and may result in flawed controls for data access [6].

Self-tracking afficionados may also be vulnerable due to the risk of unintended exposure of their data, since their data is collected continuously, from various sources, and can be aggregated by online services, such as social media channels [7]. Self-tracking has become even more popular due to the COVID-19 pandemic, allowing users to monitor their vital signs, helping government authorities to surveil citizens' mobility and trace their contacts, to monitor the spread of the disease. The proliferation of contact tracing applications led to important discussions regarding the extent to which state controls and federal regulations can impact the citizens' rights to privacy. While technology can help address the pandemic, it is unclear how to optimize its use for common benefits in a fair manner [8].

In addition to the user profile and the purposes of technology, several aspects of how data flows are also important when building effective privacy controls for digital records. This includes considering privacy controls for the data sources and systems used to process medical data [44]. Moreover, it is important to consider the devices, equipment, stakeholders, and processes employed seeking to identify privacy risks and protect user data.

First, the data sources that could pose privacy risks include systems and applications that manage protected medical data. Beyond dedicated systems used by health providers, consider also various devices and systems used by patients. These include websites, discussion forums, mobile applications, and social media channels. While some of these have medical focus, many are rather general-purpose systems employed by users to learn about medical content, exchange information with others, track health conditions, and post or discuss questions with a virtual community [48, 55].

Next, all the equipment used for data collection or processing needs to have the right privacy protections, as both physical and virtual artifacts require privacy controls. To protect these assets, a thorough risk analysis should be conducted. The duration and costs associated with such an analysis depend on the scale of the system. Generally, such analyses range from an informal internal assessment to detect potential risks to a systematic procedure carried out by a specialized service with a team of domain experts. Either way, the purpose of the analysis is to identify and mitigate vulnerabilities and breaches at the software, hardware, or operational process level.

Physical equipment that may need to be protected includes wires, ports, and drivers. While locks, latches, and keys facilitate physical safeguards, virtual applications and software, on the other hand, demand specialized systems. These include firmware and tools deployed to monitor the use of assets and control access by end users, third parties, or virtual agents. Compliance with standards and policies helps regulating access by third-party systems or external services, including cloud solutions for platforms, infrastructure, and software.

Although the patient is the main beneficiary of privacy considerations in healthcare, collaborative efforts from *multiple stakeholders* are necessary to prevent unintended disclosure and malicious use of personal data. As diverse stakeholders are involved in the data generation, analysis, and interpretation, they should be trained and qualified to manage health information with adequate privacy-preserving behaviors and attitudes. Medical practitioners, caregivers, family members, investigators, and organizations all need to take responsibility for protecting patient data from unwanted disclosure and access. Additionally, health insurance companies, clinics, pharmaceutics, and laboratories also need to actively preserve patient privacy.

To ensure users' privacy is preserved, consider different data types, information sources, and stakeholders in the entire life cycle. Data protection requires an integrative approach combining *multiple strategies* ranging from training users to deploying and testing technical controls. The training aims at raising privacy awareness, educating and informing end users about adequate behaviors when using data, equipment, systems, and resources. Technical controls aim at protecting all the assets involved and include authentication, authorization, protected network connections, obfuscation and firewalls [43].

Multiple data sources need to be considered when designing for privacy in healthcare. This includes reports written by healthcare practitioners (prescriptions of medication and therapies), caregivers (checklists and documentation), or patients (self-assessment reports and receipts). This also includes data collected in a passive or active way, from applications that use ambient sensors, to mobile applications where users report data [2, 50]. Data in various formats and modalities should be governed by privacy control mechanisms, be it imaging and signals from clinical examinations and text reports or raw data generated during clinical examinations with medical devices. Aggregated data from a patient's electronic health records (EHRs) should also be protected.

When implementing privacy controls for healthcare, concrete *artifacts* for consideration include EHRs, medical reports, notes, and prescriptions. However, not all medical data comes from health records, as information can be inferred from the user's location, lifestyle, and behaviors, among others [10]. The digital phenotype of patients can be defined based on their online behaviors, e.g., search history and social media posts [9]. On the one hand, these offer valuable information about patients' lifestyle, health status, well-being, and future condition [11]. On the other hand, this information poses new privacy risks, especially when the user-generated content becomes publicly available. Furthermore, the potential for inferences on public data increases when multiple data sources are aggregated, leading to a greater risk of identifying sensitive data, including the address, social circles, and more.

From a technical perspective, the entire system infrastructure must be considered to ensure holistic privacy controls. As Fig. 10.1 illustrates, this infrastructure is centered on the patient, but includes the devices and equipment, where data is collected, stored, or shared, like sensors, browsers, mobile applications/devices, and computers [46]. Servers, databases, hard drives, and cloud services exemplify

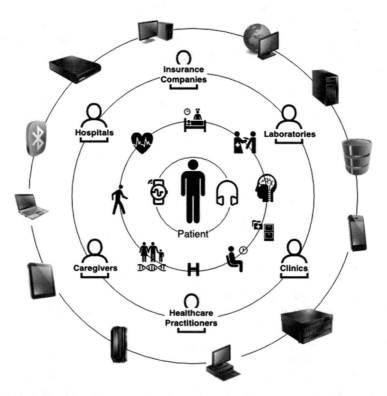

Fig. 10.1 To protect health data, privacy solutions should employ a holistic patient-centric approach considering the ecosystem of devices, data sources, and stakeholders involved in the process

applications and devices for storage purposes. Finally, network and communication protocols for exchanging information serve for data sharing and transmission.

Hardware and software solutions are part of the ecosystem for privacy-enhanced technologies. Electronic equipment, medical devices, mobile apps, and wearable technologies can be targeted when data access and sharing are enabled, posing privacy risks. The connection to the Internet exacerbates privacy risks, and special attention is needed when devices are integrated with third-party services. *Multiple stakeholders* are involved in the process of data collection, retrieval, and analysis. These are important assets for privacy considerations and include health practitioners (doctors, nurses, physicians, clinicians), service providers (therapists, dentists, caregivers), family members (relatives, guardians), and others.

In practice, examples of misuse of private data have been publicized in popular media, particularly involving private information that users were unaware of or unwilling to disclose, revealed by data analytics. A notorious case includes the 2012 "pregnancy prediction score" by Target that used the history of items purchased by a client to tailor advertisements. Targeted ads and coupons related to pregnancy and baby items were sent to a teenager. Initially, the father of the teenager complained about the incident, fearing that the advertisement could serve as a teenage pregnancy incentive. Later on, he apologized about the complaint since he realized the store had made a correct prediction about his daughter's pregnancy before it was actually disclosed [12]. Another example is the exploitation of mobile apps that track menstrual cycle of employees [47]. As reported by the press, data from the app was shared with the employer under the banner of "corporate wellness," practically revealing sensitive information about the employees' intimate lives. Even if the app usage is deemed voluntary and the data is shared in an aggregated way, there is a potential for privacy breaches related to discriminatory and abusive practices.

Genetic information publicized online thanks to the dissemination of DNA kits have become an increasing privacy concern as well. More specifically, privacy concerns emerged when genealogy findings about biological parents and abuse in fertility clinics were discovered [59]. Such genetic services can reveal confidential information to costumers through online genetic profiles, provided by services such as 23andMe and their data analysis [13, 14].

To provide definitions and concrete examples of healthcare privacy, this chapter is organized as follows. Section 10.2 illustrates the risks involved with protected health data, covering diverse information sources and the risks users face. Section 10.3 focuses on existing solutions, listing and describing the policies, principles, and regulatory tools. Section 10.4 discusses the limitations of existing approaches, presenting open questions for future research and development. Finally, Sect. 10.5 summarizes how healthcare privacy is currently managed and provides key recommendations for stakeholders.

10.2 Risks

As more patients have access to advanced healthcare services, not only more documentation from lab tests and examination results are generated, but also privacy breaches increase in risks and severity. The larger number of privacy risks can be attributed to several reasons. First, the increasing number of devices facilitates a large-scale data collection. Data collected more frequently and more continuously covers multiple information channels generating datasets are larger and have a higher inference potential with aggregated data sources. Second, interconnected devices for data collection and analysis require advanced controls to prevent unauthorized access to and inappropriate use of data. Such controls are relevant as the data is transmitted or stored, so access to storage services needs to include physical and virtual implementations. Third, current regulations and practices are insufficient for holistic privacy-preserving controls, as emerging problems are still unknown and often addressed reactively. In addition, public data analyzed at an aggregated level can lead to inference of sensitive information. An aggregated analysis, fusing data on user behavior, eating habits, and shopping, for instance, can surface valuable information about their health condition and potential illnesses, resulting in information unbeknownst to users [42, 54].

Lastly, the implementation of effective privacy controls is not trivial [3], especially when multiple data sources and stakeholders are involved, and potential problems are neither well understood nor formally characterized. Best practices, heuristics, and guidelines are often limited or lacking, tend to be complex, and costly to implement. The above challenges leave users with vulnerable systems and imminent risks of breaches. Issues in healthcare privacy include data misuse, breaches, threats, and other implications. Main risks are associated with access by unauthorized parties, inappropriate use, abuse, disclosure, or even unauthorized recording of medical data. Privacy implications affect medical data in multiple dimensions from the data to the service levels.

10.2.1 Data, Protected Health Information, and Applications

Medical records require protection against inappropriate access to prevent unauthorized access to personally identifiable, confidential, and sensitive patient information, such as address, social security number, chronic illnesses, disabilities, or diagnosed diseases. In the USA, the federal law Health Insurance Portability and Accountability Act establishes limits on health data access to protect medical data [11]. The implementation of strict controls is needed to ensure that, from a system level, the exchange of information follows appropriate policies [45, 52, 53]. Effective access control mechanisms use policies to preserve users' privacy by matching information and datasets according to the users' profiles and respective privileges. Such controls need to operate seamlessly across different medical applications, including medical imaging systems, genetic tests, and online consultations. Additionally, they need to be updated regularly to evolve as the technology advances.

10.2.2   Sources and Stakeholders

Laboratories, health providers, and clinics are considered trusted parties for health services. As the data they provide are essential to the delivery of patient care, these parties need to comply with regulations, best practices, and existing policies that govern the access control and storage practices for medical data.

Regarding online sources and public domains, when patients provide self-reported information in discussion forums, online groups, and social media posts [15], they reveal private information. While some users deliberately advocate for their conditions and become a public reference for their communities, others prefer to remain anonymous. However, oftentimes they are oblivious to and unaware of potential implications of leaving permanent digital traces, as once the information is disclosed it may be used in the future against them, for instance, in discriminatory practices related to insurance premiums or employment opportunities.

For healthcare practitioners and medical experts, online health networks are valuable for disseminating information among team members in hospitals or during epidemy outbreaks [16]. Despite users being mostly unaware of or unconcerned about potential risks [17], once the data is published online, it is impractical to control its dissemination. The risks involved are even higher when vulnerable populations are at stake (see Chap. 15), for instance, with parents sharing information about children [18] or caregivers sharing information about patients with disabilities.

Also, when multiple sources of information from different online channels are used, data can be aggregated for inference, leading to higher risks of unveiling sensitive information. If a patient posts comments and questions about their symptoms in online forums, seeking for advice from the community in a non-anonymous way, this information can be used for diagnostic purposes and also misused afterwards to potentially disadvantage the patient. This is especially risky when accounts are linked across platforms, which may lead to the unintentional disclosure of anonymized data and information. Moreover, the analysis of the user discourse has the potential to reveal age, gender, location, and medical conditions. Examples of medical topics posted in such channels include mental illnesses [11, 19], nutrition habits [9], disabilities [20], and syndromes [3]. An example of discriminatory practice and surveillance related to public posts on social media concerns the government proposal to use social media posts to detect fraud in disability payments. Not only it is unfeasible to verify whether a person is disabled from an online picture or post, but the proposal also raised questions about the legitimacy and reliability of social media posts, but the proposal also raised questions about the legitimacy and reliability of social media posts, as well as about abusive behaviors related to online contents that could harm individuals' rights to privacy [21].

Online communities and discussion forums often contain sensitive health information [15]. Although patients share information to exchange their experiences and seek for advice, they may be unaware of potential risks and misuse of the disclosed data. In these communities, nicknames are used to mask the actual identities. However, depending on the nature of the questions and answers posted, sensitive information and personally identifiable data may become inadvertently available. As Fig. 10.2 shows, PatientsLikeMe provides simple language privacy specifications that allow users to see, change, or delete their data. They can also be notified if data is stolen and request the company to stop processing their data. Notably, PatientsLikeMe does not warrant the authenticity of any user's identity or data provided by them.

Mobile health applications also pose novel privacy risks in healthcare. When users install and use an app, their personal information is often tracked, combining passive sensing (e.g., navigation and call history, location, activities) with self-reported data. As there is no legislation to regulate the usage of such data [16], there is much space for exploitative practices. For instance, the Ovia Health app has been used as a monitoring tool to track intimate fertility and pregnancy information of employees [47]. Such monitoring allows for potential discriminatory practices by employers and health insurance companies.

Another source of sensitive information is the reviews that users leave when commenting and rating mobile applications on Google Play or iTunes, or even when purchasing from e-commerce websites. Some reviews may reveal information that falls under the "protected health information" category, including medical diagnoses and health conditions. The posts are not always anonymized, and once this information is available online, there is no control over sharing and reuse of such information by untrusted parties.

10.2.3 Process and Services

The main issue with data collection through mobile sensors is associated with excessive data collection, mainly due to organizations not knowing upfront what information is useful for them. Hence, they collect more data than the application needs, planning on future opportunities for data analysis and capitalization. Despite direct use by individual users, the collected data provides valuable information about their families, relatives, caregivers, and contacts. Such individuals, despite also being affected, are neither aware nor in agreement with data collection and potential analysis for further inferences. Depending on the sensors deployed for patient monitoring (e.g., camera, GPS, and microphone), personally identifiable information of others is also collected, indirectly impacting their privacy [7].

To prevent unauthorized access during transmission, trusted protocols with authentication and firewalls need to be used. Those ensure the delivery of records and data from authentic sources to legitimate parties. When data is published, e.g., for announcements, notifications, or reports, care must be taken to properly

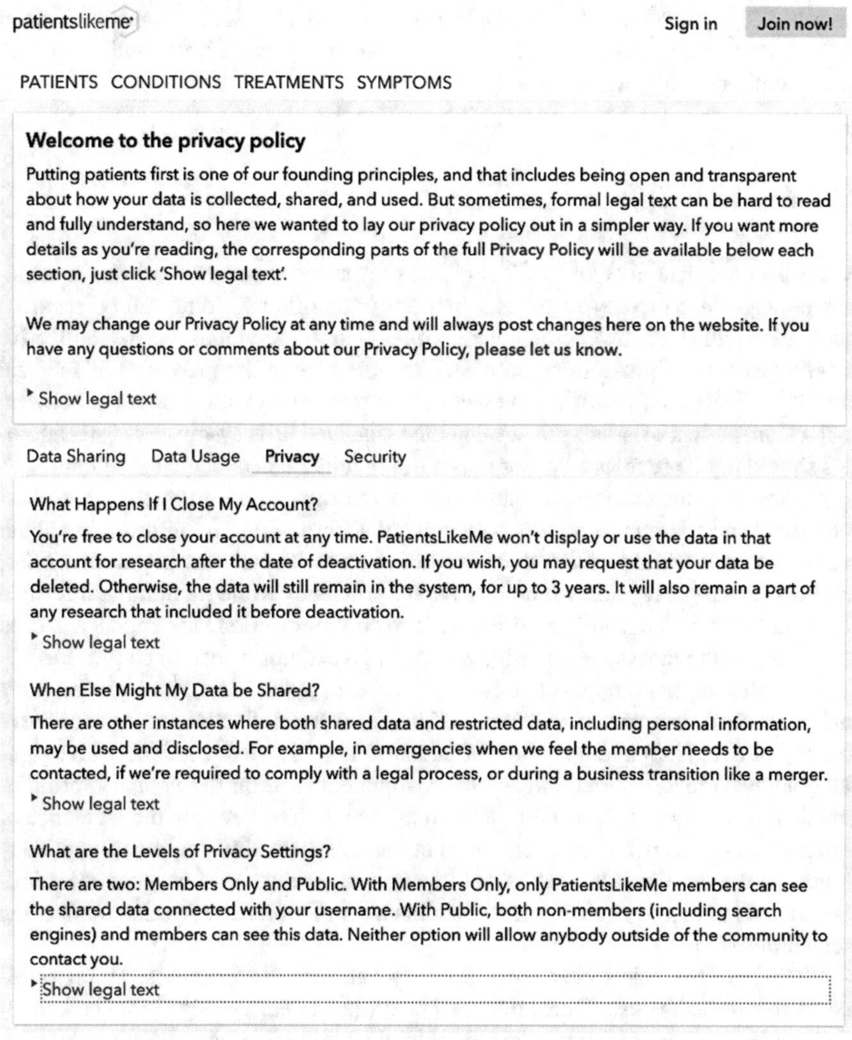

patientslikeme·

PATIENTS CONDITIONS TREATMENTS SYMPTOMS

Welcome to the privacy policy

Putting patients first is one of our founding principles, and that includes being open and transparent about how your data is collected, shared, and used. But sometimes, formal legal text can be hard to read and fully understand, so here we wanted to lay our privacy policy out in a simpler way. If you want more details as you're reading, the corresponding parts of the full Privacy Policy will be available below each section, just click 'Show legal text'.

We may change our Privacy Policy at any time and will always post changes here on the website. If you have any questions or comments about our Privacy Policy, please let us know.

▸ Show legal text

Data Sharing   Data Usage   **Privacy**   Security

What Happens If I Close My Account?

You're free to close your account at any time. PatientsLikeMe won't display or use the data in that account for research after the date of deactivation. If you wish, you may request that your data be deleted. Otherwise, the data will still remain in the system, for up to 3 years. It will also remain a part of any research that included it before deactivation.

▸ Show legal text

When Else Might My Data be Shared?

There are other instances where both shared data and restricted data, including personal information, may be used and disclosed. For example, in emergencies when we feel the member needs to be contacted, if we're required to comply with a legal process, or during a business transition like a merger.

▸ Show legal text

What are the Levels of Privacy Settings?

There are two: Members Only and Public. With Members Only, only PatientsLikeMe members can see the shared data connected with your username. With Public, both non-members (including search engines) and members can see this data. Neither option will allow anybody outside of the community to contact you.

▸ Show legal text

Fig. 10.2 Privacy policy of PatientsLikeMe including specifications of data sharing, usage, and security aspects (from https://www.patientslikeme.com/, as of November 4, 2019). The policy is copyright protected by PatientsLikeMe and used with permission

anonymize and de-identify it. In terms of access control, a combination of procedures is needed in order to (1) prevent non-authorized access to protected data, (2) avoid authentication issues, such as impersonation and spoofing attacks, and (3) ensure that users appropriately use the available privacy control mechanisms. In addition to controlling user access and privileges to prevent data access by unauthorized parties and tampering, the storage services should keep the patient's records in an encrypted format. Data disposal should also be controlled, be it through shredding physical copies (notes, printed reports, exam results, etc.) or permanently deleting digital records.

10.2.4 Trade-Offs

While the confidentiality of medical records to preserve patients' privacy is undeniable, healthcare privacy involves important trade-offs regarding safety, security, automation, ease of use, efficiency, fairness, and individual versus collective benefits. Excessive protections pose serious obstacles to the provision of medical care [22]. While confidentiality is essential for preserving the relationship between doctors and patients, patient privacy and the associated privacy-preserving technologies should not be seen as a barrier to providing reliable healthcare to patients.

Privacy controls ensure that patients have the right to be informed about their conditions and treatments so that they can act accordingly. The information about privacy controls should neither overload nor overwhelm patients. In practice, clinical decision support systems should strive for efficiency while facilitating informed decisions from patients and practitioners. The communication and language should be adapted to the literacy level of individuals, and examples need to be provided.

Fully preventing all opportunities for data access is not ideal, since practitioners and researchers can obtain valuable insight from the collective and comparative analysis of data from a large cohort of patients. The knowledge gained with aggregated analysis involves the efficacy of treatments based on the patients' profiles, genetic information, and lifestyles, as well as the relations between the incidence of certain diseases, environmental data, and cultural aspects. Fully automating privacy choices, although feasible [23], is not ideal, as algorithms rely on generalizations that can lead to biased choices and discriminatory practices, besides also reinforcing inequalities [17].

A tension also exists between the safety and security priorities, as restricted access constrains the use of data that may be critical in emergency [24]. The knowledge generated from employing different treatments and assessing their respective health outcomes is relevant to inform and improve healthcare services. At the global scale, diagnostics can also inform epidemic trends, help in disease prevention, and inform healthcare policies. Benefits for public health and medical progress are well recognized [25]; for instance, when practitioners had to address the Zika outbreak in Latin America, the Ebola crisis in Africa, and the opioid crisis in the USA, the availability of information about the cases allowed practitioners to define a contingency plan, decide on health campaigns, and plan their responses. Hence, privacy policies must be carefully established to not hinder domain advancements and facilitate healthcare delivery. Still, there are risks around healthcare privacy, and the implications go beyond data breaches, shame, and embarrassment [16, 22]. Other disadvantages include increased insurance premiums, loss of benefits, and discriminatory practices. Potential for serious harm also involves loss of insurance, unemployability, and stigmatization [25].

Among the key benefits of data sharing, we highlight the opportunity to improve patient care with more informed decisions. Datasets that are not only larger but also more diverse can help inform and enhance current healthcare practices. The inference of data generated by a large number of patients and collected longitudinally contributes to medical research advancements. Using data from multiple sources can be particularly beneficial to support personalized healthcare and precision medicine. More specifically, patients benefit if their practitioners have access to information that can help them make better informed decisions, such as the patient's history and profile, information about previous procedures, ongoing treatments, genetic information, or even potential allergies that could put the patient at risk. The analysis of individual data from multiple sources can aid in diagnostic and therapeutic decisions, better suited to the patient's needs. While record keeping and sharing foster data analysis, the optimization of current processes requires efforts to prevent breaches and vulnerabilities. On the negative side, the exchange of information across multiple parties increases the likelihood of exploitation, as the data collected and not managed according to privacy principles may be used for the patient's disadvantage by health insurance companies, employers, third-party services, and others.

10.3 Regulations

Security and compliance drivers for privacy practices and controls include regulatory mechanisms, such as standards, laws, and frameworks. Regulatory mechanisms serve different levels of care—state, federal, or continent—and include European regulations, such as the GDPR [26], US-based laws, such as HIPAA [14], or Africa-specific regulations [16]. In the USA, those mechanisms include the Protected Health Information (PHI), Health Insurance Portability and Accountability Act (HIPAA), Payment Card Industry (PCI), Federal Information Security Management Act (FISMA), and Food and Drug Administration (FDA). Such legislation is required to (1) ensure privacy, (2) improve patient care, and (3) enhance the usefulness and reliability of health information [22]. Also, their rules encourage a greater use of EHRs and other types of health information while protecting information privacy and security [27]. This section describes the main regulations addressing privacy in healthcare, including acts, legislation, rules, administrative agencies, safeguards, policies, procedures, forms, and toolkits.

10.3.1 Acts

Acts are descriptive pieces of legislation specifically applicable to circumstances and people. Acts are created in the parliament and need to be voted on by ministers before becoming laws. In the USA, three acts focus on privacy of health data,

HIPAA, HITECH, and Cures Act, whereas COPPA, FERPA, RFPA, and ADA handle tangential privacy information (education, disabilities, finances). They are defined as follows.

HIPAA The Health Insurance Portability and Accountability Act supports the sharing of health information among healthcare providers, health plans, and those operating on their behalf [28, 57]. HIPAA covers the treatment, payment, and other medical operations, besides providing channels for transmitting health information to relatives involved in the care of an individual as well as for research, public health, and other activities. Civil and criminal penalties apply when HIPAA regulations are not respected [14]. While HIPAA is a de facto standard regarding health regulation in the USA, updates are needed to ensure it also considers medical data extracted from health apps and the data collected by companies, e.g., searches for medical information [11].

HITECH The Health Information Technology for Economic and Clinical Health Act was signed in 2009 to promote the adoption and meaningful use of health information technology and EHRs [27, 41, 58]. Unlike HIPAA, HITECH is centered around digital records. Subtitle D of HITECH addresses the privacy and security concerns associated with electronic transmission of health information, through several provisions that strengthen the civil and criminal enforcement of the HIPAA rules [30] and apply violation penalties that range from US$100 to a US$1.5 million per year [29].

21st Century Cures Act (Cures Act) The Cures Act defines interoperability as the exchange and use of electronic health information, without burdening the user or blocking information access [31]. Additionally, this act facilitates the regulation of privacy controls in medical research, for instance, by waiving patients' consent when it is unnecessary and streamlining the approval processes for drugs and devices.

COPPA Enacted in 1998, COPPA limits the collection of personally identifiable information from youngsters without their parents' consent. The Commission's Rule implementing COPPA, effective since 2000, requires websites to post a complete privacy policy, notify parents about their information collection practices, and get verifiable parental consent before collecting personal information from their children or sharing it with others [32].

FERPA The Family Educational Rights and Privacy Act is a federal privacy law that gives parents protection concerning their children's education records, such as report cards, transcripts, disciplinary records, contact and family information, and class schedules [30].

RFPA The 1978 Right to Financial Privacy Act establishes specific procedures that federal government authorities must follow to obtain information from a financial institution about a customer's financial records [56].

ADA The Americans with Disabilities Act is a civil rights law forbidding discrimination acts against individuals with disabilities. ADA covers public life, jobs, schools, transportation, and all public and private places that are open to the public [39]. The law ensures that people with disabilities have the same rights and opportunities as everyone else [20]. As the technology evolves, updates were proposed to extend the protection, for instance, to prevent discrimination to deny job opportunities from individuals, whose predicted health outcomes include higher risks for disabilities [11, 40].

ACA The Affordable Care Act is a US federal status that covers health insurance plans for essential health benefits, including doctor's services, inpatient and outpatient care, prescription drug coverage, pregnancy and childbirth, and mental health services. These services are accessible for US citizens or lawful immigrants and aim at reducing healthcare costs, improving its quality, and expanding healthcare delivery to patients with a low income [33].

10.3.2   Legislation, Administrative Agencies, and Rules

Legislation consists of the enactment of the law owing to the provision of guidelines that dictate how the acts should be applied in practice. That is, legislation describes legal requirements and punishments for law violations. Legislation encompasses multiple acts. In the medical context, the Health IT Legislation includes the HITECH Act, the Cures Act, the Affordable Care Act, and the HIPAA. This legislation seeks to improve the exchange of electronic health information, by advancing interoperability, prohibiting information blocking, and enhancing the privacy of health technologies, so that multiple stakeholders, including patients, families, and healthcare practitioners, have access to electronic health information. To reinforce the legislation, regulatory agencies have been created. In the healthcare arena, the Food and Drug Administration (FDA) is a regulatory agency that enforces laws and protects public health, by ensuring the safety, efficacy, and security of drugs, biological products, and medical devices. The FDA also accepts requests for privacy acts.

While laws have legal consequences and actions associated with them, rules tend to be more flexible and carry milder consequences. Also, laws are sets of rules subject to legislative approval processes that have to be applied to everyone in a society. A rule is created by an executive branch, while a law is created by a legislative process. While the rules are enforced like laws, the laws carry a more formal connotation. In practice, both words are often used interchangeably. In the healthcare context, to regulate data and user privacy, four rules stand out.

The Privacy, Security, and Breach Notification Rules Implemented at the federal level under HIPAA, these are administered by the HHS Office for Civil Rights. Such rules establish a baseline of privacy protections and rights of patients and serve as the foundation of protections for individually identifiable health information and of individuals' rights with respect to their information [34]. These rules require that entities notify all individuals affected by a breach, informing them when an unauthorized disclosure or use of their data occurs.

The Privacy Rule Also implemented under HIPAA, this is a standard for Privacy of Individually Identifiable Health Information aimed at assuring protection to the individuals' health information, without preventing the flow of health information needed to provide quality healthcare. This rule seeks to balance appropriate usage of information with privacy protection for individuals seeking medical care [19]. This rule is applicable to healthcare providers and health plans, who should implement administrative, technical, and physical safeguards to ensure privacy of health information.

The Security Rule Also implemented under HIPAA, the rule requires entities to evaluate risks and vulnerabilities in their environments and implement appropriate security measures to prevent threats and hazards to the integrity of protected health information [34]. This rule is a national standard in the USA, affecting all entities managing protected health information. The main difference between the privacy and the security rule is that the latter deals with protected electronic health information that is created, maintained, used, or received, whereas the former ensures individuals' rights to control their protected health information.

The General Data Protection Regulation (GDPR) Implemented in the European Union since 2018, GDPR focuses on individual rights and control in a digital economy. GDPR improved the levels of transparency and fairness, informing users about the use of their data and allowing additional control. Also, it enforces that medical information is only accessible for health and social care purposes, and to address public health concerns, after the patient or their legal guardian consent. If users want to know what data is available, they can request to access it and delete it if desired. By allowing users to delete their data, GDPR also enables users to be *forgotten* [26].

GDPR provides eight rights to individual users, which are defined in Table 10.1. Notably, GDPR follows the European model, which requires approval for any data collection and usage. This opt-in strategy prohibits the reuse of data for unintended purposes as well. While the opt-in choice is frequently bypassed with dubious practices that deceive users to select the wrong choice in an interface, the "don't reuse" clause ensures that selling user data is illegal [11].

It should be highlighted that the existing rules are complementary. They have been devised to address previous incidents, and they require technology support to be implemented in medical systems. More specifically, technologists should reinforce authentication mechanisms, keep track of the users' actions, allow data deletion, and deploy careful access controls.

Table 10.1 The eight individual rights of GDPR

The right to be informed: about data collected and used
The right of access: all the data collected upon request
The right to rectification: in case personal data is inaccurate or incomplete
The right to erasure: to delete all the personal information previously collected
The right to restrict processing: to refrain further usage of data already collected
The right to data portability: allows individuals to reuse their data, by moving, copying, or transferring it across IT environments
The right to object: to stop data being used for marketing or other purposes
The rights related to automated decision making and profiling: to prevent harm from automated decision making and allow users to request human intervention or challenge a decision

10.3.3   Safeguards, Policies, Procedures, and Forms

Safeguards, policies, procedures, and forms aim at protecting the patient's privacy with concrete actions and documents.

Administrative, Physical, and Technical Safeguards These are complementary approaches combining actions, procedures, measures, and policies for protecting medical data. Safeguards involve people, information, and facilities [13]. Physical safeguards protect buildings, equipment, and systems from unauthorized access. Administrative safeguards cover actions, policies, and procedures that regulate how practitioners protect information. Technical safeguards are system controls to prevent unauthorized access due to intrusion, tampering, or inappropriate deletion. To identify pertinent actions and procedures, a risk analysis is primarily executed. Once the risks are identified and analyzed, an action plan of security measures is developed and implemented.

Technical safeguards also include principles and procedures that should be followed, for instance, to ensure accountability and anonymization. Four common types of safeguards include:

Accountability This consists of logging all the operations executed by a system, so in case of breaches, the documentation enables investigation and audit. Accountability is enforced by administrative procedures and enabled through technical and physical solutions, including log-in systems and badges.

Anonymization and De-identification of Health Information This can be ensured when the data neither identifies nor provides sufficient information to identify an individual. To de-identify information, either a qualified statistician performs data analysis to detect the uniqueness of information, or individual identifiers are removed following established heuristics. In the former approach, either additional data is included or unique values for certain records or variables are modified. In the later approach, identifiers referring to the individual's relatives, household members, and employers are also removed [19].

Individual Choice This facilitates users taking more informed decisions by ensuring that reasonable information is provided about the data collection, usage, and dissemination. Also, individuals are given the option to either protect or reveal information. To inform individuals, a consent form is distributed.

Informed Consent Form This is a comprehensive document that informs users about the risks and benefits of a procedure. Written in an accessible language, this form lets users know that they can withdraw during a treatment and whom they need to contact with questions. Informed consent is a common practice in health services explaining the risks and benefits of a procedure. Although these forms lack flexibility for negotiation, they raise user awareness of data management and provide them options to act if needed.

To help with the technical implementation of privacy and security, the NIST HIPAA Security Toolkit Application was developed by the National Institute of Standards and Technology (NIST). This toolkit, provided by the Healthcare Information and Management Systems Society, covers concrete implementations of privacy and security, supporting organizations in understanding the requirements of HIPAA, implementing these requirements, and evaluating their implementations. Although the above procedures, policies, and protocols help regulating the implementation of privacy, additional efforts by public authorities and regulatory agencies are required to enforce enactment. Joint efforts from individuals, organizations, and government also need to be combined.

10.4   Limitations and Challenges in Current Practices

The state of practice and existing legislation around privacy-preserving controls in healthcare are limited in several aspects. The limited understanding of privacy risks and the lack of support tools to implement privacy controls result in reactive measures. As technology advances and novel privacy breaches are discovered, regulatory frameworks emerge. The problem with such regulations is that they are reactive and respond to past incidents. Proactive measures are rare and the attention paid to enact privacy and confidentiality in healthcare is still limited [22]. Thus far, in practice, most actions to address privacy issues have been limited and inconsistent, increasing vulnerability risks.

The fact that the existing solutions are fragmented and not unified leads to inconsistencies between legislation and practice. No comprehensive federal law protects the privacy of health records, while state laws are scattered and inconsistent [22]. Although HIPAA regulates protected medical data, it is by no means sufficient to exhaustively address problems that emerge with novel technologies. Several important conflicts of interest exist between the parties involved, including patients, healthcare practitioners, insurers, and third-party companies. The resulting trade-offs must be carefully resolved to ensure patients' privacy. For example, the use of social media channels for medical communications may result in disclosure with third-party organizations that can capitalize on the generated information even when users are oblivious of this [16].

Open questions remain concerning data ownership and governance. While end users generate large volumes of data, the ownership of such data is unclear when regulations are lacking and policies are ambiguous. The subjective interpretation of legal documents and lack of clear resolutions by companies may result in legal disputes. Despite collecting personal data, fitness trackers and smartwatches, for instance, are neither regulated by medical policies nor have FDA approvals in the USA. Although novel technologies collect physiological and activity data from users, the devices, applications, and services remain largely unregulated from a medical standpoint.

A higher privacy risk is faced by vulnerable populations, marginalized groups, and minorities, not only because their personal data can be used as a commodity, but also because privacy-preserving controls were not devised with their involvement. Although advances in privacy solutions have increased in the recent decades, most work has been concentrated on developed nations [35] and WEIRD (western, educated, industrialized, rich, and democratic) populations [36]. Also, there is a limited understanding of cross-cultural trust [37] and privacy [16] concerns, especially among users from underdeveloped countries and low socioeconomic status where eHealth regulation is nonexistent or fragmented. In addition, in some countries, e.g., Singapore, China, and Russia, online user data is heavily regulated and sometimes controlled by the government.

For the end users, be it a patient or legally responsible individual (caregiver or guardian), there is a trade-off between benefiting from technological resources and spending time and effort to understand and set privacy controls. While the access to paper-based records is limited due to spatial restrictions, EHRs increase the risks associated with data sharing and patient privacy, mainly due to the increased amount of information being collected and stored, and the larger number of parties remotely accessing this information. While in theory, most patients and caregivers prefer to have granular control over access to their data [38], enacting such control is time-consuming and burdensome, as it is not always feasible to analyze and select the best disclosure options [29].

In summary, the main limitations and challenges faced by the current practices are:

- **Existing solutions tend to be reactive** created in response to incidents because not all concerns are foreseeable and support tools are lacking.
- **Existing solutions are fragmented**, and the lack of a unified approach leads to inconsistencies in legislation, policies, and safeguards.
- **Conflicts of interest** hinder companies and organizations from matching privacy-preserving solutions with the best interest of users.
- **Gaps exist on data governance**, and open questions remain regarding data ownership.
- **Privacy controls are devised for an average user**, and vulnerable populations and marginalized groups face higher risks.
- **Users prefer fine-grained controls**, although it is time-consuming to navigate existing policies and configure access controls.

10.5   Recommendations

Given the numerous challenges involved in the implementation of privacy controls, a set of measures is necessary to ensure that effective controls are available.

Training and education efforts are necessary to prepare the workforce and raise user awareness. All the personnel involved in data collection and management, including patients and practitioners, need to be trained on privacy practices. By raising awareness of privacy concerns, they become better prepared to keep the systems up to date and protected. Practitioners should also check that the access control ensures a proper match between the datasets and the authorized personnel given specific privileges.

Enforcement of best practices and privacy measures ensures that access controls are properly deployed. Privacy-enhancing practices across stakeholders involve understanding the benefits one can have by sharing data. Incentives, rewards, as well as violation penalties, including settlements and fines, help ensure that stakeholders comply with standards and regulatory requirements.

As Fig. 10.3 illustrates, the recommendations to effectively implement solutions for privacy-enhancing technologies in healthcare involve multiple stakeholders and devices. Such solutions cut across data processing (request, analysis, retrieval) and storage services, be those physical (servers, hard drives) or virtual (running in the cloud).

In general, the recommendations proposed to implement privacy controls include training, monitoring, compliance, and accountability. Privacy-preserving principles and laws primarily consider the transparency of data handling, the control over data access, the accountability of user actions, and the interoperability to enable exchange of data across systems and organizations [31]. Specifically, transparency informs users about how their data is handled, facilitating trust in the systems. Control allows users to select what data they agree to collect and share and how the disclosure occurs. Accountability aims at logging and monitoring the usage of data and resources by users or systems, facilitating the analysis of executed operations.

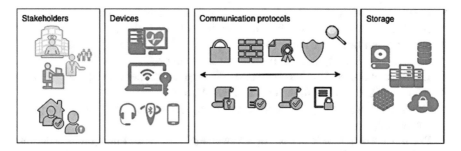

Fig. 10.3 Privacy-enhancing solutions include training various stakeholders, protecting the data storage and communication devices and infrastructure, strengthening the communication protocols, and protecting the devices and storage services

Interoperability facilitates the exchange of information, data aggregation, and analytics and also helps to ensure consistency in data sharing communication protocols.

To describe in detail the current practices and recommendations for privacy controls, the following subsections are structured per every stakeholder. The roles considered range from healthcare practitioners to third-party organizations.

10.5.1   Healthcare Practitioners

All the stakeholders involved in healthcare services generate health data and have access to patient's data from different sources, including lab results, medical imaging, and reports. When healthcare practitioners access medical records other than their own, the analysis of such external data helps to inform diagnostic and therapeutic decisions. Considering, for instance, rare diseases, it is beneficial for physicians to study health outcomes from other patients to better understand the patient's prognosis.

Practices and measures that can address privacy concerns include:

- **Educating and training workforce**. The personnel and staff managing patient data, medical equipment, and any technology involved in the data life cycle should be aware of potential risks, the legislation, and best privacy practices.
- **Certifying that personnel possess the skills needed to manage information appropriately**. The workforce should be qualified through training and evaluation sessions. Besides explaining the rationale and motivation for sharing patient data, healthcare practitioners should also clarify what data is shared, with whom, when, and for how long.
- **Performing a comprehensive risk analysis**. The analysis of risks should be conducted when a technology is introduced and also periodically to check whether upgrades or changes are needed. Such an analysis helps to detect the flaws and weaknesses of security and privacy in a healthcare facility or system and allows for defining and implementing an action plan to mitigate potential issues.
- **Conducting periodic verifications to ensure compliance with regulatory practices**. The training of the personnel and the risk analysis helps to ensure compliance. However, when relying on third-party services for data management, health providers must also ensure that these solutions are compliant with the necessary privacy requirements and regulations.
- **Selecting carefully all health providers**. Clinics, laboratories, external services, and vendors must be verified to ensure they are trusted parties that also adhere to legal requirements when handling medical data.

Some recommendations and best practices concern the communication between practitioners and patients (or legally responsible individual). In this context, healthcare practitioners including physicians should:

- **Advise patients and caregivers to adopt reliable communication channels**. For accountability and data protection, practitioners should remind patients to use trusted and secure communication channels, like tools and websites recommended by the organization for sharing sensitive information.
- **Inform patients about the choices they have regarding information sharing**. Practitioners should inform and remind their patients when they have choices concerning the disclosure of information with external parties, at different granularity levels, e.g., controlling under which circumstances laboratories and clinics may be allowed to share medical data to other organizations or stakeholders.
- **Ask patients' permission regarding the use of data and disclosing beyond the scope of the consultation**. Practitioners need to ask for patients' authorization to use their data in unconventional ways, for instance for the purpose of scientific investigation or advertisement from merchants.
- **Inform patients about consent forms and data sharing procedures**. Practitioners should allow patients or caregivers, guardians, and legal representatives to provide informed consent and authorization for data sharing when necessary.
- **Adopt accessible language and mindful approach to seek consent**. Healthcare professionals should provide patients with information related to the benefits of sharing data in a transparent and neutral way and use clear and appropriate language and tone [25].

The benefits associated with data sharing go beyond individual's advantages in the short run to collective advantages in the long run. Transparency when dealing with sharing practices of health services is essential to build trust between agencies and users and enable legitimate informed consent. Therefore, all the risks and benefits should be properly disclosed.

10.5.2 Patients and Caregivers

The benefits for patients and caregivers when sharing protected information include the knowledge gained from the exchange of information and advice received from building a network of social support. In contrast, the major drawback of sharing information is a potential loss of control over data dissemination and opportunities for misuse.

Other benefits from data sharing are large information repositories built from the aggregated data, allowing for a stronger support for evidence-based medicine, which not only advances the current knowledge on healthcare delivery but also enhances the potential for preventive and precision medicine. Preventive medicine focuses on adopting measures that either avoid the occurrence of a condition or prevent the exacerbation of symptoms when a condition has already been diagnosed.

Precision (or personalized) medicine aims at tailoring individual treatments, medical decisions, and products to the patient profile in a unique and patient-centric way.

For patients and caregivers, measures that help to protect their privacy include:

- **Installing software updates** to keep the systems in use upgraded and prevent potential attacks and vulnerabilities.
- **Using strong authentication mechanisms** by choosing strong passwords as well as two-factor authentication to log in.
- **Employing reliable communication channels**. End users should rely only on trusted channels when communicating medical information. Preference should be given to secured networks and authenticated personal devices.
- **Refraining from posting sensitive information** in online forums, public websites, social media channels, discussion boards, and online communities.
- **Assessing impacts and risks**. Patients and caregivers should note that disclosing sensitive medical data, e.g., hereditary conditions, affects not only the patient but also their relatives. To prevent mistakes, users should be aware of major privacy risks and learn the ways to prevent issues or recover from them.
- **Taking informed decisions**. Control mechanisms should ensure that patients or their guardians and caregivers are aware of the risks and benefits of data collection, monitoring, and sharing [25, 29] to select sharing preferences. If that is not the case, patients and caregivers should seek for additional clarifications.

Although training is helpful, one cannot expect end users to be privacy experts. Therefore, privacy control mechanisms should be implemented for and with end users, striving for ease of use, high usability, efficiency, and sustained adherence. Simple measures, like relying on trusted communication channels to exchange information, can help reduce the risk of unintended access. When available, privacy controls should be intuitive and transparent, proactively informing end users, and allowing them to opt in or out of data sharing according to their individual preferences. Privacy choices must allow granular controls and inform users in accessible language.

10.5.3   Insurance Companies

Electronic health records (EHRs) are medical records storing information about consultations, allergies, diagnosis, and the medical history of a patient. EHRs handled by insurance companies contain information about the financial transactions related to treatments, medical procedures, and the list of practitioners in the patient's network. To ensure privacy, the network of health providers of the insurer should encompass trusted parties, including not only practitioners, but also clinics offering examination or therapeutical services, as well as vendors of medical equipment and assistive technologies.

Another recommendation includes informing the patients about current practices around management of their health data. Terms and conditions must be made available to end users for verification. Systems from insurers should also provide interfaces for privacy controls that are easy to use, adopt, and sustain engagement. Design decisions for user interfaces and interaction must follow standard usability practices, ensuring that the settings are accessible for patients and caregivers and adequate to meet their specific health and digital literacy skills [29].

Lastly, insurance systems managing health records should give users enough flexibility for negotiation and decision making about the ways their data is shared. Flexibility includes giving users the ability to revoke or control data access by setting who has access to the data, when, and under what circumstances and conditions. In summary, the recommendations for insurance companies include:

- **Selecting trusted parties to work with**, ensuring that services in the network are reliable and comply with privacy policies
- **Ensuring compliance with existing healthcare privacy policies**, by following their guidelines and standards, conducting risk analysis and periodic assessments, providing training to personnel, and conducting compliance checks
- **Informing patients, caregivers, and legal responsible** about current privacy practices, describing in an accessible language what practices are employed to secure patients' data and not disclose it
- **Giving users control over data sharing** practices by allowing patients to select who has access to their data and under what conditions

10.5.4 Technologists

Privacy must be prioritized in the implementation of healthcare infrastructures. Rather than an add-on patchwork, privacy concerns should be thoroughly considered since the beginning of the design and development phases to ensure confidentiality, integrity, and availability of medical data. Existing systems implemented without privacy controls should be updated accordingly, to comply with recent privacy standards and policies.

To ensure privacy is preserved, a holistic approach should be adopted. Technologists need to consider the datasets in use, the entire ecosystem of devices, and the underlying systems and networks. At the data level, measures such as de-identification and anonymization have proven insufficient to guarantee that personally identifiable information is not disclosed [9]. A notorious case is the public release of the search history of 20 million search queries collected by AOL. Although the names of the users were not disclosed, the content of the queries was sufficient to trace the users' identities back. While the intention of publicly releasing the data was to support research, it ended up revealing private information, including health-related topics that users did not authorize [29]. Thus, more comprehensive and up-to-date solutions are required. Differential privacy, nudging privacy, and contextual privacy are some of the frameworks that should be adopted to facilitate the implementation of privacy-preserving technologies.

Overall, for data collection, only data essential to the analysis should be extracted, to minimize unintended disclosure risk. However, there are many benefits of scientific investigations exploring the potential of data for knowledge discovery. In these cases, patients should be informed about the data collected and given the choice to decide how it is used for scientific discoveries. In terms of implementation, a modularized architecture helps to prevent unintended access, by ensuring that certain modules of the program and application are only accessible to users with certain privileges in the system. The patient profile, for instance, could be implemented as a module, isolated from consultation schedule, medical history, etc. Regarding storage, the data should be encrypted to prevent unauthorized access and tampering. Access control mechanisms should be implemented to protect assets from unauthorized access.

At the physical level, the networks should be protected with firewalls, and the authentication mechanisms should be secured to ensure proper access control, for instance reinforcing two-factor authentication. Medical devices, such as pacemakers and defibrillators, should be subject to risk analysis and made secure to prevent attacks [24]. At the system level, access control mechanisms should ensure that only authorized personnel can access medical data upon authentication, employing highly controlled environments to avoid vulnerabilities. Also, the activity of the users should be logged, enabling auditing procedures in case a breach occurs.

Concluding the recommendations for technologists, the following are highlighted:

- **Prioritizing privacy in the design and development process** to cover it in the network, architectural, and database design and implementation in a holistic manner that spans across devices and systems
- **Adopting a modularized system architecture** to prevent access to services, resources, and data across parts of the application
- **Implementing encryption in data transfer or storage** to ensure that in case of unauthorized access during transmission, the content is not disclosed to external parties
- **Verifying the compliance of the systems** with current norms, to check whether the technology preserves data and users' privacy according to the standards and policies in practice
- **Adopting up-to-date privacy practices** to facilitate user control and ensure that the disclosed data is anonymized and de-identified as necessary

10.5.5   Regulators

In crafting the legislation, perspectives of technologists, domain experts, and legislators need to be triangulated, combining a bottom-up approach considering the needs of citizens and patients with a top-down one considering the government resources and obligations. For policy makers and regulators to decide what must be implemented in a healthcare facility to assure privacy of medical records and patients, they have to also consult with domain experts and technologists, to better understand the context in which a health service is delivered, and the capabilities and limitations of the digital realm. Altogether with legal consultants, domain experts and technologists can inform regulators on the governmental and legislation requirements for medical data.

Technologists will be aware of the potential vulnerabilities and breaches, knowing the strengths and weaknesses of the technology, and best practices to prevent problems and recover from them. Domain experts understand what data types are at stake and are familiar with the needs of patients and caregivers. Such knowledge combined helps to inform regulators in making decisions about privacy in healthcare. The technologists also need to notify regulators promptly, so that the regulators are kept up to date and they can update the legislation accordingly, when novel risks emerge, or vulnerabilities and breaches are discovered.

To facilitate this effort, the US Department of Health and Human Services' Office for Civil Rights started publishing healthcare data breach reports. By sharing what organizations were compromised, how they were affected, and the financial impacts of the attacks, the public reporting of breaches helps users to understand how their data is compromised so they take appropriate actions to prevent future problems. Additionally, it helps them to choose more trustworthy organizations. While still offering a reactive solution, breach reports inform technologists on potential issues, so that they can work on preventing, mitigating, and addressing such problems in more efficient ways by defining best implementation practices, standards, and guidelines.

Besides creating policies and guidelines, another responsibility of such stakeholders is enforcing that privacy requirements are properly addressed, to ensure that policies created for data protection and privacy are enacted. This effort should not only incentivize organizations to adopt privacy-preserving solutions but also punish organizations not compliant with current norms, standards, and policies.

In summary, the recommendations for regulators are defined as follows:

- **Communicate early with domain experts and technologists**, since their perspectives are essential to decide on the legislation and since combining a bottom-up with a top-down approach helps to holistically address privacy.
- **Enforce legislation** using proactive incentives and reactive penalties to punish organizations not conforming to existing regulations.
- **Maintain up-to-date policies** to cover emerging technologies before incidents occur, consulting with technologists.
- **Facilitate the implementation of regulations** by informing organizations, using accessible language, and making training and education available.

10.5.6   Third-Party Organizations

Third-party organizations include commercial services that may take advantage of medical data using analyses and inference for advertisement and marketing purposes. It can also include banks, e-commerce applications, or even academic institutions conducting scientific investigation. Such service providers might benefit from patient's medical data and infer medical information about patients. Such information should be protected from unintended disclosure and regulated by respective policies.

Although HIPAA protects users' data from exploitation, clinics and organizations may set up agreements with service providers. In cases when third-party services are requested, users should be informed and have the choice to not disclose information. Even though external service providers oftentimes take advantage of the data collected, in addition to complying to current regulations, third-party services must ideally:

- **Be clear and transparent** with end users about the usage of their data.
- **Maintain secure practices to manage medical information**, by informing users in advance on the use of their personal data, and obtain informed consent to authorize the use of the data.
- **Provide users with flexibility to decide on the usage of their data**, including opt-in and opt-out choices as well as the ability to withdraw the authorization for sharing at any point in time, revoking data access.

10.6   Conclusion

This chapter provides an overview of privacy in the healthcare domain, listing the dimensions that should be considered when implementing privacy-preserving controls in this domain. To address the many risks involved with handling medical data in a digital infrastructure, a holistic approach is needed, cutting across implementation phases, multiple stakeholders, and assets. Privacy-enhancing solutions need to consider the dimensions in which privacy breaches may occur, from the data collection, through processing, storage, analysis, and sharing. In addition to considering the data life cycle, such dimensions also include multiple stakeholders, equipment, artifacts, and assets, guiding not only patients and caregivers as end users, but also healthcare practitioners, providers, insurance companies, laboratories, and clinics.

Despite the undeniable importance of privacy controls when managing health data, the implementation of these dimensions is complex, several questions remain open, and numerous considerations should be taken into account to ensure that patients' data is preserved and privacy controls effectively provide them the necessary levels of transparency, control, and trust. Future research and development in the domain should ensure that patient privacy improves health outcomes and advances healthcare for patients and communities, rather than seen as a barrier impeding public health.

References

1. Lazar, A., and E.E. Dixon. 2019. Safe enough to share: Setting the dementia agenda online. *Proceedings of the ACM on Human-Computer Interaction* 3 (CSCW): 1–23.
2. Lorenzen-Huber, L., M. Boutain, L.J. Camp, K. Shankar, and K.H. Connelly. 2011. Privacy, technology, and aging: A proposed framework. *Ageing International* 36 (2): 232–252.
3. Motti, V.G. 2019, October. Designing emerging technologies for and with neurodiverse users. In *Proceedings of the 37th ACM International Conference on the Design of Communication*, 1–10.
4. Choi, Y.K., A. Lazar, G. Demiris, and H.J. Thompson. 2019. Emerging smart home technologies to facilitate engaging with aging. *Journal of Gerontological Nursing* 45 (12): 41–48.
5. Pradhan, A., A. Lazar, and L. Findlater. 2020. Use of intelligent voice assistants by older adults with low technology use. *ACM Transactions on Computer-Human Interaction (TOCHI)* 27 (4): 1–27.
6. Takemoto, M., T.M. Manini, D.E. Rosenberg, A. Lazar, Z.Z. Zlatar, S.K. Das, and J. Kerr. 2018. Diet and activity assessments and interventions using technology in older adults. *American Journal of Preventive Medicine* 55 (4): e105–e115.
7. Motti, V.G., and K. Caine. 2015. Users' privacy concerns about wearables. In *International Conference on Financial Cryptography and Data Security*, 231–244. Springer.
8. Lu, X., T.L. Reynolds, E. Jo, H. Hong, X. Page, Y. Chen, and D.A. Epstein. 2021. Comparing perspectives around human and technology support for contact tracing. In *CHI Conference on Human Factors in Computing Systems (CHI '21), Yokohama, Japan*, May 8–13, 2021. New York, NY: ACM.
9. Carrotte, E.R., I. Prichard, and M.S.C. Lim. 2017. "Fitspiration" on social media: A content analysis of gendered images. *Journal of Medical Internet Research* 19 (3): e95.
10. Abdullah, S., and T. Choudhury. 2018. Sensing technologies for monitoring serious mental illnesses. *IEEE MultiMedia* 25 (1): 61–75.
11. O'neil, C. 2016. *Weapons of Math Destruction: How Big Data Increases Inequality and Threatens Democracy*. Broadway Books.
12. Hill, K. 2012. How target figured out a teen girl was pregnant before her father did. *Forbes*. https://www.forbes.com/sites/kashmirhill/2012/02/16/how-target-figured-out-a-teen-girl-was-pregnant-before-her-father-did/#53c93a8e6668
13. Shapiro, D. 2019. How a DNA testing kit revealed a family secret hidden for 54 years. *Time*. time.com/5492642/dna-test-results-family-secret-biological-father/
14. U.S. Government Printing Office. 1996. *Insurance Portability and Accountability Act of 1996*. 104th US Congress, Washington, D.C. https://www.hhs.gov/hipaa/for-professionals/privacy/laws-regulations/
15. De Choudhury, M., and S. De. 2014, May. Mental health discourse on reddit: Self-disclosure, social support, and anonymity. In *Eighth International AAAI Conference on Weblogs and Social Media*.
16. Namara, M., D. Wilkinson, B.M. Lowens, B.P. Knijnenburg, R. Orji, and R.L. Sekou. 2018, December. Cross-cultural perspectives on eHealth privacy in Africa. In *Proceedings of the Second African Conference for Human Computer Interaction: Thriving Communities*, 7. ACM.
17. Marabelli, M., S. Newell, and X. Page. 2018. *Algorithmic Decision-Making in the US Healthcare Industry*. Presented at IFIP, 8.

18. Motti, V.G., and N. Kalantari. 2019. Understanding how social media imagery empowers care-givers: An analysis of microcephaly in Latin America. In *The 13th International Conference on Pervasive Computing Technologies for Healthcare (PervasiveHealth'19), Trento, Italy*, May 20–23, 2019. ACM.

19. Centers for Disease Control and Prevention. 2003. HIPAA privacy rule and public health. Guidance from CDC and the US Department of Health and Human Services. *MMWR: Morbidity and Mortality Weekly Report* 52 (1): 1–17.

20. Almulhem, A. 2012. Threat modeling for electronic health record systems. *Journal of Medical Systems* 36 (5): 2921–2926.

21. Brodey, D. 2019. Disability advocates poke holes in White House Plan to snoop on Facebook pages for disability fraud. *Forbes*. https://www.forbes.com/sites/denisebrodey/2019/03/11/disability-advocates-poke-holes-in-white-house-plan-to-snoop-on-facebook-pages-for-disability-fraud/

22. Goldman, J. 1998. Protecting privacy to improve health care: As the deadline for passing health privacy legislation in Congress nears, consensus is needed on a framework that values both patients' privacy and public health goals. *Health Affairs* 17 (6): 47–60.

23. Watson, J., H.R. Lipford, and A. Besmer. 2015. Mapping user preference to privacy default settings. *ACM Transactions on Computer-Human Interaction (TOCHI)* 22 (6): 32.

24. Halperin, D., T.S. Heydt-Benjamin, B. Ransford, S.S. Clark, B. Defend, W. Morgan, ...& W.H. Maisel. 2008, May. Pacemakers and implantable cardiac defibrillators: Software radio attacks and zero-power defenses. In *2008 IEEE Symposium on Security and Privacy*, 129–142. IEEE.

25. Caine, K., S. Kohn, C. Lawrence, R. Hanania, E.M. Meslin, and W.M. Tierney. 2015. Designing a patient-centered user interface for access decisions about EHR data: Implications from patient interviews. *Journal of General Internal Medicine* 30 (1): 7–16.

26. Voigt, P., and A. Von dem Bussche. 2017. *The EU General Data Protection Regulation (GDPR). A Practical Guide*. 1st ed. Cham: Springer International.

27. Goldstein, M.M., and H.T. Jane. 2010. The first anniversary of the Health Information Technology for Economic and Clinical Health (HITECH) Act: The regulatory outlook for implementation. *Perspectives in Health Information Management/AHIMA* 7 (Summer).

28. Scaraglino, P. 2002. Complying with HIPAA: A guide for the university and its counsel. *JC & UL* 29: 525.

29. Barbaro, M., and T. Zeller. 2006. *A Face is Exposed for AOL Searcher No. 4417749*. https://www.nytimes.com/2006/08/09/technology/09aol.html

30. US Department of Education. 1974. Family educational rights and privacy act (FERPA).

31. Hudson, K.L., and F.S. Collins. 2017. The 21st Century Cures Act—a view from the NIH. *New England Journal of Medicine* 376 (2): 111–113.

32. Federal Trade Commission, and Federal Trade Commission. 2016. Children's online privacy protection rule ("COPPA").

33. Blumenthal, D., M. Abrams, & R. Nuzum. 2015. The affordable care act at 5 years.

34. Office for Civil Rights. 2017. *The HIPAA Security Rule*. https://www.hhs.gov/hipaa/for-professionals/security/index.html

35. Sambasivan, N., G. Checkley, A. Batool, N. Ahmed, D. Nemer, L.S. Gaytán-Lugo, ... E. Churchill. 2018. "Privacy is not for me, it's for those rich women": Performative privacy practices on mobile phones by women in South Asia. In *Fourteenth Symposium on Usable Privacy and Security (SOUPS 2018)*, 127–142.

36. Henrich, J., S.J. Heine, and A. Norenzayan. 2010. The weirdest people in the world? *Behavioral and Brain Sciences* 33 (2-3): 61–83.

37. Berkovsky, S., R. Taib, Y. Hijikata, P. Braslavsky, and B. Knijnenburg. 2018. A cross-cultural analysis of trust in recommender systems. In *Proceedings of the 26th Conference on User Modeling, Adaptation and Personalization*, 285–289.

38. Bol, N., and J. Romano Bergstrom. 2015. Designing for vulnerable users: Illustrations (may) help understand complex health websites. *User Experience* 15.

39. Americans With Disabilities Act. 1991. Public Law 101–336. *Federal Register* 56 (144): 35,545–35,555.

40. Auxier, B.E., C.L. Buntain, P. Jaeger, J. Golbeck, and H. Kacorri. 2019, April. # HandsOffMyADA: A Twitter response to the ADA Education and Reform Act. In *Proceedings of the 2019 CHI Conference on Human Factors in Computing Systems*, 527. ACM.
41. Blumenthal, D. 2010. Launching HITECH. *New England Journal of Medicine* 362 (5): 382–385.
42. De Choudhury, M., M. Gamon, S. Counts, and E. Horvitz. 2013, June. Predicting depression via social media. In *Seventh International AAAI Conference on Weblogs and Social Media*.
43. Greene, E., P. Proctor, and D. Kotz. 2018. Secure sharing of mHealth data streams through cryptographically-enforced access control. *Smart Health*.
44. Grundy, Q., K. Chiu, F. Held, A. Continella, L. Bero, and R. Holz. 2019. Data sharing practices of medicines related apps and the mobile ecosystem: Traffic, content, and network analysis. *BMJ* 364: l920.
45. Limbago, A.L. 2019. *Combating Digital Authoritarianism: U.S. Alternative Needed to Counter Data Localization and Government Control*. The National Security Institute. Technical Report.
46. Lowens, B., V.G. Motti, and K. Caine. 2017, August. Wearable privacy: Skeletons in the data closet. In *2017 IEEE International Conference on Healthcare Informatics (ICHI)*, 295–304. IEEE.
47. Mahdawi, A. 2019. There's a dark side to women's health apps: Menstrual surveillance. *The Guardian*.
48. McHugh, B.C., P. Wisniewski, M.B. Rosson, and J.M. Carroll. 2018. When social media traumatizes teens: The roles of online risk exposure, coping, and post-traumatic stress. *Internet Research* 28 (5): 1169–1188.
49. Melton, L. Joseph. 2000. Medical privacy. *Issues in Science and Technology* 17 (1): 12–13.
50. Motti, V.G., and K. Caine. 2015, September. An overview of wearable applications for healthcare: Requirements and challenges. In *Adjunct Proceedings of the 2015 ACM International Joint Conference on Pervasive and Ubiquitous Computing and Proceedings of the 2015 ACM International Symposium on Wearable Computers*, 635–641. ACM.
51. Nurgalieva, L., A. Frik, F. Ceschel, S. Egelman, and M. Marchese. 2019. Information design in an aged care context: Views of older adults on information sharing in a care triad. In *The 13th International Conference on Pervasive Computing Technologies for Healthcare (PervasiveHealth'19), Trento, Italy*, May 20–23, 2019. New York, NY: ACM.
52. Office for Civil Rights. 2013. *The HIPAA Breach Notification Rule*.
53. O'Herrin, J.K., N. Fost, and K.A. Kudsk. 2004. Health Insurance Portability Accountability Act (HIPAA) regulations: Effect on medical record research. *Annals of Surgery* 239 (6): 772.
54. Reece, A.G., A.J. Reagan, K.L. Lix, P.S. Dodds, C.M. Danforth, and E.J. Langer. 2017. Forecasting the onset and course of mental illness with Twitter data. *Scientific Reports* 7 (1): 13006.
55. Serrano, K.J., M. Yu, W.T. Riley, V. Patel, P. Hughes, K. Marchesini, and A.A. Atienza. 2016. Willingness to exchange health information via mobile devices: Findings from a population-based survey. *The Annals of Family Medicine* 14 (1): 34–40.
56. Trubow, G.B., and D.L. Hudson. 1978. The Right to Financial Privacy Act of 1978: New protection from federal intrusion. *The John Marshall Journal of Practice and Procedure* 12: 487.
57. Department of Health and Human Services – The Office of the National Coordinator for Health Information Technology. *Understanding Electronic Health Records, the HIPAA Security Rule, and Cybersecurity*.
58. U.S. Department of Health and Human Services. *HITECH Programs*. http://healthit.hhs.gov/portal/server.pt?open=512&objID=1487&parentname=CommunityPage&parentid=28&mode=2&in_hi_userid=11113
59. Zhang, S. 2019. The fertility Doctor's secret. *The Atlantic*. https://www.theatlantic.com/magazine/archive/2019/04/fertility-doctor-donald-cline-secret-children/583249/

Chapter 11
Privacy and the Internet of Things

Heather Richter Lipford, Madiha Tabassum, Paritosh Bahirat, Yaxing Yao, and Bart P. Knijnenburg

Abstract Using networks of Internet-connected sensors, the Internet of Things (IoT) makes technologies "smart" by enabling automation, personalization, and remote control. At the same time, IoT technologies introduce challenging privacy issues that may frustrate their widespread adoption. This chapter addresses the privacy challenges of IoT technologies from a user-centered perspective and demonstrates these prevalent issues in the domains of wearables (e.g., fitness trackers), household technologies (e.g., smart voice assistants), and devices that exist in the public domain (e.g., security cameras). The chapter ends with a comprehensive list of solutions and guidelines that can help researchers and practitioners introduce usable privacy to the domain of IoT.

11.1 Defining IoT

The Internet of Things (IoT) is revolutionizing our use of computing, introducing networked devices throughout our everyday lives that collect and utilize information to provide an ever-growing number of services. Coined by Kevin Ashton during a presentation at Proctor and Gamble, the Internet of Things primarily originated

H. R. Lipford (✉) · M. Tabassum
College of Computing and Informatics, UNC Charlotte, Charlotte, NC, USA
e-mail: richter@uncc.edu; mtabassu@uncc.edu

P. Bahirat · B. P. Knijnenburg
School of Computing, Clemson University, Clemson, SC, USA
e-mail: pbahira@clemson.edu; bartk@clemson.edu

Y. Yao
Department of Information Systems, University of Maryland Baltimore County, Baltimore, MD, USA
e-mail: yaxingya@umbc.edu

B. P. Knijnenburg et al. (eds.), *Modern Socio-Technical Perspectives on Privacy*,
https://doi.org/10.1007/978-3-030-82786-1_11

with the idea of RFID tags to be used for the purpose of streamlining supply chain operation [1]. A broad definition of IoT is:

> The Internet of Things refers to the unique identification and 'Internetization' of everyday objects. This allows for human interaction and control of these 'things' from anywhere in the world, as well as device-to-device interaction without the need for human involvement

While IoT was originally conceptualized for industrial and manufacturing domains, the concept has found its place in numerous areas, ranging from public domains such as smart cities to the most intimate parts of our lives with smart homes and fitness trackers. From energy and health monitoring to remote operation and surveillance, IoT devices provide exciting services to improve our lives [2]. Yet these devices also bring unique privacy challenges due to their integration into the world around us, and the extensive amount of data that they can collect and use. We first introduce the various domains of IoT, to summarize the kinds of data they collect and their uses before delving into the challenging privacy issues that the Internet of Things raises.

Broadly speaking, there are three core domains that fit under the umbrella of IoT. They are:

- **Wearable IoT**—devices that people can wear as accessories, such as watches, for monitoring an individual's activities or vital signs.
- **Household IoT**—devices that sit in people's homes, such as smart speakers, appliances, and thermostats.
- **Public IoT**—devices that are used in public places, such as smart water meters, autonomous vehicles, and Bluetooth beacons.

11.1.1 Wearable IoT Domain

IoT-enabled wearables are internet-connected devices integrated with various sensors that can be worn as external accessories (i.e., watches, glasses, rings, etc.) or implanted in textiles such as smart shoes or jackets. Many commercially available wearables are specifically targeted for health and fitness monitoring, such as Fitbit and Apple Watch. Sensors collect the movement and vital signs of individuals, such as steps taken, heart rate, and sleep quality, in order to track activities and to help people monitor and improve their wellness and physical performance [3]. Other devices aim to help users monitor their interaction with the world around them, such as Google Glass, allowing people to capture audio and video of their daily lives. All wearable devices share a common goal of automatically and unobtrusively recording an individual's physical interaction with the world.

Despite the fact that much of this information can be related to an individual's health, research suggests that users are comfortable sharing their information with a range of other people and organizations to support their health goals because they perceive much of that information, such as step count, as not particularly sensitive [4]

11.1.2   Household IoT Domain

A smart home refers to a residence that has lighting, heating, air-conditioning, security systems, or entertainment systems which communicate with one another and work together to improve the experience and increase the comfort of the occupants. Smart home devices allow for remote monitoring and operation of parts of a home, such as the thermostat, lights, or door locks. Many smart devices aim to increase the convenience and automation of the home, such as with smart speakers and appliances. Devices can also enable safety and security monitoring, using cameras, audio, and fire or water leak sensors. Additional people and organizations may also be involved in safety monitoring, with information and devices being shared with family members, security companies, or emergency services.

The perception of the privacy of smart home data varies by device. Some information is not perceived as very sensitive, such as the status of smart lights or thermostats. Yet, video and audio from inside the home are usually considered private and users desire strong protections against recordings being accessed without their knowledge or control [5, 6].

11.1.3   Public IoT Domain

IoT technology has also gained popularity in public infrastructure through smart cities and smart buildings. Public IoT infrastructure brings a number of benefits in the management and optimization of traditional public services, such as transportation and parking, lighting, ventilation, surveillance and maintenance of public areas, and even preservation of cultural heritage. For example, the New York City Department of Transportation integrated a congestion management system to determine traffic speed at 23 intersections in Midtown Manhattan that has improved the travel time by 10% in Midtown's avenues [7]. Similar to smart homes, smart cities and buildings also provide services to monitor the security and safety of spaces and people and intelligently automate controls in response to the environment. In addition, IoT is frequently used for resource management, lowering costs by more efficiently and intelligently utilizing resources. For example, the city of Dallas, Georgia, has undertaken a smart water meter program, which helped them to detect water leaks more efficiently and minimize water loss [8].

Another emerging type of IoT device in the public domain is the autonomous vehicle, which is increasingly adopted in app-based taxi services (e.g., Uber), home delivery services, and consumer products (e.g., Tesla). Each autonomous vehicle is equipped with a large amount of sensors to collect information about the surrounding environment, including people who are walking on the street, other vehicles on the road, and nearby store information [9]. In addition, the drivers and passengers who sit in the car also face a large amount of data collection during and after their ride (e.g., vehicles may collect information about their daily schedule) [10].

11.1.4   Outline

In the following sections, we will further discuss the unique privacy challenges introduced by the use of IoT devices. To further illustrate these challenges in practice, we then discuss them in more detail through three case studies of fitness trackers, smart home voice assistants, and CCTV and surveillance cameras. While research into solutions to these challenges is still limited, we end the chapter with a discussion of potential ways to reduce the privacy risks users face and address user needs in managing their privacy with IoT.

11.2   Privacy Challenges

Similar to other technologies, IoT devices face many types of privacy issues. However, due to the volume of data collected, the ubiquitous nature of IoT devices, and their ability to blend into the background, they also introduce new challenges and greatly exacerbate existing privacy challenges when compared with traditional computing applications. In this section, we highlight the key challenges, which include the following:

- People **lack awareness** of the data practices of IoT devices and their manufacturers, due to the large amount of data involved in potentially complex ecosystems of devices, as well as the unobtrusive methods of data collection.
- The **accumulation** of large amounts of data enables the **inference** of sensitive information, unbeknownst to users.
- IoT devices can be used by **multiple users** and in environments containing **multiple other people**, increasing the complexity of privacy needs and access controls.
- IoT devices offer **limited controls** for users to manage the privacy of themselves and their information. Many scenarios and domains involve **bystanders**, who currently have **no ability to control** devices whatsoever.
- **Security mechanisms and processes** to protect the devices and data collected may not be robust or mature, putting users' privacy at risk due to attacks and data breaches.

11.2.1   No Awareness/No Interface

The decisions people make regarding their usage of a given computing device is governed by their *mental model* of the device, which is comprised of their assumptions and intuitions regarding what data they think is collected, how that data is used, how it is stored and shared, etc. This awareness is primarily based on the experiences people have with their devices over time—the kinds of exchanges they have with an application and the information involved in those exchanges. IoT devices differ from traditional computing and mobile devices in that they are more embedded into the surrounding environment, often without a dedicated screen, resembling non-computing devices and yet unobtrusively capturing and utilizing a range of information.

For instance, the "Hello Barbie" doll looks like a typical kids' toy, "Alexa" functions as a music speaker, and fitness trackers usually resemble traditional watches. Data collection is mostly invisible and automatic. Beyond the devices owned by the user, any environment they enter may potentially have devices owned by others, each collecting their own unique set of information. Together, this means that users cannot rely on their former perceptions of what interacting with a doll, a speaker, or a watch means. Users may also become habituated to their devices, and hence gradually become less aware of the pervasive data collection. In other words, users must form new mental models of IoT devices, and as these mental models are based on the incomplete information they receive from their interaction with the devices, it is not surprising that they tend to make incorrect assumptions about the privacy of their IoT devices (e.g., they may think that their child's "Hello Barbie" doll does not collect and store any data). These incorrect assumptions can lead to privacy intrusions. Alternatively, users may choose to not adopt a given device over privacy fears that arise from being uncertain about the data collection practices of the device. In this case, their uncertainty leads them to forego the adoption of technology that they would otherwise be comfortable with.

Studies of current smart home users have demonstrated that people are generally aware of the collection and use of information that is apparent in the functioning of the device [11]. For example, users understand that a smart thermostat captures temperature changes, a security camera records video, and a smart lock logs when the door is locked and unlocked. Users expect that this collected information is used by the device to properly function and provide useful services, and potentially by the manufacturers to improve their devices. Yet, while users do expect this information to be stored in the "cloud," and not on the device itself, there is little awareness over exactly what that means [11]. Users are unclear on how, where and for how long their information is stored, who it could be shared with, and what other uses could occur [11, 12]. Studies have demonstrated similar perceptions for wearable devices [13, 14]. Yet, few have studied the perceptions of IoT devices in more public settings, where users likely have less awareness of the presence of devices and little interaction with them.

The standard method for users to know about what data is collected and how it is used is the privacy policy or the end-user license agreement provided by vendors. These methods are already problematic for traditional computing devices, with few people reading them. Yet they are even more difficult to rely on for IoT devices. Studies have shown that the boxes and print materials of smart home devices rarely describe the device's data collection practices [15, 16]. As devices themselves have a small screen or no screen at all, users must instead visit a separate website or use an accompanying app to view the policy. Even if someone actively looks for information on a vendor's website, the privacy policy may provide information only about the website data practices, not the data practices regarding the device's sensor data [15]. Furthermore, the only people likely to view any sort of policy statement are those doing the setup and installation of the device. Others who are in the purview of the device (e.g., other home or building occupants) will not have this opportunity. This is particularly the case for IoT devices in public spaces, where those whose data is collected may not be aware of the existence of the device at all. As such, providing transparency regarding the ownership and policies of the data collected by IoT devices in smart buildings or public infrastructure is even more challenging.

A final challenge is the complex ecosystem in which many IoT devices are embedded. Not only the device itself exchanges information with the manufacturer; users often interact with an accompanying mobile app to access and control the device and its information, and this app itself may perform additional data collection, such as tracking the location of the user. Furthermore, devices may be interconnected with—and share data with—smart hubs and other devices, which may be built by a different manufacturer. Finally, third-party applications may operate on top of any of these platforms and involve an additional exchange of information between organizations. Even for tech-savvy users it is very difficult to fully understand how information is collected, stored, and shared by each of these entities. Yet, many users have a fairly simple service-oriented view of how different devices interact. For example, a smart home user may know that they can turn on their TV using their Google Home device, but they will have little knowledge of what information is exchanged between the TV and Google to accomplish this task [11, 17].

We summarize these challenges as follows:

- **Devices are unobtrusive** and often do not "look" like they are collecting extensive amounts of data.
- **Users do not understand the extent of data collection** and how data may be used for secondary purposes.
- **Users do not read the privacy policy** or may simply not have access to it.
- **The IoT ecosystem is complex** and understanding, let alone managing, the data collection practices of multiple actors is a huge undertaking.

11.2.2   Accumulation and Inference of Data

Another unique issue with IoT devices is the sheer volume of data that is collected, from so many different sources. Taken by itself, each individual piece of data seems innocuous—step counts or the status of a light in a house are not considered sensitive [4]. Yet over time, this accumulation of information can allow applications to learn powerful patterns of human preferences and behaviors. For example, the data from wrist-worn IoT devices such as smartwatches and fitness trackers can be used to infer users' physical activities such as walking, running, and jumping, with high accuracy [18]. While this may be somewhat expected, wrist-worn devices can even allow inferences about what the user is typing [19]. Similarly, from smart meter data, it is possible to recognize bathroom activities, cooking, and housework [20].

The threat of profiling increases when the large amount of data collected by IoT devices is *aggregated* to reveal previously inaccessible parts of people's lives. The aggregation of data from multiple devices can provide sensitive information about the users that cannot be determined from an individual data source alone. For instance, a thermostat with temperature zone control knows about the collective movement of occupants in the house. When users control the thermostat using a smartphone, then the thermostat can learn exactly who is where in the home and when. Inferences based on data aggregated from multiple devices of data can cause an unexpected revelation of users' identity, personal traits, activities, habits, preferences, sexual orientation, health status, financial situation, and more, even when data is collected anonymously [15]. A system's ability to make such inferences is beyond most users' comprehension. Indeed, even if users have some idea about the data collected by each individual device, they will likely be unable to understand the privacy implications of the aggregated data from multiple devices.

Information can even be inferred from the metadata and communication patterns of devices without gaining access to the data itself. For example, network traffic rates from a Sense sleep monitor reveal consumer sleep patterns, network traffic rates from a Belkin WeMo switch reveal when a physical appliance in a smart home is turned on or off, and network traffic rates from a Nest Cam Indoor security camera reveal when a user is actively monitoring the camera feed or when the camera detects motion in a user's home [21]. This is alarming, as Internet Service Providers (ISP) have easy access to traffic data, and the US legislature voted in 2017 to allow ISPs to use and sell the data collected from their customers' network traffic [22].

Several studies have examined users' expectations and concerns when it comes to IoT inferences. Studies of wearable devices reveal that users are concerned about sharing data with insurance companies, for example, as the information could be used to raise rates [4, 23]. While users have some expectations that their behaviors and habits could be inferred, they are unsure and lack awareness of the kinds of scenarios that are already plausible [23, 24].

The most immediate and obvious use of aggregated data is to create a reasonably accurate profile of a user for the purpose of advertising. For instance, Amazon and Google have patented the use of digital voice assistants to extract keywords from ambient speech and to use those keywords to provide relevant advertisements [25]. Studies of IoT inferences have shown that based on their experiences with web browsers and Internet applications, users do have expectations that organizations will use their information to target advertisements [11, 12]. Users are not overly concerned with such advertisements, even though they can at times be creepy. However, users are concerned that such information could also be used to manipulate their behavior; for instance, users can be influenced to buy a certain product they do not want or nudged to spend more money [26].

There are few mechanisms to educate users about the potential implications of inferred information, and few concrete threats have yet been reported. Yet, we have already seen concern and even backlash over profiling and inferences in other domains, particularly social media. For example, several scandals, such as the Cambridge Analytica scandal, have left millions of Facebook users surprised and dismayed over the use of their information to create political profiles or infer their moods outside of their awareness [27–29]. Such examples will only increase as organizations figure out how to capitalize on their IoT data.

We summarize the data accumulation and inference challenges as follows:

- **The sheer volume of IoT data threatens user privacy** as it can be used to infer users' private activities.
- **The aggregation of data across multiple devices** further increases the threat and is much harder for an end-user to comprehend.
- **Even metadata can reveal sensitive information** and such data is available to users' ISPs who are allowed to sell it.
- **Unwanted inferences are likely to generate backlash** especially if they go beyond targeted advertising (e.g., the Cambridge Analytica scandal).

11.2.3 Multiple Users

IoT devices are used by and around a variety of people. This is particularly salient for IoT devices that support smart building and city infrastructure: these devices are intended to track activities and behaviors of potentially large numbers of people. For instance, the city of San Diego has cameras built into its streetlights, which capture pedestrian traffic [30]. Likewise, driving patterns can be captured by the connected cars program piloted by New York City [31]. Even in a household setting, IoT devices capture data of a large number of people, including the multiple family members or roommates who live in the home, family and friends who visit, and house cleaners and contractors who help with maintenance. A user may also share remote access to their smart home devices with people outside of their home. For instance, neighbors could check on each other's homes in case of a fire or burglar alarm, or share access to each other's security or doorbell cameras to monitor community safety and security. Friends or family members could remotely check on pets, or let in people delivering packages, should the homeowner not be available [11]. And while wearable and health devices are primarily designed for single users, they are also commonly shared among different household members to gain their benefits without the expense of additional devices [32]. Wearable users may also share information with caregivers or doctors to receive timely medical intervention [23].

One critical privacy implication of this multi-user environment is that users may have complex preferences for how to share access to and control over their IoT devices and the collected data with others, especially if they have different social relationships with those others. For instance, if IoT devices are shared between immediate family members such as a spouse or adult children, users will likely be comfortable sharing sensitive controls (i.e., the ability to order something through the smart speaker) and information (i.e., the ability to see health profiles in fitness trackers) because of the high level of trust. However, when sharing with less trusted users (i.e., visitors, roommates, neighbors, house help) or under-aged users (i.e., kids, teenagers), people may have more restrictive access control preferences based on device capabilities and other contexts [11, 33]. For instance, home owners tend to be more comfortable sharing the live view feature of an outdoor camera with neighbors than with sharing the same capability of an indoor camera [33]. However, users may want to share that same indoor camera with neighbors when they are out of town or in case of an alarm [11].

The complexity of IoT users' access control needs can be addressed by time-based access control to share temporary access (e.g., a one-time key to drop off a package), location-based access control to share access based on the location of the user (e.g., monitoring the house when the user is away), role-based access control to grant or restrict certain capabilities for certain user roles (e.g., to prevent young children from ordering products via a smart speaker), and event-based access control to share only specific capabilities required for a particular event (e.g., to alert emergency services in case of an alarm). However, current devices are very limited in the kinds of controls they provide. Furthermore, current controls make it difficult to understand what access rights are being shared [11]. Hence, there is a risk of oversharing sensitive information (e.g., video recording of household members) or control (e.g., allowing the deletion of video recordings) with other users. This lack of transparency and existence of adequate access control mechanisms leads users to share everything with their most trusted community, often by sharing full account credentials, and to not share the device at all with people who are less trusted [11]. Yet while additional controls may enable more fine-grained access, they run the risk of introducing too much complexity, which may overwhelm users, leading instead to even more loss of user control. Hence, the challenge is to understand the most prevalent sharing scenarios and needs for different devices and platforms to decide (1) how to prioritize between different access control mechanisms for different devices and (2) how to balance users' complex access sharing requirements with their need to share devices without much effort.

Even for devices shared freely between multiple people, different users may have different preferences regarding what information and capabilities they find sensitive and how information should be shared in different contexts. To add to that complexity, users may have a different level of interaction and control of the devices. For instance, in a smart home context, admin users who set up and maintain the devices have more control and power and may able to violate the general expectations of privacy of others who have limited control over the devices [32, 34]. Resolving users' conflicting preferences regarding the use and control of shared devices remains a challenge, as does the prioritization of the privacy needs of users in different roles.

The challenges of multi-user IoT devices can be summarized as follows:

- **IoT devices are regularly used by multiple users**, even those devices that are designed with a single user in mind.
- **IoT users tend to have complex sharing preferences** that depend on their relationship with the other users.
- **Many IoT devices lack the mechanisms to support these preferences** and make it difficult to understand what is being shared with whom.
- **Reconciling the privacy needs of different users remains a challenge** that is not adequately addressed by existing IoT devices.

11.2.4 Little Control

The greatest strength of IoT lies in automation: IoT devices can take over routine or mundane tasks that would otherwise be performed by humans, thereby providing convenience. This means that to realize the full benefits of IoT, users must relinquish some level of control [35]. The tension between automation and the need for control becomes even more important in case of privacy.

A major issue with control revolves around ownership: those who interact with or are subject to the data collection practices of a device may not necessarily be the owners of the device. In addition, the owners of a device may not be the owners of the data collected by the device. Indeed, scholars studying the ownership of IoT systems have called IoT an "Imminent Ownership Threat" [36]. Their concerns revolve around questions of who has control over a smart device's actions, as well as who owns and manages the data collected by the device [37]. The latter is particularly complicated in the case of shared IoT systems. Take the case of an Airbnb host, who technically owns the smart devices installed on the rental property. Renters of the property are likely concerned about their privacy, especially in case of surveillance cameras, and may assert that they should have control over these devices for the duration of their stay. At the same time, the host would like to maintain control over their devices, for example, to ensure the safety of the property [38].

The complexity of such tensions between parties regarding the ownership of recorded data is further exaggerated in public IoT systems, mainly due to the increased number of parties who are subject to the devices' data collection practices [36, 37]. Indeed, one of the most challenging aspects of IoT is the involvement of bystanders who have no control over—or in many cases even awareness of—the devices that collect data about them and the capabilities of these devices [6]. Most IoT devices leave few opportunities for bystanders to be notified of, or give consent to, being recorded by devices in their surroundings, such as when being captured by a neighbor's smart doorbell as one walks down the sidewalk. In most cases, the only preferences a bystander may be able to express are the basic decision of whether or not to enter a space. While this is clearly an issue for smart cities, these issues can still occur with serious consequences in more intimate settings. An example is the considerable backlash over the deployment of Google Glass, as it was difficult for a bystander to determine whether they were being video-recorded by the person wearing the glasses, making those around a user feel uncomfortable [39]. While researchers have investigated a few potential technological solutions for bystanders, such as automatically obfuscating faces in videos of bystanders, there are few mechanisms or policies currently deployed to reduce these tensions between device and data owners, and the many additional people who are captured and impacted by those devices.

Even when users do have ownership of the device and access to its privacy controls, these controls are often quite limited. For example, as we discussed in Sect. 11.2.3, users may have complex needs for controlling the amount of access others have to their smart home devices. Yet, access control capabilities are often so limited, or lack transparency as to what they allow, that users provide access by simply sharing full account credentials with only their closest family and friends [11]. Other studies have shown that users often do not use existing privacy control mechanisms [40], such as the ability to review and delete recorded conversations, and may not even be aware of such mechanisms. Manufacturers of consumer IoT devices have tried to cater to this issue by providing privacy mechanisms that physically situated on the device, for example, Google Nest and Echo Dot each come with a physical button to disable microphones [41], and Facebook's Portal devices come with an integrated camera shutter or with physical camera covers [42]. These features increase the visibility of privacy capabilities and give users confidence that the mechanism is actually performing as intended. However, such physical privacy features are naturally limited in their complexity.

We summarize the challenges surrounding the lack of control in IoT systems as follows:

- **IoT systems create complex issues around ownership and control** and must find intuitive ways to address those issues.
- **IoT systems may violate the privacy of bystanders** and give them little opportunity to become aware of, let alone take control over, the collection practices that they are subjected to.
- **IoT privacy controls are often limited even for main users** leading to suboptimal privacy management practices.
- **Physical privacy controls can raise trust and awareness** but are often limited by their rudimentary functionality.

11.2.5   (In)Security of IoT Devices

IoT devices create a large number of attack vectors, resulting in many possibilities for adversaries to compromise the devices and use them for nefarious purposes. Successful attacks then compromise the privacy of device users and their information.

For example, in recent news, we saw a number of successful security attacks on smart home devices, such as the Mirai botnet (a DDOS attack on networked devices running Linux) [43], the monitoring of home occupants via their thermostat [44], the unauthorized access to google calendar information from a smart fridge [45], and the compromising of baby monitors to allow external parties to monitor live feeds, change the camera settings, and authorize other users to remotely view and control the device [46, 47]. Smart home devices, in particular, are becoming an easy and lucrative target for malicious attackers because of the availability of insecure devices and the fact that compromising one device can allow them to compromise several other connected devices in the same network.

Given that security is such a critical issue in IoT devices, it is remarkable that many devices do not have appropriate security mitigations in place. This issue has multiple root causes. The first root cause of this problem is that most IoT devices are connected directly to the Internet, which exposes them to all the network security problems of a typical online system. IoT device networks are extremely heterogeneous; they can consist of a large number of different devices, applications, and communication technologies. As such, there is not one universal security solution that can decrease or mitigate all of the security risks for all of these devices. Moreover, IoT devices typically do not have enough processing resources to support traditional security mechanisms [48]. Finally, the inter-connected nature of IoT devices contributes to their vulnerability, because even though some devices may have relatively strong security mechanisms, their security can still be compromised through other, less secure devices that they are connected to.

A second root cause is that manufacturers do not focus enough on security when developing their products—particularly for consumer-oriented devices such as those found in smart homes. Due to the novelty of the domain, many IoT devices are developed as quickly and cost-effectively as possible in an attempt to compete in the already crowded market place [49]. Security requirements are likely to take a lower priority than other features and functionality, and with less awareness of the risks consumers may not demand or pay for additional security protections. Thus, many IoT devices do not implement common security mechanisms such as encrypted communication, making them vulnerable to security attacks [50]. Many manufacturers have yet to establish mature security processes and have not yet allocated the resources needed to invest in substantial vulnerability detection and mitigation. When security is initially ignored in traditional software applications, these vulnerabilities are usually fixed over time through updates and security patches. However, not all IoT devices allow for regular and automated software updates to patch vulnerabilities [51].

Finally, another factor that makes IoT devices vulnerable to cybersecurity attacks are the users themselves. Most users of wearable and smart home devices who set up those devices are not professionals. They may not know the security risks imposed by networked devices and how to protect their devices against those risks. Indeed, some users may erroneously believe that traditional security practices, such as using strong passwords, are enough to protect them against security risks in their homes, as they do not fully understand the threats inflicted on them by their smart devices [48]. Even if users do know about security measures, these measures tend to be too complicated for them to implement correctly [11]. Finally, IoT researchers and manufacturers have not yet developed clear guidelines and best practices for users to help them employ appropriate practices, reducing their risks of security attacks [11, 17].

In summary, the security vulnerabilities of IoT devices fall along the following lines:

- **IoT devices introduce a significant security threat**, and it is therefore remarkable that most consumer-facing IoT devices lack proper security protections.
- **The heterogeneous and Internet-connected nature of IoT systems makes them difficult to secure**, and vulnerabilities in one device may leave other devices in the network vulnerable as well.
- **Market pressures and limited device capabilities make it difficult to provide proper security**, and security patches may take a long time to propagate within the network.
- **Users may not be capable of setting up their devices in a secure manner** and may not fully understand the threats caused by their IoT devices.

11.3 Case Studies

In this section we discuss three case studies and illustrate the privacy issues that have arisen in these cases. In particular, we spotlight the following three IoT devices: wearable fitness trackers, household smart voice assistants, and CCTV and smart cameras. To summarize this section:

- In the **wearable domain**, **fitness trackers** collect data that is largely considered nonsensitive, and users share their data with a variety of other people and organizations to help meet their fitness and health goals. However, users' lack of awareness of potential health-related inferences are considered more sensitive.
- In the **household domain**, **smart voice assistants** collect audio, which can be viewed as intrusive, despite controls and features that limit that collection.
- In the **public domain**, **security cameras** cause people to change their behavior when they perceive they are being watched. In public, CCTVs can result in less anti-social behavior and reduce crime. Yet, as smart cameras move into more private spaces, constantly being watched may have a chilling effect on behavior, particularly for those who lack control over the cameras.

11.3.1 Fitness Trackers

Fitness trackers are wearable devices that have gained significant popularity in recent years, with brands including Fitbit, Garmin, and Polar. Many take the form of a wrist-worn device, but they can come in a range of form factors depending on the sensors and intended usage. Apple also has fitness tracking built into the Apple watch and iPhone. The primary use of a fitness tracker is to monitor different aspects of a user's health and fitness, to motivate a more active lifestyle, to track performance, or to monitor a health condition.

A unique aspect of fitness tracker usage is that users regularly share data captured by their device with other people for a variety of purposes [52]. Users seek accountability and mutual support for their health goals by sharing their fitness progress on social media or within community forums [53]. They share health-related data with medical providers or caregivers. Employers and insurance companies may incentivize data sharing in an effort to encourage healthy behaviors through fitness campaigns [23]. Thus, users face significant challenges in managing not just the collection of their information but the sharing and use of that information with a potentially large number of other people and organizations. While most devices offer a range of sharing controls, these controls do not always provide fine-grained customization of data sharing [54].

Researchers have also demonstrated a large number of inferences that can be made with fitness tracker data. Mood, stress level, places, and sexual activity can be determined with high accuracy [18, 55, 56]. For example, in January 2018, reports revealed that fitness tracker data shared by users on Strava, a social fitness service, showed accurate locations of US military sites [57]. Despite this potential, users seem generally unconcerned about the risks of sharing their information in such a public manner. For example, research shows that users do not consider sharing one's step count with a pharmacy a cause of privacy concern. Instead, users are more concerned about managing others' impressions of them and sharing information that fits the norms of various platforms [23]. For example, someone might not want to share their lack of exercise on social media lest friends might view them as lazy.

One reason for users' high level of comfort with sharing fitness tracking data is their lack of awareness of the possible inferences that can be made with such data. Studies have demonstrated that users do not believe that certain inferences are even possible or sufficiently accurate to be useful [58, 59]. This lack of awareness may be due to a dearth in application features that can inform users about the way their information could be aggregated and used to make various inferences. Thus, users may currently be comfortable sharing their step count or heart rate but may consider it a privacy invasion if they knew that more sensitive information about their health or activity has been inferred based on this data.

Providing privacy awareness and controls for fitness trackers is challenging, though: Their often tiny screens are barely large enough to fit the necessary functional information (e.g., time, heart rate, reminders, etc.), and hence opt to leave out all other information (e.g., what data is collected, how data is handled, etc.). Even though users can often access such information, as well as some controls, through the associated apps on their smartphones (e.g., device settings) or through a corresponding web portal (e.g., privacy policy), this decoupled way of interaction makes it less appealing for users and reduces opportunities to learn about data practices.

We summarize the privacy challenges of fitness trackers as follows:

- **Users are generally comfortable sharing their data** with friends, caregivers, and sometimes even employers and insurance companies.
- **Tracker data enables a large number of inferences** that revolve sensitive information, even if the underlying data itself is not regarded as sensitive.
- **Users lack awareness of the possible inferences that can be made**, which may explain their current openness to data sharing.
- **Giving users fine-grained control is challenging** given the small form factor of most fitness trackers.

11.3.2 Smart Voice Assistants

Voice commands have become one of the most prominent modes of interacting with smart technology, particularly in smart homes. Triggered by voice commands like "Hey Google" or "Alexa," these assistants will listen to users' questions or requests. Hence, these devices continuously listen for audio cues from their surroundings to respond the moment they are called on. In response to user queries these devices can provide audio feedback and carry out a variety of actions, both virtual and physical. For instance, users can buy something from Amazon through the Amazon Echo and receive notification of packages delivered. Moreover, smart voice assistants are often connected to and used to control other smart home devices. For instance, users can use voice commands to ask their smart voice assistant to turn on their smart lights or TV.

As smart assistants are increasingly embedded in everyday conversational settings, concerns have been raised by several researchers and journalists around the devices' intrusive listening practices [40, 60]. There are general suspicions and confusion surrounding what is exactly being recorded by these devices and how the parent company handles the audio recordings. Several incidents of Amazon Echo sending sensitive recordings to someone without the owner's knowledge and approval have been in the news [61], contributing to consumer concerns. Indeed, the intrusiveness of smart assistants, their potential to violate users' privacy, and distrust of the companies that manufacture them are the main reasons reported for not adopting such devices [40, 62]. Although some companies proactively provide a set of privacy controls for smart assistants, end users are often unaware of these controls. For instance, a recent study found that most end users are not aware of their ability to view and delete the audio logs, even though those same users were not comfortable with the permanent retention of their recordings [63]. Moreover, some of the privacy controls are misaligned with users' needs. For instance, Google Home and Amazon Echo offer a physical mute button that requires different interactions than regular voice commands, and hence the button is rarely used [40].

In addition to the concern over intrusive data collection practices, smart assistant owners also face the challenge of limiting others' access to sensitive information and actions that can be performed with the device, such as buying items. For example, in Texas, a 6-year-old was able to order a dollhouse and four pounds of cookies using Amazon Echo [64]. While users can add a voice code that must be used during shopping as an extra layer of protection, many users would not think to search for this capability, and even if used, the code must be spoken aloud and can easily be overheard.

These concerns and feeling of intrusiveness may heighten as smart assistants are finding their way into our cars. There is a clear benefit to enabling car owners to control different activities in the car via simple voice commands, allowing drivers to keep their hands on the wheel at all times. Consequently, a large number of insurance providers are giving away a car-based Alexa assistant for free to their users, citing the benefit of reducing accidents caused due to texting while driving [65]. However, this trend presents privacy challenges for car passengers, particularly in the case of ride-sharing scenarios such as Uber or Lyft.

With the increasingly seamless integration of smart assistants into our daily lives, they are likely to become even more intrusive. For example, Amazon and Google have both patented mechanisms for using their digital voice assistant to extract keywords from ambient speech provide targeted advertisements [66]. In the future, a voice assistant may proactively provide assistance based on users' conversation without being invoked by the wake word [67]. Such a proactive device has a tremendous potential for helping users by providing more personalized and contextual services [35]. However, the intrusiveness of such a device calls for extensive research to identify privacy features that would allow users to enjoy these benefits without having to worry about their privacy.

The privacy challenges of smart voice assistants can be summarized as follows:

- **Smart voice assistants proactively listen for audio cues**—an intrusion that causes many to avoid adopting them.
- **Users are often not aware of existing privacy controls**, as they tend to be "hidden in plain sight."
- **Car-based voice assistants** can improve driver safety but are also intruding upon the privacy of passengers.
- **Future proactive voice assistants** have a tremendous potential to provide personalized services while at the same time further exacerbating users' privacy concerns.

11.3.3 Security Cameras

The "Watching Eye Effect" refers to the behavior modification that can occur upon the perception of being observed by something. Researchers have shown that this phenomenon can play an important role in reducing antisocial behavior of individuals in public [68, 69]. Once could argue that such behavioral modification is an unwanted intrusion into people's lives, though. Moreover, the widespread deployment of smart cameras throughout private and public spaces could lead to significant privacy concerns.

In the pre-IoT era, security cameras took the form of Closed Circuit Television Cameras (CCTVs). Research regarding the perceptions and behaviors surrounding CCTV can inform our understanding of the widespread use of cameras in smart spaces. CCTV surveillance cameras have been widely adopted by municipalities and businesses around the world to reduce crime and increase public safety. Studies suggest that CCTVs can lead to crime reduction in some cases, particularly for property crimes, and that camera surveillance is most suitable for small, well-defined areas [70], such as to reduce vehicle crimes in a parking garage.

Even when they are deployed in public spaces, CCTVs can raise a number of privacy concerns. One's autonomy and dignity can be reduced due to being under surveillance. Even when the presence of a CCTV camera is known, people typically cannot make a determination who is really behind that camera. (Not) knowing who is watching can influence how people behave. Surveillance can also have chilling effects on civil liberties and freedoms and can be particularly harmful to vulnerable populations, such as prisoners or students. Despite these concerns, the well-established use of CCTVs for public safety leads to different privacy perceptions and expectations compared to other camera-based technologies, such as smartphones or drones [71].

One challenge with CCTV is whether and how people are notified that they are under video surveillance. The most widely used way to inform people of CCTVs is to put up a sign indicating that people are within coverage of a camera. When they are clearly visible, even these notices themselves can increase the level of deterrence. However, in many cases such notices are far from effective since people rarely notice them or may become habituated to them over time. Surveillance notices also tend to provide little or no information about what happens with the captured recordings. Video technologies are also becoming smarter, with increasing capabilities toward facial and activity recognition. Again, though, surveillance notices tend to give little indication of the kind of processing that occurs, and there is typically no way for the public to access and control the data collected about them.

In recent years, IoT cameras have joined the ranks of CCTVs and are now being used throughout residential areas to provide for homeowners' security, but also collectively for neighborhood safety and security. While their motivation may be similar to CCTVs—to provide for the safety and security of one's home and belongings—this expansion of surveillance into more private spaces is likely to increase privacy risks. Privately owned IoT cameras are likely even less visible than CCTVs, with no notice at all to passersby. People will remain unaware of the extent to which they are being recorded as they drive down a road or walk down a sidewalk. Rather than prevent crime, knowledge of recording may have chilling effects on behavior in one's own private spaces. For example, residents may be less likely to speak freely in their own yard or to briefly step outside in a bathrobe if they expect to be recorded by a neighbor's camera. Finally, while cameras may be deployed by individuals on their own property, applications such as Citizens and Neighbors are enabling the sharing of videos with neighbors and law enforcement [72, 73], thereby greatly expanding the potential audience for those videos.

In summary, the privacy challenges of security cameras are as follows:

- **Being recorded can change one's behavior** which can reduce crime but may also be perceived as a violation of one's privacy.
- **People are often unaware of, or get habituated to, surveillance notices**. Such notices also typically do not reveal the identity of the recipient or how they process the recordings, and they do not allow for access and control.
- **Privately owned IoT cameras further exacerbate these privacy issues**, as they tend to inconspicuously surveil more private spaces.

11.4 Solutions and Guidelines

Much of the research examining the privacy challenges and user perceptions in IoT have resulted in recommended design guidelines for supporting users' privacy needs through privacy features and interfaces. However, there has been considerably less research into how well different kinds of privacy controls could satisfy those guidelines or into novel mechanisms that specifically address the privacy challenges of IoT. In this section, we present these guidelines along with research into related solutions, including:

- Users need **greater awareness** of the data practices of IoT devices, which can be provided, in part, by additional **privacy notices**.
- Key **privacy controls** should be provided **on the device** itself to be easily accessible to all people in the environment.
- IoT devices and applications should implement state-of-the-art measures to maintain users' **data privacy**.
- IoT devices and applications should provide **flexible privacy controls** that give users adequate choices over the collection and sharing of their data.
- Users need **community-oriented privacy features** to support the many different kinds of users that interact within an IoT environment.
- **Context-adaptive privacy mechanisms** could reduce burden on users by personalizing settings and recommendations to the users and their context.

Providing adequate privacy choices is a challenge in IoT, due to the wide variety of devices, data, and contexts of use (resulting in a complex decision landscape) along with the absence of a dedicated user interface (resulting in limited opportunities for interaction). Thus, researchers and designers need to more fully examine the design space for providing various privacy mechanisms and controls. A good example is a recent paper by Feng et al., which introduced a design space for privacy choices in which they present five key dimensions of providing meaningful privacy controls in IoT [74]. These five dimensions include choice type, functionality, timing, channel, and modality. For example, in the timing dimension, privacy choices can be delivered to users at six possible times: at setup, just in time, context-aware, periodic, on-demand, and personalized. In the remainder of the section, we provide a number of guidelines for supporting users' privacy needs, along with examples of privacy mechanisms attempting to address some of those guidelines. However, there is still significant need to expand upon these solutions to tackle the privacy issues raised above.

11.4.1   Privacy Notices and Awareness Mechanisms

One critical set of solutions to IoT privacy issues is to make users more aware of the privacy implications and risks of their interactions with IoT devices, so that they can make more informed privacy decisions. The guidelines addressing this need include the following:

- Provide privacy notices on the packaging and materials that come with the physical product, so that users can review data practices before they purchase the product and while they are first getting started setting up a device
- Provide privacy notices wherever the user may interact with the device, be that on the device, within an accompanying app, or in an online account
- Make privacy notices brief and focused around what the user would most care about or find surprising
- Make data collection and aggregation visible to the user as they interact with the device or accompanying application
- Provide periodic nudges regarding the data practices of the device, to allow users to learn more about data collection and reconsider those practices
- Provide mechanisms for users to discover what IoT devices are around them

Despite their limitations, the primary way that users learn details about the data practices of a device or application is through various privacy notices. One of the most common formats of privacy notice is the *privacy policy* available on most organizations' websites. However, current privacy policies are often lengthy and complex legal documents that contain detailed information related to a company's data practices. Research has identified many issues with such privacy policies, such as being hard to understand, time-consuming to read, and difficult to access [75, 76]. In the IoT context, many of these issues become even more prominent due to the nature of the physical devices. Unlike a website, where a privacy policy can be provided through a link on the web page, IoT devices generally have a very small screen, if they even have a screen at all. Instead, IoT device manufacturers require users to go to their product website to read privacy policies if desired, making it even more difficult for users to understand the data practices of IoT devices.

To combat this issue, Emami-Naeini et al. have proposed an IoT Security and Privacy Label [77]. The design of the label is inspired by the nutrition labels on food packages, where the key nutrition information is conveyed to the consumer in a brief, standardized format. The IoT Security and Privacy Label is designed to be placed on the package of any IoT device and contains all the key information regarding the device's data practices (e.g., data collection purposes, data storage location, data sharing practices, etc.). This would allow users to read the label before purchase and compare the practices of similar products through the label. While these labels are not yet adopted by IoT manufacturers, privacy labels are beginning to be adopted in other domains. For example, Apple recently introduced a privacy label requirement for iOS apps, based on this and prior research [78].

Researchers have also examined how to provide privacy ratings or reviews to consumers to help them make purchase or use decisions. Consumers can find many different organizations, such as Consumer Reports, that review and rate all kinds of products on a variety of dimensions. In a similar vein, for privacy, Mozilla has created an online guide called "privacy not included" where consumers can learn about the data practices and possible risks from different smart home and IoT devices, so that existing users can assess their risk, and potential buyers can decide whether and which device to buy [79].

When privacy notices are salient and easily accessible to users, they can impact decision making. Yet, users are not likely to continue to view those notices as they interact with an IoT device. Thus, a critical solution is to make data collection and use visible within the interface of the device itself. This can be accomplished by various *data views* that show an aggregate of the collected information [80], along with detailed logs that can be accessed on demand. Yet, users may not always review such information, particularly if they do not regularly interact with the app that accompanies the IoT device. Thus, devices can also periodically nudge users regarding some aspect of their data collection, to prompt them to reflect on those data practices or review them in more detail. This has been investigated outside of IoT for mobile devices, for instance, where users were provided with periodic messages about how often different apps access their location [81].

Another major awareness challenge in IoT environments is how users can learn what active devices are nearby, particularly when they are in spaces that they do not control. Thus, another class of solutions helps bystanders discover IoT devices in their immediate surroundings. For example, *IoT Inspector* provides an easy way to understand what devices are connected in an IoT environment [82]. By scanning a user's network through a web app, IoT Inspector is able to identify all devices that are connected to the user's network and provide users with information such as device names, manufacturers, and IP addresses. For example, when a user stays at an AirBnB apartment, they learn of potential data collection within the apartment by scanning the network and identifying any connected IoT devices [83]. There are several other tools that provide somewhat similar functionalities, for example, IoT Sentinel [84] and Peek-a-Boo [85].

11.4.2 On Device Controls

Many users interact with smart devices through an accompanying mobile app. Yet, controls that are on the device itself are more accessible to everyone in the environment. Thus, guidelines advise to:

- Provide visible indicators on the device itself that indicate data collection is occurring
- Provide key controls on the device hardware that limit or turn off data collection

Page et al. found that people draw from different conceptual models when it comes to interacting with IoT devices: A person drawing from an *Agentic* perspective has a higher affinity to leverage non-haptic modes of interaction, whereas someone drawing from a *User-Centric* perspective prefers to use physical buttons. Manufacturers of consumer IoT devices have tried to cater to the latter group of users by providing a limited set of physical buttons on their smart devices, for example, Google Nest and Echo Dot each come with a physical button to disable their microphone [41]. Similarly, Facebook's Portal has camera covers and a camera disable button, in addition to the microphone disable button [42]. Hardware mechanisms have the benefit of being usable by anyone around the device, providing both control and an indication of the status of the device to bystanders. They also provide an added assurance of privacy—for example, users may trust that a physical cover over a camera truly prevents recording, rather than can a digital control indicating that the camera is off.

Researchers have also examined novel approaches that interfere with or impact a device's physical ability to collect data. For example, "Alias" is a separate add-on device that paralyzes a smart voice assistant by preventing it from listening and only activates the assistant with a custom wake word from the user [86]. Others have investigated the idea of obfuscating sound at the microphone as a privacy protection [87].

11.4.3 Data Privacy

Studies have found that IoT device users are generally concerned about the data these devices collect and desire additional measures to maintain their data privacy. The guidelines for supporting this need include the following:

- Make transmission and storage of data encrypted by default
- Store data anonymously when possible
- Where possible, provide users the option to process and store data locally (e.g., inside their device, app, or home network) instead of sending it to a remote server
- Make it more difficult for manufacturers/advertisers to make unwanted inferences through novel mechanisms such as adding noise to the data

Within IoT environments, data is constantly transmitted and stored by the device itself, by accompanying app, by the manufacturer in the cloud, and everywhere in between. This data traffic often contains sensitive information, which means that each storage and transmission point creates a risk of data leakage and data breaches. Thus, users expect that organizations are utilizing reasonable practices for protecting this data from attackers and third parties. A basic step is for data-centric encryption to be in place the moment the data is created within an IoT device and at every other point where it is stored. By enforcing encryption and making users aware of it, device manufacturers can gain users' trust as well as meet regulatory standards such as the California Consumer Privacy Act (CCPA).

Although encryption is a crucial step in ensuring the security and privacy of IoT data, recent research found that in-home activities such as sleep patterns, presence, and interaction with devices can be inferred even from encrypted IoT data using a technique called *traffic analysis* [21]. There have been several attempts to prevent such inferences from occurring. For instance, Hoof et al. secured a private messaging system from traffic analysis by shaping the traffic to a predetermined rate [88]. Apthorpe et al. introduce noise to shape the IoT network traffic to limit inference from traffic rate metadata [21]. Such mechanisms should be more extensively researched to encourage adoption.

Beyond encryption, research has found that many users desire to store and process their data locally rather than on a remote server [89, 90]. This solution gives more control to end users, who could explicitly choose to share data with manufacturers or other parties only when they want the benefit that this provides. Users could also choose to apply different levels of aggregation to their data before sharing it, thereby limiting the details of what is known or stored by others. For example, a fitness tracker user may not want to share their running route, but they may be willing to share how many miles they ran to receive some service (e.g., competing with friends). IoT users may also be more comfortable with data sharing when their data remains anonymous and cannot be linked back to their real identity. However, as outlined above, users often do not realize the extent to which inferences could occur, including those that could reidentify them from seemingly anonymous information. Introducing a carefully controlled amount of noise to the data can reduce the efficacy of such inferences, without significantly reducing the usefulness of the data for its intended purposes [91].

11.4.4 Community-Oriented Controls

IoT devices are regularly shared among a number of users. Therefore, designers must take a community-oriented view of IoT devices and applications, which includes providing features and controls that enable collective usage. Guidelines include to:

- Provide flexible and fine-grained sharing capabilities to allow users to share devices with many different kinds of people

- Make transparent what is accessible when devices or data are shared with other people
- Provide mechanisms to determine how different people are using devices or accessing data
- Learn the most prevalent sharing patterns and goals to support the design of sharing and access control capabilities

While many IoT applications allow users to share devices and data with others, many studies report that users find existing sharing capabilities too limited and request more fine-grained controls (e.g. [54]). Thus, a common guideline is to allow for more flexible and fine-grained sharing with different types of recipients. This is not only true for sharing data but also for control over the devices themselves. Another key limitation is that it can be challenging to determine exactly what is shared with whom, both at setup and over time. Thus, applications need mechanisms for users to be able to determine what other users will have access to, and be able to tell who is accessing those controls or that information over time.

Even within a household, different members may have different needs that are hard to monitor and control. For example, one particular study found that and 20% of kids aged 4–11 talk to their smart voice assistant for more than 5 h per week [92]. Children may get access to inappropriate content and reveal private information during their interactions. Parents already struggle with maintaining children's online safety with traditional devices; IoT devices make the situation even more difficult, as many reside in a common space designed to be used by all household members. To limit children's access to smart voice assistants, device manufacturers already provide parental control modes such as Amazon FreeTime and the Google Family App. Researchers have also examined ways to automatically determine content that is inappropriate for certain users within voice assistant conversations, such as Skillbot developed by Le et al. [93]. While parents may aim to protect their children from inappropriate content, designers must also protect the privacy of potentially vulnerable users from others within a smart space. For example, Freed et al. examined how technology can be exploited to enable intimate partner abuse [94]. Smart devices only provide increased capability for stalking and surveillance, which few have examined.

Users may desire a range of mechanisms to share access to their IoT devices depending on contextual factors. For example, in an attempt to improve the security and privacy tensions in a multi-user smart home, Zeng et al. developed an app that includes features such as location-based access controls, supervisory access controls, the ability to ask for permission (i.e., reactive access control), along with notifications on how others users are using a device [95]. However, in their field study, they found that users did not use many of the provided access control capabilities. Arguably, despite users' stated desire for more fine-grained access control features, supporting the full complexity of users' needs could result in interfaces that are more complex than some users are willing to utilize.

To combat this problem, designers must make an effort to understand users' most important goals and their most common interaction patterns regarding IoT access control, so that they can support those goals and patterns more explicitly. For example, researchers have developed privacy-setting interfaces that are structured based on the relative importance of each contextual parameter [90, 96]. Likewise, Alqhatani et al. [23] described six particular sharing patterns of different audiences of fitness tracker information based on users' health and fitness goals. One of those patterns—sharing with healthcare providers—was not supported at all by existing devices.

11.4.5   Context-Adaptive and User-Tailored Privacy

One of the key challenges in privacy-preserving IoT is the contextual nature of privacy-related decisions and the explosion of contexts that are possible in this domain. Recent privacy regulations (e.g., California Consumer Privacy Act and General Data Protection Regulation, see Chap. 17) require by law that users can have more control over the data collected by IoT devices. Yet, providing controls that enable users to control the capture and sharing of information within every possible combination of context is simply too overwhelming. A potential solution to this problem is to provide context-adaptive and user-tailored privacy controls. More details about this solution can be found in Chap. 16; here we provide IoT-specific guidelines:

- Study the context-dependency of users' IoT privacy decisions
- Use machine learning to predict users' privacy preferences, for example, by creating comprehensive privacy profiles
- Automate the privacy practices of IoT devices based on the context and the profile of the user

A large number of studies have demonstrated that users' comfort with IoT privacy practices vary across different factors such as the type of data recorded, the location where it is recorded, who the data is shared with, the perceived value of the data, and the benefits provided by services using that data [5, 6, 63, 90, 96–101]. In the context of public IoT, Naeini et al. [5] used vignettes to study many of these factors with over 380 different use cases across 1000 users. Their results indicate that people are most uncomfortable when data is collected in their home and prefer to be notified when such collection occurs. Similarly, a survey study by Lee and Kobsa [6] found that monitoring of users personal spaces, such as their homes, was not acceptable to participants, as well as monitoring performed by the government or unknown entities. Other studies have found that people are most concerned with certain types of data, namely videos, photos, and bio-metric information, particularly when this information is gathered inside the home [5, 6, 14, 102, 103].

In a smart home setting, He et al. [90] find that when IoT devices share data with one another, users are most concerned about where that data is stored, followed by the types of devices that act as the sender and recipient of the information and the purpose of the data transmission. Significant interaction effects between sender, recipient, and purpose suggest that users have complex preferences that depend on multiple contextual parameters at once. Likewise, Barbosa et al. concluded that people's privacy perceptions regarding smart home IoT devices depend on not only the data types but also the purpose of data collection and who collect the data [104]. In another large vignette study, Apthorpe et al. [99] found that participants' acceptance of data collection and sharing was dependent on both the recipient of the information and the specific conditions under which the information was shared. Their results also suggest that users' privacy norms may change with the continued use of specific devices. Results of a different vignette survey by Horne et al. [105] suggest that those changes are not always toward more acceptance of data-sharing.

Beyond context-dependency, IoT privacy decisions also vary significantly by user [90, 96], suggesting that users must be able to make a personal decision as to whether a certain scenario warrants the collection and/or sharing of information. Unfortunately, the sheer number of contextual parameters to consider in this decision will likely substantially increase the complexity of the privacy-setting interfaces of IoT devices. In response, researchers have attempted to reduce the apparent variety of IoT privacy decisions to a small set of concise *privacy profiles* for users to choose from [90, 96, 106], thereby reducing the complexity of the privacy-setting task.

Taking this approach one step further, researchers have proposed frameworks to support IoT privacy decision-making by adapting the privacy settings to varying privacy contexts and/or by recommending users to make certain privacy decisions [6, 106–108]. More details about this user-tailored approach can be found in Chap. 16.

11.5   Conclusion

This chapter has covered the prevailing privacy challenges of IoT environments from a user-centered perspective. We have demonstrated that the introduction of sensor-based Internet-connected technologies in real-world environments—be they wearables, household devices, or devices in the public domain—exacerbate existing issues with online privacy and physical privacy and introduce new, unique challenges as well.

These challenges exist because IoT devices can inconspicuously collect vast amounts of data and perform inferences on this data to paint a detailed picture of the preferences and activities of their users (and even of bystanders). The typical lack of a comprehensive user interface reduces users' awareness of these data practices and limits their control over them—if control is even provided at all.

The resulting privacy issues are further exacerbated by the fact that existing IoT devices tend to offer limited configuration of how devices and data are shared among a community of users as well as inadequate security protections to prevent outsiders from gaining unwanted access to sensitive data and/or functionality of the device.

The final section of our chapter offers solutions and guidelines for IoT researchers and developers to increase users' awareness about and control over their privacy, both regarding the data practices of the IoT manufacturer and the use of IoT devices by multiple users. While we advocate for granular, on-device control, we also acknowledge that fine-grained control can be daunting to users. Context-adaptive and user-tailored privacy solutions may provide IoT users with adequate control over their privacy while at the same time reducing the burden of effecting this control.

The unrelenting evolution of artificial intelligence and sensor technologies, paired with the continuing miniaturization of processing and networking chips, suggests that current IoT technologies only scratch the surface of what future technologies in this realm will be capable of. For privacy researchers, it is therefore important to "future-proof" their research by not just focusing on what is currently possible with IoT technologies but to anticipate the socio-technical consequences of the imaginable. Likewise, for developers and manufacturers, it is important to acknowledge that many of the IoT devices of today will operate alongside the ones that will be created in the future, and to design the privacy mechanisms of today's systems accordingly. We hope that the tremendous benefits promised by the rise of IoT will be paired with a powerful user experience that respects the privacy of users and bystanders alike.

References

1. Ashton, K., et al. 2009. That 'internet of things' thing. *RFID Journal* 22 (7): 97–114.
2. Lee, I., and K. Lee. 2015. The internet of things (IoT): Applications, investments, and challenges for enterprises. *Business Horizons* 58 (4): 431–440.
3. Haghi, M., K. Thurow, and R. Stoll. 2017. Wearable devices in medical internet of things: scientific research and commercially available devices. *Healthcare Informatics Research* 23 (1): 4.
4. Motti, V.G., and K. Caine. 2015. Users' privacy concerns about wearables. In *Financial Cryptography and Data Security*, 231–244. Berlin: Springer.
5. Naeini, P.E., S. Bhagavatula, H. Habib, M. Degeling, L. Bauer, L.F. Cranor, and N. Sadeh. 2017. Privacy expectations and preferences in an iot world. In *Thirteenth Symposium on Usable Privacy and Security ([SOUPS] 2017)*, 399–412.
6. Lee, H. and A. Kobsa. 2016. Understanding user privacy in internet of things environments. In *2016 IEEE 3rd World Forum on Internet of Things (WF-IoT)*, 407–412. Piscataway: IEEE.
7. Nyc midtown congestion management system. https://www1.nyc.gov/html/dot/html/pr2012/pr12_25.shtml. Accessed 09 Nov 2020.
8. STAFF, W. 2020. Georgia city moves forward with extensive water loss control program. https://waterfm.com/georgia-city-moves-forward-with-extensive-water-loss-control-program/. Accessed 09 Nov 2020.
9. Bloom, C., J. Tan, J. Ramjohn, L. Bauer. 2017. Self-driving cars and data collection: Privacy perceptions of networked autonomous vehicles. In *Thirteenth Symposium on Usable Privacy and Security (SOUPS 2017)*, Santa Clara, CA, 357–375. San Francisco Bay: USENIX Association.

10. Law, B.H. 2021 What you need to know about driverless cars and privacy. https://medium.com/@baumhedlund/what-you-need-to-know-about-driverless-cars-and-privacy-8720d46e8877. Accessed 04 Nov 2021.
11. Tabassum, M., J. Kropczynski, P. Wisniewski, and H.R. Lipford. 2020. Smart home beyond the home: A case for community-based access control. In *Proceedings of the 2020 CHI Conference on Human Factors in Computing Systems*, CHI '20, 1–12. New York: Association for Computing Machinery.
12. Zheng, S., N. Apthorpe, M. Chetty, and N. Feamster. 2018. User perceptions of smart home iot privacy. *Proceedings of the ACM on Human-Computer Interaction* 2 (CSCW): 200:1–200:20. https://doi.org/10.1145/3274469. http://doi.acm.org/10.1145/3274469
13. Vitak, J., Y. Liao, P. Kumar, M. Zimmer, and K. Kritikos. 2018. Privacy attitudes and data valuation among fitness tracker users. In *iConference*.
14. Lee, L., J. Lee, S. Egelman, and D. Wagner. 2016. Information disclosure concerns in the age of wearable computing. In *NDSS Workshop on Usable Security (USEC)*, vol. 1.
15. Peppet, R. 2014. Regulating the internet of things: First steps toward managing discrimination, privacy, security, and consent. *Texas Law Review* 93: 85–179.
16. Emami-Naeini, P., H. Dixon, Y. Agarwal, and L.F. Cranor. 2019. Exploring how privacy and security factor into iot device purchase behavior. In *Proceedings of the 2019 CHI Conference on Human Factors in Computing Systems*, CHI '19, New York, NY, 1–12. New York: Association for Computing Machinery.
17. Zeng, E., S. Mare, and F. Roesner. 2017. End user security and privacy concerns with smart homes. In *Thirteenth Symposium on Usable Privacy and Security ({SOUPS} 2017)*, 65–80.
18. Kröger, J. 2018. Unexpected inferences from sensor data: a hidden privacy threat in the internet of things. In *IFIP International Internet of Things Conference*, 147–159. Berlin: Springer.
19. Wang, H., T.T.-T. Lai, and R. Roy Choudhury. 2015. Mole: Motion leaks through smartwatch sensors. In *Proceedings of the 21st Annual International Conference on Mobile Computing and Networking*, MobiCom '15, 155–166. New York: Association for Computing Machinery.
20. Srinivasan, V., J. Stankovic, and K. Whitehouse. 2008. Protecting your daily in-home activity information from a wireless snooping attack. In *Proceedings of the 10th International Conference on Ubiquitous Computing*, UbiComp '08, 202–211. New York: Association for Computing Machinery.
21. Apthorpe, N., H.D. Yuxing, R. Dillon, N. Arvind and F. Nick. 2019. Keeping the smart home private with smart(er) IoT traffic shaping. *Proceedings on Privacy Enhancing Technologies*, 2019 (3): 128–148. https://doi.org/10.2478/popets-2019-0040
22. House votes to allow internet service providers to sell, share your personal information. https://www.consumerreports.org/consumerist/house-votes-to-allow-internet-service-providers-to-sell-share-your-personal-information/. Accessed 26 Nov 2019.
23. Alqhatani, A., and H.R. Lipford. 2019. "there is nothing that i need to keep secret": Sharing practices and concerns of wearable fitness data. In *Fifteenth Symposium on Usable Privacy and Security (SOUPS 2019)*. Santa Clara: USENIX Association.
24. Gerber, N., B. Reinheimer, and M. Volkamer. 2018. Home sweet home? investigating users' awareness of smart home privacy threats. In *Proceedings of an Interactive Workshop on the Human Aspects of Smarthome Security and Privacy (WSSP), Baltimore, MD, August 12, 2018*. USENIX.
25. Home assistant adopter beware: Google, amazon digital assistant patents reveal plans for mass snooping. https://www.consumerwatchdog.org/privacy-technology/home-assistant-adopter-beware-google-amazon-digital-assistant-patents-reveal. Accessed 26 Nov 2019.
26. McStay, A. 2016. Empathic media and advertising: Industry, policy, legal and citizen perspectives (the case for intimacy). *Big Data & Society* 3 (2): 2053951716666868.
27. The facebook and cambridge analytica scandal, explained with a simple diagram. https://www.vox.com/policy-and-politics/2018/3/23/17151916/facebook-cambridge-analytica-trump-diagram. Accessed 26 Nov 2019.

28. Cambridge analytica: how did it turn clicks into votes? https://www.theguardian.com/news/2018/may/06/cambridge-analytica-how-turn-clicks-into-votes-christopher-wylie. Accessed 13 April 2021.
29. Trust in facebook has dropped by 66 percent since the cambridge analytica scandal. https://www.nbcnews.com/business/consumer/trust-facebook-has-dropped-51-percent-cambridge-analytica-scandal-n867011. Accessed 13 April 2021.
30. Smart streetlights program. https://www.sandiego.gov/sustainability/energy-and-water-efficiency/programs-projects/smart-city. Accessed 09 Nov 2020.
31. Nyc connected vehicle project. https://cvp.nyc/. Accessed 09 Nov 2020.
32. Garg, R., and C. Moreno. 2019. Understanding motivators, constraints, and practices of sharing internet of things. *Proceedings of the ACM on Interactive, Mobile, Wearable and Ubiquitous Technologies* 3 (2): 1–21.
33. He, W., M. Golla, R. Padhi, J. Ofek, M. Dürmuth, E. Fernandes, and B. Ur. 2018. Rethinking access control and authentication for the home internet of things (IoT). In *27th USENIX Security Symposium (USENIX Security 18)*, Baltimore, MD, 255–272. Berkeley: USENIX Association.
34. Geeng, C., and F. Roesner. 2019. Who's in control? interactions in multi-user smart homes. In *Proceedings of the 2019 CHI Conference on Human Factors in Computing Systems*, CHI '19, 1–13. New York: Association for Computing Machinery.
35. Page, X., P. Bahirat, M.I. Safi, B.P. Knijnenburg, and P. Wisniewski. 2018. The internet of what? understanding differences in perceptions and adoption for the internet of things. *Proceedings of the ACM on Interactive, Mobile, Wearable and Ubiquitous Technologies* 2 (4): 1–22.
36. Desai, B.C. 2017. Iot: imminent ownership threat. In *Proceedings of the 21st International Database Engineering & Applications Symposium*, 82–89.
37. Janeček, V. 2018. Ownership of personal data in the internet of things. *Computer Law & Security Review* 34 (5), 1039–1052.
38. Mare, S., F. Roesner, and T. Kohno. 2020. Smart devices in airbnbs: Considering privacy and security for both guests and hosts. *Proceedings on Privacy Enhancing Technologies* 2020 (2): 436–458.
39. Google glass users fight privacy fears. https://www.cnn.com/2013/12/10/tech/mobile/negative-google-glass-reactions. Accessed 13 April 2021.
40. Lau, J., B. Zimmerman, and F. Schaub. 2018. Alexa, are you listening?: Privacy perceptions, concerns and privacy-seeking behaviors with smart speakers. *Proceedings of the ACM on Human-Computer Interaction* 2 (CSCW): 102:1–102:31.
41. Johnson, D. 2019. How to stop your Google Home from listening to you and storing your audio data. https://www.businessinsider.com/how-to-stop-google-home-from-listening-to-me
42. PortalPrivacy, https://portal.facebook.com/privacy
43. Bertino, E., and N. Islam. 2017. Botnets and internet of things security. *Computer* 50 (2): 76–79.
44. Copos, B., K. Levitt, M. Bishop, and J. Rowe. 2016. Is anybody home? inferring activity from smart home network traffic. In *2016 IEEE Security and Privacy Workshops (SPW)*, 245–251. Piscataway: IEEE.
45. Leyden, J. 2015. Samsung smart fridge leaves Gmail logins open to attack. https://www.theregister.com/2015/08/24/smart_fridge_security_fubar/ Accessed October 4, 2021.
46. Goodin, D. 2015. Baby monitors wide open to hacks that expose users' most private moments. ars technica. 2015. https://arstechnica.com/information-technology/2015/09/9-baby-monitors-wide-open-to-hacks-that-expose-users-most-private-moments/
47. Dickson, B. 2015. Why IoT security is so critical. https://tcrn.ch/3l4FL4Z. Accessed 4 October 2021
48. Mantas, G., Lymberopoulos, D., Komninos, N. 2010. Security in smart home environment. In *Wireless Technologis for Ambient Assisting Living and Healthcare: Systems and Applications; IGI Global: Hershey, PA, USA, pp. 170–191*. DOI: 10.4018/978-1-61520-805-0.ch010

49. Braun, L. 2016. Human centered security: (How) can the typical smart home user make his home more secure?, *ResearchGate*, Aug. 2016. https://www.researchgate.net/publication/305850389_Human_Centered_Security_How_can_the_typical_smart_home_user_make_his_home_more_secure

50. Iot traffic in the enterprise is rising. so are the threats. https://www.zscaler.com/blogs/security-research/iot-traffic-enterprise-rising-so-are-threats. Accessed 13 April 2021.

51. Most iot devices are an attack waiting to happen, unless manufacturers update their kernels. https://www.techrepublic.com/article/most-iot-devices-are-an-attack-waiting-to-happen-unless-manufacturers-update-their-kernels/. Accessed 13 April 2021.

52. Lowens, B., V.G. Motti, and K. Caine. 2017. Wearable privacy: Skeletons in the data closet. In *2017 IEEE International Conference on Healthcare Informatics (ICHI)*, 295–304. https://doi.org/10.1109/ICHI.2017.29

53. Dong, M., L. Chen, and L. Wang. 2019. Investigating the user behaviors of sharing health- and fitness-related information generated by mi band on weibo. *International Journal of Human—Computer Interaction* 35 (9): 773–786.

54. Lowens, B.M. 2018. Toward privacy enhanced solutions for granular control over health data collected by wearable devices. In *Proceedings of the 2018 Workshop on MobiSys 2018 Ph.D. Forum*, MobiSys PhD Forum '18, 5–6. New York: Association for Computing Machinery. https://doi.org/10.1145/3212711.3212714

55. From cheating to pregnancy reveals, wearables know what you're doing intimately. https://www.inverse.com/mind-body/from-cheating-to-pregnancy-reveals-wearables-know-what-you-are-doing-intimately. Accessed 13 April 2021.

56. Meteriz, Ü., Fazıl Yıldıran, N., Kim J, and D. Mohaisen. 2020. Understanding the potential risks of sharing elevation information on fitness applications. *2020 IEEE 40th International Conference on Distributed Computing Systems (ICDCS)*, 464–473, doi: 10.1109/ICDCS47774.2020.00063.

57. Fitness tracking app strava gives away location of secret us army bases. https://www.theguardian.com/world/2018/jan/28/fitness-tracking-app-gives-away-location-of-secret-us-army-bases. Accessed 13 April 2021.

58. Rader, E., and J. Slaker. 2017. The importance of visibility for folk theories of sensor data. In *Thirteenth Symposium on Usable Privacy and Security (SOUPS 2017)*, 257–270. Santa Clara: USENIX Association.

59. Gabriele, S., and S. Chiasson (2020). Understanding fitness tracker users' security and privacy knowledge, attitudes and behaviours. In *Proceedings of the 2020 CHI Conference on Human Factors in Computing Systems*, CHI '20, 1–12. New York: Association for Computing Machinery.

60. 'Alexa, are you invading my privacy?' The dark side of our voice assistants. (2019). http://www.theguardian.com/technology/2019/oct/09/alexa-are-you-invading-my-privacy-the-dark-side-of-our-voice-assistants Section: Technology.

61. Amazon customer receives 1,700 audio files of a stranger who used alexa. https://www.npr.org/2018/12/20/678631013/amazon-customer-receives-1-700-audio-files-of-a-stranger-who-used-alexa?t=1570014709519&t=1570530199090. Accessed 13 April 2021.

62. Cowan, B.R., N. Pantidi, D. Coyle, K. Morrissey, P. Clarke, S. Al-Shehri, D. Earley, and N. Bandeira. 2017. "what can i help you with?": Infrequent users' experiences of intelligent personal assistants. In *Proceedings of the 19th International Conference on Human-Computer Interaction with Mobile Devices and Services*, MobileHCI '17, New York: Association for Computing Machinery.

63. Malkin, N., J. Bernd, M. Johnson, and S. Egelman. 2018. "what can't data be used for?" Privacy expectations about smart tvs in the us. In *European Workshop on Usable Security (Euro USEC)*.

64. Hey, i didn't order this dollhouse! 6 hilarious alexa mishaps. https://www.digitaltrends.com/home/funny-accidental-amazon-alexa-ordering-stories/. Accessed 13 April 2021.

65. Nationwide Insurance to Give a Million Customers Echo Auto, Doubling Amazon's In-Car User Base. (2019). https://voicebot.ai/2019/10/09/nationwide-insurance-to-give-a-million-customers-echo-auto-doubling-amazons-in-car-user-base/. Section: Alexa skills.

66. Home assistant adopter beware: Google, amazon digital assistant patents reveal plans for mass snooping. https://www.consumerwatchdog.org/privacy-technology/home-assistant-adopter-beware-google-amazon-digital-assistant-patents-reveal. Accessed 13 April 2021.
67. Tabassum, M., T. Kosiński, A. Frik, N. Malkin, P. Wijesekera, S. Egelman, and H.R. Lipford. 2019. Investigating users' preferences and expectations for always-listening voice assistants. *Proceedings of the ACM on Interactive, Mobile, Wearable and Ubiquitous Technologies* 3 (4): 1–23.
68. Dear, K., K. Dutton, and E. Fox. 2019. Do 'watching eyes' influence antisocial behavior? a systematic review & meta-analysis. *Evolution and Human Behavior* 40 (3): 269–280.
69. Mazerolle, L., D. Hurley, and M. Chamlin. 2002. Social behavior in public space: An analysis of behavioral adaptations to cctv. *Security Journal* 15 (3): 59–75.
70. McLean, S.J., R.E. Worden, and M. Kim. 2013. Here's looking at you: An evaluation of public cctv cameras and their effects on crime and disorder. *Criminal Justice Review* 38 (3): 303–334. https://doi.org/10.1177/0734016813492415
71. Wang, Y., H. Xia, Y. Yao, and Y. Huang. 2016. Flying eyes and hidden controllers: A qualitative study of people's privacy perceptions of civilian drones in the us. *Proceedings on Privacy Enhancing Technologies* 2016 (3): 172–190.
72. Brush, A., J. Jung, R. Mahajan, and F. Martinez. 2013. Digital neighborhood watch: Investigating the sharing of camera data amongst neighbors. In *Proceedings of the 2013 Conference on Computer Supported Cooperative Work*, 693–700. Ne York: ACM.
73. Ring. Ring neighborhood watch. https://shop.ring.com/pages/neighbors. Accessed 09 Nov 2020.
74. Feng, Y., Y. Yao, and N. Sadeh. 2021. A design space for privacy choices: Towards meaningful privacy control in the internet of things. In *Proceedings of the 2021 CHI Conference on Human Factors in Computing Systems*, CHI '21, New York, NY, 1–16. New York: Association for Computing Machinery. https://doi.org/10.1145/3411764.3445148
75. Luger, E., S. Moran, and T. Rodden. 2013. Consent for all: Revealing the hidden complexity of terms and conditions. In *Proceedings of the SIGCHI Conference on Human Factors in Computing Systems*, CHI '13, 2687–2696. New York: Association for Computing Machinery.
76. McDonald, A.M. and L.F. Cranor. 2008. The cost of reading privacy policies. *Isjlp* 4: 543.
77. Emami-Naeini, P., Y. Agarwal, L.F. Cranor, and H. Hibshi. 2020. Ask the experts: What should be on an iot privacy and security label? In *2020 IEEE Symposium on Security and Privacy (SP)*, 447–464. Piscataway: IEEE.
78. What we learned from apple's new privacy labels. https://nytimes.com/2021/01/27/technology/personaltech/apple-privacy-labels.htmlnytimes.com/2021/01/27/technology/personaltech/apple-privacy-labels.html. Accessed 13 April 2021.
79. Mozilla - *privacy not included. https://foundation.mozilla.org/en/privacynotincluded/. Accessed 13 April 2021.
80. Wilkinson, D., P. Bahirat, M. Namara, J. Lyu, A. Alsubhi, P. Wisniewski, and B. Knijnenburg. 2019. Privacy at a glance: Exploring the effectiveness of screensavers to improve privacy awareness. In *Proceedings of the ACM Conference on Human Factors in Computing Systems (CHI). Under Review*. New York: ACM.
81. Almuhimedi, H., F. Schaub, N. Sadeh, I. Adjerid, A. Acquisti, J. Gluck, L.F. Cranor, and Y. Agarwal. 2015. Your location has been shared 5,398 times! a field study on mobile app privacy nudging. In *Proceedings of the 33rd Annual ACM Conference on Human Factors in Computing Systems*, 787–796.
82. Huang, D.Y., N. Apthorpe, F. Li, G. Acar, and N. Feamster. 2020. Iot inspector: Crowdsourcing labeled network traffic from smart home devices at scale. *Proceedings of the ACM on Interactive, Mobile, Wearable and Ubiquitous Technologies* 4 (2): 1–21.
83. Yao, Y., J.R. Basdeo, O. R. Mcdonough, and Y. Wang. 2019. Privacy perceptions and designs of bystanders in smart homes. *Proceedings of the ACM on Human-Computer Interaction* 3 (CSCW): 1–24.

84. Miettinen, M., S. Marchal, I. Hafeez, N. Asokan, A.-R. Sadeghi, and S. Tarkoma. 2017. Iot sentinel: Automated device-type identification for security enforcement in IoT. In *2017 IEEE 37th International Conference on Distributed Computing Systems (ICDCS)*, 2177–2184. Piscataway: IEEE.

85. Acar, A., H. Fereidooni, T. Abera, A.K. Sikder, M. Miettinen, H. Aksu, M. Conti, A.-R. Sadeghi, and S. Uluagac. 2020. Peek-a-boo: I see your smart home activities, even encrypted! In *Proceedings of the 13th ACM Conference on Security and Privacy in Wireless and Mobile Networks*, 207–218.

86. Project alias. http://bjoernkarmann.dk/project_alias. Accessed 08 Jan 2021.

87. Chandrasekaran, V., T. Linden, K. Fawaz, B. Mutlu, and S. Banerjee. 2018. Blackout and obfuscator: An exploration of the design space for privacy-preserving interventions for voice assistants. Preprint arXiv:1812.00263.

88. van den Hooff, J., D. Lazar, M. Zaharia, and N. Zeldovich. 2015. Vuvuzela: Scalable private messaging resistant to traffic analysis. In *Proceedings of the 25th Symposium on Operating Systems Principles*, SOSP '15, 137–152. New York: Association for Computing Machinery.

89. Yao, Y., J.R. Basdeo, S. Kaushik, and Y. Wang. 2019. Defending my castle: A co-design study of privacy mechanisms for smart homes. In *Proceedings of the 2019 CHI Conference on Human Factors in Computing Systems*, CHI '19, 1–12. New York: Association for Computing Machinery.

90. He, Y., P. Bahirat, B.P. Knijnenburg, and A. Menon. 2019. A data-driven approach to designing for privacy in household iot. *ACM Transactions on Interactive Intelligent Systems (TiiS)* 10 (1): 1–47.

91. Chow, R., H. Jin, B. Knijnenburg, and G. Saldamli. 2013. Differential data analysis for recommender systems. In *Proceedings of the 7th ACM Conference on Recommender Systems*, RecSys '13, 323–326. New York: Association for Computing Machinery. https://doi.org/10.1145/2507157.2507190

92. Kids are spending more time with voice, but brands shouldn't rush to engage them. https://www.emarketer.com/content/kids-are-spending-more-time-with-voice-but-brands-shouldnt-rush-to-engage-them. Accessed 13 April 2021.

93. Le, T., D. Huang, N.J. Apthorpe, and Y. Tian. 2021. Skillbot: Identifying risky content for children in alexa skills. ArXiv abs/2102.03382.

94. Freed, D., J. Palmer, D.E. Minchala, K. Levy, T. Ristenpart, and N. Dell. 2017. Digital technologies and intimate partner violence: A qualitative analysis with multiple stakeholders. *Proceedings of the ACM on Human-Computer Interaction* 1 (CSCW): 1–22.

95. Zeng, E., and F. Roesner. 2019. Understanding and improving security and privacy in multi-user smart homes: a design exploration and in-home user study. In *28th {USENIX} Security Symposium ({USENIX} Security 19)*, 159–176.

96. Bahirat, P., Y. He, A. Menon, and B. Knijnenburg. 2018. A data-driven approach to developing iot privacy-setting interfaces. In *23rd International Conference on Intelligent User Interfaces*, 165–176.

97. Klasnja, P., S. Consolvo, J. Jung, B.M. Greenstein, L. LeGrand, P. Powledge, and D. Wetherall (2009). "when i am on wi-fi, i am fearless" privacy concerns & practices in eeryday wi-fi use. In *Proceedings of the SIGCHI Conference on Human Factors in Computing Systems*, 1993–2002.

98. Ghiglieri, M., M. Volkamer, and K. Renaud. 2017. Exploring consumers' attitudes of smart tv related privacy risks. In *International Conference on Human Aspects of Information Security, Privacy, and Trust*, 656–674. Berlin: Springer.

99. Apthorpe, N., Y. Shvartzshnaider, A. Mathur, D. Reisman, and N. Feamster. 2018. Discovering smart home internet of things privacy norms using contextual integrity. *Proceedings of the ACM on Interactive, Mobile, Wearable and Ubiquitous Technologies* 2 (2): 1–23.

100. Lederer, S., J. Mankoff, A.K. Dey. 2003. Who wants to know what when? privacy preference determinants in ubiquitous computing. In *CHI'03 Extended Abstracts on Human Factors in Computing Systems*, 724–725.

101. Choe, E.K., S. Consolvo, J. Jung, B. Harrison, and J.A. Kientz. 2011. Living in a glass house: a survey of private moments in the home. In *Proceedings of the 13th International Conference on Ubiquitous Computing*, 41–44.
102. Aleisa, N., and K. Renaud. 2017. Yes, i know this iot device might invade my privacy, but i love it anyway! a study of saudi arabian perceptions. In *IoTBDS 2017: 2nd International Conference on Internet of Things: Big Data and Security, Porto*.
103. Das, A., M. Degeling, X. Wang, J. Wang, N. Sadeh, and M. Satyanarayanan. 2017. Assisting users in a world full of cameras: A privacy-aware infrastructure for computer vision applications. In *2017 IEEE Conference on Computer Vision and Pattern Recognition Workshops (CVPRW)*, 1387–1396. Piscataway: IEEE.
104. Barbosa, N.M., J.S. Park, Y. Yao, and Y. Wang. 2019. " what if?" predicting individual users' smart home privacy preferences and their changes. *PoPETs* 2019 (4): 211–231.
105. Horne, C., B. Darras, E. Bean, A. Srivastava, and S. Frickel. 2015. Privacy, technology, and norms: The case of smart meters. *Social Science Research* 51: 64–76.
106. Sanchez, O.R., I. Torre, Y. He, and B.P. Knijnenburg. 2019. A recommendation approach for user privacy preferences in the fitness domain. *User Modeling and User-Adapted Interaction* 30: 513–565. https://doi.org/10.1007/s11257-019-09246-3
107. Schaub, F., B. Könings, M. Weber, and F. Kargl. 2012. Towards context adaptive privacy decisions in ubiquitous computing. In *2012 IEEE International Conference on Pervasive Computing and Communications Workshops*, 407–410. Piscataway: IEEE.
108. Sanchez, O.R., I. Torre, and B.P. Knijnenburg. 2020. Semantic-based privacy settings negotiation and management. *Future Generation Computer Systems* 111: 879–898. https://doi.org/https://doi.org/10.1016/j.future.2019.10.024, https://www.sciencedirect.com/science/article/pii/S0167739X18317035

Part III
Audiences

Chapter 12
Cross-Cultural Privacy Differences

Yao Li

Abstract As many technologies have become available around the world and users increasingly share personal information online with people and organizations from different countries and cultures, there is an urgent need to investigate the cross-cultural differences in users' privacy attitudes and behaviors in the use of these technologies. Such investigation is important to understand how users in different cultures manage their information privacy differently and to inform the privacy design for technologies that are used globally. This chapter covers major cross-cultural differences that have been reported in privacy research. Specifically, it briefly reviews the concept of culture, discusses the cross-cultural differences in privacy management, and recommends design implications on privacy design in the international context.

12.1 Introduction

Although ample research has shown that national culture influences users' privacy attitudes and behaviors in their interaction with technologies, most privacy studies and designs do not sufficiently take these cultural differences into account. Identifying such cross-cultural differences is important to inform the privacy design for technologies that are used across countries and to understand individual differences in privacy management. As more and more technologies, such as social media, shopping websites, and mobile apps, have become available worldwide, users are interacting with individuals and organizations across country boundaries. Thus, cross-cultural studies in privacy research have become increasingly important and popular in the recent decade.

While privacy regulation exists in almost every culture, the specific behavioral and psychological mechanisms that people use to regulate privacy boundaries are

Y. Li (✉)
School of Modeling, Simulation and Training, University of Central Florida, Orlando, FL, USA
e-mail: yao.li@ucf.edu

B. P. Knijnenburg et al. (eds.), *Modern Socio-Technical Perspectives on Privacy*,
https://doi.org/10.1007/978-3-030-82786-1_12

culturally unique. Since the 1960s, when privacy mostly concerned physical access to an individual's surroundings and private space, researchers had found that people in different cultures are universally aware and capable of regulating physical privacy, but their specific psychological and behavioral mechanisms vary from culture to culture [1]. For example, the Mehinacu (a tribal group in central Brazil) lived together in a small circular plaza, but used secret paths and clearings in the woods around to escape from others [2]. The Javanese families (an ethnic group native to the Indonesian island of Java) lived in unfenced homes, but they would shut people out with a wall of etiquette, such as hiding their emotional feelings [3]. A case study of Chinese families in Malaysia showed that these families maintained separation by means of cultural practices, such as strong taboos for entering others' sleeping areas, separate storage and cooking areas in different parts of the communal kitchen, and clarification of relationship status among the elderly and young, between men and women [4]. Another culture, the Ngadju Dayaks of Borneo who resided in multifamily units, maintained separate sleeping areas and possessions, ate at different times, and had strong norms against intrusion [5]. These examples illustrate how physical privacy is a culturally pervasive process that allows people to make themselves more or less accessible to others. Yet, they also demonstrate the cultural specificity of physical privacy regulation.

In the information age, the culturally distinct privacy regulatory mechanisms in users' interaction with technologies have frequently been brought up in research and news. For example, users in Western countries treat medical history as highly sensitive data compared with Eastern countries [6]. Another example is the recent launch of the General Data Protection Regulation (GDPR) in the European Union (EU) on data protection and privacy. This law significantly strengthens EU users' control over their personal data while establishing strong penalties for businesses that do not comply [7] (for a more comprehensive overview of privacy regulation, see Chap. 18). Many companies and websites changed their privacy policies and features prior to GDPR's implementation. This shows that data privacy regulatory practices differ between European countries and other countries, suggesting that multinational organizations should take cross-cultural differences into account when running technology business globally.

Based on these discussions, investigation into the concrete cross-cultural differences in users' privacy attitudes and behaviors is most warranted. Such investigation will enhance our understanding about what cultural differences exist and how such differences shape users' interaction with privacy systems. More importantly and practically, it will inform the privacy design for technologies that are used across the world. As many technologies still adopt the "one-size-fits-all" privacy design in different countries, such investigation will shed light on how to go beyond the "one-size-fits-all" privacy approach [8].

12.2 How to Study Culture

In this section, I will introduce the concept of national culture, including its definition, measurement, and influences. Culture is defined as the "collective programming of the mind that distinguishes the members of one group from others" [9]. This programming influences patterns of thinking which are reflected in people's everyday perception of various aspects of life and in the way people behave [9]. Culture is a collective concept, thus commonly used for tribes, nations, and organizations. Researchers have been highly interested in studying various aspects of country-level cultural differences, as they highlight the differences between national populations [9–11]. Although there are considerable variations among individuals in the same country, research has shown that people in the same national culture exhibit certain differences when compared with other nations [12, 13].

12.2.1 Cultural Dimensions

Many cross-cultural studies, not only in privacy but also in other domains, apply cultural dimensions to characterize national cultures, rather than other measures, such as country and language. This is because cultural dimensions are conceptual constructs that can depict the underlying patterns of how people live in different countries. These dimensions offer a way for us to classify the complex patterns of culture. Additionally, cultural dimensions explain human behaviors better than other measures, such as country and language. For example, one study has demonstrated that compared to country of residence and language, cultural dimensions are better predictors of privacy decisions in terms of prediction accuracy and variance explained [6].

Among the various country-level cultural dimensions, the majority relates the dichotomy of individualism versus collectivism [14–16]. Collectivistic cultures emphasize that groups (i.e., family, tribe, country) bind and mutually obligate individuals, whereas individualistic cultures assume that individuals are independent of one another [13, 14]. Researchers find that individualism is more prevalent in industrialized Western countries, whereas collectivism prevails in East Asian countries [17].

Researchers have also discovered other dimensions that can describe country-level cultural differences. One highly influential framework that captures these dimensions is Geert Hofstede's six dimensions of culture [9]. Aside from individualism, he also proposed power distance, masculinity, long-term orientation, uncertainty avoidance, and indulgence as cultural dimensions. Hofstede's dimensions are the result of a factor analysis at the level of country means of a comprehensive survey instrument, aiming at identifying systematic differences in national cultures. Hofstede's dimensions were first developed in the 1960s and 1970s at IBM and later enhanced by two new dimensions. Ninety-three countries have meanwhile been scored along each of these dimensions. Various studies validated the model by including other respondent groups such as students, managers, and pilots. Hofstede's most recent model identifies the following six cultural dimensions:

- **Power distance (PDI)** is the degree to which the less powerful members of a society accept and expect that power is distributed unequally. A high score of PDI indicates that people accept a hierarchical order.
- **Individualism (IND)** is defined as a preference for a loosely knit social framework in which individuals are expected to take care of only themselves and their immediate families. Low individualism is collectivism.
- **Masculinity (MAS)** represents a preference in society for achievement, heroism, assertiveness, and material rewards for success. Such a society is more competitive. Its opposite, femininity, stands for a preference for cooperation, modesty, caring for the weak, and quality of life.
- **Long-term orientation (LTO)** describes how a society maintains some links with its own past while dealing with the challenges of the present and future.
- **Uncertainty avoidance (UAI)** is the degree to which the members of a society feel uncomfortable with uncertainty and ambiguity.
- **Indulgence (IDL)** stands for a society that allows relatively free gratification of basic and natural human drives related to enjoying life and having fun. Its opposite is restraint.

In recent years, researchers have developed new dimensions that add to or reconceptualize Hofstede's dimensions. For example, Schwartz proposed dimensions such as harmony and embeddedness [11]. House et al. proposed dimensions such as assertiveness, humane orientation, and performance orientation [10]. While there are still debates about the comprehensiveness of these dimensions, they indeed facilitate our understandings about country-level cultural differences [18].

12.2.2 Cultural Differences in Behaviors

A great amount of cross-cultural research in psychology and social science has compared various aspects of behaviors among individuals with different cultures, especially between individualistic and collectivistic cultures [14–16]. One of the common approaches is to measure individual's cultural backgrounds through questionnaires and to correlate this assessment with their behaviors. Many researchers employ existing cultural questions, such as Hofstede's [9] and Triandis's [19] lists to ask participants to rate how much they agree with certain culture-related statements. Another common approach involves efforts to prime cultural values before participants perform certain behaviors. This approach usually happens in laboratory settings, where the priming techniques attempt to temporarily focusing participants' attention on different cultural values.

Regardless of the approach used to study cultural differences in behaviors, the majority of researchers have found that behaviors differ between individualists

Table 12.1 Summary of cultural differences in behaviors

Cultural differences in behaviors		
	Individualism	Collectivism
Self-concept	Defined through uniqueness and personal achievement	Defined by social roles
Social relationships	Interact with different groups and strangers; free to move to other groups	In-group over out-group relationships; stay permanently with in-groups
Attribution style	Decontextualized attribution	Contextualized attributions
Communication style	Direct; goal oriented; concern with message clarity	Indirect; concern about a target's feelings and self-presentation

and collectivists. For example, in the context of self-concept, collectivists tend to understand their self-identities based on social roles and endeavors; harmony in in-group relationships contributes to their life satisfaction [20]. In individualistic cultures, people tend to define their identities through uniqueness and personal achievement rather than social roles [21]. They feel more than collectivists that self-esteem contributes to their life satisfaction [20]. In social relationships, people in collectivistic cultures favor in-group relationships (family, friends, etc.) over out-group relationships (strangers) [22] and interact more frequently with in-group members [23]. While individualists also feel close to in-group members, they interact with more groups and expect to have more freedom to decide which groups to belong to [24]. They treat different in-group relationships in a similar manner [25] and have greater willingness to trust others—including strangers—and greater ease in their interaction with strangers [26]. In terms of attribution style, individualists are person focused and engage in more decontextualized causal reasoning, while collectivists engage in more contextualized and situated reasoning [14]. Individualists find relational and contextual information less informative or compelling than collectivists, even when contextual influences are made salient [14]. For example, individualistic adults explain behavior and outcomes more in terms of dispositions, whereas collectivists focus more on situations in describing the behavior of both themselves and others [27]. These major cultural differences in behaviors are summarized in Table 12.1.

12.2.3   Cultural Differences in Perceptions

In different cultures, some concepts can be measured in a conceptually similar manner, while other concepts may not. For example, shame and guilt are negative affect on the Positive and Negative Affect Schedule (PANAS). While they are considered as negative emotions in individualistic cultures, in collectivistic cultures, shame and guilt are somewhat positive and represent self-reflection and self-improvement instead of sheer wrongfulness [28, 29]. To examine whether people in different cultures interpret the same concepts in a conceptually similar way, researchers should perform *measurement invariance tests* in cross-cultural studies. Measurement invariance refers to a statistical property of measurement to indicate whether the same concept is measured similarly or differently across different groups. Violations of measurement invariance may preclude meaningful interpretation of measurement data.

Performing measurement invariance tests in cross-cultural studies is an important step before making cultural comparisons, including comparisons of privacy attitudes and behaviors, as different cultures may have different interpretations about the concept of privacy due to local cultural norms and practices. For example, in one study [30] that compared privacy management strategies across the USA, Singapore, and Korea, researchers found that participants in these three countries have different understandings about the meanings and the levels of information control strategies. Here I will provide the specific steps to conduct measurement invariance tests in cross-cultural studies. These steps are based on the work in [30, 31].

12.2.3.1 Step 1: Define a Factor Model Based on the Items in a Questionnaire

The measurement invariance tests start with specifying a confirmatory factor analysis (CFA). In many cross-cultural studies, concepts (in measurement models represented by latent factors) are usually measured through a number of items or statements that are rated by participants from different cultural groups through questionnaires. Researchers then conduct the measurement invariance tests on the collected ratings to these items or statements. The CFA tests whether the items in a questionnaire measure what the researcher wants to measure, as expressed in a latent factor model. Thus, in Step 1, a factor model is built and tested using CFA. This is done to ensure an overall fit of the proposed factor model.

12.2.3.2 Step 2: Configural Invariance

Next, the same factor model needs to be run separately in each cultural group. The parameters of these factor models will be completely independent from each other, but the factor structures are kept the same. This set of models is called the configural model. Validating the statistical fit of these models in each group can inform us of the configural invariance, which means whether the same factor structure is valid in each cultural group. If configural invariance is validated in this step, it means that the measured concepts have the same factor structure in the tested groups (i.e., countries). If the groups have different factor structures, then the measured concepts lack configural invariance, suggesting that group comparison cannot be conducted and that the factor model should be re-examined in each of the groups.

12.2.3.3   Step 3: Metric Invariance

In this step, the factor model should again be run separately in each group, but this time, the factor loadings should be held equal between the groups, while all other parameters are still allowed to differ between groups. This set of models is called the metric model. The metric model should be compared with the configural model in Step 2 to see if they are *not* significantly different. A lack of significant difference ensures metric invariance, which indicates that the groups attribute the same meaning to the factor. Consequently, these groups can be compared in terms of their path coefficients in a subsequent structural model.

If metric variance is not validated (i.e., the metric model is significantly different from the configural model in Step 2), then the groups may vary in terms of the relative importance of certain items in the factor model. The researchers are then advised to examine the specific content of the items that caused the invariance to understand how the perception of the factor differs between the groups. Factor loadings of these items can be freed to reinstate metric invariance; this produces a model that has *partial* metric invariance. If the number of freed items does not exceed 20% of the total number of parameters in the factor model, a path coefficient comparison of between-country causal models can still be achieved.

12.2.3.4   Step 4: Scalar Invariance

In the fourth step, the factor model should again be run in each group separately, but now both the loadings and the intercepts are constrained to be equal across groups. This set of models is called the scalar model. The scalar model should be compared with the metric model in Step 3 to see if they are *not* significantly different. A lack of significant difference ensures scalar invariance, which implies that both the meaning of the construct (the factor loadings) and the comparative baseline levels of the underlying items (intercepts) are equal across groups. Consequently, the groups can be compared on their scores on the latent variable.

Again, if the scalar model is significantly different from the metric model in Step 3, it means that two groups have disagreement on the meaning of the factors and that some differences in item scores may exist between the groups that go beyond differences reflected in the factors. The researchers are then advised to examine the specific content of the items that caused the invariance to understand why these items might differ between groups beyond their contribution to the factor score. The intercepts of these items can be freed to reinstate metric invariance; this produces a model that has partial scalar invariance. Again, the number of freed parameters should not exceed 20% of the total number of parameters in the factor model.

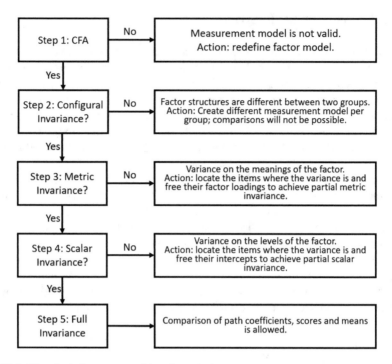

Fig. 12.1 Flowchart of measurement invariance tests

12.2.3.5 Step 5: Full Invariance

In this step, the factor model should again be run across all groups, but this time the factor loadings, intercepts, and residual variances should be held equal across groups. These models should be compared with the scalar model in Step 4 to see if they are *not* significantly different. If they are not different, the model has full invariance, which indicates that the latent factor is measured identically across groups, meaning that the groups can be combined into a single CFA. While full invariance rarely happens, the process of testing for full invariance can help us understand how factors work differently in different cultural groups.

The five steps are summarized in the following flowchart (Fig. 12.1).

12.3 Cross-Cultural Privacy Differences in Social Media

In this section, I will describe the major cross-cultural differences that have been found in privacy research in the context of social media, as social media is an important platform to study in privacy studies. Chapter 7 in this book will provide more comprehensive discussion about privacy on social media. In this section, I mainly address the cultural aspects of social media privacy.

Social media has become a global phenomenon in the last decade. Sites like Facebook, Twitter, and Instagram reach users worldwide and impact the social lives of large and diverse populations from different parts of the world. For example, as of April 2019, Facebook has 300 million users in India, making it the leading country in Facebook use over the USA, and another 100 million users spread across countries like Brazil, Indonesia, Mexico, the Philippines, Vietnam, Thailand, Turkey, and the UK [32]. Instagram is available in more than 100 countries across Asia, Europe, Africa, and North and South America. Social media users from different parts of the world have different backgrounds, expectations, norms, and experiences shaped by the cultural values where they grow up. Therefore, since many popular social media platforms have become available around the world, and since individual users' social networks increasingly include contacts from different cultures, investigations of cultural differences are needed to support privacy management for international users.

According to prior research, it was generally believed that users in individualistic cultures exhibit higher privacy concerns towards online information sharing on social media and adopt more privacy protective behaviors than in collectivistic cultures. For example, many studies reported that users in individualistic countries like the USA were highly concerned with their online privacy and aware of personal information collection on social media [33–35]. Individualistic users had the higher lack of trust in the SNS system and operator [35]. They expected more control over their information sharing [33]. They would adopt more protective self-presentation to manage their information on social media [36]. Their perceived effectiveness of privacy settings had a stronger effect on privacy control [37]. On the contrary, collectivistic users tended to be less concerned with their privacy on social media. They tended to share more information, which was largely driven by the social influence of information sharing and reciprocity in the online community [38, 39]. The group norms have a stronger effect on social rewards and privacy control under high collectivism [37]. Thus, if the members of users' social group or users' online community disclosed a lot, users would be highly likely to follow the norms. Moreover, collectivistic users were more willing to share information with a high level of intimacy, such as their personal lives and photos [36, 40]. In addition to individualism and collectivism, some studies focus on other dimensions of national cultures. For example, users in a culture with a high tendency to avoid uncertainty, such as Korea and Germany, have greater privacy concerns and awareness on social media [33, 41, 42]. They are more likely to perceive the negative outcome and impression damage from social media information sharing.

However, some recent studies have shown that cross-cultural differences in social media privacy should consider the specific information sharing context. In certain situations, collectivistic users are *not* found to be less concerned about privacy as in previous research; in those situations, they may perceive *higher* privacy risks and concerns than individualistic users. We cannot assume that users in collectivistic

Table 12.2 Summary of cross-cultural differences in social media information sharing

	Individualistic countries (e.g., the USA)	Collectivistic countries (e.g., CN)
Unknown audience	✓ Same school ✓ Friends of friends ✓ Same SNS group	✓ Friends of friends ✓ Those who share interesting posts
Known audience	✓ Employer ✓ Schoolmates ✓ Colleagues	✓ Schoolmates ✓ Acquaintance ✓ Teacher
Collective privacy	✓ Less concern about the negative impact of one's information sharing on others' privacy	✓ More concerns about the negative impact of one's information sharing on others' privacy
Privacy management strategies	✓ Individual-level privacy management strategies (corrective and information control strategies)	✓ Group-level privacy management strategies (collaborative strategies)

cultures are indiscriminately insensitive to information privacy. I will elaborate the cultural differences shown in Table 12.2 in detail in the next few sections.

12.3.1 Cultural Differences in Sharing with Different Social Relationships

Aside from group privacy, collectivistic users tend to be more cautious when sharing information with weak ties. In this section, I will describe the cultural differences when users share information with different online social relationships. These differences are found in a survey study across the USA, China, and Korea [43]. Figures 12.2 and 12.3 show how collectivism is associated with users' social information disclosure, i.e., status updates, relationship, and photos, to different types of online social relationships. In Fig. 12.2, highly collectivistic users tend to be more cautious about sharing social information with those who are from the same social network groups (green line) or the same school (orange line) than individualistic users. In Fig. 12.3, highly collectivistic users are shown to share less with colleagues (blue line) and employers (yellow line) than individualistic users. In both figures, sharing information with people who have no commonalities, who are from the same city, or who are local merchants is least acceptable for both collectivistic and individualistic users.

These findings are echoed by several other recent studies showing that collectivistic users control their privacy boundary with different online social relationships more tightly than individualistic users [44]. It is found that collectivistic users primarily use social media to maintain their existing relationships [45, 46]. Most of their online social networks tend to be close friends [40, 47]. Collectivistic

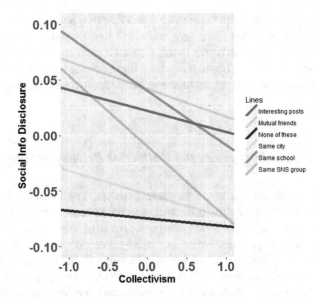

Fig. 12.2 Comparison of different types of unknown relationships

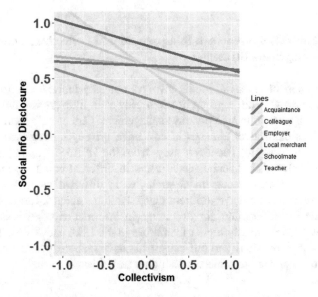

Fig. 12.3 Comparison of different types of known relationships

users also prefer to interact with offline connections belonging to the same social groups in the social media [40]. Such relationships are more likely to be their in-group members with whom they can share private information without any specific privacy boundary issues [40]. It is also easier for collectivistic users to seek social support and commitment from these close ties. Thus, they have greater trust in their online social networks [38]. Strangers and weak ties are either less likely to be part of their online social networks or are restricted from accessing to their online information sharing. Collectivistic users have higher desire to control the visibility of their information and to use anonymous or pseudonymous identities on social media [35].

12.3.2   Cultural Differences in Collective Privacy Management

The findings in this section are from several studies. The cultural differences in interpretations of the collective privacy management strategies are mainly taken from Cho et al.'s work [30], in which they perform a large survey study to gauge how social media users adopt collective privacy management strategies in three different countries: the USA, Singapore, and Korea. The cultural differences in perceptions of group privacy are mainly taken from James et al.'s work [48] and Li et al.'s work [43]. Again, both of these studies apply surveys to measure participants' perceptions about group privacy in several different countries.

12.3.2.1   Cultural Differences in Interpretations of Collective Privacy Management Strategies

Privacy management on social media involves not only individual effort but also collective processes within a group of users. However, little cross-cultural privacy literature focuses on collective privacy management. Cho et al.'s work systematically examines cultural differences in collective privacy management strategies [30]. Through a survey of Facebook users from the USA, Singapore, and Korea, this study first shows that social media users in different countries interpret the same collective privacy management strategies in different ways. For example, participants in Singapore have different understandings about information control strategies: the factor loadings for two items in information control strategies in Singapore were substantially higher than those in the USA and Korea. This might be a result of their sensitivity to self-censorship as Singaporean social media users live in a more authoritarian society with higher surveillance.

12.3.2.2   Cultural Differences in Perceptions of Others' or Group Privacy

Additionally, studies show that collectivistic users are more concerned with others' privacy and group privacy than individualistic users [48]. Compared with threats to individual privacy, users with a collectivistic cultural orientation are more likely to perceive others as being susceptible to information exposure as a result of their own Facebook activity [48]. They are more concerned whether their personal information sharing would cause negative impact on others' privacy and well-being. Moreover, users in individualistic countries rely more strongly on privacy management strategies at the individual level, such as corrective and information control strategies, to prevent personal privacy loss, while users in collectivistic countries adopt more group-level privacy management strategies, such as collaborating with each other on privacy protection and negotiating about each other's privacy boundary. This might be because collectivistic cultures place much emphasis on the good of the collective, such as their social groups and other types of in-groups. People in collectivistic cultures consider themselves as part of a group and value group welfare over their own interest. Thus, they are more concerned with the privacy protection of the group and seek more cooperation and coordination with their group members.

12.3.3   Design Implications

Generally, it is suggested that multinational social media providers should take users' cultural backgrounds into account during the privacy design process. Specifically, I make the following detailed suggestions.

12.3.3.1   Invest More Effort to Support Collective Privacy Management in Collectivistic Countries

Users in collectivistic cultures tend to be more sensitive to others' privacy and group privacy. The privacy systems in collectivistic countries should emphasize collaborative privacy management to coordinate privacy management experience between users and their online social networks. For example, privacy design can inform users of the risk their information sharing might bring to their social networks' privacy. Features like notification among users' social networks should be enabled to facilitate users to communicate with their social networks about the group privacy norms.

12.3.3.2   Differentiate Considerations in Audience Control in Different Cultures

Social media providers should focus on different factors in audience control features in different countries. It is a common practice that social media platforms provide audience control features for users to limit the people who can access to their information, such as Facebook's friend list and Google+'s circles. However, most existing audience control features are not differentiated between different cultures. Users in different cultures have different information sharing preferences with their social relationships: for instance, compared to individualistic users, collectivistic users expect more restrictive boundary regulation with their weak ties, such as employers, colleagues, and people in the same school or same social network group. Privacy designs in collectivistic countries, such as China and Korea, should therefore enable more audience control features to restrict these weak ties.

Individualistic users, on the other hand, are more open to interact with and disclose information to certain weak ties, such as people in the same social network group. They also feel comfortable to share social information with their employers. Social media platforms in individualistic countries should thus provide more opportunities for users to expand their social networks to include these relations through features like suggesting friends based on social group participation or based on professional networks. However, individualistic users feel relatively more reluctant to share with teachers. This type of relationship should thus less often be recommended as a suggested friendship, and existing relationships of this type should generally be more controlled for individualistic users.

12.3.3.3 Provide More Privacy Support to Protect Others' Privacy in Collectivistic Countries

Users' online information sharing may unexpectedly reveal others' private information. Some users will be willing to protect others' privacy by anonymizing and obscuring others' information, while some users may not even be aware of the risks exposed to others' privacy as a result of their own information sharing. In collectivistic countries, users are shown to be more sensitive to violations of others' privacy and more likely to perceive the severity of bringing negative impact on others' privacy and well-being due to their own information sharing. This is partially related with the cultural norms in promoting collective interests in collectivistic cultures. Thus, social media in collectivistic cultures should reinforce such norm commitment.

12.3.3.4 Secure Individual Privacy in Individualistic Countries

Users in individualistic cultures tend to be more sensitive to personal privacy loss. Therefore, individual-level privacy protections, such as corrective privacy management and information control, should be highlighted and enhanced. For example, based on current corrective and control features on social media, future privacy designs can incorporate more granular options for users to control their information flow and correct inappropriate information sharing. Also, privacy designs can intelligently inform users of the potential privacy loss they may experience after sharing information, so that the action of correcting can happen earlier.

Additionally, in individualistic cultures, while users are less sensitive to their violations to others' privacy as personal interests are more important, they may care about personal privacy being impacted by others' information sharing. Thus, social media in individualistic cultures should enhance features to inform the users who are negatively impacted by others' information sharing. More importantly, impacted users should be granted with more control over their personal information in others' shared content. For example, users should be granted the ability to remove their personal information in others' sharing.

12.4   Cross-Cultural Privacy Differences in Users' Information Disclosure to Organizations

As organizations increasingly conduct business globally, concerns with online data collection by organizations have extended beyond a single culture. As people in different cultures develop different values and norms, their perceptions of privacy and regulatory practices are intertwined with their cultural values and norms. Consequently, countries in different parts of the world have different regulations and policies regarding the use of consumers' personal information. Therefore, in a global market where personal data can be collected and transmitted across country borders, it is important that information privacy must be considered in an international context.

Generally, users' privacy attitudes and behaviors about information disclosure to organizations have significant grounding in their cultural values. First, individualism has a positive association with information privacy concerns [49–51]. People in individualist societies perceive higher privacy risks when disclosing personal information to shopping websites [52]. This is because individualism is associated with a strong desire for private life, freedom, and independence from others. Consequently, individuals in individualistic societies are more likely to be concerned about their personal territories and potential privacy intrusion and are thus reluctant to disclose personal information [52, 53]. They also adopt more protective behaviors, such as securing sensitive personal information [49, 54]. On the other hand, users in societies that place a high value on collectivism tend to be less sensitive to privacy concerns [55, 56]. They appear to trust data collection entities more and are more willing to share information with these entities [49, 53].

Uncertainty avoidance is another cultural value that is significantly associated with users' privacy attitudes towards personal data collection. For instance, studies have shown that uncertainty avoidance has a negative relationship with privacy concerns [49]. People in societies with a greater tendency to avoid uncertainty will perceive higher privacy risk from online information sharing and are thus less willing to disclose personal information [52, 57].

Based on these general associations between cultural values and privacy attitudes/behaviors that are well studied in previous privacy literature, a recent study discovers more concrete cross-cultural differences in users' privacy decision-making when they are asked to disclose information to organizations [6]. This study presents results from a large-scale online survey across eight countries to collect participants' responses in different data collection scenarios. In the scenarios,

Table 12.3 Summary of cross-cultural differences in disclosing personal data to organizations

	Individualistic countries (e.g., the USA)	Collectivistic countries (e.g., CN)
Usage purpose	✓ Customization	✓ Autonomously make decisions ✓ Customization
Value exchange	✓ Saving time or money ✓ Unique or compelling value	✓ Benefit the community ✓ Saving time or money ✓ Unique or compelling value
Entities	✓ Paid service ✓ Existing relationship	✓ Government
Collection methods	✓ Through computer	✓ Through mobile
Attitude	✓ Third-party accountability for data collection increases its acceptability	✓ Third-party accountability for data collection decreases its acceptability

participants were informed of whom collects their data (data collection entities), for what purpose the data is collected (usage purpose), how the data is collected (collection methods), and what values participants can get from the data collection (value exchange). Participants were then asked whether they would agree to share personal data in the scenarios (acceptability). The study shows several concrete cross-cultural differences, which are summarized in Table 12.3 to depict how users in different cultures would react in different scenarios.

12.4.1 Cultural Differences in Data Collection Entities

Figure 12.4 shows that users with different levels of individualism prefer to disclose personal information to different types of entities. People in collectivistic cultures such as China and India are relatively more accepting of data collection performed by the government than people in individualist cultures such as the USA and Canada. Data collection by users' employers is also better accepted in collectivistic cultures. People in individualist cultures are relatively more accepting of data collection when they either pay for or already have an existing relationship with the service provider. Foreign service providers are not well accepted in most of the countries.

12.4.2 Cultural Differences in Usage Purpose

Figure 12.5 shows that the probabilities of acceptability decrease more strongly in individualistic countries than in collectivistic countries when the usage purpose changes from "as I agreed" to "to autonomously make decisions for me" or "to customize the options presented to me." "To autonomously make decisions for me"

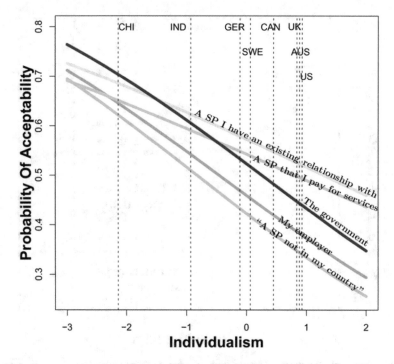

Fig. 12.4 Country comparison of acceptability in different data collection entities. SP stands for service provider

is the least acceptable usage purpose in individualistic countries, indicating that users in individualistic countries value autonomy. In collectivistic countries, such as China, "to autonomously make decisions for me" or "to customize the options presented to me" are equally accepted. "As I agreed" is the most acceptable usage purpose in all the countries.

12.4.3 Cultural Differences in Collection Methods

Collection methods describe how the data is collected by organizations. Table 12.4 describes the odds ratios of accepting data collection through mobile devices or computers. While the odds of sharing my info through mobile devices are generally lower than one, they are increasing in collectivistic countries, such as India and China, but decreasing in individualistic countries, such as the USA and Canada. This indicates that users in individualistic countries are more willing to provide personal information through computers than users in collectivistic countries.

In Table 12.5, the odds of sharing my photo or video image in public space are larger in individualistic countries, while the odds of sharing at work are larger in

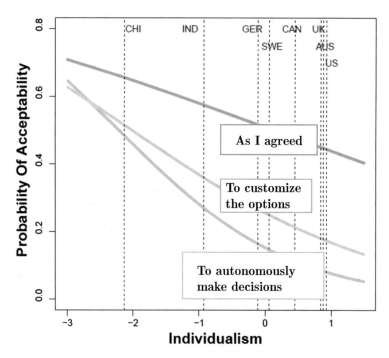

Fig. 12.5 Country comparison of acceptability in different usage purposes of data collection

Table 12.4 Comparing data collection through mobile devices and through computers

Collection methods	Relative odds of sharing my information through mobile devices, as compared to through computers				
	USA	Canada	Germany	India	China
Bank account number	0.701	0.730	0.764	0.818	0.904
Government issued ID	0.824	0.842	0.865	0.900	0.953
Medical history	0.570	0.616	0.674	0.771	0.938

Table 12.5 Comparing image collection in public space, at work, and at home

Compared to at home, odds of sharing my photo or video image	Collection methods				
	USA	Canada	Germany	India	China
	In public space				
	1.394	1.356	1.313	1.252	1.167
	At work				
	1.348	1.369	1.394	1.432	1.490

collectivistic countries. This indicates that when the data type is a photo or video image, users in individualistic countries are relatively more accepting if it is taken in public, while users in collectivistic countries accept it more at work.

12.4.4 Cultural Differences in Value Exchange from Data Collection

Value exchange refers to what value users can obtain from personal data sharing. As shown in Fig. 12.6, "saves me time or money" and "a unique or compelling value" are appealing values from data collection in both individualistic and collectivistic countries. However, "benefits the community" is more acceptable in collectivistic countries and less acceptable in individualistic countries. This indicates that users in individualistic countries cannot be swayed by benefits to the community.

12.4.5 Cultural Differences in Third-Party Accountability

Figure 12.7 describes the cultural differences in users' perception of third-party accountability—how much users regard third parties to be responsible for personal data collection. In individualistic countries, when users' perception that a third party is accountable for personal data collection increases, their acceptance of data collection generally increases as well. But in collectivistic countries, the perception of third-party accountability tends to decrease data collection acceptability. This

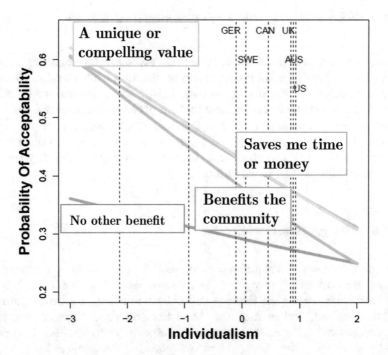

Fig. 12.6 Country comparison of acceptability in different value exchanges of data collection

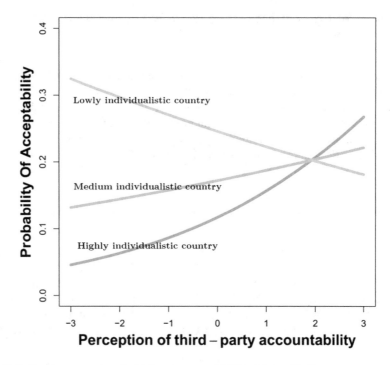

Fig. 12.7 Country comparison in third-party accountability of data collection

indicates that the attitudes towards third-party accountability regarding personal data collection have different consequences for the acceptability of data collection in different cultures. Even if users in collectivistic countries increasingly believe that third parties should be accountable for their personal data, they still find it less acceptable to disclose. In contrast, people in individualist societies are more likely to accept the data collection if the third parties establish formal agreement on the accountability regarding personal data collection, arguably because they are more comfortable with contract-based relations.

12.4.6 Design Implications

Based on the cross-cultural differences in users' data collection by organizations, we can see that users' acceptance of personal data collection is different in different cultures, even given the same data collection entities, data usage purposes, collection methods, values they can obtain from the data collection, and third-party accountability. Generally, organizations, especially organizations that operate globally, should consider users' cultural backgrounds and countries when collecting personal data and when designing privacy features to allow users to control their personal data flow. Specifically, I make the following suggestions.

12.4.6.1 Customize Data Collection Strategies in Different Countries

Users in different countries have different preferences regarding the collection of personal data. For example, users in individualist countries may find it acceptable to disclose personal data to a service provider that they pay for or have an existing relationship with. The same may be less acceptable in collectivistic countries though. Thus, service providers should take this into account when establishing privacy policies. Similarly, users in individualist countries may find it more acceptable to share their information through a computer, while users in collectivistic countries are more comfortable sharing through a mobile device. Previous work [58] has found that perceived usefulness is more important in Western culture while perceived ease of use is more important in Eastern culture. This finding may give rise to an explanation, namely, that users in individualistic countries may find computers more useful and more suited to control the disclosure of personal data, while users in collectivistic countries may view mobile devices as easier to use in data sharing. Thus, multinational organizations may need to tailor their data collection methods to different cultures in an effort to make users feel more comfortable.

12.4.6.2 Enable Different Options in Different Countries to Control Personal Data Flow

Multinational organizations can incorporate users' cultural background as an additional factor to consider in providing privacy support. For example, a site or app can determine users' country based on their IP address and use the cultural values related to the approximate location of this IP address. Combining situational cues and cultural considerations, they can then recommend customized options to users that are tailored to their specific cultural background and situation. The details of how to design user-tailored privacy support are more comprehensively covered in Chap. 16 in this book.

12.4.6.3 Differentiate Relationships Between Privacy Perceptions and Privacy Decisions in Different Cultures

The links between privacy perceptions and decisions are culturally different. Certain beliefs (e.g., third-party accountability) have opposite effects between individualistic and collectivistic cultures. This cultural variability of attitudinal effects may be related to the existence of the privacy paradox [59] (i.e., the surprisingly weak link between privacy attitudes and behaviors). It also warns practitioners that designs, policies, or technical interventions that are created to increase the acceptability of disclosure by countering such beliefs in one culture may be completely counter-productive when implemented in another culture. For example, informing users that third-party companies are accountable for the collection, access, and use of personal data in individualistic countries like the USA will make them more likely to disclose. But such intervention will have a counterproductive effect in collectivistic countries like China.

12.5 Conclusions

In this chapter, I describe a number of cross-cultural differences that exist in interpersonal privacy management on social media and consumers' management of personal data collection by organizations. Compared with the general associations between national cultures and privacy attitudes/behaviors found in previous litera-ture, the more concrete investigation presented in this chapter of how users' privacy decision-making differs in different situations in different cultures can generate many specific design implications for privacy systems, data collection strategies, and privacy regulatory mechanisms in the international context.

Future work should continue this investigation into more concrete cross-cultural differences in users' privacy attitudes and behaviors. For example, besides different types of online social networks, there might be other factors that play an important role in privacy management on social media, such as the specific content and mood in information sharing and individual personalities. These factors may act differently in different cultures.

Second, most cross-cultural privacy studies compare privacy attitudes and behav-iors at the country level. However, there are some variations in cultural values within the same country. Some people in individualistic countries may exhibit collectivistic characteristics or vice versa. Different generations and ethnic groups may have different cultural orientations. Different regions within a country may hold different traditions. Future work can further differentiate cultural groups within a country to explore the cultural differences in privacy management.

Third, emerging technologies have been increasingly available around the world, such as Internet of Things (IoT), smart devices, and augmented reality and virtual reality. For example, this book contains a chapter focusing on the details of IoT privacy (Chap. 11). Examination of the cross-cultural privacy differences in users' interaction with these emerging technologies will be necessary. The data sharing context of these technologies may be different in different countries. The cultural norms and practices may also vary from that of social media and other online systems (Chap. 5 discusses the development of privacy norms more specifically). Thus, I call for more investigation into the cross-cultural privacy differences on different technological platforms.

References

1. Altman, I. 1975. *The environment and social behavior: Privacy, personal space, territory, and crowding.* Monterey, CA: Brooks/Cole Publishing.
2. Roberts, J.M., and T. Gregor. 1971. *Privacy: A cultural view.* New York: Cornell University, Latin American Studies Program.
3. Westin, A.F. 1967. *Privacy and Freedom.* New York: Atheneum.
4. Anderson, E.N. 1972. Some Chinese methods of dealing with crowding. *Urban Anthropology.* 1 (2): 141–150.
5. Miles, D. 1970, November. The Ngadju Dayaks of Central Kalimantan, with Special Reference to the Upper Mentaya. *Behavior Science Notes* 5 (4): 291–319. https://doi.org/10.1177/106939717000500405.
6. Li, Y., A. Kobsa, B.P. Knijnenburg, and M.-H.C. Nguyen. 2017, April. Cross-cultural privacy prediction. *Proceedings on Privacy Enhancing Technologies* 2017 (2): 113–132. https://doi.org/10.1515/popets-2017-0019.
7. Weighing the Impact of GDPR. 2018. https://cacm.acm.org/magazines/2018/11/232192-weighing-the-impact-of-gdpr/fulltext. Accessed 15 April 2019.
8. Wilkinson, D., Namara, M., Badillo-Urquiola, K., Wisniewski, P.J., Knijnenburg, B.P., Page, X., Toch, E., and Romano-Bergstrom, J. 2018. Moving beyond a "one-size fits all": Exploring individual differences in privacy. In *Extended Abstracts of the 2018 CHI Conference on Human Factors in Computing Systems,* New York, NY, USA, 2018, W16:1–W16:8.
9. Hofstede, G., G.J. Hofstede, and M. Minkov. 2010. *Cultures and Organizations: Software of the Mind.* 3rd ed. New York: McGraw Hill Professional.
10. House, R.J., P.J. Hanges, M. Javidan, P.W. Dorfman, and V. Gupta. 2004. *Culture, Leadership, and Organizations: The GLOBE Study of 62 Societies.* Thousand Oaks: SAGE Publications.
11. Schwartz, S.H. 1994. Beyond individualism/collectivism: New cultural dimensions of values. In *Individualism and Collectivism: Theory, Method, and Applications,* ed. U. Kim, H.C. Triandis, Ç. Kâğitçibaşi, S.C. Choi, and G. Yoon, 85–119. Thousand Oaks: Sage Publications.
12. Hofstede, G. 2011, December. Dimensionalizing cultures: The Hofstede model in context. *Online Readings in Psychology and Culture* 2 (1). https://doi.org/10.9707/2307-0919.1014.
13. Triandis, H.C. 1995. *Individualism & Collectivism.* Boulder, CO: Westview Press.
14. Oyserman, D., H.M. Coon, and M. Kemmelmeier. 2002. Rethinking individualism and collectivism: Evaluation of theoretical assumptions and meta-analyses. *Psychological Bulletin* 128 (1): 3–72. https://doi.org/10.1037/0033-2909.128.1.3.
15. Schimmack, U., S. Oishi, and E. Diener. 2005, February. Individualism: A valid and important dimension of cultural differences between nations. *Personality and Social Psychology Review* 9 (1): 17–31. https://doi.org/10.1207/s15327957pspr0901_2.
16. Triandis, H.C., R. Bontempo, M.J. Villareal, M. Asai, and N. Lucca. 1988. Individualism and collectivism: Cross-cultural perspectives on self-ingroup relationships. *Journal of Personality and Social Psychology* 54 (2): 323.
17. Yamagishi, T., and M. Yamagishi. 1994, June. Trust and commitment in the United States and Japan. *Motivation and Emotion.* 18 (2): 129–166. https://doi.org/10.1007/BF02249397.
18. Kirkman, B.L., K.B. Lowe, and C.B. Gibson. 2006, May. A quarter century of culture's consequences: A review of empirical research incorporating Hofstede's cultural values framework. *Journal of International Business Studies* 37 (3): 285–320. https://doi.org/10.1057/palgrave.jibs.8400202.
19. Triandis, H.C., and M.J. Gelfand. 1998. Converging measurement of horizontal and vertical individualism and collectivism. *Journal of Personality and Social Psychology* 74 (1): 118–128. https://doi.org/10.1037/0022-3514.74.1.118.
20. Kwan, V.S., M.H. Bond, and T.M. Singelis. 1997, November. Pancultural explanations for life satisfaction: adding relationship harmony to self-esteem. *Journal of Personality and Social Psychology* 73 (5): 1038–1051.

21. Watkins, D., A. Akande, J. Fleming, M. Ismail, K. Lefner, M. Regmi, et al. 1998, Feburary. Cultural dimensions, gender, and the nature of self-concept: A fourteen-country study. *International Journal of Psychology* 33 (1): 17–31. https://doi.org/10.1080/002075998400583.

22. Bond, R., and P.B. Smith. 1996. Culture and conformity: A meta-analysis of studies using Asch's (1952b, 1956) line judgment task. *Psychological Bulletin* 119 (1): 111–137. https://doi.org/10.1037/0033-2909.119.1.111.

23. Gudykunst, W.B., G. Gao, K.L. Schmidt, T. Nishida, M.H. Bond, K. Leung, G. Wang, and R.A. Barraclough. 1992. The influence of individualism collectivism, self-monitoring, and predicted-outcome value on communication in ingroup and outgroup relationships. *Journal of Cross-Cultural Psychology* 23 (2): 196–213. https://doi.org/10.1177/0022022192232005.

24. Wheeler, L., H.T. Reis, and M.H. Bond. 1989. Collectivism-individualism in everyday social life: The middle kingdom and the melting pot. *Journal of Personality and Social Psychology* 57 (1): 79–86. https://doi.org/10.1037/0022-3514.57.1.79.

25. Hui, C.H., H.C. Triandis, and C. Yee. 1991. Cultural differences in reward allocation: Is collectivism the explanation? *British Journal of Social Psychology* 30 (2): 145–157. https://doi.org/10.1111/j.2044-8309.1991.tb00931.x.

26. Yamagishi, T. 1988. The Provision of a sanctioning system in the United States and Japan. *Social Psychology Quarterly.* 51 (3): 265–271. https://doi.org/10.2307/2786924.

27. Shweder, R.A., and E.J. Bourne. 1982. Does the concept of the person vary cross-culturally? In *Cultural Conceptions of Mental Health and Therapy*, ed. A.J. Marsella and G.M. White, 97–137. Dordrecht: Springer Netherlands.

28. Eid, M., and E. Diener. 2001. Norms for experiencing emotions in different cultures: Inter- and intranational differences. *Journal of personality and. Social Psychology* 81 (5): 869–885. https://doi.org/10.1037/0022-3514.81.5.869.

29. Lee, S.T.H. 2018, September. Testing for measurement invariance: Does your measure mean the same thing for different participants? *APS Observer* 31 (8): 32–33.

30. Cho, H., B. Knijnenburg, A. Kobsa, and Y. Li. 2018, June. Collective privacy Management in Social Media: A cross-cultural validation. *ACM Transactions on Computer-Human Interaction* 25 (3): 17:1–17:33. https://doi.org/10.1145/3193120.

31. Measurement Invariance - an overview | ScienceDirect Topics: https://www.sciencedirect.com/topics/psychology/measurement-invariance. Accessed: 25 May 2019.

32. Facebook users by country | Statistic: https://www.statista.com/statistics/268136/top-15-countries-based-on-number-of-facebook-users/. Accessed 24 May 2019.

33. Krasnova, H. and Veltri, N.F. 2010, January. Privacy calculus on social networking sites: Explorative evidence from Germany and USA. In *2010 43rd Hawaii International Conference on System Sciences (HICSS)*, 1–10.

34. Marshall, B.A., P.W. Cardon, D.T. Norris, N. Goreva, and R. D'Souza. 2008. Social networking websites in India and the United States: A cross-national comparison of online privacy and communication. *Issues in Information Systems* IX (2): 87–94.

35. Wang, Y., Norcie, G., and Cranor, L.F. 2011. Who is concerned about what? A study of American, Chinese and Indian users' privacy concerns on social network sites. In *Proceedings of the 4th International Conference on Trust and Trustworthy Computing* (Berlin, Heidelberg, 2011), 146–153.

36. Rui, J., and M.A. Stefanone. 2013. Strategic self-presentation online: A cross-cultural study. *Computers in Human Behavior* 29 (1): 110–118. https://doi.org/10.1016/j.chb.2012.07.022.

37. Liu, Z., and X. Wang. 2018, May. How to regulate individuals' privacy boundaries on social network sites: A cross-cultural comparison. *Information & Management.* https://doi.org/10.1016/j.im.2018.05.006.

38. Chu, S.-C., and S.M. Choi. 2011. Electronic word-of-mouth in social networking sites: A cross-cultural study of the United States and China. *Journal of Global Marketing* 24 (3): 263–281. https://doi.org/10.1080/08911762.2011.592461.

39. Posey, C., P.B. Lowry, T.L. Roberts, and T.S. Ellis. 2010, April. Proposing the online community self-disclosure model: The case of working professionals in France and the U.K. who use online communities. *European Journal of Information Systems* 19 (2): 181–195. https://doi.org/10.1057/ejis.2010.15.

40. Cho, S.E., and H.W. Park. 2013. A qualitative analysis of cross-cultural new media research: SNS use in Asia and the West. *Quality & Quantity* 47 (4): 2319–2330. https://doi.org/10.1007/s11135-011-9658-z.

41. Cao, J., and A. Everard. 2008. User attitude towards instant messaging: The effect of espoused national cultural values on awareness and privacy. *Journal of Global Information Technology Management* 11 (2): 30–57.

42. Lowry, P., J. Cao, and A. Everard. 2011. Privacy concerns versus desire for interpersonal awareness in driving the use of self-disclosure technologies: The case of instant messaging in two cultures. *Journal of Management Information Systems* 27 (4): 163–200. https://doi.org/10.2753/MIS0742-1222270406.

43. Li, Y. 2019. *Cross-cultural Differences in the Contextual Information Norms in Users' Privacy Decision-making*. UC Irvine.

44. Liu, Y., and J. Fan. 2015. Culturally specific privacy practices on social network sites: Privacy boundary permeability management in photo sharing by American and Chinese college-age users. *International Journal of Communication* 9: 20.

45. Kim, Y., D. Sohn, and S.M. Choi. 2011. Cultural difference in motivations for using social network sites: A comparative study of American and Korean college students. *Computers in Human Behavior* 27 (1): 365–372. https://doi.org/10.1016/j.chb.2010.08.015.

46. Wang, Y., Li, Y., and Tang, J. 2015. Dwelling and fleeting encounters: Exploring why people use WeChat – a Mobile instant messenger. In *Proceedings of the 33rd Annual ACM Conference Extended Abstracts on Human Factors in Computing Systems* (New York, NY, USA, 2015), 1543–1548.

47. Tsoi, H.K., and Chen, L. 2011. From privacy concern to uses of social network sites: A cultural comparison via user survey. In *Privacy, Security, Risk and Trust (PASSAT), 2011 IEEE Third International Conference on and 2011 IEEE Third International Conference on Social Computing (SocialCom)* (Oct. 2011), 457–464.

48. James, T.L., L. Wallace, M. Warkentin, B.C. Kim, and S.E. Collignon. 2017. Exposing others' information on online social networks (OSNs): Perceived shared risk, its determinants, and its influence on OSN privacy control use. *Information & Management* 54 (7): 851–865. https://doi.org/10.1016/j.im.2017.01.001.

49. Cho, H., M. Rivera-Sánchez, and S.S. Lim. 2009, May. A multinational study on online privacy: Global concerns and local responses. *New Media & Society* 11 (3): 395–416. https://doi.org/10.1177/1461444808101618.

50. Dinev, T., M. Bellotto, P. Hart, V. Russo, I. Serra, and C. Colautti. 2006. Privacy calculus model in e-commerce – a study of Italy and the United States. *European Journal of Information Systems* 15 (4): 389–402. https://doi.org/10.1057/palgrave.ejis.3000590.

51. Milberg, S.J., H.J. Smith, and S.J. Burke. 2000, February. Information privacy: Corporate management and national regulation. *Organization Science* 11 (1): 35–57. https://doi.org/10.1287/orsc.11.1.35.12567.

52. Choi, J., and L.V. Geistfeld. 2004, December. A cross-cultural investigation of consumer e-shopping adoption. *Journal of Economic Psychology* 25 (6): 821–838. https://doi.org/10.1016/j.joep.2003.08.006.

53. Miltgen, C.L., and D. Peyrat-Guillard. 2014, March. Cultural and generational influences on privacy concerns: A qualitative study in seven European countries. *European Journal of Information Systems* 23 (2): 103–125. https://doi.org/10.1057/ejis.2013.17.

54. Sawaya, Y., Sharif, M., Christin, N., Kubota, A., Nakarai, A., and Yamada, A. 2017. Self-confidence trumps knowledge: A cross-cultural study of security behavior. In *Proceedings of the 2017 CHI Conference on Human Factors in Computing Systems*, 2202–2214.

55. Chen, J.Q., R. Zhang, and J. Lee. 2013. A cross-culture empirical study of m-commerce privacy concerns. *Journal of Internet Commerce* 12 (4): 348–364. https://doi.org/10.1080/15332861.2013.865388.
56. Mohammed, Z.A., and G.P. Tejay. 2017, June. Examining privacy concerns and ecommerce adoption in developing countries: The impact of culture in shaping individuals' perceptions toward technology. *Computers & Security.* 67: 254–265. https://doi.org/10.1016/j.cose.2017.03.001.
57. Park, C., and J.-K. Jun. 2003, October. A cross-cultural comparison of Internet buying behavior: Effects of Internet usage, perceived risks, and innovativeness. *International Marketing Review* 20 (5): 534–553. https://doi.org/10.1108/02651330310498771.
58. Zhang, L., J. Zhu, and Q. Liu. 2012, September. A meta-analysis of mobile commerce adoption and the moderating effect of culture. *Computers in Human Behavior.* 28 (5): 1902–1911. https://doi.org/10.1016/j.chb.2012.05.008.
59. Norberg, P.A., D.R. Horne, and D.A. Horne. 2007. The privacy paradox: Personal information disclosure intentions versus behaviors. *Journal of Consumer Affairs* 41 (1): 100–126. https://doi.org/10.1111/j.1745-6606.2006.00070.x.

Chapter 13
Accessible Privacy

Yang Wang and Charlotte Emily Price

Abstract End-user privacy mechanisms have proliferated in various types of devices and application domains. However, these mechanisms were often designed without adequately considering a wide range of underserved users, for instance, people with disabilities. In this chapter, we focus on the intersection of accessibility and privacy, paying particular attention to the privacy needs and challenges of people with disabilities. The key takeaway messages of this chapter are as follows: (1) people with disabilities face heightened challenges in managing their privacy; (2) existing end-user privacy tools are often inaccessible to people with disabilities, making them more vulnerable to privacy threats; and (3) design guidelines are needed for creating more accessible privacy tools.

13.1 Introduction

Existing end-user privacy mechanisms are often designed without considering the wide range of user populations. As a result, these designs often made assumptions about their users that may or may not hold for underserved populations, such as people with disabilities, children, older adults, and people from non-Western developing countries. These inappropriate assumptions could lead to significant challenges for the underserved users to utilize privacy mechanisms. The difficulties in effectively using these mechanisms could in turn make the underserved users more vulnerable to various privacy risks.

Y. Wang (✉)
University of Illinois at Urbana-Champaign, Champaign, IL, USA
e-mail: yvw@illinois.edu

C. E. Price
Syracuse University, Syracuse, NY, USA
e-mail: ceprice@syr.edu

© The Author(s) 2022

293

B. P. Knijnenburg et al. (eds.), *Modern Socio-Technical Perspectives on Privacy*,
https://doi.org/10.1007/978-3-030-82786-1_13

The web browser lock icon is an example of how design may render privacy-enhancing tools unusable to someone with disabilities. The lock icon was designed to signal the use of secure (HTTPS) communication between the browser and the web server. This user interface design was built on an assumption that its users can easily recognize the icon. However, the lock icon is often inaccessible to people with visual impairments and screen reader users. CAPTCHA (Completely Automated Public Turing test to tell Computers and Humans Apart) is a similar accessibility nightmare for people with visual impairments. Even the seemingly simple Android app permission interface can be confusing to users with little technical knowledge, who may not understand what an app permission means.

While this chapter focuses on privacy needs and challenges of people with disabilities, it is worth noting that there is a fundamental issue in privacy designs that fail to consider underserved populations beyond those with disabilities. In another profound example of an underserved population (i.e., victims of intimate partner abuses), Freed et al. studied how the abusers use technologies to violate the privacy of their victims through surveillance and manipulation [1]. Traditionally, the assumption about attackers is that they do not have easy and full access to victims' devices. However, this study shows that these abusers often have full access to victims' devices. In fact, in many cases, the abusers are the legal owners of these devices [1]. This finding challenges one of the long-held assumptions about the attackers. As such, the existing protection mechanisms would fall short because their underlying assumptions no longer hold for victims of intimate partner abuses. New protection mechanisms are needed to thwart this kind of attacks by intimate partner abusers. Interested readers can refer to the chapter on privacy of vulnerable populations.

Cultural values can also have a significant impact on how people conceptualize privacy and how technologies should be designed to support their privacy management. For example, Vieweg et al. examined Arabic women's social media usage and their associated privacy concerns [2]. This research suggests that unlike social media users in the Western developed countries where the main privacy issues are centered around individuals, Arabic women are more concerned about how their social media usage might put their family reputation at risk [2]. This is a very different kind of privacy concerns (i.e., concerns about one's family more than individuals) that existing social media privacy mechanisms fall short of supporting. Interested readers can refer to Chap. 12 for a more in-depth discussion.

The commonality of these examples is that existing privacy designs tend not to be inclusive to a wide range of user groups. This leads to the conceptualization of inclusive privacy, the idea of designing privacy mechanisms that are inclusive to a wide range of users with diverse abilities, characteristics, needs, and values. The goal of inclusive privacy is desirable, ambitious but also challenging to achieve. In this chapter, we mainly explore *accessible privacy*: designing privacy mechanisms that are accessible to people with disabilities.

In the remainder of this chapter, we will first explore some example groups of people with disabilities and their privacy challenges. We will then discuss why achieving privacy is difficult as well as promising approaches towards accessible privacy. We conclude by suggesting a few future research directions.

The key takeaway messages of this chapter are:

- **People with disabilities face heightened challenges** in managing their privacy.
- **Existing end-user privacy tools are often inaccessible** to people with disabilities, making them more vulnerable to privacy threats.
- **Design guidelines are needed** for creating more accessible privacy tools.

13.2 Privacy and Underserved Populations

In this section, we will explore a few specific underserved populations and their privacy challenges and needs. When we describe people with disabilities, we follow the ACM accessible writing guide [3]. We recognize the important role that language can play in the marginalization of people as well as the language we use may or may not reflect the norms within a particular disability community.

13.2.1 Models of Disability

There are many models (certainly more than three or four) of disability that have been recognized by disability scholars, such as the medical model, the social model, and the critical realist model.

Traditionally, the medical model has been used by scientific communities, but is often considered problematic. This model sees disability as something wrong with a person that must be "fixed" and has contributed to the oppression of people with disabilities. Disability rights activists then proposed social models of disability that identify disability as socially constructed and grounded in society and culture [4]. This refers to disability as a problem with a society's lack of inclusiveness rather than a personal issue [4]. This model also has been critiqued for its emphasis on independent living (which isolates the realities of many people with disabilities who require assistance), as well as supporting "normalization" rather than celebrating or acknowledging disability pride and difference [5]. The cultural/postmodern model was created to address the medical realities, lived experiences, and social elements for some people with disabilities [5]. This model sees disability as another way of being, a cultural standpoint or lifestyle [6]. The critical realistic perspective, which emerged from disability studies and was proposed to inform accessible technology design, also centers on rich, lived experiences of individuals with disabilities [7]. Sins Invalid, a group of artists with disabilities, proposed "A Disability Justice framework understands that all bodies are unique and essential, that all bodies have strengths and needs that must be met... We understand that all bodies are caught in these bindings of ability, race, gender, sexuality, class, nation state and imperialism, and that we cannot separate them" [8]. It is important to note that these models of disability are often respected based on how an individual associates personally within these frameworks. Thus, researchers and designers need to recognize the complexity and personal tendencies and experiences attached to such models and will dissuade from bifurcating them (e.g., the medical model vs. other models).

In summary, there are many models of disabilities, such as:

- **Medical model: disability is medicalized** as being deviate from the normal biological functions [9].
- **Social model: disability is socially constructed** as being a problem with a society's lack of inclusiveness rather than a personal issue [4].
- **Critical realist model: "disability as an interaction between individual and structural factors"** where individual factors can include impairments and structural factors can include others' attitudes towards disabilities [7].

13.2.2 People with Visual Impairments

There are a wide range of disability conditions. Our first example focuses on people with visual impairments. Visual impairments exist on a spectrum, ranging from partial to complete loss of vision. In clinical settings, the term "visual impairment" refers to a "visual acuity of 20/70 or worse in the better eye with best correction, or a total field loss of 140 degrees" [10]. "Blindness" means that a person cannot see anything, whereas "low vision" denotes "sight that may be severe enough to hinder an individual's ability to complete daily activities such as reading, cooking, or walking outside safely, while still retaining some degree of usable vision" [10]. A person can have visual impairments since birth or after birth (e.g., due to accidents, medical conditions, or aging).

While computers and smartphones help improve the independence and quality of life of people with visual impairments, these technologies (particularly the mouse, visual input/output, and touch-based user interfaces) also pose significant accessibility challenges for this user group. In turn, people with visual impairments (especially those living with blindness) often use screen readers (e.g., JAWS, Window-Eyes, NVDA, VoiceOver) on their computers or phones to parse and read the information from the screen. Screen readers usually read a screen sequentially but also support keyboard shortcuts to allow users to skip certain elements of a page or extract a list of hyperlinks on a page for faster navigation. People with visual impairments (especially those with low vision) also use screen magnifiers (e.g., ZoomText, MAGic) to zoom into certain parts of the screen to make it more readable.

People with visual impairments face many accessibility challenges with information and computing technologies and are likely to struggle with current mainstream privacy user interfaces (e.g., https padlock), which heavily rely on visual representations.

Existing literature has highlighted a number of privacy concerns of people with visual impairments:

- **Shoulder surfing** (e.g., during their usage of ATM).
- **Aural eavesdropping** (e.g., screen reader reading aloud private content).
- **Asking others even strangers to read** inaccessible documents (e.g., mails).
- **Using assistive technologies can attract unwanted attention** and make people with visual impairments more noticeable to attackers.
- **Difficulty in using end-user privacy/security mechanisms** (e.g., privacy settings).
- **Taking or sharing images/videos** that might contain private or sensitive content.

These and other related privacy and security concerns/needs of people with visual impairments have been identified. Holman et al. conducted focus groups with blind users and identified their top 10 security challenges: (1) CAPTCHA, (2) auto logout, (3) auto refresh/reload webpage, (4) inaccessible PDF (i.e., the PDF is not marked up with tags that can be read by a screen reader), (5) inaccessible antivirus software, (6) auto install software, (7) auto software updates make software inaccessible, (8) SecurID (a random number display in the device used for logging in), (9) keyloggers, and (10) spams [11]. Some of these are more general accessibility issues such as inaccessible PDF; others are addressed by existing antivirus or anti-spam software. In terms of challenges related to CAPTCHA and authentication, there are a number of mechanisms proposed to improve or replace them (e.g., [12–14]).

People with visual impairments have privacy concerns about using mobile devices when they are in the speakerphone or screen-reading mode or generally in public because others can see or hear what they are speaking or doing [15–17]. People with visual impairments can wear earphones, but that is sometimes inconvenient [16] and could limit their abilities to hear or sense the nearby environment, making them vulnerable to attacks [18]. The iOS Screen Curtain allows iPhone users to blank their screen, but that does not help with the privacy issues caused by the screen-reading mode and users with visual impairments may forget to activate that feature. The use of assistive technology (e.g., a portable magnifier) could attract unwanted attention and make users more noticeable to attackers [15, 19]. People with visual impairments often have to compromise their privacy for achieving independence and/or convenience.

Ahmed et al. have conducted two interview studies specifically investigating the privacy needs and practices of people with visual impairments in online and offline settings [18, 20]. They found that these users face difficulties in detecting visual or aural eavesdropping, have physical privacy and security concerns (e.g., using ATM), and sometimes need to ask others (even strangers) to help (e.g., read documents, type pin in shopping) [20]. There are proposed solutions for specific tasks (e.g., accessible ATM [21]), but no generic solution to address the privacy risks emerged from asking others to help.

These users also report difficulties in managing their social media sharing, citing the difficulties in using the privacy settings on social media sites (e.g., Facebook) [18]. These privacy settings have been found to be difficult for social media users in general [22]. Furthermore, we have found that people with visual impairments were also concerned about online tracking (i.e., their data or web browsing activities being collected by companies or governments) [23], which has been shown as a privacy concern of the general population [24]. There are browser extensions such as script blockers (e.g., NoScript) and ad blockers (e.g., Ghostery) that block third-party content or scripts on a webpage, but they have usability issues for general Internet users [25].

A few studies have focused on privacy/security issues for people with visual impairments. Many privacy/security threats arise from the use of accessible technology, as these devices inadvertently generate new avenues for passersby to learn personal information. People with visual impairments have concerns about aural and visual eavesdropping in public when using screen readers and screen magnifiers, respectively [26–29]. Prior work also suggests that this user group may not notice privacy/security risks in their environment or inherent in the technology they use [30]. The use of accessible technologies can also draw unwanted attention and potential exploitation [31]. To mitigate some of these issues, people with visual impairments use privacy features (e.g., iOS Screen Curtain) and wear headphones to mitigate problems with screen readers [32]. Ahmed et al. identified privacy/security concerns or challenges people with visual impairments face such as difficulties verifying the security of banking or shopping websites, maintaining privacy on social media, asking strangers for help [18] and physical safety/security challenges in public spaces and at home [20]. Our most recent ethnographic research with people with visual impairments and their allies in their everyday lives found that they often work cooperatively to protect the privacy and security of people with visual impairments, yet most existing privacy/security mechanisms fall short of supporting this kind of cooperative behaviors [23].

There are a number of privacy-enhancing technologies (PETs) designed for people with visual impairments:

- **Accessible authentication** (e.g., PassChords [12], UniPass [33])
- **Accessible CAPTCHAs** (e.g., more accessible audio CAPTCHAs [34])
- **Privacy-enhancing assistive features** (e.g., Apple's Screen Curtain)
- **General assistive tools** making content more accessible and people with visual impairment more independent (e.g., screen readers)

Prior research efforts primarily those from the field of accessible computing have proposed different mechanisms to support people with visual impairments in various privacy and security-related tasks. One notable example is more accessible CAPTCHA (i.e., Completely Automated Public Turing test to tell Computers and Humans Apart) designs, for instance, using pairs of images and sounds [35, 36] as well as moving the controls for audio CAPTCHAs within the answer textbox of the authentication interface [13]. Another notable area is authentication. For instance, Azenkot et al. designed a password scheme that utilizes patterns of finger taps on a touchscreen [26]. Barbosa et al. designed a password manager that allows visually impaired users to easily transfer their login credentials from their mobile devices to web-based services [37].

Previous research has also elicited feedback on proposed solutions to physical privacy and security threats. Ahmed et al. found that their visually impaired participants appreciated the idea of devices that could detect the number of people in their vicinity, assist them with navigation, and prevent shoulder surfing attacks [18]. In their follow-up study, participants endorsed the idea of knowing others' proximity, identity, and activities, as well as inferences about the intentions of others' actions [20].

13.2.3 Are Existing Privacy-Enhancing Technologies Sufficient?

While there is not much research on the experiences of people with visual impairments in using privacy-enhancing technologies, there are anecdotes that suggest the existing PETs are insufficient for this user group. For instance, privacy/security indicators (e.g., the https lock icon in web browsers) might not be very accessible to people with visual impairments who use screen readers. Privacy settings have also been shown to be difficult for people with visual impairments [18]. Some of these are difficult to use for the broader population. It is also worth noting that some assistive technologies can introduce privacy issues. For instance, visual question and answer tools such as Be My Eyes and VizWiz [38] allow blind users to take pictures and ask questions about the pictures to crowd workers or volunteers (who can be total strangers). These pictures might contain private or sensitive content (e.g., credit cards, medicine details) [39].

13.2.4 Intersectional Privacy

Empirical research on people with visual impairments in general and their privacy and security practices in particular tend to focus on their visual impairments, which often are, however, a single aspect of their multifaceted and intersectional marginalized identities. In our own experiences of working with people with visual impairments, we found that many of them often have other aspects of marginalized identities such as other disabilities, minoritized race, and gender identities [23]. These multifaceted and intersectional marginalized identities often contribute to their challenges and influence their privacy and security practices [23].

Intersectionality is a key analytic framework proposed by Kimberlé Williams Crenshaw in the late 1980s and is situated in the lived experiences of black women, women of color, and intersecting identity structures of race, class, gender, and sexuality [40]. Crenshaw's intersectionality arose from a legal perspective regarding a case in which an African American woman sued a company for discrimination in not hiring her. The judge dismissed the case because the company claimed to hire African Americans and women. In response, Crenshaw problematized this claim because African American women have multifaced identities including both gender and racial identities, and suggested that the company did not hire African American women. Crenshaw wrote, "I used the concept of intersectionality to denote the various ways in which race and gender interact to shape the multiple dimensions of Black women's employment experiences" [40]. Among this initial definition, Crenshaw has specified three kinds of intersectionality: structural, political, and representational. Structural intersectionality refers to how "the location of women of color at the intersection of race and gender" informs identity and marginalized positions [40]. Political intersectionality highlights how "feminist and antiracist politics have, paradoxically, often helped to marginalize the issue of violence against women of color." Representational intersectionality refers to cultural norms that create certain minoritized positions regarding identities [40]. It is important to note that the concept of intersectionality encompasses many important factors beyond race and gender such as class and sexuality (e.g., used in queer studies by LGBTQ+ activists).

Since the term intersectionality has been coined, it has been adapted by a large number of feminist, critical race, critical disablity, and queer studies scholars as a research framework to examine complex identity and social structures. While retaining the black feminist foundation of this framework, critical disability scholars such as Rosemarie Garland-Thomson have proposed a disability axis on an "intersectionality nexus" which views disability not only as socially constructed but also intrinsically multifaceted [41]. In this foundational scholarship, she connects disability, race, gender, class, and queer theory [41]. Specifically, she considers disability along these complex and multifaceted elements such as political, social, and personalized understandings of disability identity [41]. As such, her ability/disability system is meant to show another identity perspective to Crenshaw's notion of intersectionality [42].

Intersectionality has been a recent topic in human-computer interaction (HCI) scholarship with the call for inclusion of critical theories such as feminism (e.g., [43]) and critical race (e.g., [44]). This line of work advocates that by using intersectional analyses, people can be better understood, thus leading to richer data and more ethical methodologies and designs (e.g., [44]). For instance, Schlesinger et al. point out that besides race, gender, and class, other dimensions such as disability or age are also good for intersectional analysis [44].

In our studies on visual impairments, we found many of our participants to have intersectional identities along with the visual impairments that shaped their experiences [23]. Therefore, we adopted intersectionality as an analytic lens to unpack the everyday privacy/security experiences of people with visual impairments. Our intersectional analysis is akin to *intracategorical intersectionality* [45], which "focuses on a single identity category...and then analyze other dimensions of identity within the target community" [44]. We focused on people with visual impairments while considering their overlapping identity dimensions (e.g., age, gender identity, and other disabilities) [23].

For instance, one of our participants unfortunately lost her sight in an accident. She is a mother and self-identifies with having bipolar disorder and a learning disability. She lives with her children and mother. She often asks their help with many things from emailing to managing her bank account. We observed that her privacy and security needs and practices were often influenced by these multifaceted and intersectional aspects of her identity. She gave a hypothetical example where it would be difficult for her to have another male friend to illustrate her inability to hide her phone conversations, which might in turn lead to misunderstanding from her boyfriend. She wants to control the visibility of the conversations on her phone herself, but she found the technologies too overwhelming to learn. There are typically functionalities such as deleting phone call records, text messages, or the contact information that allow phone owners to protect their privacy and communication on the phone. However, there is no simple one-click feature that "[hides] conversations on a phone." In practice, users need to understand and use a combination of technical features to clean their conversations (in various apps) on the phone. This participant said she had a hard time knowing and learning how to use all these features. One key insight here is that the combination and intersection of her visual impairments, bipolar disorder, and learning disability probably all played a role in her challenges in using the technologies and achieving her privacy/security goals on her own [23].

13.2.5 People with Hidden Disabilities

We use the term "hidden disabilities" as an umbrella term to cover a wide range of disabilities such as learning disabilities (e.g., dyslexia), autism spectrum, and attention deficit hyperactivity disorder (ADHD) as well as psychosocial, internal conditions such as chronic pain, and mobility disorders as well as anything "not obvious" to others. Disability and HCI research tend to focus on physical disabilities such as visual and motor impairments rather than hidden disabilities. Even fewer studies have been done to understand people with hidden disabilities and their privacy and security needs.

In our own research, we conducted focus groups with people with hidden disabilities to understand their information disclosure practices, in particular the disclosure of their disability identities. Similar to our study on visual impairments, we found that people with hidden disabilities often also have multiplicity in identity. In addition, since their disabilities are often not obviously visible to others, their (marginalized) identity disclosure is a key aspect of their everyday privacy practices.

We identified two main domains (i.e., professional and informal/social) in which our participants with hidden disabilities make decisions about whether, when, and how to disclose their disability identities. Professional domains include academic or job settings, whereas informal/social domains include online (particularly social media) and in-person settings (e.g., family and friends). We observed that our participants exhibited various types of identity disclosure behaviors in these two domains. We adopted MacDonald-Wilson et al.'s definitions for these different disclosure behaviors:

- **Forced disclosure** (e.g., students with disabilities requesting accommodations)
- **Selective disclosure** (i.e., a person with disabilities chooses when and whom to disclose which aspects of the disabilities)
- **Nondisclosure** (i.e., a person with disabilities chooses not to disclose any aspects of the disabilities)
- **Disclosure by others** (e.g., a friend or family member discloses one's disabilities often without one's permission)

Forced disclosure refers to a situation where individuals are "required by circumstances" to disclose their disability identity to another person, typically an employer or a supervisor, "or in the need for accommodation" [46]. *Selective disclosure* denotes "sharing information with specific or a limited number of people, or sharing specific or limited information with others" [46]. MacDonald-Wilson et al. also consider selective disclosure as being "used to access protections under the ADA [Americans with Disabilities Act] while minimizing risks related to stigma, and allows the person the option to 'blend in' or 'pass for normal'" [46]. *Nondisclosure* means "a choice made by individuals to keep private any information" regarding their disability identity, which they mention "may result in additional stress and lower self-esteem because one is hiding an aspect of one's life, but it also protects the individual from potential stigma and discrimination" [46].

We found that disclosure by others was more prevalent in informal social settings. For instance, one participant explained an unpleasant experience: "Yeah, I think the experiences that I have mostly had with that-with people telling other people without my permission-is with my family. I know that they have good intentions, but I'd prefer not to go to a family gathering and have everyone come up to me saying, 'Oh, I'm sorry you had a breakdown yesterday.' That's a little awkward for me, not knowing where that information is going to. I know that my mom tells her twin sister, they're really close so she feels like she can share that kind of information. But when it comes back to me, or she texts me, they have good intentions, but I'd prefer to be able to come to them when I feel like I want to." As noted, this participant did not mind sharing her disability condition but did not accept nonconsensual disclosure because she lost the agency in controlling her information.

Academic and professional settings, on the other hand, often exhibit forced disclosure or nondisclosure of their disability identities. Many of our participants felt forced to disclose their disabilities in schools to get accommodation or at workplaces to perform their work and to ensure their supervisors or colleagues that they are not lazy. For instance, one participant shared, "The other times when I've had pressure to disclose was when I was at work and I would have crazy anxiety. No one could tell because I'm extroverted introvert, no one could tell. So I'd be like, 'ok, I have anxiety.' Or I'm not meeting deadlines, and I know I have a problem, but again, I don't have a formal ADHD diagnosis so I don't really know how to explain it. There are times when I really think I've gotten in some trouble because of my disability, but I wasn't able to advocate because I wasn't able to express that, you know, I'm not lazy." Sometimes, our participants experienced the opposite where they felt "forced" not to disclose their disabilities by their families, who believed that disclosing the disabilities would, for instance, negatively affect one's chance of employment.

Our participants also disclosed specific disabilities and other marginalized identities differently. In general, the participants were comfortable disclosing their physical disabilities more than their hidden disabilities, citing stigma associated with hidden disability identity disclosure. One participant said, "I post about when I'm in pain, physically. I don't post about being emotionally in pain, but I have posted about my history with suicide a little bit." Some participants segmented social media platforms and used different platforms/accounts for different purposes. For instance, one participant had three Instagram accounts and used one of them, a private account, to relate to her disabilities. She explained, "For Instagram, I actually have three accounts for Instagram. I have a public account that I rarely ever post on, and I rarely ever look at, but it's just nice pictures of me doing things. And then I have a private Instagram account, where I follow a lot of chronic illness accounts, I don't post anything personally about my own chronic illnesses, usually, but I'll follow and comment and stuff. Then I also have a service dog one that's private where I can talk to other service dog handlers, but both of those are closed so I have control over who I allow to see those." Even though she shared nothing about her disability, she understood that the pages she follows can be visible to others and hence preferred another account rather than using the same one. Anonymity on these accounts also helped. If the target audience did not know about their real identities, the participants felt more comfortable sharing about their disability. In terms of future design, designers should explore ways to further support these users to avoid forced disclosures and to facilitate selective and nondisclosure as well as "blending in" or "passing" if these users choose to.

13.2.6 People with Other Disabilities

While there is a large body of research that demonstrates various web accessibility challenges for people with other disabilities (e.g., motor impairments, cognitive impairments), little is known about their privacy challenges and needs. There is some empirical evidence that people with Down syndrome struggle with remembering mnemonic passwords [47] and people with intellectual disabilities had difficulties remembering passwords [48]. Future research is needed to uncover additional privacy challenges for these user groups.

13.3   Why Is Accessible Privacy Difficult?

While more scholars and practitioners are starting to recognize the importance of making privacy mechanisms more accessible to a wide range of users, there are a number of challenges.

Designing accessible privacy mechanisms is difficult for a number of reasons. First, the designers need to understand the specific underserved group's privacy challenges and needs as well as their broader technology usage and social contexts. Traditional interviews and surveys are helpful, but they may fall short of providing sufficient contextual nuances of the group's everyday social settings. Ethnographic research is one way that may help fill the gap. However, conducting passive observation is also not easy for underserved populations because they are often close-knit communities that external parties including researchers may not have access to. Our experiences have been that many years of volunteering in local disability communities help us to establish trustworthy relationships with underserved groups, who were engaged in our various research efforts.

Second, there is often considerable variance within an underserved group. For instance, visual impairments range from low vision to complete loss of vision. This matters because they may have quite different technology usage. For instance, while blind users often use screen readers, users with low vision might not use screen readers and might use screen magnifiers.

Third, we need to respect and consider the complex and intersectional nature of people's marginalized identities. In our own research, we found that many of our participants with visual impairments also self-identified with other disabilities (e.g., cognitive impairments) and other marginalized identities such as LGBTQ+. Their privacy and security practices are also influenced by these multifaceted and intersectional identities. How to design to support the combinatory and intersectional nature of their privacy/security needs and practices is particularly difficult because these intersectional characteristics are complex and nuanced.

Fourth, there are a large (or even infinite) number of marginalized user groups. If the goal is to truly achieve universal design where every person is supported, then the design needs to accommodate everybody including all the marginalized user groups. Supporting the practices of one particular marginalized user group might put unduly burden or conflict with the practices of another user group. If one were to pursue a largest common denominator approach, it is unclear what design options are still available.

Last but not least, some recent work shows that even accessibility features could introduce unintended privacy/security vulnerabilities. For instance, audio CAPTCHA, which was supposed to be a more accessible alternative to image CAPTCHA, could be bypassed by over-the-counter speech recognition algorithms, effectively defeating the purpose of CAPTCHA and making the system more vulnerable [49]. Future designs that aim to improve accessibility need to go through privacy/security reviews and testing to identify any potential vulnerabilities.

In summary, some of the main challenges in designing for accessible privacy include:

- **Need to understand the target underserved users'** privacy challenges and needs.
- **There are often considerable within-group variances** of an underserved population.
- **Need to consider the complex and intersectional nature** of people's disability/marginalized identities.
- **There are a large (or even infinite) number of marginalized groups** (that one can study).
- **Assistive technologies that were designed to improve accessibility for people with disabilities might pose privacy risks** to these users.

13.4 Working Towards Accessible Privacy

Best Practices Working with people from marginalized groups is both fulfilling and challenging. Because of their marginalized identities, researchers and designers need to be extra thoughtful about how to engage with the target user groups in an ethical and empowering manner. Unfortunately, there is a dark history of marginalized groups being taken advantage of or even abused in the name of research (e.g., the abuse of people with disabilities in the Nazi experiments). Therefore, it is perhaps not surprising that marginalized groups are often close-knit and keep a distance of the outside even to academic researchers. In order to closely work with marginalized groups, researchers need to build a trustworthy relationship with the target user populations. In our own experiences of working with people with disabilities, we found that one productive way is volunteering in the local organizations that serve people with disabilities. We were able to interact/help with the local community and build relationships with them after a few years of volunteering.

It might seem trivial, but it is actually quite important to create accessible and inclusive research/study materials. When we were working with people with visual impairments, it took us a while to improve our study materials that used icons (for users with low vision) and nontechnical language in our study fliers and consent form. We also created videos with caption to explain our study. Besides, we used index cards for participants to answer Likert scale questions (i.e., pointing to a card with an answer on the table, e.g., strongly agree). The PDFs of study materials were also made accessible to screen readers. All of these efforts lowered the barriers for people with visual impairments to participate in our studies.

Research Methodologies One promising design approach in this context is participatory design [50] where the design team directly includes members of the target user population (e.g., children) who will actively engage throughout the design process. These participatory design sessions should engage a wide range of stakeholders including people from different underserved groups. These design sessions can be structured to explore everyone's own security and privacy concerns and practices, co-design, and pilot test low-fidelity designs.

Several scholars have conducted studies using a *participatory action research* method with the goal of bringing their target population to the center and empowering them to actively involve themselves in the movement for necessary change to meet their needs. Balcazar et al., for example, designed and facilitated a PAR study specifically directed at individuals with disabilities and highlighted four key principles: (1) direct participation from individuals with disabilities in problem identification and solution generation, (2) such direct interaction and involvement provides a more holistic view of the research from the perspective of individuals with disabilities, (3) the participatory action research process has the ability to raise awareness of participants' strengths, resources, and abilities, and ultimately (4) PAR is designed to improve the overall quality of life for individuals with disabilities [51]. The researchers cite examples from participants in their study to illustrate each of the four principles in action, demonstrating how each principle worked to improve participants' experiences [51]. They also address the challenges of PAR, which include difficulty developing and maintaining lasting relationships with their participants, the ability to sustain and develop the research over time, the duration of the entire research process, and the potential unintended consequences resulting from conducting participatory action research [51].

Duarte et al. conducted a study involving young forced migrants that combined participatory design and participation action research elements [52]. The authors argued that using participatory action research allowed for the inclusion of their participants in an active role regarding the conduct of the studies themselves and creating a safe space, which they realized was also a limitation of their research [52]. Used well with inclusive participatory design practices, conducting research such as this allows for participants to bring their expertise and unique needs to the forefront while fostering change that would help them in the long run.

Design Approaches *Value-sensitive design* (VSD) is a generic design approach that highlights and supports values in system design [53, 54]. Example values include user autonomy, freedom from bias, privacy, and trust [53]. VSD has been applied to assess technologies or privacy designs. For instance, Xu et al. used VSD to conduct conceptual, technical, and empirical investigations of a privacy-enhancing tool, examining how relevant theories inform the tool design, how the tool design can be technically implemented, and how end users would react to the tool [55]. In another example of using the VSD approach, Briggs and Thomas conducted workshops to understand people's perceptions of future identity technologies with six marginalized community groups: young people, older adults, refugees, black minority ethnic women, people with disabilities, and mental health service users [56]. They identified both common values and different impacting factors across these community groups regarding how people think about future identity technologies [56]. As shown in this example, VSD can be useful in identifying the underlying values that underserved user groups have and assessing whether these values have been supported in security and privacy designs.

Ability-based design proposed by Wobbrock et al., shifts the view from focusing on people's disabilities to their abilities [57]. They propose seven ability-based design principles based on their extensive experiences in designing technologies for people with disabilities. These principles include ability, accountability, adaptation, transparency, context, and commodity [57]. For instance, the principle of ability states that "Designers will focus on ability not *dis*-ability, striving to leverage all that users *can* do" [57]. The principle of accountability means that designers should change the systems rather than the users if the systems do not perform well [57]. These principles have proven valuable for designing accessible technologies for people with disabilities and should be adopted for accessible security and privacy designs that support a wide range of underserved user groups.

Ethical Considerations Some of these underserved populations may be considered vulnerable (e.g., children) and thus require the researchers/designers to be extra cautious about how to preserve these users' interests. When working with underserved populations, researchers/designers might subconsciously bring their own biases especially when they are not part of the underserved groups. Feminist scholars have proposed the notion of positionality [58], which highlights that research/design process is power laden and urges the researchers/designers to examine and mitigate their own biases. It is also worth noting that underserved populations may experience improvements of life during a study (e.g., trying out a research prototype) but they are likely to revert back to their previous life after the study, which can be frustrating to say the least. Therefore, it is important for researchers to be mindful about this ethical challenge and how to address this challenge. For instance, the researchers may consider providing their participants the option of keeping the prototype after the study.

One reoccurring theme across many of these populations is people's pursuit of different (sometimes competing) values. Accessible privacy designs need to consider the broader everyday context in which privacy and security are just two such values that people desire and people might have to trade them for other values (e.g., trust) depending on the situation.

Accessibility and Privacy Considerations Accessibility has been widely recognized as a key concern in IT and web design. Accessibility laws such as Section 508 of the Rehabilitation Act of 1973 and the Americans with Disabilities Act (ADA) in the USA may require IT and websites to be accessible to people with disabilities. These legal requirements as well as industry standards (e.g., W3C web accessibility standards) have played an important role in improving IT accessibility. Making privacy mechanisms accessible is a desirable goal, and we have seen some promising examples in technologies and laws. For instance, the California Consumer Privacy Act (CCPA) requires privacy policies or notices to be accessible. However, it is worth repeating that accessible or assistive technologies might introduce new privacy risks (e.g., making user with disabilities more noticeable to attackers). Therefore, one cannot assume that technologies designed for improving accessibility would always have a positive or neutral impact on user privacy. One ought to conduct both accessibility and privacy risk assessment when designing for accessible privacy.

13.5 Future Directions

We advocate for a list of future directions for researchers and practitioners.

Cooperative Privacy One promising direction is designing to support people especially those from marginalized groups to collaborate in privacy management. Privacy and security mechanisms are often focused on the individual's perspective, for instance, a privacy or security warning that a user can act on. In contrast, cooperative privacy fosters interdependence, which is especially beneficial for the everyday privacy management of people with visual impairment. What would a "cooperative" warning look like? Perhaps it could have built-in support for people to seek help or get feedback from others (e.g., allies), for instance, an option on the warning to ask for help. One possible cooperative privacy design could take the form of a mobile app or a website where users with visual impairments could choose to share only with specific allies they invite to the system any information about them, such as schedules and common tasks they perform. If users felt their privacy/security is at risk, they can request help from selected allies, requesting a chat session in real time where allies would be providing assistance as needed.

Users would have full control over the disclosure of any private information that they share via the system. This is just one example of a rich yet largely untapped design space for cooperative privacy and security mechanisms. These types of designs will not only be helpful for people with visual impairments and their allies but also computer users more generally (e.g., technically savvy users and novice users).

Personalized Privacy While most existing privacy mechanisms were designed to be "one size fits all," there is increasing recognition that personalized mechanisms that cater to individuals are a promising direction for future privacy design. It is particularly promising for accessible privacy because of its potential in supporting complex and intersectional nature of individuals' marginalized identities and needs.

Design Principles Since there are a large number of marginalized or underserved user groups, how can we systematically study and understand these groups as well as explore the design space? Given that there are an increasing number of scholars across multiple disciplines that are interested in designing for various specific groups, one strategy is to identify common as well as unique challenges, needs, and practices across these groups.

The goal of this research direction is to develop design guidelines for creating security and privacy designs that are accessible to different user abilities, identities, and values. This research direction can include several components. First, accessible security and privacy prototypes can be evaluated by existing design guidelines for privacy (e.g., [59]) and for accessibility and inclusion (e.g., [57]). Second, it can include other underserved populations. Given that people from different underserved groups can differ drastically, tools designed for one underserved population may or may not be directly applicable to other underserved populations. In fact, different underserved populations may need to be studied separately and inclusive design principles may be derived inductively from studying and designing for several specific populations. Third, research can seek to provide further design guidance for supporting other underserved populations based on evaluation results of accessible security and privacy prototypes.

While it is desirable to derive accessible security/privacy design patterns (i.e., what/how to do) and anti-patterns (i.e., what/how to avoid) that can be applied universally, practically this might be extremely difficult if not impossible due to the seemingly uncountable human characteristics. Partial rather than universal perspective is also valuable even though it can only be generalized to a limited number of underserved populations.

Community Building Community building is an important aspect of supporting this new wave of research. There is an emerging community of researchers and practitioners interested in accessible privacy. There are a series of workshops on inclusive privacy and security (WIPS): https://inclusiveprivacy.org/workshops.html. We discussed a wide range of user groups (e.g., children, older adults, people with disabilities, crime victims, and people who have little education or low socioeconomic status) and application domains (e.g., authentication, CAPTCHA, banking/shopping, browser security, and wearables). We also created various scenarios and conducted group design activities for these scenarios. One observation is that we still do not have a systematic methodology to support inclusive design. As discussed earlier, this is a crucial component for future research and development.

There are also an increasing number of scholars from the more traditional computer/network security community that are interested in this topic. There will be a convergence of scholars and practitioners from different fields and countries that explore different aspects of accessible privacy and security.

In summary, we advocate the following future directions:

- **Design to support both independence and interdependence** (cooperation between marginalized users and their allies) in privacy management.
- **Design to support personalized or customizable** privacy management.
- **Systematization of knowledge about the privacy challenges and needs** of different marginalized user groups.
- **Develop design principles** that can guide the development of accessible privacy mechanisms for a wide range of marginalized user groups.
- **Build a community of scholars and practitioners** from various disciplines such as disabilities, ethics, laws, cybersecurity, privacy, human-computer interaction, and design.

Acknowledgments We thank participants in our research for sharing their insights. We also thank Jordan Hayes, Smirity Kaushik, and Bryan Dosono for their assistance in the research as well as Nicholas Proferes and Bart Knijnenburg for their thoughtful feedback on earlier drafts of this chapter. This work was supported in part by the National Science Foundation (NSF Grant CNS-1652497).

References

1. Freed, Diana, Jackeline Palmer, Diana Minchala, Karen Levy, Thomas Ristenpart, and Nicola Dell. 2018. "A Stalker's Paradise": How intimate partner abusers exploit technology. In *Proceedings of the 2018 CHI Conference on Human Factors in Computing Systems, CHI '18*, 667:1–667:13. New York, NY: ACM.
2. Vieweg, Sarah, and Adam Hodges. 2016. Surveillance & modesty on social media: How Qataris navigate modernity and maintain tradition. In *Proceedings of the 19th ACM Conference on Computer-Supported Cooperative Work & Social Computing, CSCW '16*, 527–538. New York, NY: ACM.
3. Vicki, L. October 2015. Hanson, Anna Cavender, and Shari Trewin. Writing about accessibility. *Interactions* 22 (6): 62–65.
4. Shakespeare, Tom. 2006. The social model of disability. In *The Disability Studies Reader*, ed. Lennard J. Davis, 2–197. Hove, East Sussex: Psychology Press.
5. Mankoff, Jennifer, Gillian R. Hayes, and Devva Kasnitz. 2010. Disability studies as a source of critical inquiry for the field of assistive technology. In *Proceedings of the 12th International ACM SIGACCESS Conference on Computers and Accessibility, ASSETS '10*, 3–10. New York, NY: ACM.
6. Waldschmidt, Anne. 2018, June. Disability–Culture–Society: Strengths and weaknesses of a cultural model of dis/ability. *Alter* 12 (2): 65–78.
7. Frauenberger, Christopher. 2015. Disability and technology: A critical realist perspective. In *Proceedings of the 17th International ACM SIGACCESS Conference on Computers & Accessibility, ASSETS '15*, 89–96. New York, NY: ACM.
8. Sins Invalid. 2018. *Sins invalid | An unshamed claim to beauty in the face of invisibility.*
9. Corker, Mairian, and Tom Shakespeare. 2002. *Disability/postmodernity: Embodying Disability Theory*. London; New York: Continuum. OCLC: 47237980.
10. American Foundation for the Blind. Key Definitions of Statistical Terms, 2008.
11. Holman, J., J. Lazar, and J. Feng. 2008. Investigating the security-related challenges of blind users on the web. In *Designing Inclusive Futures*, ed. Patrick Langdon, CEng John Clarkson, and Peter Robinson, 129–138. London: Springer.
12. Azenkot, Shiri, Kyle Rector, Richard Ladner, and Jacob Wobbrock. 2012. PassChords: Secure multi-touch authentication for blind people. In *Proceedings of the 14th International ACM SIGACCESS Conference on Computers and Accessibility, ASSETS '12*, 159–166. New York, NY: ACM.
13. Bigham, Jeffrey P., and Anna C. Cavender. 2009. Evaluating existing audio CAPTCHAs and an interface optimized for non-visual use. In *Proceedings of the SIGCHI Conference on Human Factors in Computing Systems*, 1829–1838. New York, NY: ACM.
14. Sauer, Graig, Jonathan Lazar, Harry Hochheiser, and Jinjuan Feng. 2010, June. Towards a universally usable human interaction proof: Evaluation of task completion strategies. *ACM Transactions on Accessible Computing* 2 (4): 15:1–15:32.
15. Shaun K. Kane, Chandrika Jayant, Jacob Wobbrock, and Richard Ladner. 2009. Freedom to roam: A study of mobile device adoption and accessibility for people with visual and motor disabilities, 115–122.

16. Naftali, Maia, and Leah Findlater. 2014. Accessibility in context: Understanding the truly mobile experience of smartphone users with motor impairments. In *Proceedings of the 16th International ACM SIGACCESS Conference on Computers & Accessibility, ASSETS '14*, 209–216. New York, NY: ACM.

17. Ye, Hanlu, Meethu Malu, Oh. Uran, and Leah Findlater. 2014. Current and future mobile and wearable device use by people with visual impairments. In *Proceedings of the 32nd Annual ACM Conference on Human Factors in Computing Systems, CHI '14*, 3123–3132. New York, NY: ACM.

18. Ahmed, Tousif, Roberto Hoyle, Kay Connelly, David Crandall, and Apu Kapadia. 2015. Privacy concerns and behaviors of people with visual impairments. In *Proceedings of the SIGCHI Conference on Human Factors in Computing Systems, CHI2015*, 3523–3532. New York, NY: ACM.

19. Shinohara, Kristen, and Jacob O. Wobbrock. 2011. In the Shadow of misperception: Assistive technology use and social interactions. In *Proceedings of the SIGCHI Conference on Human Factors in Computing Systems, CHI '11*, 705–714. New York, NY: ACM.

20. Tousif Ahmed, Patrick Shaffer, Kay Connelly, David Crandall, and Apu Kapadia. 2016. Addressing physical safety, security, and privacy for people with visual impairments. In *SOUPS2016*, 341–354.

21. Cassidy, Brendan, Gilbert Cockton, and Lynne Coventry. 2013. A haptic ATM interface to assist visually impaired users. In *Proceedings of the 15th International ACM SIGACCESS Conference on Computers and Accessibility, ASSETS '13*, 1:1–1:8. New York, NY: ACM.

22. Yang, Wang, Gregory Norcie, Saranga Komanduri, Alessandro Acquisti, Pedro Giovanni Leon, and Lorrie Faith Cranor. 2011. "I regretted the minute I pressed share": A qualitative study of regrets on Facebook. In *Proceedings of the Seventh Symposium on Usable Privacy and Security, SOUPS '11*, 10:1–10:16. New York, NY: ACM.

23. Jordan Hayes, Smirity Kaushik, Charlotte Emily Price, and Yang Wang. 2019. *Cooperative Privacy and Security: Learning from People with Visual Impairments and Their Allies.*

24. Ur, Blase, Pedro Giovanni Leon, Lorrie Faith Cranor, Richard Shay, and Yang Wang. 2012. Smart, useful, scary, creepy: Perceptions of online behavioral advertising. In *Proceedings of the Eighth Symposium on Usable Privacy and Security, SOUPS '12*, 4:1–4:15. New York, NY: ACM.

25. Pedro G. Leon, Blase Ur, Rebecca Balebako, Lorrie Faith Cranor, Richard Shay, and Yang Wang. 2012. Why Johnny can't opt out: A usability evaluation of tools to limit online behavioral advertising. In *Proceeding of the SIGCHI Conference on Human Factors in Computing Systems*, Austin, Texas.

26. Azenkot, Shiri, Kyle Rector, Richard E. Ladner, and Jacob O. Wobrock. 2012. PassChords: Secure multi-touch authentication for blind people. In *Assets '12 Proceedings of the 14th International ACM SIGACCESS Conference on Computers and Accessibility*, 159–166. New York, NY: ACM.

27. Bryan Dosono, Jordan Hayes, and Yang Wang. 2015. "I'm Stuck!": A contextual inquiry of people with visual impairments in authentication. In *Proceedings of the 11th Symposium On Usable Privacy and Security (SOUPS)*, 151–168.

28. Shaun K. Kane, Chandrika Jayant, Jacob O. Wobbrock, and Richard E. Ladner. 2009. Freedom to Roam: A study of mobile device adoption and accessibility for people with visual and motor disabilities. In *ASSETS'09, October 25–28, 2009, Pittsburgh, Pennsylvania, USA*, 115–122.

29. Naftali, M., and L. Findlater. 2014. Accessibility in context: Understanding the truly mobile experience of smartphone users with motor impairments. In *Proceedings of the 16th International ACM SIGACCESS Conference on Computers and Accessibility – ASSETS 2014*, 209–216. New York, NY: ACM.

30. Brady, Erin, and Jeffrey P. Bigham. 2015, November. Crowdsourcing accessibility: Human-powered access technologies. *Foundations and Trends in Human-Computer Interaction* 8 (4): 273–372.

31. Kristen Shinohara, and Jacob O. Wobbrock. 2011, May. In the Shadow of misperception: Assistive technology use in social interactions. In *Proceedings of the 29th Annual Conference on Human Factors in Computing Systems – CHI 2011*, 705–714.

32. Ye, Hanlu, Meethu Malu, Oh. Uran, and Leah Findlater. 2014, April. Current and future mobile and wearable device use by people with visual impairments. In *Proceedings of the 32nd Annual ACM Conference on Human Factors in Computing Systems – CHI 2014*, 3123–3132. New York, NY: ACM.

33. Nata Barbosa, Jordan Hayes, and Yang Wang. 2016. Uni-Pass: Design and evaluation of a smart device-based password manager for visually impaired users. In *Proceedings of the ACM International Joint Conference on Pervasive and Ubiquitous Computing (UbiComp 2016)*.

34. Fanelle, Valerie, Sepideh Karimi, Aditi Shah, Bharath Subramanian, and Sauvik Das. 2020. *Blind and human: Exploring more usable audio CAPTCHA designs*, 111–125. Berkeley: USENIX Association. isbn: 9781939133168.

35. Jonathan Holman, Jonathan Lazar, Jinjuan Heidi Feng, and John D'Arcy. 2007. Developing usable CAPTCHAs for blind users. In *Proceedings of the 9th International ACM SIGACCESS Conference on Computers and Accessibility*, 245–246.

36. Sauer, Graig, Jonathan Lazar, Harry Hochheiser, and Jinjuan Feng. 2010. Towards a universally usable human interaction proof: Evaluation of task completion strategies. *Information Sciences* 2 (4): 15.

37. Natã M Barbosa, Jordan Hayes, and Yang Wang. 2016. UniPass: Design and evaluation of a smart device-based password manager for visually impaired users. In *UbiComp*, 49–60.

38. Jeffrey P. Bigham, Chandrika Jayant, Hanjie Ji, Greg Little, Andrew Miller, Robert C. Miller, Robin Miller, Aubrey Tatarowicz, Brandyn White, Samual White, and others. 2010. VizWiz: Nearly real-time answers to visual questions. In *Proceedings of the 23nd Annual ACM Symposium on User Interface Software and Technology*, 333–342. New York, NY: ACM.

39. Stangl, Abigale, Kristina Shiroma, Bo Xie, Kenneth R. Fleischmann, and Danna Gurari. 2020, October. Visual content considered private by people who are blind. In *The 22nd International ACM SIGACCESS Conference on Computers and Accessibility, ASSETS '20*, 1–12. New York, NY, USA: Association for Computing Machinery.

40. Crenshaw, Kimberle. 1991. Mapping the margins: Intersectionality, identity politics, and violence against women of color. *Stanford Law Review* 43 (6): 1241–1299.

41. Garland-Thomson, Rosemarie. 1997, January. *Extraordinary bodies: Figuring physical disability in American culture and literature*. New York: Columbia University Press.

42. ———. 2002. Integrating disability, transforming feminist theory. *NWSA Journal* 14 (3): 1–32.

43. Bardzell, Shaowen, and Jeffrey Bardzell. 2011. Towards a feminist HCI methodology: Social science, feminism, and HCI. In *Proceedings of the SIGCHI Conference on Human Factors in Computing Systems, CHI '11*, 675–684. New York, NY: ACM.

44. Ari, Schlesinger, W. Keith Edwards, and Rebecca E. Grinter. 2017. Intersectional HCI: Engaging identity through gender, race, and class. In *Proceedings of the 2017 CHI Conference on Human Factors in Computing Systems, CHI '17*, 5412–5427. New York, NY: ACM.

45. McCall, Leslie. 2005. The complexity of intersectionality. *Signs* 30 (3): 1771–1800.

46. MacDonald-Wilson, Kim L., Zlatka Russinova, E. Sally Rogers, Chia Huei Lin, Terri Ferguson, Shengli Dong, and Megan Kash MacDonald. 2011. Disclosure of mental health disabilities in the workplace. In *Work Accommodation and Retention in Mental Health*, 191–217. New York: Springer.

47. Ma, Yao, Jinjuan Heidi Feng, Libby Kumin, Jonathan Lazar, and Lakshmidevi Sreeramareddy. 2012, October. Investigating authentication methods used by individuals with down syndrome. In *Proceedings of the 14th International ACM SIGACCESS Conference on Computers and Accessibility, ASSETS '12*, 241–242. New York, NY: Association for Computing Machinery.

48. Buehler, Erin, William Easley, Amy Poole, and Amy Hurst. 2016, April. Accessibility barriers to online education for young adults with intellectual disabilities. In *Proceedings of the 13th Web for All Conference, W4A '16*, 1–10. New York, NY: Association for Computing Machinery.

49. Solanki, Saumya, Gautam Krishnan, Varshini Sampath, and Jason Polakis. 2017. In (Cyber)Space bots can hear you speak: Breaking audio CAPTCHAs Using OTS speech recognition. In *Proceedings of the 10th ACM Workshop on Artificial Intelligence and Security, AISec '17*, 69–80. New York, NY: ACM. Event-Place: Dallas, TX.
50. Schuler, Douglas, and Aki Namioka. 1993, March. *Participatory Design: Principles and Practices*. Boca Raton: CRC Press.
51. Balcazar, Fabricio E., Christopher B. Keys, Daniel L. Kaplan, and Yolanda Suarez-Balcazar. 1998. Participatory action research and people with disabilities: Principles and challenges. *Canadian Journal of Rehabilitation* 12: 105–112.
52. Duarte, Ana Maria Bustamante, Nina Brendel, Auriol Degbelo, and Christian Kray. 2018. Participatory design and participatory research: An HCI case study with young forced migrants. *ACM Transactions on Computer-Human Interaction (TOCHI)* 25 (1): 3.
53. Friedman, Batya. 1996, December. Value-sensitive design. *Interactions* 3 (6): 16–23.
54. Friedman, Batya, Peter H. Kahn, and Alan Borning. 2008. Value sensitive design and information systems. In *The Handbook of Information and Computer Ethics*, ed. Kenneth Einar Himma and Herman T. Tavaniessor, 69–101. Hoboken: John Wiley & Sons.
55. Xu, Heng, Robert E. Crossler, and France BéLanger. 2012, December. A value sensitive design investigation of privacy enhancing tools in web browsers. *Decision Support Systems* 54 (1): 424–433.
56. Briggs, Pam, and Lisa Thomas. 2015, August. An inclusive, value sensitive design perspective on future identity technologies. *ACM Transactions on Computer-Human Interaction* 22 (5): 23:1–23:28.
57. Wobbrock, Jacob O., Shaun K. Kane, Krzysztof Z. Gajos, Susumu Harada, and Jon Froehlich. 2011, April. Ability-based design: Concept, principles and examples. *ACM Transactions on Accessible Computing* 3 (3): 9:1–9:27.
58. Haraway, Donna. 1988. Situated knowledges: The science question in feminism and the privilege of partial perspective. *Feminist Studies* 14 (3): 575–599.
59. Nissenbaum, Helen. 2004. Privacy as contextual integrity. *Washington Law Review Association* 79: 119–158.

Chapter 14
Privacy in Adolescence

Pamela J. Wisniewski, Jessica Vitak, and Heidi Hartikainen

Abstract Late adolescence represents an important life stage where children are becoming more independent and autonomous from their parents but are not quite old enough to go out on their own. Teenagers are also avid users of mobile devices and social media and actively use their smartphones to connect with friends and share their lives. Much of the research looking at teen technology use has employed a risk-centric approach; in other words, it takes the view that teens are putting themselves at risk by sharing personal information online, so the privacy-oriented solutions typically involve parental monitoring or technology restrictions. In this chapter, we review the research on teens, technology use, and privacy and discuss why such risk-centric models may be problematic to teens' maturation. Instead, we argue that—much like it was for prior generations—risk-taking is a learning process critical to becoming a young adult and that teens do think about their privacy online, albeit in different ways than their adult counterparts. We offer design heuristics for developing tools for teens that allow for appropriate levels of risk-taking while protecting their privacy and ensuring their safety.

14.1 Introduction

The impact social and mobile communication technologies have on young people cannot be understated. Networked communication technologies are an ever-present force in the lives of nearly all teenagers; according to Pew Research, 95% of teens

P. J. Wisniewski (✉)
Department of Computer Science, University of Central Florida, Orlando, FL, USA
e-mail: pamwis@ucf.edu

J. Vitak
College of Information Studies, University of Maryland, College Park, MD, USA
e-mail: jvitak@umd.edu

H. Hartikainen
Faculty of Information Technology and Electrical Engineering, University of Oulu, Oulu, Finland
e-mail: heidi.hartikainen@oulu.fi

© The Author(s) 2022
B. P. Knijnenburg et al. (eds.), *Modern Socio-Technical Perspectives on Privacy*,
https://doi.org/10.1007/978-3-030-82786-1_14

ages 13–17 in the United States have access to smartphones, 89% go online multiple times a day—with 45% reporting near-constant connectivity [1]—and 71% use more than one social media platform [2]. Over half of teens in the United States have developed new friendships, flirted, and/or expressed romantic interest in someone through social media platforms like Instagram [3]. Common Sense Media [4, 5] reports that teens spend more than 7 h a day using screens, and the largest proportion of this time is spent on smartphones. As the Internet has become increasingly mobile and ubiquitous, teens no longer distinguish between "online" and "offline" spaces.

When describing teens and their prolific use of technology, the phrase "digital natives" [6] is often used to reference those who have grown up with modern technologies and particularly high-speed Internet access. However, this framing often incorrectly presupposes that everyone born in the twenty-first century is digitally literate and otherwise competent at technical activities, such as setting up an online account or changing privacy settings on a phone.

Hargittai [7] was one of the first scholars to note that the assumption that younger generations are inherently tech savvy is inaccurate and that web skills are not universal across all young people who use the Internet frequently. Her research showed that higher socioeconomic status, race (white or Asian), gender (male), and parental education are associated with higher levels of web skills. Hargittai suggests that most teens are more like "digital *naives*"—they are naive especially when it comes to "the critical knowledge to engage productively with networked situations, including the ability to control how personal information flows and how to look for and interpret accessible information" [8 , p. 180]. Indeed, Common Sense Media [5] found that teens and younger children (ages 10–18) possess poor digital literacy when it comes to assessing whether a piece of information is real or fake, with 31% reporting they shared a news story in the last 6 months that they later found out was untrue.

More broadly, society has also made numerous assumptions about teens and their digital privacy. For example, the assumption that teens are at extreme risk online because of their poor information disclosure decisions is prevalent in the literature (e.g., [9, 10]) and suggests that teens' lack of privacy awareness leads to serious harms, ranging from inappropriate consumer data collection to online sexual predation. Wisniewski [11] cautions that this narrative may be potentially counterproductive because it victim-blames teens for not being able to make complex privacy decisions that research has consistently shown are equally difficult for adults [12, 13]. Sonia Livingstone, a leading expert in child online safety, also argues that there is little evidence that online risks present more harm than the risks teens typically encounter offline [14]; therefore, we should be careful to not treat online risks as an epidemic that plagues our youth.

In this chapter, we unpack and scrutinize some of the assumptions regarding teens, disclosure, and privacy and evaluate whether they hold up based on empirical research with teens. In the next section, we introduce digital privacy in relation to adolescence, which is a unique and important stage of human development. Next, we show how privacy research with teens presents some unique and paradoxical challenges—between trying to give teens the privacy and autonomy they need as they transition into adulthood and using surveillance tactics to keep them safe from online risks. Then, we present recent empirical research on networked privacy and teens. We conclude this chapter with actionable guidelines for designing systems that support the privacy and online safety of adolescents.

14.1.1   The Developmental Stage of Adolescence

Section Highlights

- **Adolescence is a unique developmental life stage** where teens transition between childhood and emerging adulthood, **distancing themselves from their parents**.
- Teenage years are characterized by increased **sociality** and **peer pressure**, the need for more **autonomy** and **privacy**, as well as heightened **risk-seeking** behaviors.
- These key changes during adolescents often lead to **conflict between parents and teens**.

This chapter addresses the important—and often volatile—developmental stage of adolescence, which is characterized as between the ages of 10 and 19 by the World Health Organization [15]. However, within the digital privacy literature in the United States, the age range for adolescence is often bounded between the ages of 13 and 17 [16]. This is due, in part, to the Children's Online Privacy Protection Act (COPPA) [17], which legally protects children under the age of 13 from unfair or deceptive collection, use, and/or disclosure of their personal information by online service providers, while age 18 is the legal definition for adulthood.

During adolescence, teens are both highly social and more risk-seeking than younger children [18]; they need independence to individuate themselves from their parents [19, 20] but are less capable than adults at managing online risks without some guidance [21]. In short, adolescence is a time of great change and conflict, both physically and mentally. As Dahl [22] notes, "by adolescence, individuals have matured beyond the frailties of childhood, but have not yet begun any of the declines of adult aging" (p. 3). The high school and college years are viewed as particularly transitional periods of adolescence—what Arnett [23] has termed "emerging adulthood"—when attitudes and beliefs are maturing and teens become less dependent on their parents. In transitioning away from dependence on their parents, teens become more reliant on and influenced by their peers during this time; peer influence peaks at age 14; after that, teens start building resistance to peer influences [24].

During adolescence, many teens experiment with "risky" behaviors, including sex, drinking, and smoking, and these behaviors are sometimes perpetuated through more intense peer pressure [25]. Such behaviors often create tension in families, as teens become more secretive [26], and parents are forced to balance their concerns for their teens' safety with trusting their teens with more autonomy as they transition to young adults [27]. Some level of risk-taking and autonomy-seeking is a natural and necessary part of adolescence [28]. In fact, preventing such experiences may stunt developmental growth as teens strive to separate themselves from their parents to become well-adjusted and independent adults [18, 19, 29]. In the next section, we explain how the introduction of information and communication technologies have added to the challenges, tensions, and conflicts that arise for teens, and between teens and parents, during the unique transitional period of adolescence.

14.1.2 Adolescence as a "Privacy Paradox"

Section Highlights

- Teens' **online disclosure behavior** is often framed as **paradoxical or problematic**, putting them at greater risk for **online dangers**. Yet, adults face many of the same privacy challenges as teens.
- **Adults send conflicting messages to teens about their online privacy**. Parents may tell them to be more **private** so that they can be **safe** online and then use **privacy-invasive parental controls** to ensure their online safety.
- In order to design tools that **meet teens' privacy needs**, we need to draw from **evidence-based research**, rather than the **paternal instinct** to shield teens from all online risks.

The "privacy paradox" (as defined in Chap. X) typically describes the discrepancy between Internet users' high levels of stated privacy concerns versus their copious online disclosures [12, 30–34]. Yet, when Barnes [9] first coined the term in 2005, she specifically referred to the online dangers (i.e., sexual predators) *teens* faced because of their over-willingness to share personal information via social media; this behavior of public over-sharing was framed as paradoxical because it conflicted with teens' desire to protect their publicly posted private thoughts from their parents—a primary source of safety and protection—rather than from complete strangers.

From a developmental perspective, however, this behavior is far from paradoxical; a teen's need for autonomy from their parents is directly related to their need for privacy and respect [35]. Steeves and Regan [36] explain that young people place great social value on their online privacy and want policies that are fair and negotiable. The use of online surveillance—especially by parents [37]—can undermine trust and hinder relationship building. This is counterproductive since trust is also a critical factor in adolescents' relationship with their parents [38], where some level of monitoring and information disclosure by teens is necessary, so that parents can ensure their teen is safe from online dangers [39].

At a societal level, the trade-offs between surveillance, privacy, and safety are both controversial and complex [40, 41]. For example, in the United States, most people value their civil liberties and their right to privacy over the government's right to protect them from threats to their personal safety [42]. Yet, as adults, we do not afford the same level of privacy and personal agency to our youth, especially when trying to protect teens from online risks [43]. The "privacy as risk prevention" approach to online safety has resulted in privacy-invasive tools that allow parents to monitor and restrict their teens' online behaviors [44–46], which exacerbate the privacy tensions between parents and teens [47–51].

Furthermore, such paternalistic, restrictive, and privacy-invasive approaches to online safety have been shown to be ineffective in protecting teens from online risks, harming the trust relationship between parents and teens, and can even limit potential opportunities youth garner by engaging with others online [50, 52–55]. This fear-based approach to privacy protection of teens has led to a new privacy paradox for adolescents [43]: On one hand, adults tell teens that they need to care about their online privacy to stay safe; on the other hand, as designers and parents, we develop and use surveillance technologies that take teens' privacy away for the sake of their online safety.

To disentangle and resolve this paradox of modern adolescent online privacy, we argue that practitioners, researchers, and parents should turn to evidence-based research conducted with teens to understand how we can (1) move away from authoritarian and paternalistic models of privacy protection for teens to more resilience-based perspectives [56], (2) develop tools for teens that ensure their safety in a way that respects their privacy, (3) allow teens to engage online in ways that help them build skills and resilience related to online risks they might encounter, and (4) account for teens' developmental needs as they transition through the uniquely tumultuous period of adolescence.

14.2 Teens and Networked Privacy: Empirical Evidence

Section Highlights

- **Teens value their online privacy** and have **unique strategies** for how they manage it.
- Sometimes, teens feel **peer pressure** to make online disclosures, even when they are concerned about privacy.
- Teens' **strategies are often different** than how **adults** manage online privacy, and we need to be careful **not to make false assumptions** about **teens and privacy**.

Marwick and Boyd's [57] foundational work with teens provides pivotal insights into how teens negotiate their "networked privacy" on social media. The term "networked privacy" refers to the notion that individuals lack full control over how, when, and what personal information is shared about them online. Instead, privacy is collectively managed by individuals and others who co-own that information (cf. Sandra Petronio's Communication Privacy Management (CPM) theory [58] in Chap. 2), including service providers like Facebook and Google. Marwick and Boyd's [57] interviews with teens dispelled the myth that teens do not care about their online privacy; instead, teens go to great lengths to "be *in* public without always *being* public" (p. 1052). While teens might share frequently, this does not mean that what they share is meant for a wide audience [57].

In her book, *It's Complicated: The Social Lives of Networked Teens* [8], Boyd uncovers a range of strategies teens employ online to ensure that content can be seen by their intended audience while remaining hidden or uninterpretable by others. For example, Boyd describes a teen girl who posts song lyrics to her Facebook page. By themselves, the lyrics appear innocuous, and her mother will not worry, but her close friends immediately know the ulterior meaning—she was upset. Boyd refers to this practice as "social steganography," or hiding a message in plain sight.

Boyd's ethnographic findings are supported through large-scale studies conducted by Pew Research. Through surveys and focus groups, Madden et al. [59] found that while teens share a lot of information through social media platforms, they also take steps to manage their identity and protect sensitive information, including deleting and de-tagging content, deleting friends, deactivating their profile, using inside jokes, and using fake names and/or profile information. Privacy concerns among teens also fuel the popularity of Snapchat among this age group [1] because shared content is usually only available for a short period of time before they become inaccessible. Privacy concerns are also linked to the increasing use of "fake" social media profiles like "Finstas," where—compared to their "real" accounts—teens share less curated content with closer friends [60].

Taken together, this work confirms the central role social media plays in the modern lives of teens and highlights the interplay between sociality and privacy. The assumption that teens lack the ability to make calculated privacy decisions online has been debunked; teens do take protective measures against online risks and value their privacy, but they also value the social benefits of engaging online [8, 55, 61–63]. And even when teens are concerned about their privacy, they still report feeling pressured to make online disclosures to friends [64].

In the sections below, we discuss more recent empirical research on adolescents as it relates to their online privacy and safety. First, we explore privacy boundaries between parents and teens when negotiating technology use in the home. Then, we focus on teens themselves to show how they exhibit a markedly different privacy calculus than adults; they treat "risk as a learning process" [24], taking protective measures to recover once disclosures have escalated to the point of potentially harmful interactions. Next, we show how different parental mediation strategies (i.e., preventative versus reactive [65]) influence teen social media privacy behaviors. Finally, we conclude this section of the chapter with a discussion on the irrevocable, yet complex, relationship between privacy and online safety for teens.

14.2.1 *Privacy Turbulence Within Families*

Section Highlights

- **Technology** provides new ways for **parents to monitor teens**.
- **Parental surveillance** of teens' online behaviors **causes tensions** within families, as teens desire **autonomy** and **privacy** from their parents.

- Existing tools for **monitoring teens online** are heavily focused on **parental control**, using **authoritarian restriction** and **privacy-invasive monitoring** that negate the developmental needs of teens.
- More tools need to be developed that support **teen self-regulation**, as well as **collaborative practices** and **open communication** within families.

As noted earlier, the teen years represent an important transitional time for parent-child interactions. Adults and teenagers have strongly differing attitudes about many of the most popular apps and platforms, which can aggravate existing tensions about technology use within families. Parents may struggle to use technology themselves and to understand how and why their teenage children use it so frequently [48, 51]. Communication technologies provide new ways for parents and children to connect, as well as new ways for parents to monitor their children's online and offline behaviors. While this increased connection may help ease parental concerns, it also creates new sources of turbulence within families [66]. According to Cranor and colleagues' [51] interview study with parents and teens, teens tend to view digital spaces as "personal and private," while parents regard content shared online as "uncontrollable" and prefer to monitor or restrict it.

Parents' rules about technology use—including when teens can use technology, what content they can access, and what controls they must turn over to parents—may create tension in parent-child relationships, especially as teens approach adulthood and seek greater autonomy. According to Yardi and Bruckman [50], teens—who often have greater knowledge and skills (compared to their parents) in applying technology workarounds—may rebel against their parents' rules and engage in riskier behaviors to avoid technology constraints.

Wisniewski et al.'s [45] feature analysis of 75 commercially available parental control apps found that these tools often share fine-grained details about teenagers' smartphone use, including websites visited, calls made, texts sent (including the actual content of the message), and GPS location with parents. For example, parents may require their teen to install a monitoring app on their smartphone or use tools like "Find My Phone" to share up-to-the-minute location data with parents. Parents also may use one of the many car applications that lets them set maximum speeds and stereo volume, as well as create a perimeter zone, which notifies them if the child leaves that zone [67].

Parents often feel caught between competing desires: They recognize the need to trust and respect their children's emerging autonomy, but at the same time, they seek to preserve their teens' physical safety and emotional well-being [52, 68]. Meanwhile, teens—and especially older teens—unequivocally prefer a level of trust and privacy from their parents, rather than technologies that act to monitor and restrict their online activities. For example, Ghosh et al. [37] analyzed 736 online reviews posted by teens and younger children about parental control apps available on Google Play; 76% of the reviews gave the apps a single star rating. Children strongly disliked these apps because they were overly restrictive, invasive of their personal privacy, and negatively impacted their relationships with their parents.

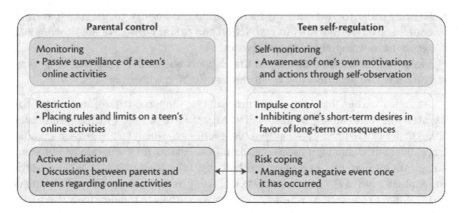

Fig. 14.1 Wisniewski et al.'s [45] teen online safety strategies framework

In light of this, we call for a paradigm shift toward family online safety apps that respect teens' privacy, help teens self-regulate their own online behaviors, and improve communication between teens and parents. In one example of this, Wisniewski et al. [45] proposed the Teen Online Safety Strategies (TOSS) framework (**Fig. 14.1**) to balance tensions between parental control and teen self-regulation. In this framework, **parental control strategies** for online safety include monitoring, restriction, and active mediation [69, 70]. These strategies were based primarily on Valkenburg et al.'s [71] foundational work, which created scales assessing three styles of parental television mediation. They have since widely been adapted for use in the context of online parental mediation [69, 72–74].

The teen self-regulation strategies were drawn from the adolescent developmental psychology literature, which considers self-regulation a "resiliency factor" [75] that protects teens from offline risks by modulating emotions and behaviors through monitoring, inhibition, and self-evaluation [76–78]. **Teen self-regulation strategies** include self-monitoring, impulse control, and risk-coping. In order for teens to effectively self-regulate their online behaviors, they must be aware of their own actions through self-observation (i.e., self-monitoring) [77, 79]. Impulse control aids in self-regulation by inhibiting one's short-term desires in favor of positive long-term consequences [80]. Risk-coping is a component of self-regulation that occurs after one encounters a stressful situation, which involves addressing the problem in a way that mitigates harm [76, 81]. It is largely influenced by teens' self-appraisals of online risk based on their frequency of Internet use, risk experiences, and observed peers' risk experiences [65, 82, 83]. The TOSS framework makes an explicit association between active parental mediation and teen risk-coping [45].

A number of researchers have called for new solutions that move away from parental control toward promoting positive parent-teen relationships and teen self-regulation of their online behaviors (e.g., [44, 46, 52, 55, 84, 85]). Human-computer interaction (HCI) researchers [85–88] have been at the forefront of this research, conceptualizing more collaborative technologies that engage parents with their children in digital rule-setting. For example, Ko et al. [87] developed a prototype called "FamiLync" that used participatory parental mediation; parents and teens engaged in co-learning activities around digital media use. This approach increased the shared understanding of smartphone use, fostered positive parent-teen relationships, and encouraged active participation in use-limiting activities, which significantly reduced overall smartphone usage [87]. Schiano and Burg [44] recently challenged interaction designers to reconceptualize parental control technologies as "collaborative self-regulation training tools" to help teach teens how to moderate their media use. Yet few, if any, technologies have been developed to help teens self-regulate and manage online privacy and/or safety risks in a meaningful way [45].

14.2.2 Risk as a Learning Process and the Suppressive Effect of Restrictive Parental Mediation During Adolescence

Section Highlights

- **Teens make privacy decisions differently than adults**. They experiment with online disclosures and **take protective measures retroactively** once their privacy concern has been triggered.
- **Parents** take both **preventative** and **reactive measures** to protect their teens online. Yet more **authoritarian measures** can have **a suppressive effect** by limiting teens' online disclosures and risk-coping skills.
- It may be beneficial to **give teens some leeway to make mistakes, learn from them, and be able to recover.**

To evaluate how teens think about and manage their privacy on social media, as well as how different parental mediation strategies affect this privacy regulation process, Wisniewski and colleagues [65, 82] conducted a secondary analysis of Pew Research dataset including teen and parent survey responses. In the first study, Jia et al. [82] compared the widely accepted concern-centric model of information privacy based on "Antecedents→Privacy Concerns→Outcomes" (or "APCO")[1] to a newly proposed "risk-centric" model of information privacy developed for teens. They confirmed that the risk-centric model was a better representation of how teens made privacy disclosure decisions on social media than the concern-centric model. Instead of privacy concerns driving teens' information disclosures or privacy protective behaviors, teens demonstrated what looked more like a risk escalation process (**Fig. 14.2** in red) in which teens first make online disclosures that render them more susceptible to experiences of risky online interactions. In turn, these risky experiences are associated with higher levels of privacy concerns, leading to privacy-preserving behaviors (e.g., advice-seeking) and remedy/corrective risk-coping behaviors (e.g., deleting content, blocking another user, deactivating their account).

---

[1] The APCO model was developed within the Information Systems (IS) field (see Chap. 3) and is typically applied to adult populations.

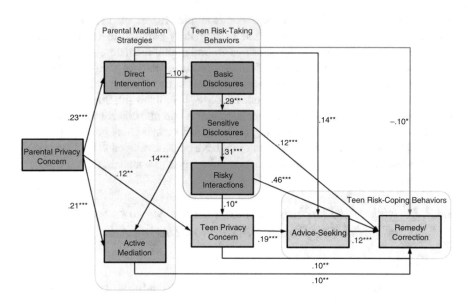

Fig. 14.2 Wisniewski et al.'s [65] preventative vs. reactive model of parental mediation

In a follow-up study, Wisniewski et al. [65] used the same dataset to determine how two different parental mediation strategies (direct intervention versus active parental mediation) affected this risk-taking process. *Direct intervention* included restrictive practices, such as using parental controls and changing the teen's privacy settings for them, while *active mediation* focused more on talking to teens about what they post online or commenting on their posts. They found **(Fig. 14.2)** that direct parental intervention reduced teens' overall information disclosures and privacy protective actions, while it was positively associated with advice-seeking. In contrast, active mediation was positively associated with more remedy/corrective or privacy protection behaviors.

In other words, direct parental intervention served as a preventative approach to privacy protection, while active mediation was more of a reactive approach, where parents engaged with teens to discuss what they are doing online and helped them recover if they did some mistakes online. When parents employed direct intervention without active mediation, this seemed to have the most suppressive effect on how frequently teens used social media and the diversity of their connections.

So while it may be possible that teens who have parents who directly intervene on the behalf of their online privacy are more discerning about the types of connections they make—in addition to reducing any possibly risky interaction online—this strategy may also reduce positive online interactions or even encourage teens to circumvent parental supervision by interacting with others more covertly through other means or platforms that are less visible to their parents.

Hearkening back to the developmental perspective on adolescence and risk-taking, these findings suggest that focusing only on shielding teens online may inhibit them from learning how to make appropriate online disclosures, learn from their own mistakes, and recover once they have encountered a privacy violation that makes them feel threatened.

14.3 Designing Sociotechnical Systems to Support Adolescence

Section Highlights

- The Internet, social media, and mobile technologies provide **both benefits and risks** to teens.
- To optimize the benefits, we must be careful **not to overly protect teens by shielding them from all risks** because these experiences help teens mature into adults.
- We need to consider the **developmental needs of teens** when we design **privacy mechanisms** for their **online safety**.

As discussed in this chapter, adolescent online safety plays a central role in adolescent privacy research. Social and mobile technologies facilitate new opportunities for teens: they can benefit from online interactions that allow them to explore their self-identities, seek social support, and search for new information [53, 89]. However, these technologies may also amplify some existing risks.

The Crimes Against Children Research Center [90] reports that one in four youth in the United States has experienced unwanted exposure to Internet pornography, one in nine has been a victim of online harassment, and one in 11 reports receiving unwanted sexual solicitations online. The rates of depressive symptoms, self-harm, and teen suicide in the United States have increased with the rise in adolescent digital media use [91, 92]; while some researchers suggest that new technologies play a critical role in these negative trends [1, 93], others have shown these claims to be overstated [94, 95].

Teens themselves are ambivalent about the effect the Internet and social media has had on their lives: about a quarter feel that social media has had mostly a negative impact on their lives, 31% think it has a mostly positive effect, and 45% are neutral [1].

Our limited knowledge about what teens are doing online, concern for the personal information they are disclosing to others, and inability to protect them from harm fosters a sense of fear and constrains our ability to design privacy and safety mechanisms for online platforms that are developmentally appropriate for empowering adolescents in a way that they become risk resilient. As Boyd aptly put it in her book:

> As a society, we often spend so much time worrying about young people that we fail to account for how our paternalism and protectionism hinders teens' ability to become informed, thoughtful, and engaged adults. [8 , p. 28]

It is clear there is a sociotechnical gap between what we know about healthy adolescent development and the current systems designed to support adolescent privacy and online safety. The current paradigm for keeping teens safe online focuses heavily on paternalistic approaches that increase parental control through authoritarian and privacy-invasive parental features that monitor and restrict a teen's online activities [45, 96–98]. Such solutions have repeatedly been shown to be ineffective, and even detrimental, to the trust relationship between teens and parents [37, 48, 52, 72, 99]. Additionally, there is little evidence that these technologies actually keep teens safe online and, more importantly, may hinder teens from learning important online safety skills and effectively managing online risks on their own [56, 96].

A more active approach, including talking to the teens about what they do online, sharing activities with them, and offering help, is linked to lower risk and harm, as well as more developed online skills [100], yet we are not currently designing tools to facilitate this process. Therefore, in the next section, we conclude this chapter with actionable guidelines for supporting online privacy and safety from an evidence-based and developmental perspective that is appropriate for the unique life stage of adolescence.

14.4 Design Guidelines for Privacy and Risk-Taking During Adolescence

Section Highlights

- A **user-centered approach** to online privacy and safety considers the needs and desire of **teens as key stakeholders**.
- Online privacy and safety tools for teens should be **developmentally appropriate** for allowing them to engage in **appropriate levels of risk**.
- Systems should **reward positive behavior** and **raise risk awareness** so that teens can become **good digital citizens** and learn how to take **privacy-preserving actions** to ensure their own online safety.
- There are **trade-offs** when designing for **adolescent privacy**, **parental control**, **online safety**, and **trust**.
- The key to **privacy design for adolescence** is helping **families negotiate online boundaries** and balance these tensions.

Drawing from the evidence-based research presented in this chapter, we provide the following privacy design heuristics for adolescence.

Take a "User-Centered" Approach to Adolescent Privacy and Online Safety
First, we should refrain from fear-based and paternalistic privacy narratives about adolescents, their digital privacy, and their online safety. When we make decisions based on fear and protectionism, we take a stronger and more authoritarian stance than we would when taking a more rational and evidence-based approach.

Further, when we design for parents without considering the needs of teens as key stakeholders in the design of technologies they will ultimately use, we are failing to take a user-centered approach to privacy design [101]. Therefore, it is important to first identify biases and assumptions about teens that are being used to design systems for them and to scrutinize these assumptions for validity.

Instead of designing for "parental control," we should design solutions that encourage teens to reflect on and self-regulate their own behaviors. Engaging teens directly as end users of online safety apps may empower them by giving them more agency and choice, thereby increasing their sense of personal autonomy and control. We should leverage user-centered techniques to better understand what safety and privacy features teens would actually find useful. Instead of assuming that teens are inherently risk seekers, a more nuanced approach would be to work with teens (e.g., through participatory design or other approaches) and ask them in what ways they feel that they need to be kept safe and then provide features teens find personally beneficial.

Some Risk Is Essential for Teen Developmental Growth We should design for features that help parents engage in conversations with their teens about their online risk-taking and risk-coping behaviors instead of concentrating on blocking all exposure to online risk. Parents should provide room for teens to make mistakes and recover from them, as this helps teens build resilience [43]. In cases where teens' perceptions of what is considered risky online behavior conflict with their parents' perception, it would be helpful to provide functionality that gives teens the possibility to negotiate the course of action with their parents [52].

For instance, instead of parental controls that unequivocally restrict teens from taking certain actions online (e.g., visiting a potentially risky website), teens might first be warned of the potential risk and be given the option to override the warning, and the software could involve the parent if the situation escalates. Allowing teens this kind of agency and choice would acknowledge that adolescence is characterized by a growing need for independence from parents but at the same time signal to teens that their parents trust them to make good decisions.

Design for Reward Instead of Punishment We should design for online environments that encourage and reward teens for positive and pro-social behavior, rather than punishing them for perceived rule violations. Wisniewski et al.'s [49, 63] diary study with parents and teens found that teens often do not tell their parents about their online risk experiences because they are concerned that their parents will punish them and/or make the situation worse.

Instead, we should consider promoting open, honest, and nonjudgmental family communication about online safety, supporting teens in a way that helps them cope with and recover from privacy violations and online risk exposure. Further, parental control software could also leverage positive reinforcement more effectively. For instance, the Screen Time Companion app[2] offers a "reward time system" that allows teens to get extra time if they meet certain criteria specified by their parents.

---

[2] https://screentimelabs.com/

Reward systems are more contextualized restraints because they provide positive reinforcement and allow teens to earn privileges, as well as their parents' trust [43].

Design for Raising Risk Awareness, Which Encourages a Protective Response from Teens When teens make online disclosures that lead to risky online interactions and increased privacy concerns, this also leads to increased privacy-preserving behaviors as well as remedy/corrective risk-coping behaviors [82]. Therefore, we should find ways to raise risk awareness through "teachable moments [102]," which has been validated as a more effective approach within educational psychology research. Havighurst's book (1953) on *Human Development and Education* explains developmental tasks must be learned at the right time so that learning can be most effective. For example, raising the risk awareness of teens in the context of a risky interaction (e.g., taking and sending an explicit photo) may be more effective than using generic warnings about appropriate sharing outside the context of that risky interaction. Therefore, we should design warning systems that make privacy risks more apparent to teens in order to enhance their privacy awareness, teach, and encourage appropriate risk-coping behaviors [102]. In this way, parental monitoring software could be transformed into online safety software to teach teens about how to manage their online interactions with others.

Design for Safety with Privacy and Trust in Mind We should consider designing features that facilitate building trust and respect teens' privacy. Most research shows teens value their privacy while interacting with others online [61, 62, 103, 104]. Teen's need for privacy is directly tied to their need for autonomy and respect [35]. In the case of families, trust is a critical factor in an adolescent's relationship with their parents [38]. Parental trust is based on knowledge of their children's past and present behavior, and information disclosure from teens is necessary for "knowing" as a form of "trusting" [39]. Inversely, trust is also tightly coupled with privacy for adolescents, where "trusting" is a form of giving a teen the space and autonomy to not disclose information [35]. Some degree of trust is needed to promote independence in teens [51]. In the context of adolescent online safety, parents have to balance their children's growing independence with their own concerns for safety [48]. Ultimately, all parents will have to rely on their teens behaving responsibly even when parents do not know where exactly they are or what they do; that is, parents just have to trust their teens' good intentions, knowing that there is a possible risk for them behaving in an unwanted way [39] While some control may be necessary, instead of risking losing their teen's trust by restricting or monitoring their technology use, parents should strive to build trusting relationships with their teens so that teens can both earn that trust and learn to self-regulate their own online behaviors into emerging adulthood [52]. Designing with privacy and trust in mind could include creating online safety apps that give parents helpful meta-level information regarding teens' online activities instead of full disclosure of what teens do online [45, 52, 96].

For example, software could provide parents with only a summary of who their teen is engaging with via their mobile device and how often, as opposed to disclosing the content of the conversations. Features such as this would contribute to maintaining a trusting relationship between family members: Parents would know when there is something to worry about, and teens would know that their parents care and have some understanding of what the teens do online and who they interact with, but teens would not need to feel like they are being spied on [55].

Support Families in Online Boundary Negotiation Privacy turbulence in families often occurs when teens do not feel like they have agency or when rules are miscommunicated, seem arbitrary, or seem overly restrictive [58]. Therefore, we should design systems that allow families to jointly negotiate and set boundaries related to technology use and renegotiate them when needed. Supporting this kind of open communication within families will help teens understand why specific rules exist, are likely to reduce uncertainty, and increase the likelihood that teens come to their parents with problems. In turn, it will help parents be less fearful about the online risks the Internet presents to their teens so that parents and teens feel empowered to leverage technology in beneficial ways. For instance, it would be beneficial to design evidence-based instructive media to educate parents and teens on digital privacy and online safety that includes how to help teens resolve privacy violations and negative online situations that *may* occur or *after* they have occurred. This approach would be analogous to providing comprehensive sex education, as opposed to abstinence-only approaches that have proven ineffective [105].

We might also reframe online safety and behaviors as joint family responsibilities, making teens and parents accountable to one another [49]. For example, accountability software detects and notifies adult peers of lapses of pornography addiction [106]. Perhaps a similar system could detect teen risk-seeking behaviors, prompt parents to inquire, encourage teens to ask their parents for advice, and even "nudge" [107] teens to change their behaviors. To close the loop, designers might also build mechanisms to keep parents accountable to teens for upholding the same moral character, teaching teens to "do as I do" instead of "as I say," emphasizing joint accountability over strict and unidirectional parental oversight. Overall, we believe these guidelines will help families reduce privacy turbulence by establishing open communication and negotiation concerning shared rules and boundaries. It would help teens build resilience to online risks while respecting teens' need for privacy, autonomy, and control.

14.5 Summary

Teen life in the twenty-first century is both very similar to and very different from that of their parents. While teens still push for autonomy and freedom to experiment and take risks, much of their behaviors are now captured on friends' smartphones, shared on social media, and archived on search engines. Much of the research and media attention on teens' technology use has focused on the risks and negative outcomes of this more public performance of adolescence, with the primary solution being more technology to closely monitor teens' behaviors. In this chapter, we argue that technology designers must push beyond authoritative approach to parenting teens in the digital age and instead recognize the importance of risk-taking during this life stage and focus on more teen-centric design solutions that encourage reflection and discussion rather than surveillance and restriction.

Acknowledgments This research was supported in part by the William T. Grant Foundation under grant number #187941 and the US National Science Foundation under grant numbers CHS-1844881 and #IIP-1827700. Any opinion, findings, and conclusions or recommendations expressed in this material are those of the authors and do not necessarily reflect the views of the research sponsors.

References

1. Anderson, M., and J. Jiang. 2018. *Teens, Social Media & Technology 2018*. Washington, DC: Pew Research Center.
2. Lenhart, A., M. Duggan, A. Perrin, R. Stepler, L. Rainie, and K. Parker. 2015. *Teens, Social Media & Technology Overview 2015*. Washington, DC: Pew Research Center.
3. Lenhart, A., A. Monica, and A. Smith. 2015. *Teens, Technology and Romantic Relationships*. Washington, DC: Pew Research Center.
4. The Common Sense Census. 2015. *Media Use by Tweens and Teens 2015*. San Francisco, CA: Common Sense Media.
5. Robb, M.B. 2017. *News and America's Kids: How Young People Perceive and Are Impacted by the News*. San Francisco, CA: Common Sense Media.
6. Palfrey, J.G., and U. Gasser. 2008. *Born Digital: Understanding the First Generation of Digital Natives*. New York: Basic Books.
7. Hargittai, E. 2010. Digital Na(t)ives? Variation in internet skills and uses among members of the "net generation"*. *Sociological Inquiry*. 80: 92–113. https://doi.org/10.1111/j.1475-682X.2009.00317.x.
8. Boyd, D. 2014. *It's Complicated: The Social Lives of Networked Teens*. New Haven, CT: Yale University Press.
9. Barnes, S.B. 2006. A privacy paradox: Social networking in the United States. *First Monday*. 11 (9): 11–15.
10. Walrave, M., and W. Heirman. 2011. Disclosing or protecting? Teenagers' online self-disclosure. In *Computers, Privacy and Data Protection: An element of choice*, 285–307. Dordrecht: Springer. https://doi.org/10.1007/978-94-007-0641-5_14.
11. Anjum, B. *Ubiquity: An Interview with Pamela Wisniewski*. https://ubiquity.acm.org/article.cfm?id=3301323. Last Accessed 29 Aug 2019.
12. Acquisti, A., and R. Gross. 2006. Imagined communities: Awareness, information sharing, and privacy on the Facebook. In *Privacy Enhancing Technologies*, 36–58. Berlin, Heidelberg: Springer.
13. Acquisti, A., and Grossklags, J. 2005. Uncertainty, ambiguity and privacy. *Presented at the Fourth Annual Workshop Economics and Information Security (WEIS 2005)*.
14. Livingstone, S., and P.K. Smith. 2014. Annual research review: Harms experienced by child users of online and mobile technologies: The nature, prevalence and management of sexual and aggressive risks in the digital age. *Journal of Child Psychology and Psychiatry* 55: 635–654. https://doi.org/10.1111/jcpp.12197.
15. 2003. Age limits and adolescents. *Paediatr Child Health.* 8: 577.
16. Pinter, A.T., Wisniewski, P., Xu, H., Rosson, M.B., Carroll, J.M. 2017. Adolescent online safety: Moving beyond formative evaluations to designing solutions for the future. In *Proceedings of the International Conference on Interaction Design and Children*.

17. Children's Online Privacy Protection Rule ("COPPA"). 2013.
18. Steinberg, L. 2004. Risk taking in adolescence: What changes, and why? *Annals of the New York Academy of Sciences* 1021: 51–58. https://doi.org/10.1196/annals.1308.005.
19. Baumrind, D. 2005. Patterns of parental authority and adolescent autonomy. *New Directions for Child and Adolescent Development.* 2005: 61–69. https://doi.org/10.1002/cd.128.
20. Youniss, J., and J. Smollar. 1985. *Adolescent Relations with Mothers, Fathers, and Friends.* Chicago, IL: University of Chicago Press.
21. Cohn, L.D., S. Macfarlane, C. Yanez, and W.K. Imai. 1995. Risk-perception: differences between adolescents and adults. *Health Psychology* 14: 217.
22. Dahl, R.E. 2004. Adolescent brain development: A period of vulnerabilities and opportunities. *Keynote Address. Annals of the New York Academy of Sciences.* 1021: 1–22. https://doi.org/10.1196/annals.1308.001.
23. Arnett, J.J. 2012. New horizons in research on emerging and young adulthood. In *Early Adulthood in a Family Context*, ed. A. Booth, S.L. Brown, N.S. Landale, W.D. Manning, and S.M. McHale, 231–244. New York, NY: Springer. https://doi.org/10.1007/978-1-4614-1436-0_15.
24. Steinberg, L., and K.C. Monahan. 2007. Age differences in resistance to peer influence. *Developmental Psychology* 43: 1531–1543. https://doi.org/10.1037/0012-1649.43.6.1531.
25. Allen, J.P., M.R. Porter, and F.C. McFARLAND. 2006. Leaders and followers in adolescent close friendships: Susceptibility to peer influence as a predictor of risky behavior, friendship instability, and depression. *Development and Psychopathology* 18: 155–172. https://doi.org/10.1017/S0954579406060093.
26. Finkenauer, C., R.C.M.E. Engels, and W. Meeus. 2002. Keeping secrets from parents: Advantages and disadvantages of secrecy in adolescence. *Journal of Youth and Adolescence.* 31: 123–136. https://doi.org/10.1023/A:1014069926507.
27. Conflict Processes and Transitions in Parent and Peer Relationships: Implications for Autonomy and Regulation – W. Andrew Collins, Brett Laursen, Nicole Mortensen, Coral Luebker, Margaret Ferreira, 1997. https://journals.sagepub.com/doi/10.1177/0743554897122003. Last Accessed 29 Aug 2019.
28. Baumrind, D. 1987. A developmental perspective on adolescent risk taking in contemporary America. *New Directions for Child Development* 37: 93–125.
29. Steinberg, L., S.D. Lamborn, N. Darling, N.S. Mounts, and S.M. Dornbusch. 1994. Over-time changes in adjustment and competence among adolescents from authoritative, authoritarian, indulgent, and neglectful families. *Child Development.* 65: 754–770. https://doi.org/10.2307/1131416.
30. Acquisti, A., and J. Grossklags. 2005. Privacy and rationality in individual decision making. *IEEE Security & Privacy.* 3: 26–33.
31. Gambino, A., J. Kim, S.S. Sundar, J. Ge, and M.B. Rosson. 2016. User disbelief in privacy paradox: Heuristics that determine disclosure. In *Proceedings of the 2016 CHI Conference Extended Abstracts on Human Factors in Computing Systems*, 2837–2843. New York, NY: ACM. https://doi.org/10.1145/2851581.2892413.
32. Norberg, P.A., D.R. Horne, and D.A. Horne. 2007. The privacy paradox: Personal information disclosure intentions versus behaviors. *Journal of Consumer Affairs.* 41: 100–126. https://doi.org/10.1111/j.1745-6606.2006.00070.x.
33. Phelan, C., C. Lampe, and P. Resnick. 2016. It's creepy, but it doesn't bother me. In *Proceedings of the 2016 CHI Conference on Human Factors in Computing Systems*, 5240–5251. New York, NY: ACM. https://doi.org/10.1145/2858036.2858381.
34. Utz, S., and N. Krämer. 2009. The privacy paradox on social network sites revisited: The role of individual characteristics and group norms. *Cyberpsychology: Journal of Psychosocial Research on Cyberspace.* 3 (2): 1.
35. Rossler, B. 2005. *The Value of Privacy.* Cambridge: Polity Press.
36. Steeves, V., and P. Regan. 2014. Young people online and the social value of privacy. *Journal of Information, Communication and Ethics in Society.* https://doi.org/10.1108/JICES-01-2014-0004.

37. Ghosh, A.K., K. Badillo-Urquiola, S. Guha, J.J. LaViola Jr., and P.J. Wisniewski. 2018. Safety vs. surveillance: What children have to say about mobile apps for parental control. In *Proceedings of the 2018 ACM Conference on Human Factors in Computing Systems*. Montréal, Canada: ACM.
38. Williams, A. 2003. Adolescents' relationships with parents. *Journal of Language and Social Psychology.* 22: 58–65. https://doi.org/10.1177/0261927X02250056.
39. Kerr, M., H. Stattin, and K. Trost. 1999. To know you is to trust you: Parents' trust is rooted in child disclosure of information. *Journal of Adolescence* 22: 737–752. https://doi.org/10.1006/jado.1999.0266.
40. Lyon, D. 2006. *Theorizing Surveillance*. London: Routledge.
41. Nock, S.L. 1993. *The Costs of Privacy: Surveillance and Reputation in America*. Piscataway: Transaction Publishers.
42. Gao, G. What Americans think about NSA surveillance, national security and privacy. http://www.pewresearch.org/fact-tank/2015/05/29/what-americans-think-about-nsa-surveillance-national-security-and-privacy/. Last Accessed 17 July 2017.
43. Wisniewski, P. 2018. The privacy paradox of adolescent online safety: A matter of risk prevention or risk resilience? *IEEE Security & Privacy.* 16: 86–90. https://doi.org/10.1109/MSP.2018.1870874.
44. Schiano, D.J., and C. Burg. 2017. Parental controls: Oxymoron and design opportunity. In *HCI International 2017 – Posters' Extended Abstracts*, 645–652. Berlin: Springer, Champions. https://doi.org/10.1007/978-3-319-58753-0_91.
45. Wisniewski, P., A.K. Ghosh, H. Xu, M.B. Rosson, and J.M. Carroll. 2017. Parental control vs. teen self-regulation: Is there a middle ground for mobile online safety? In *Proceedings of the 2017 ACM Conference on Computer Supported Cooperative Work and Social Computing*, 51–69. New York, NY: ACM. https://doi.org/10.1145/2998181.2998352.
46. Collier, A. Less parental control, more support of kids' self-regulation: Study. http://www.connectsafely.org/less-parental-control-more-support-of-kids-self-regulation-study/. Last Accessed 18 July 2017.
47. Child, J.T., and S. Petronio. 2011. Unpacking the paradoxes of privacy in CMC relationships: The challenges of blogging and relational communication on the internet. In *Computer Mediated Communication in Personal Relationships*, ed. Webb, K.W.& L., 21–40. New York: Peter Lang.
48. Erickson, L.B., P. Wisniewski, H. Xu, J.M. Carroll, M.B. Rosson, and D.F. Perkins. 2015. The boundaries between: Parental involvement in a teen's online world. *Journal of the Association for Information Science and Technology.* https://doi.org/10.1002/asi.23450.
49. Wisniewski, P., H. Xu, M.B. Rosson, and J.M. Carroll. 2017. Parents just don't understand: Why teens don't talk to parents about their online risk experiences. In *Proceedings of the 2017 ACM Conference on Computer Supported Cooperative Work and Social Computing*, 523–540. New York, NY: ACM. https://doi.org/10.1145/2998181.2998236.
50. Yardi, S., Bruckman, A. 2011. Social and technical challenges in parenting teens' social media use. Presented at the Proceedings of the SIGCHI Conference on Human Factors in Computing Systems, 1979422. https://doi.org/10.1145/1978942.1979422.
51. Cranor, L.F., A.L. Durity, A. Marsh, and B. Ur. 2014. Parents' and teens' perspectives on privacy in a technology-filled world. In *Proceedings of the Tenth Symposium on Usable Privacy and Security*. Menlo Park, CA: USENIX.
52. Hartikainen, H., N. Iivari, and M. Kinnula. 2016. Should we design for control, trust or involvement? A discourses survey about children's online safety. In *Proceedings of the the 15th International Conference on Interaction Design and Children*, 367–378. New York, NY: ACM. https://doi.org/10.1145/2930674.2930680.
53. Livingstone, S., and E. Helsper. 2010. Balancing opportunities and risks in teenagers' use of the internet: The role of online skills and internet self-efficacy. *New Media & Society.* 12: 309–329. https://doi.org/10.1177/1461444809342697.

54. Mathiesen, K. 2013. The internet, children, and privacy: The case against parental monitoring. *Ethics and Information Technology* 15: 263–274. https://doi.org/10.1007/s10676-013-9323-4.

55. Hartikainen, H., M. Kinnula, N. Iivari, and D. Rajanen. 2017. Finding common ground: Comparing children's and parents' views on children's online safety. In *Proceedings of the 31st British Computer Society Human Computer Interaction Conference*, 43:1–43:12. Swindon: BCS Learning & Development Ltd. https://doi.org/10.14236/ewic/HCI2017.43.

56. Wisniewski, P., H. Jia, N. Wang, S. Zheng, H. Xu, M.B. Rosson, and J.M. Carroll. 2015. Resilience mitigates the negative effects of adolescent internet addiction and online risk exposure. In *Proceedings of the 33rd Annual ACM Conference on Human Factors in Computing Systems*, 4029–4038. New York, NY: ACM. https://doi.org/10.1145/2702123.2702240.

57. Marwick, A.E., and D. Boyd. 2014. Networked privacy: How teenagers negotiate context in social media. *New Media & Society* 16: 1051–1067.

58. Petronio, S. 2010. Communication privacy management theory: What do we know about family privacy regulation? *Journal of Family Theory & Review*. 2: 175–196.

59. Madden, M., A. Lenhart, S. Cortesi, U. Gasser, M. Duggan, A. Smith, and M. Beaton. 2013. Teens, social media, and privacy. *Pew Research Center* 21 (1055): 2–86.

60. Dewar, S., S. Islam, E. Resor, and N. Salehi. 2019. Finsta: Creating "Fake" spaces for authentic performance. In *Extended Abstracts of the 2019 CHI Conference on Human Factors in Computing Systems*, LBW1214:1–LBW1214:6. New York, NY: ACM. https://doi.org/10.1145/3290607.3313033.

61. Davis, K., and C. James. 2013. Tweens' conceptions of privacy online: implications for educators. *Learning, Media and Technology* 38: 4–25. https://doi.org/10.1080/17439884.2012.658404.

62. Smith, P.K., J. Mahdavi, M. Carvalho, S. Fisher, S. Russell, and N. Tippett. 2008. Cyberbullying: Its nature and impact in secondary school pupils. *Journal of Child Psychology and Psychiatry and Allied Disciplines* 49: 376–385. https://doi.org/10.1111/j.1469-7610.2007.01846.x.

63. Wisniewski, P., H. Xu, M.B. Rosson, D.F. Perkins, and J.M. Carroll. 2016. Dear diary: Teens reflect on their weekly online risk experiences. In *Proceedings of the 2016 CHI Conference on Human Factors in Computing Systems*, 3919–3930. New York, NY: ACM. https://doi.org/10.1145/2858036.2858317.

64. Agosto, D.E., and J. Abbas. 2017. "Don't be dumb—that's the rule I try to live by": A closer look at older teens' online privacy and safety attitudes. *New Media & Society*. 19: 347–365. https://doi.org/10.1177/1461444815606121.

65. Wisniewski, P., H. Jia, H. Xu, M.B. Rosson, and J.M. Carroll. 2015. "Preventative" vs. "Reactive": How parental mediation influences teens' social media privacy behaviors. In *Proceedings of the 18th ACM Conference on Computer Supported Cooperative Work & Social Computing*, 302–316. New York, NY: ACM. https://doi.org/10.1145/2675133.2675293.

66. Child, J.T., and D.A. Westermann. 2013. Let's be Facebook friends: Exploring parental Facebook friend requests from a communication privacy management (CPM) perspective. *Journal of Family Communication*. 13: 46–59. https://doi.org/10.1080/15267431.2012.742089.

67. Got a teen driver? Here is tech to help keep them safe, https://www.usatoday.com/story/tech/columnist/2017/06/25/got-teen-driver-here-tech-help-keep-them-safe/103076252/. Last Accessed 29 Aug 2019.

68. Czeskis, A., Dermendjieva, I., Yapit, H., Borning, A., Friedman, B., Gill, B., Kohno, T. 2010. Parenting from the pocket: value tensions and technical directions for secure and private parent-teen mobile safety. *Presented at the Proceedings of the Sixth Symposium on Usable Privacy and Security*, 1837130. https://doi.org/10.1145/1837110.1837130.

69. Eastin, M.S., B.S. Greenberg, and L. Hofschire. 2006. Parenting the Internet. *Journal of Communication*. 56: 486–504. https://doi.org/10.1111/j.1460-2466.2006.00297.x.

70. Livingstone, S., L. Haddon, A. Görzig, and K. Ólafsson. 2011. *Risks and Safety on the Internet: The Perspective of European Children*. London: EU Kids Online.

71. Valkenburg, P.M., M. Krcmar, A.L. Peeters, and N.M. Marseille. 1999. Developing a scale to assess three styles of television mediation: "Instructive Mediation," "Restrictive Mediation," and "Social Coviewing.". *Journal of Broadcasting & Electronic Media.* 43: 52–66.
72. Duerager, A., Livingstone, S. 2012. How can parents support children's internet safety?
73. Livingstone, S., and E.J. Helsper. 2008. Parental mediation of Children's internet use. *Journal of Broadcasting & Electronic Media.* 52: 581–599. https://doi.org/10.1080/08838150802437396.
74. Mesch, G.S. 2009. Parental mediation, online activities, and cyberbullying. *Cyber Psychology and Behavior* 12: 387–393.
75. Gardner, T.W., T.J. Dishion, and A.M. Connell. 2008. Adolescent self-regulation as resilience: Resistance to antisocial behavior within the deviant peer context. *Journal of Abnormal Child Psychology.* 36: 273–284.
76. Fingerman, K.L., J. Smith, and C. Berg. 2010. Coping and self-regulation across the life span. In *Handbook of Life-Span Development.* Cham: Springer Publishing Company.
77. Kopp, C.B. 1982. Antecedents of self-regulation: A developmental perspective. *Developmental Psychology* 18: 199–214. https://doi.org/10.1037/0012-1649.18.2.199.
78. Moilanen, K.L., K.E. Rasmussen, and L.M. Padilla-Walker. 2015. Bidirectional associations between self-regulation and parenting styles in early adolescence. *Journal of Research on Adolescence (Wiley-Blackwell)* 25: 246–262. https://doi.org/10.1111/jora.12125.
79. Bandura, A. 1991. Social cognitive theory of self-regulation. *Organizational Behavior and Human Decision Processes.* 50: 248–287. https://doi.org/10.1016/0749-5978(91)90022-L.
80. Bechara, A. 2005. Decision making, impulse control and loss of willpower to resist drugs: A neurocognitive perspective. *Nature Neuroscience* 8: 1458–1463. https://doi.org/10.1038/nn1584.
81. Lazarus, R.S. 2000. Toward better research on stress and coping. *The American Psychologist.* 55: 665–673.
82. Jia, H., P.J. Wisniewski, H. Xu, M.B. Rosson, and J.M. Carroll. 2015. Risk-taking as a learning process for shaping teen's online information privacy behaviors. In *Proceedings of the 18th ACM Conference on Computer Supported Cooperative Work & Social Computing,* 583–599. New York, NY: ACM. https://doi.org/10.1145/2675133.2675287.
83. d'Haenens, L., Vandoninck, S., Donoso, V. How to cope and build online resilience? http://www2.lse.ac.uk/media@lse/research/EUKidsOnline/Home.aspx. Last Accessed 22 Oct 2019.
84. Law, D.M., J.D. Shapka, and B.F. Olson. 2010. To control or not to control? *Parenting Behaviours and Adolescent Online Aggression. Computers in Human Behavior.* 26: 1651–1656. https://doi.org/10.1016/j.chb.2010.06.013.
85. NSF Award Search: Award#1618153 – TWC SBE: Small: Helping teens and parents negotiate online privacy and safety. https://www.nsf.gov/awardsearch/showAward?AWD_ID=1618153&HistoricalAwards=false. Last Accessed 31 July 2017.
86. Hashish, Y., A. Bunt, and J.E. Young. 2014. Involving children in content control: A collaborative and education-oriented content filtering approach. In *Proceedings of the 32Nd Annual ACM Conference on Human Factors in Computing Systems,* 1797–1806. New York, NY: ACM. https://doi.org/10.1145/2556288.2557128.
87. Ko, M., S. Choi, S. Yang, J. Lee, and U. Lee. 2015. FamiLync: Facilitating participatory parental mediation of adolescents' smartphone use. In *Proceedings of the 2015 ACM International Joint Conference on Pervasive and Ubiquitous Computing,* 867–878. New York, NY: ACM.
88. Nouwen, M., JafariNaimi, N., Zaman, B. 2017, August 1. Parental controls: reimagining technologies for parent-child interaction. In *Presented at the Proceedings of 15th European Conference on Computer-Supported Cooperative Work-Exploratory Papers, Reports of the European Society for Socially Embedded Technologies.* https://doi.org/10.18420/ecscw2017-28.

89. Shapiro, L.A.S., and G. Margolin. 2014. Growing up wired: Social networking sites and adolescent psychosocial development. *Clinical Child and Family Psychology Review* 17 (1): 1–18. https://doi.org/10.1007/s10567-013-0135-1.
90. Jones, L.M., K.J. Mitchell, and D. Finkelhor. 2012. Trends in youth internet victimization: Findings from three youth internet safety surveys 2000–2010. *Journal of Adolescent Health* 50: 179–186. https://doi.org/10.1016/j.jadohealth.2011.09.015.
91. Center for Disease Control: FastStats. https://www.cdc.gov/nchs/fastats/suicide.htm. Last Accessed 24 Nov 2017.
92. Twenge, J.M., T.E. Joiner, M.L. Rogers, and G.N. Martin. 2017. Increases in depressive symptoms, suicide-related outcomes, and suicide rates among U.S. adolescents after 2010 and links to increased new media screen time. *Clinical Psychological Science*. https://doi.org/10.1177/2167702617723376.
93. Turkle, S. 2011. *Life on the Screen*. New York: Simon and Schuster.
94. Jensen, M., M.J. George, M.R. Russell, and C.L. Odgers. 2019. Young adolescents' digital technology use and mental health symptoms: Little evidence of longitudinal or daily linkages. *Clinical Psychological Science*. https://doi.org/10.1177/2167702619859336.
95. Orben, A., and A.K. Przybylski. 2019. The association between adolescent Well-being and digital technology use. *Nature Human Behaviour* 3: 173–182. https://doi.org/10.1038/s41562-018-0506-1.
96. Ghosh, A.K., K. Badillo-Urquiola, M.B. Rosson, H. Xu, J.M. Carroll, and P.J. Wisniewski. 2018. A matter of control or safety? Examining parental use of technical monitoring apps on teens' mobile devices. In *Proceedings of the 2018 CHI Conference on Human Factors in Computing Systems*, 194:1–194:14. New York, NY: ACM. https://doi.org/10.1145/3173574.3173768.
97. Stevenson, F., and M.A. Zimmerman. 2005. Adolescent resilience: A framework for understanding healthy development in the face of risk. *Annual Review of Public Health*. 26: 399–419.
98. Hartikainen, H., N. Iivari, and M. Kinnula. 2015. Children and web 2.0: What they do, what we fear, and what is done to make them safe. In *Nordic Contributions in IS Research*, ed. H. Oinas-Kukkonen, N. Iivari, K. Kuutti, A. Öörni, and M. Rajanen, 30–43. Cham: Springer International Publishing. https://doi.org/10.1007/978-3-319-21783-3_3.
99. Shin, W., and N. Ismail. 2014. Exploring the role of parents and peers in young adolescents' risk taking on social networking sites. *Cyberpsychology, Behavior and Social Networking* 17: 578–583. https://doi.org/10.1089/cyber.2014.0095.
100. Duerager, A., and Livingstone, S. *How can parents support children's internet safety?* http://www2.lse.ac.uk/media@lse/research/EUKidsOnline/Home.aspx, Last Accessed 22 Oct 2019.
101. Abras, C., D. Maloney-krichmar, and J. Preece. 2004. User-centered design. In *Encyclopedia of Human-Computer Interaction*, ed. W. Bainbridge. Thousand Oaks: Sage.
102. Havighurst, R.J. 1953. *Human Development and Education*. New York: Longmans, Green.
103. Helsper, Ellen Johanna. 2014. *Boyd, Danah: It's Complicated: The Social Lives of Networked Teens*. New Haven: Yale University Press.
104. Wisniewski, P., H. Xu, M.B. Rosson, D.F. Perkins, and J.M. Carroll. 2016. Dear diary: Teens reflect on their weekly online risk experiences. In *Proceedings of the 2016 CHI Conference on Human Factors in Computing Systems*, 3919–3930. New York: ACM. https://doi.org/10.1145/2858036.2858317.
105. Comprehensive Sex Education: Research and Results. http://www.advocatesforyouth.org/publications/1487. Last Accessed 4 Aug 2016.
106. Covenant Eyes.
107. Thaler, R.H., and C. Sunstein. 2008. *Nudge: Improving Decisions About Health, Wealth, and Happiness*. New Haven, NJ & London, U.K.: Yale University Press.

Chapter 15
Privacy and Vulnerable Populations

Nora McDonald and Andrea Forte

Abstract Vulnerable populations face unique privacy risks that not only challenge designers' preconceptions about privacy, these challenges are also frequently overlooked in decisions about privacy design and policy. This chapter defines and describes vulnerable populations and the challenges they face, as well as the research approaches that have traditionally been used to understand and design technologies that respect the privacy needs of vulnerable people. It describes how existing frameworks fail to account for the privacy concerns of people who experience heightened risk. It then introduces alternative ways of thinking about privacy that can help technologists, researchers, policy makers, and designers do a better job of serving the needs of the most vulnerable users of technology. We conclude with concrete guidance around identifying and integrating vulnerable populations into technology design for privacy.

15.1 Introduction

Section Highlights

- **We define vulnerable individuals as those who, because of their race, class, gender or sexual identity, religion, or other intersectional characteristics or circumstances**, are more susceptible to privacy violations that result in emotional, financial, or physical harm or neglect.
- **We consider some of these identities (e.g., LGBTQ, survivors of domestic abuse, and minority individuals and their intersections) in depth**, particularly the way these identities create some pressing and unique challenges.

N. McDonald (✉)
University of Cincinnati, School of Information Technology, Cincinnati, OH, USA

A. Forte
College of Computing and Informatics, Drexel University, Philadelphia, PA, USA
e-mail: aforte@drexel.edu

B. P. Knijnenburg et al. (eds.), *Modern Socio-Technical Perspectives on Privacy*,
https://doi.org/10.1007/978-3-030-82786-1_15

- **This chapter is comprised of six sections**, exploring how technologies exacerbate existing inequalities; what the specific privacy concerns and needs of certain vulnerable populations might encompass and current gaps in research; the role that social norms play in shaping privacy theory; a way forward that proposes intersectional approaches to some of the biggest challenges for vulnerable communities; and finally how technologists can identify and incorporate vulnerable populations into requirements gathering, testing, and policy making, including a thought experiment to help guide readers as they consider how to incorporate vulnerable users into their design process.

In this chapter, we define vulnerable individuals as people who are more susceptible to privacy violations that result in emotional, financial, or physical harm or neglect as a consequence of their race, class, gender or sexual identity, religion, or other intersectional characteristics or circumstances that marginalize them from society. While some legal scholars have identified misconceptions about privacy that traverse socioeconomic status, they also suggest that low-income, marginalized, and immigrant (particularly, foreign-born) communities are uniquely susceptible [1, 2] to these forms of privacy risk. We expand on this view of vulnerability to also include survivors of domestic abuse [3–5], people who have been incarcerated, immigrants [1, 6], activists, journalists [7], those who have been politically oppressed by society or their culture, those with HIV [8], LGBTQ [9–12], as well as the very young [13, 14] and very old [15], which are discussed in depth in Chapters 13 and 14. In this chapter, we demonstrate how the needs and experiences of these various identities are unique and often require different kinds of privacy protections than the general population.

Designing for privacy of *any* individuals poses considerable challenges for researchers and businesses who provide digital tools and infrastructure for users. Yet recent research on technology and privacy has surfaced what we already knew or intuited about vulnerable populations: inequalities that make people vulnerable offline are often replicated (or exacerbated) by networked technologies (cf. [2, 16–19]). The unique sensitivities that put vulnerable populations at risk frequently break designers' assumptions, which is compounded by our concern that vulnerable people are often overlooked (or not fully examined) as stakeholders in the design process—from requirements gathering, to ideation, to implementation and testing, and ultimately to policy making. In this chapter, we discuss why it is important to understand and empower vulnerable people and how to reflect their needs in policy and design.

In Chap. 2, the authors introduced various privacy frameworks applicable to digital spaces. Here, we focus on the evolution from individual-based theories, to norm-based theories, and, finally, to identity-based theories that consider structures of inequality. Identity-based theories and frameworks are useful for studying and designing for privacy with vulnerable populations because they are more attuned to the structural inequalities that make some individuals more susceptible to privacy violations. They also help explain why violations of privacy may be more dire for vulnerable individuals.

This chapter is comprised of six main sections. In the second section below, we explore how technologies exacerbate existing inequalities. In the third, we go on to explore what the privacy concerns and needs of certain vulnerable populations might encompass and discuss current gaps in research that supports more equitable and more universally effective design. In the fourth section, we review the role that social norms play in shaping privacy theory. In the fifth section, we propose intersectional approaches to some of the biggest challenges for vulnerable communities. We go on in the sixth section to give concrete examples of how technologists can identify and incorporate vulnerable populations into requirements gathering, testing, and policy making. We explore potential applications of our recommendations through a thought experiment and offer closing thoughts about current design recommendations and future challenges.

15.2   How Technology Reinforces and Promotes Inequality

Section Highlights

- **Service providers (e.g., social networks and apps) have exacerbated inequalities** by adopting policies that remove (pseudo)anonymity and potentially harm vulnerable populations.
- **In particular, the popular "real-name" policies and secondary authentication** (e.g., with email or phone) limit individuals' ability to remain anonymous. These policies result in censorship and opportunity loss and may, indeed, be easily hacked.
- **Algorithms that have become ubiquitous in our society, which profile and harm low-income and marginalized individuals,** unleash discrimination in virtually every aspect of their lives from their social networks, to their shopping, to their jobs and job searches.

We are only beginning to learn how technologies can reinforce and/or exacerbate existing inequalities. Below, we discuss three key ways technology has changed in the last decade that influence inequitable outcomes. First, policies that remove the safety of (pseudo)anonymity that may be desired by vulnerable populations. Second, one specific way that service providers (those who provide the platform and tools for online networks) regulate identity information is by requiring the use of secondary authentication (e.g., with email or phone) or real names—even requesting that users verify accounts with mobile or photo ID—which limits individuals' ability to control their privacy. These measures have become standard under the rubric of safety and security. Developers and, perhaps, others with privileged identities may take for granted that relinquishing identity information to social networks (when they request ID verification) or apps is an accepted norm. Third, algorithmic biases reinforce existing inequalities and can even propagate discriminatory practices.

Research on anonymity offers some insight into how privacy can be critical in providing opportunities for safe disclosure and interaction that are not otherwise available [20–25]. Anonymity provides avenues for overcoming ineluctable social norms embedded in existing (offline) social structures. Research on adolescents who use Ask.fm found that anonymity created opportunities for authentic self-expression and self-discovery among other social goals [26]. Pseudonymity can also facilitate self-disclosures [21, 22] on a range of topics that are critical to a person's psychological well-being [27–29], for example, by sexual abuse survivors [20] and domestic abuse survivors [25]. Environments that provide (pseudo)anonymous safe havens for identity exploration seem to be diminishing. Sites like Reddit no longer make throwaway accounts an obvious (pseudo)anonymity strategy, and subreddits regularly remove posts from new accounts, making it difficult to post (pseudo)anonymously with a throwaway account. At the same time, platforms that promote more ephemeral communications [30] are gaining in popularity.

Meanwhile, the trend toward more "authentic" [31] Internet participation requiring the use of real names raises concerns for vulnerable groups. For example, Facebook's real name policy requires that people can be identified with all content they post; because of this constraint, people may refrain from discussing sensitive topics [32]. German courts have ruled Facebook's policy illegal, finding that it surreptitiously allows Facebook to obtain users' consent to share their real names [33]. As they are currently constructed and governed, it has been argued that social platforms require vulnerable individuals to "perform" their identity according to norms that have been established by primarily white, privileged systems designers and policy makers or else risk opportunity loss [34]. In peer-production projects like open source software or Wikipedia, obscuring identity may be viewed by contributors as self-protection against opportunity loss, harassment, and threats of violence [35]. Moreover, many services require users to provide email or phone number for authentication and security. These policies are packaged as standard security measures but assume more is better to provide security and customer service. Indeed, the two-factor authentication adopted by major services like Google and Yahoo has been demonstrated to be hackable.

Additionally, government agencies can employ technologies that remove human decision-makers from social service administration, which has been shown to accelerate discriminatory practices [17]. Stereotypes about welfare recipients being "lazy" can be reinscribed in automated social welfare or healthcare systems that use failure to comply as signal of ineligibility in a way that increases the probability that welfare recipients will be rejected for beneficial services and subject to invasive visits by government officials and services [17]. For instance, Eubanks describes how a disabled girl loses Medicaid benefits for failing to cooperate in establishing eligibility—what amounts to a minor computer mistake—or how parents are flagged by social services for neglect because of an ignorant or vindictive neighbor or for failure to pay for medications: in other words, their crime was having a disabled child and being poor.

Other examples include the way in which technologies of surveillance, such as gang databases, re-encode perceptions of black and Latino young men as "deviant." That has consequences for arrests and sentencing but also affects the mindset of individuals who are criminalized [36]. Rios describes a system of ubiquitous punitive social control where family, schools, police, and prohibition systems interact to systematically criminalize marginalized youth in a way that shapes their worldview and identities [36]. Other literature also points to differences in how people engage with technologies along socioeconomic dimensions (e.g., [37, 38]). Ames and Burrell [39] found that even when trying to compensate for inequities in access to Internet technologies, individuals still face structural challenges stemming from socioeconomic circumstances, as well as bias because of their race and gender identities in their experience of technologies.

These same biases or stereotypes baked into algorithms can also undermine privacy design, for example, when low-income mothers are required to share irrelevant information about their sexual history and personal relationships as a requirement of receiving social services [16]. For example, Bridges describes how some states justify invasive questionnaires given to low-income mothers applying for benefits arguing that a history of drug abuse or domestic violence is a proxy for child neglect or abuse. Biases (including dirty policing and civil rights violations) make their way into invasive predictive policing technologies more often than not [40].

Pervasive surveillance technologies that rely on algorithms are required merely to take part in many aspects of society. Examples include systems that track individuals' online purchases [41, 42], social networks [2], job seekers [43], workplace [44, 45], and social services [2, 16, 17], and they inevitably disproportionately harm vulnerable and low-income populations.

The ways in which identities that are linked to race, sexuality, and socioeconomic status are often used to profile and punish and deny privacy rights are an insight that should lead us to consider the role that identities have in shaping vulnerable individuals' privacy needs and strategies. If we wish to develop technologies that do not exacerbate inequalities, it is critical to understand what kinds of unique privacy concerns vulnerable populations bring to their use of technology. In the next section, we will talk through some privacy concerns that can help orient technologists, policy makers, researchers, and designers to unique privacy vulnerabilities.

15.3 Who Is Vulnerable: Defining Unique Privacy Concerns

Section Highlights

- **The risks of emotional harm and physical violence loom large for LGBTQ individuals** even though the Internet has created new safe places for historically marginalized or stigmatized sexual identities.
- **Privacy is a challenge for domestic abuse victims and survivors** because it is easy for the target's partner to get access to their technology.
- **Being black and Hispanic is correlated with privacy vulnerabilities** and lack of trust in institutions that collect and store data.
- **A number of intersecting factors can compound the vulnerabilities** of already vulnerable groups.

There are many reasons why vulnerable individuals may require more privacy. In this section, we specifically consider examples related to sexuality, domestic abuse, and race that represent some of the most widespread experiences of vulnerability. Other vulnerabilities that are often adjacent include, but are not limited to, poverty, homelessness [46, 47], immigration [1, 6], stigmatized illnesses like HIV [8], and age—for instance, when it contributes to limited familiarity with scams or workplace technologies as discussed in Chap. 13. You will see that, in fact, in this section, discussions of race, ethnicity, and sexual identity (in particular) are inextricable with experiences of poverty and homelessness such that the research we cite inevitably (or unavoidably) captures those intersections. Notably, some of the most important research on privacy vulnerabilities sees poverty (in particular) and race as central [1, 2]. Privacy challenges for youth and aging populations are covered in Chapters 13 and 14.

15.3.1   Sexuality as Vulnerability

Gender identity and sexual orientation create vulnerabilities for individuals offline and online. For instance, simply being LGBTQ or female can cause individuals to seek more privacy or withdraw altogether [35, 48]. For their part, some social networks have become more inclusive when it comes to gender identification, with Facebook introducing over 50 gender options in 2014 [49] and Tinder allowing users to type in their own description of their gender identity [50]. But research has demonstrated that sexual orientation creates struggles of all kinds that require strict privacy management and even then still invite enhanced risks. That is, simply being more inclusive does not safeguard users against abuse and privacy risks. For this section, we focus primarily on LGBTQ as a vulnerability as they are often subject to the greatest harms. Other sexual preferences and gender identities exist that make people vulnerable but are not covered in this section.

LGTBQ populations are more likely to intersect with low-income populations, and these conditions of poverty are more often tied to experiences of discrimination in the workplace [51]. LGBTQ youths report overwhelmingly that they are not accepted in their community, and nine in ten experience negative messages about being LGBTQ but find that they can be more honest about themselves online (73%) [52]. For LGBTQ individuals, disclosure of sexual identity is carefully considered, and context collapse—when people from different social worlds interact, for example, when family meet friends—presents complex privacy challenges both online and offline [53].

Some research has looked at the disclosure strategies of LGBTQ young adults [10, 54] and parents [53]. Scheuerman et al. found that transgender individuals' experience of harm through social media is complex and multi-fronted arising as either targeted or incidental and both from insiders (those who are consider part of the "community") and from outsiders (those on the Internet who spread vitriol) [12]. According to Blackwell et al., LGBTQ parents worry about accidental disclosures to family, friends, and coworkers (some of whom are not even on these social networks but learn secondhand through those who are) [53]. LGBTQ parents feel both an obligation to be open about their lifestyle and an obligation to a collective social movement, to shoulder advocacy and the risk of their safety and privacy. On the one hand, broadcasting positive experiences, sharing adversity, and publicly "coming out" are all forms of advocacy—and part of an obligation to a politicized identity. On the other hand, in an environment where social views and values are in flux, "privacy stewardship" takes on greater urgency. LGBTQ parents worry that ever-shifting social views and dynamic networks leave them (and their children) susceptible to unforeseen future threats. As networks evolve, parents find themselves constantly on the lookout for "disapproval" within those social networks, and therefore, what constitutes a "safe space" online requires perpetual reassessment. Consequently, LGBTQ parents feel compelled to be both more private and more public than others.

Other studies have point to the risks faced by LGBTQ individuals that can lead to censorship online [55]. Notably, researchers in the Human-computer Interaction (HCI) and Computer-supported Cooperative Work (CSCW) community also point out that little research has focused on the specific harms transgender individuals (historically, some of the most vulnerable populations in the LGBTQ community) face online [12].

While the Internet has created new safe places for historically marginalized or stigmatized sexual identities, the risks of emotional harm and even violence loom large. Some HCI and CSCW researchers have argued that service providers consider accessibility of posts and user control [55]. According to Scheuerman et al., transgender individuals point to platforms like Twitter as examples of designs that do not take into account their needs, arguing that they allow for "trolling." They also point to the way that Facebook unwittingly (or not) can out individuals through its advertising (i.e., if others were to see their screen). While giving users greater control over their privacy settings is certainly critical, it is important that designers also not place burden on individuals to police others and safeguard themselves. Moreover, it is critical to understand these experiences from the perspective of these individuals since policies like those adopted by Twitter and Facebook (while perhaps well placed) have not offered sufficient protection from or remediation for harm.

15.3.2 Domestic Abuse as Vulnerability

One in four women and one in nine men have experienced intimate partner (physical) violence [56]. In addition to this intersection with gender, intimate partner violence may disproportionately affect LGBTQ individuals but has been somewhat little studied among this group [57]. Yet the ways in which this group has historically been underserved are most obviously in providing them with the protection they need as well as sensitivity to the nuanced issues that prevent women from seeking or finding help [58].

Domestic abuse victims and survivors represent challenging cases precisely because it is so easy for the target's partner to get access to their technology with little technological effort [4], which increasingly allows them to stalk and track. A high-profile example of design that failed to take into account potential vulnerabilities emerged in 2010 when Google introduced Buzz, a social network site that was intended to compete with Facebook. To overcome the critical mass problem of starting with an empty network, Google used frequent contacts from their other services like Gmail and chat to populate users' public list of connections. The practice of testing products only with Google employees rendered many vulnerable populations invisible in the process [59]. For example, one blogger noted that when she signed up, her abusive ex-husband suddenly had access to her location and recent online activity [60]. Users feared that contact with lawyers, doctors, psychologists, and other sensitive relationships might suddenly become public information.

Domestic abuse victims require specific technology training to ensure their physical safety [3–5]; however, designs like Buzz and the process that produced it exacerbate the problem. Google scholars note that despite the obvious life-threatening concerns, this particular group is not readily represented in technology design [5]. While domestic violence shelters have worked together with the anonymous browser, Tor, to provide victims with a reliable form of protection [3], more needs to be done to include the needs of the 10 million people in the United States who experience intimate partner violence each year [56].

15.3.3   Race as Vulnerability

Being black and Hispanic is correlated with privacy vulnerabilities and lack of trust among institutions that collect and store data and often intersects with being low income [1]. Indeed, race is at the intersection of so many central vulnerabilities that it can be hard to parse from any of those we explore in this section—and certainly with respect to amplified risk, which is why we later introduce intersectionality as such an important way of thinking about privacy. Even while the findings discussed in this section about minority populations and privacy intersect ineluctably with low socioeconomic status and other vulnerabilities, qualitative research that includes intersections of race, gender, and class/socioeconomics also seems to suggest that race alone can, for instance, impact online strategies for self-presentation and censorship [34].

Another intersection is race, crime, and socioeconomics. In their study of young people with low socioeconomic status, predominately of color, Marwick et al. (who even caveat "the pitfall of conflating race and class") find that marginalized social positions amplify risks online and contribute to avoidance of social media and self-censorship [61]. They make a parallel finding that youths of color with low socioeconomic status often experience structural racism in the form of policing and physical surveillance. Their study portrays these youth as well aware of the connection between Facebook posts and online or offline consequences (e.g., being doxed, bullied, or fired) but nevertheless prone to take the normative stance that they have "nothing to hide" [62, 63]. As a consequence, these youths self-censor or disengage altogether. Marwick et al. contrast this "individual responsibility," which makes teens censor online, with the paradoxical experience (shared by these same young adults) of being exposed to police surveillance and brutality from which there is no escape. They are aware that they have everything to fear because privacy violations are inevitable. This framing, the authors argue, helps to circumvent the "victim-blaming narrative of some media literacy efforts" that have traditionally placed responsibility on individuals to secure their privacy [61]. We echo Marwick et al. in arguing that designers should not place so much burden on users to remedy their own privacy concerns.

Recent research has suggested that people of color and people from high-crime neighborhoods may be more worried than white or higher-income counterparts about police use of social media in crime prevention [64]. Underlying these concerns is a heightened sense of fear about the repercussions of violating social norms, the consequences of being perceived of as a snitch or of information getting into the wrong hands, and abuse of power.

Yet another intersection is race and gender. Pitcan et al. [34] found that to avoid opportunity loss, black women downplay sexuality and try to otherwise appear non-threatening to avoid white American stereotypes. In their findings, white and privileged class appear inextricable, suggesting that designers need to consider how their perspective-taking shapes their designs—in this case to mitigate risks of opportunity loss for women of color.

15.3.4 Intersections of Vulnerabilities

A number of intersecting factors can compound the vulnerabilities of already vulnerable groups. Those who are LGBTQ and black are also more likely to experience violence and encounter the highest incidence of fatal violence within the LGBTQ community [65]. Black children of same-sex couples are twice as likely as black children in heterosexual households to experience poverty and over four times as likely as white children of heterosexual households [65]. LGBTQ young adults are more likely to experience homelessness than their non-LGBTQ counterparts.[1] Homelessness presents a whole host of impediments to privacy (e.g., inability to find quarters that secure physical privacy, dependence on facilities for their access to services and info, and often that access is public and potentially less secure).

---

[1] Limitations on education and income, which themselves constitute vulnerability, are also major predictors of homelessness [66]. Poverty alone goes hand in hand with certain vulnerabilities, for example, greater reliance on mobile technologies.

While the privacy concerns and needs of an LGBTQ person or a person of color are not necessarily the same as, for instance, a victim of domestic abuse, the experience of more than one of these identities increases your chances of experiencing poverty, homelessness, discrimination, violence, and other inequalities.

In the face of a growing privacy literature that focuses on technology users who are young, privileged, white, and cisgender, some researchers have undertaken the task of examining the challenges for those who fall outside of those privileged categories. Instruments for measuring technology literacy (e.g., [67–69]) have been used to explore what kinds of knowledge are associated with privacy practices (e.g., [70, 71]), which can have huge implications for vulnerable communities [6]. But this perspective potentially overlooks the way in which structural inequalities and experience conspire to make privacy threats and practices fundamentally different, not better or worse. For instance, living in poverty can amplify the consequences of a privacy violation; if, for example, a potential employer can find embarrassing (or simply unedited) information about a job seeker, the economic impact of opportunity loss may have devastating consequences for someone who is just getting by. The severity of the threat emanates not from a limited set of skills but from the condition of poverty associated with these identities. To come at privacy with a literacy framing is to suggest that if only users who are vulnerable had better skills, they would be fine, but the real difference is that privacy violations impact vulnerable groups in qualitatively different ways.

Consider the user who experiences or hears of a privacy scam that results in a loss of $4000 [71]. For someone living below the poverty line, that could be nearly half of their income. Perhaps it goes without saying that anything you do to mitigate against that threat will far surpass the type of activities we assign to the "digitally literate." These are potentially life-altering events that might leave fearful of ever using the Internet again. Measuring the effects of these events with "digital literacy" as a tool misses critical motivations and user experiences.

The experiences of those who are subject to surveillance and privacy threats on a daily basis because of their race and class can serve as a starting point for reframing privacy in ways that relieve victims of responsibility for privacy violations [61]. Instead of blaming people for the way they use limited privacy toolkits and for their reliance on shared infrastructures that mimic other oppressive systems, a growing narrative in the research literature suggests that infrastructures and services can be designed to better serve the needs of vulnerable groups. Thinking out of the box, could service providers offer insurance or compensation for users abused on their platform? The idea is not so radical given that other vendors are responsible for user experience.

15.4   Privacy, the Self and Social Norms

Section Highlights

- **Individualistic privacy theories, which focus on how people regulate information about themselves**, give way to normative approaches, ways of thinking about shared privacy expectations.
- **However, norm-based approaches overlook the increasingly ubiquitously networked environments in which we live,** in which boundaries are permeable and overlapping, and the way in which normative frames fail to meet the needs of individuals who reside outside the norm.
- **We challenge the view that privacy vulnerabilities are the result of lack of literacy** so much as sense of loss of agency and overwhelming exposure to less expensive and, by extension, vulnerable technologies, scams, predatory marketing, and exploitative sites [2].
- **Privacy threats are highly idiosyncratic**, suggesting that frameworks for addressing privacy problems should be sensitive to the stigma of vulnerable identities as well as the intersectional circumstances of individuals.

As discussed in Chap. 2 of this book, interpersonal boundary regulation [72, 73] lays a foundation for individualistic privacy theories that focus on understanding how people regulate information about the self, with an emphasis on personal exploration and self-presentation. For instance, Altman's framework of interpersonal boundary regulation characterizes privacy in an analog, pre-Internet world [72]. Taking ownership of privacy as an individual becomes more complicated as we consider the move to mediated interactions and as online systems become more complex, interconnected, and extensible [73]. Scholars have found that tending boundaries is part of everyday online practice [74], but that these strategies are complex and unique to the individual [75–80]. There is an inherent tension between the concerns of individuals seeking to protect their personal information (e.g., in order to safely self-disclose or participate in online spaces without fear of harassment) and the degree to which online platforms appear willing or able to afford those protections, leading to potential constraints on participation and self-censorship.

Approaches that emphasize social norms as a way of understanding privacy expectations are challenged by the permeable overlapping nature of online spaces. Yao explains that "in the physical world, for example, observable objects and symbols usually mark the boundaries between private and public domains, and the size of personal space can be neared in units of distance. ... in the virtual online world, the concept of 'space' is merely a metaphor ... To make things more complicated, people from different cultures, often with drastically different privacy beliefs and norms, co-occupy this abstract and metaphorical space. In such a virtual environment, the normative rules and expectations related to personal privacy are irrelevant" (p. 114) [81]. Even when privacy norms in online environments become established, they cannot take into account the values (or realities) of all individuals who inhabit them.

The difficulty of using traditional physical analogies, social norms, and common approaches like threat modeling to inform thinking about privacy for people with heightened risk is evident in the ways that technologies fail to meet the needs of vulnerable populations. For example, intimate partner violence (IPV) defies typical threat models because abusers often have access to victims' phones and can carry out injurious, albeit unsophisticated, attacks by directly accessing their devices and information, rather than through installing malicious software [4]. The challenges for IPV victims provide an analogy to the broader problems for privacy and security faced by experts: *Privacy threats are highly idiosyncratic, and as a result, so too are the specific mitigation strategies that individuals at risk must employ to counter them.* Mitigation strategies must, therefore, take account of not only the stigma or vulnerability that creates the need for heightened privacy but also other aspects of their individual circumstances, including their personal history, needs, and use of technology.

15.4.1 How Existing Privacy Frameworks Are Inadequate

The challenge of adapting a general theory of privacy in the face of rapidly changing networked information technologies gives way to new group and communitarian perspectives. For example, Lampinen et al. shift attention to the idea that boundaries are regulated as part of a group process [82–84]. Group perspectives allow participation in popular networked communities to be conceptualized as a trade-off between aspirations of personal privacy and benefits of social or participatory optimization. For example, to avoid tensions between different groups, individuals might divide the platform into separate spaces, creating private groups for some interactions. People might also self-censor or choose other channels (private or elsewhere) if they perceive a communication might be problematic.

As discussed extensively in Chap. 2, contextual integrity, an approach to thinking about privacy introduced by Helen Nissenbaum, describes privacy as a function of the social expectations of a given context, pushing beyond individual privacy to privacy as a function of norms in distinct situations [85]. Contextual integrity expands privacy theories to account for contexts in which social expectations dictate privacy violations, how information should flow, and who should have access to it. For example, Nissenbaum uses the example of healthcare environments, in which a healthcare provider may appropriately inquire about a patients' sexual behavior while that same inquiry would not be acceptable directed to the provider by the patient. Contextual integrity treats social norms as expectations of what people ought to do or what is socially appropriate to do, in contrast with a descriptive definition of norms, which are what people typically do.

Still, others point out that the two ideas (privacy and social participation) need not be positioned as alternative values if precautions are taken on an individual level. For example, when social network sites tailor privacy to fit the specific needs of individual users, they feel more socially connected [86]. This is reassuring news.

There are aspects of our identity that might stigmatize or cause users to self-censor or even abandon social networks [87, 88], and we might not be taking account of them and thus designing for them. Interestingly, scholars have argued for the queering of communitarian theories to account for unique (and radical individual identity) while also supporting local norms [89]. In our final section, we hope to resolve this tension between individual and group or communitarian needs.

What all these theories or research frameworks have in common is that they do not provide tools for considering vulnerabilities, for example, class- and race-based struggles. We are primarily concerned with theories and frameworks that directly address the privacy concerns reported by vulnerable individuals (e.g., non-white [90] and LGBTQ [91, 92]) whose vulnerability to online harassment has been documented. Only then can we design platforms that are hospitable to vulnerable individuals. We believe that frameworks that rely on social norms (e.g., that I have nothing to fear by giving up my identity to strangers) fall short because prevailing social norms assume that, for instance, one's identity does not make them the target for privacy violations that lead to threats and opportunity loss [93]. Recently scholars have questioned whether indeed frameworks based on norms about consumer pragmatism (like those introduced by Westin [94]) should not be reevaluated as stemming from vulnerabilities (particularly, socioeconomic vulnerabilities) which leads them to "misunderstand the scope of data collection and falsely believe that relevant privacy rights are enshrined in privacy policies and guaranteed by law" [95]. We hypothesize, however, that these vulnerabilities are not so much about literacies as sense of agency and overwhelming exposure to less expensive and, by extension, vulnerable technologies, scams, predatory marketing, and exploitative sites [2]. We readily give up identity information when applying for jobs and social services or simply picking up drugs at the pharmacy. As low-income, marginalized Americans, many of these activities may be more likely to take place over less secure WiFi and devices, the consequences of which are enhanced risk of privacy violations or avoidance of financial and social institutions altogether [41].

To usefully augment these theories, designers and researchers must consciously consider the experiences of those whose privacy concerns may not be captured by the prevailing "norms." Media scholar Mike Yao talks about how the invention of printing technology made it easy to disperse private information and how, later, electronic devices increased efficiency and speed of information sharing [81]. Each of these innovations required a remapping of human boundaries and a reconceptualization of personal privacy. Until now, privacy has been broadly situated as tool of withdrawal from the public eye. Yet, Yao argues, online privacy is not a normative or legal concept, but a personal, socio-technical strategy. Up until now, shifts in privacy have assumed a shift in boundaries (which could be intellectual and abstract or physical), but no such terrain exists on the Internet. The lack of legal safeguards and also the permeable, ever-changing barriers of the Internet present challenges for demarcating spheres according to old precepts having to do with physical spaces and abstractions and almost always assume boundaries to exist and be identifiable. To define a legal or technical terrain of privacy, Yao argues, would be "relatively easy," but the problem is that there is no cultural consensus, even in the United States, the constitution does not unambiguously guarantee the right to privacy.

15.5   Better Frameworks for Vulnerable Populations

Section Highlights

- **Feminist theories and queer Marxist theories** offer a useful lens through which to consider marginalized perspectives.
- **Intersectionality helps us understand marginalized identities and the ways in which they overlap to compound unique vulnerabilities in relation to systems of oppression.** It is understanding these unique relationships that, we argue, will open up designers to new ways of thinking about privacy needs for vulnerable populations.
- **Recent scholarship is increasingly drawing on feminist intersectional lenses to tackle design problems.**

In the prior section, we talked about how thinking in terms of social norms can fail to illuminate inequalities embedded in design and privacy policy. In this section, we explain how theories that specifically take up identity are critical additions to our understanding of privacy. Feminist intersectional theory is an important lens through which to consider privacy design because it focuses on identity and structures of power—the intersection of different identities and their experience of institutions that we described in Sect. 15.3. Often those experiences coincide with conditions brought on by social norms of discrimination, and these scenarios may be challenging for designers and technologists to understand and grapple with. If designers and technologists cannot imagine vulnerable users and do not seek them out during requirements gathering, then they will be left out of design and policy. We argue that designers of systems should think in terms of marginalized identities to shape (or, at very least, inform) research and decision-making.

Feminism has long been concerned with privacy [96, 97], starting with an interest in the States' role in the family and violence within the home. Recent Marxist feminist work has observed that capitalism imposes norms on counter-normative sexual identities, making them feel welcome only within a monitored sphere [98]. We see this echoed in the way that, for instance, social networks have increasingly spoken out against hate speech and bullying by portraying the victim as powerless to defend themselves while at the same time calling on the community to defend (weaker) others against attack. This kind of sanctioned, socially constructed peace-keeping does not prompt better privacy or identity protections or tools; rather it asks the community to help regulate and reform those who would openly ridicule someone. Put another way, by focusing only on monitoring, this approach side-steps design and policy-making that might protect these users at the outset.

Though feminist theories (especially those combined with queer or Marxist thought) are helpful in revealing these design tensions, intersectional theory expands the single-issue, marginalized perspective represented by feminist theories [99] to account for simultaneous identities that may not simply be additive but multiplicative in relation to systems of discrimination. Kimberle Crenshaw is credited with first introducing intersectional theory as a black feminist critique of antidiscrimination doctrine and feminist theory [100]. Crenshaw describes the social hierarchies of inequality (of the vulnerable) by describing individuals who stand on each other's shoulders, feet stacked in a deep basement. In this metaphor, Crenshaw asks us to imagine "a basement which contains all people who are disadvantaged on the basis of race, sex, class, sexual preference, age and/or physical ability. These people are stacked—feet standing on shoulders—with those on the bottom being disadvantaged by the full array of factors, up to the very top, where the heads of all those disadvantaged by a singular factor brush up against the ceiling. Their ceiling is actually the floor above which only those who are *not* disadvantaged in any way reside" [100]. This metaphor renders intersectionality as consideration for the multiplicity of vulnerabilities within the context of structures of inequality.

It is important to remember that how we investigate people's privacy concerns should take into account the defining context for intersectional identities. Taking an intersectional lens requires that we appreciate the way in which the deck can be stacked against individuals down to the basement floor and that it gets *uniquely* worse the further down you go. We propose that intersectional frameworks are often needed to address the complex layering of vulnerabilities and their consequences— for instance, the implications of being a black trans woman as opposed to just black [101]—in order to fully comprehend the nature and magnitude of risk and identify ways to mitigate risk through improved design [12].

Identity vulnerabilities and their historical relationship to policy-making are something to consider when contemplating the stakes involved with user identity information. An intersectional perspective allows us to see how multiple vulner- abilities can create heightened risks and also how policies have historically not been calibrated to address these risks—that is, exposing deeply embedded structural inequalities. In a way, it seems simple: only design that is grounded in lived political and social experience can serve the real-world needs and privacy threats faced by individuals. It is important to note that both feminist and intersectional inquiries (especially) are equipped with a critical lens that is focused on social change, power and economic structures, and empowerment and may disavow concepts that seem to perpetuate injustices the research is looking to overcome [102]. For example, feminist researchers seeking to challenge hegemonic categories of available knowledge and to privilege marginal perspectives have permission to discard traditional frameworks [103, 104]. The researchers' goal is thus to work through experience and perception and privilege the users' perspective.

Shaowen Bardzell introduces feminist design criteria that are committed to "agency, fulfillment, identity and the self, equity, empowerment, diversity, and social justice" [105]. Bardzell identifies a number of studies that integrated gender per- spectives in the study of design and highlighted opportunities to draw on feminism in design research. In particular, Bardzell argues that homes are often dominated by gender norms and that "feminist approaches can bring clarity to the way that subjectivity and experience with technology are gendered" [105]. She argues further that feminism could support inquiries into practical technology requirements while also avoiding pitfalls that propagate marginalization of women or any other group. Feminism does this through critique of dominant epistemologies, elevation of those on the margins, critical stance toward local norms, and the user identity as being prescribed by gender and other dominant norms.

Intersectional frames (maybe by contrast) invite new analytical approaches in their quest to challenge the systems that reproduce inequality [102]. Yet Schlesinger et al. find that as of 2016, identity-focused research tends only to look at one facet of identity [106] as opposed to considering where overlaps create additional vectors of vulnerabilities *and how*. What we learn from intersectional scholar Patricia Collins is that what counts as intersectionality is far from settled [102].

Recent scholarship has drawn on intersectional theories to support new ways of thinking about research and design. Blackwell et al. [107] argued for the relevance of feminist intersectional theory in thinking about HeartMob, a platform where victims of harassment can describe their experience by submitting a harassment case and then request help from volunteers. Finding that users might perceive themselves as "outsiders" because their experiences do not fit within typical categories, they contend that to fully address online harassment, platforms must consider the needs of marginalized users into the design (e.g., classification systems) and moderation policies of platforms.

15.6   Actionable Guidelines

Section Highlights

- **Designers should consider, at minimum, what kind of identity policy is reasonable for their services and what kind of vulnerable communities are part of their requirements gathering and design phases.**
- **Additionally, designers might consider how these identities might be harmed by their services and what obvious technical solutions might mitigate these harms.** Also, are there channels for experiences to be voiced? Are there opportunities to incorporate those voices into design—even after product launch?
- **Are there ways that identities intersect to create added and more complex burdens?** What are the burdens and risks and how can they be addressed?

So how can intersectional design thinking be accomplished? We see a few places to start. First, we recommend that designers actively develop personas of vulnerable users with associated key information flows and risks. Personas are a description of a fictional person that are a composite of attributes of a user segment either based on assumptions or data [108]. At minimum, we encourage designers to build personas to guide design.

We have also discussed in Sect. 15.2 the way in which technologies tend to exacerbate existing (offline) inequalities that harm vulnerable users in disproportionate ways. At minimum, we suggest designers consider the following:

- What kind of identity policy is reasonable and required for the services you offer? What are the trade-offs between anonymity, pseudonymity, and real names for users of your system?
- What vulnerable communities are you including in your requirements gathering and design explorations (e.g., minorities, LGBTQ, etc.)?

In Sect. 15.3, we talk about specific vulnerabilities and intersections and invite service providers and designers to consider how the harms potentially outweigh the benefits of "real-name" policies, when user pseudonyms connected to user histories would suffice. More broadly, we ask that designers and policy makers consider the trade-offs whenever they introduce solutions for one vulnerable population that may harm or overlook another. One way to do this may be to keep vulnerable communities engaged in the process in a way that creates a potential channel for outreach as problems arise. Further, we encourage those seeking to design systems for diverse communities to go a step further and consider the following when designing their research:

- What communities are included among your end users and who are most vulnerable? How might these vulnerable users potentially be harmed by data (e.g., "real name") policies and what are the trade-offs and possible workarounds?
- Whose voices are you hearing and whose voices are getting left out of policy and norm articulation process? Are you considering obvious technical solutions that serve your bottom line (knowing about, customizing for, creating history of, while empowering) . . . your user?
- How does your design process and outreach create comfortable opportunities for divergent opinions and experiences to be voiced? . . . When you incorporate these voices, are you giving them ample opportunity to follow design scenarios to their logical conclusion?

We have described the importance of considering the array of end users and, in particular, asking what voices have, in the past, been left out of technology and policy decisions, what the means for current design norms, and what (minimally disruptive) technical solutions might solve the problem. An important and critical step to overcoming this challenge is having designers consider or talk with users who are vulnerable and thus face privacy challenges. Another easy and obvious place to start would be to involve those with vulnerable demographics in the design process, both hiring them as designers and interviewing them as potential users. We advocate for caution, however, as this risks what queer theorist Holly Lewis describes as "tokenism" whereby "minor changes within the composition of the group . . . short-circuit the possibility of" changing the way the group interacts or solves problems (p. 68 [89]).

In Sects. 15.4 and 15.5, we talk about the inadequacy of existing frameworks and the importance of considering how identity and structures of discrimination can compound vulnerabilities. While the above questions are aimed at a more intersectional approach to design thinking, we recommend that designers and technologists also consider the following:

- What are some of the ways the identities that intersect create added burdens for users of your system? For example, it may be common practice to ensure that women are represented in design processes, but are there specific concerns from women of color, trans women, women who are living in poverty, who have survived domestic abuse, or all of the above?
- What risks does your technology introduce for people with intersectional identities?

15.6.1 A Thought Experiment

Section Highlights

- **Our thought experiment about a ride-sharing service highlights the way in which identity raises the stakes for those using services** and about the information flows that services may take for granted, especially when what works for one individual potentially harms another.
- **Intersectionality allows designers to think about facets of identity in relation to risks** created by local norms and institutions.

To help designers think through some of these questions, we developed a thought experiment using a hypothetical ride-sharing service. We chose this example because this is a technology that is not only becoming mainstream and ubiquitous, the use of location-based and identity information that has become central to these services presents obvious and not so obvious (as we will see) privacy challenges.

> **Ride sharing scenario:** Consider that you are designing a ride-share service app with a carpool feature. What information would you collect and display about users? Would you share their name with other riders? Their destination? Their Spotify playlist? All of these pieces of identity information are available on ride-sharing app, and the first two are readily shared. None of these are pieces of information that were part of the standard hailing cab services of yore, yet they have become the norm. Contextual norms dictate that we give up or confirm our name to our driver through their window, or as soon as we get in the car—much like how we used to tell a cab service where we were going at those two junctures. This is how, without a hailing signal or a yellow-checkered cab, we make sure we do not pick up the wrong person or step into the wrong vehicle. Yet when you share a ride, who has access to this information spreads and norm-based theories cannot sufficiently interrogate these seemingly benign incursions—or these shift-shaping norms.

We have been conditioned to think that our legal identities somehow make our interactions more authentic. Is there any social value in requiring real names for use of a ride-share service? When hailing a cab, was it customary to give one's name to the driver? Authentication could be separated from name identity information. What are the trade-offs of such an approach?

Further complicating this assessment is the recent murder of a student by a person posing as a Uber driver that spawned the hashtag campaign #WhatsMyName [109]. The idea behind this campaign is to encourage ride-sharing users to immediately asked drivers, "What's my name?" Although this does not specify other riders, it does swing the pendulum in the other direction where the use of name identity information is essential for safety. These types of trade-offs introduced by this incident must be part of the ongoing design and policy-making process.

Identity and experience play a huge role in driving privacy strategies [110] and in ways that are potentially at odds. For some, giving your name might be a matter of life or death; for others, the opposite might be true [111]. What is important is that we gather these perspectives and be aware of the implications for the kinds of nuanced control people need over their identity knowledge [112] even if that means that one solution for a certain group might be in opposition to another.

Consider a rider who is not just female but who has multiple vulnerabilities. How does that raise the stakes for ensuring that end user identity links were sufficiently anonymous? For example, in addition to obscuring name information, should this ride-share company provide a set of tools for riders to get picked up and dropped off near but not at their destination? The normative frame is that riders want the convenience of door-to-door service and are annoyed when they are not picked up and dropped off at the exact address. Ride-share companies do offer pick-ups and drop-offs to nearby locations, but this is for the incentive to save time and money; it is not an advertised safety feature. The designers likely did not anticipate that offering nearby location pick-up and drop-off service could potentially be a safer alternative; rather, they thought of it as a cost savings. Intersectionality allows us to think about facets of identity in relationship to risks created by local norms and institutions.

15.6.2   Reimagining Privacy for Inclusivity

Section Highlights

- **We argue for design of systems that not only provide ways to report harm but strive *not* to enable it.**
- **Intersectional identities introduce unique avenues for harm and thus require unique solutions.** The ride-sharing thought experiment usefully describes a situation where mitigating harm for one group enhances it for another and solving one problem potentially benefits a whole category of vulnerable users. These nuances present privacy design challenges, but they are surmountable.
- **We are all at risk of being the privacy "underclass"** [113]. But the privacy needs of vulnerable populations are nevertheless highly nuanced and require careful, individual attention to ensure they are addressed.
- **It is hard to know what challenges one will uncover until they use the system. We suggest designers start, however, by asking:** What are some examples of vulnerable people who may be interested in using your product, and how can you

engage them in systems design from requirements gathering to implementation and testing? How can you leave open channels for vulnerable individuals to voice their concerns as they arise?

There is ample opportunity for designers to reimagine spaces [114]. Some have suggested that designers better understand bad actors as a way of mitigating abuse and that cisgender, privileged individuals stick up for their vulnerable counterparts. In fact, addressing the abuse post hoc cannot be the only answer. We must design systems that strive to *not* enable harm (and certainly not amplify it). This requires that we radically rethink representation on social media as well as forms of participation that support different kinds of anonymity and ephemerality [30].

What the ride-sharing example illustrates is that sometimes the solution for one group is not appropriate for another. It is important that platform designers consider what tools users need to have to make sure they can make informed decisions that support their privacy goals and adequately protect them against privacy threats with research, design, and policy.

If certain classes of contributors are being excluded, or if their concerns are superseded by the concerns of a less vulnerable class of contributor, then the experiences of people with vulnerable or marginalized identities may be systematically excluded from the development of community norms and effectively rendered "invisible" on the Internet. As we come to terms with the darker implications of "surveillance capitalism" [113, 115], we might imagine that threats are also more opaque and harder to define as simply a bully, a perpetrator of hate, or an abusive domestic partner. If Shoshana Zuboff is, in fact, correct that all "users" are all the underclass (the property of tech companies), then fighting for the privacy of the most vulnerable becomes urgent for all [113]. This sets off a new "axis of inequality" which, Zuboff argues, puts at risk not just the overtly vulnerable but those not formally perceived as such. The privacy needs of vulnerable populations are nevertheless highly nuanced and require careful, individual attention to ensure they are addressed.

Privacy is the ultimate negative right. It is the right *not to* be exposed to public scrutiny, to *limit* incursions of the state or attempts of others to know what an individual is doing. There is no easy syllogism between privacy and democracy or freedom; that makes it challenging to understanding privacy. There is no universal definition of privacy. Privacy is culturally and individually defined and therefore not universally valued; nor are violations and consequences of those violations perceived or experienced by all individuals in the same way. In a society where access to technology and information requires all of us to relinquish some privacy, we must understand that the terms and conditions of that loss are inherently unequal and the consequences especially grave for some. Technology gatekeepers need to play a critical role in extending protections to those most vulnerable, guided by an empathetic and well-informed perspective on what protections are required.

There are simple steps that technologists can take to begin hearing vulnerable voices and including them in design and research. We suggest that designers ask themselves the questions we have outlined, considering broadly the way that certain design trade-offs can harm vulnerable users and also thinking more specifically about what communities are impacted by the design of specific technologies. For instance, what are some examples of vulnerable people who may be interested in using your product, and how can you engage them in systems design from requirements gathering to implementation and testing? Moreover, it is essential that designers leave open channels for vulnerable individuals to voice their concerns as they arise. It is hard to know what challenges one will uncover until they use the system. In addition to involving target vulnerable groups in prototyping and testing, they should be targeted sources of feedback for new products as they enter the market—and existing ones.

Acknowledgments This work was supported in part by the National Science Foundation grant CNS-1703736.

References

1. Madden, M. 2017. *Privacy, Security, and Digital Inequality*.
2. Madden, M., M. Gilman, K. Levy, and A. Marwick. 2017. Privacy, poverty, and big data: a matrix of vulnerabilities for poor Americans. *Washington University Law Review* 95 (1): 053–125.
3. Domestic Abuse Survivors Go "Underground" With the Tor Network. 2014. http://www.adweek.com/digital/domestic-abuse-survivors-go-underground-tor-network/. Accessed 31 Aug 2017.
4. Freed, D., Palmer, J., Minchala, D., Levy, K., Ristenpart, T. and Dell, N. 2018. A Stalker's paradise: how intimate partner abusers exploit technology. pp 1–13.
5. Matthews, T., K. O'Leary, A. Turner, M. Sleeper, J.P. Woelfer, M. Shelton, C. Manthorne, E.F. Churchill, and S. Consolvo. 2017. Stories from survivors: Privacy & Security Practices when coping with intimate partner abuse. In *Proceedings of the 2017 CHI Conference on Human Factors in Computing Systems*, 2189–2201. New York, NY: CHI.
6. Guberek, T., A. McDonald, S. Simioni, A.H. Mhaidli, K. Toyama, and F. Schaub. 2018. Keeping a low profile? Technology, risk and privacy among undocumented immigrants. In *Proceedings of the 2018 CHI Conference on Human Factors in Computing Systems*, 114:1–114:15. New York, NY: CHI.
7. Tufekci, Z. 2017. *Twitter and Tear Gas: The Power and Fragility of Networked Protest*. New Haven: Yale University Press.
8. Warner, M., Gutmann, A., Sasse, M.A., and Blandford, A. 2018. Privacy unraveling around explicit HIV status disclosure fields in the online Geosocial hookup app Grindr. *Proceedings ACM Human-Computing Interact* 2, CSCW (Nov. 2018), 181:1–181:22. https://doi.org/10.1145/3274450.
9. Blackwell, L., J. Hardy, T. Ammari, T. Veinot, C. Lampe, and S. Schoenebeck. 2016. LGBT parents and social media: Advocacy, privacy, and disclosure during shifting social movements. In *Proceedings of the 2016 CHI Conference on Human Factors in Computing Systems*, 610–622. New York, NY: CHI.
10. Gray, M.L. 2009. *Out in the Country: Youth, Media, and Queer Visibility in Rural America*. New York: NYU Press.
11. Kitzie, V. 2019. "That looks like me or something i can do": Affordances and constraints in the online identity work of US LGBTQ+ millennials. *Journal of the Association for Information Science and Technology*. https://doi.org/10.1002/asi.24217.

12. Scheuerman, M.K., S.M. Branham, and F. Hamidi. 2018. Safe spaces and safe places: Unpacking technology-mediated experiences of safety and harm with transgender people. *Proceedings ACM Human-Computing Interact.* 2, CSCW (Nov. 2018), 155:1–155:27. https://doi.org/10.1145/3274424.

13. Anjum, B. 2018, December. An interview with Pamela Wisniewski: Making the online world safer for our youth. *Ubiquity* 2018: 2:1–2:6. https://doi.org/10.1145/3301323.

14. Wisniewski, P., A.K. Ghosh, H. Xu, M.B. Rosson, and J.M. Carroll. 2017. Parental control vs. teen self-regulation: Is there a middle ground for Mobile online safety? In *Proceedings of the 2017 ACM Conference on Computer Supported Cooperative Work and Social Computing*, 51–69. New York, NY: ACM.

15. Hornung, D., C. Müller, I. Shklovski, T. Jakobi, and V. Wulf. 2017. Navigating relationships and boundaries: Concerns around ICT-uptake for elderly people. In *Proceedings of the 2017 CHI Conference on Human Factors in Computing System*, 7057–7069. New York, NY: CHI.

16. Bridges, K.M. 2017. *The Poverty of Privacy Rights*. Stanford, CA: Stanford Law Books.

17. Eubanks, V. 2018. *Automating Inequality: How High-Tech Tools Profile, Police, and Punish the Poor*. New York: St. Martin's Press.

18. Ferguson, A.G. 2017. *The Rise of Big Data Policing: Surveillance, Race, and the Future of Law Enforcement*. New York: NYU Press.

19. Noble, S.U. 2018. *Algorithms of Oppression: How Search Engines Reinforce Racism*. New York: NYU Press.

20. Andalibi, N., O.L. Haimson, M. De Choudhury, and A. Forte. 2016. Understanding social media disclosures of sexual abuse through the lenses of support seeking and anonymity. In *Proceedings of the 2016 CHI Conference on Human Factors in Computing Systems*, 3906–3918. New York, NY: CHI.

21. Joinson, A. 2001, March. Self-disclosure in computer-mediated communication: The role of self-awareness and visual anonymity. *European Journal of Social Psychology* 31 (2): 177–192. https://doi.org/10.1002/ejsp.36.

22. Ma, X., J. Hancock, and M. Naaman. 2016. Anonymity, intimacy and self-disclosure in social media. In *Proceedings of the 2016 CHI Conference on Human Factors in Computing Systems*, 3857–3869. New York, NY: CHI.

23. McKenna, K. and Bargh, J. 1998. Coming out in the age of the internet: Identity demarginalization through virtual group participation Journal of Personality and Social Psychology 75 (3): 681–694.

24. Pavalanathan, U., and M. De Choudhury. 2015. Identity management and mental health discourse in social media. In *Proceedings of the 24th International Conference on World Wide Web*, New York, NY, 315–321.

25. Schrading, N., Alm, C.O., Ptucha, R., and Homan, C.M. 2015. An analysis of domestic abuse discourse on Reddit. *Conference on Empirical Methods in Natural Language Processing*.

26. Ellison, N., L. Blackwell, C. Lampe, and P. Trieu. 2016, November. "The question exists, but you Don't exist with it": Strategic anonymity in the social lives of adolescents. *Social Media + Society* 2 (4): 2056305116670673. https://doi.org/10.1177/2056305116670673.

27. Pennebaker, J.W., and C.K. Chung. 2007. Expressive writing, emotional upheavals, and health. In *Foundations of Health Psychology*, 263–284. New York: Oxford University Press.

28. Pennebaker, J.W., J.K. Kiecolt-Glaser, and R. Glaser. 1988. Disclosure of traumas and immune function: health implications for psychotherapy. *Journal of Consulting and Clinical Psychology* 56 (2): 239–245.

29. Smyth, J.M. 1998. Written emotional expression: Effect sizes, outcome, types, and moderating variables. *Journal of Consulting and Clinical Psychology.* 66 (1998): 174–184.

30. Xu, B., P. Chang, C.L. Welker, N.N. Bazarova, and D. Cosley. 2016. Automatic archiving versus default deletion: What snapchat tells us about ephemerality in design. In *Proceedings of the 19th ACM Conference on Computer-Supported Cooperative Work & Social Computing*, 1662–1675. New York, NY: ACM.

31. Sharing to the power of 2012. *The Economist*.

32. Facebook is playing games with your privacy and there's nothing you can do about it. https://www.forbes.com/sites/thomasbrewster/2016/06/29/facebook-location-tracking-friend-games/. Accessed 18 Apr 2019.

33. German court says Facebook's real name policy is illegal. 2018. https://www.theverge.com/2018/2/12/17005746/facebook-real-name-policy-illegal-german-court-rules. Accessed 18 Apr 2019.

34. Pitcan, M., A.E. Marwick, and D. Boyd. 2018, May. Performing a vanilla self: Respectability politics, social class, and the digital world. *Journal of Computer-Mediated Communication* 23 (3): 163–179. https://doi.org/10.1093/jcmc/zmy008.

35. Forte, A., N. Andalibi, and R. Greenstadt. 2017. Privacy, anonymity, and perceived risk in open collaboration: A study of Tor users and Wikipedians. In *Proceedings of the 2017 ACM Conference on Computer Supported Cooperative Work and Social Computing*, 1800–1811. New York, NY: ACM.

36. Rios, VM. 2011. *Punished: Policing the Lives of Black and Latino Boys (New Perspectives in Crime, Deviance, and Law) – Kindle Edition by Victor M. Rios. Politics & Social Sciences Kindle eBooks* @Amazon.com. New York: NYU Press.

37. Ames, M.G., J. Go, J.J. Kaye, and M. Spasojevic. 2011. Understanding technology choices and values through social class. In *Proceedings of the ACM 2011 Conference on Computer Supported Cooperative Work*, 55–64. New York, NY: ACM.

38. Yardi, S., and A. Bruckman. 2012. Income, race, and class: Exploring socioeconomic differences in family technology use. In *Proceedings of the SIGCHI Conference on Human Factors in Computing Systems*, 3041–3050. New York, NY: SIGCHI.

39. Ames, M.G., and J. Burrell. 2017. "Connected learning" and the equity agenda: A microsociology of Minecraft play. In *Proceedings of the 2017 ACM Conference on Computer Supported Cooperative Work and Social Computing*, 446–457. New York, NY: ACM.

40. Richardson, R., Schultz, J., and Crawford, K. 2019. Dirty data, bad predictions: How civil rights violations impact police data, predictive policing systems, and justice. *New York University Law Review Online*.

41. Lanier, J. 2014. *Who Owns the Future?* New York: Simon & Schuster.

42. Newman, N. 2014. The costs of lost privacy: Consumer harm and rising economic inequality in the age of Google. *William Mitchell Law Review* 40: 2.

43. Mann, G., and C. O'Neil. 2016. *Hiring Algorithms Are not Neutral*. Brighton: Harvard Business Review.

44. Guendelsberger, E. 2019. *On the Clock: What Low-Wage Work Did to Me and How It Drives America Insane*. New York, NY: Little, Brown and Company

45. Rosenblat, A., T. Kneese, and D. Boyd. 2014. Workplace Surveillance. Data & Society Working Paper, p. 19.

46. Le Dantec, C.A., and W.K. Edwards. 2008. The view from the trenches: Organization, power, and Technology at two Nonprofit Homeless Outreach Centers. In *Proceedings of the 2008 ACM Conference on Computer Supported Cooperative Work*, 589–598. New York, NY: ACM.

47. Le Dantec, C.A., R.G. Farrell, J.E. Christensen, M. Bailey, J.B. Ellis, W.A. Kellogg, and W.K. Edwards. 2011. Publics in practice: Ubiquitous computing at a shelter for homeless mothers. In *Proceedings of the SIGCHI Conference on Human Factors in Computing Systems*, 1687–1696. New York, NY: SIGCHI.

48. Menking, A., and I. Erickson. 2015. The heart work of Wikipedia: Gendered, emotional labor in the World's largest online encyclopedia. In *Proceedings of the 33rd Annual ACM Conference on Human Factors in Computing Systems*, 207–210. New York, NY: ACM.

49. Changing Your Gender on Facebook is Easy. https://www.lifewire.com/edit-gender-identity-status-on-facebook-2654421. Accessed 02 Aug 2019.

50. Introducing More Genders on Tinder. 2016. https://blog.gotinder.com/genders/. Accessed 02 Aug 2019.

51. Lesbian, Gay. Bisexual and transgender persons & socioeconomic status. https://www.apa.org/pi/ses/resources/publications/lgbt. Accessed 29 July 2019.

52. Growing up LGBT in America: View and share statistics. http://www.hrc.org/youth-report/view-and-share-statistics/. Accessed 27 Feb 2019.
53. Blackwell, L., J. Hardy, T. Ammari, T. Veinot, C. Lampe, and S. Schoenebeck. 2016. LGBT parents and social media: Advocacy, privacy, and disclosure during shifting social movements. In *Proceedings of the 2016 CHI Conference on Human Factors in Computing Systems*, 610–622. New York, NY: CHI.
54. Duguay, S. 2016, June. "He has a way gayer Facebook than I do": Investigating sexual identity disclosure and context collapse on a social networking site. *New Media & Society* 18 (6): 891–907. https://doi.org/10.1177/1461444814549930.
55. Dym, B., and C. Fiesler. 2018. Vulnerable and online: Fandom's case for stronger privacy norms and tools. In *Companion of the 2018 ACM Conference on Computer Supported Cooperative Work and Social Computing*, 329–332. New York, NY: ACM.
56. NCADV | National Coalition Against Domestic Violence. https://ncadv.org/statistics. Accessed 18 Apr 2019.
57. NCADV | National Coalition Against Domestic Violence: https://ncadv.org/blog/posts/domestic-violence-and-the-lgbtq-community. Accessed 29 July 2019.
58. Crenshaw, K. 1991. Mapping the margins: Intersectionality, identity politics, and violence against women of color. *Stanford Law Review* 43 (6): 1241–1299. https://doi.org/10.2307/1229039.
59. Google Buzz Privacy Update. 2010. https://www.eff.org/deeplinks/2010/02/google-buzz-privacy-update. Accessed 25 Apr 2019.
60. Google Buzz privacy issues have real life implications. *TechCrunch*.
61. Marwick, A., C. Fontaine, and Danah Boyd. 2017, April. "Nobody sees it, nobody gets mad": Social media, privacy, and personal responsibility among low-SES youth. *Social Media + Society* 3: 2. https://doi.org/10.1177/2056305117710455.
62. Conti, G., and Sobiesk, E. 2007. An honest man has nothing to fear: User perceptions on web-based information disclosure. In *Proceedings of the 3rd Symposium on Usable Privacy and Security* (New York, NY, USA, 2007), 112–121.
63. Solove, D.J. 2013. *Nothing to Hide: The False Tradeoff Between Privacy and Security*. London: Yale University Press.
64. Israni, A., S. Erete, and C.L. Smith. 2017. Snitches, trolls, and social norms: Unpacking perceptions of social media use for crime prevention. In *Proceedings of the 2017 ACM Conference on Computer Supported Cooperative Work and Social Computing*, 1193–1209. New York, NY: ACM.
65. Being African American & LGBTQ: An Introduction. https://www.hrc.org/resources/being-african-american-lgbtq-an-introduction/. Accessed 25 Apr 2019.
66. Morton, M.H., A. Dworsky, and G.M. Samuels. 2017. Missed opportunities: Youth homelessness in America. In *National Estimates*. Chicago, IL: Chapin Hall at the University of Chicago.
67. Hargittai, E. 2005. Survey measures of web-oriented digital literacy. *Social Science Computer Review* 23 (3): 371–379.
68. Hargittai, E., and E. Litt. 2013, May. New strategies for employment? Internet skills and online privacy practices during people's job search. *IEEE Security Privacy* 11 (3): 38–45. https://doi.org/10.1109/MSP.2013.64.
69. Park, Y.J. 2011. Digital literacy and privacy behavior online. *Communication Research* 40 (2): 215–236. https://doi.org/10.1177/0093650211418338.
70. Kang, R., Dabbish, L., Fruchter, N. and Kiesler, S. 2015. "My data just Goes everywhere:" user mental models of the internet and Implications for privacy and security. In *Eleventh Symposium on Usable Privacy and Security SOUPS'15* (Ottawa, 2015), 35–52.
71. Vitak, J., Liao, Y., Subramaniam, M. and Kumar, P. 2018. "I knew it was too Good to be true": The challenges economically disadvantaged internet users face in assessing trustworthiness, avoiding scams, and developing self-efficacy online. In *Proceedings ACM Human-Computing Interact* 2, CSCW (Nov. 2018), 176:1–176:25. https://doi.org/10.1145/3274445.
72. Altman, I. 1975. *The Environment and Social Behavior: Privacy, Personal Space, Territory*. Brooks/Cole: Crowding.

73. Palen, L., and P. Dourish. 2003. Unpacking "privacy" for a networked world. In *Proceedings of the SIGCHI Conference on Human Factors in Computing Systems*, 129–136. New York, NY: SIGCHI.
74. Marwick, A. 2012, June. The public domain: surveillance in everyday life. *Surveillance & Society* 9 (4): 378–393.
75. Ahern, S., Eckles, D., Good, N.S., King, S., Naaman, M., and Nair, R. 2007. Over-exposed? Privacy patterns and considerations in online and Mobile photo sharing. *Proceedings of the SIGCHI Conference on Human Factors in Computing Systems* 357–366. New York, NY: SIGCHI.
76. Besmer, A., and H. Richter Lipford. 2010. Moving beyond Untagging: Photo privacy in a tagged world. In *Proceedings of the SIGCHI Conference on Human Factors in Computing Systems*, 1563–1572. New York, NY: SIGCHI.
77. Marwick, A., and Danah Boyd. 2010. I tweet honestly, I tweet passionately: Twitter users, context collapse, and the imagined audience. *New Media & Society.* 113 (1): 114–133.
78. Stutzman, F., and W. Hartzog. 2012. Boundary regulation in social media. In *Proceedings of the ACM 2012 Conference on Computer Supported Cooperative Work*, 769–778. New York, NY: ACM.
79. Stutzman, F., and J. Kramer-Duffield. 2010. Friends only: Examining a privacy-enhancing behavior in Facebook. In *Proceedings of the SIGCHI Conference on Human Factors in Computing Systems*, 1553–1562. New York, NY: SIGCHI.
80. Vitak, J., S. Blasiola, S. Patil, and E. Litt. 2015, May. Balancing audience and privacy tensions on social network sites: Strategies of highly engaged users. *International Journal of Communication* 9: 20.
81. Yao, M.Z. 2011. Self-protection of online privacy: A behavioral approach. In *Privacy Online: Perspectives on Privacy and Self-Disclosure in the Social Web*, ed. S. Trepte and L. Reinecke, 111–125. Berlin: Springer-Verlag.
82. Lampinen, A. 2015. Networked Privacy Beyond the Individual: Four Perspectives to "Sharing." In *Proceedings of the Fifth Decennial Aarhus Conference on Critical Alternatives*, 25–28.
83. Lampinen, A., V. Lehtinen, A. Lehmuskallio, and S. Tamminen. 2011. We're in it together: Interpersonal management of disclosure in social network services. In *Proceedings of the SIGCHI Conference on Human Factors in Computing Systems*, 3217–3226. New York, NY: SIGCHI.
84. Lampinen, A., S. Tamminen, and A. Oulasvirta. 2009. All my people right Here, right now: Management of Group co-presence on a social networking site. In *Proceedings of the ACM 2009 International Conference on Supporting Group Work*, 281–290. New York, NY: ACM.
85. Nissenbaum, H. 2010. *Privacy in Context: Technology, Policy, and the Integrity of Social Life.* Stanford Law Books.
86. Wisniewski, P., A.K.M.N. Islam, B.P. Knijnenburg, and S. Patil. 2015. Give social network users the privacy they want. In *Proceedings of the 18th ACM Conference on Computer Supported Cooperative Work & Social Computing*, 1427–1441. New York, NY: ACM.
87. Baumer, E., P. Adams, V.D. Khovanskaya, T.C. Liao, M.E. Smith, V. Schwanda Sosik, and K. Williams. 2013. Limiting, leaving, and (re)lapsing: An exploration of Facebook non-use practices and experiences. In *Proceedings of the SIGCHI Conference on Human Factors in Computing Systems*, 3257–3266. New York, NY: SIGCHI.
88. Rainie, L., A. Smith, and M. Duggan. 2013. *Coming and Going on Facebook | Pew Research Center.* Washington, DC: Pew Research Center.
89. Lewis, H. 2016. *The Politics of Everybody: Feminism, Queer Theory and Marxism at the Intersection.* London: Zed Books.
90. Duggan, M. 2017. *Online Harassment 2017.* Washington, DC: Pew Research Center.
91. Hamidi, F., M.K. Scheuerman, and S.M. Branham. 2018. Gender recognition or gender reductionism? The social Implications of embedded gender recognition systems. In *Proceedings of the 2018 CHI Conference on Human Factors in Computing Systems*, 8:1–8:13. New York, NY: CHI.

92. 2017. *Discrimination in America: Experiences and Views of LGBTQ Americans.* National Public Radio, the Robert Wood Johnson Foundation, and Harvard T.H. Chan School of Public Health.
93. McDonald, N., B. Mako Hill, R. Greenstadt, and A. Forte. 2019. Privacy, anonymity, and perceived risk in open collaboration: A study of service providers. In *CHI Conference on Human Factors in Computing Systems Proceedings (CHI 2019).* New York, NY: CHI.
94. Hoofnagle, C., and Urban, J. (2014, June). Alan Westin's privacy Homo Economicus. *Wake Forest Law Review* 49: 261.
95. Urban, J.M. and Hoofnagle, C.J. 2014. The privacy pragmatic as privacy vulnerable. Technical report #ID 2514381. Social Science Research Network.
96. Gavison, R. 1992. Feminism and the public/private distinction. *Stanford Law Review* 45 (1): 1–45. https://doi.org/10.2307/1228984.
97. Richardson, J. (2014, December). Spinoza, feminism and privacy: Exploring an immanent ethics of privacy. *Feminist Legal Studies; Dordrecht,* 22(3):225–241. http://dx.doi.org.ezproxy2.library.drexel.edu/10.1007/s10691-014-9271-3.
98. Fraser, N., Bhattacharya, T. and Arruzza, C. 2019. Feminism for the 99%. Verso.
99. Hartsock, N.C. 1983. The feminist standpoint: Developing the ground for a specifically feminist historical materialism. In *Discovering Reality*, 283–310. Boston, MA: Reidel Publishing Company.
100. Crenshaw, K. 1989. Demarginalizing the intersection of race and sex: A black feminist critique of antidiscrimination doctrine. *University of Chicago Legal Forum* 1989 (1): 139–167.
101. The Report of the 2015 U.S. Trangender Survey: 2016. http://www.ustranssurvey.org/. Accessed 21 Apr 2019.
102. Collins, P.H. 2015. Intersectionality's definitional dilemmas. *Annual Review of Sociology* 41 (1): 1–20.
103. Bardzell, S. 2010. Feminist HCI: Taking stock and outlining an agenda for design. In *Proceedings of the SIGCHI Conference on Human Factors in Computing Systems*, 1301–1310. New York, NY: SIGCHI.
104. Bellini, R., A. Strohmayer, E. Alabdulqader, A.A. Ahmed, K. Spiel, S. Bardzell, and M. Balaam. 2018. Feminist HCI: Taking stock, moving forward, and engaging community. In *Extended Abstracts of the 2018 CHI Conference on Human Factors in Computing Systems*, SIG02:1–SIG02:4. New York, NY: CHI.
105. Bardzell, S. 2010. Feminist HCI: Taking stock and outlining an agenda for design. In *Proceedings of the SIGCHI Conference on Human Factors in Computing Systems*, 1301–1310. New York, NY: SIGCHI.
106. Schlesinger, A., W.K. Edwards, and R.E. Grinter. 2017. Intersectional HCI: Engaging identity through gender, race, and class. In *Proceedings of the 2017 CHI Conference on Human Factors in Computing Systems*, 5412–5427. New York, NY: CHI.
107. Blackwell, L., Dimond, J., Schoenebeck, S. and Lampe, C. 2017. Classification and its consequences for online harassment: Design insights from HeartMob. *Proceedings of the ACM on Human Computer Interaction.* 1, CSCW (Dec. 2017), 24:1–24:19 https://doi.org/10.1145/3134659.
108. Personas. https://www.interaction-design.org/literature/book/the-encyclopedia-of-human-computer-interaction-2nd-ed. Accessed 26 July 2019.
109. Salam, M. 2019. #WhatsMyName stresses safety for Uber riders. *The New York Times.*
110. Kang, R., S. Brown, and S. Kiesler. 2013. Why do people seek anonymity on the internet?: Informing policy and design. In *Proceedings of the SIGCHI Conference on Human Factors in Computing Systems*, 2657–2666. New York, NY: SIGCHI.
111. Chang, E. 2019. Opinion | what women know about the internet. *The New York Times.*
112. Marx, G.T. 1999. What's in a name? Some reflections on the sociology of anonymity. *The Information Society* 15 (2): 99–112.
113. Zuboff, S. 2019. *The Age of Surveillance Capitalism: The Fight for a Human Future at the New Frontier of Power.* New York: PublicAffairs.

114. Dourish, P. 2006. Re-space-ing place: "Place" and "space" ten years on. *Proceedings of the 2006 20th Anniversary Conference on Computer Supported Cooperative Work* (New York, NY, USA, 2006), 299–308.
115. Gandy, O.H. 2017. Surveillance and the formation of public policy. In *Surveillance & Society Biennial Conference 2017.*

Part IV
Moving Forward

Chapter 16
User-Tailored Privacy

Bart P. Knijnenburg, Reza Ghaiumy Anaraky, Daricia Wilkinson,
Moses Namara, Yangyang He, David Cherry, and Erin Ash

Abstract Modern information systems require their users to make a myriad of
privacy decisions, but users are often neither motivated nor capable of managing
this deluge of decisions. This chapter covers the concept of tailoring the privacy
of an information system to each individual user. It discusses practical problems
that may arise when collecting data to determine a user's privacy preferences,
techniques to model these preferences, and a number of adaptation strategies that
can be used to tailor the system's privacy practices, settings, or interfaces to the
user's modeled preferences. Throughout the chapter, we provide recommendations
on how to develop user-tailored privacy solutions, depending on the requirements
and characteristics of the system and its users.

16.1 Introduction

As our digital and personal lives become increasingly intertwined, the frequency
with which we encounter privacy decisions is on the rise. Moreover, given the
complexity of modern information systems, users often report feeling helplessly
overwhelmed by the privacy decision-making required to effectively manage the
boundaries around the collection and use of their personal information.

In this chapter we present User-Tailored Privacy (UTP) as a means to reduce
the burden of privacy decision-making. Combining the best aspects (and avoiding

B. P. Knijnenburg (✉) · R. G. Anaraky · D. Wilkinson · M. Namara · Y. He
School of Computing, Clemson University, Clemson, SC, USA
e-mail: bartk@clemson.edu; rghaium@clemson.edu; dariciw@clemson.edu;
mosesn@clemson.edu; yyhe@clemson.edu

D. Cherry
Computer Science Department, Morehouse College, Atlanta, GA, USA
e-mail: David.cherry@morehouse.edu

E. Ash
Department of Communication, Clemson University, Clemson, SC, USA
e-mail: ash3@clemson.edu

B. P. Knijnenburg et al. (eds.), *Modern Socio-Technical Perspectives on Privacy*,
https://doi.org/10.1007/978-3-030-82786-1_16

367

the downsides) of the existing privacy management paradigms of "notice and choice" and "privacy nudging" (see Chap. 2 for an overview of existing paradigms), the concept of UTP can be implemented alongside technical privacy-preserving solutions (see Chap. 8) and Privacy by Design (see Chap. 2) to provide a system whose privacy settings are tailored to the level of privacy each individual user is most comfortable with.

In the remainder of this section we first critically appraise the shortcomings of existing privacy management paradigms. In Sect. 16.2 we outline the UTP framework, which consists of three phases that will be discussed in subsequent sections: Measuring users' privacy preferences (Sect. 16.3), modeling these preferences and the appropriate decision context (Sect. 16.4), and adapting the system according to these models (Sect. 16.5). We conclude with an overview of the various goals UTP can accomplish if implemented correctly (Sect. 16.6).

16.1.1   The Limitations of Technical Solutions to Privacy

Engineers tend to consider technical solutions to privacy problems, which broadly fall into two categories: Architectures, platforms, and standards designed specifically to minimize data leakage (including distributed architectures, portable user profiles, and client-side personalization techniques that provide limited access to and "linkability" of user data [1, 2]), and algorithmic techniques for data protection (including anonymization, obfuscation, differential privacy, and homomorphic encryption [3, 4]). These solutions have numerous well-documented limitations: Distributed architectures [1] and encryption [3] are notoriously slow, client-side personalization leaves users vulnerable to data loss and theft [2], and providing full anonymity or even pseudonymity is often not feasible in modern information systems [5].

A notorious example of the latter is the case where Netflix released anonymized user data as part of a contest to improve its recommendation algorithm. Soon after the release of the data, researchers were able to de-anonymize the data by cross-referencing anonymous user ratings with IMDb profiles [5]. In response, a closeted lesbian mother sued Netflix, alleging that the de-anonymization procedure could "out" her based on her viewing behavior [6].

Importantly, technical privacy-preserving solutions do not apply to social networking applications, where disclosure is at the heart of the functionality of the application. In such applications, it is not the disclosure of the information per say that users are worried about, but rather the determination of *who* has access to the disclosed information [7].

Moreover, while technical solutions provide some protection against privacy violations, the existence of such protection does in itself not necessarily mean that users will disclose more information. For example, work on client-side personalization shows that users' perception of the privacy afforded by this technology is modest and has only a very slight impact on their subsequent sharing decisions [2]. In other cases, the use of the technical solution itself is cumbersome, and many users avoid it (see Chap. 8). Hence technical solutions to privacy must be supplemented with socio-technical solutions.

16.1.2   The Limitations of Privacy by Design

As discussed in Chap. 2, Privacy by Design is a design philosophy in which privacy aspects are addressed early in the system design and development process [8]. Privacy by Design is often regarded as an alternative to outfitting a system with a vast array of privacy settings. Unfortunately, the existence of privacy settings is inevitable in many modern information systems, for two important reasons. First of all, the functionalities embedded in many modern information systems, such as social networking and personalization, are not feasible without data collection [9, 10]. In these cases, privacy and functionality are in direct opposition, and a decision must be made regarding how much data collection is justified to provide a certain level of functionality. Second, users tend to differ extensively regarding this decision. The goal of the system is to ensure that all users' privacy preferences are adhered to without limiting certain users' ability to use the system to the fullest extent [11].

16.1.3   The Limitations of Notice and Choice

Where privacy is in direct opposition with system functionality and users differ in the amount of privacy they prefer to trade off for functionality, privacy experts argue that users must be given controls (e.g., "privacy settings") as a means to effect this trade-off, as well as a certain amount of information that will help them operate these controls [12]. The idea of "notice and choice" is also at the heart of existing or planned regulatory schemes (see Chap. 18).

Unfortunately, for most modern information systems, privacy notices fall prey to the "transparency paradox" [13]: notices that are sufficiently detailed to have an impact on people's privacy decisions are often too long and complex for people to read. Moreover, notices may actually decrease disclosure, even if they are supposed to indicate positive privacy protection practices [14, 15]. For example, e-commerce practitioners have documented several cases where privacy seals *decrease* conversion rates rather than increasing them [16, 17]. Finally, the effect of notice may be very fleeting: even the slightest distraction can easily nullify any effect of privacy notices [18]. Indeed, while many people claim to read online privacy policies [19], many do not actually read them [20] or do not read closely enough to understand them [21].

Likewise, users of modern information systems tend to fall prey to the "control paradox," which states that users claim they want full control over their privacy but often do not actually take control, even when it is offered [22]. Indeed, many users tend to pay little attention to privacy seals [23], social navigation cues [24], privacy assurances [25], and permission requests [26].

Finally, many researchers no longer believe that users always make "calculated" privacy decisions, but often employ heuristic decision strategies instead (see Chap. 4). As such, even if users do take control over their privacy, it is not certain that they will do so effectively.

16.1.4   The Limitations of Privacy Nudging

Privacy nudges attempt to relieve some of the burden of privacy decision-making by making it easier for users to make the "right" decisions regarding their privacy [18, 27, 28]. Traditionally, nudges have been defined as covert changes to the structure, framing, and defaults of a decision environment, but in the field of privacy they have also been used to describe designs that steer users in a desirable direction in a more overt manner [27].

Ample research has demonstrated that the more overt nudges like justifications [24, 29], privacy seals [30], and audience/sentiment feedback [28, 31] fail to have a consistent effect on users' disclosure and privacy concerns. Moreover, while the traditional nudges have been found to be more effective [32], they have typically only been tested for behavioral impact, disregarding the question of whether they reduced users' privacy concerns or their privacy decision burden [33]. Indeed, researchers worry that defaults may threaten consumer autonomy, especially when they work outside of users' explicit awareness [34].

16.1.5   A Case for User-Tailored Privacy

We summarize the problems with existing privacy solutions as follows:

- **Technical solutions cannot always effectively be implemented**, hence they must be complemented with user-centric solutions.
- **Privacy by Design is not universally applicable**; it fails when privacy and functionality are not in conflict, and when users differ in their inherent trade-off between privacy and functionality. In these cases, privacy settings are inevitable.
- **Notice and choice assume that users will take control over their privacy**. In reality, they often fail to take control effectively, either due to a lack of motivation or ability.
- **Privacy nudging takes a one-size-fits-all approach to privacy**, and by making universal assumptions regarding the "best" privacy decisions, they threaten user autonomy.

User-Tailored Privacy (UTP) acknowledges the need for privacy settings, but rather than putting the full burden of managing these settings on the user, it uses *personalized* nudges to simplify and/or automate part of these privacy management responsibilities. As such, it takes into account both the wide variety in users' privacy preferences and their inability to effectively implement these preferences themselves in the context of complex modern information systems.

The concept of tailoring privacy to users' needs was first explicitly discussed by Kobsa in his keynote to the 2001 *User Modeling* conference [35]. Since then, the idea has been explored in several areas of computing.

One existing application of UTP makes user-tailored suggestions for privacy settings or permissions. In this light, Liu et al. [36] developed a profile-based personalized privacy assistant for smartphone app permissions. The app groups users into different profiles based on their privacy preferences. Based on these profiles, the assistant recommends permission settings that the user could change. User study results show that the recommendations were adopted by the majority of users. And that the recommendations led to more restrictive permission settings without compromising on user comfort with these configurations.

UTP can also recommend Web sites or applications to users, based on their adherence to the user's privacy preferences, for example, in the context of an app store. The idea of automated evaluation of the privacy practices of Web sites or applications has a long history that started with the invention and eventual demise of P3P [37]. Several studies have looked into evaluating Web sites or applications from a privacy perspective [38], and some have found that users who have access to such evaluations may end up paying a premium for privacy [39]. While these studies provided users with privacy information about the Web site or app, none of these studies took an active approach to provide privacy-based *recommendations*. UTP could leverage the generated privacy descriptions (cf. [38]) and provide automatic recommendations.

In a social networking setting, UTP has been used to help users decide what information should be shared with whom. For example, Fang and LeFevre use hierarchical clustering on social network structures to predict the most suitable audience for users' personal information [40], Ravichandran et al. [41] demonstrated how a small number of default policies can accurately capture most users' location-sharing preferences, and Knijnenburg and Jin recommend audience-related sharing settings for a location-sharing service [42].

Finally, research has shown that social network users employ privacy management strategies that go beyond selective information sharing (see Chap. 7). Recent work shows that social network users can be classified into six profiles when it comes to these privacy boundary management strategies [43]—a few studies have demonstrated how UTP can leverage these profiles to adapt the privacy-setting interface of the social network to highlight the user's most-used privacy functionalities [44, 45].

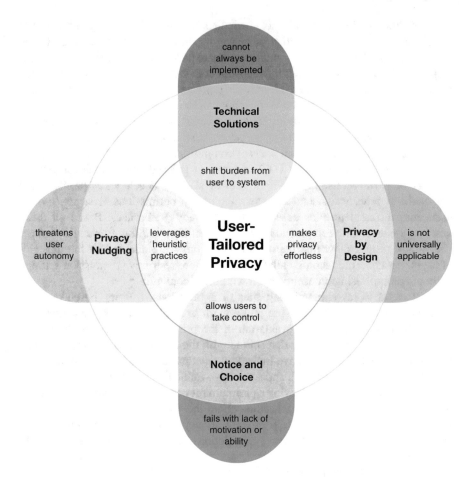

Fig. 16.1 Roots of the UTP approach

Beyond these existing applications of UTP, we note that the idea is rooted in decades of user-centered privacy research as it builds upon the strengths of existing privacy paradigms while avoiding the aforementioned limitations (see Fig. 16.1):

- Like other technical solutions, it leverages computational power to help users manage their privacy, thereby shifting some of the burden from the user to the system.
- Like Privacy by Design, it aims to make privacy "effortless."
- Like notice and choice, it allows users to take control over their privacy.
- Like nudging, it acknowledges (or even leverages) users' heuristic decision-making practices.

In the following sections, we describe UTP in more detail and give advice regarding its implementation.

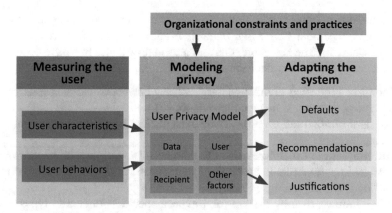

Fig. 16.2 Overview of UTP framework

16.2   The UTP Framework

UTP is an approach to privacy that models users' privacy concerns and provides them with adaptive privacy decision support. With UTP, a system measures user privacy-related characteristics and behaviors, uses this as input to model their privacy preferences, and then adapts the system's privacy settings to these preferences (see Fig. 16.2). UTP solutions attempt to provide the right amount of privacy-related information while allowing users to maintain control, without being misleading or overwhelming.

The following three steps are common among the many variations of UTP; in the following sections we describe each of these steps in more detail:

- **Measure user characteristics and behavior** in order to tailor the provided support to the user and the context of the decision.
- **Model users' privacy decisions using machine learning algorithms** and then plan adaptations based on this model. Models can be built based on direct observation of users' behaviors or via inference from their attitudes.
- **Adapt the system to the users' privacy concerns**. UTP can adapt the system's privacy settings, justifications, privacy-setting user interface, and/or personalization procedure.

16.3   Measuring the User

The first step of UTP is to model users' privacy decisions. Users vary extensively in their privacy decisions; no two people make exactly the same privacy decisions, and even for the same person the decision tends to depend on the context.

The dynamics of contextually determined privacy norms are the central topic of Nissenbaum's popular *Contextual Integrity* framework (see [13], covered in more detail in Chap. 2). The key contextual and personal variables that have been shown to influence users' privacy decisions are:

- **The data requested (What)**—Users' privacy behaviors and decisions vary by the type of data that is being collected [46, 47].
- **The user him/herself (Who)**—There exist distinct profiles of privacy behaviors among users [47, 48].
- **The recipient of the information (To whom)**—The recipient of the information plays an important role in users' disclosure decisions as well, both in "commercial" and "social" settings [49–51].
- **Other factors, usually system- or purpose-specific**—In certain types of systems, privacy preferences depend on other contextual factors [52–54].

The system should identify as much of these contextual and personal variables as possible to be able to accurately model users' privacy decision.

16.3.1   The Data (What)

Each data category has a different degree of sensitivity. Research shows that the least sensitive types of information are first name, email address, physical characteristics (age, gender, height), and interests and preferences, while the most sensitive types of information are contact information (aside from email address), financial information, information regarding sex and birth control, and social security number [33, 55]. These attitudinal results have been confirmed behaviorally [2, 29, 43].

Beyond these general rankings, research has found that privacy behaviors are multidimensional, meaning that disclosure is more complex than a single tendency, but also not completely unstructured [47, 48]. The differences between the uncovered dimensional structures also show that the underlying dimensionality of disclosure behaviors varies by context.

16.3.2   The User (Who)

Users differ in their level of privacy concern and behavior. Most privacy surveys report sizable standard deviations in their estimates of disclosure tendencies and privacy behaviors [47, 56]. Moreover, research shows that using machine learning techniques, users can be sorted into groups that demonstrate similar behaviors. These "privacy profiles" can be built on top of the dimensions of "what" (see above) or based directly on their privacy-setting behaviors [48]. For example, Fig. 16.3

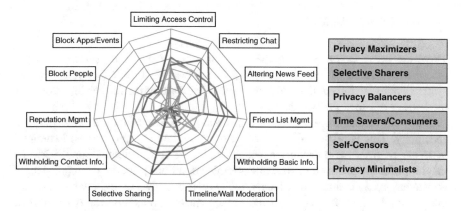

Fig. 16.3 Facebook users' privacy management strategies

shows the profiles related to a number of personal privacy management strategies uncovered by Wisniewski et al. [43].

As explained in Chap. 12, there also exist differences in privacy behavior based on universal cultural dimensions. Notably, Li et al. demonstrate that if UTP takes culture into account, this will likely result in a significant improvement in the accuracy of privacy predictions [57]. Finally, at the individual level, demographic differences and differences in personality have been used to predict users' privacy concerns in prior research. The most prominent demographic characteristics that affect privacy behavior are age, gender, education level, rural/urban background, and income level [58]. Results regarding personality seem rather inconsistent, though [59].

16.3.3 The Recipient (To Whom)

The recipient of the information is another important variable affecting users' privacy decision-making. Whereas decisions regarding people as recipients are usually governed by social conventions, decisions about applications as recipients are governed by information privacy concerns [7, 47]. Similar to the "what" and "who" aspects, recipients can be clustered into groups or "circles" [49, 50]. This approach imposes some structure on the effect of recipient, and these decisions are mainly moderated by the degree the user trusts those recipients [60].

16.3.4   Other Factors

There are other factors such as the location, time of day, the usefulness of the information, and users' emotion [52–54]. The relevance of these factors differs per system, so researchers and practitioners should study them to further improve their predictions of users' privacy decisions.

Many contextual influences on privacy concerns and behavior are due to purpose specificity. This is related to the concept of contextual integrity, which is defined in terms of informational norms which render certain attributes appropriate or inappropriate in certain contexts, under certain conditions [13]. For example, people will be less likely to share their location with their employer at night, when they are not on the job. As such, UTP can leverage the logic of purpose specificity to improve privacy predictions.

16.4   Modeling Privacy

Researchers and practitioners interested in implementing UTP can model users' privacy preferences using off-the-shelf machine learning algorithms. In doing so, they should consider the potentially dynamic aspect of users' privacy decisions (i.e., their privacy preferences may change over time), the way the algorithm may balance the cost of over- versus under-disclosure, the potential trade-off between privacy and other user and/or system goals, and the impact of traditional machine learning problems like overfitting and the cold start problem.

16.4.1   Types of Input

There are two ways to model users' privacy preferences: direct observation of user behaviors and inference from users' attitudes. The most rudimentary privacy decision behavior is users' decision to disclose or withhold information (or, analogously, to allow or reject a certain collection or sharing of data to occur automatically). Such behaviors have been successfully used in user privacy modeling [36, 40, 41, 53, 54, 61]. Some platforms (especially social networks) may offer users a plethora of features to control various aspects of their privacy. Users' use of such controls has been modeled successfully as well [43]. Moreover, when UTP gives users explicit privacy recommendations, users' acceptance or rejection of these recommendations can be another important user modeling input, especially when it is combined with other data [62].

Users' privacy preferences can also be measured directly [42, 48, 61]. While attitudinal data are generally more difficult to collect than behaviors, they are often more stable and precise, because behavior tends to fall prey to heuristic influences.

Likewise, users' privacy preferences can be derived from their traits, such as their culture, demographics, job title, or personality, although these relationships are often weaker [48, 53, 57, 63].

Aside from users' preferences, context is an essential user-modeling input for UTP, as privacy decisions are likely to be heavily context-dependent. It is important to automatically include context in UTP's user model, as the absence of contextual information would likely increase the number of times users have to interact with their privacy settings [64].

Contextual variables can introduce a large amount of sparsity to a user model or result in overfitting. Luckily, various mechanisms exist that allow a recommender system to integrate contextual variables without significantly reducing the amount of data available for each prediction context [54]. Another way to prevent overfitting and sparsity is to have a psychological theory behind the measurement of certain contextual variables [53]. An example of this is Toch et al.'s [65] realization that entropy is the most important aspect of location sensitivity and Li et al.'s [57] finding that country-level cultural variables are a better predictor than country itself.

In sum, we recommend the following practices for gathering input data:

- **Model users' decisions** to disclose/withhold information, to allow/reject tracking, and to use/avoid privacy features.
- **Collect implicit feedback** on privacy recommendations provided by UTP.
- **Elicit privacy attitudes/preferences** to factor out the influence of heuristic decision-making.
- **Collect user traits** to kick start UTP's user model.
- **Take context into account** when modeling users' privacy preferences.
- **Respect the user's privacy** in gathering all this input data.

16.4.2   Algorithms

Algorithms can calculate privacy recommendations using one of two methods: "collaborative filtering" methods, which rely on other users' behaviors, and "case-based reasoning" methods, which rely on the target user's behavior only.

Collaborative filtering leverages other users' privacy behaviors to help predict the current user's privacy preferences [36, 54]. An example is the nearest neighbor approach, where the target user's behaviors are matched with other users' behaviors in an attempt to find the users who are most similar to the target user. Once a set of nearest neighbor users has been found, any unknown preferences of the target user can be predicted using the preferences of these neighbors. This approach is called "user-based collaborative filtering," as opposed to "item-based collaborative filtering," which applies the same approach to the items instead of the users.

Privacy recommendations that are based on collaborative filtering can "leak" information about users' privacy preferences, and thus create security violations. For example, if a hacker has access to users' privacy settings, they may be able to derive from these settings what kind of information users find most sensitive. Zhao et al. propose a system that treats users' privacy recommendations themselves as sensitive information, and in response, they build a differentially private privacy recommender using standard data obfuscation techniques [66].

Case-based reasoning applies contextualized rules to decide on the best outcome in a given situation [57, 61, 64]. The rules can be based on common sense (e.g., recommendations could be predefined for various types of applications) or based on (past) data of other users (e.g., past user data could be used to establish a "privacy score" for each type of app, which then informs future recommendations). Regardless, one benefit of case-based recommendation is that the system does not require "live" user data (which reduces the chance of "privacy leaking") and can easily be implemented on the client side (which voids the need for user data to be shared with the recommender) [67].

Personalized case-based reasoning systems are usually profile-based, where the specific set of rules to apply to the target user's behavior depends on the profile that was assigned to them. Profiles turn the user modeling from a multidimensional tracking problem into a simpler classification problem [48] and offer personalization without requiring a central server to calculate the recommendations. A downside of case-based privacy recommendations is that its rules are static: unless the algorithm behind the rules is re-trained, the rules will not change even if users' behavior evolves.

Finally, in predicting users' privacy preferences, it is important to keep the user "in the loop" regarding the origin of and reasoning behind these predictions. UTP should therefore adopt explainable and user-controllable algorithms, even if this is at the cost of prediction accuracy. The following practices are recommended in this regard:

- **Make it easy for users to give preference input** or explicit feedback, so that they can control and, where needed, correct the recommendations [62].
- **Build conversational recommenders** that engage in a dialogue with users to uncover their privacy preferences [68].
- **Implement explanations** as a means to increase users' understanding of the recommendation process, their trust in the quality of the recommendations, and their perception of competence and benevolence of the system [69].

16.4.3 The Adaptation Target: What Should UTP Try to Accomplish?

Once the user's privacy behavior or attitude is known, the question remains how UTP should adapt to this behavior/attitude. This can be done in several ways:

- **Match the user's current behaviors**—this alleviates their decision-making burden, especially when done through automation.

- **Recommend practices that dovetail with users' current behavioral patterns**—this solidifies their behavioral practices. It is best to use suggestions or highlights to make such recommendations.
- **Move beyond current behavioral patterns**—this encourages exploration and self-actualization. Research shows that users appreciate such a personalized educational approach, especially when it is done through active, well-explained recommendations [45].

Note that these suggestions pair each recommendation target (match, dovetail, move beyond) with a particular recommendation method (automate, highlight, explain). Other pairings may not work well. For example, actively recommending users privacy behaviors that they already engage in can be regarded as redundant or a nuisance [45]. Likewise, pushing users beyond their current behavioral patterns without careful explanation can cause reactance (see Sect. 16.7.2).

16.5 Adapting the System

While most existing work on UTP covers the modeling aspect, it is of utmost importance to also cover various ways in which systems can leverage these user privacy models to provide user-tailored privacy decision support. Particularly, this section covers the following adaptations:

- **Intelligent privacy settings**—These adaptations alleviate the burden of privacy decision-making, either through fully automated adaptive defaults or adaptive nudges in the form of highlights or suggestions.
- **Augmented privacy notices**—These adaptations inform users about the reasons behind a recommendation or act as a nudge that gives users a rationale for engaging in a privacy-related behavior. More complex justifications can educate users about the risks and benefits involved in a privacy decision.
- **Adaptive privacy-setting interfaces**—These adaptations restructure the user interface of the system to make certain privacy actions easier to accomplish.
- **Privacy-aware personalization**—These adaptations influence the types of personalization a system can engage in based on the collected user data, thereby preventing potential unwanted inferences to be made.

16.5.1 Intelligent Privacy Settings

The most commonly studied application of UTP is "adaptive privacy settings." These are essentially adaptive versions of nudges or defaults [34]. Unlike traditional nudges and defaults, they consider the crucial role of the user and decision context, thereby limiting threats to user autonomy.

Adaptive default settings make it easier for users to choose the right settings, since most settings will already be aligned with their preferences [70]. A large number of existing works on privacy prediction assume that users will benefit from this relief in privacy-setting burden, but very few works test whether users indeed appreciate—and go along with—such adaptive defaults. Early work in this regard by Namara et al. suggests that UTP should implement a "hybrid" adaptive privacy-setting procedure, along the following guidelines [45]:

- **Automatically apply settings to alleviate users** from frequent privacy behaviors but avoid automating decisions with far-reaching consequences.
- **Highlight suggested settings to reduce users' cognitive burden** in a subtle but useful manner.
- **Suggest privacy settings to keep users involved in their privacy decisions** but avoid making suggestions with awkward social consequences.

Finally, in cases where settings and/or disclosure requests are presented in a sequential manner, the order of sensitive versus less sensitive requests has an impact on disclosure [29]. For example, disclosure rates are lower when asking less sensitive questions first, and sharing rates in social networks are higher when users are asked to share with weaker ties first [51]. Generally speaking, disclosure is higher for information that is requested first, so UTP can adapt the order of sequentially presented settings and information requests to prioritize the disclosure of certain types of information.

16.5.2 Augmented Privacy Notices

A justification is usually accompanied by a recommended setting or action and provides a succinct reason to engage or not engage in the recommended privacy-related behavior. In general, justifications seem to have no positive effect on users' privacy decision-making [29, 71], but justifications that are adapted to the user seem to have a positive effect [63]. Moreover, context-relevant justifications are likely more effective if shown when users are actually in the process of making a decision, rather than "post-hoc" [26]. And finally, justifications can be used to frame a privacy decision, which can significantly influence the level of disclosure, with negative framing leading to significantly lower levels of disclosure than positive framing [71]. As such, we make the following recommendations:

- **Make justifications context-relevant**—This helps users understand the purpose of the request or decision.
- **Time justifications carefully**—Justifications should only happen in situations where they may have a short-term (e.g., impact the user's decision) or long-term (e.g., increase the user's privacy knowledge) impact.
- **Tailor justification types** (explanation, usefulness, or social norm) to the user's personal characteristics.
- **Leverage the framing of justifications** to adaptively influence disclosure.

Fig. 16.4 Bringing certain privacy features to the forefront: (**a**) Users can directly change the audience of a post with toggle buttons, without having to use the standard drop-down list. (**b**) A more prominent design for blocking apps, events, and people that is displayed directly in the notifications

16.5.3 Adaptive Privacy-Setting Interfaces

Privacy features are often difficult to access, and they create an unwieldy "labyrinth" of privacy functionality that users find difficult to use [72]. UTP can be used to tailor the design of the interface itself to the user. This approach, labeled User-Tailored Privacy by Design (UTPbD) [43], emphasizes features the user is expected to use most often and de-emphasizes features they only seldom use (see Fig. 16.4). UTPbD can be implemented in two ways:

- **A direct application of UTPbD** involves profiling the users of a system based on their privacy behaviors, and then tailoring the privacy controls of the system in a way that changes their salience depending on the profile of the current user.
- **An extrapolated application of UTPbD** involves turning the profiles uncovered in a baseline system (e.g., Facebook) into "personas" to develop privacy design guidelines for a yet-to-be-implemented system that is envisioned to have similar privacy features (e.g., a new social network).

The latter approach may not result in a user-tailored solution per say, but it uses the "measure" and "model" aspects of the UTP framework for persona development.

16.5.4 Privacy-Aware Personalization

UTP models should not only acknowledge and account for potential differences in users' attitudes toward data *collection*, but also data *use*. The latter is particularly important in systems that use users' data to personalize their content or its presentation. In providing a personalized experience, such systems may make unexpected (or unwanted) inferences about the user. As such, users may prefer that the system *not* use (a subset of) their data for certain personalization purposes. To address users' preferences regarding the use of their data for personalization purposes, UTP can be used to adapt a system's personalization procedures to the users' data use preferences.

Particularly, UTP can be integrated into a dynamic privacy-enabling user modeling framework. Wang and Kobsa developed such a framework to consider prevailing privacy laws and regulations based on the country of residence of the user [73]. Our suggestion is to support a much more granular level of personalized constraints based on UTP: Users' privacy preferences as modeled by UTP can serve as a basis to determine whether certain types of inferences or data use should be allowed and disallowed for each particular user.

16.6   What Should Be the End-Goal of UTP?

UTP can serve multiple goals. While UTP has traditionally been envisioned to alleviate the user's privacy decision-making burden, UTP can also support users by taking on a "teaching role" and giving them the tools they need to decide for themselves how to meet their privacy goals. To further complicate things, UTP can take the privacy requirements of the recipient of the information, other users, and the community or organization in which it operates into account as well. Below, we discuss these goals in more detail and outline strategies for reconciling conflicting goals among multiple stakeholders.

16.6.1   Support the User

The main goal of UTP is to support the user. However, in providing such support we should note that users have conflicting motivations and goals in making such privacy decisions. For example, users of recommender systems, the goals of privacy, and recommendation quality are in conflict, and the balance depends on what level of recommendation quality is considered "acceptable" and what kind of tracking users consider to be "comfortable." It will be up to system designers to decide which of these goals to prioritize and what policies to adopt. In this regard, collecting more data (see Sect. 16.3) will help the system to identify the conflicts and the contexts of each decision.

Finally, a conflict exists in that users usually claim to want control over their privacy, without wanting to spend a significant amount of time on setting privacy settings [22]. UTP can help users by automating their privacy decisions, but this could eventually result in users who are disinterested and ill-equipped to set any settings manually. This could in turn result in an erosion of user autonomy [74] which can cause severe privacy violations. Hence, we make the following recommendations:

- **Make most of the individual privacy decisions automatically**—Given the complexity of the privacy trade-offs in most systems, this is the only way to avoid overwhelming users.
- **Allow the user to control the general rules by which these decisions are made**—Arguably, users will be much better equipped at making higher-level privacy decisions, rather than lower-level individual settings.
- **Where appropriate, raise exceptions to ask for user feedback**, and incorporate such feedback into the user privacy model maintained by UTP.
- **Allow users to share their "stewardship" over their data** with a trusted third party.

16.6.2   Teach the User

In addition to alleviating the user's decision burden, UTP adaptations can also be used to teach the user about privacy based on their behavior and current level of knowledge. This way, UTP allows users to decide for themselves how to meet their privacy goals. The field of recommender systems has shown that explanations increase users' understanding of the recommendation process [75]. Hence, they ascertain that users are actively involved in the decision process, which is instrumental in increasing their understanding and teaching them about their privacy. We recommend two useful venues for such explanations:

- **Provide personalized privacy "tips"** that highlight users' inconsistent behaviors and bring them to their attention.
- **Use tailored privacy education** to give users more confidence in their overall privacy strategy and to support the evolution of this strategy.

Ghaiumy Anaraky et al. [71] introduced tips in a privacy decision-making scenario and demonstrated that combined with other nudges they can affect disclosure behavior. Privacy tips are envisioned to work particularly well when users exhibit inconsistent privacy-related behaviors (e.g., withholding a piece of information from a colleague, while at the same time posting it on a public site), or when users fail to engage in synergistic privacy behaviors (e.g., grouping Facebook friends into circles, but not using these circles to selectively target posts to specific audiences) [43]. UTP can personalize the tips to these occasions, which should increase the effectiveness of privacy tips and minimize the chance that they will be ignored.

In contrast, privacy education works best when recommending actions outside the user's current purview. This helps users to adopt new privacy protection strategies. Note, however, that education is not effective for the practices the user already engages in, nor for practices the user has decided they do not want to engage in. UTP can actively avoid these situations as a means to optimize the effectiveness of privacy education.

16.6.3   Help the Recipient

UTP can also advocate for the recipient of the user's information, or even society at large. For example, an app that tracks epidemics will function better if users are willing to share their health status and location, and this would allow authorities to appropriately allocate resources to mitigate or prevent outbreaks. In this case, the privacy of each individual user is in conflict with the success of the application and its benefit for society. As such, governments (or, in a corporate context, the user's employer) may mandate certain data collection practices (e.g., reporting job training results) or even prohibit certain disclosures (e.g., for mission-critical data to be shared on public servers).

In case the user's privacy is in conflict with organizational or societal goals or regulations, it is important to increase user trust in the recipients of data, if their long-term data disclosure is to be maintained. Therefore, we make the following recommendations:

- **Make sure that users never feel pressured to provide sensitive data**—In these cases, they are likely to provide fake data instead.
- **Use justifications** to explain why certain organizational or legal constraints are in place.
- **Utilize collected data in a way that aligns with users' expectations** with regard to the purposes of disclosure.

16.6.4   Reconciling the Differences

In some cases, UTP must make trade-offs to reconcile the preferences of stakeholders with conflicting goals (e.g., users, recipients of data, other users, the organization). The field of group recommender systems has studied various ways to integrate the preferences of multiple stakeholders in the recommendation process [72]. A useful ethical principle for reconciling the goals of multiple stakeholders is to always put the end-user first, using the principles of fairness [76] and reciprocity [77]. However, these principles do not give sufficient recourse in cases of organizational constraints (which often cannot be traded off against users' preferences) or conflicts between users (who may have equal stake in the management of a piece of co-created data). We recommend the following practices in reconciling the conflicting goals of multiple stakeholders:

- **Develop UTP as a multi-stakeholder recommender system** if it is likely that there exist multiple conflicting goals around privacy.

- **Put the end-user first** and apply the principles of reciprocity and fairness to reconcile conflicting goals among multiple stakeholders.
- **Honestly inform users about the optimization strategy** of UTP, that is, to explain to them how different conflicting internal and external goals are taken into consideration.
- **Allow users to reflect upon UTP's privacy policies at a meta level**—UTP can manage the user's privacy settings, and users can manage the principles by which UTP operates to reconcile multi-stakeholder differences.

16.7 Problems That May Arise When Implementing UTP

16.7.1 Problems Related to Privacy Modeling

Potential problems related to modeling users' privacy decisions should be considered when implementing UTP. For instance, due to the privacy paradox [78], there will likely be a difference between UTP user models that are based on users' and models that are based on their attitudes or preferences of input is more suitable for privacy modeling purposes.

Likewise, typical metrics of prediction accuracy such as F1 and AUC treat "false positives" and "false negatives" as equally bad, but this may not be desirable in privacy prediction settings. To complicate matters, privacy decisions are rarely made in isolation but usually considered as a trade-off with other goals. In making this trade-off, one would have to decide whether the trade-off should be a compensatory (linear) trade-off or a non-compensatory (threshold-based) trade-off. Moreover, it requires estimates of the decision options in light of these various goals, which can be either derived from objective system parameters or subjective user experiences [79].

Most user-modeling systems have a problem of overfitting: the more granular a user's contextual preferences get, the less data the predictions will be based on [54]. Privacy prediction needs a certain amount of input before it can determine the user's privacy preferences. Without input, it is impossible to create an accurate user model. In the user modeling community, this problem is known as the "cold start" problem.

Finally, we must acknowledge the fact that privacy recommendations can have a persuasive effect on users [42], which may result in "positive feedback loops" of users accepting a suboptimal privacy recommendation and thereby reinforcing the user model in the wrong direction.

To overcome these problems, we recommend that UTP should be implemented using a layered and gracefully degrading approach:

- **Start with simple "smart profile"-based approaches** [61] when implementing UTP in new systems, then move to more complex user privacy modeling solutions once more user modeling data is available.

- **Study the relative cost of over-disclosure versus under-disclosure** and build this cost into the UTP algorithms.
- **Trade-off privacy with other user goals**, such as the goals of the system, the institution, and other users.
- **Couch the recommendation logic in psychological principles** to prevent overfitting [53].

Combining simple and complex user modeling within the same system allows for "graceful degradation" of the user modeling approach. For example, a collaborative filtering recommender will not work when too little user data is available or when the user is offline. In such cases, the system can fall back on a profile-based approach or even just recommend the settings of the average user.

Finally, to ascertain the quality and validity of the UTP module, it should be evaluated using the "layered evaluation" approach [80], which allows input, processing, and output procedures to be evaluated separately.

16.7.2   Problems Related to Adapting the System

Adaptations span a variety of "degrees of automation," which present problems for implementing UTP: fully automated UTP can be overly persuasive and difficult to control, while low-automation UTP can be a burden on the user.

Users may show reactance toward adaptations, especially in domains where adaptations are not expected—privacy is one such domain. In this case, it is better to start off with a less automated approach. Once users have gained enough trust in the privacy adaptation procedure, they may choose to accept subsequent adaptations automatically, thereby reducing their decision-making burden [45].

Adaptations that users may find unexpected should be explained to the users to allow them to judge the integrity, benevolence, competence, accuracy, and overall usability of the adaptations [69]. However, it is important to avoid pressuring users into accepting adaptations that they might not want to accept [81]. Users should be given various options to choose from to possibly empower them to make better decisions on their own.

Given these potential problems, we make the following recommendations:

- **Find the optimal adaptation method** with regard to the goals of UTP, be it automation, awareness, guidance, or education (see Sect. 16.6).
- **Give users explicit suggestions if they are unfamiliar with a privacy feature**—This allows for the adaptive behavior to be explained, which can increase trust.
- **When users use a feature frequently, use the fully automated approach**—Users in this situation are willing to give up some control in return for the significant reduction in the burden that this approach offers them.

16.8   Conclusion

In this chapter we introduced the concept of User-Tailored Privacy (UTP) as a means to support the privacy management practices of the users of modern information systems. We hope that our recommendations will help researchers and practitioners to implement UTP in their systems.

We made a case for UTP by highlighting the shortcomings of technical solutions, Privacy by Design, notice and choice, and privacy nudging. We recommend that researchers and practitioners should not avoid these existing practices, but rather complement them with the personalized approach afforded by UTP.

We then defined UTP as a "measure, model, adapt" framework. And covered each of these steps separately:

- We argued that in measuring privacy, researchers and practitioners should acknowledge the plurality and multidimensionality of users' privacy decision-making practices. They should also note that the variability of users' practices can often be captured by a concise set of "privacy profiles" and that data recipients can often similarly be grouped into a number of groups or "circles."
- In modeling privacy, we particularly noted that matching the users' current privacy practices may not always be the best modeling strategy; in certain cases, UTP should recommend complementary practices, while in other cases UTP can completely move beyond users' current practices. Researchers and practitioners should carefully balance these various approaches. Moreover, since privacy modeling may not always be successful, UTP should be implemented as a layered and gracefully degrading modeling component.
- In adapting privacy, we argued that UTP can personalize the privacy settings of an application, the justification it gives for requesting certain information, its privacy-setting interface, and its personalization practices. Researchers and practitioners should carefully balance proactive and conservative adaptation strategies in order to reduce users' burden but at the same time give them sufficient control and reduce undue persuasion.

Finally, we argued that researchers and practitioners should carefully consider the various goals that UTP can support. They should acknowledge that UTP must reconcile users' potentially conflicting goals, and they should balance the goal of replacing the users' privacy decision-making practices with the longer-term goal of teaching them about privacy. Moreover, researchers and practitioners should consider that UTP's support can help other stakeholders in the privacy decision-making process as well. Regarding this, they should carefully consider how to reconcile the potentially conflicting goals of these various stakeholders.

While we were able to leverage existing work to make extensive recommendations regarding the implementation of UTP, we must at the same time acknowledge that UTP is still a relatively novel and underexplored solution to users' privacy problems. As such, we encourage privacy researchers to investigate UTP in its various incarnations and to contribute to the growing body of literature around this topic. We hope that this chapter provides a starting point for them as well, as we have highlighted gaps in existing research throughout the chapter.

References

1. Berkovsky, S., Y. Eytani, T. Kuflik, and F. Ricci. 2006. Hierarchical neighborhood topology for privacy enhanced collaborative filtering. In *Proceedings of PEP06, CHI 2006 Workshop on Privacy-Enhanced Personalization*, Montreal, Canada, ed. Kobsa, A., R. Chellappa, and S. Spiekermann, 6–13. http://www.isr.uci.edu/pep06/papers/PEP06_BerkovskyEtAl.pdf.
2. Kobsa, A., H. Cho, B.P. Knijnenburg. 2016. The effect of personalization provider characteristics on privacy attitudes and behaviors: An elaboration likelihood model approach. *Journal of the Association for Information Science and Technology*. https://doi.org/10.1002/asi.23629, http://onlinelibrary.wiley.com/doi/10.1002/asi.23629/abstract.
3. Nikolaenko, V., S. Ioannidis, U. Weinsberg, M. Joye, N. Taft, and D. Boneh. 2013. Privacy-preserving matrix factorization. In *Proceedings of the 2013 ACM SIGSAC Conference on Computer & Communications Security*, CCS '13, 801–812. New York, NY: ACM. http://doi.org/10.1145/2508859.2516751
4. Dwork, C., and M. Naor. 2008. On the difficulties of disclosure prevention in statistical databases or the case for differential privacy. *Journal of Privacy and Confidentiality* 2 (1). http://repository.cmu.edu/jpc/vol2/iss1/8.
5. Narayanan, A., and V. Shmatikov. 2008. Robust de-anonymization of large sparse datasets. In *2008 IEEE Symposium on Security and Privacy*, 111–125. IEEE. https://doi.org/10.1109/SP.2008.33.
6. Singel, R. 2009. Netflix spilled your brokeback mountain secret, lawsuit claims, Dec 2009. http://www.wired.com/2009/12/netflix-privacy-lawsuit/?+wired27b+%2528Blog+-+27B+Stroke+6+%2528Threat+Level%2529%2529/.
7. Lederer, S., J.I. Hong, A.K. Dey, and J.A. Landay. 2004. Personal privacy through understanding and action: Five pitfalls for designers. *Personal and Ubiquitous Computing* 8 (6): 440–454 (2004). https://doi.org/10.1007/s00779-004-0304-9, http://www.springerlink.com/index/10.1007/s00779-004-0304-9.
8. Cavoukian, A. 2010. Privacy by Design. Information and Privacy Commissioner of Ontario, Canada. http://www.privacybydesign.ca/content/uploads/2010/03/PrivacybyDesignBook.pdf.
9. Awad, N.F., and M.S. Krishnan. 2006. The personalization privacy paradox: An empirical evaluation of information transparency and the willingness to be profiled online for personalization. *MIS Quarterly* 30 (1): 13–28.
10. Strater, K., and H.R. Lipford. 2008. Strategies and struggles with privacy in an online social networking community. In *Proceedings of the 22nd British HCI Group Annual Conference on People and Computers*, 111–119. Swinton: British Computer Society.
11. Hann, I.H., K.L. Hui, S.Y. Lee, and I. Png. 2007. Overcoming online information privacy concerns: An information-processing theory approach. *Journal of Management Information Systems* 24 (2): 13–42. https://doi.org/10.2753/MIS0742-1222240202, http://mesharpe.metapress.com/openurl.asp?genre=article&id=doi:10.2753/MIS0742-1222240202.
12. Taylor, D., D. Davis, and R. Jillapalli. 2009. Privacy concern and online personalization: The moderating effects of information control and compensation. *Electronic Commerce Research* 9 (3): 203–223. https://doi.org/10.1007/s10660-009-9036-2.
13. Nissenbaum, H. 2011. A contextual approach to privacy online. *Daedalus* 140 (4): 32–48. https://doi.org/10.1162/DAED_a_00113.
14. Gardner, J. 2012. 12 Surprising A/B test results to stop you making assumptions. http://unbounce.com/a-b-testing/shocking-results/.
15. Pollach, I. 2007. What's wrong with online privacy policies? *Communications of the ACM* 50 (9): 103–108. https://doi.org/10.1145/1284621.1284627.

16. Aagaard, M. 2013. How privacy policy affects sign-ups surprising data from 4 A/B tests. http://contentverve.com/sign-up-privacy-policy-tests/.

17. Bustos, L. 2012. Best practice gone bad: 4 shocking A/B tests. http://www.getelastic.com/best-practice-gone-bad-4-shocking-ab-tests/.

18. Adjerid, I., A. Acquisti, L. Brandimarte, and G. Loewenstein. 2013. Sleights of privacy: Framing, disclosures, and the limits of transparency. In *Proceedings of the Ninth Symposium on Usable Privacy and Security*, SOUPS '13, 9:1–9:11. New York, NY: ACM. https://doi.org/10.1145/2501604.2501613.

19. Milne, G.R., and M.J. Culnan. 2004. Strategies for reducing online privacy risks: Why consumers read (or don't read) online privacy notices. *Journal of Interactive Marketing* 18 (3): 15–29. https://doi.org/10.1002/dir.20009.

20. Jensen, C., C. Potts, and C. Jensen. 2005. Privacy practices of internet users: Self-reports versus observed behavior. *International Journal of Human-Computer Studies* 63 (1–2): 203–227. https://doi.org/10.1016/j.ijhcs.2005.04.019, http://www.sciencedirect.com/science/article/pii/S1071581905000650.

21. Pan, Y., and G.M. Zinkhan. 2006. Exploring the impact of online privacy disclosures on consumer trust. *Journal of Retailing* 82 (4): 331–338. https://doi.org/10.1016/j.jretai.2006.08.006, http://www.sciencedirect.com/science/article/pii/S0022435906000558.

22. Compano, R., and W. Lusoli. 2010. The policy maker's anguish: Regulating personal data behavior between paradoxes and dilemmas. In *Economics of Information Security and Privacy*, ed. Moore, T., D. Pym, and C. Ioannidis, 169–185. New York, NY: Springer. https://doi.org/10.1007/978-1-4419-6967-5_9.

23. Larose, R., and N.J. Rifon. 2007. Promoting I safety: Effects of privacy warnings and privacy seals on risk assessment and online privacy behavior. *Journal of Consumer Affairs* 41 (1): 127–149. https://doi.org/10.1111/j.1745-6606.2006.00071.x, http://onlinelibrary.wiley.com/doi/10.1111/j.1745-6606.2006.00071.x/abstract.

24. Besmer, A., J. Watson, and H.R. Lipford. 2010. The impact of social navigation on privacy policy configuration. In *Proceedings of the Sixth Symposium on Usable Privacy and Security*, Redmond, Washington, 7:1–7:10. https://doi.org/10.1145/1837110.1837120.

25. Metzger, M.J. 2006. Effects of site, vendor, and consumer characteristics on web site trust and disclosure. *Communication Research* 33 (3): 155–179. https://doi.org/10.1177/0093650206287076.

26. Felt, A.P., E. Ha, S. Egelman, A. Haney, E. Chin, and D. Wagner. 2012. Android permissions: User attention, comprehension, and behavior. In *Proceedings of the Eighth Symposium on Usable Privacy and Security*, SOUPS '12, 3:1–3:14. New York, NY: ACM. http://doi.org/10.1145/2335356.2335360.

27. Acquisti, A. 2009. Nudging privacy: The behavioral economics of personal information. *IEEE Security and Privacy* 7:82–85. https://doi.org/10.1109/MSP.2009.163, ACM ID: 1685896.

28. Wang, Y., P.G. Leon, A. Acquisti, L.F. Cranor, A. Forget, and N. Sadeh. 2014. A field trial of privacy nudges for facebook. In *Proceedings of the 32nd Annual ACM Conference on Human Factors in Computing Systems*, CHI '14, 2367–2376. Toronto: ACM. https://doi.org/10.1145/2556288.2557413.

29. Knijnenburg, B.P., and A. Kobsa. 2013. Making decisions about privacy: Information disclosure in context-aware recommender systems. *ACM Transactions on Interactive Intelligent Systems* 3 (3): 20:1–20:23. https://doi.org/10.1145/2499670, http://bit.ly/tiis2013.

30. Rifon, N.J., R. LaRose, and S.M. Choi. 2005. Your privacy is sealed: Effects of web privacy seals on trust and personal disclosures. *Journal of Consumer Affairs* 39 (2): 339–360 (2005). https://doi.org/10.1111/j.1745-6606.2005.00018.x.

31. Jedrzejczyk, L., B.A. Price, A.K. Bandara, and B. Nuseibeh. 2010. On the impact of real-time feedback on users' behaviour in mobile location-sharing applications. In *Proceedings of the Sixth Symposium on Usable Privacy and Security*, Redmond, Washington, 14:1–14:12. https://doi.org/10.1145/1837110.1837129, http://portal.acm.org/citation.cfm?doid=1837110.1837129.

32. Johnson, E.J., S. Bellman, and G.L. Lohse. 2002. Defaults, framing and privacy: Why opting in opting out. *Marketing Letters* 13 (1): 5–15. https://doi.org/10.1023/A:1015044207315, http://www.springerlink.com/content/vrf4lmw6jgnq3pvd/abstract/.
33. Knijnenburg, B.P. 2015. A user-tailored approach to privacy decision support. Ph.D. thesis, UC Irvine.
34. Smith, N.C., D.G. Goldstein, and E.J. Johnson. 2013. Choice without awareness: Ethical and policy implications of defaults. *Journal of Public Policy & Marketing* 32 (2): 159–172. https://doi.org/10.1509/jppm.10.114, http://search.ebscohost.com/login.aspx?direct=true&db=bth&AN=91886736&site=ehost-live.
35. Kobsa, A. 2001. Tailoring privacy to users' needs (invited keynote). In *User Modeling 2001*, ed. Bauer, M., P.J. Gmytrasiewicz, and J. Vassileva, 303–313. No. 2109 in Lecture Notes in Computer Science, Springer. https://doi.org/10.1007/3-540-44566-8_52.
36. Liu, B., J. Lin, and N. Sadeh. 2014. Reconciling mobile app privacy and usability on smartphones: Could user privacy profiles help? In *Proceedings of the 23rd International Conference on World Wide Web*, 201–212. WWW '14, International World Wide Web Conferences Steering Committee, Republic and Canton of Geneva, Switzerland. https://doi.org/10.1145/2566486.2568035.
37. Cranor, L.F. 2002. *Web Privacy with P3P*. Sebastopol, CA: O'Reilly & Associates, Inc.
38. Harkous, H., R. Rahman, and K. Aberer. 2016. Data-driven privacy indicators. In *Twelfth Symposium on Usable Privacy and Security (SOUPS 2016)*. Denver, CO: USENIX Association. https://www.usenix.org/conference/soups2016/workshop-program/wpi/presentation/harkous.
39. Egelman, S., J. Tsai, L.F. Cranor, and A. Acquisti. 2009. Timing is everything? The effects of timing and placement of online privacy indicators. In *Proceedings of the 27th International Conference on Human Factors in Computing Systems*, 319–328.
40. Fang, L., and K. LeFevre. 2010. Privacy wizards for social networking sites. In *Proceedings of the 19th International Conference on World Wide Web*, WWW '10, 351–360. New York, NY: ACM. http://doi.org/10.1145/1772690.1772727.
41. Ravichandran, R., M. Benisch, P. Kelley, and N. Sadeh. 2009. Capturing social networking privacy preferences. In *Privacy Enhancing Technologies*, ed. Goldberg, I., and M. Atallah. Lecture Notes in Computer Science, 1–18. Vol. 5672. Berlin: Springer. https://doi.org/10.1007/978-3-642-03168-7_1.
42. Knijnenburg, B.P., and H. Jin. 2013. The persuasive effect of privacy recommendations. In *Twelfth Annual Workshop on HCI Research in MIS* (2013)
43. Wisniewski, P.J., B.P. Knijnenburg, and H.R. Lipford. 2017. Making privacy personal: Profiling social network users to inform privacy education and nudging. *International Journal of Human-Computer Studies* 98: 95–108. https://doi.org/10.1016/j.ijhcs.2016.09.006, http://www.sciencedirect.com/science/article/pii/S1071581916301185.
44. Wilkinson, D., S. Sivakumar, D. Cherry, B.P. Knijnenburg, E.M. Raybourn, P. Wisniewski, and H. Sloan. 2017. User-tailored privacy by design. In *Proceedings of the Usable Security Mini Conference*, USEC '17. San Diego, CA: Internet Society. https://doi.org/10.14722/usec.2017.23007.
45. Namara, M., H. Sloan, P. Jaiswal, and B.P. Knijnenburg. 2018. The potential for user-tailored privacy on facebook. In *2018 IEEE Symposium on Privacy-Aware Computing (PAC)*, 31–42. IEEE.
46. Spiekermann, S., J. Grosslags, and B. Berendt. 2001. E-privacy in 2nd generation e-commerce: privacy preferences versus actual behavior. In *Proceedings of the 3rd ACM conference on Electronic Commerce*, 38–47. ACM.
47. Olson, J.S., J. Grudin, and E. Horvitz. 2005. A study of preferences for sharing and privacy. In *CHI'05 Extended Abstracts on Human Factors in Computing Systems*, 1985–1988. ACM (2005)
48. Knijnenburg, B.P., A. Kobsa, and H. Jin. 2013. Dimensionality of information disclosure behavior. *International Journal of Human-Computer Studies* 71 (12): 1144–1162.

49. Kairam, S., M. Brzozowski, D. Huffaker, and E. Chi. 2012. Talking in circles: Selective sharing in google+. In *Proceedings of the SIGCHI Conference on Human Factors in Computing Systems*, 1065–1074. ACM (2012)
50. Watson, J., A. Besmer, and H.R. Lipford. 2012. + Your circles: Sharing behavior on google+. In *Proceedings of the Eighth Symposium on Usable Privacy and Security*, 12. ACM.
51. Knijnenburg, B.P., and A. Kobsa. 2014. Increasing sharing tendency without reducing satisfaction: Finding the best privacy-settings user interface for social networks. In *International Conference on Information Systems (ICIS)*
52. Benisch, M., P.G. Kelley, N. Sadeh, and L.F. Cranor. 2011. Capturing location-privacy preferences: quantifying accuracy and user-burden tradeoffs. *Personal and Ubiquitous Computing* 15 (7): 679–694.
53. Dong, C., H. Jin, and B.P. Knijnenburg. 2016. PPM: A privacy prediction model for online social networks. In *International Conference on Social Informatics*, 400–420. Springer
54. Xie, J., B.P. Knijnenburg, and H. Jin. 2014. Location sharing privacy preference: analysis and personalized recommendation. In *Proceedings of the 19th International Conference on Intelligent User Interfaces*, 189–198. ACM.
55. Wang, Y., G. Norcie, and L.F. Cranor. 2011. Who is concerned about what? A study of American, Chinese and Indian users privacy concerns on social network sites. In *International Conference on Trust and Trustworthy Computing*, 146–153. Springer. https://doi.org/10.1007/978-3-642-21599-5_11.
56. Ackerman, M.S., L.F. Cranor, and J. Reagle. 1999. Privacy in e-commerce: Examining user scenarios and privacy preferences. In *Proceedings of the 1st ACM Conference on Electronic Commerce*, EC '99, 1–8. Denver, CO: ACM Press. https://doi.org/10.1145/336992.336995, ACM ID: 336995.
57. Li, Y., A. Kobsa, B.P. Knijnenburg, and M.C. Nguyen. 2017. Cross-cultural privacy prediction. *Proceedings on Privacy Enhancing Technologies* 2017 (2): 113–132.
58. Hoy, M.G., and G. Milne. 2010. Gender differences in privacy-related measures for young adult facebook users. *Journal of Interactive Advertising* 10 (2): 28–45. https://doi.org/10.1080/15252019.2010.10722168.
59. Page, X., B.P. Knijnenburg, and A. Kobsa. 2013. FYI: Communication style preferences underlie differences in location-sharing adoption and usage. In *Proceedings of the 2013 ACM International Joint Conference on Pervasive and Ubiquitous Computing*, 153–162. ACM (2013). http://dl.acm.org/citation.cfm?id=2493487
60. Mesch, G.S. 2012. Is online trust and trust in social institutions associated with online disclosure of identifiable information online? *Computers in Human Behavior* 28 (4): 1471–1477. https://doi.org/10.1016/j.chb.2012.03.010, http://www.sciencedirect.com/science/article/pii/S0747563212000763.
61. Bahirat, P., Y. He, A. Menon, and B. Knijnenburg. 2018. A data-driven approach to developing IoT privacy-setting interfaces. In *23rd International Conference on Intelligent User Interfaces*, IUI '18, 165–176. Tokyo: ACM. http://doi.org/10.1145/3172944.3172982.
62. Kelley, P.G., P. Hankes Drielsma, N. Sadeh, and L.F. Cranor. 2008. User-controllable learning of security and privacy policies. In *Proceedings of the 1st ACM Workshop on Workshop on AISec*, AISec '08, 11–18. New York, NY: ACM. http://doi.org/10.1145/1456377.1456380.
63. Knijnenburg, B.P., and A. Kobsa. 2013. Helping users with information disclosure decisions: potential for adaptation. In *Proceedings of the 2013 International Conference on Intelligent User Interfaces*, 407–416. ACM.
64. Pallapa, G., S.K. Das, Di Francesco, M., and T. Aura. 2014. Adaptive and context-aware privacy preservation exploiting user interactions in smart environments. *Pervasive and Mobile Computing* 12: 232–243.
65. Toch, E., J. Cranshaw, P.H. Drielsma, J.Y. Tsai, P.G. Kelley, Springfield, J., L. Cranor, J. Hong, and N. Sadeh. 2010. Empirical models of privacy in location sharing. In *Proceedings of the 12th ACM International Conference on Ubiquitous Computing*, 129–138. ACM (2010).

66. Zhao, Y., J. Ye, and T. Henderson. 2014. Privacy-aware location privacy preference recommendations. In *Proceedings of the 11th International Conference on Mobile and Ubiquitous Systems: Computing, Networking and Services*, 120–129. ICST (Institute for Computer Sciences, Social-Informatics and Telecommunications Engineering).

67. Bradley, K., R. Rafter, and B. Smyth. 2000. Case-based user profiling for content personalisation. In *International Conference on Adaptive Hypermedia and Adaptive Web-Based Systems*, 62–72. Berlin: Springer.

68. Cranshaw, J., J. Mugan, and N. Sadeh. 2011. User-controllable learning of location privacy policies with Gaussian mixture models. In *Proceedings of the Twenty-Fifth AAAI Conference on Artificial Intelligence*, AI '11, San Fancisco, CA, 1146–1152. http://www.aaai.org/ocs/index.php/AAAI/AAAI11/paper/viewPDFInterstitial/3785/4052.

69. Wang, W., and I. Benbasat. 2007. Recommendation agents for electronic commerce: Effects of explanation facilities on trusting beliefs. *Journal of Management Information Systems* 23 (4): 217–246. https://doi.org/10.2753/MIS0742-1222230410.

70. Dinner, I., E.J. Johnson, D.G. Goldstein, and K. Liu. 2011. Partitioning default effects: Why people choose not to choose. *Journal of Experimental Psychology: Applied* 17 (4): 332–341. https://www.learntechlib.org/p/64714/.

71. Anaraky, R.G., T. Nabizadeh, B.P. Knijnenburg, and M. Risius. 2018. Reducing default and framing effects in privacy decision-making. In *SIGHCI 2018 Proceedings*.

72. Madejski, M., M. Johnson, and S. Bellovin. 2012. A study of privacy settings errors in an online social network. In *Fourth International Workshop on Security and Social Networking*, SEC-SOC '12, Lugano, Switzerland, 340–345. https://doi.org/10.1109/PerComW.2012.6197507

73. Wang, Y., and A. Kobsa. 2013. A PLA-based privacy-enhancing user modeling framework and its evaluation. *User Modeling and User-Adapted Interaction* 23 (1): 41–82. https://link.springer.com/article/10.1007/s11257-011-9114-8.

74. Knijnenburg, B.P., S. Sivakumar, and D. Wilkinson. 2016. Recommender systems for self-actualization. In *Proceedings of the 10th ACM Conference on Recommender Systems*, 11–14. ACM.

75. Gedikli, F., D. Jannach, and M. Ge. 2014. How should I explain? A comparison of different explanation types for recommender systems. *International Journal of Human-Computer Studies* 72 (4): 367–382.

76. Ekstrand, M.D., R. Joshaghani, and H. Mehrpouyan. 2018. Privacy for all: Ensuring fair and equitable privacy protections. In *Conference on Fairness, Accountability and Transparency*, 35–47. http://proceedings.mlr.press/v81/ekstrand18a.html

77. Pai, P., and H.T. Tsai. 2016. Reciprocity norms and information-sharing behavior in online consumption communities: An empirical investigation of antecedents and moderators. *Information & Management* 53 (1): 38–52. https://doi.org/10.1016/j.im.2015.08.002, http://www.sciencedirect.com/science/article/pii/S0378720615000865.

78. Norberg, P.A., D.R. Horne, and D.A. Horne. 2007. The privacy paradox: Personal information disclosure intentions versus behaviors. *Journal of Consumer Affairs* 41 (1): 100–126 (2007). https://doi.org/10.1111/j.1745-6606.2006.00070.x, http://onlinelibrary.wiley.com/doi/10.1111/j.1745-6606.2006.00070.x/abstract.

79. Knijnenburg, B.P., E.M. Raybourn, D. Cherry, D. Wilkinson, S. Sivakumar, and H. Sloan. 2017. Death to the privacy calculus? In *Proceedings of the 2017 Networked Privacy Workshop at CSCW*. Social Science Research Network, Portland, OR, Feb 2017. https://papers.ssrn.com/abstract=2923806.

80. Paramythis, A., S. Weibelzahl, and J. Masthoff. 2010. Layered evaluation of interactive adaptive systems: Framework and formative methods. *User Modeling and User-Adapted Interaction* 20 (5): 383–453. https://doi.org/10.1007/s11257-010-9082-4.

81. Bösch, C., B. Erb, F. Kargl, H. Kopp, and S. Pfattheicher. 2016. Tales from the dark side: Privacy dark strategies and privacy dark patterns. *Proceedings on Privacy Enhancing Technologies* 2016 (4): 237–254. https://doi.org/10.1515/popets-2016-0038. https://www.degruyter.com/view/j/popets.2016.2016.issue-4/popets-2016-0038/popets-2016-0038.xml?format=INT.

Chapter 17
The Ethics of Privacy in Research and Design: Principles, Practices, and Potential

Lorraine Kisselburgh and Jonathan Beever

Abstract The contexts of sociotechnical privacy have evolved significantly in 50 years, with correlate shifts in the norms, values, and ethical concerns in research and design. We examine these eras of privacy from an ethics perspective, arguing that as contexts expand from the individual, to internet, interdependence, intelligences, and artificiality, they also reframe the audience or stakeholder roles present and broaden the field of ethical concerns. We discuss these ethical issues and introduce a principlist framework to guide ethical decision-making, articulating a strategy by which principles are reflexively applied in the decision-making process, informed by the rich interface of epistemic and ethical values. Next, we discuss specific challenges to privacy presented by emerging technologies such as biometric identification systems, autonomous vehicles, predictive algorithms, deepfake technologies, and public health surveillance and examine these challenges around five ethical principles: *autonomy*, *justice*, *non-maleficence*, *beneficence*, and *explicability*. Finally, we connect the theoretical and applied to the practical to briefly identify law, regulation, and soft law resources—including technical standards, codes of conduct, curricular programs, and statements of principles—that can provide actionable guidance and rules for professional conduct and technological development, codifying the reasoning outcomes of ethics.

L. Kisselburgh (✉)
Purdue University, Center for Education and Research in Information Security, Burton Morgan
Center for Entrepreneurship, West Lafayette, IN, USA
e-mail: lorraine@purdue.edu

J. Beever
Department of Philosophy, Center for Ethics, University of Central Florida, Orlando, FL, USA
e-mail: jonathan.beever@ucf.edu

© The Author(s) 2022
B. P. Knijnenburg et al. (eds.), *Modern Socio-Technical Perspectives on Privacy*,
https://doi.org/10.1007/978-3-030-82786-1_17

17.1   Introduction

Privacy is an ethical issue. Almost every chapter in this volume takes on these issues to some degree, whether in the broader context of cultural norms (Chap. 5), the professional context of codes of ethics (e.g., Chap. 6), as cultural values (Chap. 12), or as an implicit good in the discussions of privacy enhancements or violations (Chap. 8). This chapter develops a typology of the ethics of privacy, emphasizing the roles and responsibilities of the researcher. We draw a parallel between the ethics of design and the landscape of privacy research, arguing that a structured reflexive approach to ethical decision-making is required in the complex and changing landscape of contemporary privacy practices, problems, and policies.

To begin, we take a historical approach to typologizing the ethics of designing technologies for privacy. In this first section, we outline key terms as a means of grounding our discussion on a carefully defined sense of ethics and understanding of the moral agents and patients involved. The next section examines the eras of privacy research from an ethics perspective, arguing that ethical values within privacy discussions have and are again shifting, reemphasizing the need to continued development of ethics literacy in this area. We articulate a strategy of ethical decision-making by which decision-makers can thoughtfully adjudicate among conflicting values within privacy debates. That decision-making strategy can help us reframe contemporary privacy challenges, the target of our fourth section, by drawing attention to changes in the ethical landscape. Next, we outline emerging ethical challenges, arguing that historical/traditional conceptualizations of privacy limit our ability to consider privacy issues of contemporary technologies in the AI era and beyond. Finally, we consider some implications for an ethically literate perspective on privacy practice and policy.

17.2   Eras of Privacy Ethics

We begin with an outline of eras of privacy research from an ethics perspective, arguing that the ethical issues around privacy discussions have and are again shifting, reemphasizing the need to continued development of ethics literacy in this area.

17.2.1   Research Ethics and Emerging Technologies

In the context of research and design, ethics is concerned with the moral issues that arise during or as a result of research activities, as well as the ethical conduct of researchers. Discussions of ethics are scaffolded from issues within research practices ("research ethics" or "responsible conduct of research") and the societal and environmental implications of that research ("broader impacts"). This scaffolding of ethics is historically driven: a result of notorious unethical research practices in the early twentieth century.

Notably, the revelation of bioethical scandals such as the Guatemala STD studies and the cultivation and dissemination of the HeLa cell line in the United States led to the realization that clear measures were needed for the ethical governance of research to ensure that people, animals, and environments are not unduly harmed in research. Yet when US physicians experimented on Guatemalan prisoners of color, women, and children without consent [1], the ethical concern was not *merely* about the physical harms involved. Similarly, the use of Henrietta Lacks' genetic material without her consent was not *merely* about disrespecting her autonomy (see [2, 3]). Importantly, these and other cases of unethical research involved an ecosystem of ethical concern based on what we owe each other. What has become known as *bioethical principlism* [4] defines four key universally applicable principles: non-maleficence (avoiding harms), beneficence (doing good), justice, and respect for autonomy. In the context of research, all four principles are in play together outlining the complex landscape of rights and responsibilities. Thus, the harms done to research subjects in Guatemala or to Henrietta Lacks and her family posed ethical challenges to individuals' rights, broadly construed, and can be seen through the lens of privacy.

As bioethics has evolved in the US context, its principles have come to mark out a broad ethical territory that is not only about the research practice itself (say, extracting biological samples from human subjects in the clinic) but also about the design of processes that lead up to, frame, and fall out from those practices. Emphasis on the processes of design draws attention to the *reflexivity* between normative principles and the context in which they are applied (see [5]). A *reflexive*[1] principlism [6] is analogous to the design process in that they both rely on a cyclical application and analysis of principles considered through constraints of particular stakeholders or audience and specifics of the real-world context.

Stakeholders in ethics play roles either (or both) as moral agents or (or and) moral patients. Moral agents have the capacity and therefore the responsibility to act ethically, and moral patients have moral rights based on some capacity or characteristic they have. As bioethical principlism has evolved alongside the technologies with which it interfaces, those relationships among agents and patients have become more diverse and more complicated. Theoretical and practical concerns about physical harms became the impetus for the wider net of research ethics cast to focusing broadly on the implications of technology practices on lived experience. Contemporary research ethics (see [7]) marks out the points of intersections among the human interests and technological influences. But as the technology landscape continues to evolve and integrate into the experiences of living entities (human

---

[1] We take *reflexion* to be an unconscious habituated response, whereas *reflection* is a conscious, deliberate process of thinking about what one is doing. Both are necessary conditions of robust ethical decision-making.

and nonhuman alike), the ethics of research and design also continues to evolve. Each part of research ethics continues to get both more complicated and more interconnected as emerging technologies break down the spaces between them. As an example, consider the collection and sharing of human genetic information, which puts individual and public health considerations up against individual rights and privacy concerns. Issues like these are the direct result of the information technologies, economies, and ecosystems that have so rapidly evolved since the mid-twentieth century. With this evolution, careful ethical distinctions—say, between physical, dignitary (psychological or emotional), and informational harms—play increasingly important roles in conversations about the collection, curation, and use of information.

17.2.2 Changing Contexts of Concern

The terrain of research ethics drives ethical concern about privacy not only historically but also in the contemporary context. Yet what is ethically salient about privacy changes with the social and technological context [8]. We argue that the context under which privacy has been considered has shifted in the past several decades as a direct result of the influences of information technologies. We identify five privacy paradigms that have shifted the ethical salience of privacy research from merely a focus on the human individual through a future of privacy discourses among artificial systems apart from human experiences (Fig. 17.1). These paradigms intersect in robust ways; yet it is helpful to think about them as expansions to more clearly engage relevant privacy practices and policies.

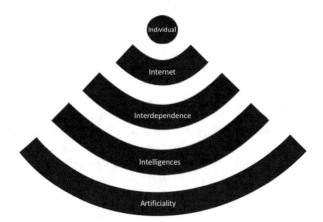

Fig. 17.1 Expansions of privacy contexts

17.2.2.1   Privacy 1.0

In what we might call *Privacy 1.0*, ethical attention was focused on risks of dignitary harms[2] to the individual citizen. In the US context, ethical concerns about privacy have a long history (see [1]). The ethical focus of Privacy 1.0 was codified in legal precedence in what has become known as the "Katz test," proposed by US Supreme Court Justice Harlan in his concurring opinion in the 1967 Katz v. United States case. There, Harlan proposed a two-part test of privacy: that "a person have exhibited an actual (subjective) expectation of privacy and, second, that the expectation be one that society is prepared to recognize as "reasonable" [9]. This legal ruling solidified an ongoing social debate about the rights of citizens to be legally (and ethically) protected against *unreasonable* breaches of their privacy. For example, if a citizen has a conversation in her home with doors and shutters closed, she has evidenced an expectation of privacy that is arguably reasonable—even if someone else can overhear that conversation from the sidewalk outside. Yet if the doors and shutters are thrown wide, there is no such evidence and, therefore, arguably less legal protection for her privacy. So while it had been seen as reasonable for conversations taking place within one's home to be protected as private, it was at that time much less clear how far that protection extended or what constituted *reasonableness*. For our purposes, this legal ruling is less important than the core framing question to which it gives voice: namely, what kinds of information are protected as private and in what contexts?

17.2.2.2   Privacy 2.0

As information technologies quickly expanded in the mid twentieth century, ethical concerns about privacy expanded in reaction. The rise of Internet technologies brought into stark relief what we will call *Privacy 2.0*, expanding concerns about dignitary harms from a local to a global level. The Privacy Act of 1974 [10] in the United States codified privacy concerns in the emerging information age, at least in the context of information collected, maintained, used, and disseminated by federal agencies. That Act mandated limits on transmission of information about individuals, offering baseline protections for information privacy. Responding to tensions among ethical values related to economy, access, and privacy in the emerging information age, legislation like the Privacy Act pushed the focus of the ethics of privacy from the individual to the Internet, expanding the scope of privacy concerns. Importantly, this shift in focus pushed back the locus of ethical inquiry from a view of the isolated individual agent and toward the individual's information.

Information philosopher Luciano Floridi, in his 2013 *Ethics of Information*, argued for an informational interpretation of the self and, therefore, a focus on

---

[2] Dignitary harms differ from physical harms in that they are not bodily but psychological or, in our current context, informational.

informational privacy. In his view, privacy researchers distinguish among four types: physical, mental, decisional, and informational ([11], p. 230). Floridi offers the example of a typical human moral agent [12], Alice, to help make these distinctions. Alice's **physical** privacy is contingent on constraints on her embodied experience, including sensory or mobility interference. When we get ready for a Zoom meeting, we might each demand this kind of physical privacy in asking to be allowed to dress or frame the scene offline rather than sitting in front of the camera. But privacy for Floridi's Alice also includes **mental** privacy, or freedom from psychological interferences to her mind and mental states. While an individual preparing for a Zoom meeting might request physical privacy, they may have no similar desires concerning mental privacy; indeed, perhaps they are on the phone with a colleague talking about structure for the meeting. Alongside physical and mental privacy, Alice is also owed or at least has the capacity for **decisional** privacy. Alice's decisional privacy requires autonomous decision-making, free from interference by others. Finally, Floridi circles back around to the idea of **informational** privacy, or freedom from restrictions on facts—what Floridi calls "epistemic interference" (p. 230). These four categories define the horizon of Alice's privacy landscape, acting as the parameters for discussions about what we owe her, morally. Now, Floridi's broader argument concerning informational privacy is that what he calls "old" information, and computing technologies (ICTs) reduce this kind of privacy, whereas new ICTs can either decrease or *increase* informational privacy. Floridi notes that "solutions to the problem of protecting informational privacy can be not only self-regulatory and legislative but also technological, not least because information privacy infringements can more easily be identified and redressed, also thanks to digital ICTs" (p. 236). While he argues against our reading this claim as an "idyllic scenario" (p. 236) of technological optimism, the idea that increases in quality (scope), quantity (scale), and speed[3] of informational technologies will *equitably* increase opportunities for benefits and harms is difficult to evidence.

This account is important in that it addresses multiple aspects of the ethics of privacy. First, Floridi argues for an expansion of the *scope* of privacy concerns, from individual to information through Internet technologies. Second, Floridi argues for a change in the *scale* of privacy concerns, suggesting that information technologies, *ceteris paribus*, are value neutral in that they can either decrease or increase privacy thanks to the scale, scope, and speed of information exchange they enable. Floridi's ontological account of ICTs reframes traditional discussions of privacy ethics and policy by baselining out both human individuals and computational technologies as the same kind of entities, namely, informational entities. Imagine here the difference between slander in a local newspaper in the 1950s compared to slander on global

---

[3] There are several similar descriptions of digital data. Analyst Doug Laney introduced "three V's" of data – volume, variety, and velocity – in a 2001 report [13]. A 2015 National Institute of Standards and Technology (NIST) report defined a six-part parallel description of data that included validity, velocity, veracity, vertical scaling, volatility, and volume [14].

social media in the early 2000s. Privacy concerns are broader and potentially more significant under the 2.0 paradigm than under its 1.0 predecessor.

17.2.2.3   Privacy 3.0

The changes in scope, scale, and speed of information transfer enabled by contemporary information technologies have pushed privacy concerns from extensions of my information to networks of my information, or from internet to *interdependence*. Interdependence, or the networking relations of information that constitute each individual, shifts the burden of privacy further from the isolated individual (whether local or global) to the network of information to which that individual is connected and through which that individual is constituted [15]. This shift from Privacy 2.0 to Privacy 3.0 is ontologically uncomfortable, since many of us are culturally habituated into a worldview that privileges the view that the individual somehow stands alone. Floridi's Alice stands for just such a traditional individual moral agent from Privacy 2.0. Yet extensions of information through both digital and analog environments challenge this worldview.

   In a recent book looking at interdependence through the lens of film, Beever argues that another Alice—this one from the science fiction film series *Resident Evil* [16]—represents this relational paradigm of privacy concerns. Here, Alice exists as a cloned instance of some original Alice and is constituted as a complex amalgam of technologies, an inherited set of information, and unique lived experiences and interpersonal connections. Alice is not Alice *except* for these relationships: indeed, in this fictional context, there is nothing essential to her character about her physical form or, even, her genetic information. This film series is compelling because it complicates and extends the realities of interdependence to show us moral threat in the digital extensions of the self: "interdependence with other information flows like the virus is interdependent with the host" (p. 186). We need not stretch to the science fictional to understand this paradigm shift of privacy concerns. Consider, as a real-world example, the myriad roles that genetic information plays in our understanding of who we are and how we relate. A single sample can share with others information about our relational selves that we did not yet know. Similarly, algorithms that drive our digital platforms deny or define our choice of relations (whether social media streams, the Internet access, or shopping choices), defining who we are by what we know and to whom we have access. In this Privacy 3.0 paradigm, informational interdependence governs new responses to our core question: "what kinds of information are protected as private and in what contexts?" (e.g., [17–19]). Committed to an information ontology but also an epistemic and ethical position that our relations constitute what we know and what we value, the response to this question is now broader and more complicated.

17.2.2.4   Privacy 4.0

Across privacy paradigms, the onus of ethics has been on the definition and defense of human individual rights regarding their information. Changes to the technological landscape and, in turn, the speed, scope, and scale of digital information were the predominant focus, while the moral target remained the same. In what we call Privacy 4.0, it is the target of ethical inquiry that changes. Here, artificial intelligence systems present a potentially novel kind of ethical agent: a nonhuman nonorganic agent that conflates the categories of the previous privacy paradigms. AI systems thread together individual agency, Internet big data technologies, and interdependence. In so doing, they offer a new space of ethical discourse between human agents and these nonhuman artificial agents. Ongoing efforts to define what constitutes "ethical" AI have led to a convergence around five ethical principles: transparency, justice, non-maleficence, responsibility, and privacy [20]. There are clear parallels here between this set of normative principles and the principles of bioethics; justice and non-maleficence remain key ethical principles. Yet in the place of autonomy and beneficence stand transparency, responsibility, and privacy, emphasizing the focus on information structures, use, and representation. In Privacy 4.0, human individuals and AI systems are combined together as two types of information systems. Human individuals play roles in this ethical landscape not only as users (moral patients) but as collaborating moral agents, designers, and developers of artificial information systems. Developing reflexivity in the analysis and application of these principles is just as important as it is within the Privacy 1.0 paradigm. But reflexivity takes on new meaning as an encoded ability of complex information systems.

17.2.2.5   Privacy 5.0

As we look toward the future of the ethics of privacy, we envision a Privacy 5.0 paradigm in which the reflexive process of ethical decision-making takes place between two artificial information systems. In this paradigm, the human agent is wholly excluded, having participated (perhaps) as the designer of a now wholly autonomous artificial agent. While this paradigm is still largely the stuff of science fiction, it is visible on the horizon of our technological development. Thinking about the value of privacy as something understood and negotiated outside of the participation and direct guidance of human moral agents enables us to think proactively about practices and policies around privacy now.

The five paradigms of privacy laid out in this section reframe the complex stakeholder or audience roles present in an increasingly complex information economy. They serve as a heuristic by which to assess ethical practices around privacy, like the practice of informed consent, which may apply in one paradigm but seem outmoded in another. The intersections among paradigms create new research contexts, new social interactions, and new uncertainty that can lead us to renegotiations of legal and regulatory frameworks related to privacy.

17.3   Ethical Decision-Making and Key Issues

In the previous section, we argued that changing paradigms of privacy, enabled by continued development of information technologies, challenge the roles and natures of stakeholders. These challenges reshape the ethical terrain of privacy concerns, adding complexity to analyses of what or whom matters morally and why. In this section, we turn from the theoretical and conceptual concerns to the practical, asking "How do the changing paradigms of privacy challenge our models of ethical decision-making?"

Models of ethical decision-making (EDM) emphasize the procedure of reasoning through complex ethical issues, taking into account not only philosophical concerns about values and value conflicts but also the epistemic or factual context in which those value relations play out (see [21] for a review). Generally speaking, ethical decision-making describes a series of steps to be taken, often in cyclical series, until a decision is reached:

1. Identify the problem.
2. Review the facts.
3. Identify the values at stake.
4. Identify the relevant ethical guidelines (codes or theories).
5. Enumerate consequences, outcomes given the context.
6. Decide on a best course of action.

Ethical decision-making is a dynamic, iterative process that starts with developing ethics sensitivity, or the ability to see a problem as an ethical problem in the first place and to judge its intensity ([22], p. 159). An ethical issue is not identified or evaluated in a vacuum, so the problem is always grounded in epistemic constraints (the *facts*) and assessed through utilization of the tools of normative ethics to get at values and their conflicts (the *values*). The values landscape is informed by normative theories, or structured approaches to how, why, and under what circumstances values apply. Contemporary approaches to EDM often take a pluralistic approach, relying not on a single normative approach (like *either* utilitarianism *or* deontology) but on their fit given the epistemic and ethical context (see [23]).

The reasoning process is not algorithmic but a part of this richly dynamic EDM process, with a goal of producing a pragmatic, context-informed decision. The iterative nature of EDM is itself pragmatic in the same way as is the design process: both recognize that changing constraints or actualization of outcomes might shift the parameters of the decision. *Good* ethical decision-making, then, is the result of practice, or developing the right habits and experiences to work through the process reflexively.

Complexity in ethical decision-making is clearly seen when applied to questions of privacy. For example, should someone submit a cheek swab to a genetic information corporation? With limited ethical sensitivity, we might not be attuned to the ethical tensions between access to, say, some details about our ancestry and the ways in which my information will be digitized and monetized. But without a robust understanding of relevant business models, digital information policies and practices, and social context, worrying about our data is ungrounded.

Ethical decision-making is a process of application of the principlism we outlined in the last section. Indeed, principlism does not offer a decision-making process but, instead, "an analytical framework of general norms . . . that form a suitable starting point for reflection on moral problems . . . " ([4], p. 13).[4] Principlism enters the EDM process directly at steps three and four, where adjudication among values meets the context in which it applies. Ethical principlists have argued that the process of specification and balancing principles in context moves principlism from theory to practice (see [5]). Yet EDM is guided by ethical principles; indeed, without them, it would be simple decision-making. Also essential to the process is the targets, or stakeholders. Ethical decision-making both applies *to* moral patients (those individuals who matter, morally) and is applied *by* moral agents (those individuals capable of making ethical decisions). We turn next to this relationship between patients and agents in the context of privacy paradigms, distinguishing between modes of ethics reception and ethics transmission.

17.3.1   Principles and Patients: Reception

The four ethical principles of principlism offer a pluralistic approach to the major normative theories in ethics: beneficence and non-maleficence considering consequences or utility of actions, and justice and autonomy worrying about rights and duties of individuals who matter morally, otherwise known as *moral patients*. Too much of ethics of technology work has focused too heavily on consequences. For example, much of the early discussion around the ethics of self-driving cars has drawn on trolley problem variants to consider strategies for dealing with the consequences of decisions by the system: does it protect the driver, one or another type of pedestrian, the manufacturer's reputation, etc. [24]? That focus is important here, since it empowers ethical decision-making to focus on consequences for moral patients. But it is also insufficient as it leaves out broader questions of rights.

Privacy concerns are concerns about both the ethical consequences of actions and the rights of the user, stakeholder, or audience. Breaches of privacy can lead to significant dignitary harms by failing to acknowledge or uphold the right to privacy of the individual. Consider the example of Internet of Things (IoT) devices in the home. When my IOT devices are listening to my choices and using those for marketing purposes, they present me with tension between two competing ethical values: access and privacy. I might value access at the expense of privacy and, say, not even read the disclosures that come with my devices. Or I might value privacy

---

[4] The authors add, " . . . in biomedical ethics," unnecessarily, on our view, since we argue principlism applies to any discipline or professional that utilizes a version of the design process.

at the expense of access and not allow IOT devices access to my information in the first place. There is less risk to physical Privacy (think Privacy 1.0) than there is risk to informational privacy (think Privacy 2.0+). Thus, privacy concerns are different ethical concerns than other technology-related ethical issues precisely because they are informational.

Without understanding both why a moral patient would value privacy and what consequences breaches of privacy might have, we moral agents cannot effectively evaluate the moral salience of those devices. A recent article in Canadian Bar Association's *National* magazine has received considerable attention for asking the question: "should we recognize privacy as a human right?" [25]. Its author notes that while Canada has introduced legislation to strengthen its consumer privacy protections, it does not "explicitly recognize privacy as a human right, nor does or [sic] give precedence to privacy rights over commercial considerations" (ibid). Whether privacy should be taken up as a basic human right is contingent on its moral salience which, again, is contingent on our understanding of the complex epistemic and ethical contexts in which it functions.

We can think of these ethical tensions and practical responses as on the *receiving end* of ethical discourse. That is, as we focus on the consequences of privacy application or breach, we evaluate the moral patient receiving benefits or harms or negotiating impacts to fairness or free action.

17.3.2   Action and Agents: Transmission

On the *sending end* of ethical discourse, the discussion shifts from outcomes to agency and intention, or from conduct to character. Ethical concern lies not with the moral patient but instead with the moral agent. What responsibilities or duties does the moral agent have vis-à-vis privacy? Questions of character are the focus of *virtue ethics*, one of the oldest normative theories in western philosophical ethics. Reflexive principlism does not emphasize virtue ethics within its pluralism. Rather, one of its designers, Tom Beauchamp, argued that virtue ethics and principlism were complementary [26]. He argues that "virtue theory is of the highest importance in a health-care context because a morally good person with the right motives is more likely to discern what should be done, to be motivated to do it, and to do it" (pp. 194–5). In the same way we have proposed to extend biomedical principlism to other design-based disciplines, we likewise extend Beauchamp's argument. We agree that in design-based contexts, "morally good" agents are more likely to engage in ethical decision-making and act rightly.

A principles-based approach to EDM offers an ethical orientation to real-world problems but is incomplete without complementarity from a theory of the virtue of the agents involved. Virtue ethics complements principlism in the EDM process specifically because privacy stakeholders propose to treat human participants and artificial information systems as collaborating moral agents. Thus, we must be able to evaluate both the receiving and the transmission ends of ethical action.

To situate the idea of the sending end of ethics in a practical context, consider the ethics of digital breast imaging. Medical science continues to prove the benefits of early-detection mammography. Yet there are risks involved, as with any medical procedure, including a low risk of psychological stress from false positives, the even lower risk of physical harm from the mechanical procedure itself, or privacy risks from failure to keep confidential the resulting images. But federal regulations like the US Health Insurance Portability and Accountability Act [27] might offer protection and legal recourse against these types of physical harms, so from individual and public health perspectives, the benefits of digital breast imaging significantly outweigh its harms.

Yet this analysis is over-simplified given the complexity of privacy paradigms. The contemporary landscape of breast imaging involves not traditional mammography but digitally stored and transferred AI-analyzed medical imaging. AI systems continue to be developed for screening, diagnosis, risk calculation, clinical decision support, and management planning [28]. While these advances in health-care technology show promise [29], they also promise peril. The ways that AI systems handle privacy concerns are twofold: First, value priorities are encoded by human designers into the algorithms used by the system; then the system prioritizes that set of values in its learning processes. Thus, privacy concerns here involve potentially *two types* of moral agents on the sending end of ethics: the human and the artificial. While current AI systems are limited in this moral capacity [30], the future of AI development leaves open that Privacy 5.0 door.[5] Privacy policies and practices will have to adapt in order to continue to uphold privacy as a fundamental right [31].

17.3.3   Privacy's Network and Hub

The reception (involving moral patients) and transmission (involving moral agents) of privacy ethics through the process of ethical decision-making rely on the ongoing specification and balancing of principles. The speed and scale of technology development challenge the goal of cultivating ethical reflexivity: habituation is hard under conditions of change. Thus, ethical decision-making around privacy-in-design will continue to demand epistemic and ethical vigilance.

If we think of the hub of privacy ethics as the ethical principles and epistemic value contexts, then its network is the landscape of specified ethical issues (see Table 17.1). The importance of the principlist framework is that it provides a shared normative framework across the various disciplines, professions, and governance bodies with a stake in discussions of privacy. The work of balancing and specifying principles allows several perspectives on what is most ethically salient about, say,

---

[5] We note that we have offered several medical ethics examples in our discussion so far because those carry significant ethical salience. But our analysis applies broadly to many case contexts involving information systems and value relations with which they interact.

Table 17.1 Ethical principles, cases, human rights, and key privacy concepts

Ethical principle	Autonomy	Justice	Non-maleficence	Beneficence	Explicability
Dimensions	Respect for human dignity, human determination, and oversight; respect for person; right to be left alone; freedom from intrusion	Fairness, equality (non-bias), diversity	Prevention of harm; protection of vulnerable populations; robust, safe, secure	Societal well-being, social impact	Transparency, intelligibility, accountability, traceability
Use cases	Autonomous vehicles, facial recognition, biometric databases	Algorithmic bias; social credit scoring; robot judges, predictive policing	Deepfakes, disinformation, ethnic surveillance	Privacy by design, ICT4All, AI4Good, pandemic health, sustainability	AI black boxing, predictive algorithms
Key privacy concepts	Agency, consent, confidentiality; freedom from intrusion	Due process, right to access, correct, redress	Security; minimization of data, use, and purpose	Data protection	Access, audit, accountability, transparency
Universal Declaration of Human Rights	Respect for human dignity, freedom from arbitrary interference, protection of identity, freedom to make decisions	Non-discrimination, liberty, right to justice, equality, right to remedy	Freedom from arbitrary detention, freedom from arbitrary interference	Responsibility to community	Rights to access public documents, rights to public goods

the principle of non-maleficence in any particular context. By requiring ongoing ethical discourse, principlism empowers collaborative decision-making.

But as privacy paradigms advance, privacy as a value appears more and more in conflict with other values, including access, interaction, and engagement with other information systems. Beyond risk and harm analyses, beyond questions of consent, and beyond aged questions of agency and autonomy, the concern is that *privacy is dead*. In making this claim, we channel Friedrich Nietzsche who, in the late nineteenth century, made a similar claim about God [32]. Nietzsche's acerbic claim was that what we had taken to be God had become, in his view, unbelievable. The death of that particular metaphysical belief was the result of human scientific and technological advancement, which brought into question the religious metaphysic that had guided much of western society. Without that grounding in a view of God, Nietzsche worried that what was left was nothingness: *a void of meaning*. When we say that privacy is dead, we suggest that what we have taken to be privacy no longer has meaning, thanks to tremendous changes in the technology landscape. Privacy is unbelievable because human existence in current (and future) privacy paradigms is defined by how we manage, not restrict, access. And so privacy, like God for Nietzsche, has become a mere simulacrum of doctrine and concept. Thinking about privacy as a practical possibility for which societies can legislate protections is now naive. Contemporary work on privacy continues to reshape the concept as an important if complicated value in the human experience.

17.4 Reframing Privacy Ethics: Emerging Ethical Challenges

Recognizing the broadened social and technological contexts that have shifted the ethical salience of privacy concerns from the individual to interdependent networks and to futures of artificiality and the decision-making frameworks that can assist us in asking what or whom matters morally and why, we turn now to discuss specific emerging ethical challenges pushing us to reconceptualize privacy ethics. We anchor this reconception of privacy in a foundation of universal human rights, recognized throughout the world with the establishment of the Universal Declaration of Human Rights [33] and encoded in international law and treaties. These rights are legally enforceable and provide clear consequences for violations. They include specific reference to concepts associated with privacy, including a respect for human dignity, freedom of the individual to make decisions for themselves and be free from intrusion and intervention, respect for justice and due process, a commitment to equality and non-discrimination, and the right of citizens to access and participate in their governing processes and public services.

Following the ethical framework outlined in the previous section, in this section, we discuss specific challenges to privacy presented by twenty-first-century emerging technologies in order to illustrate the ways in which the contexts for privacy violations have become more complex. We organize these discussions around five ethical principles: *autonomy*, *justice*, *non-maleficence*, *beneficence*, and *explicability*.

While we continue to address concepts traditionally associated with privacy, such as anonymity, confidentiality, consent, right to correct, and minimization of scope, we argue here that privacy threats now encompass broader ethical concerns. Specifically, we suggest that ethical concerns in privacy must now shift:

- Beyond a focus on data protection of individuals to consider multifaceted and ubiquitous forms of surveillance as intrusions that violate respect for one's *dignity*
- From consent of individuals to a concern for human *agency* and *autonomy*
- From a focus on individual due process to a consideration of social fairness, non-discrimination, and *justice*
- From individual risk assessments to also consider safety, robustness, and the protection and inclusion of vulnerable populations as *non-maleficent* goals
- Beyond the individual or singular context of intrusion or data collection to consider collective responsibilities for environmental, social, and cultural well-being aligned with *beneficent* goals
- Beyond limits of scope and purpose to also consider data integrity, provenance, and accountability for *explicability* in the processes of algorithms, modeling, and data use

17.4.1 Autonomy as Dignity: From Data Protection to Multifaceted Forms of Intrusion

For the past 50 years, starting with the advent of computer systems used to store electronic records about individuals in financial, health, educational, and other sectors, the primary focus of privacy concerns has been the protection of data used in order to ensure that individual rights to privacy are not violated. Those concerns remain today, but they are complicated by the multiple forms of data that are now collected (e.g., numeric, text, voice, image, biometric) as well as the many technological means for doing so. We now live in a world filled with video cameras, facial recognition systems, RFID chips, electronic toll collectors, smartphones with location tracking, and voice-activated networks in our homes and automobiles. This modern context enables large-scale ubiquitous multimodal surveillance of users and citizens in public as well as in spaces traditionally considered to be private and free from intrusion: our cars, homes, and bedrooms. These new contexts suggest that ethical concerns in privacy must now shift beyond a focus on data protection of individuals to consider multifaceted and ubiquitous forms of surveillance as intrusions that violate respect for one's dignity, as an expression of individual autonomy. That includes concerns about privacy of one's *person*, *identity*, as well as one's *information*.

For example, facial recognition technologies (FRTs) used in public spaces present unique challenges for privacy. Using biometric data and processes to map facial features from image or video data, facial recognition systems attempt to identify individuals by matching their image against stored data. Biometric identifier data (fingerprints, iris, and face images) raise specific privacy concerns because they are uniquely identifiable, highly sensitive, and hard to secure. And if captured and misused, biometric data cannot be changed or uncoupled from an individual's identity [34]. When used by government or other institutional authorities to identify, track, and surveil citizens or institutional members, FRTs create fundamental imbalances in power and can be used as a means of social control, a form of digital authoritarianism [35].

For example, FRTs in China are an integral part of a social scoring system used to monitor and assess citizen behavior in public spaces and assign consequences when behaviors fall outside acceptable boundaries [36]. Similarly, the use of biometric identification systems in India's Aadhaar [37]—a centralized database that collects biometric information from 1.35 billion citizens, including fingerprints, iris scans, photographs, demographic information, and a unique 12-digit identifier—has raised significant concerns about the unprecedented access to and power over citizens given to government [38].

Because FRTs often operate continuously, invisibly, ubiquitously, and automatically, concerns about the risks of intrusion increase due to the large amounts of data collected, when data is collected without the knowledge or consent of the subject, and when human determination is removed from the equation. In addition, concerns about the accuracy, reliability, and security of FRTs—including false positives and negatives (e.g., for women and persons of color; [39])—have led some companies and countries to call for moratoriums on the use of FRTs in public spaces [40]. The specific risks of structural violence [41] resulting from the use of technologies to categorize individuals, monitor their movements, and mete punishments lead to clear potential loss of freedoms of movement, intrusion, and liberty.

17.4.2   Autonomy as Agency: From Consent to Access

A second, prominent privacy concern has centered around the expectation of *knowledge and consent* of an individual when her person or information is accessed. Individuals who provide permission to be searched or have their information collected are presumed to give *informed consent*—a fundamental assumption that individuals have the right to decide when, what, and how much information about themselves will be shared [42] or that they have *agency* in the decisions that are made on their behalf (see [43] on proxy consent; [44] on deferred consent). Consent and agency have formed the core elements of research ethics practice (see Common Rule) as well as terms of service used in many industries.

Yet while our early conceptions of consent were based on individual transactions, today's ubiquitous, invisible, and large-scale data collection practices mean consent is not only difficult, it is largely no longer meaningful [45]. For example, when withholding consent equates to being denied access to services and goods provided through such platforms (e.g., without an Aadhaar ID, one cannot receive social support services), or when the terms of service agreements are inauthentic because they are too complex to be understandable or disguise exceptions that allow data sharing [46], consent as a means to respect and protect the rights of individuals to control their information becomes meaningless.

We argue that respecting autonomy in new privacy eras must shift away from consent and toward access, since self-governance is as much contingent on access (to *read*) as it is contingent on permission (to *be read*). This balance between read and write is essential in the context of information systems. We must ask not only *What is the role that individuals play in determining how data are used?* but also *What level of control do humans maintain in automated systems?* and *How are systems designed to gauge individual tolerance for trusted systems and to adjust if a potential intrusion (or trust-eroding event) is imminent?*

The ethical concern here focuses on tensions around autonomy between consent and agency. In addition to having the capability to act on the basis of one's own decisions and ensure that individuals are not placed at risk when sharing information [47], we must also have the agency to intervene when engaging with automated systems or decision-making algorithms that make determinations about us.

One example arises in self-driving vehicles. Because these systems are designed with granular levels of autonomy in decision-making and responses to environmental stimuli, they must also be designed to learn and adopt the values of the community in which they are installed. This is essential not only for trustworthiness but also to ensure the preservation of human determination. Thus, critically important is an iterative design process that continually assesses ethical consequences of design choices, follows *ethically aligned* standards [48], and ensures that individuals are able to determine the values and rules used in the process. Centering humans and their values in the loop is a key part of *human-centric computing* [49, 50], where technological devices, algorithms, and systems are designed with consideration of the human impact, and human values are centered in the design process (see also *value-sensitive design* [51] and *privacy by design* [52]).

17.4.3 Justice: From Material Risk to Fairness and Due Process

In light of growing evidence and concerns about unfairness in technologies and algorithms, there have been many recent calls to reorient and broaden ethics discussion about emerging technologies like AI, as one that is defined by *justice*, including social, racial, economic, and environmental justice [53, 54]. Others have taken up these concerns as *information justice* (e.g., [55, 56]) or *algorithmic justice* [57] (see https://www.ajl.org/).

These discussions focus on the technical mechanisms needed to address questions of fairness, bias, and discrimination in algorithmic systems, as well the consequences suffered by individuals and groups from inaccurate, unfair, or unjust systems. With the deployment of predictive algorithms and machine-learning models as decision-support systems across many sectors—e.g., financial, health, and judicial—these consequences are of great concern [58].

For example, the work of Buolamwini and Gebru [39] revealed that a widely used facial recognition system was largely inaccurate in identifying darker-skinned females, with error rates close to 35%, compared to 1% for lighter-skinned males – suggesting that automated facial analysis algorithms and datasets can produce both gender and racial biases. Similarly, a widely used predictive algorithm used by judicial courts in the United States to predict recidivism rates for sentencing decisions was found to be more likely to incorrectly label Black defendants as higher risks compared to White defendants [59]. These cases illustrate the larger societal risks that arise from algorithmic decisions that lead to systematic bias against individuals within groups with protected social identities like race, gender, and sexuality [60, 61].

Even for non-marginalized populations, algorithmic bias can lead to decisions that limit opportunities, intentionally or not. When Amazon attempted to address gender gaps in its hiring, they implemented an applicant screening algorithm to predict applicants likely to match the qualities of past successful candidates [62]. But when the outcome widened gender gaps, they realized the dataset used to train the model included primarily successful *male employees*, thus making it less likely that *female applicants* would match the ideal [63]. In this case, the problem was not inaccuracies in the data or model but rather what was *missing*: there was insufficient data about females to model a fair representation of their goals [64].

Algorithmic bias has due process implications as well. For example, automated performance evaluation systems for public school teachers in California, New York, and Texas led to termination decisions, without informing the employees such tools were being used or providing meaningful opportunities for scrutiny and accountability. Such secret black box systems, especially in public agencies, generate a number of ethical concerns [65, 66].

On a societal level, the use of social credit scoring systems (SCS) also carries the potential for large-scale systematic violations of privacy and human rights. In China, a government-mandated SCS was implemented to strengthen social governance and harmony [67]. Every citizen was assigned a "trustworthiness" score, calculated from an algorithmic assessment of data from medical, insurance, bank, and school records; credit card and online transactions; satellite sensor data; mobile phone GPS data; and behavioral data from public cameras. Authorities use these data and the social credit score to evaluate and hold citizens accountable by imposing sanctions that range from restrictions on travel, bans on employment in civil service and public institutions, disqualification of children from private schools, and public disclosure of ratings on national websites [68]. Thus, the stakes of large-scale state surveillance include significant loss of freedoms of movement, employment, education, and reputation [41].

17.4.4 Non-maleficence and Beneficence: From Individual Risk to Collective Societal Good

17.4.4.1 Non-maleficence

Privacy ethics have long included attention to assessing the risk for individuals and adequately consider the safety, robustness, and protection of vulnerable populations. Indeed, much of the legal discourse about privacy protection and rights centers on the harmful consequences suffered when privacy is violated. However, harm remains narrowly defined and allows violations to go unpunished. In this section, we argue that broadening the ethical focus to one of *non-maleficence* — a call to ensure that our research conduct and technological designs also consider potential harms to society at large—provides an opportunity to broaden concerns beyond individual risk assessments to consider and assess long-term social, intellectual, and political consequences.

At the intersections of humans and technologies, there are significant privacy concerns, in particular for the young (Chap. 14 this volume), the vulnerable (Chap. 15, this volume) and the marginalized, that are exacerbated with contemporary technologies. Of specific concern are tools of authoritarian regimes that have clear and dangerous consequences when individuals can more easily be identified and targeted [35]. For example, it has recently come to light that facial recognition and other surveillance technologies are being used to identify, persecute, and imprison members of the Uyghur population in China [69]. Members of this community are considered enemies of the Communist Party and subjected to incarceration and, by some reports, torture, sterilization, and starvation. The determination of whether Uyghurs are imprisoned is built upon a massive system of government surveillance both in public spaces using a network of CCTV cameras equipped with facial recognition software as well as private spaces using spyware installed on smartphones, allowing the government to trace location, communication, and media use [70].

Another example of malicious, harmful technology is illustrated in the case of deepfake technologies. Deepfake technology uses machine learning algorithms to combine images and voices from one person into recordings of another to create a realistic impersonation that is difficult to detect as inauthentic. Doctoring images is not new, nor are harmful lies. But as Floridi [71] notes, deepfake technologies can also "undermine our confidence in the original, genuine, authentic nature of what we see and hear" (p. 320).

The sophisticated digital impersonation made possible with modern deepfake technologies is realistic and convincing in a way that carries the potential for significant harms. Typically created without the knowledge or consent of the individual and often in negative or undesirable situations, they present significant ethical violations and a wide array of harms. These harms include *economic* harms from extortions under threat to release the videos; *physical* and *emotional* harms from simulated violence and dignitary or *reputational* harms that include relationship loss, job loss, and stigmatization in one's community; and even *societal* harms when important political figures are depicted in damaging contexts, election results are manipulated, or trust is eroded in critical institutions [72]. As more of our identities shift into digital spaces, this array of harms is informationalized or spread beyond the bodily self to the networks of information that extend us digitally [15]. Thus, the potentials for harm are significantly amplified in a networked information environment context that facilitates wide distribution, viral spread, and infinite persistence of access.

17.4.4.2 Beneficence

If non-maleficence asks moral agents merely to avoid harms, the principle of *beneficence* shifts our focus to a positive account of doing good. Beneficence implies a balancing of tensions between individual and collective concerns to consider how we can design and conduct our research with a specific goal to benefit the well-being of society. This requires moving beyond the individual in a singular context of intrusion or data collection to consider collective responsibilities for environmental, social, and cultural well-being aligned with beneficent goals.

In the research context, this means asking not only *How do I avoid risks?* but also *How can I modify how I conduct my work so that it generates social good and contributes to well-being?* In the industry context, there have been growing movements to promote the specific design and deployment of technologies to serve broader social good—ICT4All and, for example AI4Good—particularly focusing on technologies to contribute to the social and economic development of underserved populations and countries [71]. Other calls have come from disciplines like human-computer interaction to discuss emerging policy needs for culturally sensitive HCI, accessible interactions, and the environmental impact of HCI [73].

The principles of non-maleficence and beneficence intersect as privacy practices and policies continue to negotiate value tensions between avoiding harms and managing risk and active engagement in developing or protecting privacy concerns. One example is the technologies and applications developed to minimize the risk and spread of infection during the COVID-19 pandemic. In order to manage the highly infectious disease, public health officials around the world raced to create technological and data analysis capabilities, including contact tracing, symptom tracking, surveillance, and enforcement of quarantine orders—typically enabled through mobile phones [74]. These health surveillance systems provide important capability to mitigate and manage the risks to global public health during the pandemic but also raise concerns about potential individual and societal-level privacy violations, both short term and long term. They seek to balance potential privacy harms against the good of public health.

Short-term concerns focus on the sharing of highly sensitive health, location, and behavioral data, complicated with disclosures of infectious health status. Long-term concerns center around the ambiguous end point for data collection and concerns that once allowed in order to mitigate a temporary emergency, surveillance will become permanent. Unfortunately, these concerns are warranted based on the history of previous surveillance activities enacted during crises: In the United States, there have been over 30 national emergencies declared providing emergency powers, including the domestic and international surveillance activities put in place after the September 11 terrorist attacks [75]. Balancing the clear long-term societal benefit of technologies to manage critical infection spread and reduce deaths and health-care costs, with short-term risks of disclosing sensitive personal information and long-term risks of continuous health surveillance, illustrates the ethical tensions of crisis contexts.

17.4.5 Explicability: From Data Transparency to Process Intelligibility

Ethical values are always tightly coupled to epistemic values, or values about what and how we know. Privacy ethics have long focused on the important epistemic principles of *transparency* (i.e., providing notice to individuals regarding the collection, use, and dissemination of personally identifiable information), as well as *accountability* (i.e., holding accountable compliance with privacy protection requirements) [76]. In the modern era, where the workings "inside the box" of complex systems are often invisible or unintelligible to most, these principles must be broadened to include requirements for *intelligibility (how does it work?)*, along with clear provenance of the data and people involved (*who is responsible for the way it works?*) [77].

Collectively this principle has been termed *explicability*, or the ability to obtain a clear and direct explanation of a decision-making process [71], cf. [78]. Explicability is especially salient in the case of algorithms and machine learning procedures and ensures individuals the right to know and understand what led to decisions that have significant consequence in their liberty, employment, and economic well-being: freedoms that are fundamental human rights protected by law.

Furthermore, as Floridi and Cowls [77] explain, explicability actually complements (or *enables*) the other principles: In order for designers and researchers to not constrain human *autonomy* and "keep the human in the loop," we must know how the technologies might act or make decisions (instead of us) and when human intervention or oversight is required; to assure *justice*, we need to be able to identify who will be held accountable and explain why there was a negative consequence, when there are unjust outcomes; and to adhere to values of *beneficence* and *non-maleficence*, we must understand how such technologies will benefit or harm our society and environment (p. 700).

Pasquale's *Black Box Society* [65] makes clear that algorithmic decision-making produces morally significant decisions with real-life consequences in employment, housing, credit, commerce, and criminal sentencing often without offering an explanation for how such decisions were reached. Civil society advocates have warned that "many of these techniques are entirely opaque, leaving individuals unaware whether the decisions were accurate, fair, or even about them" [79].

For example, algorithms are used in the criminal justice system to predict the probability of recidivism for individuals in parole and sentencing decisions. One such tool, the Correctional Offender Management Profiling for Alternative Sanctions (COMPAS), has been used in more than 1 million cases since 1998, yet research indicates the accuracy of predictions made by the algorithm is no more accurate than those made by people without criminal justice expertise [80]. Furthermore, although individuals are more likely to trust the accuracy of computational tools, research indicates the COMPAS tool led to racially-biased outcomes: it overestimated the rate at which Black defendants would reoffend and underestimated the rate at which White defendants would [59, 81]. Furthermore, when defendants challenged the decisions, they were unable to receive an explanation about the information used in the decision because the COMPAS creators claimed the algorithm was proprietary information [82]. In doing so, they violated the defendant's right to due process.

The factual context of a particular privacy problem is a key element of specifying ethical principles. The epistemic context is always tightly coupled to the ethical. In privacy eras of varying complexities, the explicability of data has an impact not only on the reception of ethics but also on the transmission: especially when artificial agents are included in those contexts. Like other ethical principles, the epistemic principle of explicability takes on an increasingly complex role. Whether in the context of predictive algorithms, surveillance by autonomous systems, or any other information context, epistemic values no longer merely focus on replicability or accuracy but instead on validity, transparency, and comprehensibility.

Emerging ethical challenges to core ethical principles shift the way principles are specified and balanced, adding complexity to their scope and focus. These challenges have direct implications for research policy and practice.

17.5   Guidelines for Research and Practice

In this next section, we connect the theoretical and applied to the practical, considering how an ethics literate perspective on privacy can inform the future of related policy and regulatory discussions (see [83]). While having the tools to engage with ethical principles has utility in the face of emerging technologies and unformed social norms, researchers and practitioners are still well served with additional resources for guidance in ethical decision-making.

Having worked through the reasons and justifications offered by ethical principles and frameworks, one might still ask how that work connects, practically, to our world bound by law and policy. Law and regulation provide actionable guidance and rules for professional conduct and technological development, codifying the reasoning outcomes of ethics. For example, the Privacy Act (1974), [27, 84] provide federal law to govern the collection, use, and dissemination of personally identifiable information in federal, health insurance, and telecommunication records in the United States; the Illinois Biometric Privacy Act (2008) extends protections to residents of the state of Illinois for biometric data; and the GDPR [85] provides regulatory protection of personal data for citizens of the European Union (see Chap. 18 for a review).

In research practice in the United States, ethical conduct for federally funded research involving human participants is guided by the Belmont Report [86], which applies the principles of beneficence, justice, and respect for persons to research practice. To assure compliance with these ethical guidelines, the Common Rule [87] codifies federal regulations for the protection of human subjects, with additional protections for vulnerable populations. Industry researchers are also typically required to abide by institutional policies or guidelines established for ethical practice (e.g., [88–90]).

Laws and regulations provide specific rules for ethical conduct and practice but can be dated in their relevance to today's technological contexts. Nearly 50 years have passed since the earliest privacy laws, and 30 years since the publication of the Common Rule, so there are inherently *gaps* in the relevance of legal and ethical guidelines established when computational technologies were in their infancy. Furthermore, the development of new law or international treaties takes time, resources, and significant negotiation, which means that "hard law" often lags behind the pace of development for innovative technologies (the "pacing problem"; [91]). For example, governments around the world are working to develop policy for the governance of AI technologies, as industries race to become global leaders in this field. Still others, such as the United States, have not yet passed comprehensive privacy legislation to address the unique challenges of modern contexts and technological capabilities.

These *gaps* in codified law and regulatory guidelines create challenges for researchers and designers when the technologies being tested and implemented are not specifically addressed. As we move into new eras, new contexts and technologies create new uncertainties in ethical decisions. However, "soft law" can fill the gaps until such hard codes are in place, or even where hard laws and regulations are in conflict with one another [91]. Wallach and Marchant [92] note that soft law measures—including technical standards, codes of conduct, curricular programs, and statements of principles—can also be promulgated by many stakeholders including "governments, industry actors, nongovernmental organizations, professional societies, standard-setting organizations, think tanks, public–private partnerships, or any combination of the above" (p. 506). Thus, soft law serves as an important complement to hard-coded law and regulation—particularly when norms and technologies are still developing.

17.5.1   Technical Standards

In some cases, there are government or industry *standards* available to provide specific guidance. For example, the National Institute of Standards and Technology

(NIST) in the United States provides industry standards for technologies, including a *privacy framework* guidebook for enterprise risk management [14]. In addition, the Institute of Electrical and Electronics Engineers (IEEE) professional society is a leading source for standards for emerging technologies with over 1300 standards [48] such as one for *data privacy* (P7002), recommended practice for *inclusion, dignity, and privacy in online gaming* (P2876), and one under development for *biometric privacy* (P2410). They have also published a resource guide for *ethically aligned design* for human well-being in autonomous and intelligent systems (IEEE EAD 2017).

17.5.2   Statements of Principles

Another set of resources are available in the form of *statements of principles* developed by scientific societies (e.g., ACM, AAAS, IEEE), civil society organizations (e.g., Electronic Privacy Information Center), think tanks (e.g., AI Now Institute), or government agencies. These principles are amalgams of value concerns identified by members of a specific community. One well-known set of principles for privacy researchers are the *Fair Information Practices* first published in 1973 through the US Department of Health, Education, and Welfare [76]. These included the now familiar concepts of *notice, consent, access, security*, and *redress* and laid important groundwork for subsequent legislation. The ACM professional society for computer scientists also releases regular policy statements on emerging technologies (see https://www.acm.org/public-policy), such as its *Statement of Privacy Principles* [93, 94], which outlines foundational principles of *fairness, transparency, collection limits, control, security, data integrity and retention*, and *risk management.*

Most recently, a number of principles have been released to address ethics for AI technologies (see [20]). The most significant is the Principles on AI released by the international Organisation for Economic Co-operation and Development [95]. These guidelines identified five values-based principles for trustworthy AI that closely align with *beneficence, justice, transparency, security*, and *accountability*. The OECD principles were subsequently endorsed by the G20 leaders in 2020, providing an important international agreement. In addition, global technology industries, such as Google, Microsoft, and IBM, have also contributed AI Principles to communicate to their clients and employees that their practices and technologies will be designed and implemented in ways that are trustworthy and adhere to consensus principles [88–90].

17.5.3   Codes of Conduct

Codes of ethics and professional conduct can also provide helpful guidance regarding practices specific to your profession. Some spell out clear consequences for conduct outside the bounds of acceptable behavior and practice (e.g., loss of funding, loss of rights to conduct research, loss of licensure, or loss of employment). For example, the ACM Code of Ethics [93] includes seven ethical imperatives and 18 professional responsibilities for those practicing in computer professions, including *respect for privacy and confidentiality*, *avoid harm*, *be fair and not discriminate*, and *contribute to human well-being* that again resonate with the principles outlined in this chapter [96].

17.5.4 Curricular Programs

Finally, curricular innovations are another approach under the umbrella of soft law. Public attention to questions of privacy and information ethics more generally has yielded calls for parallel attention to ethics education curricula at the collegiate level, in disciplines of computer science, engineering, and data science. To date, disciplines have been slow to integrate ethics modules or courses into their undergraduate and graduate curriculums (cf. [97, 98]). However, some early examples include the PRIME Ethics program developed for graduate students in science and engineering [12], which combines the reflexive principlism framework with discipline-specific case studies to strengthen ethical reasoning skills [99, 100]. In computer science, colleagues are beginning to develop ethics education activities for CS courses [101], and other universities, such as the Markkula Center for Applied Ethics, have developed ethics education modules for data ethics, software engineering, and technology practice (see https://www.scu.edu/ethics/ethics-resources/ethics-curricula/).

17.6 Conclusion

In this work, we asked: *What are the ethics of conducting privacy research and technology design, what new challenges do we face with next-generation technologies like AI, and how do the core questions we have relied upon for decades change in these new contexts?* To answer those questions, we argued that the contexts of sociotechnical privacy have evolved significantly in 50 years, with correlate shifts in the norms, values, and ethical concerns, and this has yielded significant eras of privacy (from 1.0 to 5.0), each with a broadening field of ethical concerns. We discussed these emerging ethical issues and introduced a *principlist framework* for privacy researchers to guide ethical decision-making. To summarize, we discussed that:

- Contexts of privacy have expanded from individual (1.0) to internet (2.0), to interdependence (3.0), to intelligences (4.0), to artificiality (5.0).

- Effective ethical decision-making (EDM) approaches are pluralistic, involving interface among ethical and epistemic principles as privacy paradigms evolve.
- Contemporary relationships between moral patients (receivers) and moral agents (transmitters) are shaped by digital information.
- Principles are reflexively applied in the ethical-decision making process.

We then discussed specific emerging privacy challenges and used the principlist framework to reframe privacy concerns amidst these emerging contexts and ethical questions, organizing the discussions around five ethical principles. To summarize, we discussed that:

- *Autonomy* shifts from data protection to multifaceted forms of intrusion and access.
- *Justice* shifts from material risk to fairness and due process.
- *Non-maleficence* and *beneficence* shift from individual harms to collective societal good.
- *Explicability* shifts from data transparency to process intelligibility.

Finally, we noted that while having the conceptual and reasoning tools to engage with ethical principles has utility in the face of emerging technologies and unformed social norms, researchers and practitioners are also well served with additional resources for guidance in ethical decision-making. We then briefly discussed soft law resources that can provide practical guidance in ethical decision-making, including technical standards, codes of ethical conduct, curricular programming, and statements of principles.

As researchers, we have an ethical obligation to ensure our research practice does not create undue intrusion on the people involved and that our results advance scientific knowledge to inform better practice. As designers, we have an ethical obligation to ensure the algorithms, applications, devices, and platforms we design yield intelligent agents that act and behave morally and contribute to the larger social good.

The notion of privacy is not dead but instead reborn in new form in the digital era: a fundamental human right deserving of protection and possibly under greater threat than any time of modern technological development. Striving for control of our own information, the right to manage it, strategies for understanding it and applying it fairly, and policies and practices to balance its harms and benefits will continue to be key foci of the ethics of privacy. But the mechanisms for intrusion on one's space, person, and identity are vastly more complex today than they were in the eras of Warren and Brandeis [102] and Westin [42], and the ethical concerns that come into play when we consider privacy ethics have now also broadened. Guidance for ethical decision-making, grounded in ethical principles, is a necessary tool in this challenging future.

References

1. Spector-Bagdady, K., and P.A. Lombardo. 2013. "Something of an adventure": Postwar NIH research ethos and the Guatemala STD experiments. *The Journal of Law, Medicine & Ethics* 41 (3): 697–710. https://doi.org/10.1111/jlme.12080.
2. Hudson, K.L., and F.S. Collins. 2013. Family matters. *Nature* 500 (7461): 141–142. https://doi.org/10.1038/500141a.
3. Skloot, R. 2018. *Immortal Life of Henrietta Lacks*. New York, NY: Crown.
4. Beauchamp, T.L., and J.F. Childress. 2019. *Principles of Biomedical Ethics*. 8th ed. Cambridge, UK: Oxford University Press.
5. Richardson, H.S. 2000. Specifying, balancing, and interpreting bioethical principles. *The Journal of Medicine and Philosophy* 25 (3): 285–307. https://doi.org/10.1076/0360-5310(200006)25:3;1-h;ft285.
6. Beever, J., and A.O. Brightman. 2015. Reflexive principlism as an effective approach for developing ethical reasoning in engineering. *Science and Engineering Ethics* 22 (1): 275–291. https://doi.org/10.1007/s11948-015-9633-5.
7. Steneck NH. 2019. *Introduction to the Responsible Conduct of Research*. Office of Research Integrity, Department of HHS. https://ori.hhs.gov/ori-introduction-responsible-conduct-research. Accessed 19 Feb 2021.
8. Nissenbaum, H.F. 2010. *Privacy in Context: Technology, Policy, and the Integrity of Social Life*. Stanford, CA: Stanford University Press.
9. 398 U.S. 347. 1967. *Katz v. United States, 389*. Retrieved from https://supreme.justia.com/cases/federal/us/389/347/.
10. 5 U.S.C. Sec 552a. 1974. *The Privacy Act of 1974*. Retrieved from https://www.justice.gov/opcl/privacy-act-1974
11. Floridi, L. 2015. *The Ethics of Information*. Oxford, UK: Oxford University Press.
12. Brightman, A., J. Beever, J. Hess, A. Iliadis, L. Kisselburgh, M. Krane, M. Loui, and C. Zoltowski. 2016. PRIME ethics: Purdue's reflective & interactive modules for engineering ethics. In *Infusing Ethics into the Development of Engineers: Exemplary Education Activities and Programs*, ed. National Academy of Engineering, 39–40. Washington, DC: National Academies Press.
13. Laney D. 2012. *Deja VVVu: Gartner's Original "Volume-Velocity-Variety" definition of big data*. https://community.aiim.org/blogs/doug-laney/2012/08/25/deja-vvvu-gartners-original-volume-velocity-variety-definition-of-big-data. Accessed 18 Feb 2021.
14. ———. 2018. *Privacy Framework*. National Institute for Standards and Technology. https://www.nist.gov/privacy-framework. Accessed 18 Feb 2021.
15. Kisselburgh, L. 2011. Privacy in networks. In *Encyclopedia of Social Networks*, ed. G. Barnett and J.G. Golson. Sage.
16. Beever, J. 2021. *Philosophy, Film, and the Dark Side of Interdependence*. Lanham, MD: Lexington Books.
17. Caine, K., L. Kisselburgh, and L. Lareau. 2011. Audience visualization influences online social network disclosure decisions. In *CHI EA 2011: Proceedings of the 2011 Annual Conference on Human Factors in Computing Systems*, 1663–1668. New York: ACM.
18. Kisselburgh, L. 2012. Privacy and social media ecologie. In *CSCW'12 Conference on Computer-Supported Cooperative Work*. New York, NY: ACM.
19. Lipford HR, Wisniewski P, Lampe C, Kisselburgh L, Caine K (2012) Reconciling privacy with social media. In *Proceedings of the 2012 Annual Conference on Computer-supported Cooperative Work Companion*, pp. 19–20.
20. Jobin, A., M. Ienca, and E. Vayena. 2019. The global landscape of AI ethics guidelines. *Nature Machine Intelligence* 1 (9): 389–399. https://doi.org/10.1038/s42256-019-0088-2.
21. Cottone, R.R., and R.E. Claus. 2000. Ethical decision-making models: A review of the literature. *Journal of Counseling and Development* 78 (3): 275–283. https://doi.org/10.1002/j.1556-6676.2000.tb01908.x.

22. Tuana, N. 2014. An ethical leadership development framework. In *The Handbook of Ethical Educational Leadership*, ed. C.M. Branson and S.J. Gross, 153–175. Hoboken, NJ: Taylor and Francis.
23. ———. 2007. Conceptualizing moral literacy. *Journal of Educational Administration* 45 (4): 364–378. https://doi.org/10.1108/09578230710762409.
24. Kuebler S, and Beever J. 2019 Who should self-driving cars be programmed to protect? UCF forum 339.
25. Smith A. 2020. Should we recognize privacy as a human right? In *National Magazine*. http://nationalmagazine.ca/en-ca/articles/law/in-depth/2020/should-we-recognize-privacy-as-a-human-right. Accessed 16 Feb 2021.
26. Beauchamp, T.L. 1995. Principlism and its alleged competitors. *Kennedy Institute of Ethics Journal* 5 (3): 181–198. https://doi.org/10.1353/ken.0.0111.
27. The Health Insurance Portability and Accountability Act of 1996 (HIPAA; Pub.L. 104–191, 110 Stat. 1936, enacted August 21, 1996).
28. Carter, S.M., W. Rogers, K.T. Win, H. Frazer, B. Richards, and N. Houssami. 2020. The ethical, legal and social implications of using artificial intelligence systems in breast cancer care. *The Breast* 49: 25–32. https://doi.org/10.1016/j.breast.2019.10.001.
29. Gao, Y., K.J. Geras, A.A. Lewin, and L. Moy. 2019. New frontiers: An update on computer-aided diagnosis for breast imaging in the age of artificial intelligence. *American Journal of Roentgenology* 212 (2): 300–307. https://doi.org/10.2214/AJR.18.20392.
30. Brožek, B., and B. Janik. 2019. Can artificial intelligences be moral agents? *New Ideas in Psychology* 54: 101–106. https://doi.org/10.1016/j.newideapsych.2018.12.002.
31. Bari, L., and D.P. O'Neill. 2019. Rethinking patient data privacy in the era of digital health. *Health Affairs*.
32. Nietzsche F. 2016/1885. *Thus spake Zarathustra: A book for all and None*. Thomas common (trans. https://www.gutenberg.org/files/1998/1998-h/1998-h.htm. Retrieved 1 May 2021.
33. United Nations. 1948. *The Universal Declaration of Human Rights*. https://www.un.org/en/universal-declaration-human-rights/. Accessed 19 Feb 2021.
34. Kak A. 2020. *Regulating Biometrics: Global Approaches and Urgent Questions*. AI Now Institute. https://ainowinstitute.org/regulatingbiometrics.pdf. Accessed 18 Feb 2021.
35. Polyakova A, and Meserole C. 2019. *Exporting Digital Authoritarianism: The Russian and Chinese Models*. Brookings Institute. https://www.brookings.edu/wp-content/uploads/2019/08/FP_20190827_digital_authoritarianism_polyakova_meserole.pdf
36. Kostka, G., L. Steinacker, and M. Meckel. 2020. Between privacy and convenience: Facial recognition technology in the eyes of citizens in China, Germany, the UK and the US. *SSRN Electronic Journal*. https://doi.org/10.2139/ssrn.3518857.
37. Banerjee, S., and S. Sharma. 2019. Privacy concerns with Aadhaar. *Communications of the ACM* 62 (11): 80–80. https://doi.org/10.1145/3353770.
38. Ranganathan, N. 2020. The economy (and regulatory practice) that biometrics inspires: A study of the Aadhaar project. In *Regulating Biometrics: Global Approaches and Urgent Questions*, ed. A. Kak, 52–61. New York: AI Now Institute.
39. Buolamwini, J., and T. Gebru. 2018. Gender shades: Intersectional accuracy disparities in commercial gender classification. *Proceedings of Machine Learning Research* 81: 1–15.
40. Pasquale, F. 2018. When machine learning is facially invalid: Observations on the use of machine learning and facial inferences to classify people using inexplicable data. *Communications of the ACM* 61 (9): 25–27.
41. ———. 2020. *New Laws of Robotics Defending Human Expertise in the Age of AI*. Cambridge, MA: Harvard University Press.
42. Westin, A.F. 1970. *Privacy and Freedom*. New York: Atheneum.
43. Saks, E., L. Dunn, J. Wimer, M. Gonzales, and S. Kim. 2013. Proxy consent to research: The legal landscape. *Yale Journal of Health Policy, Law, and Ethics* 8 (1): 37–92.
44. Levine, R.J. 1995. Research in emergency situations. The role of deferred consent. *JAMA-J Am Med Assoc* 273 (16): 1300–1302. https://doi.org/10.1001/jama.273.16.1300.

45. Nissenbaum, H.F. 2018. Stop thinking about consent: It isn't possible and it isn't right. *Harvard Bus Review*, 19–22.
46. Fiesler, C., N. Beard, and B.C. Keegan. 2020. No robots, spiders, or scrapers: Legal and ethical regulation of data collection methods in social media terms of service. *Proceedings of the International AAAI Conference on Web and Social Media* 14: 187–196.
47. Friedman, B., and H. Nissenbaum. 1996. User autonomy: Who should control what and when? In *CHI '96: Conference Companion on Human Factors in Computing Systems*. New York: ACM.
48. IEEE. 2018. Ethically aligned design: A vision for prioritizing human well-being with autonomous and intelligent systems. https://standards.ieee.org/content/dam/ieee-standards/standards/web/documents/other/ead_v2.pdf. Accessed 18 Feb 2021.
49. Dow K, and Hancock M. 2018. *Injecting Ethical Considerations in Innovation via Standards – Keeping Humans in the AI Loop*. IEEE Insight. https://insight.ieeeusa.org/articles/standards-address-ai-ethical-considerations/.
50. Shneiderman, B. 2020. Bridging the gap between ethics and practice. *ACM Transactions on Interactive Intelligent Systems* 10 (4): 1–31. https://doi.org/10.1145/3419764.
51. Friedman, B., and P.H. Kahn. 2007. Human values, ethics, and design. In *The Human-Computer Interaction Handbook: Fundamentals, Evolving Technologies and Emerging Application*, ed. A. Sears and J.A. Jacko, 2nd ed., 1177–1201. Boca Raton: CRC Press.
52. Cavoukian A. 2009 Privacy by design: The seven foundational principles. https://iapp.org/resources/article/privacy-by-design-the-7-foundational-principles/. Accessed 18 Feb 2021.
53. Ada Lovelace Institute. 2020. Examining the black box: Tools for assessing algorithmic systems. https://www.adalovelaceinstitute.org/report/examining-the-black-box-tools-for-assessing-algorithmic-systems/. Accessed 18 Feb 2021.
54. Hao K. 2021. *Deepfake Porn Is Ruining Women's Lives. Now the Law May Finally Ban It*. MIT Technology Review. https://www.technologyreview.com/2021/02/12/1018222/deepfake-revenge-porn-coming-ban/. Accessed 15 Feb 2021.
55. Butcher, M.P. 2009. At the foundations of information justice. *Ethics and Information Technology* 11 (1): 57–69. https://doi.org/10.1007/s10676-009-9181-2.
56. O'Neil, C. 2018. *Weapons of Math Destruction: How Big Data Increases Inequality and Threatens Democracy*. London: Penguin Books.
57. Re, R.M., and A. Solow-Niederman. 2019. Developing artificially intelligent justice. *Stanford Technology Law Review* 22: 242.
58. Binns, R. 2018. Fairness in machine learning: Lessons from political philosophy. *Proceedings of Machine Learning Research* 81: 149–159.
59. Angwin J, Larson J, Mattu S, Kirchner L. 2016. *Machine Bias*. ProPublica. https://www.propublica.org/article/machine-bias-risk-assessments-in-criminal-sentencing. Accessed 18 Feb 2021.
60. Noble, S.U. 2018. *Algorithms of Oppression: How Search Engines Reinforce Racism*. New York: New York University Press.
61. Ferguson, A.G. 2019. *Rise of Big data policing: Surveillance, race, and the future of law enforcement*. New York, NY: New York University Press.
62. Hamilton, R.H., and W.A. Sodeman. 2019. The questions we ask: Opportunities and challenges for using big data analytics to strategically manage human capital resources. *Business Horizons* 63 (1): 85–95. https://doi.org/10.1016/j.bushor.2019.10.001.
63. Reuters. 2018. Amazon ditched AI recruiting tool that favored men for technical jobs. In *The Guardian*. https://www.theguardian.com/technology/2018/oct/10/amazon-hiring-ai-gender-bias-recruiting-engine. Accessed 18 Feb 2021.
64. Williams, B.A., C.F. Brooks, and Y. Shmargad. 2018. How algorithms discriminate based on data they lack: Challenges, solutions, and policy implications. *Journal of Information Policy* 8: 78–115. https://doi.org/10.5325/jinfopoli.8.2018.0078.
65. Pasquale, F. 2016. *Black Box Society: The Secret Algorithms that Control Money and Information*. Cambridge, MA: Harvard University Press.

66. Reisman D, Schultz J, Crawford K, and Whittaker M. 2018. Algorithmic impact assessments: A practical framework for public agency accountability. In *AI Now Institute*. https://ainowinstitute.org/aiareport2018.pdf. Accessed 16 Feb 2021.
67. Botsman R. 2017. *Big Data Meets Big Brother as China Moves to Rate Its Citizens*. WIRED. https://www.wired.co.uk/article/chinese-government-social-credit-score-privacy-invasion. Accessed 18 Feb 2021.
68. Chen, Y., and A.S.Y. Cheung. 2017. The transparent self under big data profiling: Privacy and Chinese legislation on the social credit system. *SSRN Electronic Journal* 12 (2): 25–27. https://doi.org/10.2139/ssrn.2992537.
69. Mozur P. 2019. *One Month, 500,000 Face Scans: How China Is Using A.I. to Profile a Minority*. The New York Times. https://www.nytimes.com/2019/04/14/technology/china-surveillance-artificial-intelligence-racial-profiling.html. Accessed 18 Feb 2021.
70. Roberts, S.R. 2020. *The War on the Uyghurs China's Campaign Against Xinjiang's Muslims*. Manchester, UK: Manchester University Press.
71. Floridi, L., J. Cowls, M. Beltrametti, R. Chatila, P. Chazerand, V. Dignum, C. Luetge, R. Madelin, U. Pagallo, F. Rossi, B. Schafer, P. Valcke, and E. Vayena. 2018. AI4People—An ethical framework for a good AI society: Opportunities, risks, principles, and recommendations. *Minds and Machines* 28 (4): 689–707. https://doi.org/10.1007/s11023-018-9482-5.
72. Citron, D.K., and R. Chesney. 2019. Deep fakes: A looming challenge for privacy, democracy, and national security. *California Law Review* 107: 1753. https://doi.org/10.2139/ssrn.3213954.
73. Kisselburgh, L., M. Beaudouin-Lafon, L. Cranor, J. Lazar, and V. Hanson. 2020. HCI ethics, privacy, accessibility, and the environment: A town hall forum on global policy issues. In *CHI2020: Proceedings of the 38th Annual CHI Conference on Human Factors in Computing Systems*. Honolulu, HI: ACM.
74. Li, T. 2020. Privacy in pandemic: Law, technology, and public health in the COVID-19 crisis. *SSRN Electronic Journal* 52 (3). https://doi.org/10.2139/ssrn.3690004.
75. Boudreaux, B., M.A. Denardo, S.W. Denton, R. Sanchez, K. Feistel, and H. Dayalani. 2020. Data privacy during pandemics: A scorecard approach for evaluating the privacy implications of COVID-19 mobile phone surveillance programs. RAND Corporation.
76. U.S. Department of Health, Education and Welfare. 1973. *The Code of Fair Information Practices*. Secretary's advisory committee on automated personal data systems, records, computers, and the rights of citizens viii.
77. Floridi, L., and J. Cowls. 2019. A unified framework of five principles for AI in society. *Harvard Data Science Review* 1 (1). https://doi.org/10.1162/99608f92.8cd550d1.
78. Robbins, S. 2019. A misdirected principle with a catch: Explicability for AI. *Minds and Machines* 29 (4): 495–514. https://doi.org/10.1007/s11023-019-09509-3.
79. The Public Voice. 2018. *Universal Guidelines for AI*. https://thepublicvoice.org/ai-universal-guidelines/. Accessed 19 Feb 2021.
80. Dressel, J., and H. Farid. 2018. The accuracy, fairness, and limits of predicting recidivism. *Science Advances* 4 (1): aao5580. https://doi.org/10.1126/sciadv.aao5580.
81. Barocas, S., and A.D. Selbst. 2016. Big Data's disparate impact. *California Law Review* 104 (3): 671–732. https://doi.org/10.2139/ssrn.2477899.
82. Loomis v. Wisconsin, 881 N.W.2d 749 (Wis. 2016), cert. denied, 137 S.Ct. 2290 (2017).
83. Diamantopoulou and King, this volume.
84. The Family Educational Rights and Privacy Act (FERPA) of 1974 (20 U.S.C. § 1232g; 34 CFR Part 99).
85. European Parliament and Council of European Union. 2016. *Regulation (EU) 2016/679*. ("General Data Protection Regulation"). Retrieved from https://eur-lex.europa.eu/legal-content/EN/TXT/HTML/?uri=CELEX:32016R0679&from=EN
86. National Commission for the Protection of Human Subjects of Biomedical and Behavioral Research. 1979. *The Belmont Report: Ethical Principles and Guidelines for the Protection of Human Subjects of Research*.

87. 45 CFR Part 46. 1991. Federal policy for the protection of human subjects ("the Common Rule").
88. IBM. 2018. *IBM'S Principles for Data Trust and Transparency*. IBM. https://www.ibm.com/blogs/policy/trust-principles/. Accessed 15 Feb 2021.
89. Microsoft. 2018. Responsible AI principles from Microsoft. https://www.microsoft.com/en-us/ai/our-approach-to-ai. Accessed 18 Feb 2021.
90. Pichai S. 2018. AI at Google: Our principles. https://www.blog.google/technology/ai/ai-principles/. Accessed 18 Feb 2021.
91. Marchant, G.E. 2011. The growing gap between emerging technologies and the law. In *The Growing Gap Between Emerging Technologies and Legal-Ethical Oversight: The Pacing Problem*, ed. G.E. Marchant, B.R. Allenby, and J.R. Herkert, 19–33. Cham: Springer.
92. Wallach, W., and G. Marchant. 2019. Toward the agile and comprehensive international governance of AI and robotics. *Proceedings of the IEEE* 107 (3): 505–508. https://doi.org/10.1109/jproc.2019.2899422.
93. Association for Computing Machinery. 2018. ACM code of ethics and professional conduct. https://www.acm.org/code-of-ethics. Accessed 18 Feb 2021.
94. USACM. 2018. Statement on the importance of preserving personal privacy. In *Association of Computing Machinery*. https://www.acm.org/binaries/content/assets/public-policy/2018_usacm_statement_preservingpersonalprivacy.pdf. Accessed 15 Feb 2021.
95. Organisation for Economic Co-operation and Development. 2019. Principles on artificial intelligence. https://www.oecd.org/going-digital/ai/principles/. Accessed 18 Feb 2021.
96. Gotterbarn, D., A. Bruckman, C. Flick, K. Miller, and M.J. Wolf. 2018. ACM code of ethics: A guide for positive action. *Communications of the ACM* 61 (1): 121–128. https://doi.org/10.1145/3173016.
97. Beever J, Kuebler SM, Collins J (2021) Where ethics is taught: An institutional epidemiology. *International Journal of Ethics Education* 6 (2): 215–238.
98. Karoff P. 2019. *Harvard Works to Embed Ethics in Computer Science Curriculum*. Harvard Gazette. https://news.harvard.edu/gazette/story/2019/01/harvard-works-to-embed-ethics-in-computer-science-curriculum/. Accessed 15 Feb 2021.
99. Hess, J.L., J. Beever, C.B. Zoltowski, L. Kisselburgh, and A.O. Brightman. 2019. Enhancing engineering students' ethical reasoning: Situating reflexive principlism within the SIRA framework. *Journal of Engineering Education* 108 (1): 82–102. https://doi.org/10.1002/jee.20249.
100. Kisselburgh LG, Hess J, Zoltowski C, Beever J, Brightman AO (2016) Assessing a scaffolded, interactive, and reflective framework for developing ethical reasoning skills of engineers. In *Proceedings of the 2016 American Society for Engineering Education*, New Orleans.
101. Skirpan, M., N. Beard, S. Bhaduri, C. Fiesler, and T. Yeh. 2018. Ethics education in context: A case study of novel ethics activities for the CS classroom. In *Proceedings of the 49th ACM Technical Symposium on Computer Science Education*. New York: ACM. https://doi.org/10.1145/3159450.3159573.
102. Warren, S.D., and L.D. Brandeis. 1890. The right to privacy. *Harvard Law Review* 4 (5): 193–220. https://doi.org/10.2307/1321160.

Chapter 18
EU GDPR: Toward a Regulatory Initiative for Deploying a Private Digital Era

Vasiliki Diamantopoulou, Costas Lambrinoudakis, Jennifer King, and Stefanos Gritzalis

Abstract Nowadays, people and enterprises put effort in protecting systems and applications that handle personal data and also in protecting digital footprints, and they realize that the concept of privacy protection is continuously evolving, depending on each environment. Admittedly, there is a plethora of digital products or services that necessitates the provision of personal data.

The GDPR came into effect to establish a more concrete framework for the protection of EU citizens' personal data. The impact of this regulation goes beyond the boundaries of EU in two ways. Firstly, the GDPR acts as a facilitator of non-EU enterprises that wish to do business and interact with EU citizens. Secondly, the GDPR, due to its wide applicability and generality, can be used as a basis and inspiration for other countries to establish their own data protection regulations and legal frameworks.

This chapter consists of guidance for organizations to be able to reach compliance with the GDPR, regarding the protection of the personal information they process. Also, this chapter presents the impact that the GDPR has brought to the global landscape, because of its wide territorial scope and the expanded approach of the various definitions of data protection concepts being used.

V. Diamantopoulou (✉)
Department of Information and Communication Systems Engineering, University of the Aegean, Samos, Greece
e-mail: vdiamant@aegean.gr

C. Lambrinoudakis · S. Gritzalis
Department of Digital Systems, University of Piraeus, Piraeus, Greece
e-mail: clam@unipi.gr; sgritz@unipi.gr

J. King
Stanford Institute for Human-Centered Artificial Intelligence, Stanford University, Stanford, CA, USA
e-mail: kingjen@stanford.edu

© The Author(s) 2022
B. P. Knijnenburg et al. (eds.), *Modern Socio-Technical Perspectives on Privacy*,
https://doi.org/10.1007/978-3-030-82786-1_18

427

18.1   Introduction

The necessity of preserving individuals' privacy is becoming of utmost importance as technology advances [1, 2]. Organizations serving every sector must respect the personal data they process, demonstrating compliance with the corresponding regulatory schemas, according to the territory they act and to the individuals' origins. However, the concept of the protection of privacy is treated differently according to the specific context in which it is applied. The legal sector, like the Information Technologies (IT) sector, also has to deal with the problem of defining and dealing with the concept of personal data protection. The global landscape is changing step by step, developing regulatory frameworks aligned with the dramatically increased technological advances [3–5]. The European General Data Protection Regulation (GDPR) [6] is the "golden standard" in Data Protection Law globally, with various countries around the world implementing or amending local legislation in the areas of data protection and privacy, based on a core set of principles in common with the GDPR. We expect that the regulatory schemas around the world will contribute toward a harmonized addressing of the protection of personal data.

This chapter concerns both the scope of privacy protection and the policies and regulatory framework that ensure it. Personal data, which concerns every piece of information that is related to a natural person, has received increased attention lately, mainly regarding its protection. The level of protection that is demanded is determined by the type of processing applied to the data, its combination with other information, and by the environment in which it is used and evaluated. Today, the possibilities of collecting, processing, disseminating, and correlating the information generated by the information and communication systems in general-as well as the possibility of using, exchanging, and correlating the data collected for multiple and different purposes than those for which they were collected. This directly affects the life and communication of individuals, their personality, and their habits, and has also highlighted the qualitative dimension for the risks of natural persons. We are now aware that the increase in the processing capabilities of personal information is related inversely proportional to the ability of the person to supervise the use of information relating to them.

The issue of privacy is not a new matter of concern for the "Information Society," nor is it a unique one. It is related to the social environment; its size, structure, and nature; and the emergence of new social spaces and fields of activity of people [7, 8]. New communication technologies change the reality and the notion of "private" and "public." These new technological advances include the Internet of Things, behavioral marketing, the use of Big Data, and blockchain technology. In addition to the above, and to a much greater extent, the available communication and expression platforms offered through Web 2.0 have been enriched, with platforms such as social platforms, e-participation platforms, consultation sites, and more.

This chapter presents the impact that the GDPR has brought to the global landscape. In many cases (countries), it is obvious that the GDPR acts as an inspiration for the development of other legal frameworks, being used as an international model, due to its wide territorial scope as well as the expanded definitions of data protection concepts (being used). From a business perspective, the GDPR has strengthened the control of the consumers over their data, adding rights that they can exercise to protect their personal data and helping in raising awareness on the use of this data. Also, the GDPR puts in place requirements for data controllers and data processors, such as data protection-by-design and data protection-by-default, implementation of appropriate technical and organizational controls that ensure the security of their information systems, and recording of processing activities, to name a few. Finally, the GDPR activates the "consent" that the data subject/consumer has to provide to the data controller in order for the latter to process the personal data of the first. All these requirements act as control elements for every data subject that is related to the EU. Consequently, organizations that act on a worldwide scale are enforced to apply all the privacy requirements enforced by the GDPR, making GDPR a facilitator for the protection of data subjects' personal data in a broader level of applicability.

This chapter aims at the analysis of privacy concerns from the legal perspective in order for organizations, private or public ones, to be able to be compliant with the GDPR, regarding the protection of the personal information they process. To this end, we proceed in the next sections with the analysis of the GDPR, and specifically, by focusing on the main changes of the regulation compared with the previous European Directive 95/46/EC [9], highlighting the major changes in the legal framework. Moreover, we provide a "to do list" describing ten discrete steps for compliance of data processors and data controllers who process EU citizens' personal data. Finally, we present the current status of the global legal perspective, emphasizing the influence of the GDPR to other legal frameworks around the world.

18.2   Data Protection in EU

To further government protection of individual privacy, more than 20 years ago, the European Union aligned data protection standards within the countries—Member States in order to facilitate cross-border data transfers internally in the EU. At that time, national data protection laws provided considerably different levels of protection and could not offer legal certainty neither for individuals nor for data controllers and processors. In 1995, the European Community therefore adopted Directive 95/46/EC [9] of the European Parliament and of the Council of 24 October 1995 on the protection of individuals with regard to the processing of personal data and on the free movement of such data (hereafter, Data Protection Directive). The aim of this directive was the harmonization of the protection of fundamental rights of individuals with regard to data processing activities, ensuring, in parallel, the flow of personal data between EU Member States in a free and unobstructed way. However, the continuous growth and evolution of technology have taken place at such a pace that the existing legal frameworks had become obsolete, calling for an adaptation of the corresponding legislation. The GDPR that replaces Directive 95/46/EC builds on the principles and rules of the pre-existing Directive, but it is differentiated in the volume of the enhancement of the rights of the Data Subjects, it appoints responsibility to the data controllers and processors for the protection of personal data they keep, by bringing forth the concept of self-regulation and accountability, and it increases the sanctions related to the violations of its provisions. Detailed analysis of the new concepts the GDRP brings is provided in Sect. 18.2.2.

In addition to the Data Protection Directive, the ePrivacy Directive 2002/58/EC provides data protection rules for telecommunications networks and internet services. This Directive is due to be repealed by the ePrivacy Regulation. The European Commission adopted a proposal for ePrivacy Regulation on 10 January 2017; it is currently under discussion in the European Parliament and the Council of the European Union. These Directives have emerged as necessary tools to use in the internal market in which goods, services, capital, and people should move freely.

18.2.1 General Data Protection Regulation (EU) 2016/679

The GDPR is a new regulation, which brings new obligations, new rights to the world formed by Information and Communication Technologies, and the globalization of information flows and services. The orientation of the Regulation is to support the security of personal data so that it can then support citizens' rights. It lays down the requirements for the protection of individuals with regard to the processing of personal data and the free movement of such data. It is mandatory for public and private organizations that manage personal data of European citizens. The aim is for citizens in the European Union to gain (more) control of their personal data.

18.2.2 Introduction of the New Concepts of the GDPR

The new Regulation is based on the concept of privacy as a fundamental human right [10, 11]. The EU's landmark in the evolution of its privacy framework is an attempt to change data controllers' and data processors' mentality about the uncontrolled processing of individuals' personal data they process. Additionally, the use of IS's for unknown (i.e. other than those clearly stated) purposes is a major problem for democracy in an information society. Consequently, the implementation of the GDPR is not tertiary, and it is of major importance for the citizens' own life; this orientation was given by the European Parliament.

Many of the concepts of the GDPR are not new ones but have their origin in the replaced Directive 95/46/EC. One of the main drivers of the new regulation can be considered the need for modernization. The use of new technological achievements has invaded individuals' lives and threaten their privacy. New or advanced online services and technologies have been introduced, such as social networks, location-based services, cloud computing, data processing, and storage capabilities, to name a few. As an outcome of this technological invasion, decisions can be taken based on the automated processing of personal data, ignoring transparency and fairness. Another driver for the GDPR can be considered the control over individuals' personal data and the self-regulation of organizations, as an answer to the complexity of the previous regulatory environment (e.g. notification to several data protection authorities). Additionally, the territorial scope of the GDPR has changed, since its applicability concerns not only EU countries but every organization that processes EU residents' personal data. All these issues have been taken into consideration in the various articles of the GDPR, and appropriate actions are enforced in order to protect individuals' personalities.

In particular, the major breakthroughs of the GDPR are summarized in the following list:

- **Definition of Personal Data**. Additionally to the definition of personal data presented in Directive 95/46/EC which mentions that it is any information relating to an identified or identifiable natural person (i.e. the data subject), the GDPR has added *location data, an online identifier*, as well as factors specific to the *genetic identity* of a natural person, besides physical, physiological, mental, economic, cultural, or social identity, already included in Directive 95/46/EC.
- **Definition of Special Categories of Personal Data**. In special categories of personal data, GDPR includes the processing of *genetic data* and *biometric data for the purpose of uniquely identifying a natural person*, apart from personal data revealing racial or ethnic origin, political opinions, religious or philosophical beliefs, or trade union membership, data concerning health or data concerning a natural person's sex life or sexual orientation, already included in Directive 95/46/EC.
- **Data Controller's responsibilities**: The GDPR describes precisely the term of the data controller as well as its roles and responsibilities. Compared with Directive 95/46/EC, where they are the ones who must implement appropriate technical and organizational measures to protect personal data against accidental or unlawful destruction or accidental loss, alteration, and unauthorized disclosure or access, the data controller shall now implement appropriate technical and organizational measures to ensure and to be able to demonstrate that processing is performed taking into account the *nature, scope, context*, and *purposes of processing* as well as *the risks of varying likelihood and severity for the rights and freedoms of natural persons*. Moreover, data controller shall implement appropriate data protection policies, in relation to processing activities.
- **Jurisdiction**: This point presents another dimension in the territorial scope of the application of the Regulation, since it applies, now, to the processing of personal data in the context of the activities of an establishment of a controller or a processor in the European Union, *regardless of whether the processing takes place in the Union or not*. This requirement relates with processing regarding *the offering of goods or services, or the monitoring of their behavior as far as their*

behavior takes place within the Union. To this end, every organization around the world that processes personal data of EU citizens must comply with the GDPR, regardless of their place of establishment.

- **Consent Management**: The way the data subject is providing their consent to anyone asking to process their personal data has now changed: consent should be freely given, specific, informed, and unambiguous. Consent should be given *by a statement or by a clear affirmative action.* In this way, the data subjects are given the opportunity/ability to gain control over the management of their data, and the controllers can manage the provided consent as a proof for their legal processing. It is worth noting in this point that the consent should concern a specific data processing activity, clearly described to the data subject. If, for any reason, the data controller wishes to use a data subject's personal data for a different data processing activity, this should be described as a consent related to the new processing activity.
- **Breach notification**: In Directive 95/46/EC, there wasn't any reference regarding the notification of the supervisory authorities when a data breach occurs. The GDPR describes this process as an obligation assigned to the data controller, highlighting the short time period that they should react, by informing the supervisory authorities *without undue delay and, where feasible, not later than 72 h after having become aware of it.* Reference is also made to the notification of data subjects, if there is a risk for their rights and freedoms.

The GDPR does not introduce many substantially new concepts, but it increases the compliance requirements of data controllers and data processors. Moreover, this regulation encourages the use of certification schemes like ISO 27001 [12] to serve the purpose of demonstrating that the organization is actively managing its data security in line with international best practices.

18.2.3   Ten Steps for Compliance of Data Processors and Data Controllers

GDPR extends the scope of existing legislation to all EU or non-EU controllers who process personal data of citizens of the EU Member States and imposes compliance on a sufficiently rigorous legislative framework. With the enforcement of the Regulation, companies face new data protection obligations, as well as a reinforcement of pre-existing obligations under the GDPR. The very wide scope of application of the GDPR is based mainly on the intention to capture the challenges of the global economy, the new emerging technologies, and the new business models that organizations apply [13].

Moreover, the impending fines imposed by the GDPR have been significantly increased, reaching up to €20,000,000.00 or up to 4% of the total worldwide annual turnover (GDPR/Art. 83, Sec. 5) Thus, it is imperative for the companies to carefully reorganize their internal data protection procedures in order to reach compliance with the GDPR [14].

The following ten steps can be considered as the basis to achieve compliance with the requirements of the regulation:

1. **Privacy awareness—readiness of the organization**. Probably this is the most critical point. Organizations should consider compliance with the GDPR as a systematic action, that is supported by appropriate for the needs, the volume, and the culture of the organization planning. In this step, focus should be given to the human resources of the organization as the success of it is based on the awareness that will have been achieved among the employees, the third parties, and any other associate of the organization. Moreover, organizations have to be prepared that the project of compliance with the GDPR is an ongoing process that potentially can increase the workload.

   - All business processes associated with personal data have to be assessed and potentially redesigned based on the preservation of individuals' privacy.
   - The organization should implement an organizational framework according to which there will be roles with responsibilities for the protection of personal data. The framework should include at least the roles of the data protection officer, the information systems' lead developer, the information technology (IT) manager, and the information systems auditor.
   - The organization should conduct an assessment of all important "gaps" related to the requirements of the GDPR, taking into account the required data protection policies, documentation, and implemented security measures.

2. **Develop and maintain Record of Processing Activities** The organization should recognize the processing purposes that it serves and all related processing activities, paying attention to the fact that many of them may not be immediately visible, such as document archive, staff file, customer file, electronic application files, contact files for communication purposes, security files-camera material, online access logs, etc. Each processing activity should be distinguished per processing purpose.
   Then the organization should explore whether there is an obligation to maintain a record of processing activities (GDPR/Art. 30), although it is certainly a good practice to do it. An obligation exists if the organization employs more than 250 persons or if processing poses a risk to the rights of the data subjects or if it involves special categories of personal data (i.e., "sensitive" data) or data relating to criminal convictions. The development of a comprehensive inventory of enterprise information resources (data inventory) and the implementation of an appropriate data classification scheme are proposed. The information to be kept includes:

   - Contact details of the Data Controller, its representative, and the appointed DPO-if any
   - The processing purposes

- A description of the categories of Data Subjects
- A description of the categories of personal data
- Whether the organization transfers data to non-EU countries
- The deletion deadline for each data category and the legal basis for this decision
- A general description of the technical and organizational security measures taken by the organization

3. **Designate a Data Protection Officer (DPO)** The obligation to designate a Data Protection Officer applies to:

- All public authorities or bodies, except for courts acting in their judicial capacity (GDPR/Art. 37a). Examples of this category are ministries, hospitals, telecommunications, and transport.
- Organizations that perform regular and systematic monitoring[1] of data subjects on a large scale (GDPR/Art. 37b). Examples of this category are security service providing companies, call centers, marketing companies, etc.
- The core activities of the organization consist of large-scale processing of special data categories (GDPR/Art. 37c). Examples of this category are clinical studies companies and research centers.

The senior management designates a Data Protection Officer, a competent person reporting directly to the senior management without receiving any instructions on how to perform their tasks as a Data Protection Officer. The senior management shall ensure that the Data Protection Officer is not dismissed or penalized for performing their tasks. The Data Protection Officer should have direct access to the senior management, and the data subjects of the personal data should have clear access to the Data Protection Officer. The Data Protection Officer may also have other responsibilities, but the organization ensures that no "conflict of interests" arises due to these additional professional duties and obligations. The Data Protection Officer is responsible for all matters relating to the protection of personal data in the organization. Therefore, he/she must have access to all databases and organization's systems. The Data Protection Officer is bound by terms of confidentiality.

The role of the Data Protection Officer is to advice the data controller/processor, organize training/awareness programs, act as an internal auditor on personal data issues, and monitor compliance with legal requirements. Furthermore, the Data Protection Officer is the point of contact with the data protection authorities as well as with the data subjects.

---

[1] This activity can refer either to online monitoring, such as location tracking services, or processing that aims to define a particular behavior or the subject of the personal data for advertising purposes, such as behavioral advertising, and data subject's profiling based on specific personal data, such as identification of consumer identity, preferences, favorite stores (profiling).

The Data Protection Officer should have the following knowledge and skills:

- Specialized knowledge of the legal framework for the protection of personal data at national and European level.
- Basic knowledge of Information Security and Information Systems in order to be able to understand, design, and supervise the implementation of a personal data protection program.
- Communication skills and persuasion in order to be able to report directly to senior management and persuade them to support the compliance and personal data protection program.
- Appropriate experience to coordinate the internal team dealing with the personal data protection program, as the team leader.

The specialization level of the Data Protection Officer is not explicitly defined in the GDPR but it should be proportional to the risk level of the organization, as well as to the level of complexity of the organization's business processes and the volume of the processing of personal data.

The organization assigns to the Data Protection Officer the following responsibilities:

- To represent the organization vis-à-vis the authorities, national and European.
- To advise the senior management on data protection issues.
- To suggest the appropriate data protection policies directly to senior management.
- To monitor and harmonize the operation of the organization, when acting either as a Data Controller or as a Data Processor with regard to the policies, practices, and methodologies of processing, storing, and transferring personal data.
- To protect the organization when acting either as a Data Controller or as a Data Processor from the risks of getting penalized with the substantial and heavy administrative fines provided by the Regulation.
- To ensure the support of the senior management and the required budget for implementing the data protection program.
- To develop the data protection program and the data protection policy and supervise their implementation, to evaluate the degree of participation and success, and to make the necessary corrections where necessary.
- To establish an inventory of Personal Data categories that relates to the type of personal data, the way the data is stored and processed, the time allowed for their retention, and the methodology for deleting or destroying them.
- To assess and advise on a case-by-case basis for establishing a Data Protection Impact Assessment Method and performing Privacy Impact Assessment.
- To coordinate the interdepartmental collaboration with the Human Resources, Information Security, Information Systems, Legal and Regulatory Compliance, and Marketing and Procurement departments to

create a sustained corporate data protection culture as a valuable corporate asset.

- To design and implement internal training programs and maintain the required training completion records by department/group of employees.

Finally, the organizational structure of the organization should reflect the distinct role of the Data Protection Officer.

4. **Ensure consent of data subjects when necessary** The organization must record the legal basis for the processing of the data. When consent is the legal basis for the processing of personal data, it must be provided by the Data Subject. The data controller must be able to prove that:

- They have obtained the consent of the data subjects.
- The consent is "free."
- The consent is specific and explicit for a well-defined processing purpose.
- The consent has been obtained with a clear positive action (e.g., filling in a box when visiting a website, selecting desired technical settings for a service, etc.). Silence, pre-filled boxes, or inactivity should not be taken as consent.
- For underage persons the consent is considered to be "valid" when the child is at least 16 years of age. Otherwise, consent must be given by the person who has parental responsibility.

Prior to the consent process, the organization must inform the Data Subject, at least for all the essential elements of the processing:

- The identity and contact details of the Data Controller
- The identity and contact details of the Data Protection Officer
- Third parties and recipients potentially involved in data processing
- The purposes and legal basis of the processing
- The period of data retention
- The intention of cross-border transfer
- The Data Subject's rights

This information should be in visible form, easily accessible, and understandable so that the Data Subject has a real choice. Moreover, the consent procedure must be user-friendly to avoid ambiguities. The Data Subject must be able to withdraw its consent at any time. However, it must be ensured that the Data Subjects have access to their current status of consent at any time and can change their settings or withdraw their consent completely. So far, numerous fines have been imposed on various organizations across Europe and beyond, because of their inadequacy to prove that they have obtained the consent of the data subject in a free and unambiguous way.[2] For example, consent should not be requested via a document that also includes other matters (e.g., general Terms and Conditions) as this should be regarded as "blurring" the consent.

---

[2] https://gdpr-fines.inplp.com/list/.

An entity must be capable of providing a proof of validity of obtained consent, otherwise the legal requirement for GDPR compliance is not met [15].

5. **Apply privacy-by-design and privacy-by-default principles** The protection of personal data and privacy can be improved and enhanced by designing information systems in a way that reduces the degree of invasion in privacy. Privacy by design, or Data Protection by Design (GDPR/Art. 25), is an approach that requires the integration of the key protection parameters by the controller into existing wider project management and risk management methodologies and policies. GDPR provisions facilitate this direction by requiring controllers (companies, organizations, etc.) to ensure that the protection of users' privacy is a basic parameter in the early stages of each project and then throughout its life cycle [16, 17]. To achieve that it is important to consider issues like state-of-the-art technology developments, cost of implementing the protection measures, nature—scope—context and purposes of processing, and minimization of threats against the rights and freedoms of individuals from processing. In this area belong a series of methodological frameworks [18–22] and tools [19, 23–25] that help analysts, designers, and developers to develop IS's that privacy will be a built-in and not an add-on feature as it happens many times.

Privacy, in order to be included as a concept in the software development cycle, should be transformed into a technical requirement. Thus, during the development of new IT systems, the organization should identify technical ways for the protection of personal data. To this respect, the Information Systems Development Officer consults the Data Protection Officer and opts for a development method that supports the identification and modelling of data protection mechanisms during the analysis of the overall system's specifications prior to the implementation.

As far as the privacy by default approach, it requires to ensure that, by definition, only the personal data necessary for the specific purpose is processed, and at the same time it is necessary that the "default" settings of the applications be as privacy-friendly as possible.

Based on the above, the organization shall ensure, when procuring new systems, that appropriate technical ways for the protection of personal data are followed. The Information Systems' Lead Developer seeks advice from the Data Protection Officer and ensures that each procurement notice for a new IT system includes in the obligations of the contractor the identification and modelling of personal data protection standards and the integration of specifications into the new system during development. The organization's Information Systems vendors must demonstrate that they have applied the principles that the law requires in the solutions to be used by the organization. This requires special attention when recording specifications and evaluation criteria for the acquisition of a new Information System.

6. **Protect processing of personal data—conduct Data Protection Impact Assessment**

The organization must plan the protection of personal data, taking into account the risk of processing to the rights and freedoms of natural persons, and the nature, scope, context, and purposes of the processing. While Directive 95/46/EC implies the requirement for risk management procedures, GDPR clearly proposes the implementation of management processes that will facilitate the objective assessment of risks in order to determine whether the data processing operations involve a risk or a high risk for the natural persons (GDPR/Art. 35).

A data protection impact assessment, and hence, the criticality of data shall (in accordance with the GDPR) particularly be required in the case of:

- A systematic and extensive evaluation of personal aspects relating to natural persons which is based on automated processing, including profiling, and on which decisions are based that produce legal effects concerning the natural person or similarly significantly affect the natural person (e.g., user profiling by web search activity monitoring for targeted advertising and promotion of products and services (hotels, restaurants, etc.))
- Processing on a large scale of special categories of data referred to in Article 9(1), or of personal data relating to criminal convictions and offences referred to in Article 10 (e.g., processing of patients' medical records (special category of personal data) from healthcare organizations, including medical history, illnesses, and patient care)
- A systematic monitoring of a publicly accessible area on a large scale (e.g., traffic monitoring for informing drivers of the fastest route, residence entries' monitoring, and public transport entrance)

The concept of risk management becomes even more clear in GDPR since it imposes the requirement for an impact assessment (when a type of processing, in particular using new technologies and taking into account nature, scope, context, and processing purposes, is likely to cause a high risk to the rights and freedoms of natural persons), a very risk-centric process.

In general, Impact Assessment is one of the most useful tools for identifying and assessing risks to privacy when a controller employs new technologies, products, or services. To this end, a variety of methodologies have been proposed, several of which are also included in the guidelines of the Article 29 Working Party [26]. However, data protection impact assessment processes are not included in most risk management standards, are often not embedded in an organization's broader risk management framework, and are even less relevant to an organization's internal business processes [27]. Taking into account the systems' and threats' continuous evolution, risk management "necessitates" the identification of appropriate controls. The processing of personal data, hierarchy, and the management of risks have to be examined in a way that optimizes the cost and contributes to the most suitable decision-making, aiming at protecting personal data. Impact assessment contributes to the application of privacy principles, in a way that the data subjects are able to preserve control of their personal data.

An integrated risk management process should support the ability to control and limit the risk at all levels, while assessing how the impact of a specific risk compares with the consequences that may be caused by some other risk. Risk management, in the framework of privacy protection, can have many common elements with risk management for the protection of personal data in an organization (e.g., security, information systems, etc.). Their successful combination allows optimization of resources (human and technical) and better risk management [28].

The Data Protection Impact Assessment (DPIA) should provide:

- A systematic description of the processing activities envisaged, the purposes of the processing and its legal basis
- An assessment of the necessity and proportionality of the processing activities
- A risk assessment on the rights and freedoms of data subjects
- The anticipated risk mitigation measures

while in terms of the protection (security) of the processing activities it is necessary for the organization to propose the appropriate/suitable technical and organizational measures. Indicatively:

- Pseudo-anonymization and encryption
- Ensuring privacy, integrity, availability, and reliability
- Restoration of availability and access in the event of an incident
- Testing, assessing, and continually evaluating the effectiveness of the protection measures

7. **Develop Data Protection Policy** Organizations need to update/enhance their data protection policies in relation to the existing legal framework. The data protection policy generally includes the purpose and the objectives set by the management with regard to the protection of personal data, as well as the instructions, procedures, rules, roles, and responsibilities related to the protection of such data. The implementation of the data protection policy is binding for all employees and associates of the organization. This means that compliance with the procedures and directives it provides is mandatory for all employees and associates of the organization directly or indirectly involved in the operational processes involving the processing of personal data. With the help of the data protection policy, the organization seeks to achieve the following goals:

- The protection of natural persons whose personal data is processed by the organization.
- The identification of the risks involved in the processing of personal data by the organization.

- The implementation of rules and techniques in order to satisfy the legitimate rights of the natural persons whose personal data is processed by the organization.
- The compliance with the requirements set by the European and national legal framework.

The data protection policy attempts to define commonly accepted principles, ways, and responsibilities governing the processing of personal data. The data protection policy is not only about technical or organizational issues, but it treats both categories with the same attention.

A data protection policy should provide information on:

- The legal basis for the processing (which "complicates" the information as it requires legal analysis)
- The time frame that the processing/storage will take place
- The existence of any automated decision-making process, including profiling, with information on possible consequences
- Data collected from other sources
- The Data Protection Officer's data
- The procedures employed in order to satisfy all data subjects' rights

The data protection policy is not a static document but should be kept as up to date as possible and adjusted in line with the changes of IS and the technical and social environment. It is also updated in the event of major changes to the organization or its IT systems.

8. **Data breach** The organization is considered as being aware of a data breach after it is has been confirmed that an event that results in undermining of personal data has occurred. The timely detection and evaluation of a data breach incident are extremely crucial. It should be noted that the Data Controller is considered aware of the breach only after the initial investigation of the event (which must begin as soon as possible) and upon its classification as an incident. Whether it is immediately clear that personal data is at stake or whether this conclusion takes some time to achieve, emphasis must be given to direct action to investigate the incident in order to determine whether there has actually been a violation of personal data. As soon as the short investigation period has passed, and the Data Controller has confirmed the incident, it is deemed to be aware and then notification to the supervisory Authority is required (GDPR/Art. 33). When the Data Processor detects the breach, it should promptly notify the Data Controller of the violations. This notice must be "immediate" to help the Data Controller comply with the time commitments. Moreover, if the Data Processor offers services to more than one Data Controllers, it must report the incident and details about it, to each of them.

A prerequisite to achieve the timely detection of a breach is to make clear what constitutes it, since what may be considered a breach for one organization may not for another. It will be beneficial for an organization to have a list of events that are considered as breaches so as not to lose time by investigating these events in real time. For example, any successful SQL connection from an IP outside a known and pre-defined IP range, or if any file is being accessed from a file server outside business hours.

When a potential data breach occurs, and provided there is a risk for natural persons, the organization, when acting as a Data Controller, must inform the competent supervisory authority *without delay and, if possible, no later than 72 h from the time it occurred.*

The organization must design procedures that describe how it communicates with the Supervisory Authority and the information that will be communicated to them. The organization must state:

- The nature of the violation, including, if possible, the categories and number of affected Data Subjects, and the categories of data
- The name and contact details of the Data Protection Officer
- The possible impact of the violation
- The controls taken or proposed to be taken to address the breach

In addition, the organization must inform the Data Subjects for the violation of their data, if the data breach may pose a high risk to their rights and freedoms. Thus, the organization must design procedures that describe how it communicates with the Data Subjects and the information that will be communicated to them. This information must be concise, transparent, comprehensible, and easily accessible. The organization must use clear and plain language, especially when the information concerns children. The procedures should include providing information through hardcopy forms, electronic announcements, or even orally once the identity of the Data Subject has been confirmed.

9. **Organizations operate in more than one EU Member States**
   If the controller is active in more than one Member States, the country of the main establishment should be designated (GDPR/Art. 51). This article spares the organization the requirement to get to grips with several different laws of the various countries of the organization's activity. Thus, in the case of cross-border processing, the "one-stop-shop" mechanism [29, 30] is supported by the implementation of the GDPR, ensuring the cooperation between the corresponding Data Protection Authorities of each country.
   The data protection authority of the country that the organization has its main establishment is considered as the Lead Supervisory Authority for the organization. This is identified as the organization's central administration in the EU unless decisions about the purposes and means of processing of personal data are taken in another establishment and that establishment has the power to implement those decisions. If the organization processes data in order to fulfill an obligation under the national law of an EU Member State, only the DPA of that EU Member State is competent.

For the identification of the above, it is therefore important for the organization to clearly determine:

- The place/country of the main establishment (headquarters)
- Potential other facilities within EU
- The place/country where the basic decisions for processing are taken (in the headquarters or not)
- The existence of joint data controllers

10. **Transfer personal data to non-EU countries**
    In cases where the data controller must transfer personal data to non-EU countries, it is required to ensure that this transfer is conducted with respect to the legal requirements being imposed by the GDPR (GDPR/Art. 44). Transfer of personal data to a third country or an international organization is realized under the following conditions:

- Transfers subject to appropriate safeguards: EC has decided that the third country, a territory or one or more specified sectors within that third country, or the international organization in question ensures an adequate level of protection (GDPR/Art. 45). EC has already recognized the appropriateness of some countries around the world,[3] with this list being updated.
- Transfers subject to appropriate safeguards: The data controller or data processor has provided appropriate safeguards (GDPR/Art. 46), and on condition that enforceable data subject rights and effective legal remedies for data subjects are available:

    - Binding corporate rules (GDPR/Art. 47)
    - Standard data protection clauses (EC) (GDPR/Art. 46)
    - Codes of conduct (GDPR/Art. 40)
    - Certification mechanism (GDPR/Art. 42)

Then it is important to assess and select an appropriate transmission mechanism and also to explore whether it has an obligation to inform the persons whose data will be is transferred.

18.3 Global Privacy Landscape

The demand for the protection of personal data is not limited to Europe. Citizens and consumers around the world are increasingly demanding privacy. And in turn, companies are recognizing that providing strong privacy protection gives them a competitive advantage as confidence in their services increases. Many, especially those with global reach, are under pressure to align their policies with the GDPR,

---

[3] https://bit.ly/2XR5TSE.

not only because they want to do business in Europe, but also because the GDPR has become the "golden standard" in Data Protection Law globally.

The quintessence of the global impact of the GDPR is encapsulated in this rule: the GDPR applies to any entity doing business in the EU regardless of whether the service provider has a presence in the EU or the recipient of the service is an EU citizen or resident.[4]

The global significance of the GDPR is exemplified by the fine of 50 million Euros that the French National Data Protection Commission (CNIL) imposed for its violation on the global tech giant Google. The CNIL enforcement action focused in particular on the GDPR's transparency and consent requirements and at the same time provided useful guidance on how to design privacy policies.[5]

Furthermore, in recent years, increasing numbers of countries around the world have implemented new or amended legislation in the areas of data protection and privacy, based on a core set of principles in common with the GDPR. These include, inter alia, the recognition of data protection as a fundamental right; the adoption of overarching legislation in the field; the existence of enforceable individual privacy rights; and the setting up of an independent supervisory authority.[6] Of new or modernized laws that overlap up to 80% with the GDPR, a few have been enacted as recently as 2018, such as the Brazilian General Data Protection Law[7] that is very closely modeled on the GDPR or India's Personal Data Protection Bill[8] (to be enacted) that contains GDPR-inspired provisions around consent and the right to be forgotten.

On January 23, 2019, the EU Commission adopted its adequacy decision on Japan, allowing personal data to flow freely from the EU to Japan on the basis of mutually agreed data protection standards. In addition, and for the first time in the history of EU adequacy discussions, Japan is also granting an equivalent status to the EU, thus creating the first mutual system for data flows. This is also the first adequacy decision granted on the basis of the GDPR.[9]

---

[4] Article 3 GDPR. See also Recital 24 of the GDPR clarifies that tracking individuals on the Internet to analyze or predict their personal preferences—as many websites and apps do—will trigger the application of EU law.

[5] https://www.cnil.fr/en/cnils-restricted-committee-imposes-financial-penalty-50-million-euros-against-google-llc.

[6] In 2015 the number of countries that had enacted data privacy laws stood at 109, a significant increase from 76 in mid-2011. As of May 2019, the number has climbed to more than 120 countries.

[7] The Brazilian General Data Protection Law "Lei Geral de Proteçao de Dados" (LGPD) was adopted on August 18th and will come into force in early 2020. See the English translation in https://iapp.org/media/pdf/resource_center/Brazilian_General_Data_Protection_Law.pdf.

[8] https://www.meity.gov.in/writereaddata/files/Personal_Data_Protection_Bill,2018.pdf.

[9] Commission Implementing Decision (EU) 2019/419 of January 23, 2019, pursuant to Regulation (EU) 2016/679 of the European Parliament and of the Council on the adequate protection of personal data by Japan under the Act on the Protection of Personal Information (Text with EEA relevance), OJ L 76, 19.3.2019, p. 1–58 ELI.

Following a review of the Privacy Shield (the framework arrangement between the European Union and the USA to enable the transfer of personal data between the two) by the European Data Protection Board (EDPB)10 and a formal complaint by the French digital rights group, La Quadrature du Net, the General Court of the EU on July 1st and 2nd of 2019 struck down the Privacy Shield, ruling it insufficient in terms of data protection according to EU law. As such, international companies cannot rely merely on the Privacy Shield and must separately determine whether their data privacy practices adhere to the GDPR.

Privacy shield was meant as a placeholder (SCC) to allow for transfer to the USA in light of government surveillance. It got contested in Schrems I, Schrems II and La Quadrature du Net. In Schrems II, the CJEU decided that privacy shield did not apply because surveillance is not limited to strictly necessary and proportional, and there is no judicial redress. This means that companies cannot rely on privacy shield for transfer to USA and other countries as well, and must determine whether surveillance (or other practices) meets these limitations and requirements, set up legal export mechanisms. If not, additional protections are required (e.g. encryption), or transfer must be suspended.

Especially for countries with a surveillance regime that is incompatible with the GDPR requirements for privacy and due process. Get transparency from and control over the importer, so that the exporter can verify GDPR compliance.

Despite the worldwide influence of the GDPR, as of 2021 the USA remains disconnected from the global conversation on privacy. The California Consumer Privacy Act (CCPA), which went into effect in January 2020, was spurred by growing consumer unease with data collection. Like the GDPR, it provides certain rights to consumers-including the right to information and access to personal data, the right of erasure, and the right to opt-out-and, at the same time, greatly expands the definition of personal data.[10] However, the law is limited in its scope (it applies to businesses with a gross annual revenue of $25MM USD; or, drives 50% of their revenue from data sales of California residents; or, businesses that buy, receive, or sell the personal information of 50,000 or more California residents, households, or devices) and only provides rights to California residents. While other US states have attempted to pass similar legislation, these efforts as of yet have been unsuccessful. These attempts also highlight the divergence of agreement in US discussions around data privacy. Despite widespread consumer interest and attention from legislators, discussions at the US federal level continue to stall. However, if enough US states are successful in their efforts to pass privacy legislation, this will put pressure on federal legislators to harmonize the varying laws. Additionally, a second California privacy law, the California Privacy Rights Act (CPRA) that was approved by voters in November of 2020 and set to go into effect in 2023, may further increase this urgency. The CPRA also establishes the first US state-level regulatory agency

---

[10] For the CCPA core requirements, see https://www.dataprotectionreport.com/2018/06/california-passes-major-privacy-legislation-expanding-consumer-privacy-rights/ or https://oag.ca.gov/privacy/ccpa.

devoted to overseeing California's privacy laws, and once established, may even exceed the size of the Federal Trade Commission's privacy and consumer protection division, responsible for enforcing consumer privacy protections across the entire USA.

Based on the recent examples referred to above, it is expected that the GDPR will continue to operate as a trigger for non-EU countries to adopt much higher data protection standards than they do today. This, in turn, should lead to greater upward convergence of data protection principles internationally, at both bilateral and multilateral levels—a goal which is in the interest and to the benefit of citizens and businesses alike wherever they are in the globalized world. Released from the bottle, the privacy genie isn't likely to be returned. Even companies that may not directly engage in business with the EU would be wise to be aware of the GDPR's provisions and consider proactive compliance in anticipation of continued international adoption of its core principles.

18.4   Conclusions

The protection of personal data is becoming an issue that now, more than ever, affects all organizations around the world. The global scene has changed dramatically during the last few years because of the vast technological advancements affecting every sector. To this end, the reforming of the existing regulatory schemas in order to capture the mechanisms and the technologies that are used for the processing of personal data was of utmost importance. European Commission with the GDPR aimed to define a harmonized framework of action with respect to individuals' privacy. Existing national laws were too difficult to be controlled, leaving room for derogations. After the establishment of the GDPR, other nations followed this example, either by being based on this regulation and developing their own (i.e., LGPD of Brazil), by establishing frameworks in alignment with the European regulation in order to be able to transfer personal data (i.e., Privacy Shield, between EU and USA), or by demonstrating that they have undertaken all the necessary actions,[11] ensuring an adequate level of protection.

---

[11] https://ec.europa.eu/info/law/law-topic/data-protection/data-transfers-outside-eu/adequacy-protection-personal-data-non-eu-countries_en.

Compliance with the GDPR comprises a challenging project for organizations for a series of reasons; the complexity of business activities and the duplication of data (in different information flows or even entire departments within an organization) are the most important ones. However, even if organizations need to comply with the GDPR, they lack guidelines that could help them into reaching compliance. There are already products being developed that can be used toward this compliance; however, none of the current technical solutions is able to capture the current security status of an organization, identify the gaps, assess the criticality of the processing activities and the personal data that they use, provide concrete solutions tailored to each organization to finally fortify its processes, and guarantee the protection of individuals' personal data [31]. The "ten steps for compliance" list that is provided in this work aims to facilitate data processors/controllers toward their compliance. Of course, if organizations have already been certified under a specific certification schema (e.g., ISO 27001), they have already satisfied a part of the requirements that the GDPR requests, which means that less effort is required [32].

References

1. Solove, D.J. 2004. *The Digital Person: Technology and Privacy in the Information Age*. Vol. 1. NyU Press.
2. DeVries, W.T. 2003. Protecting privacy in the digital age. *Berkeley Technology Law Journal* 18: 283.
3. Goddard, M. 2017. The EU general data protection regulation (GDPR): European regulation that has a global impact. *International Journal of Market Research* 59 (6): 703–705.
4. Safari, B.A. 2016. Intangible privacy rights: How Europe's GDPR will set a new global standard for personal data protection. *Seton Hall Law Review* 47: 809.
5. Greengard, S. 2018. Weighing the impact of GDPR. *Communications of the ACM* 61 (11): 16–18.
6. European parliament. 2016. Regulation (EU) 2016/679 of the European parliament and of the council of 27 april 2016 on the protection of natural persons with regard to the processing of personal data and on the free movement of such data, and repealing directive 95/46/ec (general data protection regulation).
7. Acquisti, A., S. Gritzalis, C. Lambrinoudakis, and S. di Vimercati. 2007. *Digital Privacy: Theory, Technologies, and Practices*. CRC Press.
8. Gritzalis, S. 2004. Enhancing web privacy and anonymity in the digital era. *Information Management & Computer Security* 12 (3): 255–287.
9. European commission. 2017. Directive 95/46/ec of the European parliament and of the council. http://eur-lex.europa.eu/legal-content/EN/TXT/?uri=CELEX:31995L0046, Accessed 14 May 2017.
10. Warren, S.D., and L.D. Brandeis. 1890. Right to privacy. *Harvard Law Review* 4: 193.
11. Westin, A.F. 1968. Privacy and freedom. *Washington and Lee Law Review* 25 (1): 166.
12. ISO/IEC. 2013. ISO 27001:2013 information technology—security techniques—information security management systems—requirements. Tech. Rep.
13. Voigt, P., and A. Von dem Bussche. 2017. The EU general data protection regulation (GDPR). A Practical Guide. 1st ed. Cham: Springer International Publishing.
14. Lambrinoudakis, C. 2018. The general data protection regulation (GDPR) era: Ten steps for compliance of data processors and data controllers. In *International Conference on Trust and Privacy in Digital Business*, 3–8. Springer.

15. Fatema, K., E. Hadziselimovic, H.J. Pandit, C. Debruyne, D. Lewis, and D. O'Sullivan. 2017. Compliance through informed consent: Semantic based consent permission and data management model. In *PrivOn@ ISWC*.
16. Cavoukian, A., et al. 2009. Privacy by design: The 7 foundational principles. Information and Privacy Commissioner of Ontario, Canada. Vol. 5.
17. Langheinrich, M. 2001. Privacy by design principles of privacy-aware ubiquitous systems. In *International Conference on Ubiquitous Computing*, 273–291. Springer.
18. Deng, M., K. Wuyts, R. Scandariato, B. Preneel, and W. Joosen. 2011. A privacy threat analysis framework: Supporting the elicitation and fulfillment of privacy requirements. *Requirements Engineering* 16 (1): 3–32.
19. Bijwe, A., and N.R. Mead. 2010. Adapting the square process for privacy requirements engineering. Technical Note.
20. Kalloniatis, C., E. Kavakli, and S. Gritzalis. 2008. Addressing privacy requirements in system design: The Pris method. *Requirements Engineering* 13 (3): 241–255.
21. Jensen, C., J. Tullio, C. Potts, and E.D. Mynatt. 2005. Strap: A structured analysis framework for privacy. Tech. Rep., Georgia Institute of Technology.
22. Islam, S., H. Mouratidis, C. Kalloniatis, A. Hudic, and L. Zechner. 2012. Model based process to support security and privacy requirements engineering. *International Journal of Secure Software Engineering (IJSSE)* 3 (3): 1–22.
23. Kalloniatis, C., E. Kavakli, and E. Kontellis. 2009. Pris tool: A case tool for privacy-oriented requirements engineering. In *MCIS*, 71.
24. He, Q., A.I. Antón, et al. 2003. A framework for modeling privacy requirements in role engineering. In *Proc. of REFSQ*, 137–146. Vol. 3.
25. Liu, L., E. Yu, and J. Mylopoulos. 2003. Security and privacy requirements analysis within a social setting. In *Proceedings of 11th IEEE International Requirements Engineering Conference*, 151–161. IEEE.
26. Party, D.P.W. 2017. Guidelines on data protection impact assessment (DPIA) and determining whether processing is "likely to result in a high risk" for the purposes of regulation 2016/679.
27. Wright, D., K. Wadhwa, M. Lagazio, C. Raab, and E. Charikane. 2014. Integrating privacy impact assessment in risk management. *International Data Privacy Law* 4 (2): 155–170.
28. Notario, N., A. Crespo, Martín, Y.S., Del Alamo, J.M., Le Métayer, D., T. Antignac, A. Kung, I. Kroener, and D. Wright. 2015. Pripare: Integrating privacy best practices into a privacy engineering methodology. In *2015 IEEE Security and Privacy Workshops*, 151–158. IEEE.
29. Tambouris, E., and M. Wimmer. 2005. Online one-stop government: a single point of access to public services. In *Electronic Government Strategies and Implementation*, 115–144. IGI Global.
30. Sedek, K.A., S. Sulaiman, and M.A. Omar. 2011. A systematic literature review of inter-operable architecture for e-government portals. In *2011 Malaysian Conference in Software Engineering*, 82–87. IEEE.
31. IAAP. 2018. Privacy tech vendor report. Tech. Rep.
32. Diamantopoulou, V., A. Tsohou, and M. Karyda. 2019. General data protection regulation and iso/iec 27001:2013: Synergies of activities towards organisations' compliance. In *International Conference on Trust and Privacy in Digital Business*. Springer.

Chapter 19
Reflections: Bringing Privacy to Practice

Jennifer Romano and Liz Keneski

Abstract We interviewed a panel of 13 applied researchers to understand why applied and academic privacy researchers do not collaborate more often. While many agree about the benefits of collaboration, they simply do not collaborate due to real and perceived barriers, such as timelines, goal differences, and data-sharing difficulties. We synthesize the findings and provide actionable recommendations to help bridge the gap between academic and applied research.

19.1 Introduction

In our work across academic and applied settings—from research agencies to in-house research teams, from scrappy start-ups to established organizations—we have identified a hole. Academics and applied researchers are not collaborating, and those collaborations that exist are rare. The collaborations are rare enough that we, and the editors of this book, decided to raise awareness by publishing this book. We hope you, the reader who has made it to the final chapter, agree.

One might wonder why bridging applied, or "industry," and academic privacy research is an important issue. As the other chapters in this book have demonstrated, academics are tackling big, important privacy issues. However, they are not necessarily the same big, important privacy issues that we in industry attempt to tackle. We believe it is essential to work together:

1. **In order for applied privacy researchers to utilize the foundation that privacy academics have built.** This can inform our very fast-moving applied work.

J. Romano (✉)
Google, New York City, NY, USA
e-mail: jennifer@romanocog.com

L. Keneski
Facebook, Boston, MA, USA
e-mail: lizkenes@fb.com

B. P. Knijnenburg et al. (eds.), *Modern Socio-Technical Perspectives on Privacy*,
https://doi.org/10.1007/978-3-030-82786-1_19

449

2. **In order for privacy academics to understand the problems that applied industry is facing.** This can make academic research farther reaching and applicable to real-world problems.

In order to provide a broad and balanced opinion informed by diverse experiences, we believe collaboration is essential. Industry folks are moving fast and are often thinking about issues in an applied context, which sometimes varies from academic researchers. Academics, on the other hand, have the wealth of knowledge from both their own past work and that of others and the time to ponder issues at length. It is only by collaborating that we can get these diverse viewpoints in the same room.

> There is a lot of distance between privacy in the books and privacy on the ground. Scholarly debate about privacy is important—it helps guide discussion.
> – Trevor Hughes, International Association of Privacy Professionals

In an effort to share the landscape, we believed it was important to talk to fellow applied researchers working outside of academia and to synthesize their views alongside ours. We conducted one-on-one interviews with a panel of 13 applied researchers who have engaged in academic collaborations and/or other cross-industry research endeavors. Further, we solicited input and feedback from the Privacy Research Teams at Google and Facebook. What follows in this chapter is a synthesis based on these researchers' and our experiences, advice, and hopes for the future of privacy research across academic and applied contexts.

Our panel consisted of:

- **Anja Dinhopl:** Google Privacy Safety & Security Team. Anja is a UX research manager at Google, responsible for ensuring that privacy settings are communicated in the most understandable and intuitive way to users under the age of 18. Anja previously worked at Facebook, leading a research team focused on understanding how children, teenagers, and families use and get the most from online services.
- **Carol Smith:** Carnegie Mellon University's Software Engineering Institute. Carol worked previously at Uber ATG (self-driving). In a 20-year career spanning work across multiple industries and now working in academia, Carol has a unique point of view between them. Since 2015, her work with AI systems has increased her concerns about preserving privacy. In response, she has been developing methods and tools to support responsible system development.
- **Gretchen Gelke:** Google Privacy and Data Protection Office (PDPO). In her 20+ year career, Gretchen has worked in industry, healthcare, government, and educational settings, conducting and leading research efforts on a range of topics. Privacy, security, and safety themes have always been a part of her research, ultimately leading her to specialize in privacy and security UX at Google, an area of research that is significantly benefited by the work happening across domains, to include academia and industry.
- **Heather Desurvire:** Google Ads; Interactive Media and Games Department at the University of Southern California. Heather's prior work involved game

companies through her agency User Behavioristics, such as EA, Disney, Blizzard, and King.

- **Janaina Pantoja:** eBay. Janaina worked previously at Walmart. Janaina is a former neuroscientist and has over 15 years of professional experience across design and academic research. She manages a team of design researchers at eBay, and prior to that, she led strategic research initiatives at Walmart. Janaina strives for social impact with her work and is energized by connecting with people and their stories. Janaina is the vice president of the User Experience Professionals Association.
- **Janice Tsai**: Google. Janice is a privacy engineer on the Android Security and Privacy team; a former research scientist at Mozilla, working on voice and emerging technologies; and a privacy and ethics manager at Microsoft working in marketing, Microsoft Research, and Windows.
- **Jofish Kaye**: Mozilla. Jofish previously worked at Yahoo and Nokia. Jofish ran a team building a privacy-preserving open-source voice assistant, Firefox Voice, as well as running the Mozilla Research Grants program.
- **Jules Polonetsky:** Future of Privacy Forum (FPF). Jules serves as CEO of the Future of Privacy Forum, a Washington, D.C.-based nonprofit organization that serves as a catalyst for privacy leadership and scholarship, advancing principled data practices in support of emerging technologies. Jules previous roles have included serving as Chief Privacy Officer at AOL and before that at DoubleClick, as Consumer Affairs Commissioner for New York City, as an elected New York State Legislator and as a congressional staffer, and as an attorney. Jules is a co-editor of *The Cambridge Handbook of Consumer Privacy*, published by Cambridge University Press (2018).
- **Julie Schiller:** Google NBU. Julie worked previously at Facebook. Julie works as part of the Next Billion Users initiative (https://nextbillionusers.google/) and has previously worked on research questions around identity, security, and effects of digital advertising. She shares her work regularly at conferences and journals and finds the partnership of academia and industry to be a powerful structure to create thoughtful technology.
- **Kat Lo:** Content Moderation Lead, Meedan; Affiliate, UC Irvine Center for Responsible, Ethical, and Accessible Technology. Kat worked previously at Instagram. Kat works with civil society groups, academia, and targets of online harassment to increase transparency of content moderation processes, accessibility to industry expertise, and efficacy of advocacy for human rights issues in social media product development.
- **Katie Giari:** Google Ads. Katie works on enterprise ad products at Google. She focuses on strategic projects, such as understanding the needs of Gen Z content creators and the impact of privacy regulations on the ads industry.
- **Rebecca Destello:** Facebook; University of Washington. Rebecca is a Research Manager at Facebook where she leads teams who work on projects aimed to improve the quality of experiences in Facebook's Community products. Rebecca also serves as an Affiliate Faculty member at the University of Washington's Human Centered Design & Engineering (HCDE) department where she has been

teaching graduate students in user-centered design, design thinking, research, usability testing, and web design since 2012.

- **Trevor Hughes:** International Association of Privacy Professionals (IAPP). Trevor leads a professional association of over 70,000 privacy professionals and provides oversight of the large research and editorial agenda at IAPP.

And us!

- **Jennifer Romano:** Google Ads; University of California, Berkeley Extension; University of Maryland. Jen leads a UX team at Google who focuses on privacy and innovation in the ads industry, and she teaches at UC Berkeley Extensiton and University of Maryland. In her prior role at Facebook, she led UX research for privacy products on the Privacy and Trust team. She bridges the gap between academic and applied researchers by teaching and coaching budding UX'ers as well as organizing events and discussions around the topic.
- **Liz Keneski:** Facebook. Liz leads the Privacy Research Team, a part of Facebook's broader Privacy arm. Her team studies foundational privacy topics, such as consumer privacy attitudes, feelings and behaviors, privacy user experiences, employee privacy decision-making and execution, and external privacy expert understanding and partnership.

19.2   Why Industry-Academic Partnerships Are Valuable

19.2.1   Applied Research Benefiting from Academic Research

Applied researchers often need to move quickly—our science is in service of informing upcoming decisions about products, programs, policies, etc., and those outcomes come with hard deadlines. However, this also means that we cannot always comprehensively investigate a given topic from "top to bottom" due to time constraints. Industry benefits from working with academics because it can create the opportunity to look at a problem more objectively and over a longer term. In order to benefit from this long-term academic thinking, the work that applied researchers and academic researchers do together needs to be scoped to occur over several years—a true long-term partnership.

> The deep knowledge and experience in the specific space is so good for us. We get deeply expert in one space, but then we get moved to another space and become an expert at that. We are never deeply understanding a space like academics.
> – Rebecca Destello, *Facebook*

Another way that applied researchers can benefit from academic research is via academics' expertise in working with particular topics or sensitive populations (e.g., older adults, teens and children, people experiencing cyber abuse). As discussed in Chap. 15, vulnerable populations face unique privacy risks that not only challenge designers' preconceptions about privacy but also are often overlooked in decisions about privacy design and policy. Further, existing frameworks often overlook the privacy concerns of people who experience heightened risk. Applied sectors have a vested interest in serving diverse consumers or clients well; however, that doesn't always mean that the right course of action is for applied researchers, many of whom have more generalized research experience, to reach out directly to potentially vulnerable populations for research. Rather than industry trying to break into communities, it's better to work with people who are trusted in those environments. Many times, those are the academics.

> At Walmart, I studied how people budget in preparation for holiday shopping. I learned that people usually set a budget for different categories, ranging from bills and rent to savings, entertainment and "me-money." Some people used envelopes for cash for food, bills, transportation, etc. to categorize expenses. Customers part of a different segment did not use envelopes, but they also had ways to categorize and control expenses, for example, one checking account and three savings accounts—one for emergency, one for kids education, and one for monthly unexpected events like if the washer broke. People had a way of controlling their budget, whether physical or in their heads. While analyzing the data I collected, I did a quick review and learned about a solid concept in the literature, called 'mental accounting,' that described exactly what I had been seeing in my studies.
> – Janaina Pantoja, *eBay*

19.2.2 Academic Research Benefiting from Applied Research

Some of the problems applied research is positioned to solve can benefit academics because of the potential for impact. Many of these problems are the exact "big questions" that motivate academics to study privacy in the first place—e.g., How should technology companies protect the privacy of potentially vulnerable people? How should governments collect census data in ways that promote necessary social programs but also responsibly collect, use, and store sensitive data? How should IoT technologies provide in-home, everyday value to people's lives while also protecting their privacy? Academics' opportunity for impact in the applied sector—to influence the experiences of billions of people's lives on a daily basis—is unparalleled.

Another way that academics can benefit from such collaborations is access to resources. Despite developing rigorous theory-derived hypotheses in academia, academic researchers sometimes lack the resources to appropriately test their hypotheses with large enough or diverse enough samples. One way that academic researchers may benefit from applied research is to capitalize on the possibility to (a) collaborate, and thus have access to larger samples (with appropriate privacy protections), and/or (b) bidirectionally replicate work with multiple samples across academic and applied settings. In addition to sheer sample size, an additional benefit of applied research is the ability to access diverse, global samples through resource-intensive methods.

19.2.3 How Academics Can Best Contribute to Applied Outcomes

Until there is a direct application for academic research results and they influence our ability to build something, they simply won't be used. This means that in order for applied researchers to benefit from academic privacy research, it is paramount that academic researchers do not just imply or suggest how their work "might" or "could" be applied, but they need to take the next step to *understand* and to *collaborate with* the industries they seek to influence.

This type of impact starts with academics gaining as much context as possible about the applied sectors they seek to influence. Industry researchers do not have unlimited manpower, technology, etc., to create the solutions academics are calling for, and this lack of consideration for the business reality of solving real-world problems can make implementing academics' recommendations untenable. Academics should reach out to applied researchers and ask questions about how their work can influence applied outcomes. Then, they can incorporate that knowledge into their future research and especially into their recommendations for applied sectors.

19.2.4 Successful Relationships

Some have mastered this, and it is up to the rest of us to learn and follow suit. For example, Anja Dinhopl, a UX Research Manager at Google, shared an example of a successful partnership between applied researchers and academics. For research she conducted, she collaborated with academics for foundational work that she and her team then wanted to build on, rather than starting from scratch. She said that the applied team was "able to move much faster than most industry groups." She also argues there need to be feedback mechanisms between communities, industry researchers, and academic researchers. Ideally, this would include a way to share back to the community and a *stronger commitment* for industry to share with academia and legislatures and maybe even competitors. This can be done via white papers, collaborative meetings, conferences, published articles and blogs, and more. There is a need to give transparency of *why* we are doing what we are doing, and with that comes building on existing research. We cannot simply conduct research in a silo, but we must share with other researchers and organizations so others can learn as well.

Heather Desurvire from Google also shared an example of a successful partnership. When she conducted game user research, she saw a need for partnering on a recurring problem in many games she worked on. While she ran a research agency, she recognized that she was answering the same problems: AAA game companies were producing games that were showing the same critical player issues over and over. For example, the game tutorials were consistently too open world or too pedantic—neither are optimal for learning the tools to play the game. There was a need in industry to find a more principled way to create optimized designs. And the only way to do so properly and to have impact industry-wide was to understand the principles behind optimizing the player experience. Heather was able to offer consistent insights to all the game studios. She partnered with academics she had met at conferences, through her association with USC and a fruitful collaboration with the Microsoft games research group who were also geared toward raising the bar for all game studios via shared knowledge. Heather conducted theoretical work with authors and academics and shared it back to the game companies. Together, they came up with principles. They then had the task of actually applying them. This occurred eventually via publications in conferences and game research books, as well as teaching them to up-and-coming game designers, as a faculty member at USC's Interactive Media and Games department. An example of a play principle they developed is: (1) the game presents overarching goals early as well as short-term goals throughout play, (2) the game does not put any unnecessary burden on the player, (3) mechanics are easy to learn but hard to master, (4) the player should not lose any hard won items, and (5) the game world reacts to the players and remembers their passage through it.

Another way Heather bridged the gap was to take a faculty position, teaching future game publishers game user research. By having future designers understand the player experience, it was a "way to plant a seed on how to optimize player experience by teaching them the concepts." To Heather, planting the seeds was a way of raising the bar. And she has been teaching now for over a decade and has seen those seeds flourish in industry. In fact, many game researchers in the gaming world, who were there since the beginning, came from academia. That bridge happened naturally in the gaming industry, as a result of this dual focus. Heather and these others helped define and pioneer the game research methods that are now industry standard.

Ideally we should work towards a multi-partnership—academia, government, non-profits, and industry. Academia is known for methods, detailed inquiry, and long-term goals. Applied research focuses on how findings impact prioritization and development of products, programs, processes, etc. Government makes the rules, but may wrestle with the right approach when designing privacy experiences is a complicated endeavor without obvious answers. Government agencies may not always trust companies to come up with design principles, but overly detailed mandates can also be problematic or restrict innovative problem-solving. While academics, policy folks, and industry researchers seem to have conflicting interests, they actually are all working toward common goals of helping people benefit from using products while protecting their privacy. Each sector differs in how they prioritize and work toward these goals. We simply have a fundamentally different way of framing things. But in the end, we are all working toward the same outcomes and can help one another get there if we work more closely together.

> Companies face a variety of commercial, legal, ethical, and reputational risks that serve as disincentives to sharing data for academic research, with privacy—particularly the risk of reidentification—an intractable concern. For companies, striking the right balance between

the commercial and societal value of their data, the privacy interests of their customers, and the interests of academics presents a formidable dilemma.

To help support data sharing for research by companies, we have developed model contracts, a special ethics review committee for projects not covered by IRB review and an award to honor successful industry-academic teams that collaborate using company data safely. We hope this will move the ball forward.

– Jules Polonetsky, *Future of Privacy Forum*

19.3 Why These Partnerships Are Challenging

So why don't more of us foster these relationships? Why aren't all applied researchers partnering with academic researchers? There are many reasons, but one that stands out to us and many in our panel is **timelines**. Simply put, the timelines that academic researchers and applied researchers work with are different. Applied researchers are moving quickly, sometimes conducting a project from start to finish in just a few weeks. Academic researchers, on the other hand, take much longer in order to conduct research that can lead to publication of peer-reviewed results. Projects can last anywhere from a few months to many years. This discrepancy poses a bit of a problem. It is harder to adopt what you learn in academia in industry because we need to do it fast—we aim to solve immediate problems.

In addition, because academia aims for knowledge that is generalizable and scrutable by third-party reviewers, there is a general sense that there are **so many steps** one has to go through to conduct academic research, such as IRB approvals, statistical testing, theoretical validation, and generalization rather than focused and contextual findings. Heather Desurvire from Google serves as a bridge herself, and she shared a story about her experiences working with a new field: "Academia funded the research, and the work was adopted because the field was brand new. There were no real methods in industry. We applied what we learned in academia in industry." But it was not always easy, and everything was not readily accepted. "Some work was criticized as not statistically valid, and some qualitative research was looked down upon." But she did not stop. While the early work received some initial criticism, over time the qualitative work was appreciated for its depth, and the academic partners utilized it. It is often important to use both qualitative and quantitative work together, for example, when studying gaming and the player experience: "You can look at quant, but need the qual to understand WHY. This was taking place in industry, not academia. Academia did the theoretical work, not the applied work." And if it is not something you can eventually use, why is the work being conducted at all?

Applied researchers are working on improving products, and while time and other constraints play a role, is it simply that applied researchers don't care about the theoretical work? Well, not necessarily. Gretchen Gelke started working on privacy at Google about 3 years ago. Prior to this role, she worked on security software, hardware, and smart devices—privacy and data have been key issues for her for a long time. Compared to other companies, her privacy specialty was never really the focus of her role ... until Google, where she realized her specialty was an asset. The team she joined, while very applied, was also extremely academic. They focused on products (e.g., helping users find privacy settings) and also foundational research both across Google and externally. The team is frequently asked to present the foundational work to product teams to inform thinking and inspire change in products, overarching strategy, or to inform entirely new directions. The team hired people with PhDs in privacy and security to help inform policy and set context for the product changes being recommended. These efforts were critical for Google. Having the academics in house helped the team make *better* applied product decisions.

Unfortunately, applied research teams reinvent the wheel constantly—conducting research that has likely already been conducted in academia or by previous colleagues. Sure, it would be easier to go to someone who has done the work, but we want to make sense of it too. So how do we stop reinventing the wheel and shift to doing this together?

So what do we do? Do we abort the mission of trying to bridge? Of course not; we certainly don't think so (or we would not be writing this chapter). We believe that collaborations are essential for building on existing work and applying that work to real-world problems. Academic researchers have been studying many of the things we are grappling with in applied research for years! We need to figure out how to make those timelines match up. If we have problems we are interested in examining in a year or two, it would be nice to be able to predict that so academics could get a head start. Applied researchers need to be proactive, *to predict future needs*, to move earlier to foster those collaborations.

19.4   Actionable Strategies for Making These Partnerships Work

In order to properly bridge, we believe that industry researchers need to be mindful about what academic institutions are worried about, and academic researchers need to be mindful about what industry researchers are worried about. We need to make sure the collaboration is good for both sides. We believe we need to also work against some of the biases, for example, the incorrect stereotype that companies do not *actually* want collaboration, they just want to be told they are right. We believe we need to build a strong relationship model that simply does not exist for most of us right now. So how do we actually DO that? How do we better understand and communicate with each other? We have identified some actionable strategies that have worked for us and our panel, and here we synthesize them for you, the reader who would like to implement these strategies.

19.4.1 Provide Funding Sources

We heard time and again from our panel that one way that applied privacy researchers learned about academics' work is through participating in industry-funding programs (e.g., serving as a reviewer for proposals to a private sector research grant). Relevant research may be discovered this way, and to further academic research so that we can all make more progress, industry should help fund it. This helps academics accelerate their work, which also helps industry get to results quickly. For instance, rooted in the advocacy of internal researchers, Facebook launched a new research funding proposal to fuel academic research on inclusive privacy (see https://research.fb.com/programs/research-awards/proposals/peoples-expectations-and-experiences-with-digital-privacy-request-for-proposals/). As a part of this funding, awarded academic researchers provide updates to Facebook research partners throughout the progression of the research so that those working on related, applied questions at Facebook can benefit quickly from the latest results. Additionally, the academic researchers can learn from how their industry counterparts are considering using the research to shape product development in order to make their work and its implications more valuable to the applied sector upon publication. Touchpoints should be created during academic-industry partnerships so that applied researchers and academics can learn from one another.

Likewise, Mozilla has funded privacy research grants over the last several years with diversity and transparency at the heart of this program. Privacy research that resulted from this funding led to direct impact on Mozilla's products such as changes to what Mozilla displays when one uses private browsing mode. In addition to funding research practices, funding academics in nontraditional ways can also greatly contribute to productivity and mutual benefit, such as providing funds for childcare over the course of the grant.

Sure there are existing grants, but are they good enough? A true program/collaboration would involve long-term relationships, like conferences or "labs" that connect academia and industry, and they would involve ongoing commitments, not just a project in a single point in time. Current grants are often perceived as pertaining to a specific topic and project goal. We need to foster relationships and open the time and space for ongoing relevant questions. Companies can also give money to foundations or other organizations who can then determine and fund research based on their own values. This type of intermediary can be important to be sure the results are not influenced or perceived to be influenced by the industry group who is funding the work.

19.4.2 *Invest in the Next Generation of Scholars*

Applied researchers can align their efforts with privacy academics' overarching goals by investing in the next generation of privacy scholars. Because academic researchers spend a great deal of time mentoring and teaching students, focusing joint energy on bolstering student skills and experiences will foster better collaborations with applied researchers, not just now, but into the future. For example, many large technology companies fund capstone course projects for graduate and undergraduate students studying computer science. Students receive a real-world problem that applied researchers are currently facing and are provided resources to study related concepts and report back with proposed solutions at the end of the semester. Importantly, these courses allow for cross-academia and applied sector collaboration during which both applied researchers and professors provide guidance to students.

Applied researchers should be actively involved in the training of future privacy researchers in academia, regardless of whether students end up going into applied or academic careers. Providing students with context about applied problems, solutions, and careers will ultimately strengthen their research and impact across privacy science as a whole. For example, both Facebook and Google invest in conducting "Research Jams" and other collaborative hands-on workshops with industry researchers and students at different universities aimed at developing rigorous applied research plans about privacy topics. These events provide students with exposure to solving applied problems through research as well as to applied research career trajectories.

> In my work, I get to partner with professors and students on projects—they do research on their own, and I bring it together for our government customers. I advise on the work, and sometimes collaborate, but there is still separation. The strongest partnerships I've seen between academic and industry partners are through CMU's Human-Computer Interaction Institute's Capstone courses. As both a teacher and an advisor, I've been thrilled to observe student teams successfully collaborating with corporations and nonprofits to improve all types of experiences. In these situations, they are sharing and learning from each other resulting in positive outcomes including employment for graduates.
> – Carol Smith, *Carnegie Mellon University*

19.4.3 *Sharing Work*

Both academic researchers and applied researchers need to find ways to regularly and relevantly share their work with one another. Academic privacy researchers should consider publishing summaries of their work for mainstream audiences, send relevant papers to applied researchers they have previously connected with, and present at both academic and applied research conferences. We may need more and new mechanisms to do this well. For instance, perhaps we need to expand the open source and open data movements into the privacy sector and create shared repositories of both academic and applied research *by topic*. Although there are challenges to doing so (e.g., private sector confidentiality), there are ways to start to build these bridges. For example, the Facebook Privacy Research Team has partnered with Trust, Transparency, and Control Labs to share privacy research insights with external audiences so all can learn from one another. In addition to these types of forums being useful for sharing results across academia and applied research, applied researchers across different companies and industries, in and of themselves, also benefit from shared knowledge bases.

Members of our panel described times when academic partnerships hadn't worked out, when there were concerns or disagreements in how results would be shared at the end of a project (e.g., one academic wanted to publish based on collaboratively collected data without having the partner applied researcher review the final product). These disagreements can lead and have led to collaborations failing. Thus, it's vital that applied researchers scope collaborative or funded academic research projects with publication as the ultimate goal and that both sides of any collaboration talk openly about and agree to publication guidelines (in writing) at the very beginning of the project.

Lastly, academics can help make their work more applicable in industry settings by ensuring insight-based recommendations are actionable, plausible, and in digestible language for non-scientists. This allows applied researchers to easily translate academic findings and implications into design and engineering "languages" for stakeholders on the ground who might be implementing academics' suggestions.

> Provide a '5 things you need to know about privacy' document that accompanies any academic publication. This type of document is not about dumbing down the work; rather, it is a way to translate the work for all to read, like how we should explain concisely and clearly to our users!
>
> – Julie Schiller, *Google*

19.4.4 Sharing Data and Resources

It would be remiss to not identify one of the ways that privacy academics consistently ask for partnership with applied researchers—they request data to be shared with them for their own use and analysis. On the surface, this may seem like a simple ask. However, the sensitivity of sharing consumers' data from a business or clients' data from a nonprofit generates, ironically given the topic of study, a number of privacy considerations that need to be addressed (e.g., Has consent been obtained? Can data be effectively deidentified? Will the analyses directly benefit consumers/clients?). Sometimes it is easy to answer all these questions and other necessary questions with "yes." For example, Facebook has provided aggregated and de-identified data sets to academics working on research for social good. But sometimes the answers to the privacy questions above are more fuzzy, and in those cases, applied researchers simply cannot justify sharing data.

The best practice here is not to ask these questions post hoc but instead to define how data can be shared at the beginning of a collaboration so the right security and privacy measures can be put in place. This will allow academic and applied researchers to work together to determine what inputs are essential to project goals and then work from there to determine if, when, and how data sharing will be executed.

One technique to include more academic work in applied research is to include a literature review as the foundational part of setting up projects. Julie Schiller, a UX Research Manager at Google, thinks that those who have academic training can bridge by "using the skills we were taught academically to give a thorough overview of existing work for the team to better understand the project and broader problem." Janaina Pantoja, a UX Researcher and Manager at eBay, starts most of her research with literature reviews. She takes advantage of the huge amount of research that has already been conducted on e-commerce, in general, and on eBay, in particular: "If I don't take the time to understand what is in the literature, I may not be able to synthesize and analyze my data properly. Sometimes it is about language gap— we study topics that others might have studied outside of industry, and there are concepts and terms that have been formalized elsewhere ... sometimes you are saying the same thing that was said in academia already."

One might think that adding literature reviews to the process is time-consuming and inefficient. What many applied researchers may not know is that it actually does not take that much extra time to conduct the literature reviews that Julie and Janaina find so valuable. Many articles are publically available on Google Scholar, ResearchGate, and at local libraries, and conducting a literature review upfront can save you time later.

Collaborating with academics for literature reviews is an excellent way to bridge the gap. Academics can recommend the articles to read to get up to speed quickly on a topic. In fact, putting out a little bit of funding for various literature reviews might be a good way to incentivize academics (likely students) to do this. New students are always looking for new topic areas, and this is a mini step toward shared knowledge and better partnerships without having to have done a lot of research in the area already and without having to commit to the area just yet.

> This is why they hire us—to know the rigor and then to make those short cuts, in ways that do not detract from the proper study.
> – Janice Tsai, *Google*

Similarly, another way to bridge is to have academics join industry. They can bring the rigor that is second nature to them to industry and teach industry folks to slow down just a bit and learn from what already exists in academia. We have seen this type of cross-over to be very successful at organizations like Facebook and Google, who often hire academics or sponsor them for a period of time (e.g., a sabbatical). Employing academics and grad students as interns and student researchers to move projects/programs forward is also a way to bridge.

The editors of this book have been working on bridging academia and industry for a few years now with a number of initiatives, including:

- Networked Privacy workshop at CSCW conference, Portland Oregon in 2017 (Xinru, Pam, Bart, Jen)
- Facebook Research Speaker Series panel, "Talking with the Experts: A Panel Discussion about Individual Differences in Networked Privacy," at Facebook, Menlo Park, CA in 2017 (Jen, Xinru, Pam, Bart)
- UXPA panel, "Unique Challenges of Researching Individual Differences in Online Privacy," at UXPA conference, Puerto Rico in 2018 (Jen, Xinru)
- Bridging Industry and Academia to Tackle Responsible Research and Privacy Practices Summit at Facebook, NY, in 2018 (Jen, Xinru, Pam, Bart)
- Industry and Academia Privacy Symposium at Bentley University, Waltham, MA, in 2019 (Xinru, Pam, Jen)
- Presentation "Creating a Gateway for Purposeful Privacy Design" at IAC conference, Orlando, FL, in 2019 (Xinru, Pam)
- Article "Designing for Social Technologies: Responsible Privacy Design" UXPA Magazine in 2019 (Xinru, Pam, Bart) (https://uxpamagazine.org/designing-for-social-technologies-responsible-privacy-design/)
- Presentations at various conferences attended by applied researchers such as User Experience Professionals Association International Conference (UXPA), Information Architecture Conference (IAC), and Grace Hopper Celebration (GHC), as well as local ACM Special Interest Group on Computer-Human Interaction (SIGCHI) events

This book is another step in the direction of getting academics and applied researchers collaborating, sharing, and sitting at the same table, thinking about and working on the same problems together. We believe that it is essential for us to work together to accomplish greater impact through more comprehensive work. What will you do to build a bridge?

Printed in the United States
by Baker & Taylor Publisher Services